JEWS IN THE SOVIET UNION

The USSR, 1939–1945

International USSR Border
Borders of the Soviet Republics
Annexed by the USSR, 1939-41
Furthest German Advance into the USSR
60°N
Bering Sea
120°E
OCEAN
140°E
100°E
Magadan
SIBERIA
RUSSIA
Sea of Okhotsk
OCIALIST REPUBLICS
PACIFIC OCEAN
Birobidzhan
140°W
Lake Baikal
Irkutsk
Vladivostok
40°N
MONGOLIA
Sea of Japan
KOREA
160°W
CHINA
0
500 Miles
0
600 Kilometers
LUCIDITY INFORMATION DESIGN, LLC

THE EUGENE SHVIDLER PROJECT FOR THE HISTORY OF THE JEWS OF THE SOVIET UNION

JEWS IN THE SOVIET UNION

A HISTORY

GENERAL EDITORS: GENNADY ESTRAIKH AND DAVID ENGEL

Volume 1:
Revolution, Civil War, and Consolidation, 1917–1930
Elissa Bemporad

Volume 2:
Dictatorship and Terror, 1930–1939
Deborah Yalen and Arkady Zeltser

Volume 3:
War, Conquest, and Catastrophe, 1939–1945
Oleg Budnitskii, David Engel, Gennady Estraikh, and Anna Shternshis

Volume 4:
Post-War Hopes and Continued Terror, 1945–1953
Anna Shternshis

Volume 5:
After Stalin, 1953–1967
Gennady Estraikh

Volume 6:
The Final Years, 1967–1991
Zvi Gitelman

JEWS IN THE SOVIET UNION
A HISTORY

WAR, CONQUEST, AND CATASTROPHE 1939–1945

Volume 3

OLEG BUDNITSKII, DAVID ENGEL,
GENNADY ESTRAIKH, AND ANNA SHTERNSHIS

NEW YORK UNIVERSITY PRESS
New York

NEW YORK UNIVERSITY PRESS
New York
www.nyupress.org

Please contact the Library of Congress for Cataloging-in-Publication data.
ISBN: 9781479819430 (hardback)
ISBN: 9781479819454 (library ebook)
ISBN: 9781479819447 (consumer ebook)

New York University Press books are printed on acid-free paper, and their binding materials are chosen for strength and durability. We strive to use environmentally responsible suppliers and materials to the greatest extent possible in publishing our books.

Manufactured in the United States of America

10 9 8 7 6 5 4 3 2 1

Also available as an ebook

With deep gratitude to Eugene Shvidler,
whose generosity made possible the research and
preparation of this NYU study.

CONTENTS

FOREWORD TO *JEWS IN THE SOVIET UNION: A HISTORY*

DAVID ENGEL AND GENNADY ESTRAIKH

This volume is part of a six-volume comprehensive history of Jews and Jewish life in the Soviet Union, from the establishment of the Russian Soviet Republic in late 1917 through to the Union's formal dissolution on 8 December 1991. The project was launched in 2015 under the auspices of New York University's Global Network for Advanced Research in Jewish Studies, thanks to a major gift from Eugene Shvidler. It has been carried out by an international team of scholars—authors, consultants, archivists, and librarians—based in North America, Israel, and Europe, including several former Soviet states.

The scholars have worked to fill a major need in the study of both Soviet and Jewish history. The prominence of Jews among Soviet elites during certain intervals in the USSR's seven decades, along with pressures to remove them from elite ranks during others, has long been noted as a significant factor in Soviet politics, but the extent of such prominence, pressure, and significance has yet to be explored in detail. Similarly, the Jews of the Soviet Union, though numbering about 20 percent of the world's Jewish population for most of the twentieth century and ranking second or third among Jewish communities defined by geopolitical boundaries, have yet to be incorporated significantly into a broader Jewish historical narrative.

Reasons for both phenomena can be found in the very histories from which Soviet Jews have been largely absent. For Soviet ideologues and policymakers, the Jews of their country resisted easy categorization. From a

Marxist point of view, their status was confusing. Were they a fully-fledged nation? If so, how were Soviet Jews connected to Jews elsewhere in the world, including Palestine, later Israel? Without a clear ideological lens through which to regard them, certain aspects of their situation in the USSR could not be readily explained. How, for example, to account simultaneously for their prominent role in many domains of Soviet life, most notably during the 1920s and 1930s, on the one hand, and for the unofficial but universally evident restrictions imposed, increasingly from the late 1940s, on their educational choices and career paths, on the other? How did it happen that Jews, many of whom had once been enthusiastic supporters of the Soviet way, sought to leave the country in growing numbers during its final three decades? Why were Jews allowed, at various times and with varying degrees of willingness or reluctance, to emigrate, whereas the vast majority of Soviet citizens were not afforded a similar possibility? The state's guardians preferred to leave such questions in repose. As a result, historians living in the Soviet Union (and, after 1945, in the Soviet-dominated countries of eastern Europe as well) were strongly discouraged from taking up such an ideologically treacherous subject.

For historians of the Jews, Soviet Jewry presented a different set of anomalies. The Soviet state purported to act in accordance with a unique set of principles that, its leaders and advocates promised, would offer Jews greater physical safety, material security, and psychological peace of mind than would any alternative set of principles guiding other contemporary states or political movements, including those associated with liberal democracy and with Zionism. The principles' uniqueness made the USSR seem an outlier in the political history of modern Jewry. Moreover, in the highly charged atmosphere of the Cold War, those principles became associated with forces hostile to the countries in which most historians of the Jews resided. Consequently, the handful of Western scholars who displayed sustained interest in Soviet Jewish history tended to investigate the negative, tragic aspects of that history that eventually impelled many Jews to want to depart the country, leaving more quotidian, less dramatic, less controversial, and more successful parts of the story largely in the dark.

Lack of sources for studying those parts of the story compounded the problem. As long as the Soviet Union existed, it severely restricted Western scholars' access to relevant documents in Soviet libraries and archives. Only after its demise did scholars begin to grasp the breadth and depth of the materials they had once been unable to consult. During the three decades that have passed since then, many of those materials have been brought to light. Moreover, the passage of time has been both long enough to offer researchers sufficient distance for evaluating this massive documentary record and short enough to allow them still to benefit from the living memories of the large number of Jews who directly experienced the Soviet regime. Those memories have been and continue to be tapped by several large-scale oral history projects. Thus a critical mass of new source material appears to have made possible a synthesis of the Soviet Jewish past with a degree of accuracy, inclusion, understanding, and refinement unachievable even a generation ago. That is the outcome the current project has sought.

The project's findings suggest that the results of the Soviet Union's approach to matters of Jewish concern and the attitudes of different parts of the heterogeneous Soviet Jewish population toward the Soviet Union were mixed. At first many Jews were great supporters of the new regime that replaced the oppressive tsars. Yet it was not long before Soviet Jews faced the dismantling of their religious life. Some aspects of Jewish culture were suppressed, while others were promoted. For some Jews, these features of life under the Soviets were profoundly distressing, for others less so. Some found ways to maintain certain religious and cultural practices despite official disapproval. At the same time, the regime pursued policies that helped some Jews achieve Soviet-style prosperity and reach the highest levels of Soviet society, though often simultaneously heightening tensions between Jews and some of their non-Jewish neighbors. After 1941 the Soviet Union fought the Nazis and sheltered Jews who had escaped to the East, with Soviet Jews playing a significant role in the war effort. Shortly thereafter, however, the regime intensified its own repression of the sharpened Jewish consciousness that World War II had aroused. Even under those conditions, Soviet Jews developed multiple mechanisms for excelling in this difficult environment and for preserving a Jewish identity. Some Jews became dissidents, campaigning for the right to emigrate and contributing to the Soviet regime's eventual downfall. Other Jews strove to prosper within the Soviet system, despite difficult circumstances. Some of them were more successful than others.

Accordingly, the authors of the six volumes have tried to present the multiple, changing situations in which Soviet Jews found themselves over seven decades and more as much as possible through the eyes of all the various actors in those situations, Jewish and non-Jewish alike. In doing so, their aim has been to help readers understand how the various ways in which different groups of Jews adjusted to the policies and practices of the Soviet regime at different times could make sense to their members and how the changing policies that the regime adopted at different times could make sense to the regime itself in changing contexts. They have not sought to take sides in the debates of the times they explore, to evaluate the actions or attitudes of the participants, or to identify heroes and villains. Instead they have endeavored to fathom and to represent an intricate, multifaceted history as fully and fairly as available documents and available space allow.

EDITORS' NOTE

Volume 3 of *Jews in the Soviet Union* concerns the shortest time span of any volume in the series—a mere six years, from 1939 to 1945. No matter how brief, however, that interval was arguably both the most difficult and the most consequential in the entire history not only of Soviet Jewry but of the Soviet Union overall. In 1939 and 1940 the USSR added about 20 percent to its land area, expanding to the borders that would define it through to its end. More than two million Jews inhabited the new territories, increasing the Soviet Jewish population by two-thirds. But the increase was tragically short lived. A massive invasion of the USSR by Nazi Germany and its allies, beginning in 1941, led to the deaths of 60 percent of the Jews under Soviet rule over the next four years. The truncated and disfigured Soviet Jewish community that emerged from the Holocaust years was marked by trauma, whether suffered directly under German or Romanian occupation, in combat through service in the Red Army, or in the Soviet interior as refugees. The experience of war and mass death would shape the contours of Soviet Jewish life for decades to come.

The volume is the product of four hands. David Engel is primarily responsible for the first three chapters, which deal with the newly acquired lands and the occupied territories, and for the prologue. Oleg Budnitskii is similarly responsible for chapter 4, on Jews in the Red Army, and for the appendix; Gennady Estraikh for chapter 5, on the Jewish Anti-Fascist Committee; and Anna Shternshis for chapter 6, on Jews in the Soviet rear. The editors have endeavored to link the chapters into a coherent narrative by adding brief connective material, as well as to achieve a unified format and writing style.

Place names have been rendered according to the official gazetteers of the states that held internationally recognized sovereignty over them as of 1 January 1939: hence Lwów, Wilno, and Cernăuţi instead of the current Lviv, Vilnius, and Chernivtsi. Places are called by the official name in force at the time referred to in the text: hence, for the years 1939–45, Kuibyshev, not Samara; Stalingrad, not Volgograd or Tsaritsyn. Standard English names are used for major capital cities (Moscow, Warsaw, Bucharest). Individuals' names are rendered as the individuals were accustomed to Romanize them. Absent evidence of preference, names are transliterated according to the language in which the person wrote most frequently. Languages using Cyrillic alphabets are generally transliterated according to Library of Congress standards, except for omission of diacritics that the Library uses and of some hard and soft signs (mostly in the notes). Yiddish is transliterated according to the system adopted by the YIVO Institute for Jewish Research, Hebrew according to an internal scheme that aims for a reasonable balance between the most common orthographically and phonetically based systems currently in use. Deviations may occur at times; readers who spot them have read carefully, and we are grateful for their attention to detail.

PROLOGUE

Though few could know it at the time, a laconic announcement at the bottom of the back page of *Pravda* on 4 May 1939 heralded a new era in the history of Soviet Jews:

> The Presidium of the Supreme Soviet of the Union of Soviet Socialist Republics has released Comrade M. M. Litvinov from the duties of People's Commissar for Foreign Affairs of the USSR, at his request.[1]

In fact the foreign minister had not asked to leave his post; he had been cashiered by the general secretary of the Communist Party, Josef Stalin, ostensibly for his "disloyal attitude" toward the regime but more likely because the Soviets' geopolitical calculations had begun to push their foreign policy in a new direction.[2] Their reorientation altered the course of world history. It also had profound implications for millions of Jews in the USSR and abroad. Replacing the country's chief diplomat was hardly the greatest of those implications, but it was the first to show its face.

The ousted foreign minister, Maxim Maximovich Litvinov, had been a Soviet Jewish success story. Born Meir Wallach in 1876 to a religious, Yiddish-speaking merchant family in the heavily Jewish manufacturing town of Belostok (since 1921 Białystok, Poland),[3] he had enlisted in the tsarist army, only to be discharged (by his account) after refusing to fire upon striking workers.[4] Shortly thereafter he had joined the fledgling, clandestine Russian Social Democratic Workers' Party. He had served time in a tsarist prison; escaped; fled to Switzerland; become a protégé and trusted confidant of Vladimir Lenin; followed Lenin into the Bolshevik faction; smuggled literature, agents, and arms to Bolshevik cells in Russia; and represented his party at the International Socialist Bureau in London. In the British capital he had developed contacts with local businessmen and government officials that he had used to aid the Bolshevik cause. He had also married an English Jewish woman (the novelist Ivy Low), started a family, and become a British subject.[5] Multilingual, erudite, at home among the European political class, Litvinov had emerged after the Bolshevik revolution as a principal exponent and interpreter of the Soviet cause in the West. Since 1930 he had distinguished himself at home and abroad as his country's most visible spokesman in the international arena. No Jew anywhere had ever held such a high-profile position on the modern world stage for so long.[6] For a Jew from the Russian Pale, Litvinov's rise had been conspicuous and heady. At the time, such an ascent had arguably been possible only in the Soviet Union.[7]

But times had changed. A goal of Soviet diplomacy during the late 1920s and the early 1930s had been to normalize relations with the world's great powers. The Soviets had hoped that acceptance by the international community would allow them to divert state resources from defense toward economic development, helping them consolidate their rule at home. Their efforts had been sufficiently successful to mitigate Soviet fears of active Western efforts at regime change.[8] Still, memories of the Russian Civil War, when military forces from eleven countries, including Britain, France, the United States, and Japan, had intervened against the Bolsheviks, continued to stoke mistrust of the West's ultimate intentions.[9] Suspicions had acquired renewed force when the Nazi regime took power in Germany in 1933. The Nazi leader, Adolf Hitler, had long made clear not only his ideological abhorrence of Bolshevism but also his determination to gain new territories for his country at Soviet expense.[10] His rhetoric had stoked anxiety among Soviet leaders that the states that had tried to crush the Bolsheviks fifteen years earlier would now take up their crusade once again, this time with Germany as a powerful new ally.[11]

Litvinov had designed a strategy for confronting the threat. The plan had called for the USSR to present itself as a responsible member of the international community, in contrast to Nazi Germany, which threatened the peace not only of the Soviet Union but of the entire world.[12] Litvinov had hoped that Britain, France, and the United States would acknowledge the threat and would join the Soviets in a multilateral agreement for collective security, in which each would regard an attack on one as an attack on all, and all together would contain Germany's drive to expand.[13] For six years he had pursued that hope with vigor, bringing the USSR into the League of Nations in 1934 (less than a year after Germany left the world body) and winning applause for his eloquent speeches at League meetings.[14] But by early 1939 Soviet leadership circles had concluded that his strategy had failed. Britain and France still seemed to reject any alliance with the USSR. The Soviets thus felt a need for additional options in confronting the German menace and for new leadership to pursue them. Litvinov had to go.[15]

That Litvinov was a Jew probably did not play the decisive role in his ouster; his perceived failure would surely have sufficed to bring him down sooner or later. His departure did, however, eliminate a potential difficulty after the Soviets finally gave up on collective security and negotiated with Germany for a pact of mutual neutrality. Those negotiations were led by Litvinov's successor, Viacheslav Mikhailovich Molotov (1890–1986), a man quite different from Litvinov in background, education, and experience.[16] In the past Molotov had condemned discrimination against Jews in government service (he was married to a Jewish woman, Polina [Perl] Zhemchuzhina, who had held several key positions in the Soviet administration, including a ministerial post). Nevertheless, on his first day in office he reportedly promised his successors to "tear out that kike's [Litvinov's] wasp nest by the roots."[17] Years later Molotov recalled that Stalin himself had ordered him to "purge the [Foreign] Ministry of Jews."[18] The ostensible anti-Jewish turn did not necessarily reflect any consistent ill will either man held toward Jews as such; had such animosity governed personnel decisions in Stalin's state in the 1930s, Litvinov and other members of the Jewish elite could not have risen as far as they did. Still, Stalin doubtless understood that a Jewish foreign minister could make it more difficult to pursue one option that some Soviet officials had been suggesting for several years—a political agreement with the Nazis.[19]

Thus, though few Soviet Jews appear to have sensed it at the time, Litvinov's dismissal in May 1939 signaled that Nazi Germany was now to become a factor in their history. Over the next six years the German role would only grow. From mid-1939 through mid-1945 the experience of Jews in the Soviet lands would be shaped by people taking direction not only from Moscow but from Berlin as well. Decisions rooted in both places would combine to make those years the fulcrum of Soviet Jewish history.

1

NEW LANDS, NEW SUBJECTS

The first German decision affecting Soviet Jewish life was to seek rapprochement with Moscow.

The idea crystallized in spring 1939 in response to the same developments that prompted the Soviets' interest in resetting relations with Germany. For both sides, the newfound search for cooperation followed departures by Poland and Britain from earlier tendencies in their foreign relations. Poland was central to Nazi geopolitical thinking, thanks largely to its position between Germany and the USSR. The Nazis had long coveted Soviet territory.[1] Initially Hitler had anticipated that Poland might be induced to help Germany acquire it.[2] In January 1934, Germany and Poland signed a nonaggression pact, followed by economic and cultural agreements. From Poland's perspective, the pact's great advantage was that it shifted Germany's immediate attention away from its demands for revision of the border between the two countries. The Nazi regime also saw to it that attacks on Poland in the German press were muted and promised to take Poland's interests into account in formulating its policies toward other countries, including the USSR.[3]

From time to time Poland took concrete advantage of this seemingly favorable German attitude, as in 1938, when it exploited German pressure upon Czechoslovakia to seize a strategically important border area from its southern neighbor.[4] Jewish issues also played a notable role in Polish-German relations, with many of Poland's 3.5 million Jews attributing what they perceived as an increasingly hostile public climate in their country largely to the growing amity between the two states.[5] Already in June 1936 Poland's prime minister endorsed a campaign of economic pressure against Jewish Polish citizens aimed at driving as many of them as possible abroad.[6] Subsequent moves to exclude Jews from the civil service, the free professions, the universities, political life, and even citizenship, punctuated by outbreaks of mass violence, generated widespread disquiet among Polish Jews over their future.[7]

Noting this feature of Polish policy, German observers expected the so-called Jewish question to become a matter for ongoing Polish-German collaboration. They were thus taken aback when, in late fall 1938, Poland rejected Germany's offer of a "basic settlement of issues" (*Gesamtlösung*) between the two states, including frontier guarantees, a twenty-five-year treaty of friendship, "joint action in colonial matters, the emigration of Jews from Poland, and a joint policy toward Russia on the basis of the Anti-Comintern Pact."[8] The German government had not grasped how determined Poland was to maintain a position of "balance" (*równowaga*) between Germany and the USSR—to avoid close association with either and to hold both equally at arm's length.[9] Following the Polish rebuff, the Germans tried to push the Poles off balance by intimidation. On 15 March 1939 they overran Czechoslovakia (violating the vaunted Munich Peace Pact they had signed six months before). A week later they seized the disputed territory of Memel (Klaipėda) from Lithuania, as if to warn that they could take land from Poland in the same way.

Their moves did not move the Poles. Instead they impelled Britain to guarantee that "in the event of any action which threatens Polish independence . . . , His Majesty's Government would feel themselves bound at once to lend the Polish Government all support in their power."[10] Evidently Britain now believed that the Nazi government was bent upon an aggressive agenda that demanded confrontation if it was to be contained. Poland became Britain's containment boundary.[11]

The British guarantee to Poland, followed by French endorsement, sent German strategic planners back to the drawing board. The new situation reminded many Germans of the world war of 1914–1918, a trauma still within recollection of most adults. In that catastrophic confrontation Britain and France had combined with Russia to force Germany into an unsustainable two-front conflict. To forestall a similar scenario now, German strategists looked to drive a wedge between the Western powers and the USSR. In Litvinov's time possibilities for turning the Soviets had appeared virtually nil. But on the day the Soviet foreign minister's dismissal was announced, the German chargé d'affaires in Moscow speculated about a new opportunity:

> Sudden change [in leadership at the Soviet Foreign Ministry] has caused great surprise here, since Litvinov was in the midst of negotiations with the English delegation.... Since Litvinov had received the English Ambassador as late as May 2..., his dismissal appears to be result of spontaneous decision by Stalin. The decision apparently is connected with the fact that differences of opinion arose in the Kremlin on Litvinov's negotiations. Reason for differences of opinion presumably lies in deep mistrust that Stalin harbors toward the entire surrounding capitalist world. At last Party Congress Stalin urged caution lest Soviet Union be drawn into conflicts.[12] Molotov (no Jew) is held to be "most intimate friend and closest collaborator" of Stalin. His appointment is apparently to guarantee that the foreign policy will be conducted strictly in accordance with Stalin's ideas.[13]

German documents do not disclose how important it was to this diplomat's superiors that control of Soviet foreign policy now lay in the hands of "no Jew." They do show, however, that regular high-level overtures from Germany to the USSR followed in short order. For their part, *Soviet* archives indicate that for two months and more Moscow received the overtures with reserve.[14] The Soviets evidently believed—ironically, given Litvinov's fall—that Britain's newfound readiness to confront Germany meant that the strategy of collective security might succeed after all. Accordingly, Molotov embarked upon intense negotiations for a "triple alliance" linking Moscow, London, and Paris in a mutual military assistance pact against Berlin.[15] As late as 4 August 1939, Germany's ambassador to the Soviet Union reported his "overall impression," gained from a seventy-five-minute conversation with the foreign minister: "[T]he Soviet Government is at present determined to sign with England and France if they fulfill all Soviet wishes."[16]

Nevertheless, the Soviets kept options open. In mid-August Poland, still adhering to the strategy of "balance" and determined to stay out of the Soviet camp no less than the German, indicated that it would not allow the Red Army to enter Polish territory to help it fight a German attack. When

Britain backed Poland's stance, the Soviets suspended talks.[17] Finally, on 22 August, Molotov informed British and French negotiators that his government would sign a nonaggression pact with Germany.[18] The following day he and Stalin met German Foreign Minister Joachim von Ribbentrop in Moscow, where the diplomats signed the Treaty of Non-Aggression between Germany and the Union of Soviet Socialist Republics—later dubbed the Ribbentrop-Molotov Pact.

Some of the pact's terms were published immediately. Neither state would attack the other, "either individually or jointly with other powers." Each would remain neutral should another state attack either one. Neither would join any alliance directed against the other. Both would coordinate their foreign policies with one another "on problems affecting their common interests."[19] The language was the language of peace, but, as many observed at the time, the agreement actually invited war.[20] German leaders, like the German public at large, saw that their country was now unlikely to encounter any serious military obstacle to eastward expansion and would not face a future two-front struggle.[21] Accordingly, when German troops moved against Poland on 1 September, few anywhere were surprised.

By contrast, hardly anyone appears to have expected *Soviet* troops to make a similar aggressive move. At 4:00 a.m. on 17 September, upward of six hundred thousand Red Army soldiers crossed the USSR's western border, advancing by nightfall a reported sixty kilometers into Polish territory.[22] The invasion was undertaken to secure the provisions of a secret protocol the Soviets had insisted be added to the nonaggression accord.[23] The protocol acknowledged distinct German and Soviet "spheres of influence" in the nine hundred kilometers that separated the USSR from Germany—lands the Nazis coveted, belonging not only to Poland but to Lithuania, Latvia, and Estonia as well.[24] It thereby set limits to Germany's planned eastward advance, keeping Nazi troops as far as possible from the Soviet heartland.

At the time the protocol was signed the Soviets likely had no concrete scheme for exercising influence within their sphere. However, Germany's rapid military advance against unexpectedly weak Polish defenses (which deterred Britain and France from intervening) impelled the Soviet government to send troops of its own to keep German forces from occupying more territory than the agreement allowed.[25] By 28 September the Red Army had accomplished its mission, and a new German-Soviet Boundary and

Friendship Treaty formally repartitioned Poland between the two powers. The new demarcation line was set along the San, Bug, and Narew rivers, leaving nearly two hundred thousand square kilometers of Polish territory and upward of thirteen million people under Soviet control.[26]

The region that came into Soviet hands included some 1.5 million Jews.[27] Thus, in one fell swoop, the number of Jews subject to Soviet rule grew by nearly 50 percent. The Jews of the new western territories had spent the previous two decades in a nation-state with a capitalist economy (albeit a relatively poor one in which much of the political leadership regarded Jews as an unwelcome outgroup). As a result they had not experienced the massive reshaping of political, economic, social, and cultural norms that the Soviet regime had engineered. They would experience it now. Their encounter with the Soviet state—a by-product of the high-level intergovernmental geopolitical maneuvering that launched the Second World War—would add new layers of complexity to the already intricate history of Soviet Jewry.

Soviet archives have yet to disclose a comprehensive plan for ruling the newly conquered territories. In fact, no plan may ever have been articulated. Nevertheless, some basic lines of thinking can be inferred from the ways in which the new rulers established control over the territories and their residents.

Three features of the region confronted the Soviets as they constructed their occupation regime: the lands were poor, ethnically mixed, and subject to intense conflicts over who should rule them. All three characteristics reinforced one another. Between 1914 and 1918 (as most of the territories' adults could recall) German, Austrian, Russian, and Romanian armies had trudged back and forth over the area's length and breadth, exhausting its resources and trying the physical and mental stamina of its inhabitants. No sooner had those forces retreated, unable to control the space between them, than troops from two new states—Poland and Soviet Russia—continued the fight, contested in the north by a third new state (Lithuania) and in the south by two aborted ones (the Ukrainian and West Ukrainian National Republics).[28] In 1921 the Peace of Riga ended the fighting by partitioning the disputed lands, but not before the territories on the Polish side of the partition line (the ones the Soviets would seize in 1939) saw nearly 4.5 million hectares of agricultural land removed from cultivation, 2.5 million hectares of forest destroyed, and 4.5 million farm animals lost. Fires consumed valuable property, while the contending armies stripped factories of machinery and raw materials, destroyed railways and bridges, and confiscated rolling stock.[29] Eighteen years later, much of the region still struggled to surmount the previous war's devastation.

Ethnic politics exacerbated the struggle. The 1921 Riga line that the Soviets violated in 1939 lay well east of what Western policymakers called the "Polish ethnographic frontier." The term evoked an imaginary line east of which peasants more likely observed the Orthodox Christian or Greek Catholic rite than the Roman Catholic one and where the local vernacular was more likely written in Cyrillic than in Latin characters. Most people who cared about such things habitually identified the Roman rite and Latin letters as Polish (ignoring a concentration of Roman Catholic peasants in the area's far northeastern reaches whose vernacular, usually labeled Lithuanian, was written in the Latin alphabet but was not intelligible to speakers of any of the region's Slavic-based languages). An eastern church rite and Cyrillic letters, by contrast, invited a variety of designations, including Ukrainian, Ruthenian, Byelorussian, Russian, or simply "local" (*tutejszy* in the argot of Polish bureaucrats). The boundaries between the groups were neither incontestable nor impermeable.[30] Still they were sufficiently clear to identify approximately two thirds of Poland's residents as members of an ethnic Polish community whose needs and interests the Polish state had been created to serve. The remaining third, though citizens of Poland with equal individual civic and political rights, found themselves in the position of minority stockholders in a corporation they could never hope to direct: one beholden entirely to the majority owners, who for their part felt no obligation to consider the minority shareholders' desires in formulating company policy.[31] These non-Polish minorities were concentrated in what Poles called their "eastern borderlands" (*kresy wschodnie*)—the country's poorest and least developed region.[32] Not surprisingly, when two decades of Polish state economic programs failed to close the material gap between the borderlands and the ethnic Polish heartland to the west, many in the minority communities regarded themselves as victims of willful government discrimination.[33]

Sources are insufficient to determine how many of the region's thirteen million residents had become so disgruntled with the Polish regime by 1939 as to wish its replacement, let alone the extent to which disgruntlement was apportioned among the different ethnic groups. In fact, no one knows precisely how many people in the territories counted themselves as Poles and how many identified with a minority community. It was clear to virtually all observers, however, that disaffection was likely to be greatest among the minorities and that those groups, taken together, outnumbered Poles by a substantial margin.[34] Little wonder that the Soviets seized upon interethnic tensions as a lever for consolidating their rule and as an argument supporting their right to do so.

In some ways the Soviets' tactics marked a return to practices of the 1920s, when the state had actively fostered ethnic self-consciousness among borderland minorities.[35] At that time large parts of the territories east of the Riga partition line had been incorporated into the USSR as the Ukrainian and Byelorussian Soviet Socialist Republics.[36] The existence of theoretically sovereign units in which Ukrainian and Byelorussian served as official languages alongside Russian gestured to local inhabitants that the new Soviet Union would not be a Russian nation-state.[37] It also signaled to the Western powers that the USSR would protect the welfare of its ethnic minorities more satisfactorily than would its Polish antagonist. Now the Soviets repeated those messages. They had crossed the Riga line, they declared publicly, to assist their Ukrainian and Byelorussian "blood brothers," whose security had been jeopardized by the Polish state's collapse.[38] They offered ostensible assistance first by annexing the newly acquired territories to the existing Ukrainian and Byelorussian republics, proclaiming in effect that members of those groups need no longer feel themselves excluded from political power (while tacitly abrogating the Riga treaty at the same time).[39] That message was reinforced by the appearance of new newspapers in Ukrainian and Byelorussian and by the introduction of Ukrainian as a language of instruction at all levels of education.[40] Materially the Soviets instituted a land reform that redirected economic resources away from (mostly Polish) estate owners, state officials, and monasteries toward Ukrainian and Byelorussian peasants.[41] They also created opportunities in urban areas for unemployed peasants, offering them jobs and housing,[42] largely at the expense of several hundred thousand Poles (the dominant element in cities and towns), and perhaps many more, deported to the Soviet interior in four mass expulsions between February 1940 and June 1941.[43] Such demographic engineering helped the Soviets underscore their message that they had not usurped the annexed territories but had restored them to their rightful owners.

Still, strategists in Moscow could hardly be certain that these manipulations would turn Ukrainians and Byelorussians into enthusiastic Soviet patriots. In fact, some of their moves might well have given their ostensible beneficiaries cause to suspect long-range Soviet intentions. The deportations of Poles, for one, actually pointed to greater continuity with the violent repression of national groups that characterized the 1930s than with the affirmation of national cultures common a decade earlier.[44] The Stalinist regime that took shape after 1928 aimed first and foremost to transform the USSR into a self-sufficient socialist industrial power. To that end it worked to maximize central Soviet control over all aspects of life within its borders by all means necessary, even to the point of extreme brutality. Neither its rapprochement with Nazi Germany nor the westward expansion that resulted from it diverted it from that goal. Consequently, none of the measures the Soviets now undertook ostensibly in defense of their "blood brothers" could mask the fact that they had annexed Western Byelorussia and Western Ukraine less in order to transfer hegemony from one local ethnic group to another than to exploit the area over which they held sway. They had come as conquerors, not as liberators; they looked primarily to recast political, economic, and social relations in the annexed regions in the Soviet mold, to make those territories fully a part of the Soviet empire, and to tap their resources to the maximum in service of the regime's fundamental purpose. Potential resistors to their rule and to their plans needed to be eliminated, no matter what their ethnic background. As a corollary, though playing upon ethnoreligious sensibilities and antagonisms may have been a useful tactic in the early stages of Soviet rule, its value as a long-term strategy was limited.

Not surprisingly, then, class, vocation, and political orientation appear to have governed the fate of the territories' inhabitants under Soviet rule more than ethnicity.[45] In early 1939 the USSR had launched the Third Five-Year Plan for National Economic Development, which declared the country's "principal economic task" to be "*to overtake and surpass . . . the most highly developed capitalist countries of Europe and the United States.*"[46] Only now, the plan's architects declared, could such an ambitious goal be set because "socialist society" had already been built.[47] That success had resulted largely, to their minds, from the collectivization of Soviet agriculture—the mass removal of the peasantry from individually owned holdings to large-scale cooperative or state-owned farms—which was supposed to have made it possible to sustain a large industrial workforce. In 1939 they declared that process nearly complete everywhere within the Soviet realm.[48] The extension of Soviet rule into the newly acquired territories thus meant not so much redistribution of privately owned farms and their transfer from one ethnic group to others as the end of private proprietorship altogether and the reshaping of the countryside after the Soviet fashion. Accordingly, in January 1940, the new authorities introduced the first collective farms into the region, effectively vitiating their promised land reform.[49]

That situation augured ill for those same Byelorussian and Ukrainian peasants whose welfare the invaders professed to cultivate. During the previous decade few peasants had proved eager to relinquish their plots, tools, and livestock to the state. Consequently, collectivization had been accomplished largely through coercion, often accompanied by violence.[50] There was no reason to suspect that it could be carried out any more peacefully in the newly annexed territories than it had been anywhere else. Moreover, in 1932–1933 state repression of peasant resistance had brought catastrophic famine to Eastern Ukraine, adding fuel to what several Soviet officials described as a Ukrainian anti-Soviet, "counterrevolutionary" movement.[51] The famine had been widely reported throughout Western Ukraine (then under Polish rule) and among Ukrainian communities abroad. It had also been the subject of several Ukrainian-language memoirs and novels published during the 1930s.[52] That literature powerfully reinforced what had been since at least the late 1920s a growing conviction among Ukrainians outside the Soviet Union not only that the Soviets were enemies of the Ukrainian nation but that Ukrainian interests were best served by alliance with the most extreme anti-Soviet forces in Europe, located at the far right of the political spectrum.[53] In short, in the newly annexed territories the Soviets faced a potentially recalcitrant, even rebellious population, one unlikely to be assuaged by the sops they offered to the communities on whose behalf they claimed to have incorporated the territories into the USSR.[54]

In this complex socioeconomic and ethnopolitical matrix, the territories' 1.5 million Jews were, for the Soviets, a population of secondary importance. Generally regarded by their neighbors as a group unto themselves—not Ukrainians, Byelorussians, or Poles—they counted neither among the peoples the invaders had purportedly liberated nor among the former masters with a rival claim to rule. Neither peasants nor landlords, they did not figure centrally in the conquerors' vision of the new social order they hoped to construct. On the other hand, they were highly visible—10 percent of the region's total population, a third to half of its urban residents, the dominant force in the overwhelmingly agricultural economy's commerce, industry, and finance. That presence had long made them something of a wild card, as it were, in relations among the territories' contending ethnic groups.[55] It also meant that they possessed a notable share of the territories' liquid (not landed) wealth.[56] Consequently their new Soviet rulers could be expected to court both their assets and their endorsement.

Initially, though, it was not clear, either to policymakers or to their targets, which aspects of the Jews' existence would move the new masters to what actions. Nor was it obvious how their actions would affect the Jews newly transferred to their rule.

Since coming to power the Soviets had developed a general blueprint for dealing with Jews under their control. That blueprint continued to govern both the new rulers' perceptions of the Jews they encountered in the annexed lands and the ways in which they tried to derive maximum advantage from the Jews' presence. Nevertheless, the new context in which those Jews became part of the Soviet sphere meant that the calculus of advantage might well differ from the one that had shaped the blueprint during the previous two decades.[57]

The Soviet model deviated radically from the state policies and practices to which Jews in the annexed territories had become accustomed under Polish dominance. To begin with, it incorporated Jews into the Soviet polity not only as individual citizens but as members of a recognized "nationality"—something similar to a status many Jewish political parties and movements had long demanded of the Polish state, to no avail.[58] That recognition, in turn, entitled Jews to benefits difficult to achieve in Poland, especially state support for Jewish cultural and educational institutions. Additionally, Jews were offered unrestricted merit-based access to higher education and to the elite ranks of Soviet society. Public expressions of hostility toward Jews, including derogatory ethnic slurs, were also officially proscribed, as was invidious discrimination in employment—again in marked contrast to Poland, whose government had actively, even aggressively, prodded masses of Jews to leave the country.[59] On the other hand, in return for support and protection, Jews needed to conform to a set of state-dictated norms for public behavior. Those norms reflected the USSR's foundational ideological commitment to Marxist-Leninist doctrine as interpreted by Stalin and expressed in its latest plans for economic development. They included contempt for private ownership, exaltation of the state and its leaders, valorization of the "toiling masses," militant atheism, rejection of the Hebrew language and its literary tradition, and disavowal of ties with Jews abroad.

The Soviets imposed these norms with vigor in their new domains of Western Byelorussia and Western Ukraine. The available evidence, however, suggests that the manner of implementation varied widely from place to place.[60] Variation appears to have depended largely upon how local officials thought Jews under their control might contribute to achieving the Soviet leadership's broad economic and political aims. The evidence also points to many divergent perspectives from which Jews regarded their new situation, based largely on geographical location, socioeconomic situation, sex, political background, religious orientation, and age.

Such divergence should not be surprising, for the Jews of the former Polish borderlands were a heterogeneous socioeconomic group. According to the Polish census of 1931 (the last statistical measure before the Soviet conquest) more than 70 percent of the region's "occupationally active" Jews earned their livelihoods in commerce or industry, against less than 7 percent who sustained themselves by working the land.[61] Those figures revealed a social structure profoundly different from that of the predominantly agricultural non-Jewish population.[62] Yet they also masked a wide range of income sources and levels. A majority (56 percent) of the occupationally active were classified as self-employed or as "entrepreneurs," while 23 percent earned wages or salaries, and nearly as many were unemployed.[63] Fewer than 10 percent of the self-employed operated businesses that employed other workers.[64] The rest sold goods or services individually; most were small shopkeepers, traders in the local market, or independent artisans. By some measures they earned a bit less on average than their non-Jewish neighbors.[65] For many, economic distress became more acute over the following decade; by 1937 as many as 40 percent of Jewish families in some parts of the borderlands were requesting financial assistance from their local Jewish communities.[66] On the other hand, income inequality among Jews was conspicuous: a mere two hundred families accounted for more than 5 percent of all Jews' earnings.[67] Those families included owners of some of the largest industrial enterprises and commercial houses in the annexed territories.[68]

Jewish-owned big businesses appear to have caught the attention of Soviet officials from the outset, for their assets were of clear immediate value. Not surprisingly, their owners were among the first Jews both to lose their property to the Soviet state and to feel its repressive sting.[69] In Białystok—where in the year before the outbreak of war 110 textile mills, nearly all Jewish-owned, produced goods valued at 40 million Polish złoty (about $7.5 million at the time, more than $135 million in 2018), 20 percent for export[70]—the first weeks of Soviet control brought nighttime seizures of plants and homes belonging to large factory owners and merchants. Some of the erstwhile proprietors were left to run their former concerns under state supervision; others found themselves subject to police surveillance, their freedom of movement limited, the threat of arrest as "class enemies" ever present.[71] A similar fate befell owners of the oil fields and petroleum refineries in the East Galician towns of Drohobycz and Borysław, of whom Jews comprised the lion's share.[72] Soviet economic planners now counted oil extracted from those wells toward the Third Five-Year Plan's ambitious goals for petroleum production.[73] In Równe, the largest city in Volhynia and a major transportation hub, the Soviets moved first against the warehouses of wealthy wholesale merchants, mostly Jews, whose inventories were shipped eastward to mitigate the chronic shortages of consumer goods that were a regular feature of the Soviet economy.[74] In all these places Soviet officials evidently sought first to commandeer Jewish-owned assets and to transfer them eastward in service of the regime's overall economic plan.

These early assaults on large-scale manufacturers and merchants, however, affected only a relatively small number of Jews in places where significant industry was present. The far greater number of Jewish small business operators, spread over nearly six hundred cities, towns, and villages throughout the new territories, appear often to have been of less immediate concern to Soviet authorities. In some places local officials shut down retail stores and artisan workshops by force and confiscated their stocks of goods and tools, but elsewhere they waited for the shops to wither away gradually.[75] Either way, over the winter of 1940 many thousands of independent Jewish shopkeepers, grocers, haberdashers, bakers, butchers, tailors, cobblers, furriers, and other small-time merchants and craftsmen who for decades had comprised the most visible denizens of the local marketplaces that punctuated the former Polish countryside found that they could no longer maintain their independence. Even where direct coercion was absent these retailers and artisans were done in by the inexorable encroachment of the Soviet system upon the economic relations that had hitherto enabled their livelihoods. The goods they sold and the raw materials from which they fashioned their wares had been supplied in considerable measure by the same large manufacturers and wholesalers whose production schedules and distribution networks the Soviet authorities now controlled. The authorities had little interest in sustaining the dominant Jewish occupations, for those occupations fit neither with the Soviets' grand ideological vision nor with their more immediate economic strategy.[76] Consequently, Jewish-owned small businesses could only exhaust their existing inventories, with no hope of restocking their shelves. When those inventories vanished, businesses closed.[77]

Additional factors hastened their liquidation. In the immediate aftermath of the conquest, Red Army soldiers, flush with ready cash from three months' advance pay, exploited the relative abundance of consumer items in the territories to stock up on products unavailable closer to home, creating a run on stores.[78] Increased demand for dwindling supplies brought a temporary spike in prices, inviting the regime to institute price controls and to tax proceeds from sales at confiscatory rates.[79] To increase the purchasing power of soldiers, officials, and other Soviet citizens who came to Western Byelorussia and Western Ukraine from farther east, the Soviet authorities proclaimed the ruble legal tender. Though officially the Soviet currency had traded at virtual parity with the Polish złoty since the late 1930s, in fact the złoty had bought considerably more in prewar Poland than had the ruble in the USSR.[80] Effectively, then, residents of the incorporated territories were compelled to sell their merchandise to bearers of Soviet currency at a considerable discount. In late December 1939 the Polish currency was eliminated altogether, wiping out the savings of many small business owners and forcing them into ranks of the proletariat.[81]

Still, the consequences of these practices were not quite as universally catastrophic as they might have been under a different regime. Fortunately for the newly declassed proprietors, the Soviet Union staked its claim to the superiority of its economic system upon its ability to provide gainful employment for all workers. Soviet economic planners were also keen to increase production in the new territories, both to foster the Five-Year Plan and to supply the military and civilian personnel sent to rule them. As a result, the state often preferred to reorganize, combine, and even expand bankrupt businesses instead of closing them, engaging some of their former owners as salaried managers and creating new jobs for once-independent shopkeepers and tradesmen looking for work.[82] Additional opportunities came from expanded state investment in the region's infrastructure and industrial development, which included vocational training courses for one-time retailers hoping to refashion themselves into skilled laborers or factory administrators.[83] Moreover, like most residents of the annexed regions, Jews were generally permitted, sometimes even encouraged, to take jobs within the prewar boundaries of the USSR, especially in industrial areas like the Donets Basin.[84] Alternatively, artisans could continue to ply their trades by contributing their tools and machines to one of the dozens of craft-based collectives (*arteli*) that supplied consumer goods and services in larger and smaller towns.[85] Public administration was another promising field, as the Soviets replaced the erstwhile Polish civil service, from which Jews had been largely excluded, with one in which Jewishness proved no barrier, at least in the lower ranks.[86] In short, most of the Jews who had lost their former sources of livelihood in the new socialist economy found new ones. Even many who had been unemployed or living close to subsistence could now count upon a regular income.

Assurance of a job, however, did not always guarantee what jobholders considered adequate compensation. Contemporary letters from Jews, along with later memoirs and testimonies, often recount severe difficulties making ends meet.[87] Official prices of basic items were high compared to most wages; in many places an average employee's monthly salary was quickly consumed by rent and a minimal diet, with little to spare for clothing or shoes, let alone rudimentary items for daily activities.[88] Additionally, supply at official prices in state-owned stores was spotty—a consequence of the same regime-instigated practices that emptied Jewish businesses of their stocks. Long lines for a daily-changing inventory of available products became commonplace, as did hoarding and a market for contraband, where demand could be met at prices well above official levels.[89] Housing also became an increasingly scarce commodity, in part because the new regime was administered largely by thousands of veteran Soviet bureaucrats and officers—commonly labeled *vostochniki* ("easterners") by locals, as distinguished from indigenous *zapadniki* ("westerners")—who required suitable accommodation. Jews were often forced to share living space with Soviet officials; sometimes they were even evicted from their dwellings on false pretenses to make room for *vostochniki* who coveted their homes.[90] Many Jews thus blamed the Soviets for making their lives more difficult. On the other hand, state subsidies for housing, electricity, and running water, together with free medical care and discounts for members of *arteli*, offset the cost of living and improved conditions for some.[91] Women sometimes felt compelled to join the workforce in order to help support their families, noting that the Soviet doctrine that "anyone who does not work does not eat" did not apply only to men.[92]

On balance, these manifold changes in their economic lives and material circumstances brought satisfaction to some Jews, discontent to others. Most, evidently, learned over time to manage under the new system, even if grudgingly.[93] For the many who had lived at or below subsistence level under Polish rule, as well as for many young people whose chances of finding gainful employment in the prewar Polish labor market had appeared bleak, the new Soviet economic regime relieved much anxiety for the future. For those who had lost their businesses and been forced into the ranks of the proletariat, by contrast, Soviet rule was widely associated with diminished well-being and loss of control over their lives. One contemporary observer estimated the first group, "for whom a piece of dry bread every day is an improvement," at 30 to 35 percent of the Jewish population of the annexed territories. The remainder, he ventured, were likely to suffer, while the benefit to their poorer fellow Jews would probably diminish over time:

> 60–65 percent of Jews [in the prewar borderlands] . . . had both bread and butter, and often a piece of meat and once a year a pair of shoes or a suit of

> clothes. That is on average. 10–15 percent had more than their fill to eat, more than one pair of shoes, more than one suit of clothes a year. It would not have bothered me . . . had [the government] taken from the rich and given to the poor. The unfortunate thing about Soviet Russia, though, is that it does a splendid job carrying out the first part of that formula and an awful one . . . with the second.[94]

The observer's comment impugned the Soviet regime in general, not its attitude toward Jews as such. Indeed, those Jews in the annexed regions who found themselves worse off economically under Soviet rule suffered for the most part more on account of their occupation and social position than in consequence of their ethnoreligious identity. To the extent that they clashed with Soviet authorities *as Jews*, they did so outside of their workaday lives.

Clash was imminent, for example, for the one third or more of the region's Jewish population who found meaning in traditional religious observance.[95] The regime confronted all religious organizations aggressively and stigmatized most public religious expression, whether Christian, Jewish, or Muslim.[96] The Yiddish-language press, now entirely government controlled, conveyed that stigma to Jews throughout the new territories, especially before Jewish holidays.[97] So, too, did the state-owned enterprises that employed most Jews, whose work schedules generally made it impossible to refrain from labor on the Sabbath and festivals.[98]

Yet although religious behavior was vocally discouraged and tangibly encumbered, it was not prohibited altogether. Officially the Soviet state considered religious belief a private matter and professed to allow its individual expression as long as it involved no political activity.[99] Among Jews the Soviets appear to have aimed less at spreading ideologically inspired defiance of religious norms than at exploiting Jewish piety for pecuniary gain. Although many synagogues were forcibly converted to other uses, some continued to exist, almost always in return for payment of heavy taxes upon the property they occupied and upon the remuneration their congregations paid rabbis.[100] Moreover, whereas under Polish rule synagogues had been operated by state-recognized Jewish religious communities, now (somewhat incongruously in the Soviet system) they could exist only as private bodies maintained voluntarily by their own members. The former communities (which, as erstwhile public corporations, had owned considerable property, including cemeteries, ritual baths, study houses, social halls, and their own headquarters) were systematically liquidated and their assets seized.[101]

Jews for whom religious observance was important appear to have found ways to cope with the new conditions that governed it. Although private kosher slaughterhouses could not operate legally, former ritual slaughterers were often hired in state-owned abattoirs, where they were able, in some places at least, to slaughter and prepare a small quantity of meat according to Jewish law.[102] Similarly, communal bakeries for Passover *matsot* were closed, but Jews sometimes managed to persuade local millers to produce kosher flour, with rabbis supervising production and baking, often done in private homes.[103] Jews did the same with citrus growers in the Caucasus, who supplied etrogim for the Sukkot holiday.[104] Attendees at Jewish burials in newly nationalized cemeteries could recite traditional funeral prayers as before, although graveside services were often shortened.[105] Rabbis continued to oversee ritual circumcision and Jewish marriage ceremonies, which remained legal.[106] They also advised Jews how to say essential prayers on Jewish holidays even when they were required to work.[107] Hasidic *rebbes* sometimes lowered their profiles and moved the seats of their courts for fear of police repression, but their followers continued to seek their counsel and aid when possible.[108]

It is difficult to ascertain how many Jews used such adjustments to retain earlier patterns of religious practice and how many became less observant in response to impediments under the new regime. According to some sources, older people made up most of the first category, younger ones the second.[109] Others, by contrast, point to sustained or even increased synagogue attendance across different age groups.[110] Some Jews evidently felt constrained to compromise their religious convictions; others reported no such pressure.[111] Students and teachers from some of the great Talmudic academies (*yeshivot*) in the annexed territories appear to have found the antireligious atmosphere so demoralizing that they fled Soviet territory, hoping to reconstitute their schools elsewhere.[112] Others continued to operate, dispersed, or went underground.[113] On the whole, Jewish religious behavior appears to have varied significantly from place to place along lines that are not easily explained.

Nevertheless, synagogues in general may well have witnessed increased activity, not only on holy days but throughout the week, for once other Jewish communal bodies were dismantled, they became the primary location where Jews gathered licitly. The Soviets eliminated not only all other *religious* institutions that the official Jewish communities had managed under Polish rule but also the imposing network of voluntary economic, social, cultural, and educational organizations that had enabled those of the region's Jews who wished to do so to live within a self-contained Jewish society.[114] The broad functions those organizations had performed—caring for the sick, assisting the poor, housing orphans, teaching children, training youth for employment, providing opportunities for recreation—were now taken over by state institutions, which served Jews and non-Jews alike. In those institutions Jews came together with their Polish, Byelorussian, and Ukrainian neighbors to a far greater degree than they had before. Socializing with other Jews or discussing matters of communal concern thus happened most easily in synagogues, aiding (perhaps unwittingly) their function as the hub of Jewish *social* life.

Yet though synagogues were licit, they were not necessarily safe. In some places Soviet security forces, fearing that Jewish houses of worship were liable to become foci for "anti-Soviet activity," placed them under surveillance. A Jew from Drohobycz reported, for example, that his son-in-law, who served as rabbi of the town's central synagogue, was regularly summoned to local NKVD headquarters, where officers demanded information on political activity by worshipers, sometimes under threat of execution.[115] Rabbi Aharon Rokeah, leader of the Hasidic dynasty of Belz, felt compelled to move his court several times during the summer of 1940 and to limit the number of followers who could gather there, mainly in response to police pressure.[116] Pressure appears to have increased beginning in February 1941, following the establishment of a new state undercover investigative agency, the People's Commissariat for State Security (*Narodnyi Komissariat Gosudarstvennoi Bezopasnosti*—NKGB). Agents from this organization infiltrated synagogues in search of evidence that, in the words of a May 1941 NKGB report from the venerable Jewish community of Pińsk, "the Jewish clergy and mainly yeshiva students" had formed a subversive movement threatening Soviet authority:

> Highlighting the interests of the Jewish religion, the representatives of the clerical counterrevolutionary underground have launched active anti-Soviet activity

> among the backward strata of the Jewish population and especially among the youth, forming a bloc in support of their hostile aims with other counterrevolutionary nationalist elements and clerical counterrevolutionary formations. Presenting themselves as defenders of the Jewish religion and of the interests of the Jewish people . . . , the clericalists are conducting an uncompromising struggle with the Soviet authorities and are expressing harmful attitudes to the effect that Jews [in the USSR] have been ruined. The clericalists are working actively against the Soviet authorities, spreading libels against the party, against the Soviet government, and against the living conditions of the workers under Soviet rule . . . , while summoning the backward strata of the Jewish people to a fight against the Soviet authority.[117]

The report quoted statements from local rabbis casting doubt upon the beneficence of the Soviet regime, its staying power, and its ability to improve the lives of the people it governed. It indicated that it had opened files on those Jewish leaders in order to build criminal cases against them. However, at the time the report was filed all of the persons of interest named in it remained free. It cannot be known whether the investigations would have led to any eventual concrete action: one month after the report was composed, invading German forces ousted the Soviets from Pińsk, confronting the town's Jews with a threat of an altogether different order.

Ironically, the activities the report described point to another reason why synagogues may have grown in importance for religious and nonreligious Jews alike. There were, to be sure, other physical and virtual spaces, including schools, theaters, and newspapers, where Jews could come together as Jews. But synagogues ostensibly concerned themselves only with private matters. Hence they did not demand explicit state approval to exist. Nor was the state inclined to operate them directly. That is why the authorities needed undercover agents to keep track of doings they could not otherwise check. By contrast, the Soviets regarded educational and cultural institutions as powerful public instruments for ideological indoctrination and political socialization. Hence they actively and openly supervised and regulated the operation of those bodies to a degree never attempted with synagogues. Controlling school curricula, literary and artistic production, and information about current affairs were, to their minds, far more important than preventing religious practice in their ongoing effort to reconcile a critical mass of their subjects to the Soviet system.

In that context the Yiddish language offered a vehicle for winning Jewish hearts and minds. Schools became a key venue for demonstrating ostensible official support for the lingua franca of east European Jewry and, by extension, recognition of Jews as a legitimate national minority. In contrast to Poland, where parents wishing to teach their children in that language could do so only at their own expense,[118] the 1936 Constitution of the USSR guaranteed all Soviet citizens the right "to instruction in [tuition-free public] schools using their native language."[119] Practically, this provision meant that the state would establish and operate schools with a particular language of instruction wherever a sufficient number of parents demanded them. Accordingly, schooling in Yiddish was widely available in the annexed territories' towns and cities, where Jews tended to live in concentrated Jewish neighborhoods. Many more Jewish children were taught in that language than had been under Polish rule.[120]

The regime also offered encouragement to dozens of Yiddish-language writers and theater artists in the annexed territories. These cultural figures—among them some of the best-known names in Polish Jewry—were invited to apply for membership in the Byelorussian and Ukrainian Writers' Unions. Those admitted received a monthly stipend of between 200 and 600 rubles, consistent with the earnings of skilled workers and professionals, with additional payment for pieces accepted for publication.[121] During the year and a half following the Soviet conquest, state publishing houses issued fourteen new works written in Yiddish by writers from Western Byelorussia and Western Ukraine, with print runs twice the size afforded established Soviet Yiddish writers.[122] Actors, directors, and set designers found work in state-sponsored Yiddish theaters in Białystok, Lwów, and Tarnopol, as well as with smaller troupes in Przemyśl, Drohobycz, and other Western Ukrainian towns.[123] Renowned Jewish performers and literati from Poland who had fled eastward to escape German rule, including actress Ida Kamińska, playwright and critic Alter Kacyzne, and comedians Szymon Dzigan and Izrael Szumacher, now featured prominently in Soviet Jewish theatrical life.[124] A chair in Yiddish was established at Wilno University.[125]

Yet over time it became evident to many Jews that such gestures toward their cultural sensibilities actually served as a smokescreen for propaganda among the Jewish population. In truth Yiddish under Soviet rule proved less a vehicle for free expression of those sensibilities than a means for the authorities to inculcate the state's new norms. Yiddish-language schools taught a state-imposed curriculum that did not differ significantly from the one used in schools employing Ukrainian, Byelorussian, Polish, or Russian. They were not permitted to teach Jewish history and religion or Hebrew language and literature. Nor were they allowed to mark the Sabbath or Jewish festivals. Jewish schools that under Polish rule had employed Hebrew as the language of instruction, along with schools affiliated with Jewish religious movements—both of which had enrolled many more children than Yiddish-language schools in the 1930s[126]—were forced to adopt the new general program of study.[127] A number of students in such schools later recalled with shock not only how language and curriculum changed overnight but how their teachers and headmasters, fearing to confront the new regime, made themselves into mouthpieces for the official line.[128] Educators evidently understood that challenging the regime over the instruction of youth was liable to endanger both them and their pupils.[129]

Perhaps these facts explain why Yiddish-language schools in Western Byelorussia and Western Ukraine lost enrollment over time.[130] For Jewish parents, the only added value such schools could offer was as vehicles for transmitting Jewish culture; absent instruction in that culture, they gave parents little reason to prefer them over schools that taught in one of the local languages. Indeed, for Jews who hoped to take advantage of the opportunities for upward mobility that the Soviet regime allowed, an education in Yiddish had notable disadvantages. Admission to higher education demanded command of Russian at a level few young people raised in independent Poland possessed. Jobs in public administration required both Russian and Ukrainian or Byelorussian, as did skilled positions in industry. Consequently, parents in many nominally Jewish schools, especially those that had formerly taught in Hebrew, eventually requested that at least some instruction be carried out in a local non-Jewish language. Authorities were generally happy to oblige.[131]

Similar resignation to what common argot dubbed "Soviet reality" appeared among purveyors of the Yiddish word in print and on stage. They discovered that the regime was no more committed to broad freedom of artistic expression in that language than in any other. In fact, cultural activity in Yiddish was constrained in many ways. Acceptance into a writers' union turned out to involve close inspection of the applicant's life and family history, as revealed in a questionnaire, a personal interview with a government functionary, and sometimes even a public hearing.[132] Admission was selective: of 226 applicants in Białystok during the first two months of Soviet rule, only 66 were permitted legally to ply their craft.[133] Common wisdom among writers and artists held any hint of a "bourgeois" past or of noncommunist political activity in Poland to be automatic disqualifiers.[134] Nor did union membership guarantee publication or production; state censors alone determined what cultural products saw the light of day. Journalists actually found fewer opportunities to earn a living from writing, with but a single Yiddish-language newspaper, *Bialystoker shtern*, serving the new territories for most of the period of Soviet rule.[135] Yiddish theater companies were mostly allowed to produce translations of European plays chosen for what government supervisors took to be their positive message for Soviet citizens.[136] Thus it became clear in Yiddish literary and theatrical circles that ideological and moral pliability were the first requirements for those who wished to continue to write or perform. Cabaret humorist Szymon Dzigan even recalled an explicit warning from a state supervisor: "Our reality compels us to do many things. Understand this, and you will live longer."[137]

The official did not specify what those things were, but his admonition left no doubt that failure to recognize them could bear dire consequences. Dzigan and his colleagues knew well the fate of Moshe Kulbak and Izi Kharik, two of the USSR's most celebrated Yiddish poets, who in 1937 ran suddenly afoul of the authorities and perished in Stalin's purges.[138] Under such a formidable shadow many Jewish artists appear to have had difficulty finding their bearing. Actress Sheyne-Miriam Broderzon noted in retrospect, "for people who didn't live in the Soviet Union at the time it is hard to comprehend . . . the attitude toward Jewish writers and culture producers . . . , [which] changed from day to day."[139] Broderzon's husband, poet and theatrical entrepreneur Moshe Broderzon, warned that efforts to stay on the right side of the regime bred opportunities for hacks who made a "wordhive" (*shraybarnie*) of *Bialystoker shtern* and "informed openly and shamelessly ... upon real writers."[140] According to Sheyne-Miriam, "people were afraid to speak [their minds] even to their closest friends"; there was no one, she complained, "with whom I could share my ... thoughts."[141]

Some artists found themselves unable to function in such a situation. These abandoned writing and performing for what one of them, journalist Jacob Kahan, called "quiet, nonpolitical jobs in the civil service."[142] Others, like the poet Maurycy Szymel, whose work had appeared earlier in publications with a bourgeois Zionist bent, underwent a conversion sufficient to permit him a platform in the Kiev-based Yiddish journal *Sovetishe literatur*.[143] Another Lwów-based poet, Rachel Korn, was actually appointed to the municipal *soviet* despite her background as the child of landowners and her marriage to a labor Zionist.[144] So, too, was Ida Kamińska, whose international stature made her an attractive figure for the regime to showcase and allowed her to reach a satisfactory modus vivendi with a succession of state supervisors.[145] But most who were not already committed communists struggled to navigate among the formidable conflicting demands of art, hunger, state, conscience, and peer relations. Their artistic sensibilities compelled them to produce art; their need to feed and clothe themselves and their families impelled them to seek compensation for their product. They could do so, however, only insofar as the state believed their output advanced its purposes.

Yet what the state believed in that regard appears to have changed from moment to moment. Novelist Moshe Grossman tried to navigate what he called the "zigzags" of Soviet demands as a writer for *Bialystoker shtern*, but by spring 1940, after successive rejection of pieces he thought ideologically sound, he gave up his position and his salary, sending his wife and child to live with a relative in a "hovel" (*alker-shtibl*) in the provincial town of Baranowicze.[146] Dzigan and Szumacher, along with Moshe Broderzon, their longtime mentor, found that they could perform comedy routines skewering capitalist failures in Poland, Britain, France, and the United States as long as they avoided mentioning Germany and "took the Soviet people very seriously." Evidently they could tolerate the obligatory encomium to Stalin at the end of their act as long as they could perform material "written with a skilled pen."[147] Still, they could not escape the threats of denunciation and sudden official displeasure, and they took care to adjust their behavior accordingly.[148] Anyone in power, they feared, might one day interpret the very act of writing or performing in Yiddish as an expression of Jewish "nationalism"—an offense for which "Soviet reality" demanded grievous punishment.

Actually Jewish nationalism extended well beyond the relatively small circle of Yiddish literati. The multiethnic character of the newly acquired territories and the contest among its various groups for hegemony had historically encouraged the region's Jews to assert particular group interests instead of identifying with any larger ethnic or civic community. As a result, the former Polish *kresy* had been for decades a primary breeding ground for two mass political movements, the Bund and Zionism, both of which asserted as first principles that Jews constituted a nation and were entitled as such to determine their own political future.[149] Together the two movements arguably claimed the loyalties of a plurality, perhaps even a majority, of the region's Jews.[150] Bundists—members of the General Federation (*Bund*) of Jewish Workers in Poland—imagined that future as an autonomous constituent of a multinational socialist state in eastern Europe. Zionists envisioned the eventual concentration of all the world's Jews in a "home in Palestine secured by public law." They differed among themselves, however, over the nature of the state and society to be established there: some favored capitalist liberal democracy, others various shades of socialism, still others a rabbinic theocracy.[151] But Bundists and Zionists alike claimed a measure of collective Jewish self-direction that Soviet political theory did not allow.[152] The Soviets needed to disengage their newly acquired Jews from that claim.

They did so by turning the state's repressive power against the leadership of both movements. The Bund was decapitated swiftly: Soviet police seized its two senior figures, Henryk Erlich and Wiktor Alter, even before the Red Army had completed military operations in eastern Poland.[153] By December 1939 virtually all key members of Bund local committees in the major towns of the annexed territories sat in Soviet jails.[154] Zionists, by contrast, were targeted with less urgency and less thoroughness, perhaps because, whereas the Bund had consistently opposed the Comintern and the USSR, some socialist Zionist parties (then the dominant force in the movement) had once flirted with the possibility of establishing a Soviet-style regime in Palestine and affiliating with the world communist movement.[155] Nevertheless, several prominent Zionists were arrested or banished from their homes, and Zionist groups, even the most pro-Soviet, were forced underground.[156] By late 1940, Zionist leaders who had escaped Poland in the early days of the German occupation noted an urgent need to "rescue . . . our people in the Russian occupation zone" from imminent danger.[157]

For neither movement, however, do repressions appear to have extended below the top leadership levels: rank-and-file members were for the most part not molested for their political affiliation.[158] To be sure, the Soviets limited the freedom of many ordinary Zionists and Bundists, along with Jews of virtually every political and religious affiliation and social class, during their twenty-one-month hegemony in Poland's former eastern territories. But most of those encumbered Jews were not political targets. The Soviets moved against them less in order to consolidate their power, to extract wealth, or to impose their norms—as they had in the economic, religious, cultural, and political realms—than to solve an acute problem created by their newfound friendship with Nazi Germany.

The German forces that invaded Poland in September 1939 attacked civilians as well as soldiers. Jews were a notable target. Some evidence suggests that the violence had a strategic aim—to remove Jews from large swaths of Polish territory as a prelude to German settlement.[159] Strategic or gratuitous, it prompted mass Jewish flight. Some took to the roads after experiencing German brutality firsthand, others hoping to avoid it.[160] Flight increased after 7 September, when Poland's government left Warsaw for Romania and Polish radio advised military-aged men to gather east of the Bug and San rivers, where the Polish Army hoped to regroup.[161] It continued apace after Soviet troops entered the fray ten days later. By December somewhere between 145,000 and 300,000 Polish Jews whose homes were elsewhere had taken refuge in lands under Soviet control.[162]

For several weeks the Soviets allowed refugees into those lands virtually unimpeded. From late October, however, with solidification of the new German-Soviet frontier, they blocked border crossings, forcing Jews fleeing the Germans to enter illegally.[163] Refugees, it turned out, complicated their plans for exploiting the new territories. Usually arriving without money or possessions, following an extended and often torturous journey,[164] they drew away resources the new rulers would surely rather have directed toward broader policy aims.[165] Housing needs were especially pressing. Białystok, a primary destination, counted thirty-three thousand refugees in November 1939, increasing the total municipal population by more than a third and the Jewish population by four fifths.[166] Such growth not only exceeded available residential space; it bred clashes with *vostochniki*, whose needs trumped those of recently arrived foreigners.[167] The refugee influx thus presented the new Soviet administration with some of its severest challenges in the early months of its rule.[168]

Soviet authorities worked along multiple fronts to mitigate difficulties. In some places local officials established municipal aid committees, which offered palliative relief to refugees while simultaneously supervising their movement.[169] Some encouraged refugees to work wherever they could find employment, even arranging for railroads to transport them gratis in search of jobs.[170] From late October 1939 state spokesmen urged refugees to apply for work elsewhere in the USSR.[171] Yet although the seeming offer of, as one applicant put it, "a normal life and an end to homelessness" appears to have appealed to many,[172] not enough took it up to alleviate the refugee burden in the state's eyes.[173] Not surprisingly, the Soviets eventually concluded that the flow of refugees into the country had to be stopped.

Doing so, however, strained relations with Germany, which hoped to extrude as many Jews as possible from its realm and eyed Soviet territory as a potential address.[174] Soviet archives suggest that possibilities for moving large numbers of Jews from Poland to the USSR may have been discussed during talks over the Boundary and Friendship Treaty of 28 September 1939.[175] That agreement included a "confidential protocol" stipulating cooperation between the two states in transferring "persons of German descent" from the Soviet to the German zone and "persons of Ukrainian or Byelorussian descent" in the opposite direction.[176] German negotiators appear to have believed that the latter groups included Jews. Accordingly, Germany resisted when, from November, Soviet soldiers, enforcing the newly closed border, began returning Jewish refugees to German-held territory.[177] Sometimes both sides used armed force to push Jews in the desired direction. Such confrontations were dangerous for both parties, inviting German and Soviet troops to fire upon one another.[178] In response, the two governments created a joint commission to supervise population transfers, but the commission failed to settle the dispute.[179] When German officials formally requested it in February 1940 to "organize resettlement of the Jewish population . . . to Birobidzhan and to Western Ukraine," the Soviets refused.[180] The standoff demanded resolution.

Germany moved to defuse the confrontation by suspending plans for mass extrusion to the USSR in favor of alternate destinations.[181] The Soviets, realizing they could not rid themselves of Jewish refugees, decided to send them far away. To justify deporting large numbers and to identify who should stay or go, they devised an elaborate set of ruses, widely dubbed "passportization."[182]

Passportization aimed ostensibly to clarify the refugees' legal status. On 29 November 1939 the Presidium of the Supreme Soviet in Moscow had granted Soviet citizenship to everyone legally present in the conquered former Polish territories on the day of their formal incorporation into the Ukrainian or Byelorussian Soviet Socialist Republics.[183] The decree applied to all ethnic groups. It also encompassed refugees who had entered the territories before the establishment of the joint German-Soviet commission on population transfer in mid-November.[184] However, the new Soviet citizens had not been required to exchange their old Polish identity documents for Soviet ones (passports).[185] Only in February 1940, after refusing the German request to admit more refugees, did Soviet officials announce the *possibility* (not the requirement) of obtaining Soviet papers, making it appear that accepting Soviet citizenship was optional.[186] They also intimated that refugees not wishing to become Soviet citizens could apply to return to their former homes in Poland, now under German control.[187] Both suggestions were disingenuous: the Soviets could not give permission to enter the German zone, while refusing a passport was tantamount to lèse-majesté. But creating the illusion of choice gave Soviet authorities a basis for deciding the fate of each refugee. Those who asked to leave the USSR were marked for deportation, while those choosing a passport were required to submit extensive biographical details, providing the NKVD, which supervised the passportization process, with valuable data for surveillance.[188]

Documents brought to light after 1992 show that at least some Soviet bureaucrats expected many refugees to apply to return to German-controlled territory, hinting that passportization may have been designed initially to ferret out an "alien element" seemingly unfit for Soviet citizenship.[189] Actual numbers may have been even greater than anticipated. Precise figures are not known, but virtually all witnesses reported that more than half of the Jews who had once sought sanctuary in Soviet-held lands now preferred the German zone.[190] The phenomenon must have sorely embarrassed the Soviets. The USSR had justified its annexation of the former Polish borderlands by claiming that the annexed territories' non-Polish residents would prefer Soviet to Polish (or German) rule. The movement of refugees into its territories could only have strengthened its claim. Hence the government had offered them terms essentially equal to those governing all Soviet citizens. Yet within months of entry masses of Jews appeared to have turned their backs upon the Soviet enterprise in favor of a Nazi regime that marked them for violent persecution. Not only did their choice seem to lack gratitude; it was easily interpreted as downright hostile. No wonder one senior Soviet official pronounced himself "pained" by the "enormous queues" he saw waiting to sign up for "return to Polish territory."[191]

That so many would prefer German to Soviet rule also left other Jews, fellow refugees included, incredulous. Tania Fuks, a journalist from Łódź who fled to Lwów in 1939, reported asking Jews in repatriation lines, "Have you thought about how you will look in a yellow patch?" referring to the special mark Jews in German-occupied Poland had been obligated to wear since December 1939.[192] Still, she recalled, "people had their reasons":

> Most of the refugees . . . were men who fled during the first days of the war, leaving wives and children behind. They remembered their homes as they had left them: warm, clean, intact. Here, by contrast, they found themselves in oppressive conditions, filth and hunger. Most had no livelihood, or their livelihood was inadequate. Everyone had an excuse: I left my parents there, my wife and children; at least there I will have a roof over my head, a shirt on my back. No one imagined that the home "there" was no longer a home.[193]

Other observers shared Fuks's impression,[194] but it captured only part of the story. True, family considerations did play a central role in decisions about moving into and out of the Soviet zone. In the days following the September 1939 German invasion, men of military age were called to join Polish army units forming in the east. Those who heeded the call expected to return home once fighting ended; instead, by late September, they found themselves under Soviet control, separated from their families against their will. Even those who fled later to Soviet-held areas were often men convinced that the Nazis posed a danger only to them, not to women or children. Many of these male refugees evidently hoped to send for their families once they were safely settled, but difficulties finding work and housing rendered them unable to do so before borders were closed. Nevertheless, many families crossed the border together, sometimes to be separated only after entering the Soviet zone.[195] Many joined extended family already living in the annexed territories. Some, including women, fled only after their homes had been destroyed.[196] Yet even among families and women, some registered to return to the German side.[197] They were evidently impelled by the thought that, as Moshe Grossman put it, "accepting Soviet citizenship meant staying here [in the USSR] forever."[198] Indeed, Soviet citizens were enjoined from leaving the USSR without state permission. Many refugees, men and women alike, undoubtedly believed that as long as they could live and work on Soviet soil without carrying Soviet identity documents, their sojourn was temporary, and they could remain for as long as they wished. That belief appears often to have been coupled with an expectation (derived, perhaps, from analogy to the First World War) that Germany would eventually be defeated. Once Germany no longer occupied Poland, refugees anticipated being able to determine for themselves where they would continue their lives. Passportization, with its requirement to choose between Soviet citizenship and return to German-controlled territory, rendered that belief untenable. Future options were no longer open; carrying Soviet papers meant a permanence many refugees were not ready to accept.[199] Although some Jews may have joked that under the Nazis "we had been sentenced to death, but now [under the Soviets] our sentence has been commuted—to life imprisonment,"[200] many seem to have been prepared to gamble that they would outlive the would-be Nazi executioner. Imprisonment under the Soviets, by contrast, was irreversible.[201]

The gamblers learned quickly that prison was not a metaphor. In June 1940, police and NKVD agents seized some seventy thousand to seventy-eight thousand Jews, mostly refugees who had applied to travel to the German zone or had refused Soviet passports, dispatching them deep into the Soviet hinterland.[202] Technically these were not convicts but exiles, under NKVD supervision but free to move within limited range. Some were sent to "special settlements," mainly in Siberia, where heavy labor in forests and mines was compulsory. Others counted as "free exiles"; they lived in ordinary towns and villages, usually in more hospitable climes, including Central Asia, and could earn their livelihoods in any available legal manner, required only to report periodically to the local police.[203]

It seems that, virtually to a person, the deportees were convinced they had been dealt a grievous blow. Observing the flight from Warsaw in November 1939, diarist Chaim Kaplan—a Hebrew teacher and grammarian, hardly a communist—praised God for "preparing the remedy before the plague," or as he put it, "Were it not for Soviet Russia we would simply choke to death" under the German heel.[204] "The Soviets," he declared, were the sole light in a world of darkness: "[they] say, 'Come! We'll give you work. Just be with us!'" This attitude, he noted, was in sharp contrast to "America and England, the rich democracies, who closed their gates to refugees from Germany and turned a deaf ear to their heart-rending cry in their hardest hour."[205] The magnitude of such expectations could only amplify the refugees' eventual disaffection, but forced banishment to the USSR's harsh inner reaches, with no hope of release,[206] surely seemed at the time the unkindest cut of all. For a few, like film actor Zishe Katz who hanged himself after learning he would be sent away, it was a fate worse than death.[207]

Yet, as Tania Fuks observed with hindsight, "One can never know, especially in wartime, what lies ahead, for good or ill."[208] In the end, deportation turned out to be a life saver, sparing deportees nearly certain death at Nazi hands. In June 1940, however, no one could anticipate the horrors to come later under Nazi rule.

Thanks to ongoing turns in German-Soviet relations, a small proportion of refugees managed to avoid the passportization dilemma altogether, while a much larger number, along with Jews from other regions bordering the USSR, became part of the Soviet realm.

Even after the two countries collaborated in Poland's dismemberment and concluded a treaty of friendship, Soviet leaders continued to worry that Germany still coveted their land. In particular, they were concerned that the Nazis might overrun the Baltic region, placing their forces dangerously close to Leningrad. The USSR had addressed the issue in the negotiations for the

Ribbentrop-Molotov Pact, which secretly gave it a free hand in Latvia, Estonia, and Finland, and again in discussions over the Boundary and Friendship Treaty, which added Lithuania to the Soviet sphere. But it remained for them to establish their prerogatives in practice. Accordingly, once fighting in Poland approached the end, they pressed their Baltic neighbors to allow the Red Army to establish bases on their territories.[209] Estonia and Latvia gave in quickly, while Finland balked, forcing the USSR into a four-month war that exposed severe weaknesses in its military capacity. Lithuania, by contrast, found a way to turn old border disputes and competing Soviet and German interests to its advantage. Together with the USSR, Lithuania had long contested Polish sovereignty over some 32,250 square kilometers along its southeastern border, including the city it called Vilnius (Polish Wilno). When the Soviets conquered that area, Lithuania demanded that it be given control. The Ribbentrop-Molotov Pact had acknowledged "the interest of Lithuania in the Wilno area," but in return for moving Lithuania from the German to the Soviet sphere of influence, the Boundary and Friendship Treaty replaced that provision with a stipulation that it cede the Suvalkija region, along Lithuania's southwestern border, to Germany. In negotiations among the three parties, Lithuania managed not only to delay action on the German claim but to obtain some seven thousand square kilometers of the Wilno region, including the city itself, as reward for accepting twenty-five thousand Soviet troops on Lithuanian soil.[210]

Wilno's transfer was announced on 10 October 1939 and completed eighteen days later, just as the USSR was closing its border to refugees from German-occupied Poland. During that interval, and for two months thereafter, the city offered Jews an alternative to both German and Soviet rule.[211] The Wilno option proved especially attractive to those whose political, economic, or religious past exposed them to arrest or to persecution in the USSR. All told, some 14,000 to 15,000 former Polish Jews—at least 30 percent from the Soviet zone—fled to independent Lithuania, including nearly 4,000 Zionist activists, 2,600 yeshiva students and rabbis, 600 Bundists, and 100 writers, artists, actors, and musicians.[212] Though living conditions were generally harsh, most appear to have believed that their existence in Lithuania was less precarious than under the Soviets, let alone under the Nazis.[213] About four thousand Jews even managed to take advantage of Lithuania's neutrality and transportation connections to escape beyond the Nazi and Soviet realms altogether. Many traveled to the Far East via the Trans-Siberian Railway, using transit visas supplied by Japan's consul in Kaunas, Chiune Sugihara.[214]

But the Lithuanian haven was short-lived. Germany's successful spring 1940 offensives against Denmark, the Low Countries, and France intensified Soviet fears that the Nazis might soon reactivate their aggressive aims in the east.[215] Moscow's response was to create additional buffer zones, besides the former Polish *kresy*, along its western borders. In June 1940 the Soviets occupied Lithuania, Latvia, and Estonia, installing subservient governments that quickly acquiesced to incorporation into the USSR.[216] Later that month they forced Romania, which had recently made friendly gestures toward the Third Reich, to cede some fifty thousand square kilometers in Bessarabia and northern Bukovina, along the border between the two countries.[217] The Baltic and Romanian annexations brought more than nine million people under Soviet rule, including some 570,000 to 650,000 Jews.[218] These included perhaps as many as 70,000 additional Jewish refugees who fled from other parts of Romania during the second half of 1940, most of them driven out by Romanian mobs blaming them for the Soviet incursion.[219] By summer 1940 the USSR governed well over five million Jews—more than any other country, a third of world Jewry.[220]

For the most part, the Soviets took charge of their Bessarabian, Bukovinian, and Baltic Jewish subjects much as they had in the *kresy*, confiscating wealth, restructuring occupational patterns and consumption habits, discouraging religious practice, and permitting limited schooling and cultural expression in Yiddish while offering new educational opportunities and career paths and a buffer against the harshest expressions of popular antagonism. Some divergence from place to place was noticeable, the result of local officials' different applications of policy or of variations in wealth or occupational distribution. Lithuania and Latvia became home to more Yiddish-language newspapers and theaters than the more populous Western Byelorussia and Western Ukraine, while Jewish lawyers in Bukovina, who dominated the legal profession there, faced stiffer competition for admission into attorneys' guilds than they did elsewhere.[221] Most strikingly, unlike with regard to Poland, the USSR extended Soviet citizenship to all Jewish refugees who entered its territory from Romania.[222] Those discrepancies, however, do not appear to have skewed Jewish responses to Soviet rule in the erstwhile Romanian and Baltic territories; like in the former Polish lands, reactions appear to have varied according to each Jew's personal situation and vantage point.[223]

Instead, the most consequential difference between the way Jews in the 1940 additions experienced Soviet rule and the way in which Polish Jews experienced it nine months earlier reflected the different circumstances of Soviet occupation. The regime's claims to have liberated subject nationalities were far weaker than they had been in 1939.[224] Its policies and practices in the 1940 additions thus displayed no overt ethnic dimension. They had seized those territories for geostrategic reasons; as a result their actions there concentrated first upon eliminating putative security threats.[225] That focus meant that political repressions were felt more immediately by a broader range of Jewish activists and communal workers. In particular, leaders of the right-wing Zionist youth movement Betar, especially strong in the Baltics, were arrested quickly, along with prominent religious leaders.[226] By June 1941, following intelligence reports of an impending German invasion,[227] security fears prompted deportations encompassing, for the first time, Jews who were not refugees but bona fide residents of the annexed territories. During the night of 13–14 June, NKVD agents rounded up approximately twenty-two thousand local Baltic, Bessarabian, and Bukovinian Jews, dispatching them to the Soviet interior as "socially dangerous elements."[228] A week later the practice was extended to the former Polish territories, when the last of the four mass expulsions of Polish citizens likely included significant numbers of Jews.[229]

Whether even greater numbers would have been deported in subsequent weeks and months cannot be known. As with so many Soviet actions in the lands acquired since 1939, Germany brought deportations to an abrupt end.

Germany was the catalyst for numerous fateful changes in the lives of Jews under Soviet rule following its tenuous rapprochement with the USSR. The changes were most emphatic for the two million or more Jews who encountered the Soviets as a by-product of the evolving relations between Moscow and Berlin. The three million Jews who had been governed by the USSR since its inception also felt the impact of that evolution, though less directly and less obviously than did their fellow Jews in the newly acquired lands. Effects on their lives appear to have been more emotional than material. Unlike Italy or Hungary, whose increasingly close ties with Germany during the 1930s found expression in legislation reflecting the Nazi anti-Jewish Nuremberg Laws of 1935, the Soviets did not deviate from their long-standing commitment to guarantee legal and social equality for Jews, to protect their physical safety, and to suppress public expressions of hostility toward them. As a result, the trends that had marked Soviet Jewish life over the previous decade—urbanization, upward mobility, occupational diversification, linguistic assimilation, acquisition of secular education, abandonment of traditional religious norms, and entry into elite ranks in many branches of Soviet society, to name the most immediately apparent—appear to have continued apace during the twenty-one months of Soviet-German cooperation.[230] Nevertheless, the USSR's diplomatic turnabout of 1939 gave some observers at home and abroad pause to wonder whether a parallel volte-face might soon be in store for Jewish policy:

> Only a short while ago it was so clear, so definitely certain, that as long as the Soviets held power, the Jews were secure at least in their persons, their political and economic equality ironclad, their equal social status absolute. But on the day when Stalin concluded his agreement with the greatest enemy of the Jewish people . . . the situation of Soviet Jews was shaken. True, there are no explicit signs of change in how the authorities or the Communist Party relate to Jews, but the security and confidence that once prevailed has vanished like smoke, as if a worm has begun to gnaw away at . . . the former calm. One does not need to have a Jewish nose . . . to sense that something has happened or is about to happen in Soviet Russia. . . . An agreement with Hitler, especially an agreement that has held now for more than a year and that requires expressions of sympathy and spiritual kinship, must change something. . . . One hopes that the clouds will roll away and the storm will pass. But the uneasiness that has overtaken Jews throughout the world and that is eating at the soul of Soviet Jewry has, sadly, a solid basis in fact.[231]

Before the German invasion, most of what was feared did not happen. Although commentators have detected hints of Nazi influence upon Soviet behavior toward Jews from mid-1939, beginning with Stalin and Molotov's reported resolution to rid the Foreign Ministry of Jews,[232] several facts suggest that no purge took place. Shortly after taking office Molotov appointed a Jew as his deputy—Solomon Lozovskii, the senior member of the Central Committee of the Communist Party of the Soviet Union—and another Jew, Konstantin Umanskii, as ambassador to the United States. Jews also continued to serve in and to be appointed to other key state, party, diplomatic, and military positions. Among them were Lev Mekhlis, deputy minister of defense and state controller; Semen Ginzburg, minister of construction; Semen Dukelskii, minister of the navy; Ivan Maiskii, ambassador to Great Britain; and Mikhail Kaganovich, aviation minister. Kaganovich was the older brother of Lazar Kaganovich, arguably Stalin's most valued lieutenant during the years of the German rapprochement and beyond.[233] In 1940–1941 more Jews still occupied high-level government positions than in any other country. If Stalin ever felt an impulse to adjust the ethnoreligious composition of his regime to satisfy Nazi preferences, he does not appear to have acted upon it.[234]

Some German visitors to the USSR even demonstrated surprise over the regime's continued tolerance of Jews in positions of authority. A newspaper correspondent from Berlin, for example, wondered about a Jewish defense lawyer she observed in a criminal trial. When her Soviet interlocutor, an official of the All-Union Society for Cultural Relations with Foreign Countries, explained that "in our country one is not embarrassed to be a Jew" and that actions that bred dissension between Jews and other groups were treated as illegal acts, she expressed amazement: "This means that I cannot abuse someone on the street by using the curseword … 'Jew'?" You can, her interlocutor replied, "but you risk having to answer for this before a court." She concluded that Russians were incapable of comprehending "what is happening in Germany with respect to the Jews."[235]

Yet the Soviets made no significant effort to help their own citizens understand what German rule meant for the Jews subject to it. Here lay what may have been the most tangible negative consequence for Jews of the USSR's transformation from Germany's foe to its strategic partner. The September 1939 Boundary and Friendship Treaty obligated the Soviet government to "tolerate … no Polish agitation which affects [German] territories."[236] Soviet leaders evidently interpreted the obligation to imply a ban upon any public expression portraying Germany in an unfavorable light.[237] Accordingly they withdrew two popular locally produced films about the persecution of German Jewry, *Professor Mamlock* and *The Family Oppenheim*, from cinemas.[238]

More significantly, they disallowed publication of news about German anti-Jewish actions in occupied Poland. When, for example, Moshe Grossman showed the editor of *Bialystoker shtern* a yellow patch given him by a recent refugee, the editor implored Grossman to prepare an article about it, but party officials forbade publication. "That is the policy now," Grossman remembered the editor explaining; "a higher necessity."[239] As a result, facing the German invasion, Jews and non-Jews throughout the USSR were not especially well informed when evaluating their position.

The information they did possess originated mostly in refugee stories and in letters sent to refugees by friends and family members left behind in the German zone. It was transmitted mainly between individuals by word of mouth. From the queues of refugees who applied to return to their former homes in the German zone it can be inferred that such information did not consistently convey a sense of imminent life-threatening danger from German rule.[240] To be sure, Germany had not yet embarked upon deliberate, systematic murder of Jews; it would do so only following its invasion of the USSR in June 1941.[241] Nevertheless, at the time of passportization, in mid-1940, Jews in several cities in German-occupied Poland, including some two hundred thousand in Łódź, had been enclosed in ghettos, while more were being impressed for forced labor and faced a starvation-level food supply.[242] Soviet citizens could not discuss these facts in a public forum. Nor could they speak openly about the enclosure of 400,000 Warsaw Jews in a ghetto in November 1940 or about the nearly 14,000 Jewish deaths in the city from hunger and disease during the first half of 1941.[243] How such discussions might have affected refugees considering whether to return to the German-occupied zone of Poland cannot be determined. Nor can it be known how lack of information influenced Soviet Jews' perceptions of their situation when Germany attacked the USSR.[244] Still, it is clear that those perceptions were not informed by knowledge that Soviet authorities would no doubt have disseminated widely before September 1939.

The availability of information to veteran Soviet Jews was further encumbered by restrictions upon travel from the annexed lands into pre-1939 Soviet territory. Transfer of information about Jews across the erstwhile border thus took place most easily at the elite level, where delegations of Soviet Jewish writers, artists, and educators were dispatched regularly to meet with their colleagues in the incorporated regions as part of the state's effort to inculcate Soviet norms among its new subjects.[245] Such meetings offered articulate Jews from the new territories opportunities to discuss their experience with Soviet rule and to inquire about future prospects. It appears that at least one of the expeditions—a February 1940 journey to Western Byelorussia that included chairman of the Jewish Section of the Soviet Writers' Union Isaac Nusinov, director of the Moscow Jewish State Theater Solomon Mikhoels, and renowned Yiddish writer Peretz Markish—considered the plight of Jews under Nazi domination. Following that encounter, the three Jewish cultural luminaries, all well connected to the highest levels of the Soviet regime, addressed a letter directly to Stalin, informing him that "the [Jewish] masses in the liberated districts, along with hundreds of thousands of refugees, [who have become] loyal patriots of their new Soviet homeland . . . , are living through a tragedy whose like is unknown in the history of the Jewish people" because of their "blood ties with the three million [*sic*] Jews remaining in the German zone of influence." The letter called for "urgent measures" to address their predicament.[246]

The document was remarkable for its audacity. Not only did it offer unsolicited policy suggestions; it evoked an ethnic solidarity that the Soviet regime had worked for at least a decade to attenuate.[247] Interaction with Jews who had not faced similar pressures—whom a contemporary called "more conservative, more stubbornly Jewish, less inclined to give up their own way of life"—may well have ignited that sense of belonging to a wider Jewish world and a resolve to advance collective Jewish interests.[248] So too may have the observation that the Ribbentrop-Molotov Pact carried a different meaning for Soviet Jews and non-Jews. For the Soviet population at large the agreement with Nazi Germany signaled primarily reduction of the immediate threat of war. Among Jews, by contrast, the thought that their country had suddenly befriended the bitterest and most implacable foe of Jews everywhere, reversing its long-standing excoriation of Hitler and all he stood for, appears to have been a source of intense emotional pain. For some the pain was rendered especially sharp by the fact that they were officially enjoined from expressing it publicly. Artists and writers who had thought themselves thoroughly integrated and accepted into Soviet culture and society now began to sense a new distance between them and their non-Jewish peers.[249]

That perception seems to have been somewhat less acute among another category of veteran Soviet Jews that came into direct contact with Jews from the annexed territories—civil servants, party functionaries, and military personnel posted to the new lands.[250] The few available sources suggest that meetings with their "more conservative" fellow Jews may have generated in them a modicum of nostalgia for dimly remembered folk customs.[251] More likely, though, their own impact on those "more stubbornly Jewish" Jews was greater. Jewish officers and government officials were not a common sight for Jews from the new lands; such positions had been largely closed to them under their former rulers. Now, as one of them recalled, "when among the soldiers of the Red Army we encountered a Jew who spoke to us in Yiddish, we felt ten feet tall."[252] Such soldiers became effective spokesmen for the new regime, persuading Jews that Soviet troops were, in the words of a diarist from Wilno, "entirely different from any other military force."[253] Even the appearance of a Jew conducting a Soviet military orchestra reportedly brought expressions of delighted disbelief from Jews who flocked to a concert in newly occupied Białystok.[254]

That the Soviets permitted Jews to wield public authority, that they appeared committed to ending hostile discrimination in the new territories,[255] and, most obviously, that they punished opponents brutally, undoubtedly gave many Jews from those areas powerful impetus to rethink their purported conservative disposition and to adjust to the new Soviet reality. Indeed, for all the multiple hardships, pressures, and vexations the new regime created, sometimes extreme, the large majority appear to have done precisely that. Of more than two million Jews who came under Soviet authority in 1939–1940, fewer than 140,000 (7 percent) encountered the state's coercive apparatus. More than half of those were refugees, not residents of the annexed regions. Active resistance to Soviet rule in those regions was minimal, as were efforts to maintain Jewish communal institutions underground.[256] In short, most Jews who became part of the Soviet orbit after 1939 were neither inclined nor able to move their brethren on the other side of the former border to become any "more stubbornly Jewish" than the Soviet regime allowed. But on the other hand, neither their experience nor the post-1939 policies of the Soviet government appear to have moved veteran Soviet Jews to become any less Soviet.

Ironically, the regime's ability to induce accommodation and to retain loyalty would prove fateful for both new and veteran Soviet Jews after June 1941, when the Moscow-Berlin rapprochement met a violent end.

2
DISFIGUREMENT

Neither Germany nor the USSR expected the Ribbentrop-Molotov Pact to endure. For the Germans the agreement was primarily a device to avoid fighting on two fronts. By summer 1940, with France defeated and the British Army pinned back beyond the English Channel, the western front had collapsed. The eastern front could now be safely reopened. Recognizing the new reality, German military planners began in July 1940 to design an assault aimed at capturing the vast "new living space" the Nazi Party had eyed since assuming power in 1933. Before the month was out, the invasion had been set for the following spring.[1]

The Soviets grasped Germany's grand design but not its operational plans. They appear to have believed that Germany would be ready to attack only in 1942, by which time, they anticipated, Soviet forces would be formidable enough to stop any German advance in its tracks. Consequently not only were Soviet planners caught by surprise when, before dawn on 22 June 1941, Germany, with no prior ultimatum or declaration of war, launched a coordinated ground-air attack across the Soviet frontier; the plans they had made to ward off the invasion proved inadequate for the military situation they faced.[2]

The invading German force numbered more than three million. German allies—Finland, Hungary, Romania, and Slovakia—supplied an additional 650,000 to 850,000 troops.[3] The assault, termed Operation Barbarossa, may well have been the largest ever mounted to date.[4] Its immediate objective was to destroy the Soviet military and to topple the Soviet regime. It was designed to do so within a few months. After achieving that objective, German leaders planned to reduce the population of the captured territories by tens of millions through deportation, starvation, and mass murder, opening vast new territories for German settlement.[5]

In the end, the invasion accomplished none of its goals. It was defeated in a protracted, agonizing struggle in which the Soviet state and Soviet society mounted the superior war effort. But Soviet armed forces needed three years to drive the invaders back across the Ribbentrop-Molotov line and another year to reach Berlin and dismantle the Nazi Third Reich. During those years, on the way to failure, Germany precipitated violent death on an unprecedented scale. Some eighteen million soldiers fell or went missing in battle, ten million of them from the Red Army.[6] Perhaps another fourteen million civilians perished in the USSR as a result of German actions, including an estimated 7.4 million murdered outright.[7] In all, the Soviet Union lost 12 to 14 percent of its population, a quarter to a third of its wealth.[8]

Jews' proportionate losses were even more staggering: some 2.8 million met premature deaths within the June 1941 Soviet boundaries in consequence of the German onslaught.[9] Upward of 200,000 were soldiers or partisans killed in the course of military service; they numbered approximately three eighths to one half of the 400,000 to 540,000 Jews who bore arms against Germany on the Soviets' behalf.[10] Of the remainder, the overwhelming majority were slain by German army, police, and security units or by associated military or paramilitary forces.[11] In short, more than half the Jews living in Soviet-controlled territories in June 1941 died as a result of events set in motion by the German invasion. Those Jews, who comprised around 2.7 percent of the territories' residents, accounted for some 12 percent of all Soviet military and nonmilitary deaths and upward of 35 percent of civilian murder victims.[12]

On 9 May 1945, after Stalin proclaimed final victory in what he dubbed the Great Patriotic War, the acclaimed Russian writer and Jewish public figure Ilya Ehrenburg,[13] whose wartime reportage had made him perhaps the most prominent face of the Soviet anti-Nazi struggle at home and abroad, penned a short verse to express "the bewilderment, the anxiety that lurked somewhere deep inside" him, together with the exultation he felt now that "the blaze of the rockets had faded out":

> A poet spoke of them in bygone times: they awaited one another for many a long day, and when they met they did not recognize one another in the heavens

> which know no sorrow. Not in paradise, but on this vast tract of earth, where at every step there is sorrow, sorrow, sorrow, I awaited her, as one waits only when one loves; I knew her as one knows only oneself; I knew her in blood, in mud, in grief. The hour struck. The war ended. I made my way home. She came towards me, and we did not recognize each other.[14]

The unrecognized figure, Ehrenburg wrote, was "Victory," whose arrival he had awaited through four years of cruel hardship, only to find himself bewildered upon its appearance. No doubt his perplexity also reflected the baleful realization that those years had disfigured Soviet Jewry beyond recognition.

Disfigurement was far less than Germany wished for Jews in the heady summer and fall of 1941, when its soldiers and soldiers of its allies encircled and eliminated ten Soviet armies and occupied lands from the Gulf of Finland in the north to the Sea of Azov in the south, besieging Leningrad and threatening Moscow.[15] Among the German leadership, expectations of the USSR's imminent collapse abounded, making plans for mass German settlement seem ripe for immediate implementation.[16] The area designated for future German colonization was precisely the one in which Soviet Jews were most densely concentrated. German plans for that region thus implied that Jews would suffer deportation, starvation, and mass murder no less, and likely much more, than Soviet residents generally.[17]

In fact, Jews were far more vulnerable than others. Nazi planners, beginning with Hitler himself, considered them a problem not only (and not even primarily) because they inhabited space intended for German settlers. They were an ideological problem as well. Hitler saw Jews as parasites in the most literal sense—pernicious creatures incapable of independent existence, who survived only by stealing food from others. To facilitate such theft they had, Hitler claimed, concocted the doctrine of Bolshevism, which not only legitimized expropriation but, by advancing (the Jew) Karl Marx's notion that "the history of all hitherto existing society is the history of class struggle," caused the nations of the world to ignore the vital necessity of defending the national food supply from Jewish attack. The Jews of the USSR were surely the most pernicious of all, he reasoned, for they had delivered the world's largest country into Bolshevik hands. Hence Operation Barbarossa entailed not only a conventional war to control territory but also a two-track ideological war against both the citadel of Bolshevism and the Jews, who used the citadel to bleed humanity dry. For Hitler, successful prosecution of both tracks was the Third Reich's chief raison d'etre.[18]

German military planning documents connected the two wars explicitly. On 3 March 1941, Alfred Jodl, chief of operations in the Armed Forces High Command, recorded Hitler's comment on the initial draft sketch of the invasion: the Nazi leader expressly designated the upcoming fight "a conflict between two worldviews" and demanded that "the Jewish-Bolshevik intelligentsia ... be removed."[19] Army field commanders were informed of this aim no later than early May; some had already decided to transmit it to their soldiers.[20] On 4 June divisional commanders were ordered to advise all troops that the campaign, described as a war against the "disintegrative [Bolshevik] worldview and its carriers," would involve "ruthless and energetic measures against Bolshevist agitators, guerrillas, saboteurs, [and] Jews."[21] At the same time Germany's minister of public enlightenment and propaganda, Josef Goebbels, and the country's chief of press, Otto Dietrich, prepared to trumpet the upcoming war as a fight against "Stalin and his Jewish men behind the scenes."[22]

Actually, even before the invasion began some German planners may already have been looking to extend the war against the Jews beyond the horizon of the conventional war and its immediate aftermath. By the eve of Barbarossa German military conquests had placed an estimated 3.4 million Jews under control of the Third Reich, of whom nearly three million resided either in places with German majorities or in areas slated, like the USSR, for eventual German colonization.[23] Nazi doctrine held those Jews unfit by nature to inhabit German "living space." Accordingly, leaders of the Third Reich had long sought to push Jews out of lands where Germans resided or could be expected to reside in the future. Initially they had hoped that by creating unbearably harsh conditions for Jews under their rule, they could induce mass emigration. However, by late 1939 the unwillingness of potential receiving countries to accept the growing numbers of would-be refugees generated by German expansion into Austria, Czechoslovakia, and Poland persuaded some key Nazi officials that the Reich needed to control a territory to which Jews could be deported en masse.[24]

The immense expanse of the Soviet Union could meet that need. For purposes of German settlement Nazi planners focused for the time being on the most easily habitable European Soviet territories only.[25] That focus left the five thousand kilometers from the Ural Mountains to the Bering Strait, along with European Arctic regions, available for other uses, including as a site for resettling the tens of millions of inhabitants of non-Arctic Soviet Europe that the Germans intended to displace. The 3.4 million Jews outside the USSR whom the Nazis looked to extrude could easily be added to that number. In fact, the idea appears long since to have occurred to some German diplomats: Soviet documents hint that as early as September 1939 the two countries may have discussed possibilities for shipping Jews from German-occupied Poland to the Jewish Autonomous Region centered in Birobidzhan, located on the Soviet border with Manchuria (then controlled by Japan).[26] At the time nothing had come of that idea.[27] Now, however, with the USSR's collapse anticipated in short order, the thought resurfaced.[28] One month into the invasion, Hitler himself intimated to his ally, Slavko Kvaternik, commander-in-chief of the armed forces of the recently installed German puppet regime in Croatia, that the mass transfer of every Jew from Europe to Siberia was about to begin.[29]

Before it could begin in earnest, however, the captured Soviet lands needed to be pacified. The Germans expected resistance to follow their victory—chiefly, as the order of 4 June 1941 had intimated, from "Bolshevist agitators, guerrillas, saboteurs, [and] Jews."[30] If these threats to order were not eliminated, they might well encumber, and perhaps even thwart, the complex mass population transfers the Germans had in mind. As a result, initial German operational plans regarding Soviet Jews reflected less grand schemes for the future than perceived short-term security demands. Though all Jews were dangerous in Nazi eyes, some were more immediately dangerous than others. These would be targeted at once, the rest addressed when circumstances allowed.

Well before the invasion, its strategic architects had outlined pacification procedures. Primary responsibility for securing the military's gains was entrusted to four Special Task Forces (*Einsatzgruppen*) under supervision of the SS—a vast extragovernmental imperium with its own elite paramilitary force, recruited from the Nazi Party's most ideologically committed members that controlled, among other things, all police, investigative, and security activities in the Third Reich and its conquered territories.[31] Created in March 1941 in response to Hitler's demand for "removal" of the "Jewish-Bolshevik intelligentsia,"[32] the *Einsatzgruppen* were charged with carrying out "certain special security-police duties which are outside the army's domain." Specifically, they were to advance just behind the moving battlefront in order "to discover and stamp out anti-German . . . movements . . . in the army's rear area." In order to accomplish this task they were empowered "to take administrative measures affecting the civilian population . . . on their own responsibility," free from military oversight except "in those areas where their deployment may affect [military] operations adversely."[33] Military leaders appear to have bridled at this infringement upon their authority in a battle zone.[34] Nevertheless, they understood that the ideological nature of the coming campaign required that the SS assume a leading role in the fight against the Reich's ideological enemies. Accordingly they resolved, in the words of the army's chief of the general staff, Franz Halder, to "do their share in the ideological struggle."[35] On 13 May 1941 the chief of the Armed Forces High Command, Wilhelm Keitel, signed a series of orders requiring soldiers to employ "the most extreme means" against Soviet civilians who resisted them and exempting them from punishment for doing so, "even if the act they committed was regarded at the time as a crime or a military infraction."[36]

Still, the instructions to both the *Einsatzgruppen* and the military lacked detail. The "administrative measures" to be undertaken against civilians were not specified. Nor were the "most extreme means" by which they were to be applied. Notably, Jews were nowhere mentioned in them directly.[37] In fact, it was only ten days into the invasion, on 2 July 1941, that Reinhard Heydrich, the second-ranking figure in the SS, who oversaw *Einsatzgruppen* operations, explicitly designated a few relatively small segments of the civilian population for execution: "officials of the Comintern (together with professional Communist politicians in general); top- and medium-level officials and radical lower-level officials of the [Communist] Party; central committee and district and subdistrict committees; People's Commissars [i.e. government ministers]; Jews in Party and State employment; and other radical elements (saboteurs, propagandists, snipers, assassins, inciters, etc.) insofar as they are . . . no longer required to supply information on political or economic matters."[38]

Heydrich's written order most likely set only a minimum expectation, identifying first-priority targets; it did not explicitly preclude more extensive killings of broader segments of the Soviet Jewish population should opportunities present themselves to carry them out.[39] That killing Jews as such was acceptable, even desirable, had long featured in the ideological training of SS personnel;[40] that masses of Jews in Poland should be put to death immediately instead of being held for eventual removal to a distant location had already been broached within the SS in 1940.[41] Nevertheless, even in the enthusiasm of Germany's early battlefield successes, Heydrich could not be certain when his troops might be able to kill beyond the circumscribed range of targets he had specified for immediate liquidation. The *Einsatzgruppen* comprised only three thousand men—one tenth of 1 percent of Germany's total invading force.[42] As mobile units they depended upon the army for transport and logistical support, as well as for access to areas close to the rapidly advancing front lines. But the army, although instructed by the Armed Forces High Command to execute all Jews among the Soviet *soldiers* it took prisoner, was not expected initially to dispatch its own personnel for killing *civilian noncombatants* at a time when it needed all available troops to accomplish its primary military objective.[43] In short, during the first weeks of Operation Barbarossa, Germany lacked the necessary manpower to fight its ideological war against Jews to the fullest. If it was to pursue that war beyond Heydrich's stated limited aims while the assault was still in motion, it would need help from forces beyond those at its immediate disposal.

On the eve of Operation Barbarossa and during its first weeks, certain key German planners, including Heydrich himself, expected those forces to come largely from disgruntled local elements in the lands Germany intended to conquer. Ever since Germany and Poland had fallen out in late 1938, German propaganda had represented the Nazi regime as a champion of the "subjugated" and "enslaved" peoples to Germany's east, especially of the Lithuanian, Byelorussian, and Ukrainian minorities living under Polish rule, to whom the peace settlements following the First World War had denied residence in "their own state."[44] High-ranking Nazis expected that Germany could continue to exploit that self-proclaimed advocacy to advance their strategic aims even after Soviets had replaced Poles as ostensible enslavers and placed Latvians, Estonians, and Romanians under their oppressive thumb as well. Accordingly, on 20 April 1941, his fifty-second birthday, Adolf Hitler appointed his longtime Nazi Party comrade Alfred Rosenberg, a Baltic German educated in the Russian language, to head a newly created Office for the Central Consideration of Matters Relating to the East European Region (*Dienststelle für die zentrale Bearbeitung der Fragen des osteuropäischen Raumes*), with a mandate to "draw up comprehensive guidelines . . . for this whole Russian question." Rosenberg was to take into account, among other items, "the racial and historical situation in the Baltic provinces," "the Ukraine in its struggle against Moscow," and "the mindset of the Russian soldiers and ordinary citizens under great stress."[45] In a speech delivered two days before the invasion to Nazi officials most closely involved in planning the fate of Soviet territories about to fall into German hands, Rosenberg defined Germany's "political task" in eastern Europe as "to reactivate the aspirations of all these peoples for freedom in a clever form that will secure the aim and to channel them into a definite statelike form (*ganz bestimmte staatliche Form*)—that is, organically to cut statelike structures (*Staatsgebilde*) out of the enormous territory of the Soviet Union and to build them up against Moscow, in order to liberate the German Reich from the eastern nightmare for centuries to come."[46]

Curiously, in his lengthy text Rosenberg mentioned Jews only in passing, but he, along with virtually all of the top Nazi leadership, imagined masses of Balts, Slavs, and Romanians suffering under a Judeo-Bolshevik regime. Intelligence sources had informed them since shortly after conclusion of the September 1939 Boundary and Friendship Treaty that in the territories the USSR had taken from Poland, "the Russians are placing the Jews in leading positions everywhere."[47] Reports prepared for various branches of the German security apparatus indicated that Jews were supervising non-Jews in forced labor projects, that Soviet security forces had given Jews arms, that Jews made up at least half of NKVD and police personnel, that "numerous Jewish women are finding employment as aides in [government] offices," and that in general Jews were acting as "propagandists for Bolshevism" and "props for the [Soviet] regime."[48] To be sure, some intelligence sources painted a more complex picture of ethnic relations in the new territories, diminishing the Jewish role in the Soviet administration and stressing that "only the lowest of the Jewish proletariat is satisfied with the current Bolshevik regime."[49] Evidently, however, readers of the reports gave greater credence to evaluations that confirmed their ideological biases. That inclination was reflected in a set of policy documents prepared by Rosenberg's staff as preparations for Operation Barbarossa were becoming concrete:

> Fundamentally, with respect to all measures it must be kept in mind that the population in general sees the Germans as liberators from the Jewish Bolshevist government. Capital is thus available that we can use to advantage by skillfully propagating the [ostensible] objectives [of the invasion]. . . . The entire population surely will welcome our understandable portrayal of the Jews as the chief culprits.[50]

That assessment led the staff to an ominous operative conclusion:

> The Jewish question can be solved to a significant extent by giving the population free rein for a certain length of time after we occupy the country. . . . The propaganda should emphasize that the clique in the Kremlin is nothing but a group of Jewish criminal despots who are exploiting the peoples of the Soviet Union. Their only goal is to stay in power; they are not interested in the welfare of the peoples. . . . The propaganda must again and again emphasize that the German army comes as a liberator from Bolshevism and from Jewry and bears no hostility toward the population, which, on the contrary, is to be brought out of hardship and misery into a decent existence. . . . The people itself will probably deal with its real oppressors, for it should be generally assumed that the population, especially in Ukraine, will proceed to large-scale Jewish pogroms and murders of Communist functionaries. In short, it would be advisable to leave the reckoning with the Bolshevist-Jewish oppressors in the hands of the population itself.[51]

Of course, Rosenberg and his staff, like the rest of the Nazi regime, were no more "interested in the welfare of the peoples" than they supposed the Soviets to be. The Nazi regime had no intention of promoting independence for any ethnic group to Germany's east; it coveted Soviet-held territories for German settlement and enrichment alone. The "state-like structures" to which Rosenberg referred were, as his speech made clear, actually colonial protectorates, each governed by a German "commissioner" taking orders from Rosenberg himself, with internal administrative divisions determined by German fiat and political organization by a local population dependent entirely upon German consent.[52] Consequently, Rosenberg's staff warned not only that the local population could be "given free rein" only for "a certain length of time" but also that "during the fighting, nothing must be said about the political program of the future configuration, because if it becomes known, pro-German sympathies would likely diminish considerably."[53] Meanwhile, the sole basis for cooperation with any local ethnic groups was to remain the struggle against "the treachery and blood guilt of Bolshevism, with special emphasis on the role of the Jews."[54]

Reinhard Heydrich appears to have endorsed reliance upon non-Germans to kill masses of Jews, although he raised additional qualifications to the ones that Rosenberg's office had adumbrated. At a meeting with the heads of the four *Einsatzgruppen* and their immediate subordinates on 17 June 1941, five days before the invasion was launched, he indicated how he wished SS and military personnel to engage local groups prepared to assist:

> The efforts at self-purging (*Selbstreinigungsbestrebungen*) by anticommunist or anti-Jewish circles in the new territories about to be occupied are not to be hindered. On the contrary, they are to be given free rein by all means, without leaving a trace [of our own involvement]. They should be intensified if need be and guided into the correct channels, without enabling these local "self-defense circles" later to refer to any directives or to any acknowledged political assurances. Because, for obvious reasons, such an approach is possible only during the first period of military occupation, the *Einsatzgruppen* and *Einsatzkommandos* of the SP and the SD[55] should strive insofar as possible, in consultation with military headquarters, quickly to introduce at least one advance detachment in the newly-occupied territories in order to set the necessary work in motion. Only members of the SP and the SD who have the necessary political instincts should be selected to lead such advance detachments. The creation of *permanent* self-defense associations with a central leadership is to be avoided in all cases, but it is useful to allow local pogroms to proceed.[56]

Heydrich appears to have foreseen two pitfalls for Germany's occupation strategy should non-Germans be called upon, as Rosenberg envisioned, to bear the initial brunt of the anti-Jewish war. First, leaving the "reckoning with the Bolshevist-Jewish oppressors in the hands of the population itself" ran the risk of releasing uncontrolled mob violence—not an entirely welcome scenario for an occupying regime seeking to establish order in enemy territory. As he indicated in his written instruction to the *Einsatzgruppen* commanders of 2 July, "the immediate general operational aim is the political pacification of the new territories to be occupied, meaning, at its most essential, [pacification] from a security-police perspective."[57] Hence his insistence that "advance detachments" of German security personnel try to retain as much control as possible over local "efforts at self-purging."[58] German control was also important, he thought, in order to prevent popular violence against Jews from developing what seemed to him too pronounced a political dimension for the local populations involved. Heydrich and other top Nazi planners evidently agreed with Rosenberg and his staff that Ukrainian, Byelorussian, Lithuanian, and Latvian organizations were liable to demand German acquiescence to their respective national political aspirations as a reward for active participation in the killing of Jews. For the Germans, such support was out of the question. Accordingly, Heydrich insisted that German forces direct aggression by local populations "into the correct channels," away from the hands of groups expecting political quid pro quo. He also warned, like Rosenberg, that local violence against Jews would serve German interests "only during the first period of military occupation," when *Einsatzgruppe* personnel would be available to supervise it before moving on as the military front advanced eastward. He feared, no doubt, that the longer such violence continued without proper control, the more forcefully the perpetrators were liable to advance political claims.[59]

German planners thus found themselves searching for assistance from agents who would display an unlikely combination of characteristics. Apparently they imagined helpers who would form themselves—perhaps spontaneously, perhaps at German suggestion—into large, ad hoc mobs with no permanent leadership. The mobs would be motivated primarily neither by desire for material gain nor by an expectation of emotional satisfaction from gratuitous violence but by a political passion powerful enough to impel them to murder on a massive scale; yet at the same time they would express no concrete political aims of their own. Instead they would turn to

German forces for direction, acquiescing to whatever role German commanders assigned them in the new Nazi order. They would be ferocious, merciless, and lethal, but they would also display sufficient self-control so as not to threaten German-imposed discipline and order. These, evidently, were the "correct channels" the Germans sought.

Unsurprisingly, the German forces that took part in the invasion of the USSR found such ideal assistants few and far between. In fact, beginning less than a month into the invasion, daily compilations of reports assembled in Berlin from dispatches by the four *Einsatzgruppen* and their constituent *Einsatzkommandos* reveal steadily growing despair over what seemed to them the widespread reticence of local Baltic and Slavic populations to turn their apparently powerful animosity toward their Jewish neighbors into murderous mass violence.[60] "The Latvians," according to information sent on 16 July 1941 from *Einsatzgruppe A*, which accompanied Army Group North (*Heeresgruppe Nord*) from East Prussia through the Baltic regions on the way to Leningrad, "have been, so far, absolutely passive in their anti-Semitic attitudes, not daring to take action against Jews."[61] A week later *Einsatzgruppe B*, attached to Army Group Center (*Heeresgruppe Mitte*), which headed through Byelorussia toward its objective of Smolensk, complained that "the White Russians [*sic*] remain undecided whether to carry out pogroms."[62] *Einsatzgruppen C* and *D*, detailed to Army Group South (*Heeresgruppe Süd*) and together responsible for the Ukrainian lands, recorded similar observations. A report from 5 August noted that although "in general the population harbors a feeling of hatred and rage towards the Jews and approves of the German measures (establishing ghettos, labor units, security police, procedures, etc.)," it was nevertheless "not able by itself to take the initiative in regard to the treatment of the Jews."[63] The same conclusion was restated four days later: "Carefully planned attempts made at an earlier date to incite pogroms against Jews have unfortunately not shown the results hoped for."[64] The following month, on 12 September, the situation appeared unchanged: "The population is always grateful for our treatment of the Jewish question," but "almost nowhere could the population be induced to take active steps against the Jews."[65] A comprehensive summary of all *Einsatzgruppen* activities through 31 October 1941 reinforced the general conclusion across all fronts:

> Now as before it must be confirmed that the population is refraining from any self-help action *vis-à-vis* the Jews. Even though the population reports uniformly about the terror from the Jews to which they were exposed during the Soviet regime, or it complains about new encroachments by the Jews, it nevertheless turns out in no way to be prepared for pogroms. The *Einsatzgruppen* ... are thus moving ahead with increasingly sharp action against the Jews, which necessitates their intervention in the most diverse areas.[66]

Large comprehensive data sets culled from tens of thousands of extant depositions and memoirs offered by Jews, Germans, and others who were present in the hundreds of former Soviet, Polish, and Baltic cities, towns, and villages that fell under German control beginning in the second half of 1941 largely reinforce such impressions.[67] Those first-person accounts relate events and experiences from more than seventeen hundred locations in the territories seized during Operation Barbarossa in which Jews resided at the time of the invasion, yet in fewer than two hundred of them does it appear that those experiences included violence by local mobs formed ad hoc and asserting no claim to permanent authority in their communities—at least of sufficient magnitude to feature prominently in witnesses' testimonies.[68] Moreover, in only about half of these places did unorganized mob violence claim Jewish lives; in the rest rioters concentrated upon plundering and vandalizing property, sometimes (although not always) beating and humiliating Jewish owners in the process. The total number of Jewish lives claimed by such local mob violence in all of the lands that German forces conquered during the summer of 1941 probably did not exceed thirty thousand—fewer than 1 percent of the Jews who fell under German control during those months—and it may well have been smaller, perhaps by as much as a third.[69] True, the pace and scale of murder by their neighbors arguably placed the brief interval in question among the most catastrophic for Jews in their entire history, rivaling the aftermath of the First World War.[70] To Germans, however, the returns on the "capital" Rosenberg had identified in the local view of "the Germans as liberators from the Jewish Bolshevist government" seemed meager indeed—so great was the gap between any of the manifold tribulations the region's Jews had suffered in earlier generations and the total destruction contemplated by the Nazis.[71]

To be sure, there were some cities and towns—maybe two dozen in all—in which deaths at mob hands were reported to have exceeded one hundred or where more than half of local Jewish residents were reported murdered by crowds of fellow townspeople. The most thorough killings appear to have taken place in some of the smallest communities. A surviving witness from Touste,[72] a town of fewer than fifteen hundred just west of the pre-1939 border between Soviet Ukraine and Polish East Galicia, recalled that local marauders slaughtered nearly all of its hundred or so Jewish residents.[73] Wąsosz, south of Grodno in the Białystok district, was home to fewer than five hundred Jews among some two thousand inhabitants; on 5 July 1941 a group of local thugs reportedly murdered all but fifteen Jews in their homes, raping women and mutilating their bodies in the process.[74] Two days later, in the nearby town of Radziłów (Jewish population fewer than one thousand), a large mob, encouraged and armed by a recently arrived *Einsatzkommando* detachment, herded the lion's share of the town's Jews into a barn and set them afire.[75] A similar scenario was repeated on 10 July in neighboring Jedwabne; after a spectacular conflagration, no Jews remained there.[76]

By contrast, most mob attacks produced proportionately few casualties, even in small settlements. In Wizna, less than ten kilometers south of Jedwabne, on 24 June 1941, a group of local thugs beat three of the six hundred to seven hundred Jewish inhabitants to death; two days later they locked twenty more in a blacksmith shop, where a German threw a bomb, killing them all. However, the remaining 97 percent of the town's Jews evidently managed to flee to other nearby locations.[77] Around the same time the Volhynian Jewish agricultural colony of Ignatowka, with a population of no more than five hundred, was attacked by nearby villagers. Five Jews died in the raid, but the attackers appear to have coveted the Jews' livestock and agricultural equipment more than their lives.[78] In another Volhynian town, Włodzimierzec, with twelve hundred to fifteen hundred Jewish residents, a local gang killed two Jews who tried to resist plunderers.[79] Farther south, peasants from the countryside raided the Galician town of Bóbrka on 2 July 1941, robbing Jews, beating them, and burning their homes, but of the more than two thousand Jews who lived there at the time, no more than sixty died.[80] To the north, in Anykščiai, Lithuania, on the day of the German invasion, a group of peasants raped and murdered a Jewish girl on a bicycle, but the town's two thousand remaining Jews were spared any further violence from their neighbors.[81] In another Lithuanian town, Viekšniai, an armed band, led by the schoolmaster, was evidently satisfied to kill only the rabbi and a few others among the six hundred local Jews.[82]

Mobs in some cities and larger towns claimed many more Jewish lives; however, in all but a handful of locations they left alive many more than they killed. Only four places saw a thousand Jewish dead or more. Three were in Galicia—Lwów, Tarnopol, and Złoczów; the fourth, Kaunas, had been independent Lithuania's de facto capital. These locations alone may have accounted for as many as two thirds of all murders resulting from local action in what German observers appear to have regarded as the "correct channels," but local perpetrators contributed to the deaths of no more than 10 percent, and most likely far fewer, of the total number of their Jewish inhabitants.[83] By contrast, Jews in many more of the most populous and prominent communities that fell under German control in 1941, including Białystok, Brześć, Grodno, Pińsk, Równe, Słonim, and Wilno in the former Polish *kresy* and Gomel, Kharkov, Kiev, Minsk, Vinnitsa, Vitebsk, and Zhitomir to the east of the Riga line, do not appear to have recorded any notable murderous attacks by mobs of their neighbors. Jews in some of these cities and towns did suffer traumatic violence shortly after falling into German hands, but Germans themselves were the direct perpetrators, and the violence followed patterns different from those displayed by local mobs.[84] Mobs were absent in large expanses of the countryside as well. By all accounts the territories of the pre-1939 Ukrainian, Byelorussian, and Russian Federated Soviet Republics captured during the course of Operation Barbarossa—home to more than two million Jews in more than three hundred locations at the moment of invasion[85]—were almost entirely free of the sort of crowd-led street violence the Germans preferred. If German planners had initially anticipated, in Rosenberg's words, that "the Jewish question can be solved to a significant extent by giving the [local] population free rein" to carry out "large-scale Jewish pogroms," these returns sufficed to disabuse them of their hope.

Another discovery added to their disillusionment. It turned out that Rosenberg and other German leaders who shared his expectation were not mistaken that significant organized elements among the Baltic and Slavic populations under Soviet rule were prepared to help German forces rid their countries of Jews, but they had already evidently decided to demand a political reward in return. Even before the invasion began, and again in its immediate aftermath, the Lithuanian Activist Front (*Lietuvos Aktyvistų Frontas*—LAF), the Latvian Thunder Cross (*Pērkonkrusts*), the Estonian Liberation Committee (*Eesti Vabastamise Komitee*), and the Organization of Ukrainian Nationalists (*Orhanizatsiya Ukrains'kykh Nationalistiv*—OUN) all issued statements greeting the prospect that the Nazi regime would bring about a "final settling of accounts" with "communism, Jewry, and their allied organizations and states."[86] However, as Heydrich had feared, those statements stemmed precisely from the sort of "*permanent* self-defense associations with a central leadership" whose creation he had proscribed. The Lithuanian Activist Front asserted authority throughout the country already on 22 June, immediately after German aerial bombardment had induced Soviet troops and officials to withdraw from Kaunas, two days before German forces entered the city. To fill the power void the Soviets had left, LAF proclaimed a provisional Lithuanian government, taking to the radio to promise renewed Lithuanian independence and broadcasting instructions to fly the national flag.[87] Similarly, on 30 June, the day the German army captured Lwów, the majority wing of the Organization of Ukrainian Nationalists (OUN-B), meeting in the city's historic residence of the Austrian governors of Galicia, declared the establishment of a sovereign Ukrainian state. The group announced the formation of a "Ukrainian *Wehrmacht*" the following day.[88]

Both LAF and OUN-B evidently hoped that the advancing German forces would welcome them as worthy and reliable partners in the Nazi-led European New Order—as independent allies, like Slovakia and Croatia, ready to advance key Nazi policy aims while retaining political authority over their respective national territories.[89] One of those aims was the elimination of Jews from the spaces the national movements sought to control. Accordingly, no doubt to strengthen its pro-Nazi bona fides, a well-known, high-ranking Lithuanian military officer proclaimed that for every German soldier killed in the course of the campaign to expel the Soviets, one hundred Jews would be executed.[90] At the same time, men in Kaunas wearing uniforms or insignias of a progovernment Lithuanian militia began to take

Jews into custody, rousting them from their homes or seizing them in the streets.[91] Acting with a similar purpose in Lwów, OUN-directed militias began from the first to impress Jews for compulsory labor service and to expel them from administrative positions.[92] They also rounded up Jews, herding them brutally to central locations where they were publicly humiliated and compelled to perform demanding and demeaning physical tasks.[93] The most prominent locations were three prisons where Soviet forces, before their retreat, had murdered between two thousand and three thousand prisoners whom they could not or would not take with them.[94] Ukrainian forces made Jewish men remove the corpses and forced women to clean them. When the work was done, militiamen shot many of the male victims.[95]

However, though the perpetrators in the two capitals may have expected German rewards for their bold moves, the Germans in charge of the war against the Jews gave them no support. Quite the contrary: once LAF and OUN-B presented their bills for anti-Jewish service, as it were, German officials refused to pay, telling their would-be organized Lithuanian and Ukrainian nationalist supporters, in effect, that their service was neither welcome nor necessary. They also took action to make certain that similar bills would not be presented in the future. In Kaunas they contracted with an independent militia, not connected with LAF, led by a former Lithuanian army officer and newspaper editor, Algirdas Klimaitis—who, it appears, sought only personal blandishments and made no political demands—to take the lead in moving against the city's Jews. The head of *Einsatzgruppe* A, Franz Walter Stahlecker, who first approached Klimaitis about organizing attacks, later reported to Heydrich the reasons why he had done so:

> In Kaunas four larger groups of guerrilla groups had formed, with which the advance commando immediately made contact. A unified leadership of these groups did not exist. Rather, each attempted to outstrip the other and to gain the closest possible connection with the Wehrmacht, in order to take part in future military action against the Soviet army and thereby to strike a blow on behalf of the eventual reconstitution of Lithuania and the establishment of a new Latvian [*sic*] army. While assigning the partisans[96] a military task was not to be considered for political reasons, a capable auxiliary squad about 300 men strong soon came to be formed out of the reliable elements among the undisciplined partisan groups, leadership of which was placed in the hands of the

> Lithuanian journalist Klimatis [*sic*]. This group has subsequently been engaged in pacification work, not only in Kaunas itself but in numerous places in Lithuania, and has carried out the tasks assigned it, particularly the preparation of and assistance in major liquidation operations under the regular supervision of the *Einsatzkommando* without any significant breaks. The rest of the partisan groups were disarmed smoothly.[97]

Only by coopting locals not affiliated with their country's national movement and placing them under strict German supervision, Stahlecker suggested, could Heydrich's encouragement of "self-purging" be successful. To be sure, he noted, with evident satisfaction, that on the night of 25 June Klimaitis had successfully "eliminated" (*beseitigt*) more than fifteen hundred Jews, "set a number of synagogues on fire or destroyed them by other means, and burned down a Jewish residential quarter of around 60 houses." The Lithuanian and his band had, according to the German commander, killed another twenty-three hundred Jews in similar fashion on subsequent nights, and they had done so without leaving a trace of "any German instruction or of German agitation." Nevertheless, he warned, relying on Lithuanian assistance to organize anti-Jewish mobs was not a viable strategy for the long term: "It was obvious that possibilities for carrying out progroms [*sic*] presented themselves only during the first days after occupation."[98] Evidently the new German authorities regarded retaining a monopoly on the legitimate use of force in Lithuanian territory as more valuable than whatever they might gain by licensing autonomous Lithuanian nationalists to attack Jews on their own authority. Accordingly, the progovernment Lithuanian militias were disarmed, bringing local "self-purging actions" to an end. In early August the occupiers induced the provisional Lithuanian government voluntarily to disband; a month later they outlawed LAF altogether.[99] Meanwhile, Lithuania was subsumed, together with Latvia, Estonia, and portions of present-day Belarus, into a new civilian administrative unit, *Reichskommissariat Ostland*, ruled by *Reichskommissar* Hinrich Lohse, who reported to Alfred Rosenberg's Reich Ministry for the Occupied Eastern Territories. These moves effectively clarified to Lithuanian nationalists that no matter how aggressively they acted against their country's Jewish population, they had no hope of turning their actions to political advantage.

OUN-B faced an even harsher reaction. On 2 July 1941, less than two days after the organization proclaimed Ukrainian independence despite an explicit German warning not to do so,[100] *Einsatzgruppe C* reported that although "some elements of the Bandera group [i.e. OUN-B] ... have organized a militia force and a municipal office ..., the *Einsatzgruppe* has created a counterbalance to the Bandera group, a Ukrainian self-policed city administration" under German control. The report noted also that "further measures against the Bandera group, in particular against [OUN-B leader Stepan] Bandera himself, are in preparation."[101] Those measures were revealed in short order. German authorities in Lwów quickly shut down the self-proclaimed, OUN-B led independent Ukrainian government.[102] On 5 July German police took Bandera, on his way to Lwów to assume control of the new state, into custody; when he refused to retract the proclamation of independence they transferred him to a Berlin prison.[103] A similar fate befell the acting government leader in Lwów, Yaroslav Stets'ko, four days later.[104] On 16 July Adolf Hitler himself ordered the separation of what had been the prewar Polish districts of Lwów, Tarnopol, and Stanisławów from the territories over which OUN-B had claimed sovereignty and their assignment to the German-occupied Polish *Generalgouvernement*. In August Alfred Rosenberg created *Reichskommissariat Ukraine*, a German-controlled civil administration parallel to *Reichskommissariat Ostland*, ruled by *Reichskommissar* Erich Koch, who served simultaneously as Nazi *Gauleiter* in East Prussia and as head of the civil administration in the Białystok district (which had been annexed to East Prussia shortly before). Even more than in the Baltics, the new German administrative arrangement effaced old ethnopolitical boundaries: *Reichskommissariat Ukraine* joined part of the pre-1939 Ukrainian Soviet Socialist Republic (SSR) with the onetime Polish provinces of Volhynia and Polesie, along with bits of the pre-1939 Soviet Byelorussian SSR.[105] Simultaneously the Germans shut down all Ukrainian political activity, outlawing the display of Ukrainian flags and the singing of the Ukrainian anthem.[106]

Control over actions against Jews in Lwów appears to have been one of the earliest points of German-OUN conflict, as German forces moved quickly, over OUN-B opposition, to direct the initial Ukrainian nationalist-led assaults into what they considered the "correct channels." By 2 July *Einsatzgruppe C* had not only created, as it reported, a "self-policed city administration;" it had also managed to subordinate under its command militias that only a day earlier had acted in the name of independent Ukraine.[107] It also evidently succeeded in activating a large crowd of townspeople not associated with OUN to assist in locating Jewish targets. On 3 July one of its constituent units, *Einsatzkommando* 5, reported that "the population is greatly excited: 1,000 Jews have already been forcefully gathered together."[108] A subsequent report, summarizing the first three weeks of German occupation, repeated the observation, noting that local inhabitants "rounded up about 1,000 Jews and took them to the [Soviet] prison, which has been occupied by the *Wehrmacht*."[109] The reports adumbrated a different role for the local population from the one initially suggested by Rosenberg and Heydrich. Locals were not to be given "free rein" to "purge" their own environment through "large-scale Jewish pogroms." Instead they were to play a closely supervised role as assistants to German formations, identifying Jews, gathering them together, and delivering them into German hands for execution. From 3 July on, murders of Jews in Lwów generally followed this pattern: local militias supported German killing operations, but they were not under OUN command. Their support was often brutal in the extreme, to an extent the Germans did not require, but German personnel directed the actual shooting of the victims.[110]

A similar pattern dominated elsewhere as well, although in some regions local militias that German authorities considered reliable were entrusted with a more direct role in the killing process. In Latvia, for example, Stahlecker turned, as he had in Lithuania, to a local entrepreneur of violence—Viktors Arājs, a former provincial police officer and a Soviet-trained attorney who, together with a motley group of four hundred to five hundred eager anti-Soviet fighters, had occupied the Riga police headquarters following the withdrawal of Soviet forces and armed his comrades with weapons seized from a nearby armory—to organize a popular uprising against the city's Jews.[111] Arājs's men themselves carried the brunt of the attacks, with little assistance from others, local or German: on 4 July 1941 they locked Jewish worshipers inside synagogues and set the buildings on fire, killing four hundred to five hundred.[112] They also rousted Jews (mostly men, but some women as well) from their homes, imprisoning some in dungeons, impressing others for forced labor, all the while humiliating, beating, abusing, and torturing their captives mercilessly. They then transported most of the prisoners not selected for work details to a forest on the outskirts of town, where, following instructions by German security personnel, they shot each one from behind.[113] *Einsatzgruppe A* reported on 16 July that twenty-three hundred Riga Jews were murdered in this fashion.[114]

Yet even after Arājs and his men had completed their task, some thirty thousand Jews remained in the Latvian capital. They epitomized the fundamental problem that became apparent to the Germans at the outset of their campaign against the USSR: catch-as-catch-can "self-purging" actions, no matter how reliable the executioners, no matter how cruel their deeds, could, at their most effective, reach only a small proportion of Soviet Jewish targets. As a result, throughout the summer, as German forces pushed ever deeper into Soviet territory, the heads of the *Einsatzgruppen* worked with SS leaders in Berlin, military commanders in the field, and their local accomplices to increase efficiency and to expand the scope of their murder operations.

How did it happen that German planners misconstrued the readiness of Slavs and Balts under Soviet rule to kill their Jewish neighbors? After all, their sense that those groups shared the Germans' loathing of their Soviet masters and agreed with Nazi leaders that the USSR was at bottom a Jewish enterprise dedicated to exploiting them for the Jews' own nefarious purposes was hardly without foundation. Quite the contrary: it reflected attitudes that permeated some (though not all) of the groups' leadership circles since September 1939. Members of those elite circles had served as informants for various German intelligence services during the years of the Ribbentrop-Molotov Pact, and information they provided had helped Germans confirm their own perception that the masses recently conquered by the Soviets blamed Jews especially for their misfortune.[115] That perception, moreover, was consistent with a European-wide stereotype of "Judeo-Bolshevism" that predated the formation of the Nazi Party—a stereotype fueled in turn by long-standing prejudices rooted in religiously grounded suspicions and sociopolitical antagonisms that had beclouded the relations between Jews and non-Jews in the region for centuries.[116] Only two decades earlier, after the First World War, fear of a "Judeo-Bolshevik" conspiracy had helped spark a wave of armed popular and military attacks upon Jews throughout the lands to the east of the Riga line. Those attacks had been both numerous (some fifteen hundred incidents were recorded in Ukraine alone between 1918 and 1920, in upward of thirteen hundred individual locations[117]) and deadly, claiming, by some accounts, as many as two hundred thousand Jewish lives—perhaps the largest concentrated mass killing in Jewish history to date.[118] If fearful anticipation of Bolshevik hegemony yet unknown had produced so savage an anti-Jewish reaction, German leaders might well have reasoned, how much more likely was an even more lethal response to the actual experience of Soviet repression? Such, it seems, was the conclusion they drew from what their Slavic and Baltic informants told them during the months leading up to Operation Barbarossa.

In hindsight, the conclusion appears to have rested upon a mistaken premise. Evidently the masses of Slavs and Balts depicted by their elites as ripe for vengeance upon their Jewish tormentors either did not, on the whole, perceive the Soviet-Jewish nexus as those who claimed to speak for them did, or they were not sufficiently outraged by it to murder their neighbors en masse. On the heels of their forces' incursion into Soviet territory, German propagandists, following the guidelines of Rosenberg's staff, distributed copious posters, flyers, broadsheets, and newspapers in local languages throughout the newly occupied territories labeling the Soviet Union "a Jewish state" in which "the Jews and their Bolshevik henchmen profited and luxuriated at the expense of workers and peasants" and exhorting readers to "throw the Jews out," for "Jews have no place among you." "Jews and their Bolshevik henchmen," inhabitants of the territories were told, had "brought you blood, tears, and hunger . . . , drawn your blood to the last drop . . . , taken bread from your granaries . . . , informed upon you and sent millions of you to starve in exile . . . , [and] tortured millions of you to death in NKVD cellars."[119] Yet all the incitement did not move nearly enough Poles, Ukrainians, Byelorussians, Russians, Lithuanians, Latvians, or Estonians to act toward Jews as the Germans wished.

At the time, German observers attributed what they saw as local passivity to a fear that the Soviets would soon return and allow Jews to exact revenge from all who had abused them.[120] Such a fear would have been consonant with the experience of most of the region's residents, who had seen their lands change hands multiple times during the previous quarter century. Nevertheless, other, more complex, considerations may well have played an equal or greater role. After all, the people from whom the Germans solicited assistance—the non-Jewish peasants, teachers, officials, judges, blue- and white-collar workers, small business owners, priests, pharmacists, doctors, lawyers, and local gentry who lived side-by-side with Jews in cities, towns, and villages throughout the region—knew their Jewish neighbors from sources besides German propaganda. Their attitudes toward Jews were shaped not only by ethnopolitical grievances or by religious preconceptions but also by the cumulative weight of ongoing day-to-day civic and personal interactions with individuals they often knew by name. Jews and non-Jews habitually came together in the marketplace, but they also met routinely in schools, cinemas, town councils, hospitals, fire brigades, lending libraries, beauty pageants, dance halls, sporting fields, and, increasingly among young people, one another's homes.[121] Soviet efforts at socioeconomic engineering expanded sites of contact to the industrial and agricultural workplace, where the economic relationship between Jews and non-Jews was recast from the transactional exchange between sellers and buyers to the cooperative activity of fellow team members working side by side to advance their unit's output.[122] East of the Riga line those efforts had been underway for some two decades when the Germans arrived. They had contributed, among other things, to rates of intermarriage approaching or exceeding 20 percent in the pre-1939 Soviet areas that fell under German occupation.[123] More significantly, they had led, by many accounts, to a marked lessening of perceptions among non-Jews of Jews as significantly divergent: "If work needed to be done in the field," one non-Jewish member of a collective farm recalled, "they called us both out, there was no difference."[124] Prospects that neighbors will deliberately harm one another can reasonably be expected to decline as they come to regard themselves more as sharing common circumstances than as separated by ethnic or religious boundaries. The relative rarity of lethal mob attacks upon Jews in Eastern Ukraine, Eastern Byelorussia, and the portions of Soviet Russia under German rule may reflect such a rising feeling of commonality.[125]

Soviet socioeconomic engineering had a much shorter history west of the Riga line and in the Baltics, but even in those regions there is evidence that the integration of workplaces, schools, and social service networks that the Soviets introduced contributed to the formation of new interethnic friendships, especially among the young.[126] In another sense as well, the short period of Soviet rule may have reshaped intergroup relations in ways that the Germans did not anticipate. When their lands became part of the USSR, residents could not have known how long they would be subject to Soviet authority. That authority could not simply be rejected or ignored in the expectation that it would pass quickly. On the contrary, because the new regime swiftly asserted control over virtually all aspects of daily life, all who hoped to secure life's basic necessities for themselves and for their families needed to come to terms with it. Hence, unless individually targeted for removal, most teachers, whatever their ethnoreligious affiliation, continued to teach in the new Soviet schools, postal workers continued to sort mail in the new Soviet post office, doctors and nurses continued to tend the sick in the new state-run hospitals, and clerks continued to file papers in the new government offices.[127] On the whole, Jewish patterns of accommodation to the demands of daily life Soviet style do not appear to have differed significantly from those of non-Jews, at least below the upper ranks of government and economic administration. At the higher ranks, moreover, Jews do not appear to have been disproportionately represented in most places.[128] In other words, the perception that Jews had profited uniquely from the Soviet regime in a manner that proved the regime's fundamentally Jewish character—the perception conveyed to German intelligence by Slavic and Baltic elite informants, which German planners believed would move Slavs and Balts to murderous mass violence against their Jewish neighbors—did not match the experience that many ordinary Slavs and Balts lived from day to day. Of course, stereotypes like "Judeo-Bolshevism" can easily shape perceptions of experience, and inaccurate, myth-driven perceptions often propel behavior more readily than perceptions rooted in facts not refracted through a mythical lens. But it is not necessarily the case that they *must* do so invariably. The unexpectedly low incidence of lethal anti-Jewish mob violence committed by local populations during the initial weeks following the launch of Operation Barbarossa may well testify to the existence of counterweights to the tendency to blame Jews for the misfortunes of Soviet rule, counterweights sufficient to stay the hands of at least some of the people the new German conquerors initially counted upon to carry the initial burden of mass killing.

The empirical data required to test that possibility probably do not exist; what made some non-Jews in some places murder Jews during the summer of 1941 while many others in many more places did not do so is a question most likely beyond the reach of scholarly investigation. Clearly, to understand any individual attack as a simple act of revenge for Soviet oppression in general or for perceived Jewish support for the oppressive regime—let alone as an outburst of elemental hatred, whether endemic in the peoples of the region or a product of recent history—will not do: an explanation must suggest why such emotions not only surfaced but manifested themselves murderously precisely where they did and not elsewhere. Plausible correlations with possible causative factors—population, age, and occupational distribution; occurrence of previous mob riots; length of interval between Soviet withdrawal and German conquest; presence and types of German forces in situ; incidence of violent crime; ownership of taverns; number and types of churches or newspaper circulation, to name but a few of dozens imaginable—have yet to be located.[129] It does appear that Germans often succeeded in arousing violence in especially emotionally loaded situations, as in the places where they discovered the bodies of prisoners murdered by Soviet security forces while leaving town, but even in many of those places the discovery was not the sole reported trigger.[130] In the end it may well be that much local violence against Jews, perhaps even most, was at bottom more interpersonal than intercommunal, with individuals taking advantage of what they presumed was their Jewish neighbors' lack of protection to settle private scores, enrich themselves, or release pent-up frustrations at the expense of the most vulnerable people in their immediate vicinity.[131] In such cases personal interventions and histories of face-to-face interactions were likely often crucial in determining whether local tensions flared into a murderous mob attack or remained below the threshold of mass intercommunal violence.[132] Invidious representations of Jews, whether ancient or of recent vintage, may have justified such attacks after the fact, but they do not appear *by themselves* to have turned masses of eastern Europeans into ardent coexecutioners of Nazi anti-Jewish designs.

To be sure, bonds of day-to-day association, even of friendship, especially recently formed ones, are hardly permanent, and some Jews recalled that they broke quickly once Soviet control vanished. "The same comrades who had worked with me—not simple people, but [educated ones like] the chief bookkeeper [in my factory] and the engineer who had been under my supervision (and also my neighbor)—no longer recognized me," recollected a Jewish woman from Minsk who had worked her way through the ranks to an administrative position in a cooperative manufacturing plant. Though she remembered no workplace friction at all before the German invasion, on the day the war broke out "they started to make trouble." Only then, she observed, "did we feel the difference."[133] Another Minsk Jew reported that his closest friend, a Byelorussian, with whose family he had spent many happy hours, immediately volunteered to serve the Germans: he "took off [his] mask . . . when the war began . . . and showed right away who [he] really was."[134] Jews in locations throughout the USSR feared attacks from their neighbors after German rule was in place.[135] But whatever augmented antipathy was noted within the pre-1939 Soviet borders revealed itself during the war's first weeks mostly in verbal taunts or in claims of privilege at Jewish expense. Sometimes it escalated to robbery and plunder but hardly ever to murderous independent mob violence.

Whatever the reason, as they pushed forward into Soviet territory during the summer of 1941, the German units charged with prosecuting their country's war against the Jews found themselves no less in need of assistance than they had been when Operation Barbarossa began.

Another potential source of assistance lay with two of Germany's allies, Hungary and Romania, whose forces joined in the invasion of the USSR and occupied parts of Soviet territory. Hungary had obtained a common border with the Soviet Ukraine as a result of its March 1939 annexation of the former Czechoslovak province of Subcarpathian Rus'[136] and the Soviet takeover of East Galicia from Poland the following September. Beginning on 27 June 1941, five days after the beginning of the German invasion, and continuing over the next two weeks, infantry units of the Hungarian Carpathian Army Group advanced along the Stryj and Borżawa rivers, turning east at Skole toward Stanisławów and beyond, while motorized and cavalry brigades moving northeast through the Tartar Pass captured Kołomyja and Tłuste, then crossed the Zbrucz River (the former Polish-Soviet border), taking the East Ukrainian town of Kamenets-Podolskii and portions of the surrounding countryside. By 9 July it occupied more than twenty thousand square kilometers of the Ukrainian SSR, with more than a hundred thousand Jewish inhabitants. Romania, for its part, attacked the Soviets together with the Germans, mobilizing two full armies (some 325,000 troops) to reconquer Bessarabia and Northern Bukovina (lost to the USSR a year earlier) by the end of July. Romanian forces then continued into pre-1940 Soviet territory, with the intention of helping Germany fulfill its strategic aim of annihilating the USSR. By the end of August they controlled upward of forty thousand square kilometers between the Dniester and Bug rivers, formerly parts of Soviet Ukraine and Moldova,[137] extending northward from the Black Sea, and they had laid siege to the seaport of Odessa. Once they completed the conquest of that metropolis on 16 October, they controlled the fate of perhaps as many as 600,000 Jews who had once lived under Soviet rule (including more than 300,000 residents of the pre-1939 USSR).[138] Both Hungary and Romania were thus both in a position to advance Germany's anti-Jewish designs substantially.

Hungary proved of little value in this regard. Its alliance with Germany did not require it to commit troops to the invasion, and its government anticipated little strategic benefit from doing so. It had become involved in the fighting of its own volition following a curious incident five days into the German advance that left doubt as to both Germany's and the USSR's intentions toward it, but, reflecting lack of public excitement, it prosecuted its war effort with little enthusiasm. Germany soon concluded that Hungary's contribution to the war effort brought more trouble than it was worth. By November Hungarian troops abandoned the battlefield temporarily, with German agreement.[139] Meanwhile, though, occupying Hungarian military units, unwilling to tolerate disorder, had frequently restrained or even suppressed local elements attacking Jews.[140] They were evidently unconcerned with Germany's war against the Jews and indifferent toward its wish to see those elements encouraged.[141]

Romania helped the Germans much, much more.[142] Unlike Hungary, its motivation to assist was strong. The Romanian Leader,[143] Ion Antonescu, had taken power in a September 1940 coup d'état thanks in part to German support, and he saw himself beholden to German desires. He also regarded a German alliance as the key to regaining the territories his country had lost to the Soviets the previous June. Hence he enthusiastically committed Romanian forces to Germany's invasion of the USSR.[144] Moreover, he displayed considerable sympathy for Germany's approach to Jewish matters. Even before learning of plans for Operation Barbarossa, his government, extending the practice of earlier regimes, moved to deny the country's nearly eight hundred thousand Jewish residents[145] access to an ever-growing range of civic benefits, public spaces, and means of livelihood through legislation adapting German models to local conditions.[146]

Antonescu's campaigns against both Jews and the USSR enjoyed widespread popular approval. They gave expression to a common attitude that placed Jews among the "foreigners" from whom, according to virtually all of the country's major political groups, Romania needed to be freed.[147] Such aggressive sentiments had been turned against Jews with particular vehemence following the loss of Bessarabia and Northern Bukovina, which many Romanians tended to blame in large measure on a purported universal Jewish affinity for the Soviet regime. At the time, in 1940, the Romanian Army, looking to repair the damage to its public standing brought about by its failure to defend the country's borders, had spread reports of widespread Jewish perfidy and collaboration with the Soviet invader.[148] In response, mobs in several locations, not only in the provinces lost to the Soviets but in parts of the Romanian heartland as well, had joined retreating military units in torturing and executing alleged Jewish traitors. In some places, including the Moldavian cities of Galați and Dorohoi, military-incited popular riots had claimed several hundred Jewish lives.[149] Now, in the summer of 1941, with the lost provinces returned to Romanian rule, the army, the police, and much of the populace were poised to give the remaining traitors their due. The Romanian government egged them on. On 3 July 1941, Deputy Premier Mihai Antonescu (by some accounts a distant relative of his namesake, the Leader) told a gathering of military and civilian administrative personnel assigned to Bessarabia and Bukovina that the country now found itself in "the most favorable and the most expansive historic moment" for "purifying our nation of all those elements foreign to its soul." "In order not to miss" this one-time opportunity, he declared, an "action of ethnic purification" must be undertaken, involving "removing or isolating Jews in labor camps," along with "forced migration of the Jewish element... across the border."[150] Five days later Ion Antonescu not only told his cabinet of his personal support for forced migration, he authorized troops to "shoot with machine guns" to make it happen.[151]

The day after the Leader's remarks, Romanian troops and civilians began the work of "ethnic purification" in Bessarabia and Northern Bukovina with a vengeance. The chief of the Romanian general staff instructed a senior commander to organize teams of soldiers to agitate among peasants, so that in villages throughout the reclaimed provinces the populace would "remove [Jews] on its own, by whatever means it finds most appropriate and suited to the circumstances."[152] With such clear political direction, and supported by the German *Einsatzgruppe D*,[153] local villagers and gendarmes worked together with the army systematically to rid the provinces of all Jews.[154] In the countryside, home to more than a quarter of the Jews in Bukovina and perhaps as much as half of Bessarabian Jewry,[155] wholesale murder of men, women, and children appears often to have been the method of first resort. As early as 30 June 1941, after communicating with Romanian soldiers still at a distance from their location, peasants in the central Bessarabian village of Ghirovo arrested nearly all local Jews and suspected communists, awaiting the arrival of Romanian and German troops. Once the military completed conquest of the area, on 3 July, a local gendarmerie executed all in custody.[156] A similar scenario took place a day later in Ciudei, Northern Bukovina: a Romanian military unit shot some 450 of the village's Jews, who had earlier been driven into the local jail by a peasant mob. Only a few families managed to escape.[157] Around the same time virtually the entire Jewish communities of Ropcea, Iordăneşti, Pătrăuţi, and other nearby rural locations in Northern Bukovina were annihilated.[158]

In larger towns Romanian and German forces faced more complex logistical problems, but even there they managed, often with local assistance, to murder large numbers in short intervals. Over three days, between 7 and 9 July, Romanian soldiers, together with local residents, killed nearly 1,000 of the approximately 4,000 Jews of the northern Bessarabian town of Noua-Suliţă, burning down half of the Jews' homes in the process.[159] In nearby Hotin, 2,000 of the town's 5,700 Jews were shot by Romanian troops as a German military unit looked on.[160] The two largest cities of the recovered lost provinces, Chişinău, capital of Bessarabia, and Cernăuţi, capital of Bukovina, also witnessed cooperative Romanian-German, military-civilian efforts to kill large numbers of Jews during the first days after resumption of Romanian control. In Cernăuţi, the first ten days of Romanian rule (5–15 July) brought death to 3,500 of the city's 50,000 Jewish residents.[161] In Chişinău the toll and the pace of death were greater still: some 10,000 of the city's Jews, who had numbered upward of 60,000 on the eve of Operation Barbarossa, were murdered between 17 and 24 July, the first week of Romanian control.[162]

The precise number of Jews murdered in Bessarabia and Northern Bukovina during Antonescu's "ethnic purification" campaign has not been determined, in part because the total elimination of the Jewish population in numerous villages left no survivors, and hence no trace.[163] The most thoroughly considered estimates to date place the death toll during July and August 1941 at between forty-five thousand and sixty thousand, with the actual figure more probably closer to the higher end of the range.[164] The number is staggering: in the first two months of Germany's active ideological war against the Jews, between one fifth and one fourth of the Jewish population of Bessarabia and Northern Bukovina was annihilated, mainly by a German ally, with relatively little expenditure of resources by the Germans themselves.[165] The Romanian government, in other words, with its military capacity and its ability to rally masses to a mission of national liberation, showed itself a far more useful source of assistance in the German project of killing Jews than did the Slavic and Baltic populations that had fallen under Soviet rule in 1939 and 1940. To be sure, German observers were not always entirely satisfied with Romanian performance. Reports from *Einsatzgruppe D* complained periodically about what German officers perceived as the venality, inefficiency, and insubordination of Romanian soldiers. They also sometimes chided Romanians for attacking all Jews indiscriminately instead of directing their fire first against Jewish leadership groups. In other instances, however, effective cooperation was noted.[166] In any event, the *Einsatzgruppe* reports do not appear to have detected any lack of popular will to kill of the sort they recorded among local Slavs and Balts.

Nonetheless, the articulated goal of the Romanian state was not necessarily to kill the Jews of Bessarabia and Northern Bukovina but to isolate them from Romanians and to remove them from Romanian territory.[167] In larger towns and cities, Romanian forces learned, there were simply too many Jews for outright total murder to bring about those goals as quickly as the regime evidently desired. Accordingly Romanian officials soon adopted the directions that Mihai Antonescu had suggested on 3 July—placing Jews in labor camps and forcing them across the border. The latter course received the greater emphasis. During the second half of July the Romanian army began marching Jews from various locations in the newly regained lost provinces to concentration points on the Dniester River with the intent of pushing them into parts of Soviet Ukraine recently occupied by their own and German forces. Twenty-five thousand—some 10 percent of all the Jews present in the two provinces at the beginning of Germany's invasion of the USSR—were transported across the river on 24–25 July. However, the German military authorities in charge of the occupied region balked at accepting them. After three weeks in which the deportees were detained in a barbed wire enclosure in the middle of a field, German troops pushed them back onto Romanian territory—but not until one third or more had been shot or had perished from starvation.[168] In light of the German response, additional deportations that Romanian authorities had begun in the interval were halted, and the deportees moved to larger towns, where they were concentrated in confined spaces until an opportunity to move them across the river arose. Sometimes deportees were forced to walk for weeks on end until they arrived at the concentration point, often far from home. Many died en route; survivors later recounted being deprived of food, water, and shelter while their captors and civilians along the route beat, plundered, raped, and killed with impunity.[169] By the end of August, some seventy-five thousand to eighty thousand Jews in Bessarabia and Bukovina had been incarcerated in eight large urban ghettos or transit camps, awaiting the outcome of German-Romanian negotiations over the possibility of deportation beyond the Dniester.[170]

The negotiations concluded on 30 August 1941 with assignment of Soviet territory between the Dniester and the Bug to Romanian administration. Deportations resumed shortly thereafter, this time with no German opposition. Romania dubbed the region "Transnistria" and designated it a target for eventual colonization by Romanians within and beyond the state's borders.[171] Meanwhile it would serve as the place where the Antonescus' program of "ethnic purification" would be consummated.

When Romania assumed control, Transnistria had already been ravaged by two months of heavy combat, in which the local Jewish population had sustained considerable losses. Some had been direct casualties of military action: soldiers fell fighting the combined German-Romanian invasion, while civilians perished in aerial and artillery bombardments. Others had tried to flee the battle zone, only to be captured and shot by German or Romanian soldiers. Still others had fallen victim to targeted executions by

Einsatzgruppe D, carried out according to Reinhard Heydrich's original instruction to concentrate first upon Jewish members of the Soviet state and Communist Party apparatus.[172] The precise number of losses from each source during the period of German control in such prominent Jewish communities of the region as Ananyev, Balta, Berezovka, Bershad, Bratslav, Dubossary, Mogilev-Podolskii, Odessa, Shargorod, Tiraspol, Tulchyn, and Yampol has not been determined, but figures compiled from multiple sources suggest that of the more than three hundred thousand Jews resident in the area in 1939, upward of one-third were no longer present when the Romanian administration began.[173] Shortly before departing, German forces began concentrating those who remained into half a dozen ghettos in the larger towns.[174]

During fall 1941 the Romanian authorities continued the ghettoization process, greatly increasing the number and type of restricted spaces in which local Jews were confined. In addition to urban ghettos, concentration camps were established in one-time *sovkhozy*, and punitive labor colonies came to dot the countryside.[175] At the same time the Romanian regime deported between 120,000 and 180,000 Jews from Bessarabia and Bukovina into the Transnistria zone.[176] Damage from the recent fighting having decimated the available housing stock, both sets of Jews were forced into spaces largely unfit for human habitation, often devoid altogether of enclosed shelter and sanitary infrastructure. Mass death from exposure and disease was the result: perhaps as many as half of Transnistria's Jews died "naturally," as it were, by the end of 1941.[177]

The spread of disease worried local Romanian officials, for infection-producing microbes could not be counted on to respect ghetto boundaries. Nevertheless, officials' pleas notwithstanding, deportations continued apace. By December 1941, the prefect (supervisor) of Golta County in eastern Transnistria, Modest Isopescu, who had watched the number of Jews in his district grow from fifteen thousand to more than one hundred thousand after warning Bucharest that "new convoys of kikes (*jidani*)" would only spread further infection,[178] decided that immediate danger of epidemic made radical action imperative. On 13 December he ordered all Jews in the town of Golta shot. A week later he extended the order to the entire population of the concentration camp at Bogdanovka—forty-eight thousand people. On 21 December his command was carried out. Most of the victims were marched to a nearby forest, where they were shot one by one in an operation that extended over several days. Those too feeble to march were burned alive in the camp stable. The Jews of two other nearby camps, at Domanevka and Akmecetka, were murdered shortly thereafter.[179]

Fall 1941 and winter 1942 also witnessed the near total obliteration of the remaining Jewish population of Odessa, one of the largest aggregations of Jews in a city occupied by hostile forces during the Second World War.[180] Odessa had withstood a siege of some two and a half months before falling to the Romanian and German armies in mid-October. The long interval between invasion and conquest, together with the ongoing availability of a supply and evacuation route through the Black Sea, no doubt contributed to the ability of perhaps as many as half of the city's approximately two hundred thousand Jews to escape before the siege was broken.[181] The hundred thousand or so who remained were subjected immediately to a campaign of killing as extensive as any attempted to date anywhere within the Nazi orbit. On the day they entered the city, 16 October, a unit of *Einsatzgruppe D*, working with a company of Romanian intelligence officers, began hunting suspected communists, mainly intellectuals and mostly Jews. Over the next day as many as eight thousand were shot.[182] On 18 October occupation authorities ordered all Jews to register with the police; the more than sixteen thousand who complied found themselves shoved into the central prison and surrounding streets, which became a temporary concentration camp.[183] Their fate, and the fate of all other Jews in the city, was determined five days later, after a booby trap exploded in the headquarters of the Romanian Military Command, killing the city's newly appointed chief military administrator along with sixty other officers and enlisted personnel.[184] Ion Antonescu himself responded by ordering drastic repressions: two hundred communists for every officer and one hundred for every enlisted man were to be executed; one member of each Jewish family was to be taken hostage (along with all communists in the city); all Jews who had fled to Odessa from Bessarabia were to be put to death; and all who could not be shot or hanged immediately were to be "placed inside a building that will be mined and detonated . . . on the day of the burial" of the dead Romanian soldiers.[185] The orders were carried out in spirit if not precisely to the letter, with the brunt of punishment falling upon Jews, communist or not. At least twenty thousand Jewish men and women were either shot in place or herded into warehouses, where they were strafed by machine guns and their bodies burned.[186] The tens of thousands of Jews who managed to escape the initial retaliatory murders were concentrated shortly thereafter in the heavily damaged suburb of Slobodka, awaiting deportation to an unknown destination. An eyewitness described the scene:

> There were no lodgings to be had in Slobodka. People crowded around in the streets. The sick groaned and fell straight to the ground. Romanians rode straight over them with their horses. All around you could hear the sobbing of hungry, freezing children, cries of terror, pleas for mercy. These were covered over by shouts from Romanians: "Kike, get out of the way." People would scatter like a frightened herd of sheep. That year Odessa had an unusually harsh winter. Already on the evening of the first day frozen bodies were falling on the streets of Slobodka. On the first night you could hear the completely desperate cries of the deportees who had been chased onto the train that would take them away.[187]

The witness expressed envy for the Jews who had been killed at once: she thought their end preferable to the lingering death that awaited the remainder.[188] Over the next four months they would be dispatched to camps in Golta County. Some perished on the way; most died shortly after arrival. Within 120 days, one of the proud citadels of Soviet Jewry ceased to exist.

The Antonescu regime seems to have understood intuitively what the Nazi regime learned from experience—that for killing not merely large numbers but large percentages of enemy populations, forces armed, trained, and commanded by a state were far more effective than ad hoc mobs or militias not beholden to state authority. Accordingly, in mid-July 1941, the highest-ranking German planners, including Hitler himself, set about making certain that not only the *Einsatzgruppen* but the entire German occupation apparatus, military and civilian, would dedicate itself to the maximum extent possible to the Nazi ideological anti-Jewish war. A crucial planning meeting took place on 16 July at Rastenburg, East Prussia, where the Nazi dictator had recently built a command post (the infamous Wolf's Lair) for directing Operation Barbarossa. There the *Führer* informed Alfred Rosenberg, along with Hermann Göring, Hitler's deputy; Wilhelm Keitel, his chief military officer; and his party and state chiefs of staff, Martin Bormann and Hans Lammers, that "we are performing and can [continue to] perform all necessary measures … for occupying, securing, and establishing order in a region," including "shooting, population transfer, and so forth." "The Russians [*sic*]," he continued, "have given an order for a partisan war behind our front."[189] Germany could now use the Soviet partisan campaign to justify "extirpating whatever places itself against us." The quickest way to pacify the conquered regions, he concluded, was "to shoot to death anyone who even looks at us sideways." Moreover, he insisted, Germans alone would take up arms against opposing forces.[190] Apparently Rosenberg's earlier expectation that locals could be counted upon to do the bulk of the necessary killing, at least of Jews, no longer figured in Nazi strategy.[191]

One key Nazi leader was absent physically from the Rastenburg meeting—Heinrich Himmler, chief of all SS and police operations throughout the entire German Reich, to whom Heydrich, among others, reported directly. Nevertheless, the meeting established that he would play the same role in the newly occupied Soviet lands that he played throughout the entire German Reich: through the SS and police formations at his command, he would continue to supervise and coordinate all matters pertaining to internal security[192] Himmler moved quickly to consolidate his position, placing an additional 16,500 men, including 11,000 SS personnel and 5,500 members of the Order Police,[193] at the disposal of his three personal representatives in the east, Higher SS and Police Leaders (HSSPF) Friedrich Jeckeln, Erich von dem Bach-Zelewski, and Hans Adolf Prützmann.[194] The additions brought the total force under the three senior SS figures' direct command to thirty-five thousand—more than ten times the men available to the *Einsatzgruppen*.[195] In turn, Jeckeln, Bach-Zelewski, and Prützmann designated nearly all the new forces to the war against the Jews, no doubt at the behest of Himmler, who evidently sensed that Hitler's comments at Rastenburg implied stepping up the pace of that campaign.[196] Himmler moved again to increase the pace on 25 July with an order to enlist local populations in auxiliary police formations. "The task of the police in the occupied eastern territories," he explained, "cannot be accomplished with the manpower of the police and SS now deployed or yet to be deployed."[197]

Not that the *Einsatzgruppen*'s initial contribution to the campaign had been meager: from the first week of Operation Barbarossa through late July 1941, an interval of five weeks, they murdered at least thirty thousand Jews all along the battlefront.[198] In the larger cities and towns they did so most commonly by kidnapping Jews, usually but not always working-aged men, from their homes or in the streets, gathering them in a jail or a temporary camp, marching them by groups to a remote site on the town's outskirts, and shooting them, either one-by-one with rifles or all at once with machine guns. In some places they proceeded according to Reinhard Heydrich's mandate to concentrate first upon Jews in Soviet employ; in others they were less discriminate—individual unit commanders seem to have found considerable room for interpretation and initiative. Often they were assisted by local militias that had been subordinated to German command: those groups helped identify Jewish houses, prepare the killing sites, guard Jews as they were brought to them, and in some cases even fire the fatal bullets. Sometimes commanders of *Einsatzgruppe* units used large-scale kidnappings and executions to co-opt the fervor of local mobs and militias.[199] In Kaunas, for example, beginning on 30 June 1941 and continuing over the next week, Lithuanian auxiliaries recently placed under the supervision of *Einsatzkommando* 3 brought thousands of Jews to the Seventh Fort, one of twelve nineteenth-century citadels ringing the city, where *Einsatzkommando* personnel and Lithuanian riflemen gunned down nearly all of the five thousand male internees together with some of the women.[200]

The most extensive early *Einsatzgruppe*-led operation took place in Wilno from 4 to 20 July 1941, when *Einsatzkommando* 9 and Lithuanian auxiliaries mowed down at least five thousand Jews (and by some estimates as many as ten thousand) in the abandoned foundations of an unfinished Soviet oil storage facility in the wooded suburb of Ponary (Paneriai).[201] But such a thorough action strained available manpower to the limit, and even after it was completed, some 80 to 90 percent of Wilno's Jews remained alive. The *Einsatzgruppen* were thus at first only moderately more effective than local mobs at killing Jews. They were preferable, to be sure, for their political loyalties were unquestioned. But their small size, along with their task of moving forward together with rapidly advancing troops in order to pacify newly conquered areas, prevented them from reaching many Jewish settlements or from remaining in any one place long enough to produce more decisive results. Himmler's moves in mid-July sought to rectify this deficiency by expanding the range and type of forces devoted to murder en masse.

Actually, some Order Police and SS units not commanded by the *Einsatzgruppen* had already demonstrated their readiness to kill Jews with abandon. In Białystok, on 27 June 1941, immediately after German troops entered the city, the commander of Police Battalion 309, Major Ernst Weis, instructed his men to roust Jews from their homes (often pointed out to them by local non-Jews) and to assemble them in the marketplace or in the nearby courtyard of the Great Synagogue. The collection process was carried out with much gratuitous cruelty. Some of the assembled were taken away in small groups to be shot at various points around town. Others, estimated at seven hundred to eight hundred, were locked in the synagogue and burned alive after the building was doused with gasoline and set ablaze. The fire spread to the wooden houses of the surrounding area, which was heavily populated by Jews. Meanwhile, elsewhere in the city, a German detachment shot all patients in the Jewish hospital. All told, the Jewish death toll on the first day of German occupation alone reached 2,000 to 2,200.[202] A second police-led murder action in Białystok, less spectacular but better organized and more lethal, took place on 12 July, when more than a thousand members of Police Battalions 316 and 322 were assigned to arrest Jews (now easily identifiable because they had been forced to wear an identifying mark) on the street and in their homes. The Jewish men who were caught were marched to a stadium in the southwestern part of town, then transferred in small groups by truck to an abandoned Soviet antitank ditch, where shootings continued into the next day. Between three thousand and four thousand Jews perished at the hands of a force ostensibly meant to preserve public safety.[203]

Around the same time, Police Battalion 307 joined with SS troops to carry out an even more catastrophic slaughter in Brześć. Over the course of several days battalion members escorted between forty-five hundred and six thousand Jewish men to an execution site south of town, where SS soldiers shot them, and policemen buried the bodies. Here, however, SS personnel also rounded up and murdered women and children as well—perhaps as many as four thousand.[204] Thus, in less than a week, German SS and police units not part of the *Einsatzgruppen* murdered as many as half of the town's

Jews.[205] It was the largest proportional cull of a Jewish community achieved by German forces up to that time.

The killings at Brześć pointed to the enhanced returns that extension of responsibility for the war against the Jews beyond the four small *Einsatzgruppen* could produce. Although comprehensive figures are not available, it seems clear that the returns grew as additional SS and police forces hitched themselves to the campaign. *Einsatzgruppe C*, for one, reported that during August 1941 alone "the units of the Higher SS and Police Chiefs … shot a total of 44,125 persons, mostly Jews."[206] The actual number was likely much higher. It is known that more than seven thousand Jews were killed by five Order Police Battalions commanded by HSSPF Jeckeln during the final twelve days of the month[207] and that Jeckeln's counterpart Bach-Zelewski boasted that by the end of the month's *first week* the number of dead in his territory already exceeded thirty thousand, of whom Jews comprised 90 percent.[208] It is not clear whether Bach-Zelewski's total included the nine thousand Jews of Pińsk murdered by bullets from the Second SS Cavalry Regiment between 5–8 August.[209]

During the final week of August, German mass killing reached a new order of magnitude, when Jeckeln orchestrated the murder of nearly twenty-four thousand Jews in Kamenets-Podolskii over a mere three days. His excuse was an action by Germany's ostensible Hungarian ally. Kamenets-Podolskii was among the southern Ukrainian towns Hungary had occupied during Operation Barbarossa's opening phase.[210] Though Hungary did not seek permanently to annex any Soviet territory, it did seize upon its temporary occupation to eliminate what it regarded as an unfortunate by-product of its annexation of Subcarpathian Rus' nearly three years earlier. That area was home to upward of a hundred thousand Jews, about 13 percent of the total population.[211] Keen to Magyarize the new acquisition to the maximum, the Hungarian rulers looked to expel as many non-Hungarians as they could. Their incursion into Soviet Ukraine gave them the opportunity to do so. Beginning on 12 July 1941, in response to an order from Budapest, local Hungarian officials expelled at least seventeen thousand Jews, along with an unknown number of Roma, into the occupation zone.[212] More than ten thousand arrived in Kamenets-Podolskii before 15 August, when the German authorities in Ukraine, who had no intention of yielding any part of its jurisdiction to permanent Hungarian control, told the Hungarians to stop.[213] Hungary agreed, but it refused to take back any of the Jews it had already deported.

The Hungarian refusal infuriated the German military command in the region, which had been charged with carrying out the imminent planned incorporation of Kamenets-Podolskii into the civilian-run *Reichskommissariat Ukraine*. Even at an early stage of the expulsions, after only three thousand Jews from Subcarpathian Rus' had arrived, army officials had complained that "feeding [the deportees] is proving enormously difficult" and that "danger of epidemic also exists."[214] Neither the army nor the incoming civilian administration appears to have had a clear idea how to obviate these problems.[215] Jeckeln showed them the way. With no *Einsatzgruppe* units in the vicinity, he brought an SS company under his own direct command together with Order Police personnel and regular German and Hungarian army troops to shoot not only all of the Subcarpathian deportees but between three fifths and two thirds of Kamenets-Podolskii's more than twelve thousand local Jews between 26 and 28 August. The second day of the operation alone claimed more than eleven thousand victims, more than double the highest number German forces had ever killed on a single day in one location. The proportional loss to the Jewish community now surpassed that of Brześć as the greatest recorded so far, as was the proportion of women and children among the murdered.[216]

The massacre in Kamenets-Podolskii demonstrated that during August Germany had acquired what it had lacked at the start of its invasion of the USSR: the capacity to annihilate with great speed virtually all Jews in any town of comparable or smaller size, using only its own personnel. Between late August and the end of September that capacity was employed to liquidate, completely (or nearly completely), four medium-size Jewish communities in Ukraine—Berdichev, Kherson, Nikolaev, and Zhitomir—and three more in the Baltics—Daugavpils, Panevėžys, and Ukmergė. The limited aims that Heydrich had set for the *Einsatzgruppen* in his instruction of 2 July 1941 clearly no longer applied.[217] Nor was the military as reticent as it had once been to devote resources to the murder of civilians. Two months after the onset of Barbarossa, the German state stood poised to eradicate Soviet Jewry altogether.

It did not succeed. Though millions of Soviet Jews were murdered, the massive Jewish settlement in the Soviet Union did not vanish: when the last German troops retreated behind the Ribbentrop-Molotov line in winter and spring 1944, the Jews of the USSR, numbering two million strong,[218] still constituted the second-largest aggregation of Jews in a single state anywhere in the world, dwarfing all others save the United States. True, their losses at German hands had been horrendous, their trials hellish, their trauma profound. The Germans had disfigured their community severely. But they had failed to bring about the "complete and immediate 100 percent clearing of the Jews" of which the architects and the executioners of killing operations had spoken in summer 1941.[219]

Germany failed in the first instance because its war against the USSR, upon which the war against the Jews depended, did not proceed as planned. The Barbarossa blueprint had foreseen the rapid destruction of the Red Army, leading quickly to the fall of a now defenseless Soviet state. Initial developments on the battlefield had looked promising from the German perspective: rapid advances by German forces during the war's first two weeks, which encircled and destroyed multiple Soviet armies and brought German tanks to the banks of the Dvina and the Dnieper rivers (in some places nearly seven hundred kilometers into Soviet territory), had led Army Chief of Staff Halder privately to declare victory as early as 3 July.[220] No doubt that expectation of imminent triumph ranked high among the factors that had encouraged Himmler to divert personnel from front to rear areas in order to hasten the murder of Jews. But by the time Himmler did so, in the middle of the month, Halder and other top military figures had begun to sense that the Soviets were not yet ready to abandon the fight.[221] Red Army soldiers fought on with unanticipated resolve. Contrary to German expectations, most sectors of the country's two-hundred-million-strong citizenry (about twice the population of Greater Germany and its allies put together) remained loyal to the regime. That loyalty helped the Soviets mobilize effective replacement troops as needed despite staggering battlefield casualties. The country's unparalleled strategic depth permitted relocation of factories far into the Soviet interior, where they continued to produce essential military equipment and supplies. Counterattacks on the flanks and determined resistance at the center, especially at Smolensk on the road to the Soviet capital, impeded German progress, claiming losses far heavier than expected and taxing manpower reserves to the limit. "One is gradually becoming aware that the eastern campaign is no stroll to Moscow," wrote Propaganda Minister Goebbels in his diary on 24 July. Two days later, Hitler himself complained that "the Russians . . . simply do not know when they are defeated." The Soviets, German leaders now thought, would not fall in a matter of weeks; the war would continue into spring 1942 at least.[222]

As it turned out, by that time the Germans had managed to advance only another three hundred kilometers eastward. Except in the southern sector—the Donbass and North Caucasus regions—that was as far as they got. They came close to Moscow, even closer to Leningrad, but they conquered neither. In November 1942 the Red Army began pushing them back relentlessly toward Berlin. By June 1944 no German soldiers remained on Soviet soil. Hitler's vision of a German "Garden of Eden . . . in the newly-won eastern territories," voiced at Rastenburg in the first flush of battlefield success, could not be consummated.[223] His dream of an *Ostraum* empty of Jews was part of that larger vision. Both faded together.

More than any other factor, it was the frustration of the Barbarossa plan in late summer 1941 and German responses to it that shaped Soviet Jewry for the next three years and beyond. At that point, with troops exhausted, supplies depleted, and ranks worn thin, German strategists faced a stark choice: replenish frontline units and regroup quickly for a massive, all-out September assault upon Moscow, where the Soviets had concentrated the bulk of their forces, in the hope of delivering the Red Army a fatal blow before winter, or prepare first economically for a longer conflict by turning simultaneously south, toward the Ukrainian breadbasket, the Donbass coal mines, and the Caucasian oil fields, and north, toward the Baltic, to keep Soviet submarines away from bases where they could interfere with vital iron ore shipments from neutral Sweden. Hitler's generals urged the first course, but the *Führer*, convinced (perhaps rightly) that they did not grasp the economic imperatives of contemporary warfare, dictated the second.[224] On 21 August he ordered Army Group Center's premier armored units to turn south toward Kiev. Although the move spared Moscow (for the moment, the Germans thought), it broke the back of Soviet resistance in northern and central Ukraine, until then the most difficult regions for German forces to subdue. The Ukrainian capital fell on 19 September, opening the road to the strategic resources southeast.

Kiev's fall also paved the way for what was perhaps the largest single massacre of Jews in one city anywhere at any time, not only at Nazi hands but in all of Jewish history. The trigger resembled the one that would prompt the slaughter of Odessa Jewry a month later: booby traps exploded in former Soviet government offices that had been expropriated by the German army. In response, Army and SS leaders determined to execute every Kiev Jew within reach. On 28 September all Jews in the city and its surrounding areas were ordered to report the following day to a street corner near the Jewish cemetery. At least half the estimated sixty thousand to seventy thousand Jews who had not escaped before German occupation did so. Some were moved, no doubt, by the death penalty attached to failure to appear. Others evidently believed that they would be resettled in another location or preferred German custody to the mercies of the newly created Ukrainian police force under German command. In the event they were marched a short distance to a shallow ravine called Babii Yar ("Grandmother's Gulch"), where between thirty-three thousand and thirty-six thousand Jewish men, women, and children were felled by gunfire within forty-eight hours.[225] A combined effort by units of *Einsatzgruppe C*, Police and Waffen-SS battalions under Jeckeln's command, companies of the regular army, and local auxiliary police, unprecedented in its intensity, generated murder at several times the pace later reached at the killing centers at Auschwitz and Treblinka.[226] Hunts for the remainder continued throughout autumn, until by the end of 1941 only a handful of Jews in the city remained alive in hiding.[227]

On the other hand, the German turn south spared Moscow's more than a quarter of a million Jews a similar fate.[228] After its success in the battle for Kiev, in whose defense the Red Army suffered more than seven hundred thousand casualties,[229] Germany turned its attention once again to the Soviet capital. Now, though, autumn rain and snow, which turned roads to deep mud, joined ongoing troop fatigue, supply difficulties, and Soviet resistance to encumber progress. Though the Germans came close enough to impel the Soviets to remove the government a thousand kilometers east to Kuibyshev, in early December they suspended their campaign until the following spring.[230] They would never come closer. Moscow remained unconquered, its Jews living through the war, like their non-Jewish fellow Muscovites, beyond the Germans' direct reach. Their chances of outliving the German onslaught were thus more or less equal to those faced by their non-Jewish neighbors.

The same was true of the 200,000 to 275,000 Jews of Leningrad,[231] although the day-to-day experience of all residents of the USSR's second city was immeasurably harsher than what was felt in the capital, and the chances of dying from German action were greater by far. Initially Germany had counted upon Finnish assistance to take the city, and it had deployed its troops in the north accordingly. When Finland halted its advance after recovering the territories it had lost to the USSR in March 1940, the Germans adjusted their strategy.[232] On 8 September 1941, two days after the Finns announced they would not join a German assault, Germany, lacking sufficient strength to conquer Leningrad without moving troops from the south (where they were preparing for the assault upon Kiev), placed the northern metropolis under siege. The Germans expected to starve the city's 3.5 million people to death. They nearly succeeded: in 872 days of German encirclement, before the Red Army broke through on 27 January 1944, some 630,000 to 800,000 residents perished from hunger, cold, and disease, with another 17,000 dying from aerial and artillery bombardment.[233] It is likely impossible to determine how many among them were Jews. Nor is information available about how they coped with the bitter conditions—whether Jews possessed any advantages or disadvantages in procuring food or shelter or in escaping the city, whether they developed their own communal networks for self-help, or whether ties among them grew stronger or weaker in the face of an adversity they faced together with their neighbors. Clearly Jews had a vital interest in doing what they could to help Leningrad avoid falling into German hands. Nevertheless, evidence suggests that some non-Jews perceived them as privileged and that verbal expressions of hostility became more frequent in factories, on the street, and in communal housing. Disparaging remarks about Jews have been discovered in several private diaries that recorded the siege. Such expressions appear to have troubled officials, who were charged with the supremely difficult task of maintaining social solidarity under conditions of extreme deprivation. But in the end, no indication has yet turned up to suggest that Jews faced any serious threat from any part of the city's population.[234] If then, Jews' experiences in besieged Leningrad, including their losses, resembled those of non-Jews more or less, it seems reasonable to estimate that the German blockade cost somewhere between forty thousand and seventy thousand Jewish lives. It was a grievous loss indeed, but not a mortal blow to a major Jewish center.[235]

The Soviets' ability to halt the German advance while maintaining their authority along the front in the face of constant German attempts to undermine it spared not only the half million or more Jews in the USSR's two largest cities but another 350,000 Jews living in the parts of the Russian Federation and in the other Transcaucasian and Central Asian Soviet Republics (Armenia, Azerbaijan, Georgia, Kazakhstan, Kyrgyzstan, Tajikistan, Turkmenistan, and Uzbekistan) that German forces did not reach.[236] As a result of the German invasion these Jews would eventually assume a more prominent position in the collective Soviet Jewish profile than they had occupied earlier, when seven tenths or more of the Jews in the pre-1939 Soviet territories continued to inhabit the historically dense regions of Jewish settlement that fell under German control. A small minority, including the fourteen thousand Jews in the city of Gorkii, and the seven thousand in Saratov, lived in locations within aircraft range and were exposed to heavy German bombing, but they did not become targets of any direct German action *as Jews*. Nor did any other Jews east of the front lines. Their encounter with the Nazi war against the Jews came instead indirectly, through service in the Red Army and in war industries[237] or through contact with some 1.2 to 1.25 million Jews from parts west who managed to outrun the invaders and find shelter in places the Germans did not reach.[238]

Those Jews would constitute the bulk of Soviet Jewry after 1944. Some of them fled eastward on their own; others joined the state-organized evacuation that transported perhaps 16.5 million Soviet citizens—mostly government and party officials, managers and workers in vital war industries, military-aged young people, important scientists, leading intellectual and cultural figures, and their families—away from places deemed in danger of falling under German control.[239] The progress of the German invasion was a primary determinant of Jews' ability to leave those areas. During Operation Barbarossa's opening weeks—when German forces, moving with seemingly preternatural speed, encircled towns, wrought havoc on the roads, and disoriented a regime and a population caught entirely unprepared, first by the invasion itself, then by its evident success—escape proved far harder to achieve and evacuation far harder to organize than they did once the enemy advance had slowed. Consequently, the percentage of people able to move eastward tended to vary directly with their homes' distance from the advancing front line, the time it took German armies to reach them, and their proximity to the Soviet interior. In the former Polish *kresy*, in Lithuania, and in the westernmost reaches of eastern Belarus, almost all of whose territory was within German grasp by the end of the first week in July, only about 5 percent of Jews managed to get away. Latvia was also overrun during the first fourteen days, but because it was closer to Red Army positions, more than one sixth of that country's Jews were able to find shelter behind the Soviet lines. For all of the annexed territories together, the escape rate was approximately 7 percent.[240] By contrast, Jews whose towns fell after 10 July, the large majority of them within the USSR's pre-1939 boundaries, often found significantly greater chances to leave.[241] More than half the Jews of Vitebsk escaped, half from Vinnitsa, two thirds from Dnepropetrovsk, 85 percent from Smolensk, and more than 90 percent from Gomel. Of the Jews in pre-1939 Soviet territories occupied by Germany before August 1941, fewer than 40 percent avoided occupation. In territories occupied later the proportion rose to 65 percent.[242]

Evacuation interacted with military developments to influence the course and the extent of killing in complex ways. The influences did not always reinforce one another. On one hand, evacuation brought German killing operations numerically diminishing returns as the battlefront moved east. "It is hardly possible at present," reported *Einsatzgruppe B* from Smolensk on 4 September 1941, "to continue the number of liquidations on the same scale as before, since the Jewish elements are to a great extent missing."[243] But as Jewish ranks became progressively thinner in the front areas, where mobile killing units were concentrated, wholesale destruction of entire communities became a simpler task requiring smaller forces. Had, for example, all 130,000 or more Jews living in Kharkov in June 1941 stayed in the city when it fell to the German army four months later, the relatively small detachments from *Sonderkommando* 4a, the SS, and the military police that rid it of Jews during the last days of the year and the first days of 1942 would hardly have sufficed for the job. By that time, however, only about twenty thousand Jews remained to be killed, making it possible to accomplish the job with considerably fewer personnel than had been employed in Kiev in early autumn.[244] The Germans' cost-benefit calculus in late 1941 thus favored attending first to Jews closest to their front lines. And so the

Germans did, increasingly employing regular army units in the process.[245] By the end of the year the areas under German military occupation (those farthest to the east, which did not become part either of *Reichskommissariat Ostland* or of *Reichskommissariat Ukraine*) were virtually free of Jews, as were southeastern Ukraine and much of Eastern Byelorussia. Most Jews from those areas had fled or been evacuated, but various combinations of German forces had murdered more than half a million.[246]

By concentrating on the front areas, though, the Germans postponed action against more than a million Jews to the rear who had been passed over both by local mobs and militias and by the executions of the invasion's first month. In early August at least 80,000 Jews remained alive in Lwów; 43,000 in Białystok; 40,000 in Wilno; 35,000 in Kaunas; 29,000 in Riga; 12,000 in Tarnopol; 10,000 in Brześć; and 6,000 in Złoczów—that is, after the forces that had visited catastrophic violence upon these Jewish communities in June and July had moved on. Other large and mid-sized communities were still more or less intact, having lost only relatively small numbers of Jews targeted as potential sources of resistance or as examples made to terrorize others into submission. Upward of 75,000 Jews continued to live in Minsk; 40,000 in Stanisławów; 22,000 in Równe; 20,000 in Grodno; 18,000 each in Łuck, Pińsk, and Vinnitsa; 15,000 in Słonim; 14,000 in Kowel; and 10,000 each in Baranowicze, Nowogródek, and Proskurov. Hundreds of thousands more continued to inhabit more than a thousand localities, with Jewish communities numbering from a few hundred to ten thousand, spread throughout the former Polish *kresy*, the Baltic regions, and the westernmost reaches of pre-1939 Soviet Byelorussia and Ukraine. Initially the Germans had not paid these Jews much heed: if local mobs did not murder them all immediately, they evidently assumed, German forces would dispose of them once the Soviet regime collapsed. At that time they appear still to have equated complete disposal with removal to Siberia.[247] However, by August it looked increasingly to German strategists that the lands east of the Urals would not come into their hands anytime soon. Total murder of all Jews in the rear areas offered an alternate means of disposal, but the security, police, and military forces required to complete the job were still needed close to the front. As a result, the Germans were now compelled to consider how best to manage those Jews until the time for final reckoning arrived.

It turned out that the army had already laid the groundwork for management. Before civilian rule was instituted in most of the occupied territories in late August 1941, the military had assumed responsibility for day-to-day administration, including maintenance of order and control of the local population. In conjunction with that task, individual army commanders frequently imposed decrees upon local Jews imitating practices the Nazi civil administration had adopted in western and central Poland beginning in 1939. Jews under those commanders' control were forced to identify themselves with a yellow star attached to their clothing. In most locations they were also forbidden to travel, were impressed for forced labor, and were subjected to various additional encumbrances and humiliations. Military officials generally supervised the appointment of Jewish councils (*Judenräte*) or councils of elders (*Ältestenräte*) to head Jewish communities, to transmit German orders, and to enforce Jews' compliance with them.[248] Whether the commanders who introduced such measures meant them from the start as steps toward immediate mass murder or merely as practical administrative devices, their actions made it easier to locate Jews once the time to kill arrived.[249]

Until that time came, military considerations appear initially to have been paramount in shaping German behavior. Those considerations stemmed from a strategic decision German planners had made before launching their invasion of the USSR—to sustain their soldiers from the occupied territories' own resources instead of transporting food and supplies from Germany.[250] Needs for history's largest-ever invasion force would at first be massive, but planners anticipated they would diminish sharply once the Soviets were no more.[251] However, once it became clear that Soviet collapse was not imminent and that troop strength would need to be maintained or even increased for many months, plans for feeding, housing, and clothing German soldiers had to change. In particular, local demand for indigenous resources could be met only after German requirements had been satisfied. Local inhabitants who helped supply German needs might be tolerated, but local inhabitants who might take food or shelter from German personnel had to be removed.[252]

With regard to Jews, German calculations pulled in two opposite directions at once. On one hand, as overwhelmingly artisans, professionals, managers, and (still, in the annexed territories) merchants, with few farmers among them, Jews consumed much more food than they produced. On the other hand, living off the land involved exploiting precisely the essential services of day-to-day life that local Jews, especially in small towns, were best positioned to provide, from repairing boots, uniforms, and machinery to cutting hair and tending to the acutely ill. More generally, their labor could be of value to Germans in maintaining the productivity of local industries that supplied day-to-day German needs, as well as in constructing the roads, barracks, and fortifications required for the ongoing war effort. The balance between the two factors varied from place to place and from time to time, depending upon local conditions and the progress of the war. As a result, local military commanders and civilian officials were often the ones who determined when, which, and how many Jews in their jurisdictions would be maintained and how many would be put to death.

In the Baltic regions the balance inclined more often than not toward immediate wholesale murder. The German authorities there were charged with supplying the nine hundred thousand men of Army Group North as they advanced upon (and later besieged) Leningrad. By mid-July the demands of the troops had exhausted available food reserves, while local peasants were unable to produce sufficient surpluses to feed the soldiers, themselves, and a nonagricultural population of more than eight hundred thousand. To solve the problem, multiple civilian, SS, and military officials came to the simultaneous conclusion that "useless eaters" (*unnütze Esser*) should be eliminated immediately.[253] Jews, of course, along with Soviet war prisoners, were to Nazi minds the most obvious candidates for liquidation. Accordingly, beginning in August 1941, Jews in town after town throughout Lithuania and Latvia were assembled, beaten, marched or driven to a remote location, shot, and buried in shallow pits hastily dug for the purpose. An eyewitness described a typical wholesale murder operation in the provincial town of Święciany, north of Wilno, which took place on Saturday, 27 September 1941:

> All of the Jews were driven ... into the market place.... Those who didn't leave their houses quickly enough were brutally beaten.... They left five families of "useful Jews" behind in town.... At 11 am ... the Jews assembled at the market place and were taken away, in columns.... The sick, elderly and weak ones were taken on wagons.... All of the Jews in the towns of Shventzionys [*sic*] County were assembled at [a] military estate that Saturday; they were kept there for

> twelve days, under terrible conditions. On Wednesday, October 8, 1941, the shootings began. In the course of three days about 8,000 Jews were shot. Their corpses were thrown into a long mass grave, in a sandy forest. . . . The mass grave was 170 meters long and 10 meters wide.[254]

Contrary to the practice of *Einsatzgruppe A* during its initial sweep, in which young, educated men were the primary targets, now all Jews, including women, children, and older men, were fair game. By the end of 1941 these mass murder operations claimed upward of 120,000 victims in Lithuania, another 70,000 in Latvia. Between 40,000 and 50,000 Jews, mostly younger men and women deemed employable in local German-run war-related enterprises, together with their families, were left behind. They were concentrated almost entirely in a handful of urban centers, principally Wilno, Kaunas, and Šiauliai in Lithuania, and Riga in Latvia.[255] Nearly all other Jewish settlements in the Baltics were destroyed.[256]

Three factors helped Germany annihilate more than three quarters of Baltic Jewry within four months during late summer and fall 1941. First, a third or more of the region's Jews lived in rural areas, where commerce, not artisanry, provided their main source of livelihood.[257] Because German forces in the Baltic regions turned out not to require masses of hands and backs for large-scale military construction projects, Jewish men lacking skill at a craft, let alone women and children, were immediately expendable in German eyes. Moreover, Jews in the Lithuanian and Latvian countryside were divided from the outset into groups small enough to be managed by relatively few soldiers, policemen, or SS agents, facilitating rapid wholesale liquidation of their communities. Finally, Germans found significant support for their murderous endeavors among the local population. As a result, they were able to delegate many aspects of the killing process, often including actual shooting, to specially recruited killing squads like the Arājs group or the Lithuanian National Labor Defense Battalion, as well as to local police units under German supervision.[258] The ability to call upon large-scale local assistance proved especially crucial in concentrated killing operations in major urban centers, like the murder of nearly ten thousand Jews in the Ninth Fort at Kaunas on 29 October 1941 and of twenty-four thousand in the Rumbula forest outside Riga on 30 November and 8 December.[259]

Elsewhere, different factors led to different outcomes. In the area the Germans called White Ruthenia (*Generalkommissariat Weißruthenien*)—the largest administrative division of *Reichskommissariat Ostland*, which combined portions of the former Polish provinces of Białystok, Nowogródek, and Wilno with parts of the Minsk *oblast* of the pre-1939 Byelorussian SSR—significantly more skilled Jewish manual and industrial workers were available than in the Baltic regions to produce for Germany's war needs. They constituted the overwhelming majority of such workers on both sides of the 1939 Soviet border.[260] Additionally, the Jews of White Ruthenia were less scattered in small rural settlements than were Jews to the north.[261] Many more Jewish artisans lived in mid-sized towns or in large urban centers than in Lithuania or in Latvia, making it more difficult to eradicate entire communities in a single blow. And the local assistance needed to carry out such wholesale eradications in larger locations was not nearly as readily available as it was in the Baltic countries. Whereas five battalions of local police (*Schutzmannschaften*)—perhaps as many as three thousand men—served the German occupiers in the city of Wilno in November 1941, and another five in Kaunas, the district administrator (*Gebietskommissar*) of Baranowicze could call upon a force of only 250 local policemen in his entire jurisdiction.[262] Under such circumstances, the balance of costs and benefits between clearing their bailiwicks of Jews entirely and maintaining large numbers of Jewish workers indefinitely appeared to most German civilian and military officials in White Ruthenia to favor maintenance, at least until a local non-Jewish workforce could be cultivated. The *Gebietskommissar* of Lida, Hermann Hanweg, explained his approach to *Generalkommissar* Wilhelm Kube in a comprehensive report on economic and security arrangements in his district:

> Creating a healthy manufacturing sector is complicated by the fact that the artisans are focused on speculation and trade. . . .[263] Aware of the inability of local artisans to produce all the necessary commodities for my own staff, for the *Wehrmacht* officers, and for other civilian authorities, I created an enterprise in which only Jewish specialists work. After exhausting the entire Jewish workforce, I intend to turn these [facilities] into fully-equipped workshops for training [non-Jewish] artisans under the guidance of a German master.[264]

Evidently Hanweg's thinking was widely shared, for nearly two thirds of the Jews in White Ruthenia lived at least into 1942.[265] Wholesale liquidations in the area during 1941 were confined to a relatively small number of communities with Jewish populations under one thousand.[266] In a few larger towns local officials separated workers from ostensible "unnecessary gluttons" (*unnotige Fressern*) and, if the necessary personnel could be assembled, ordered the latter shot: *Gebietskommissar* Gerhard Erren, for example, was able to call upon SS, army, and police units in the area to murder 9,000 to 10,000 of the 16,000 Jews in Słonim on 13–14 November 1941.[267] But in other places, like Slutsk, south of Minsk, *Gebietskommissar* Heinrich Carl actually opposed offers from police under the command of HSSPF Bach-Zelewski to render their jurisdictions "free of Jews" (*judenrein*), warning of severe damage to the war economy as a result:

> On 27 October [1941] ... a lieutenant from Police Battalion 11, coming from Kaunas, appeared, presenting himself as the adjutant of the Battalion Command of the Security Police. The lieutenant stated that his battalion had received an order to liquidate all the Jews in Slutsk within two days.... I immediately raised a vigorous protest, stressing that the liquidation of the Jews of Slutsk must not be carried out arbitrarily. A large portion of the Jews in the town are skilled workers or their families. We simply cannot do without these skilled workers; they are indispensable to the functioning of the economy. I pointed out that there are virtually no skilled workmen among the so-called White Ruthenians, so that eliminating all the Jews will paralyze the most important factories all at once.[268]

The incident in Slutsk reflected a fundamental tension within the Nazi regime over the implications of eliminating all Jews from the captured Soviet territories as well as contention over its priority. On one hand the ideological demand to vanquish the Jewish parasite once and for all, which the Nazi leadership had defined not only as a central war aim but as a reason for the Third Reich's very existence, encouraged as rapid and complete a killing operation as possible. The SS, in particular, as the chief prosecutor of the ideological war against the Jews, was eager to mount such an operation without delay. On the other hand, as an inspector in the army weapons office informed the office's commander, General Georg Thomas, in early

December 1941, "Eliminating [the Jews] must have profound economic repercussions, affecting even the military directly."[269] Accordingly, many within the army and the civil administration, concerned first with successfully completing the battle to topple the Soviet Union, preferred to exhaust the Jews' labor potential before consigning them to death. In early 1942 Alfred Rosenberg, the Nazi official responsible for *Reichskommissariat Ostland* and *Reichskommissariat Ukraine*, pushed back directly against SS efforts to accelerate the killing process, claiming that he and the civil administrators that reported to him were in the best position to balance ideological and military demands:

> In which specific form and at what speed ... the extraction of the Jews ... is to be carried out ... can only be subject to the political decision of the *Reichskommissare* and *Generalkommissare* [and not of the SS]. It is self-evident ... that the segregation of the Jews, as a *political* consideration, must take precedence over all *economic* considerations. Nevertheless, *initially* wartime economic measures in the occupied eastern territories must still be factored in. It is thus the political duty of the German administration ... to replace Jewish craftsmen to the greatest possible extent with Ukrainians, Belorussians, etc., who are to be trained.[270]

The weapons inspector put it even more bluntly: "If we shoot the Jews to death," he asked rhetorically, "who is supposed to produce things of economic value?"[271] At the time no one in the Nazi regime appears to have had a persuasive answer. Hence in 1941 economic considerations tended to prevail: large numbers of Jews outside the areas of military occupation, the Baltics, and the eastern portions of *Reichskommissariat Ukraine* were put to work, sometimes in factories near home, sometimes in more distant labor camps. As a result, a significant majority of Jews in these areas remained alive even after six months of savage German rule had claimed more than 1.2 million lives.[272]

Over the next year, however, a unified response to the inspector's conundrum emerged, making 1942 the *annus horribilis* of Soviet Jewish history.

The response did not address the conundrum directly; instead it dismissed it as unimportant.

The dismissal followed a fundamental strategic reassessment following Germany's declaration of war against the United States on 11 December 1941. For two years Germany had tried to hold off such a fight, knowing that it would reinstate the two-front conflict German planners had long feared. However, growing US material support for the British and Soviet war efforts had persuaded Hitler that a battle was inevitable. When Japan bombed Pearl Harbor, forcing the United States into all-out war in the Pacific, the Nazi dictator and his generals saw an opportunity: they could hold the Americans at bay in Europe while continuing to concentrate their forces against the USSR. If a two-front war had to be fought, these seemed like the most favorable conditions for fighting it.[273]

Still, as 1941 turned to 1942, Germany's military situation was not good. Its declaration of war on the United States came amidst a massive Soviet counterattack, launched six days earlier. The offensive sent German armed forces into disarray, to the point where, on 19 December, Hitler appointed himself army commander-in-chief. His act rallied the troops: he ordered them to hold the line, and they did. Over the next six weeks the Red Army failed to dislodge them, despite a concerted effort and superior strength.[274] However, Germany emerged from its crisis still needing to plan for a conflict far more protracted and extensive than the one it had imagined in September 1939 or in June 1941.

Plans developed even as the Soviet winter offensive was being rebuffed. They addressed material concerns—food, fuel, and manpower to meet the needs both of Germany's military and of its civilian population.[275] But they also involved clarification of fundamental war aims. From the outset those aims had been both territorial and ideological. At first achievement of the main ideological aim—eradicating Jewish Bolshevism root and branch—was predicated upon conquering Jewry's territorial fortress, the USSR.[276] But with conquest delayed, and with Germany now facing the United States and the USSR together, the Nazi calculus changed. The new Soviet-British-American Grand Alliance persuaded many within the Nazi regime, including Hitler himself, that Jews actually ruled all three countries.[277] By mobilizing the most powerful of its client states, Jewry—so it appeared to Nazi leaders—had escalated its conflict with the Third Reich to a new and unprecedentedly urgent level. Now that the Jews "have imposed the [worldwide] war on us," Hitler explained to Rosenberg, "they should not be surprised if the consequences hit them first." The consequences to which Hitler referred, as Rosenberg well understood, were "the annihilation of Jewry."[278] Henceforth that aim would be elevated to the highest priority, to be pursued with the utmost vigor and without delay, whatever economic or military difficulties such pursuit might generate.[279] The question of who would "produce things of economic value . . . if we shoot the Jews to death" no longer mattered.[280] All Jews needed to be eliminated immediately, come what may.

Near total elimination in all areas under German control took nearly two more years to achieve. The reason appears to have been chiefly the sheer numbers of Jews involved. Practical obstacles actually turned out to be fewer than anticipated. To begin with, the many Jewish workers that had been employed as heavy laborers were easily killed upon exhaustion and replaced with non-Jews.[281] Demand for *skilled* Jewish labor thus proved less acute than many Germans had initially estimated. Additionally, the northern and central fronts remained fairly static throughout 1942, allowing mobile units initially charged with pacifying newly conquered territories in those regions to be redeployed to rear areas, where they could concentrate upon wholesale liquidation of Jewish settlements. At the same time, in 1942 police in Byelorussia and Ukraine stepped up recruitment to local *Schutzmannschaften* nearly tenfold, providing the German killers with far greater support than they had enjoyed in 1941.[282] German efficiency also increased dramatically in spring and summer 1942, when gas chambers at Bełżec, Sobibór, Majdanek, and Treblinka commenced operation. Instead of being executed by shooting squads, several hundred thousand Jews from the Galicia and Białystok districts, the Baltics, and the former Polish *kresy* (along with many more from central Poland), were dispatched by rail to these mass killing centers, where they were asphyxiated upon arrival.[283] The so-called second sweep of German forces through areas where substantial numbers of Jews remained, during the spring, summer, and autumn of 1942, brought about the deaths of some 1.1 million Jews. By the end of the year, when the Red Army began to reacquire lost lands and to push German forces westward, only 250,000 at most remained alive anywhere in the German-occupied territories of the USSR.[284]

The year 1942 also brought death to tens of thousands of Jews along the eastern Black Sea coast and in the Kuban and North Caucasus regions, which Germany overran in summer of that year.[285] Among those threatened with murder in this campaign were some three thousand to five thousand so-called Mountain Jews (*Gorskie Evrei*)—non-Ashkenazi Jews, indigenous to the region, who spoke Judeo-Tat, a religiolect of the Tati-Persian language.[286] Yet despite their self-identification as Jews, 75 to 80 percent of them managed to escape the Nazi killing campaign, mainly because German authorities were unable to decide whether they ought to be counted as Jews at all. Some Nazi officials placed them in the same category as Karaites, followers of the eighth-century Jewish teacher Anan ben David. Karaites assigned exclusive religious authority to the Hebrew Bible; they rejected the rabbinic tradition expressed in the Talmud and (especially in modern times) separated themselves from Jewish communities. Nazi scholars who studied the issue generally determined that the policies of the Third Reich regarding Jews did not apply to them, allowing some nine thousand to ten thousand Soviet Karaites to escape death at German hands.[287] When German forces encountered the Mountain Jews, they questioned whether that community might be similarly exempt, for the dress, manners, and cuisine of these Jews, like that of the Karaites, associated them more with the peoples of the Central Asian steppe than with the Jews of Europe (even though, unlike the Karaites, they accepted rabbinic authority). That doubt evidently saved the large majority, with only members of *kolkhozy* with a significant Ashkenazi Jewish presence falling victim to the murder campaign.[288]

Of course, the legal loophole that saved Karaites and most Mountain Jews was available only to them. For all other Jews virtually the only way to subsist legally under German rule by mid-1943 was as a worker in a small number of factories or labor camps operated by the SS, by the German state-run construction and engineering conglomerate Organisation Todt, or by a handful of private employers who had persuaded local occupation officials to allow them to make use of a limited number of Jews on an ad hoc basis. Such positions had been dwindling steadily throughout the year; they would vanish altogether before the Red Army pushed the Germans back across the Riga line beginning in January 1944. As part of Germany's retrenchment, on 21 June 1943, Heinrich Himmler ordered all Jews in *Reichskommissariat Ostland* placed in concentration camps under direct SS supervision, with "unnecessary" Jews to be "evacuated to the East"—a euphemism for deportation to a killing center.[289] The order appears to have been carried out without significant opposition; the entire Nazi regime was now evidently determined to salvage at least one accomplishment—the eradication of all Jews under its control—from its impending military debacle. During summer and fall 1943, all who still remained in the few significant Jewish settlements left not only in *Ostland* but throughout the German-occupied USSR—Białystok, Lida, Lwów, Minsk, Riga, Šiauliai, and Wilno—were either resettled in large labor camps, transported to a killing center, or shot to death.[290] The workers selected for the camps were regularly culled. Some who lived into 1944 were removed to concentration and labor camps in Germany with the retreating German armies; the rest were murdered on the spot. By the time Soviet forces regained control of all of their post-1939 territory in July 1944, they found no more than ninety-thousand Jews—about 3 percent of the number who had fallen under German or Romanian occupation, not including evacuees. More than half had spent the war under Romanian rule, where the authorities lacked both the ideological impetus and the political will to turn mass murder into total eradication.[291] The others had survived in hiding, under cover of false identity, or with partisan groups.[292]

One of the Jews who emerged from hiding was physician Baruch Milch. Posted by the Soviets to Tłuste in East Galicia in 1940, he had managed to take advantage of his professional expertise to hold on legally under German control, until his town's Jewish settlement was liquidated in May 1943. Though his wife and son perished, he found shelter in a series of nearby farmhouses and stables for nine months, until Soviet troops arrived. During the interval he recorded his thoughts and experiences in a diary. In one of his final entries, on 26 March 1944, he described his first confrontation with the disfigurement of his world that all survivors had now to face:

> I became weak when I passed by the house where I had once lived with my family. The roof had collapsed . . . ; the door and windows were no more. There was nothing inside, because after my departure the local residents had plundered everything. . . . The town looked unrecognizable. . . . Almost all the Jewish houses were in ruins; here and there smoke was rising from a few houses recently set on fire or bombed. The few isolated Jews who made their way to town from various hiding places greeted each other with tears in their eyes, as if they had returned from the netherworld. They looked like corpses exhumed from the ground. I rarely recognized people who greeted me. Even though they

> used to be my patients, I had to ask, "Who are you? What is your name?" They were in rags and barefoot. Young people had grown gray, lost all their teeth; girls had gone bald. All related different stories about the hell they had lived through and how they had miraculously survived.

He kissed the first Soviet soldier he saw "like my own brother." Still, he noted plaintively, only a handful of his Jewish brothers—"Mohicans," he called them—remained to tell their tales.[293]

3
SPACES FOR SURVIVAL

Different survivors encountered disfigurement differently, but their tales shared a common feature. All survived because they found spaces where their would-be killers could not reach them. Milch's spaces were among the most constrained: an attic, a hayloft, a subterranean pit, where he hid like a hunter's quarry. Others were less confined, and day-to-day life was less onerous. All were obtained, in some measure at least, through decisions Jews took at different moments during the war. Those decisions helped shape how Soviet Jewry would reconstruct itself once the German menace had passed.

Locating any safe haven invariably involved imposing obstacles, high risk, and intense existential fear. Such was the case even in what turned out to be the least confining, least onerous, safest havens of all—the ones in the Soviet interior, beyond German-controlled territory. Masses sought those spaces with vigor from the outset. More than a quarter of Soviet Jews found them.[1] It is not known how many more tried and failed. However, if eyewitness accounts offer any reliable indication, abortive attempts were numerous, especially in the border areas, where German bombs fell from the earliest moments of fighting.

The aerial assault was terrifying; it destroyed homes and buildings, claiming life and limb. "Already in the first hour of war there are casualties," wrote Moshe Margolis, a young diarist from Włodzimierz in Volhynia. The shock sent masses to the highways, Jews and non-Jews alike. "The road ... to Łuck is full to overflowing with hundreds and thousands of fleeing refugees," Margolis indicated in his entry for the first day of hostilities, "some on foot, some in trucks or other vehicles, all filled to capacity."[2] Różka Korczak, a seventeen-year-old Zionist youth movement activist in Wilno, observed a similar sight the following day:

> The intense bombardment does not cease. The city is consumed in flames. Ashes are all that is left of houses. Cultural treasures are reduced to rubble.... An enormous human wave is moving through the city.... It doesn't seem stoppable. Everyone to the East! To Minsk! Individuals are running away, dozens, hundreds. Anything to be far from here!... Thousands of Wilno Jews have just one desire, one goal: to get away. To get away from here! Not to fall into [the enemy's] hands.[3]

Few got far. The experience of Avraham Golub, a lawyer from Kaunas, was typical:

> I... tried to flee northward on a bicycle. The traffic was heavy. German Messerschmitts strafed the refugees and the Red Army units, which were retreating without putting up any real resistance. I felt like a hunted animal in a forest going up in flames. I continued on the bicycle and on foot, from village to village, with no food and almost without sleep, until German bombs destroyed the road.... The escape route was blocked. I had no choice but to retrace my steps back to [Kaunas].[4]

Physical impediments drove Golub back where he started. Upon returning he learned of human dangers as well. "The Germans," he recounted, "[had been] joined by gangs of Lithuanians, which had sprung up in every forest and village."[5] Survivor testimonies from dozens of larger and smaller locations, not only in Lithuania but throughout the border regions, recount both German roadblocks and ambushes by local militias set to harass retreating Soviet troops. These units fell upon civilian refugees as well, whether fleeing their homes or, like Golub, attempting to return to them.[6] Early in the fighting even *Soviet* forces guarding the former Riga frontier foiled some Jewish flight attempts by enforcing restrictions upon movement from the territories annexed in 1939 and 1940 to the pre-1939 USSR.[7] Not until the German army effectively erased the old border in early July did this impediment vanish. By then, though, it was too late for all but a handful to escape the annexed regions.

Those who avoided literal roadblocks faced hurdles less tangible but no less real. Transportation was a formidable problem. Trains seemed the surest means of escape to most, but not all could find space on them. Although the USSR possessed an extensive rail network, many Jews in smaller towns and villages lacked immediate access to it.[8] Even where trains were plentiful in peacetime, war made them scarce. The army needed them to move troops, including new recruits, to their posts. "There are still trains" in Wilno, Różka Kurczak recorded, but "people must push their way [onto them], mixing with the army, stricken with fear bordering on madness."[9] Actress Ida Kamińska was performing in Równe, a major rail junction, when German bombs began to fall; yet, as she recalled, she and her troupe had to flee on foot, hoping to pick up a train en route, no matter where it was heading. They succeeded, but only after a trek of several days in the hot summer sun punctuated by short rides on wagons or in trucks. They spent nights in houses when they could and in municipal parks when they couldn't. Three months pregnant, she described her condition when she finally boarded a train for Kiev as "more dead than alive."[10]

Kamińska eventually wandered from Kiev to Poltava to Kharkov to Baku and on into Central Asia.[11] Her experience on the road was a common one among the small percentage of Jews from the western territories that succeeded in escaping; journeys unfolded unpredictably, usually in broken segments that did not always pull in the same direction.[12] In Kamińska's case, though, the difficulties she encountered are surprising. Given her fame and the favor the Soviets had shown her,[13] she might have expected some official assistance. After all, the Soviet regime was keen to remove all resources potentially valuable to the Germans—physical, organizational, and human alike—from areas liable to fall under enemy control. To that end, from the war's first week, the state organized massive road and rail convoys to carry heavy industrial equipment from dismantled factories, along with the personnel needed to reassemble and operate it, as far to the rear as required. Senior state and party officials were also offered places on the evacuation transports, as were prominent scientists, intellectuals, and figures essential to operating the USSR's leading educational, cultural, and research institutions. Families of top-priority evacuees were permitted to accompany them.[14] By all indications Jews who belonged to those categories (which the Soviets had long since opened to them) found space on the transports to the same extent and on the same basis as others of comparable rank and privilege; they experienced neither discrimination nor preferential treatment.[15] Thus, for example, the day after the war began, a large group of Yiddish writers from Białystok was offered a car of its own on a hastily organized train for important cultural figures, and organizers worked to bring eligible Jews to the departure platform.[16] But practice did not always follow policy, as Kamińska, for one, soon discovered. Procedures for implementing the broad strategic aims of evacuation crystallized only gradually during late June and early July.[17] Meanwhile, with bombs falling and canons ablaze, military and civilian officials in the western border areas and beyond could hardly attend to everyone who wanted to flee, including, sometimes, individuals and families (of all ethnic backgrounds) entitled to precedence according to policy guidelines. As a result, many—Jews and non-Jews alike—did not wait for an official invitation; like Kamińska, they attempted to evacuate themselves—if necessary, even entirely under their own power.[18]

Nevertheless, the fact that trains continued to move away from the war zone at all—whether to transport troops, remove civilians, or simply avoid falling into German hands—coupled with the general confusion and the absence of clear evacuation procedures, appears to have enabled many would-be self-evacuators to latch on to official civilian or military transports without explicit authorization. "While the Soviets were evacuating their personnel, we sneaked aboard their train cars," reported Shlomo Mann and Yisrael Glazer, two Zionist activists who had fled from German-occupied Poland to Lithuania in 1940 and now found themselves running from the Germans again.[19] Alexander Prużański, a physician from Lida who had been dispatched to Minsk in 1940, recollected that when a German aerial attack began, he and some of his hospital colleagues, sensing that "everybody was on his own," simply climbed onto a train standing far from the station and waited for it to leave, without investigating its destination. Eventually the train brought him to Leningrad, even though he carried no travel authorization.[20] Testimonies are replete with similar stories of Jews reaching diverse locations, some just behind the front lines, some deep in Central Asia or Siberia, because they found places on trains they had no formal permission to board.[21] On the other hand, efforts to do so were not always successful. Transports were all too often packed to overflowing.[22] Hence, whether a refugee trying to board a train at a station or along the way managed to do so depended mainly upon the attitudes of loading supervisors and train crews. Railroad personnel often made policy for themselves. In some places they evidently kept men off trains in order to make room for women and children;[23] in others, even local Soviet officials were reportedly unable to influence decisions about who traveled onward and who remained behind.[24] Sometimes well-placed bribes of cash, liquor, or jewelry helped grease a transport's wheels for those with the means and the knowledge to distribute them properly.[25]

In the end, the ability to gain space aboard a train proved essential to finding safety in the Soviet interior: there was simply no other way to outrun the German advance. But the trains did not always bring their passengers to safety. German strategy included bombing rail lines, and German planes routinely attacked convoys traveling along them. The writers' train from Białystok, for one, faced frequent bombardment: actress Sheyne-Miriam Broderzon,[26] one of its passengers, recalled that "time and again we had to jump from the train car and seek cover in the fields, clutching the ground hard so the German pilots wouldn't see us."[27] The passengers on that transport escaped injury, but travelers on other trains were not always so fortunate. Mann and Glazer reported coming across identification cards belonging to some of their Zionist comrades who had boarded a different train: "Their train was bombed, and all were killed."[28] Fear of a similar fate evidently persuaded some to prefer travel by foot or cart along back roads, moving only by night, when bombing ceased.[29] These, however, became easy prey for the German commandos and local militias working to secure the countryside.[30]

Flight thus always involved multiple risks. So, too, though, did remaining in place. But at the beginning of the war hardly anyone was in a position to determine which risks were worth taking and which were not. No one could predict the war's eventual course. In fact, many were initially unsure about the precise source and extent of danger and about the relative efficacy of various possibilities for avoidance. Many Jews appear to have thought at first that they needed to find only short-term shelter from immediate war damage, expecting Soviet forces to repel the German attack quickly.[31]

These people looked not to trains or to highways to carry them far from the scene of battle but to nearby villages for places to stay until the Soviets reestablished their authority and rebuilt their towns.[32] "None of us could have imagined that the Soviet Union was so weak," observed humorist Szymon Dzigan.[33] "We were certain that all of [the country's] wealth was being invested in the army."[34] Consequently, military withdrawal from a town was widely interpreted at first as merely a tactical retreat in preparation for a massive thrust into enemy territory. I. B. Gertsovich, a Jewish employee of a Minsk newspaper, described a conversation that took place in his office while German bombs fell:

> We, like many others . . . , were educated by the newspaper. . . . We read that we would reply to the attack with an attack three times as big, that dealing with the enemy would be a piece of cake, that we would go all the way to Berlin, that the war meant a world revolution. This was the popular formula at the start of the war, and that is why we thought that any day now we would head westward on the offensive. And we firmly believed it.[35]

To be sure, even a temporary withdrawal of Soviet forces frightened many Jews. It scared them, however, not primarily because it invited *German* occupation but because it created a power vacuum that hostile *local* elements might fill to the Jews' detriment. Jews in the former Polish *kresy* recalled similar *interregna* following the First World War and again in September 1939. During those unsettled times, forces associated with rival ethnic groups had fought one another for control of cities, towns, and entire regions, with Jews often caught in the crossfire.[36] Now, after two years during which Soviet manipulations of the annexed territories' complex ethnic politics had often exacerbated intergroup tensions, talk of a new round of violence abounded in many places even before German troops had arrived.[37] A Jew from Tłuste in East Galicia, Yehoshua Shechner, opened his wartime diary with a description of the trepidation such talk engendered in his community:

> Groups of Ukrainians began to gather on the outskirts of town. Those Ukrainians incited the local residents against us while expressing hatred toward the Soviets. Every petty hooligan made so bold as to threaten every Jew on the street with words like, "Hitler is coming, and he'll put an end to you!" No

> wonder that among Jews, fear grew from moment to moment. The feeling was that the Ukrainians' words were not just idle talk and that an explosion was drawing near.[38]

Jacob Shkolnik, a Riga Jew whom the Soviets had appointed comanager of a factory, faced an even more direct, personal danger:

> When I came to the factory ... on 27 June [five days before German forces entered Riga], I saw that two gallows had been erected. A female worker explained to me tearfully that "one is for you and the other is for [the Latvian communist factory manager]." I went away and recounted the story. I was told to leave, "but don't make any noise."[39]

Acute threats like these from known assailants, which raised their heads even before German rule had begun, appear at times to have pushed the perils of the impending German arrival away from the forefront of consciousness. Baruch Milch, like Shechner a resident of Tłuste, avoided the menace of a local mob by hiding with his family in the cellar of an acquaintance's farmhouse. He stayed there three days and nights while local "dark elements prowled the town, joining peasants from surrounding villages in robbing and stripping bare whomever they could." But once looting subsided he did not try to run farther or to hide for a longer period. To be sure, by his account, he considered both options. He knew, he wrote retrospectively, "that things were very bad for the Jews under Hitler, that various surprises were in store for us," even that "there will be murders with many victims." But at the time those perils seemed sufficiently distant for him to reject "voluntary exile."[40] According to Shechner, most of the town's Jews reached the same conclusion.[41] Evidently they preferred to deal with the most imminent dangers as they occurred instead of formulating a long-range survival strategy from the outset.

Jacob Shkolnik, facing a potentially lethal mob of his own workers, appears similarly to have concentrated upon the most immediate source of adversity, to the exclusion of others still more distant from him. He took a horse and wagon from the factory and set out with his wife and children, evidently with no particular destination in mind. On the road he heard shooting, which persuaded him to improvise. By chance he came upon a doctor acquaintance who, "as a supervising physician, had a bus at his disposal." He decided to entrust his family to the doctor's care, believing, no doubt, that on his own he could evade a concrete, present menace from his neighbors more easily and with less risk to his loved ones, even though he did not know what the doctor had in store for them.[42] First he would look for a way out of the imminent jeopardy facing him and his family. He would deal with the future consequences of his actions as they appeared.

Even Jews who feared a long, painful German occupation from the outset, and decided immediately to flee as far from the front lines as they could, soon discovered that they needed to adjust on the fly. Jews from Lithuania, Byelorussia, and the Białystok area tended at first to set out toward Minsk.[43] However, German bombs falling from the first day of the war raised flames visible at some distance from the city. The sight of the burning capital evidently persuaded many that "there is no point heading there while the bombing is going on."[44] But alternate escape routes could be found only through trial and error. Evacuees often learned to their dismay that "at any time the Germans may catch up to them or surprise them from the front or outflank them, cutting off the road after capturing a strategic bridge deep inside [Soviet] territory."[45] Would-be escapees generally did not know that from the first day of fighting German planes dropped paratroopers far behind the front lines, allowing them to capture points east before places farther west.[46] Many found themselves unable to advance as a result. Some managed to return to their places of origin; others chose to remain where they had been stopped.[47] Dzigan described their position: "No matter where they tried to run from the war, the war ran after them."[48]

Jews who took flight may or may not have considered such possible outcomes, but they were clearly undeterred by them. By contrast, many who remained behind envisioned the hazards of refugee life as even greater than the hazards of German rule. Fifteen-year-old Icchak Rudnicki, who fled southward from Święciany on the fourth day of war, recalled that "at the last minute" his uncle tried to dissuade him from leaving. "He argued that we have no chance to get away, that the Lithuanians are liable to kill us on the road, making it better to stay here. In his opinion, under German rule we could expect a ghetto, forced labor, misery, and degradation. . . . But all of this is better than dying on the road."[49] Some Jews imagined a German regime no worse than the relatively benign one they had known during the

First World War.[50] Others feared what might await them to the east. Leon Kahane, nineteen-year-old son of a well-to-do businessman from Tarnopol who had moved to the nearby town of Mikulińce after being dispossessed by the Soviets, remembered years later that "my parents, who were not 'kosher' as far as the Russians were concerned, decided to stay in [town] and leave the future to fate." His parents ignored the example of their neighbors who, after hearing local non-Jews warn of a bloodbath once the Germans arrived, attached themselves to retreating Soviet columns.[51] A Hasid from Bobruisk reportedly dug in his feet even more emphatically: "They can carry me away like an animal carcass, but I will never go to 'them'; I'm not moving from here no matter what."[52] Some associated movement eastward with the mass deportations the Soviets had carried out shortly before the German invasion, concluding that "if we are destined to die, better here [under the Germans] than in Siberia."[53] And some were simply too exhausted to move. The librarian Herman Kruk, a prominent Bund member who had undergone a harrowing, five-week journey from Warsaw to Wilno in September-October 1939, told his diary on 23 June 1941, "No more strength to take the walking stick in hand and set out again on the road.... The heavy shoes are off, the rucksack is unpacked."[54]

Perhaps many of the Jews who unpacked their rucksacks and awaited German rule with resignation might have been more inclined to take up the walking stick had they known the Germans would soon undertake to kill every man, woman, and child among them. At the time, however, no information was at their disposal from which they could reasonably infer such a prognosis.[55] The conquerors, after all, neither publicized their designs nor telegraphed their blows. Thus the expectation of a harsh but ultimately survivable existence reflected in Rudnicki's recollections (and in many others)[56] could have been founded only upon observations of the Jews' lot in other parts of the Nazi empire. At first those observations came mainly from reports by refugees from the German-occupied zone in Poland; after the refugee flow from that region was throttled in late 1939,[57] they were based largely upon letters from the German zone, which continued to arrive by regular post up to the outbreak of the German-Soviet war. Evidently it was from letters sent by his family in Warsaw that Rudnicki and his uncle learned of the compulsory labor service the Nazis had forced upon Polish Jews and of the ghetto regime in Europe's largest Jewish community.[58] There was no way they could have been aware of more. Since the Ribbentrop-Molotov Pact the Soviet government had suppressed news Germany did not wish to become widely known,[59] but even had it not done so, the government likely possessed no intelligence that might have led to a different outlook for the future.[60] Even the Polish underground, with a broad network of informants close to the Nazi occupation authorities, concluded in spring 1941 that Germany aimed "to wrench the Jews from the general society" and "to isolate and divide them from the Polish population" by "locking them up in a massive prison under the threat of hunger, epidemics, cultural backwardness, as well as unceasing aggression."[61] It did not anticipate the systematic murder on which the Germans would soon embark. There is no evidence that those who fled held a substantially different assessment.[62] On the contrary, Rudnicki and his uncle do not appear to have disagreed about German intentions. Their disparate operational conclusions stemmed rather from differing evaluations of identical data. For them, as for many who debated whether to stay or to leave, determining the relative risks and possible rewards associated with fleeing or remaining in place involved weighing perceptions of both the Soviet and the German regimes and their armies together with individual and family circumstances, the physical and social environment, the availability of transportation, and the course of battle. The balance appears to have varied widely from place to place: whereas Rudnicki recalled "many hundreds" who tried (mostly without success) to flee Święciany as he had, Yehoshua Shechner recorded "only a few [communist] activists from among the local Jews" in Tłuste joining evacuating Soviet personnel.[63]

In general, the farther east a community was situated, even within the territories annexed to the USSR after 1939, the more the balance shifted toward trying to leave. In Volhynia, for example, escape attempts were an estimated three times more frequent in the parts of the province east of Krzemieniec, Równe, and Sarny than to their west.[64] At least eight times more Jews attempted to flee the pre-1939 Byelorussian SSR than the Polish provinces incorporated in the republic in that year.[65] *Within* pre-1939 Soviet Byelorussia escape attempts may have been as much as seven times more frequent in the republic's easternmost areas than in its westernmost ones.[66] Fewer than 4 percent of Jews appear to have tried to escape from the former Polish province of East Galicia.[67] By contrast, *successful* escapes alone from the Zhitomir District of *Reichskommissariat Ukraine* have been estimated at nearly 50 percent.[68]

These substantial differences cannot be explained by supposing that Jews farther east had greater knowledge or understanding of German designs upon them than did Jews closer to the point of German attack. Nearly all who fled, successfully or not, did so before German forces occupied their towns. Consequently, only German actions in locations captured before their own could have influenced their decisions. But those actions took place behind the nether side of a war front. In the fog of battle, with communication disrupted, information did not flow readily over any distance, let alone from one side of the front to the other. And even if Jews on the Soviet side had been in a position to receive information from Jews in German-occupied territory during summer and fall 1941, when flight and evacuation had reached their peak, they would have heard primarily about the "ghetto[s], forced labor, misery, and degradation" Rudnicki's uncle anticipated. There were, to be sure, several places in which Germans carried out the sort of "murders with many victims" that Milch feared, but even those operations, not yet the norm, were not widely known even close to the places where they occurred.[69] And the worst apprehensions of Milch and of Rudnicki's uncle had not moved them from their homes in any event.[70] Perhaps not surprisingly, then, the same sort of dismissals of the severity of the German threat were heard among veteran Soviet Jews who refused to move east as among similarly reluctant Jews from the western borderlands.[71]

The pattern of Jewish flight attempts seems instead more satisfactorily explained by two other considerations: augmented hope for success and diminished fear of Soviet reality. Both of these considerations were, to a significant degree, products of distance from the front. Distance bought Soviet authorities additional time to organize comprehensive evacuations. Beginning in mid-July, considerably more railroad cars were placed at the disposal of local officials in still-unoccupied areas of heavy Jewish settlement than had been at hand farther west. Many of those officials made intensive efforts to increase access to the transports.[72] These transports, in turn, were less likely to be intercepted on the ground or bombed from the air the farther German forces had to travel to reach them and the more dispersed the routes they traveled.[73] What had been significant impediments and deterrents to flight in regions closer to the September 1939 border thus became less so farther east. The strategic depth the USSR acquired via the events of September 1939 thus became a lifesaver for Jews to the east of the former Riga line.

Moreover, Jews from the pre-1939 USSR were more familiar with the Soviet system than were Jews who had known it for only one or two years. Veteran Soviet Jews, especially younger ones who had grown up within the Soviet system, surely knew of the regime's oppressive face, but for most of them the opportunities for social advancement and the protections from the ill effects of long-standing group prejudices that it offered appear, by all available indications, to have elicited in them more assurance than distrust.[74] As a result they were, on the whole, no doubt less uneasy about placing their security in the hands of Soviet officials than were Jews from the newly incorporated western lands, many of whom had learned to distrust the intentions of rulers who had only recently expropriated their property, dismantled their communal structures, and deported members of their families.[75]

In the end, neither Jews who fled nor Jews who remained behind could be certain what awaited them. Their decisions were often less the result of informed calculation than of circumstance. For some, circumstance pointed to what would be a fortunate direction; for others it was ruinous. Choices made on the spur of the moment bred a succession of unintended consequences. What journalist Tania Fuks[76] observed of herself applied to virtually all Jews who sought a safe space in which to pass the storm: "I came through every time not thanks to my foresight that doing some particular thing would turn out better for me, but precisely the opposite: I wanted to do something, and by accident I had to do something else, and the something else was good for me."[77]

The faith that veteran Soviet Jews who boarded evacuation trains tacitly placed in the country's governors set them apart not only from their fellow Jews in the borderlands but also from non-Jewish Soviet citizens who calculated the regime's debits and credits differently.[78] The brutal repressions of the 1930s had left many Soviet residents apprehensive of their rulers' intentions toward them. The rout of the Red Army during the war's first weeks sowed even deeper doubt, not only about the regime's concern for their welfare but about its very ability to shield them from harm. For more than a decade, and with redoubled force since the Nazi rise to power in Germany, Soviet leaders had explained to their people that the stringent political controls, painful material deprivations, violent social upheavals, harsh limitations upon personal freedom and cultural expression, and bloody purges that characterized their rule were all vital to supplying the Soviet homeland with the resources it required to defend itself against a hostile capitalist world. They had also portrayed their military as the world's strongest, capable of repelling any attack. When an attack came, Foreign Minister Molotov promised that "our valiant army and navy and the brave falcons of the Soviet air force . . . will deal the aggressor a crushing blow."[79] But once it became clear that crushing blows had been dealt *by* the aggressor instead of *to* it, faith not only in the current Soviet leadership but in the entire Soviet system and the worldview that sustained it became, even for ardent communists, increasingly difficult to maintain.[80]

Official evacuation efforts added a further dimension to systemic mistrust. Especially in the war's early stages, many took evacuation as evidence of panic in the leadership. Others saw it as proof of cowardice and moral bankruptcy: evacuation seemed an opportunity for officials and members of the elite to save their skins while abandoning the rest to their fate. More practically, fear of becoming a refugee at the mercy of a state that was neither a competent nor a beneficent protector appears to have deterred many among the Soviet population at large from joining the eastward exodus. Some even equated evacuation with expulsion and protested it vigorously. For others it offered final confirmation of the regime's incorrigibly oppressive nature, from which only a German victory could redeem them.[81]

The extent of these sentiments is difficult to gauge, as is their impact. They were not exclusive to non-Jews; a number of Jews, most of them highly acculturated figures from large cities, expressed them as well.[82] Ultimately they were not powerful enough to impede seriously the state's ability to mobilize masses for a successful war effort. Nevertheless, government promotion of evacuation from the war zone appears to have exerted a destabilizing effect upon Soviet society. That destabilization, in turn, helped open the door to expressions that challenged, among other things, the place of Jews within it.

The challenge echoed German war propaganda. German radio broadcasts and leaflets dropped over Soviet territory proclaimed the fighting an act of Soviet aggression undertaken at the behest of a "Jewish plutocracy," with whom "Bolshevism" purportedly colluded in "treasonous cooperation."[83] Germany, so the line went, had no quarrel with the Russian people or with any other national group within the USSR except "Jews and their Bolshevik henchmen."[84] The depiction evidently resonated sufficiently among the Soviet population for the NKVD to inform Stalin himself in July 1941 and again in September of increasing expressions of hostility toward Jews among all social classes.[85] Those expressions were often tied to evacuation. One police intercept quoted in the September NKVD report recorded a retired Russian professor complaining that "there are no Jews at the front; they have all run away to any place where everything will be quiet."[86] The notions that the "USSR is not a Russian country, it's a Jewish country" and that Russian draftees were being sent "to defend the kikes" simultaneously fed and were fed by a widespread perception that "the Jews have fled."[87] At least once, anger at Jews' seeming privilege and lack of patriotism spilled over into popular violence even before the Germans arrived. On 16 October 1941, the day major central government offices began their move from Moscow to Kuibyshev, crowds of enraged citizens intercepted evacuating vehicles and dragged Jews from them. Calls of "Beat the Jews" and "Kill the Jews" were recorded.[88]

Such behavior, both verbal and physical, was punishable under Soviet law.[89] For two decades leading organs of the regime had condemned it, and Soviet courts had prosecuted it with varying degrees of vigor.[90] Records from one Regional Court show that prosecutions continued throughout the war, although with diminishing frequency and severity of punishment as the war progressed.[91] Now, however, state legal and party political protections appear to have lost much of their deterrent effect: hostility toward Jews could evidently be expressed publicly with little fear of adverse consequences.[92] Even party members were noted openly hurling insults at Jews, while their party organizations let the incidents pass.[93]

The apparent willingness of some authorities to acquiesce to at least some expressions of enmity toward Jews—expressions they would likely have condemned and penalized only months before—is probably best understood as part of the regime's broader response to the surge of popular disgruntlement that surfaced in the wake of the German invasion.[94] Facing a massive invasion, the USSR could tolerate nothing less than full mobilization of all available human and economic resources. Under the circumstances, though, coercion and terror could bring only diminishing returns as vehicles for social discipline: after all, people executed or imprisoned for political crimes could neither fight nor produce for the war effort. Instead the regime required as close to universal popular support for its conduct of the war as possible. To gain such support it was vital to persuade all segments of the public that the state and its military were fighting to defend what its citizens supposedly valued most—home, hearth, motherland, and a unique way of life that only a state whose foundations rested firmly upon authentic native traditions could preserve. Accordingly, while still preaching solidarity among all Soviet ethnic groups and condemning German anti-Jewish pronouncements as directed against the foundations of the USSR as a whole, the state and party leadership coalesced during the opening months of the war around a program of domestic propaganda that portrayed the Soviet Union less as a revolutionary departure from any hitherto-known political arrangement than as the contemporary embodiment of the soul of "Mother Russia," the instrument of defense for all who lived within its borders, their material possessions, and their cultural patrimony.[95] Themes of class warfare were now subsumed within a rhetoric of national solidarity. The day after the invasion *Pravda* proclaimed a "victorious patriotic war for the motherland, for honor, for freedom," echoing the popular description of Russia's heroic stand against Napoleon in 1812.[96] Stalin adopted the characterization in a radio address on 3 July:

> The enemy is cruel and relentless. He aims to conquer our lands, which are soaked with our sweat, and to take away our grain and our oil, which we have harvested by our labor. He aims ... to destroy the national culture and the national sovereignty of the Russians, the Ukrainians, the Byelorussians, the Lithuanians, the Latvians, the Estonians, the Uzbekis, the Tatars, the Moldavians, the Georgians, the Armenians, the Azeris, and the other free peoples of the Soviet Union.... Therefore [the war] is a matter of life or death for the Soviet state, of life or death for the Soviet peoples, a matter of whether the Soviet peoples remain free or fall into slavery.... Many thousands of workers, *kolkhoz* farmers, and members of the intelligentsia are joining with the Red Army in the war against the invader. The masses of our nation will rise up in their millions.... We must arouse all working people to put their lives on the line, defending

> their freedom, their honor, and their motherland in our patriotic war against Germanic Fascism.[97]

One purpose of such locutions was undoubtedly to push back against assertions that the USSR was "not a Russian ... [but] a Jewish country."[98] Such sentiments, the regime worried, undercut popular willingness to defend the Soviet state, for they misled the masses into swallowing the German line that communists and Jews were the invaders' sole targets.[99] Inducing the masses to put their lives on the line for the Soviet cause thus seemed to demand that the regime distance itself from anything that might smack of undue solicitude for Jews and their particular plight. To appear more Russian, the Soviets had to appear less Jewish. Thus it was surely not by accident that Jews were not enumerated in Stalin's list of threatened peoples, even though they were more numerous than half of them.[100] Nor is it surprising that state authorities would now be less keen to employ the legal system to shield Jews from popular enmity or to employ public media to counter unfounded charges that Jews habitually shirked their military obligations. On the contrary, basic facts about Jewish service in the Red Army (let alone facts about Jewish casualties) that might have refuted such charges appear generally, perhaps even systematically, to have been hidden from public sight.[101] Indeed, throughout the war the Soviets more often than not eschewed public domestic references to Jews as a distinct group for whom the Germans had designated an especially maleficent fate. Although the official press frequently mentioned mass German killings of Soviet citizens, Jews were for the most part counted among their total number of victims, even when the sources that informed the press reports stated explicitly that the operations were directed specifically against Jews.[102] In principle, as far as the leaders of the USSR were concerned, the German invaders threatened all Soviet citizens equally with obliteration, regardless of ethnic origin.[103] To be sure, this line did not preclude reporting specific items of information about murder operations in which Jews were killed. In the event, no explicit Soviet policy about how to speak of Jews killed by Germans, whether within the USSR or beyond its borders, was ever articulated, and from time to time press items appeared highlighting mass Jewish death at German hands.[104] Nevertheless, a concern over appearing overly solicitous of particular Jewish concerns appears to have shaped official Soviet representations of German occupation for its duration and beyond, even though throughout the conflict Soviet officials steadily accumulated information testifying that Jews were subjected to far more brutal Nazi policies and practices than any other constituent peoples of the USSR.[105]

In the final analysis, the Soviet leadership's evident resolve to distance itself from association with Jews or Jewish interests left it unwilling not only to punish expressions of anti-Jewish hostility but to take any steps to address the extraordinarily urgent needs of its Jewish citizens under German rule. Throughout the years of occupation and murder, it would issue no instruction to non-Jewish citizens to render assistance to Jews under immediate threat of annihilation, no order to its partisans behind the German lines to interfere with murder operations, no direction to party or Komsomol members in the underground about how they might help Jews remain alive. Protecting civilians in general who had fallen into German hands was not a significant Soviet war aim; protecting or assisting Jews under German rule figured even less in Soviet strategy. Jews who boarded the evacuation trains may have demonstrated faith in their country's rulers, but their fellow Jews who remained in the German-occupied areas would not be able to count on aid from their government any more than other Soviet citizens in finding space to withstand their would-be executioners, no matter how exceptional their plight.

The first problem for Jews hoping to withstand German rule was to fathom the depth of the danger that faced them and to determine what they needed to survive. Only then could they search sensibly for a secure space in which to lead their lives.

The first weeks of war encumbered their thinking. The heat of battle sent some to the roads, but others preferred shelters nearby. "The earth shook with the heavy air and artillery bombardments, as if flung about by a volcanic eruption," noted Avraham Golub of Kaunas on 7 July 1941. "Now [the Jews] are cooped up in cellars and other hideouts, trembling at every sound coming from the outside."[106] Shimon Redlich, six years old when German planes shelled his hometown of Brzeżany on 28 June 1941, recalled years later that after his family's Sabbath meal was interrupted by "a powerful explosion, followed by the sound of broken glass . . . , everybody was running downstairs into the cellar," where they listened to "the terrifying sequence of whining sounds followed by heavy thumps all through that dreadful night" and for two more nights afterward.[107] Some Jews remained in their shelters after military action gave way to local violence and German pacification efforts. David Kahane, a rabbi from Lwów, noted that "from Tuesday through Sunday [1 through 6 July 1941] I hid in the basement of my apartment . . . , well camouflaged by a wooden wall."[108] But bunkers made poor observation points. Kahane, for one, was hiding from German and Ukrainian press-gangs gathering Jews to exhume the bodies of prisoners murdered by Soviet forces when they withdrew from the city, evidently unaware that those actions and their attendant turbulence had come to an end three days before.[109] Danger, it turned out, was not easily assessed from below ground, nor were opportunities to escape: a woman from Bobruisk did not learn of the first evacuation train leaving the city because she had taken shelter from German bombings.[110]

Watching through a window above ground did not make correct assessment easier. Maurycy Allerhand, a renowned professor of law at Lwów's Jan Kazimierz University and a former president of the city's Jewish community, recorded in his diary that "on 1 July 1941 I saw from my apartment . . . how Ukrainians were beating Jews with clubs and whips." He noticed "an old Jew falling on the ground" but could not tell whether "he had died or merely fainted." The Ukrainians—he deduced their ethnic identity "from the blue and yellow bands they wore on their left arms" and from the language of their curses—seemed to him interested mainly in gratuitous brutality and plunder. By 3:00 p.m., he noted, all was quiet.[111] Although he could discern that at least one of the beaten Jews was being led in the direction of Brygidki Prison (where the Soviets had massacred several thousand inmates), he appears to have had no sense of the destination's significance, even though it was located only a block from his home. He thus remained blind to the rioters' motives. Nor was he aware that Jews brought to Brygidki were being put to death by *German* soldiers, that similar mobs had formed in other parts of the city, that Germans were executing Jews at other prisons, or that violence continued elsewhere in town well beyond the time when calm had been restored in his neighborhood.[112]

Even what must have seemed like the best vantage points did not offer clarity. Later that afternoon two German soldiers and a civilian "of unknown ethnicity" took Allerhand from his apartment to the newly established local headquarters of the Secret State Police (Gestapo). There, a high-ranking military officer, apparently under the false impression that Allerhand still served as community president, instructed him to prepare a report on the city's Jewish institutions as they had functioned under Polish rule. Allerhand complied.[113] From his encounter he concluded that "the German authorities have a plan to resurrect the Jewish community for the purpose of imposing on the Jews a special tax."[114] If he suspected anything more ominous, his diary did not reflect it. On the contrary, his interrogator "made a favorable impression" upon him: the German officer appeared to be "objective in his administrative duties," interested "in hearing only the truth." In fact, the Jewish professor evidently felt sufficiently secure to challenge the German on two fundamental points of Nazi ideology—the nature of Jewish identity and the relative degree of favor shown by the Soviets to Jews, Ukrainians, and Poles. From his account of the conversation it seems that Allerhand viewed Ukrainians, who beat Jews and asked questions later, as a far greater menace than the new German rulers, with whom it was possible to argue reasonably.[115]

Allerhand may well have been the first Jew anywhere in any territory the Germans took from the Soviets to speak directly with a senior German administrator. Similar conversations must have occurred in short order in other locations where officials appointed Jewish councils to transmit and enforce their orders.[116] Only one other, though—in Kaunas on 7 July 1941—is known to have produced a substantial record at the time it occurred.[117] On that day, following a week in which Lithuanian auxiliaries under German command had incarcerated several thousand Jews in the city's Seventh Fort and executed the men among them,[118] German soldiers brought five prominent Jewish public figures, including two rabbis, to local Gestapo headquarters, where the commanding officer presented them with a choice:

> Total disorder and unrest prevail in the city. I cannot allow this situation to continue. I will issue orders to stop shooting. Peace and order must return to the city. The Lithuanians have announced that they no longer wish to live together with Jews; they demand that the Jews be segregated in a Ghetto. The choice is up to the Jews—either the present situation with the disorder and the bloodbath, or leaving the city and moving into the Ghetto.... You must go

> to the ghetto. . . . There is plenty of room for you there. . . . You can take your belongings with you; there you will be free to establish your community life.

The commander also promised that if his Jewish interlocutors took responsibility for moving Jews into the ghetto—designated for the impoverished suburb of Vilijampolė, across the Neris (Vilija) River from the city center[119]—he would order the release of some three thousand women and children who remained in custody in the Seventh Fort.[120]

The Jewish leaders in Kaunas appear to have come away from their encounter with many of the same impressions that Allerhand took from his. They, like their counterpart in Lwów, were persuaded that whereas locals sought only to "vent the rage which has accumulated in their hearts over . . . the Soviet rule in their country . . . by oppressing the Jews,"[121] Germans were a force for order with whom reasonable negotiation was possible.[122] They too saw locals as independent actors instead of as accessories to German-ordered anti-Jewish actions.[123] And although, unlike Allerhand, they were presented with the Germans' first substantial demand upon the local Jewish population, they too left with no clear sense of German thinking beyond the immediate term.[124] They may not even have understood who was in control. Once the meeting concluded, two of them tried to persuade Lithuanian leaders to call off their partisans without the promise of a ghetto. Only after determining that the Lithuanians would not listen did they conclude that "the state of affairs . . . gave us no option but to leave the city and move into the Ghetto."[125] Even a month later Avraham Golub, a close confidant of the Jewish spokesmen and the one who recorded their dealings, found the situation "confusing" and the ghetto order lacking any purpose beyond "to humiliate, to offend, and to cause distress."[126]

Such confusion likely stemmed less from failure to see what lay in plain sight than from cognitive dissonance. The stereotype that juxtaposed the rational, orderly German with the benighted Slavic or Baltic peasant driven by blind, violent emotion evidently carried wide purchase among Soviet Jews, especially among the many with personal memories of a relatively benign German occupation during the First World War, which contrasted with simultaneous recollections of the murderous locally driven upheavals that followed.[127] Disassociating Germans from the violence that beset Kaunas and Lwów during the first days of occupation accorded with that preconception; the greater visibility of locals than of Germans among perpetrators in the streets no doubt reinforced it. But as days passed, Jews in both places encountered German authorities in ways that did not match their impressions. In Kaunas, where the meeting on 7 July had ended with what the Jewish leaders took as the German commander's promise to expand the boundaries of the future ghetto beyond what he had originally proposed, subsequent petitions for modification were summarily denied.[128] More ominously, although the ghetto had initially been represented as a protective measure against Lithuanian assaults, Lithuanians and Germans alike remained free in practice to harass, rob, and murder.[129] On 4 August Golub noted in his diary that "the food supply deteriorates daily" and that "all the efforts ... to change the course of events, to blunt their edge, had proved futile." The community, he concluded, was "helpless."[130]

In Lwów, Allerhand's initial surmise that the Germans would impose a special tax upon Jews came true a month later, when the recently appointed Jewish council was ordered to pay twenty million rubles (nearly $4 million) for war damage repair.[131] Still, he remained certain that his own personal possessions would remain inviolable: "If the Bolsheviks respected the property of a university professor," he wrote in his diary, "how much more so the Germans."[132] Shortly thereafter his apartment was confiscated, along with his furnishings and his library. When he asked the police officer who sealed the apartment for permission to take his books, the officer told him, "It is no longer your library ..., and in any event, you won't be alive much longer." He took the hint and went into hiding—perspicaciously, it turned out, for the next day police sought him at his son's apartment with an arrest warrant. Neither he nor any of his acquaintances, he wrote, understood any longer what the Germans were after.[133]

If community elites could not understand, how were ordinary Jews to make sense of what they saw? Community leaders who spoke with German officials could at least gauge the distance between German word and deed; Jews without such access had no grounds for comparison. Comparison may have prompted initial confusion, but it also offered an extra bit of experience and an additional point of reference from which to assess the situation. Most Jews, by contrast, could assess from German deeds alone, whether observed directly or reported secondhand.

Those deeds generally included one or another permutation of a standard set of initial orders, usually proclaimed by a local military governor within days of occupation: in most places Jews were required to wear identifying badges, register their addresses, surrender radios, and perform labor on demand; they were forbidden to travel, change their residences, sell their wares in the marketplace, use sidewalks, or initiate contact with their non-Jewish neighbors. They were also subjected to food rationing, with daily allotments less than those of non-Jews and obtainable only in segregated queues. The appointment of Jewish councils also usually followed quickly upon conquest.[134] By contrast, it was unusual for Jews to be restricted, as in Kaunas, to an enclosed ghetto. Ghettos began to proliferate only in late summer or fall 1941. In some locations they were used to concentrate the Jewish labor pool, but in most they served simply as short-term holding pens for Jewish communities awaiting liquidation. In fact, in many places they were created only in 1942, after most Jews had already been murdered.[135] In any event, ghettos appear to have existed in fewer than half of the Soviet Jewish communities that fell under German rule.[136]

To date, direct evidence of how Jews understood these decrees and administrative measures at the time they were first pronounced remains extremely sparse. All of the measures, though, were consistent with the expectation of a harsh but ultimately bearable rule that seems to have underlain some Jews' decisions not to flee the German conquest. It appears safe to assume that few Jews changed their evaluation in response to them. Even in towns where *Einsatzgruppen* and other police and SS formations had carried out an initial round of killings it remained possible to incorporate events into the common frame of reference, at least for a while.[137] Many executions were targeted at people with connections to the Soviet regime or who belonged to leadership strata; Jews not part of the target groups could conclude that they had done nothing to bring a similar fate upon themselves.[138] Even more indiscriminate, larger-scale killings, like the murders of Jews from Wilno at Ponary in early July 1941, took place far from public view.[139] Germans generally announced that the Jews selected for them were being taken to work at a distance and would return once their assignment was completed; absent clear evidence to the contrary, the German claim appears to have made initial sense to virtually all who heard it.[140] Moreover, in most of those early actions the tasks of rounding up Jews and herding them to the killing sites were assigned to local auxiliaries, making murder appear an initiative of the Jews' neighbors, not of the conquerors. Germans might acquiesce to the violence, which they portrayed as a spontaneous local reaction to Jewish complicity with Soviet rule, but few Jews seem at first to have taken killing as an essential aspect of the occupation regime. That conclusion was only reinforced in the many locations where an initial killing operation was followed by intermittent lulls in which daily life appeared to follow a bearable, if bitterly harsh, routine.[141]

A pattern of alternating violence and calm unfolded in most places over the first several months of German rule. Two aspects of it proved especially distressing. The first was the seeming impossibility of avoiding spaces associated with serious physical harm. Some Jews hoped at the outset that their homes might offer shelter from the ravages being visited upon them. In Shpola, a community of some twenty-five hundred Jews located ninety kilometers east of Uman in Central Ukraine, a resident reported that "houses echo with the thud of hammers; locks, windows, doors are being repaired, reinforced with iron bars to withstand violent attacks."[142] But sooner or later dwindling larders forced Jews into the streets in search of food and work. Virtually everywhere, Jews who ventured outdoors wearing identifying armbands were fair game for attackers, extortionists, forced labor details, and random killings. Few, though, were prepared to go outside without them, for if caught they would be shot.[143] And homes were hardly inviolable: Germans and locals could enter them at will, appropriating possessions, taking inhabitants into custody, raping, or even murdering them.[144] Some, particularly men, thought for a while that safety came with a job, but they learned quickly that even with an official work certificate from their Jewish council or from a German official, they could be "snatched on their way to work and taken to [prison]."[145] David Kahane from Lwów summed up the situation four months into German rule:

> The fall passed with affliction and suffering.... It was hard to stay at home; the air was stale with the smell of rot; there was no place to sit; it was impossible to concentrate. Ten times each day we would hide in the basement from fear of sundry kidnappers. But we were [also] afraid to go out into the street. We were disconsolate: "The sword brings death from without and terror from within." You can't sit at home, but you can't go outside.[146]

A second source of desperation was the seeming randomness of German actions. In his journal, Yehoshua Shechner recorded a series of occasions, beginning in September 1941 and extending into the following year, in which his entire community feared imminent complete liquidation. Jews had been told by local peasants and by German soldiers passing through town that Jews in nearby locations had already been murdered en masse, while "local Christians who had a connection to the German authorities" spread rumors that "Gestapo personnel were supposed to come to our area together with Lithuanian murderers in order to carry out a mass killing here." The rumors put Jews on edge: "It was enough for an automobile to appear in the streets for panic to set in immediately." Each such appearance passed without incident, but the reprieve offered no comfort. Shechner noted that "fear and trembling" continued to grip the community, stemming from "fundamental uncertainty." "You are living in darkness," he wrote. "You do not know what to expect. Who can know what will happen tomorrow or even in a few hours?"[147]

Tremors born of anxiety were noted throughout the occupied Soviet Jewish world. Yitskhok Rudashevski, a thirteen-year-old diarist from Wilno, summarized his community's situation in late summer 1941, some ten weeks into the German occupation: "We do not know what is in store for us . . . ; the Jews in our courtyard are in despair."[148] Adult Jews with far greater political savvy found themselves equally at a loss. Hersz Smoliar, a veteran communist activist and former political prisoner in Poland, editor of the Yiddish-language newspaper *Bialystoker shtern* and a prominent figure in the Byelorussian Writers' Union, had missed an evacuation train and walked to Minsk instead. He could adduce only one parallel to the situation he encountered during his first month in the Byelorussian capital—an earthquake he had felt in Crimea two decades before. "People ran in panic from place to place, without knowing how to save themselves," he recounted. What called that parallel to mind, though, was not so much the event's initial force as its aftershocks: "The quake came back again and again, sometimes with greater energy, sometimes with less." The repeated blows had cut the area off from the outside world, rendering everyone around him powerless to act. He felt the same in 1941: "My entire life experience could not tell me what to do."[149]

Options were few. Most Jews appear at first to have considered them tactically, as ways to live through the next immediate aftershock of conquest, more than as strategies for outlasting occupation altogether. Most also seem to have thought about them from the perspective of their individual situations rather than as remedies for their communities as a whole.[150]

Finding protection from aftershocks as they occurred required a way to predict their occurrence. In some places, reported Blanca Rosenberg, a former law student from Kołomyja in East Galicia, "People always seemed to know when a [killing] action was going to occur."[151] In truth, their knowledge was imperfect at best. It was usually drawn from local non-Jews, with whom some level of interaction remained possible nearly everywhere, despite German efforts at separation. These non-Jewish informants were hardly ever privy to German plans; instead they inferred a likely killing operation from changes in German personnel or from activity clearing nearby forests or digging pits. Sometimes such occurrences presaged catastrophe, but they also often prompted false alarms. Failed predictions, in turn, bred disgruntlement and distrust in information sources. David Kahane was only one of many who complained.[152] Yehoshua Shechner, who took each alert seriously, soon acquired an invidious reputation as a panic monger when his frequent warnings, which set his fellow Tłuste Jews to running "like dazed mice," did not materialize.[153]

Still, the price of ignoring a true warning could have severe consequences, impelling Jews to cultivate spaces where their pursuers would not find them easily. Shechner found open fields expedient: expecting the killers to be concentrated in town, he would run in the dark to a nearby pasture, lying flat on the ground among the tall grass until immediate danger passed.[154] Among Jews in larger settlements, concealed hideouts, commonly called *meliny* (singular *melina*), were more frequent.[155] In his diary entry for 12 July 1941 Herman Kruk, the Wilno librarian, described how he prepared his secret quarters: "In the house, I found a mezzanine, blocked it up with old baskets, machinery, and an old broken cupboard, and arranged it all so that before anything happens, we go up there, the ladder is taken away and hidden, and we, my brother-in-law and I, the landlady's son, and somebody else we dragged along, stay there until the danger is past."[156] Shimon Redlich from Brzeżany recalled moving among several *meliny*, including "a small space behind a closet" and "a well-camouflaged double attic next to the hot tin roof" of his apartment building, which housed many of the building's residents.[157] But *meliny* were not available to all. Infants and very young children, in particular, were often not welcome because, as Miriam Tokarski, a young mother from Minsk, recalled, "They would betray the hideaway." She could find refuge only by sneaking with her child through the barbed-wire ghetto fence whenever she suspected danger, risking certain death if they were caught.[158] Nor could *meliny* relieve their occupants of worry. Redlich remembered a time when "loud footsteps and shrill German voices were nearly on top of us."[159] Różka Kurczak, recording how the German police in Wilno used dogs to sniff out Jews in hiding, concluded that "sitting in a *melina* and the constant waiting are driving people to insanity."[160] Within days of preparing his loft, Kruk realized that he had yet to find a satisfactory solution for his predicament. He wondered, "Can we hold out like this for long?"[161]

Some sought more permanent security by running farther afield. On 26 September 1941, after "Lithuanian police and German SS-men" told the Jews of Święciany that the next day they would be deported to Poligon, a nearby military base, for assignment to labor details, Icchak Rudnicki and eleven other young men decided to flee to Byelorussia, where, they had heard, Jews continued to live in their own homes, "and their situation was better than in Lithuania."[162] They set off by night with no particular destination in mind, no contacts, not even a map. They needed to avoid not only German patrols but local peasants, whom the Germans had promised to reward for handing over Jewish fugitives. At first they headed southeast, toward Minsk, but found the route dangerous. Then they turned east toward Głębokie, on the road to Vitebsk, arriving after close encounters with police and with peasant pursuers that claimed four from their group. The eight who arrived safely found shelter with local Jewish families. Rudnicki's hosts led him to work in a bakery—a job that helped him set aside additional bread for them. But he did not feel secure, especially after Głębokie Jews were forced into a ghetto. A young man from Święciany, who had escaped Poligon, arrived in town and reported that although most who had been sent to the military base had been killed, many (including members of Rudnicki's family) had been released. Rudnicki then decided to go home. He thought that Święciany, where a mass killing had already taken place, would now be safer than Głębokie, where the community remained intact. On a night in late December 1941 he snuck back into the town he had left three months before.[163]

According to Rudnicki, hundreds of Święciany Jews fled in similar fashion.[164] There is corroborating evidence of traffic between the Wilno region and northwestern Byelorussia in response to the varying intensity of killing in each area.[165] It is not known how many survived in this manner, for how long, or how extensive such behavior may have been in other parts of the German-occupied USSR.[166] Clearly, though, the sort of positional arbitrage that Rudnicki practiced—changing locations according to differences in estimated danger—was available to relatively few. Travel featured deadly hazards at every turn, even for a young, healthy man like Rudnicki, whose physical appearance and command of languages helped him pass as a non-Jew when needed. Finding food, shelter, and work in a new location required cooperation from local Jews, who placed themselves in mortal danger by offering assistance. Sometimes such cooperation had to be bought, putting it out of reach for Jews without means.[167] And the best outcome possible was continued life as a slave, not knowing any better when and where the next possibly lethal blow might fall. In late 1941, when murder still seemed to nearly all Jews a sporadic danger instead of an integral aspect of German hegemony threatening them immediately and directly, the risks of moving must have looked greater than the rewards.

So too at the time did the risks of seeking shelter from non-Jews or trying to live among them under a false identity. Hiding required a hider, but hosts who were both willing and able to offer safe haven were hard to find.[168] Moreover, even though most Jews had non-Jewish acquaintances in their towns and in the surrounding countryside, they generally favored alternate means of evasion to seeking non-Jewish assistance, at least until their own deaths appeared imminent. The reasons were numerous. Families often preferred to remain together, but rarely could they expect accommodation under a single roof. Neighbors they turned to might demand payment, a prospect that deterred Jews of lesser means. Neighbors might also betray them, fearing the capital penalties attached to harboring Jews in an unauthorized residence. Even when Jews were sufficiently confident of their contacts not to fear denunciation, some were loath to expose them to danger. Some also feared depending for their most basic needs upon people who owed them no obligation.[169] Initial refusals sometimes led to abandoning further efforts.[170] In any event, protectors could not guarantee protection for the long haul. Hence, it seems, Baruch Milch, who had found shelter with a peasant family to elude local violence in Tłuste in the early days of the German-Soviet war, did not pursue a similar arrangement to avoid the vagaries of German rule for many months, until no alternative remained.[171]

Passing as a non-Jew entailed peril of similar magnitude. It demanded a face without stereotypically Jewish features, full unaccented control of the local language, and intimate familiarity with Christian religious ritual. Adults could hope to acquire only the last on short notice. There is evidence that some tried to do so: in fall 1941 a Polish writer from Lwów observed among Jews a new "demand for catechism books, missals, instruction manuals for learning the [Roman] Catholic faith." But he also noted that most who sought instruction did not plan to make immediate use of their new knowledge.[172] They dared not try without a document attesting to Aryan origins. The most reliable of these—birth certificates of Christians who had moved elsewhere—were scarce and prohibitively expensive. Mechanisms for forging passable false papers came into being only with time: obtaining them usually entailed significant risk, and in the end they hardly offered a solid sense of security.[173] Shmerke Kaczerginski, a young communist poet from Wilno, obtained papers in September 1941 after a non-Jewish acquaintance threatened to inform the Germans of his whereabouts. With them he traveled through much the same territory as Rudnicki, but he still felt "a ten thousand-eyed death" pursuing him at every turn. "I was all right as long as I didn't meet anyone," he recalled, but he could not avoid what seemed like a constant series of close calls. After seven months he, too, like Rudnicki, gave up and returned home. Only "among [his] own," he remarked ironically, where he did not need "to hide [his] eyes from passersby lest they see [his] Jewish sorrow" did he feel truly "free."[174]

Unlike Rudnicki and Kaczerginski, most Jews who stayed in the German zone appear to have believed that the key to living through their desperately uncertain situation lay in their own communities. The belief gained credence in regions where, beginning in late 1941, German administrators slowed killing operations in favor of maintaining a Jewish workforce.[175]

Sometimes—in Kaunas, for example—the German in charge actually announced a change in policy, which Jews gradually confirmed through observation.[176] More often Jews were left to notice the change on their own. Herman Kruk wrote in his diary on 12 January 1942 of signs that Wilno Jews were "entering a new age"; four days later he observed that "lately it has been relatively calm."[177] "Relatively" was an apt modifier. To be sure, in many cities and towns where significant numbers of Jews had yet to be murdered, large-scale killings ceased for months, sometimes even for a year or more. Nevertheless, the harsh regimen of repression continued throughout. Food, housing, clothing, and medical care remained everywhere meager and difficult to procure. Workers labored solely for German benefit, often without compensation, at best for a pittance, with no protection from arbitrary dismissal or abuse. Death was still the penalty for violating basic ordinances, and German officials applied it to individuals without mercy. Nevertheless, the sense that the most brutal, arbitrary, and unpredictable aspects of German rule had passed helped Jews in some places think more strategically than before about obtaining and distributing life's basic necessities. In those places Jews were assisted by community-based plans for withstanding a German regime that had now seemingly granted them a tiny space for survival.

Comparative studies of scattered small and medium-sized towns in the former Polish *kresy* have pointed to additional factors that may have encouraged or discouraged strategic thinking and communal self-help in different locations. Varying policies concerning food supply implemented by different local German officials proved of paramount importance. In communities like Krzemieniec in Volhynia—where twelve thousand Jews were permitted to draw water from only three wells during restricted hours, official rations dropped to as low as fifty grams of bread per day, a tightly sealed ghetto limited opportunities for food smuggling, and the annualized death rate from starvation alone exceeded three hundred per thousand in 1942—few Jews had peace of mind to think beyond their next bite.[178] By contrast, in Baranowicze—a community of roughly the same size—rations were slightly more plentiful and supervision of ghetto boundaries less stringent. There the local Jewish council managed to organize a network for procuring additional resources and distributing them among community members, substantially reducing hunger and mortality.[179]

The character of local Jewish leadership could also be decisive. Effective leadership required the ability to organize communities for collective self-help under conditions where both energy and manpower for organization were largely lacking. The repeated blows of the occupation's initial months had bred widespread mental exhaustion. People who had become accustomed, in Yitskhok Rudashevski's words, to "dying like sheep, unconscious of [their] tragic fragmentation, [their] helplessness," were not easily mobilized for collective action.[180] Soviet reality may have exacerbated communal torpor. Hersz Smoliar observed that "Soviet people had been habituated over the years to receiving commands, orders, and slogans exclusively from above."[181] But few were in a position to command Jews seeking direction. The Soviets had dismantled the organizations and institutional frameworks that had once trained a Jewish communal leadership. Jews within the USSR's pre-1939 boundaries had been instructed with steadily mounting force over the previous decade to take cues from state and party figures who, even if Jews themselves, professed no particular Jewish loyalty or interest.[182] According to Smoliar, they continued to look to the same figures under German rule, believing—falsely, it turned out—that some had been placed undercover in order to subvert the new regime.[183] In the territories acquired after 1939 the Soviets had driven away the top ranks of autonomous Jewish political parties.[184] The Germans, for their part, were obviously keen to suppress any independent Jewish initiative aimed at sustaining long-term communal welfare; those who seemed inclined to encourage such initiative became targets for quick execution.

Nevertheless, the standard German practice of utilizing a Jewish council to mediate between local officials and Jewish communities automatically created a new potential leadership stratum. Most council heads did not fulfill that potential. Many were executed when Germans deemed them insufficiently pliant; others used their positions to promote their personal welfare at communal expense. But in a significant number of locations councils managed for a while to keep the German wolves from the door while winning respect and cooperation from their charges. In places with well-regarded official leaders, a satisfactory relationship with the authorities, and minimally adequate food supplies, various strategies for collective survival crystallized.[185]

One such strategy came to be dubbed "rescue through work."[186] An early, terse articulation came from a member of the Białystok Jewish council in November 1941: "Those who will not report to work will be destroyed in the end."[187] The assumption was that if Germans perceived Jews as a valuable economic resource, they would maintain them at an adequate level. The council's deputy chairman, Efraim Barasz, justified the assumption in a June 1942 speech to his community:

> Special means must be taken so that our 35,000 residents will have the right to claim toleration. We have turned all residents into a useful element. Our security is proportional to our labor output.... Seeing our output, the German authorities are taking the machines we need from German concerns outside the ghetto and giving them to our factories.... All the German delegations [that have visited the Jewish factories] have been satisfied with our work.... The result of those visits is an ongoing improvement in the [German] attitude toward us.... Instead of forced levies, deportations, etc. we are receiving subsidies for our enterprises, for the [communal] kitchen, for job training, hospitals, and industry. Even more important than the material aspect is the good attitude toward us.[188]

Similar approaches were adopted in Wilno, Kaunas, Šiauliai, Grodno, and Równe, among other places.[189] Unlike Białystok, none of these had a large manufacturing base upon which to build. Nevertheless, leaders in all these communities managed both to establish Jewish-run workshops (from which different branches of the German administration purchased services and supplies) and to persuade local and German-run enterprises to hire Jewish workers. Payments to Jews in cash and kind were low, but they undoubtedly helped create sufficient surplus to assist materially in the ongoing battle against starvation.[190] They also helped support a meaningful measure of community-based health care and mutual aid, along with religious, educational, and cultural activities. Wilno, in particular, maintained a range of heavily patronized cultural institutions, including a theater, an orchestra, a library, and art exhibitions, all underwritten largely by the Jewish council.[191]

It is not clear what drove the community leaders who adopted the strategy to do so. Some may have expected eventual German defeat. For them, rescue through work promised a way to buy time until liberation. Others undoubtedly saw it simply as a desperate, last-ditch effort to hold on, the most logical way to behave in the conditions in which they were forced to exist. Barasz, for his part, appears to have believed that his program could actually guarantee satisfactory relations over the long haul. There is fragmentary evidence that he had an inkling of the divisions that surfaced in late 1941 within the German hierarchy between ideological and pragmatic approaches to Soviet Jewry.[192] The relative calm many Jews noticed around the same time no doubt persuaded him that the pragmatists had won. Evidently, though, he did not understand that the divisions concerned short-term adjustments to the military situation only, not the fundamental ideological goal of eventually ridding the occupied territories of Jews once and for all. Consequently, rescue through work could succeed only as long as battlefield developments dictated temporary suspension of the Nazi war against the Jews.

In the end, rescue through work did bring notable short-term benefits to communities that accepted the idea. The enhanced food supply that it provided and the community services that rested upon it undoubtedly bolstered the physical and psychological health of ghetto residents. In December 1942 a grateful consumer of culture in Wilno ventured that thanks to his community library, "our hope increases that we will survive this journey … and reach the oasis of freedom."[193] Far more was needed for survival, of course. Nevertheless, the strategy arguably delayed the final liquidation of at least some communities where it was applied. Moreover, Jews from those places had greater chances, perhaps thanks to enhanced physical and mental health, of avoiding death by working in a labor camp instead of being murdered on the spot.[194]

Still, mass killing resumed in stages between mid-1942 and late 1943, even where rescue through work had appeared to succeed for a while. When it did, leaders were hard pressed to explain the development, not only to the many Jews who had found hope in their message but to themselves as well.[195] The desperation of early occupation returned. "Recently everything has pointed toward one thing," wrote the Wilno ghetto librarian Kruk in his diary on 31 March 1943, after the last remaining Jews in nearby Oszmiana and Święciany were sent to Ponary—"tremble for tomorrow."[196] A week later he noted a return to the tactical, individual orientation of the occupation's early days:

> All who still live and walk the streets . . . are truly lost and helpless; everyone is waiting . . . for liquidation. Most workers don't go to work. Those who do, don't really work. Nothing is in your head—anyway, it is all coming to an end! . . . In the chaos, in the horrifying shudder of events, anything seems likely. All rumors come together, and no one can deny them. . . . A lot of people spent the night in melinas [*sic*]. In some homes, people don't get undressed. All night long, they work with spades, digging melinas and underground passages.[197]

In the same entry Kruk mentioned that "the FPO is fully prepared." He referred to the *Fareynikte partizaner organizatsye* (United Partisan Organization), a small group of perhaps three hundred people, mostly in their twenties, that for a bit more than a year had offered Wilno Jews an alternative strategy to rescue through work.[198] The strategy was first articulated publicly in a manifesto dated 1 January 1942: "The sole answer to the murder is—armed rebellion."[199] It was predicated—as its author, Abba Kovner, a Sevastopol-born, Wilno-raised artist, poet, and Zionist youth leader,[200] explained—upon the intuition that everywhere within the Nazi orbit Jews faced "a total system" aimed at "absolute, total annihilation," from which "there is no rescue." "Perhaps individuals or hundreds" would outlive the oppressor, Kovner prophesied, but "for the millions, for the Jewish people under the yoke of Nazi occupation" all that remained was "to save our human dignity and the dignity of the people by waging war against the murderous foe."[201] Three weeks later, members of three Zionist parties came together with local Jewish communists to form an underground combat organization that would "prepare mass armed resistance to any attempt to liquidate the ghetto."[202]

Kovner had no illusions: "There is no hope of victory, no chance even for a real battle." Any effort to take up arms, he expected, would be "nipped in the bud . . . , precipitat[ing] the end [of Wilno Jewry] before its time."[203] Armed revolt, in other words, was not a strategy for saving lives. Nevertheless Różka Korczak, a member of his movement, saw in the effort the only possible wellspring of future hope:

> Every people has its sources of heroism . . . that nourish future generations. . . . Our people is experiencing a catastrophic bloodbath. It major portion, European Jewry, is facing extinction. . . . But we still hope that the *entire* people has

> not yet reached its end.... What will nourish our [future] generations ... if our people's history is only one of slaughter, of extermination, of helplessness? Our task is to inject into our history a new sound, to give it new content, so it will be about more than tragedy. Our history should also be about the struggle for heroism, self-defense, fighting for life ..., death with honor. If we see our task in this light ..., we will remain true ... to our responsibility as the vanguard of our people.[204]

Few Jews saw things this way; most preferred the prospect of continued life (however nasty, brutish, and short) to precipitous death (however noble), and they shunned leaders who made no pretense to save them. During 1942 similar groups planning a heroic last stand at the moment of liquidation formed in fewer than one hundred towns throughout the USSR. Hardly any counted more than fifty members.[205] In a handful of smaller locations they actually put their arms to use, attacking troops trying to lead the last Jews away.[206] But in cities and larger towns proponents of armed revolt often faced opposition from the majority, effectively setting their plans to naught.[207] Such was the case in Wilno. On 1 September 1943, with the "executioners at the ghetto gate," Kovner's FPO issued a call to "take up arms in your own defense." Only a small group of young people enlisted for the fight. That day, one FPO member died exchanging fire with a German patrol, but the encounter did not rally ghetto residents to the flag. The next day, FPO disavowed further action in the city. Shortly thereafter its remaining members evacuated to a nearby forest, hoping to continue their fight alongside Soviet partisans.[208]

Until that time FPO, despite its name, had resisted fighting the Nazis as part of the broader guerrilla war the Soviets had been supporting since Operation Barbarossa's early days.[209] Although the group sought Soviet support and expressed readiness to assist other partisan units, it insisted on remaining inside the ghetto until the ghetto ceased to exist.[210] It also refused to aid Jews trying to escape the ghetto before the final battle in order to join partisan groups on their own, maintaining that "going to the forest at this time means looking for *individual safety*," whereas FPO would defend only the collective life and honor of the Jewish people.[211] Such extreme subordination of the individual to the collective was exceptional among groups espousing armed revolt.[212]

In other locations Jewish leaders placed the partisan struggle at the center of their defense strategies and made helping individual Jews find shelter among partisans one of their primary purposes. Baranowicze, Kaunas, Lida, Minsk, and Słonim—all, surely not by coincidence, in Lithuania and Byelorussia, the most heavily forested parts of the German occupation zone—were standouts.[213] The strategy crystallized first in Minsk, where in mid-August 1941 a small group of veteran Jewish communist activists, headed by Hersz Smoliar, met to discuss the brutal, often deadly German raids that had beset the ghetto with alarming frequency since its establishment a month before. The group concluded that the ghetto was not a safe place, that Jews could find protection only on the "Russian side" of the city, and that the group's first duty was to spread that message.[214] During the fall the members' political contacts led them to other cells on both sides of the ghetto fence, all awaiting orders from higher party ranks to organize an underground. When orders failed to arrive, the groups decided together to take the initiative. Heavy Jewish involvement in the Minsk underground's formation and the promise that the ghetto might serve as a source of armed manpower for partisan formations led it to adopt rescue of Jews as an aim, alongside participation in the Soviet anti-German war effort.

Initially the underground concentrated on stealing and stockpiling weapons (mostly from a German armory and from a buried Soviet cache) and on sabotage operations. When the first contact with a partisan detachment was established in September, underground leaders persuaded the Minsk Jewish council to support it with funds and supplies. Contact was soon lost—one of the strategy's many hazards—but in early 1942 it was reestablished and strengthened. At the same time Jewish underground members established seven camps of their own in nearby forests, where, beginning in March and continuing for eighteen months thereafter, an estimated ten thousand Jews found space to remain alive. To be sure, nearly half perished in battle or from harsh conditions in the forest (including attacks by peasant bands or anti-Soviet guerrilla groups), but fifty-four hundred returned to Minsk after the Red Army recaptured the city in July 1944.[215]

These returnees constituted by far the largest group of survivors from a Soviet Jewish community under German rule—about 7 percent of the Minsk ghetto population, more than three times the survival rate in the German occupation zone as a whole.[216] Organized efforts in other towns to move Jews from ghettos to safety with partisan detachments were not nearly as successful: the combined total of Jews from Baranowicze, Kaunas, Lida, and Słonim who survived with partisans in the forest is estimated at no more than 1,650.[217] A much larger number of Jews from these and other nearby locations—perhaps as many as sixteen thousand—fled to the forest and joined partisan units on their own.[218] Some of these units, like those of Yehezkel Atlas and Tuwia Bielski, were commanded by Jews.[219] However, not all partisan formations, even the Jewish-led ones, regarded rescuing Jews as an essential purpose. For Atlas, the partisan movement existed to fight Germans; any activity that did not advance that mission directly, including assisting Jews without arms, was discouraged.[220] For Bielski, by contrast, assisting Jews appears to have outweighed all else; not only did he offer his protection to all who reached him, but he also sent messengers to nearby ghettos to bring Jews to his base.[221] As a result, besides a partisan unit, he oversaw the largest of what came to be called "family camps"—groups of Jewish men, women, and children of all ages determined to eke out an existence under cover of the forest, far from German eyes, for as long as necessary. Family camps are estimated to have held between seven thousand and ten thousand Jews. Though it is not known how many of them lived to the end of the war, testimonies of survivors suggest that mortality was high.[222]

Still, it appears that Jews had the greatest chance to survive in places where some of them banded together to create living spaces for themselves and others in remote locations that German forces did not entirely control. It seems, moreover, that the earlier that strategy was adopted, the greater its chances for success. In Minsk virtually all leadership groups agreed to pursue it nearly from the outset, whereas elsewhere forceful advocates espoused salvation through work and armed insurrection in situ for many months, until their futility became apparent. The agreement in Minsk was likely facilitated by the unusual absence of a sustained suspension of major killing operations in late 1941 and early 1942, during which alternative communal strategies gained traction elsewhere.[223] It may also be that Germans made less of an effort in Minsk than elsewhere to camouflage their murders, making it easier for Minsk Jews to accept the underground's determination that "the ghetto means extinction; we must break out of the ghetto walls."[224] And, possibly, the large presence in the Minsk underground of Jews from the annexed territories helped others overcome the purported Soviet habit of waiting for orders from above.[225]

But in the end the Minsk strategy could succeed only where sustainable remote locations that Germans did not entirely control—dense forests—were plentiful and close at hand. That condition prevailed widely in only one part of the German zone—the upper basins of the Nieman and Pripyat rivers in Byelorussia and northern Volhynia.[226] Elsewhere, even where community perceptions and inclinations were favorable, it could not be pursued to much effect.[227] Consequently, once alternative strategies lost credence, the large majority of Soviet Jews were left to scramble for individual safe spaces on their own. Locating such spaces invariably required the assistance of willing non-Jews. Some Jews could turn to non-Jewish acquaintances; others depended upon chains of relationships. Rosa Leikina, a physician from Dnepropetrovsk, was hidden in a hospital laboratory by a colleague.[228] David Kahane found refuge in the home of the Ukrainian Greek Catholic archbishop of Lwów, Andrey Sheptytsky, whom he met through a Ukrainian priest with whom he had a long-standing working relationship.[229] Shimon Redlich's family was taken in by a Ukrainian woman who knew a Polish locksmith who had once worked for Redlich's grandfather.[230] Where relationships were absent, Jews could be reduced to pounding on doors, begging for admission.[231] Lucky ones encountered saviors; the rest tried to hide in farm enclosures, gullies, or open fields. Leon Rosen from Buczacz, who spent four months crouching in a goat pen, eventually gave up: "I must hand myself in to the Gestapo and ask them to shoot me," he wrote in an October 1943 farewell letter to his children, who had somehow been safely sheltered. "I can no longer endure these conditions."[232]

No place of concealment was ever secure. There does not appear to be any way to know how many Jews in hiding were discovered and killed, how many were betrayed by their hosts, how many took ill and died while in hiding, or how many, like Rosen, simply gave up the ghost. When Red Army soldiers arrived in town after town on their triumphant westward march in 1943 and 1944, only a few thousand Jews were left to greet them. It would remain to the Jews among those soldiers, along with those who had escaped the territories under Nazi rule, to join the survivors in reconstituting Soviet Jewry.

4
THE FRONT

"The first Soviet soldier I encountered was an officer, a major," wrote Baruch Milch in his journal entry for 26 March 1944, the day the Red Army drove German forces from Tłuste, where for the past ten months he had been hiding from the Nazi onslaught. "I kissed him like my own brother, as I had promised myself I would."[1] He did not say whether the officer was a Jew, but the probability was far from negligible.[2] A week earlier Soviet troops had entered Cernăuţi, where Solomon Shapiro was among the fourteen thousand Jews who had remained in the city under Romanian rule.[3] Jewish soldiers stood out among Shapiro's liberators:

> On the morning of 19 March 1944 a rider on horseback galloped through the ghetto. This advance Soviet scout was the first herald of our release. Cautiously we came out of our hiding places.... That evening infantry and artillery units began their first patrols.... There were many Jewish soldiers in the column that advanced past our location. They broke ranks, hugged and kissed us, and told us that we were the first living Jews they had met since setting out from Stalingrad.[4]

At least four hundred thousand Jews, perhaps many more, fought the Germans as part of the organized Soviet effort to repulse the Nazi onslaught.[5] Some 40 percent of them are estimated to have perished on the front lines or as prisoners of war.[6] In other words, at least a quarter of a million Soviet Jews who lived through the years of the German invasion were veterans who had put their lives on the line in defense of the Soviet state. These Jews made up more than one eighth of the immediate postwar Soviet Jewish population. Consisting mostly of men and women in their twenties and thirties entitled (in theory, at least) to the elevated status Soviet leaders claimed to bestow upon the country's demobilized soldiers, they would exert an outsized influence upon the Soviet Jewish community for decades to come.[7] Their experiences with the Soviet military bore heavily, in turn, upon the direction in which their influence would lead.

The history of Jews' relationship with the Soviet military offers a striking indication of the far-reaching transformation Soviet rule brought to their community. In Imperial Russia Jews had associated military service by and large with government repression. The 1827 conscription order of Tsar Nicholas I, which envisioned a twenty-five-year term of duty in the army as a tool for converting Jews to Russian Orthodoxy and authorized the effective abduction of male Jewish children into special military preparatory academies (*Kantonistskie shkoly*—"Cantonist schools"), left a heavy mark on communal memory, vividly reflected in Jewish literature written in Hebrew, Yiddish, and Russian.[8] Even after the term of duty was reduced to five years in 1874, Jews remained subject to numerous restrictions and a generally hostile atmosphere.[9] Accordingly they continued to regard military service as a thing to be avoided; fear of the draft became a significant motive for emigration. The thought that a Jew might reach officer rank or pursue a military career had been virtually inconceivable.[10]

The formation of the Red Army in 1918 and its successful defense of the revolution during the civil war that tore the country apart over the next two years changed the picture radically. The army's principal organizer and guiding spirit, Leon Trotsky, was himself a Jew, as were several members of the Revolutionary Military Council that supervised army operations. At the end of 1919, more than three hundred Jews served as high-ranking political officers (commissars) in Red Army units—about 10 percent of all holders of such positions.[11] More notably, over the course of the civil war, growing numbers of Jews joined combat units on the Red side. Many were mobilized through Jewish political parties, including the Bund and socialist Zionists, who noted that "the counterrevolutionary forces threatening our country are also antisemitic, and threaten to destroy and wipe out the Jewish proletariat and the laboring Jewish masses."[12] Not that hostility toward Jews was absent from Red Army ranks, but, unlike their opponents, Red Army leaders moved actively to suppress it, even to the point of publicly executing soldiers who engaged in anti-Jewish violence. That fact appears to have moved even completely apolitical Jews, who at the beginning of the civil war had shown no attraction to the Bolsheviks, to see support for the revolutionaries as a matter of life and death.[13] In the Red Army, Jews enjoyed possibilities for promotion and advancement as career officers never available to previous Russian Jewish generations. A notable number took advantage of the opportunity, eventually displaying not inconsiderable talent as military leaders.[14]

One who took advantage was Yakov Kreiser. Born in 1905, the grandson of a former Cantonist school graduate who had served a full twenty-five-year term in the Imperial Russian army and had achieved the rank of sergeant (*feldfebel*), Kreiser told an interviewer in 1942 that he had joined the Red Army in February 1921. His motivation was a beating he had suffered sometime earlier at the hands of a member of the (White) Cossack Cavalry Corps commanded by General Konstantin Mamontov, who had captured Kreiser's home city of Voronezh in September 1919 and had become notorious for leading massacres of Jews during the civil war.[15] Remaining in service once the war was over, he rose through the ranks into increasingly responsible command positions. To be sure, his ascent was slow—perhaps, he ventured, because his father's occupation, a shopkeeper who sold used clothes, made his social origins suspect. Nevertheless, he distinguished himself at every level, receiving the Order of Lenin in 1936—a rare achievement. In March 1941 he was appointed commander of the elite First Moscow Proletarian Division; two months later he was promoted to the rank of colonel.

Receiving such a high award was unusual for anyone at the time, but the sight of a Jew rising to such a rank was not. During the 1920s and 1930s, military service had become a normal, even prestigious, Jewish profession. In fact, Jews in the army exceeded their share in the general population by a considerable margin: the 1926 census reported that Jews comprised 2.1 percent of soldiers, as opposed to only 1.7 percent of Soviet residents—a difference of nearly 25 percent.[16] The margin was even greater in the higher ranks: Jews made up 4.6 percent of all senior officers in 1926, 10.3 percent in 1929.[17] Jews were also far more likely to pursue military careers than were non-Jews: by the mid-1930s some 40 percent of Jewish army personnel were career soldiers, compared with 19 percent overall.[18] Of the eighty-five members of the Defense Ministry's Military Council (an advisory body of senior military figures) in 1936, 12 (14.1 percent) were Jews.

The Great Terror of 1937–1938 significantly changed the picture, especially at the highest levels. Nine of the twelve Jews in the Military Council were shot; one more committed suicide on the eve of his imminent arrest. Of the two survivors, one was executed in 1941, while the other was sentenced to ten years in penal camps. One hundred eighty Jewish officers holding a rank equivalent to general suffered repression in one form or another.[19] Nevertheless, these repressions do not appear to have been aimed at clearing the higher military levels specifically of Jews. Unlike ethnic Poles, Germans, Latvians, and some other minority groups, Jews in the military seem to have been targeted less on a national than on a generational basis, similar to Russians. The main aim of the military purges was evidently to eliminate officers who had served long enough to contradict Stalin's claim that he was the true creator of the Red Army and the hero of the civil war's most crucial battles. Thus all members of the Military Council, who were by definition among the army's most senior officers, were targeted to more or less the same extent, regardless of ethnicity.[20] The lack of specific anti-Jewish animus is also indicated by the late-1937 appointment of Lev Mekhlis, a Jew (and one-time Labor Zionist) who had formerly served as editor-in-chief of *Pravda* and as secretary to Stalin, to head the Red Army's Political Directorate—the body to whom commissars reported and the office charged with maintaining ideological purity among military leaders and with reporting deviations to the state and party agencies of repression.

In any event, even after the bulk of the repressions had been carried out, Jews remained well represented and highly visible in the army's upper echelons. In May 1940, when, as part of an overall military reorganization, the ranks of general and admiral were introduced, twenty-five Jews were named to them.[21] A relatively large number of Jewish colonels, majors, and captains provided a reservoir for replenishing and augmenting that number; between 1940 and 1945, 229 Jews became generals.[22] In addition, a new conscription law, enacted on 1 September 1939 (the day Germany invaded

Poland), reduced the draft age from twenty-one to nineteen, or eighteen for high school graduates, meaning that students who enrolled in institutions of higher education in 1939, who had previously been exempt, became immediately subject to induction. A relatively large proportion of Jews belonged to this group, a situation that would soon lead to an increased Jewish presence among enlisted men as well.[23] When Germany launched Operation Barbarossa on 22 June 1941, Soviet Jews were poised to play a notable role in defense of their Soviet homeland.

For the many Jews in uniform when Germany invaded, and for the many more mobilized during the following weeks, defending their homeland along with themselves and their families offered by itself a sufficiently powerful motivation for service, without adding any particularly Jewish concerns. The large majority of them were Soviet-style "new Jews" in most every respect; they had grown up under Soviet rule and been socialized to Soviet reality. During the previous two decades their families had migrated conspicuously from the former tsarist Pale of Settlement to the great cities of the Soviet heartland. The Russian Soviet Federated Socialist Republic, which consisted almost entirely of territories where Jews, with limited exceptions, had been forbidden to reside before 1915, was home to nearly one million Jews in 1939, while another quarter of a million Jews inhabited parts of the Ukrainian SSR that had once been beyond the Pale. All told, on the eve of the German incursion more than 43 percent of Soviet Jews lived far from the western districts of the USSR where the cultural patterns traditionally associated with east European Jewry had their strongest root.[24] A majority of Soviet Jews now named Russian, not Yiddish, as their native language, including 80 percent each in Moscow and in Leningrad, and more than three quarters in Kharkov.[25] The rapid German conquest of the western districts during the summer of 1941 meant that the more highly acculturated Jews to the east, especially those who resided in places like Moscow and Leningrad, which German forces never occupied, would make up a disproportionately large share of the Jewish soldiers. These Jews were on the whole less likely to share the mistrust and alienation from the regime that had become increasingly evident among other sectors of Soviet society over the previous decade (and among Jews from the former Polish,

Romanian, and Baltic territories annexed to the USSR in 1939); in many respects they could be counted among the most quintessentially "Soviet" of Soviet citizens.[26] Thus the day following the German invasion, when *Pravda* announced that "the Soviet people (*sovetskii narod*) is marching toward a victorious patriotic war for the motherland, for honor, for freedom," virtually all could identify without hesitation.[27]

Identification with the Soviet people did not necessarily preclude a sense of membership in a Jewish group, but it complicated that sense considerably. Evidence of complication appears in diaries kept by a number of Jewish veterans of that war. One, David Kaufman (later to gain fame as a poet under the pen name David Samoilov, in homage to his father, Samuel), began recording his thoughts and experiences while still a teenager during the 1930s. In late 1935, aged fifteen, he noted that despite his father's efforts to instill in him a "spirit of nationalism" from early childhood by telling him stories from the Hebrew Bible, "the nationalist in me turned out insignificant, even though I am not devoid of a certain national pride and self-esteem."[28] Three months later he remarked that "essentially I don't have a nation. The spirit of Jewishness (*evreistvo*) is foreign to me, incomprehensible, distant. I am an internationalist by conviction, and in spirit as well." Nevertheless, in the same entry he observed that "something brings me closer to these people." "My people's language is not mine," he wrote, "nor is its spirit, but its heart is my heart.... Should misfortune befall it, I will not walk away but will bravely accept all suffering together with my brothers."[29]

At times the Jewish sensibilities of the "new" Soviet Jews were put to the test by encounters with the "old" Jews of the annexed territories, who had known Soviet rule for only a brief interval. Some, like thirty-year-old Boris Tartakovskii from Meshcherskoe, near Moscow,[30] had run into them during the interval between annexation and war. In February 1941 Tartakovskii, then a graduate student in history at Moscow State University, had made an academic trip to Lwów, where he recalled the unfamiliar sight of "Biblical-looking Jews with sidelocks (*s peisami*) and gray beards" near the university campus. He was reminded of those images eight months later when, now a Red Army political instructor stationed in Stalingrad, he observed similar figures among crowds of evacuees "filling the streets, crowding in shops, pushing in queues to drink soda water." The sight not only repelled him; it generated musings about the meanings of Jewishness and about the future of the Jewish group:

> Alien and exhausted, they carry their bags, wandering around the marketplace of the enormous city on the Volga. How far they have betaken themselves from their native places. Every now and then you hear the grating Jewish manner of speech. Involuntarily you come to think all about Jurenito[31]—his pronouncements about the fate of the Judean tribe (*suzhdeniia o sudbakh iudeiskogo plemeni*). Truly, the entire fate of this unfortunate but talented people pushes you into mysticism, toward Zionism. Nevertheless, its future lies in assimilation. If you don't have your own territory you must not try to hold onto all of your own national habits and prejudices. That is reactionary and utopian.[32]

Another soldier, Private Mark Shumelishskii, a thirty-one-year-old technician in an artillery unit, also encountered "Jews from Lwów" in another location on the Volga, not a large city but a small village.[33] For him, "Lwów" probably served as a metonym for all Jews from the annexed territories. The western Jews he met were living several families to a room in barracks, working rather unhappily as lumberjacks. The Soviet soldier was harsh in his judgment:

> In the past they were probably petty traders or owners of small stores or workshops. They are typical Polish Jews who have yet to be touched by the assimilatory influence of Soviet culture. They stay close to one another, but they don't seem to live together terribly amicably. Everyone wants to grab a better piece of the pie. Their income comes primarily from selling things to one another. [They have taken up work as] lumberjacks evidently only in order to gain rights. They have been forced [into this situation]. This entire building, swarming with animated and noisy inhabitants, makes an extremely unpleasant impression. These people have not yet understood that it is altogether proper for Jews to be lumberjacks.[34]

The comments of Tartakovskii and Shumelishskii suggest that they were prompted to think about Jewish matters initially more as a result of contact with other Jews, including civilians, than through hostile encounters with their non-Jewish comrades in the ranks. That view coincides with a large proportion of Jewish veterans' postwar testimonies, which speak of widespread camaraderie among combat troops and claim that soldiers tended to ignore ethnicity. "We really had no time to discuss these things—whether one was Jewish, or Tatar, or Russian," recalled former serviceman Misha Yablonovski. "We had to look out for each other, such is the way of war."[35] But evidence from the war years themselves, though not plentiful,[36] presents a more complex picture. Some Jewish diarists reported being subject to insults or to overhearing them more or less frequently, but others mentioned no such problems.[37] Most who entered the military as committed Soviet internationalists and patriots appear to have remained so throughout their service. Nevertheless, it seems that many also developed new understandings of themselves as Jews. Those understandings were not uniform, nor were the circumstances that produced them. Both are best grasped through individual histories.

Boris Slutskii, a twenty-two-year-old graduate of the Moscow Institute of Law and the Gorky Literary Institute at the time of his induction on 13 July 1941, served first as a military investigator, later as a propaganda officer in a unit charged with demoralizing the enemy. He fought on multiple fronts, taking part in the expulsion of the occupiers from Ukraine, then advancing through Bulgaria, Hungary, Romania, and Yugoslavia before ending the war in Austria. During his service, in 1943, he joined the Communist Party. Following his discharge he took up a literary career, eventually becoming (along with his contemporary, David Kaufman-Samoilov) one of the foremost representatives of what came to be called the "war generation" of Soviet poets.[38]

In 1945, shortly after returning from the front, Slutskii penned a series of "notes on the war," never published during his lifetime.[39] In them he ventured that during the conflict "thousands of Jews who fought on the front lines were given the distinct feeling that their nation (*natsiia*) was not . . . working hard enough" for victory. Jews who heard this comment from others, he suggested, felt "shame and anger" as they resolved to sacrifice themselves in order "to make up for the absence of their compatriots from the forward lines."[40] Slutskii may well have been describing his own emotions, for the wartime Jewish question seems to have worried him more than anything else. He related, among others, a story about "Gershelman, a Jew" who had survived under German occupation. Married to a Russian woman, he had, according to Slutskii's account, forgotten before the war that he was a Jew. During the war, however, he had been compelled to wander in search of shelter because former colleagues, neighbors, acquaintances, and even his wife's brother not only refused his entreaties but attempted to turn him over to the Germans. Still, Gershelman told Slutskii, "ten times more" people helped him than tried to sell him out. But in the story Gershelman recounted he did not name ten times as many rescuers as betrayers. Perhaps Gershelman, speaking to an officer he didn't know, felt obliged to draw an ideologically "correct" conclusion from his misfortunes. But Slutskii drew a different conclusion: this and many other similar stories that he heard undermined his confidence in the purported internationalism of the Soviet people.[41]

Another experience late in the war reinforced that conclusion in his eyes. "In Austria," he wrote, "I came across [someone who] assessed the attitude of Russians toward Jews differently [from Gershelman]." She was a Jewish woman from Vienna who had been hidden by Styrian peasants for two years, out of what she called "peasant decency" and pity for her three-year-old son. He described her as "a drab woman, with flabby skin and dull red . . . hair." She told him that while in hiding she had often listened to the radio and had heard about the Red Army's advance. "I was waiting for you," she declared, imagining liberation. But when the army arrived she encountered it in an altogether different face: "All my life I have loved only one man, but now I have to sleep with every soldier who passes through the village, whenever I'm told."[42]

There was nothing unusual about such a story in those days, but Slutskii gave it a particular interpretation, one not immediately apparent in the situation. After all, the soldiers did not rape the woman because she was Jewish; for them she was a German-speaking Austrian, and as such she was free for the taking. Yet Slutskii appears to have felt the incident painfully: it showed him that the attitude of Russians toward Jews had changed for the worse during the war years (or perhaps that it had become more permissible to demonstrate a hostility that had formerly been suppressed). He explained the change by noting that "the Russian peasant has established [what is for him] an indisputable fact: he fights more than anyone else, better than anyone else, more loyally than anyone else." The authorities, he added, encouraged this attitude: "The war brought us widespread nationalism in its nastiest, most aggressive, most chauvinistic variety." As a result, when the different peoples of the Soviet Union met one another during the war, "they did not always improve their opinions of one another." The Soviets' vaunted "friendship of nations" collapsed: "Once there was internationalism, then there was internationalism minus the Fritzes [Germans], but now the glorious legend that 'there are no bad nations, only bad people and classes' has finally collapsed. Too many [nations] have been subtracted."[43]

These realizations appear to have knocked Slutskii off balance. He addressed the charge that Jews were not "working hard enough" as soldiers by arguing that even if Jews were underrepresented in the infantry,[44] they made up a notable stratum within the artillery, the combat engineers, and other technical units, which were composed mainly of proletarians. Certain groups of soldiers had noticed this Jewish participation, he claimed, creating positive feelings toward Jews in parts of the army. He also posited that negative feelings toward Jews "gradually came to naught" in the officer corps, where Jewish staff officers, artillerymen, engineers, and political workers were valued.[45] Of course, there was no way to measure the phenomena Slutskii claimed to observe. It seems, though, that in 1945 he still sought to place his thoughts about Jews within a Marxist framework, an effort visible in the following account:

> One of the few Jewish men who returned to Sombor [then Yugoslavia, since 1992 Serbia], the son of a wealthy merchant, transferred his property to the Communist Party of Yugoslavia. People said that his sister had protested vigorously. This example demonstrates the existence of two streams within contemporary Jewry—the stream of those who build capitalism and the stream of those who seek to bring it down.[46]

Several years later Slutskii composed a verse entitled "About the Jews," where he wrestled with what had become his Jewish dilemma:

Evrei khleba ne seiut,	Jews don't plant any crops—
Evrei v lavkakh torguiut,	Jews do deals in their shops;
Evrei ran'she lyseiut,	Jews prematurely go bald,
Evrei bol'she voruiut.	Jews grab more than their own.

Evrei - liudi likhie,	Your Jews are conniving bastards:
Oni soldaty plokhie:	He is not much good in the army:
Ivan voiuiet v okope,	Ivan in a trench doing battle,
Abram torguiet v rabkope.	Abram doing trade at the market.
Ia vse eto slyshal s detstva,	I've heard it since I was a child,
Skoro sovsem postareiu,	And soon I'll be past any youth,
No vse nikuda ne det'sia	But I can't find a place to hide
Ot krika: "Evrei, evrei!"	From the cries of "The Jews, The Jews!"
Ne torgovavshi ni razu,	Not a single deal have I pulled,
Ne vorovavshi ni razu,	Never stolen and always paid,
Noshu v sebe, kak zarazu,	[But I carry within myself this accursed race
Prokliatuiu etu rasu.	Like an infection—MG].
Pulia menia minovala,	From the war I came back safe
Chtob govorili nelzhivo:	[To prove that what they say is right—MG]:
"Evreev ne ubivalo!	"No Jews got killed! None!
Vse vorotilis' zhivy!"[47]	They all came back, every one!"[48]

Slutskii's notes reveal that ongoing complaints about the Jews' collective military record came together in his mind with meetings with Jews who had survived the Nazi Holocaust both within the USSR and without, and especially with their descriptions of the behavior of Soviet non-Jews toward them, to crack for him the framework of proletarian internationalism that had marked the outlook of his early years. However, they did not break the framework altogether. Slutskii used poetry to confront hostile stereotypes while affirming membership in a Jewish group that he saw as part and parcel of the Soviet fabric. Other soldiers, by contrast, responded to offensive comments by consciously concealing their Jewishness. Nineteen-year-old Sergeant Vladimir Gelfand saw combat action around Kharkov and Stalingrad and spent several months in a military hospital recovering from wounds in late 1942 and early 1943.[49] There, he recounted in his diary, "The people (not all, to be sure) blame the Jews for everything." "I am attacked the most," he complained; "they take out their anger on me and shout 'kike' (*zhid*) at me with derision, curse me and never give me a chance to speak or to say a word while they defecate on my bed and soil it."[50] He had experienced similar affronts, along with several beatings, even before being drafted and had evidently developed a strategy for dealing with them.[51] Noting that his "appearance and speech do not betray the Jew in me," he preferred not to betray it voluntarily.[52] His experience following induction reinforced the wisdom of that approach: whenever he shared feelings of shame and humiliation with fellow soldiers he found himself facing even greater unpleasantness, sometimes even genuine suffering. On one occasion, some two months after joining the army, he even introduced himself as the child of a Georgian mother and a father who claimed to be Russian.[53] Jewishness, it seems, was becoming an increasing source of pain. "Why am I a Jew?" he wrote after leaving the hospital for an officers' training course. "Belonging to the Jewish nation is my consistent scourge, my unending torment, from which there is no salvation.... Why do I, like so many others, find myself sometimes having to hide my origins?"[54]

One year younger than Gelfand, Private Yakov Forzun, a machine gunner, suffered repeated severe wounds, spending more than a year in hospitals between his August 1942 conscription and his medical discharge in early 1945.[55] During his final six-month hospital stay, in Furmanov, northeast of Moscow, he found himself mistaken for a Ukrainian and heard the usual talk about Jews not fighting. His response, told to an interviewer from the Commission of the USSR Academy of Sciences on the History of the Great Patriotic War (the so-called Mints Commission)[56] around the time of his discharge, resembled Gelfand's:

> While I was in the hospital, they told me that Jews were not visible at the front, that the Jews were hiding. I didn't raise any objection to them, because ... if you tell them anything, they'll kill you in the first battle. So for that reason I decided not to tell them anything. In that respect it was very bad in the hospital. I spent a lot of time in hospitals, and the conversation there was all the same: the Jews don't want to fight. The patients conducted themselves badly. They didn't know my nationality, and they began to say that the Jews did not want to fight, only to hide in the rear. They talk[ed] and I remain[ed] silent; I ma[d]e no response.

Forzun was not a timid man; in combat he had distinguished himself for bravery. Indeed, his exploits on the battlefield eventually spoke for him in a manner available only to a few. At the time his final hospital stay began, he had been nominated for the title of Hero of the Soviet Union. Accordingly, he explained, "I kept waiting for news of my award to arrive; then they would see whether Jews wanted to fight or not. After the order for my award was read out, everyone shut up. No one said anything any more." Absent the prestigious decoration, however, he appears to have been intimidated by "the many criminals who had been released from prison," who had "ended up at the front and later in the hospital."[57]

Forzun and Gelfand reacted similarly to similar situations, but their backgrounds were hardly similar at all. Gelfand, raised in Dnepropetrovsk, was in all respects a typical "new" Soviet Jew. Forzun, by contrast, was the product of a *shtetl* (Korostyshev, near Zhitomir). He described his upbringing as one of extreme poverty, exacerbated by the great Ukrainian famine of 1932–1933, which, he told his interviewer, had left him and his sister swollen from hunger. He had studied only in Yiddish-language schools through the fourth grade, first in his native town, later in Stalino, where his father had moved in search of work. Although he eventually learned to read in Russian, he reported having had few books to read. In short, the opportunities for upward mobility that so many young Soviet Jews of his generation enjoyed appear to have passed him by.[58] Yet for all of the differences between his early life and Gelfand's, their respective brushes with prejudice did not move either man to a more assertive self-identification as a Jew. Gelfand, better educated and with future literary aspirations,[59] expressed his aversion to such identification in an unmistakable internationalist idiom: "Why do nations exist at all?"[60] Fozun was less articulate; he accepted his lot as is, without complaint. For him, the Red Army had offered a way out of a life that he described simply as "bad." After the war he went to work as a plant foreman in Zhitomir, joining the Communist Party in 1961.[61]

Other Jewish soldiers, though, looked askance at such a reaction. Sergeant Boris Komskii, an infantryman from Kiev, of the same age cohort as Gelfand and Forzun,[62] kept a diary while fighting in some of the war's bloodiest engagements, including the hellish Battle of Kursk in July and August 1943, in which virtually all of his comrades were killed.[63] In early January 1945, in the small Polish village of Nowe Malinowo, just west of the September 1939 Boundary and Friendship Treaty line,[64] he met a middle-aged former partisan who, recognizing Komskii as a fellow Jew, confided that "terrible antisemitism" (*zhutkii antisemitizm*) among his comrades-in-arms had induced him to hide his nationality. Komskii disapproved; the soldier's effort, he admonished him, was useless:

> His name is Ilia Cherepakha, from Byelorussia. That's where the Germans caught up with him. His entire family, 35 people, had perished. He himself had been shot twice,[65] but he had remained alive and had crawled out from under the corpses at night. His wife was a Ukrainian. She [then] married a Vlasovite.[66] The two of them went around pillaging; later they left for Germany. He himself had joined a partisan platoon: "We drank their blood. I avenged my family in full. . . ." [He said that] there was a lot of antisemitism among the partisans as well. A Jew who had held an officer's rank wouldn't be appointed to a [command] post. Only once the front got closer did the situation begin to change. He related many facts about his life in the partisans as well as about now, in the army, and I regretted telling him [that he was concealing his identity] in vain. What moral right do I have to lecture and to judge the actions of a person who has seen and experienced a thousand times more than I have? I cannot justify people who deny their own nationality. But still, "A person is given life only once. . . ."[67] And he had lost it twice.[68]

Komskii had heard derogatory remarks about Jews earlier, including recently from his direct superior.[69] Nevertheless, this Communist Party member, who as a schoolboy had written for a newspaper of the Party children's organization, Pioneer, found "absolutely no reason" to hide that he was a Jew.[70] After the war he remained in the army as a journalist, publishing widely on military and patriotic themes. After retiring with the rank of colonel, he became editor of a Russian-language Jewish newspaper in post-Soviet Ukrainian Lviv.[71] Until his death in 2011 he bemoaned the demise of the USSR.[72]

Still other soldiers came through the war with feelings and observations that made them even more difficult to place on a Jewish-internationalist spectrum. In his diary entry for 19 November 1943, for example, twenty-one-year-old Sergeant Naum Rosenberg, a combat engineer from Pavlograd, near Dnepropetrovsk, who had fought on the southwestern, Don, and Stalingrad fronts,[73] expressed concern over "how far this hatred and contemptuous attitude toward the Jews has eaten its way" into Soviet society.[74] Over the next six months, as he proceeded westward with the advancing Soviet forces, he encountered disdain many times. "There is a widespread opinion among the people (*narod*) that all Jews are afraid of death, afraid to fight, in a word—cowards," he wrote in early March 1944.[75] Six weeks later, after taking part in driving German forces from Krzemieniec, where he found no Jews remaining out of the fifteen thousand who, he thought, had lived there before the war, he was even more emphatic: "Hatred and scorn for the Jews flows in the blood of the Russian people."[76] He did not report trying to conceal his own identity, but neither was he proudly defiant. Instead, he sought an explanation that would help him rebuff the prejudice he encountered and bear the insult he felt acutely, yet allow him to go on not only fighting but believing in the Soviet experiment:

> The mere fact that there are such [biased] opinions is painful. But it is even more painful to admit to myself that to a certain degree they are true. Deprived of a fatherland (*otchizna*) . . . , torn away from their maternal soil, not having to give their lives for their soil, for their Motherland (*Rodina*), for more than two thousand years, the large majority of Jews have ceased to be brave people. Having had to struggle for its existence within other nations for two thousand years, having withdrawn within itself, [having endured] the contempt and fear of other peoples, dislike and hatred toward them— these are the elements (far from all) that have formed the characters [*sic*] of the Jewish nation (*natsiia*). History shows that those Jews who found a homeland for themselves or who made transforming the state their goal in life—those Jews proved themselves worthy of their ancestors at the time of the destruction of Jerusalem and their dispersion across the globe. This cannot be denied.[77]

Such worthy Jews might not dispel prejudice, he averred: even though more than a hundred of them had been named Heroes of the Soviet Union, partisans had still refused to accept Jews into their ranks. "Obviously," he deduced, "they [the partisans] were afraid of [the Jews'] abilities."[78] Nevertheless, his understanding of Jewish history guided him to a clear operative conclusion:

> To live simply and honestly and to fulfill my obligation to Stalin—he is my Motherland. I am a man of the world, but maybe I don't belong to this world. I was accepted into the party as an equal; to my mind I too belong to it and to no

> one else. It's hard not to have a motherland and a people (space on earth and a tribe of one's own), but for me Russia is a good place to find shelter, while the Jewish nation is not entirely native. I was brought up in a semi-Jewish family, on Russian soil; the party—the Central Committee—is my Motherland and my people (*narod*).[79]

After the war Rosenberg became a career officer in the Red Army, retiring in 1974, aged fifty-two, with the rank of colonel.[80]

Individual life histories testify to a range of experiences and responses, but they cannot locate a center of gravity within the range. Evidence is insufficient, for example, to determine how likely any individual Jewish soldier was to face the calumny and discrimination recorded by some diarists, let alone in which ranks, units, or branches of the military they were more or less present. Nevertheless, besides Jewish complaints, a few extant letters and diary entries from non-Jews of different social backgrounds show that fighting together did not necessarily remove prejudices or foster intergroup solidarity among all soldiers.

Dmitry Finenko, a thirty-seven-year-old collective farmer from Sovetskaia, a village in the North Caucasus, was drafted into the army on 24 August 1941. On 10 September he wrote to his wife:

> Lena, are they taking the Jews to the front or not? If not, then beware of them. Why do they eat our bread? Why are they so shifty? Lena and all Red Army women, demand that all products from the *kolkhoz* [are distributed] according to the rules, in return for days worked, for Jews also in return for days worked. Don't give in yet to these violations. Write to us in our unit. We'll pass the letters on to the commissars.[81]

Finenko's resentment toward Jews was palpable. Evidently a number of Jewish evacuees had appeared in his village and been allocated produce from his *kolkhoz*, yet there were hardly any Jews among the residents of his rural region who had been called up for military service. He, however, had been drafted and sent to the front, even though he had no teeth. "The commissars don't accept [excuses from] anyone," he wrote in the same letter;

"even the crippled aren't released" from service. "I am completely worn out; my head hurts from anemia."[82] Still, after only a month and a half of training, he and his fellow draftees were thrown into battle. He sent what would be his last letter to his family from Rostov-on-Don on 18 October 1941; four days later he was reported missing in action.

Around the same time a wounded soldier, also thirty-seven years old, named Piotr Platonovich Yagupov came to visit the writer Nikolai Verzhbitskii in his Moscow apartment. Verzhbitskii recorded in his diary Yagupov's long, tortured monologue, in which the soldier recounted the horrors he had faced during the recent bloody German encirclement and bombardment of Viazma (between Smolensk and Moscow, a key point on the German army's march toward the capital). He complained bitterly about lack of adequate equipment and provisions and castigated what he called the "idlers" he encountered who abandoned their posts and refused to perform essential tasks. In that context he commented that "the Jews aren't ready to fight; they have all left for Kuibyshev" (the city on the Volga River to which the Soviet government had retreated shortly after Viazma fell).[83] Here, too, the charge of Jewish malingering came amid a litany of grievances aimed at various targets.

To be sure, Finenko and Yagupov had not received a Soviet education; they had come of age in prerevolutionary times. Perhaps, then, they were unthinkingly reproducing a lingering Russian social practice of blaming personal misfortune upon Jews. But there is also evidence of similar disparagement in the diaries of two younger, new-style Soviet military officers from the educated stratum. In both cases mentions of Jews were altogether peripheral to the diarists' concerns. Nevertheless, they reveal a persistence of scorn and disparagement that Soviet socialization had evidently not managed entirely to erase.

Georgii Slavgorodskii, born 1914, a teacher of Russian literature, gave Jews little attention and hardly saw them as a major problem, but it seems he could not refer to them at all without attaching some derogatory epithet. He used the demeaning sobriquet "Abrasha" as an uncomplimentary eponym for all Jews, even misspelling the name in a manner that mocked a stereotypical Jewish accent.[84] He called a doctor in a hospital "a Jewish woman who resembles a hound dog."[85] Even one of his comrades in arms, with whom he regularly discussed "friendship and collegiality, generosity and parsimony, individualism and sociability," did not escape a gratuitous sneer: "I do not like this frivolous, sloppy, vain Jew."[86] A perception that Jews were absent from the ranks does not appear to have driven Slavgorodskii's attitude; rather he was more likely to interpret his encounters with Jews through the lens of older stereotypes.

Similarly, Nikolai Belov, an engineer who advanced from the rank of captain to lieutenant colonel, revealed animus toward Jews in the course of deteriorating relations with his commanding officer, Colonel Vladimir Gruzenberg. Though initially complimentary toward him, as time went on he began to call Gruzenberg "Abram" and "a mangy, rotten Jew" (*parshivyi evrei*).[87] On 22 March 1944 he complained to his diary that "I can't live with Gruzenberg; I want very much to be transferred away from him." He attributed his difficulties to Gruzenberg's apparent Jewish origins, ostensibly revealed by his surname: "I've had enough of these Bergs." But Gruzenberg was not the sole Jewish object of Belov's ire. Earlier, on 3 December 1943, he noted, "Today I traveled with Lieutenant Colonel Yukhatskii and [with] Vysotskii (two Abrams) for the final investigation" of a failed mission. On 21 January 1944 he generalized about all Jews: "Every day I have a scandal with an Abram. I hate them. All together it is not without reason that everyone tears into them."[88] Ironically, though, Colonel Gruzenberg's personal documents listed him as a Russian, not as a Jew.[89] Moreover, Gruzenberg signed several documents nominating Belov for various decorations and awards. Hence it seems that Belov, like Slavgorodskii, carried long-standing biases against Jews into the army; his views were not influenced by the actual behavior of Jews with regard to military service.[90]

These examples suggest that attitudes toward Jews in the army reflected attitudes permeating Soviet society more broadly. To be sure, many veterans posited in retrospect a sharp difference between the two environments, placing hostility exclusively in the rear and asserting its absence from the front; but such a clear division is highly implausible. Front and rear were not separated from one another by an impenetrable wall; they were rather two closely connected social spheres that interacted regularly with one another. Soldiers traveled in both directions: reinforcements were brought to the front from the rear; the wounded were treated in the rear and returned to the front upon recovery; front soldiers sent and received letters to and from the rear. Expressions of hostility toward Jews became markedly more frequent and more forceful in the rear during the months following the German invasion, and agencies of the state became less emphatic about enforcing existing prohibitions upon them.[91] Such developments could not have helped but resonate on the front lines as well.

Still, no matter how broadly or how deeply Jewish soldiers may have felt such repercussions, no evidence indicates that Jews' motivation to fight was impaired by it to any degree. Quite the contrary, as the Red Army gradually pushed German forces out of the occupied areas during 1943 and 1944, and Soviet troops uncovered the horrific losses and wholesale devastation brought by Germany's war against the Jews of those regions, many Jewish soldiers appear to have found new reasons to fight on.

That the Nazis harbored savage intentions toward Jews was no secret to Red Army fighters. The German invaders used leaflets rained down upon Soviet troops from the air explicitly to incite them to murderous anti-Jewish violence. Many Soviet soldiers recalled one in particular: "Beat the Jewish *politruk*; his mugface is asking for a brick."[92] On occasion, Stalin himself referred in public speeches to Nazi animus toward Jews. On 6 November 1941, for example, as part of observances marking the twenty-fourth anniversary of the Bolshevik revolution, he announced that "the Hitlerites . . . organize medieval pogroms against the Jews, just like the tsarist regime." He likened the Nazis to the Black Hundreds who had rampaged against Jews in the Russian Empire in an effort to prop up a brutal autocracy; they were, in his words, "the most vicious reactionaries" and "enemies of democratic freedoms." When his speech was published in *Pravda*, his characterization of the Nazis as "the party of medieval reaction and Black Hundred pogroms" was highlighted in large type.[93]

Indeed, despite the regime's insistence in principle that all Soviet citizens were threatened with annihilation,[94] soldiers with a particular concern for Jews (along with other readers of Soviet newspapers) could find, from time to time, information on the progress of the German anti-Jewish war. For instance, when the Red Army retook Rostov-on-Don in November 1941 after the city had fallen briefly to German forces,[95] a correspondent for *Izvestiia*, the official daily of the Soviet government, reported on the "special attention" Jews got from the Germans, "just like everywhere else":

> The Jews . . . were subjected to particular humiliation and insults. They were permitted to move about in the streets only between the hours of 6 am and 2 pm. . . . The fascist Black Hundreds brought the full weight of their accumulated experience to bear here. From the beginning they ordered all Jews to sew a yellow star on their sleeves and to draw the same star on the doors of their dwelling places. After branding them with identifying marks, they lightened their own burden by setting Jews to do all the dirty work. Later they announced the general registration of all Jews living in Rostov. The mass slaughters of Jews in Kiev and Odessa[96] also began with general registration. In Rostov, too, the fascist pogromists were preparing yet another annihilation of tens and thousands of people. Fortunately they did not have time. [Nevertheless], the fascists had organized a place for the annihilation in Rostov. They placed three commandos in the city, who began shooting right away.[97]

A broader warning about what Germans had done to Jews in the USSR and elsewhere—and what the remaining Jews throughout Europe could anticipate if Germany were not quickly defeated—appeared on the front pages of *Pravda*, *Izvestiia*, and other large-circulation newspapers, including military and regional publications, on 19 December 1942, one day after the Soviet press had published a statement from the Allied governments condemning the Nazi regime's "bestial policy of cold-blooded extermination."[98] The announcement, from the Information Bureau of the People's Commissariat for Foreign Affairs, spoke of a "cannibalistic plan, developed by Hitler at the beginning of this year, that seeks to concentrate about four million Jews in eastern Europe, primarily in Poland, for the purpose of putting them to death." Most of the article was devoted to the persecution and the extermination of the Jews of Europe, but it offered concrete data about murders of Soviet Jews as well:

> In Riga the Nazis have shot more than 60 thousand Jews, including many brought in from Germany. . . . Entire families have been shot. Children have been ripped from their mothers' arms and been either murdered or cast alive into previously prepared pits . . . , all before their [mothers'] eyes. At present there are no more than 400 Jews in Riga, living in a ghetto enclosed with barbed wire that no one is allowed to enter. This group of Jews, condemned to hunger, is slowly perishing. In Wilno, Swięciany, and other cities of the Lithu-

> anian SSR, both the local Jews and those brought from Germany have been annihilated almost entirely. Those who have managed to escape the murder actions are hiding in forests, living like hunted beasts, ill clad, dying of hunger and disease.... There is evidence that... the Hitlerites are carrying out their plan for the total annihilation of all Soviet citizens of Jewish nationality.... Over a period of only two days—26–27 August [1942]—the German fascist pogrom makers have created bloody slaughterhouses in the following places in the Ukrainian SSR: in Łuck, 20,000 Jews have been shot...; in Sarny, where in the spring of this year... 18,000 Jews were executed, over 14,000 more Jews were brought together from surrounding small towns and rural areas and put to death...; 850 Ukrainians and 1,600 Jews were shot in Rokitno.... In the two cities of Kiev and Dnepropetrovsk, more than 60,000 people were murdered during the first months of occupation alone.[99]

As the tide of battle turned in 1943, advancing Red Army troops were able to confront evidence of German atrocities with their own eyes. Some of what they witnessed in once-populous Jewish communities now decimated not only made its way into newspaper reports but attracted comment from prominent Soviet literary figures. Thus, for example, on 5 August 1943 *Pravda* published an article by the popular historical novelist and science fiction writer Aleksei Tolstoi—a member of the Extraordinary State Commission for the Establishment and Investigation of the Crimes of the Fascist German Invaders and their Accomplices, established by the Council of People's Commissars in November 1942 for the purpose of gathering evidence to be used in future trials of Germans responsible for atrocities and in support of Soviet claims for war damage compensation[100]—offering his eyewitness testimony from an official trip he had made to the North Caucasus a month earlier "in order to compile material evidence... of the traces of German crimes." Tolstoi reported that the Germans had killed "the entire Jewish population" of the area, "most of whom were wartime evacuees from Leningrad, Odessa, Ukraine, and Crimea":

> There were many educated people here, professors, doctors who had been evacuated together with their academic institutions. The Germans began their preparations for mass killing from the very first days of their occupation. They organized Jewish Committees, ostensibly in order to resettle the Jews in the

> underpopulated districts of Ukraine. At the same time they created unbearable, humiliating living conditions for them.... The old, the young, the infirm ..., all were sent for hard labor on the land, without pay and with no bread ration. They had to wear a yellow star on their sleeves; they were forbidden to enter public eating facilities, stores, or [other] public spaces, and they were enjoined from leaving town. That way, when "resettlement day" finally came, the Jews ... gathered together with their families, carrying 20 kg. of baggage per person and provisions for two days.... Around one o'clock a train carrying around 1,800 people passed the station at Mineralnye Vody and stopped by a field.... "Get out, jump to the ground," the Germans accompanying the train shouted. [The Jews] began to become uneasy. The members of the Jewish Committee ... calmed them.... Ten minutes later a staff car showed up with the Gestapo chief.... The command was given, "Strip naked." ... Then the people understood that their lives were over.... Those who tried to run away were gunned down [by soldiers in] a few automobiles circling the field. It isn't easy to kill 1,800 people by standing opposite them and mowing them down. The shooting lasted from one o'clock until evening.[101]

In short, information about the Nazi extermination of the Jews was available in the USSR. However, the matter was far from being a central concern of the Soviet press. After all, Soviet propaganda placed special emphasis on the common suffering of all the peoples of the USSR under occupation.[102] As a result, many—perhaps even the majority—of Soviet Jews perceived the Nazis' anti-Jewish war as part of the overall catastrophe of the occupied areas. In any event, the publications in which information about the murder of Jews appeared did not reach the majority of Red Army soldiers. As a result, Jews in the Red Army often did not realize the scale of mass killing until the war's later stages; nor did they understand the basic nature of German policy and attitudes toward the Jewish people. "Why don't the Germans like the Jews?" asked Jewish soldier Yuri Osipov in a 1942 letter to Ilya Ehrenburg—naively, it seems.[103] Twenty-year-old Sergeant Noson (Nathan) Epstein told an interviewer in May 1943 about a conversation he had had with a group of German prisoners two months earlier. "How many Jews are there in your army?" he recalled asking.[104] Another soldier who often spoke with German prisoners, twenty-three-year-old Boris Itenberg (later to acquire fame as a prolific historian), recounted in an August 1944 letter to his parents how he would ask Germans why they don't like Jews in order to practice his German-language skills. One day, he wrote, "a thirty-six-year-old Fritz, a gardener by trade, began to tell me enthusiastically . . . : 'When Hitler came to power, most banks, industrial plants, factories, and other commercial establishments were owned by the Jews, and for that reason, in order to seize all this, they began to shoot the Jews and put Germans in their place.'" "Is that close to reality?" he wondered in the letter, as if searching for a materialist explanation for the Nazi annihilation of the Jews.[105]

But what newspapers failed to convey, personal experience often provided. By the time Itenberg posed his questions, many Jewish Red Army soldiers, especially those from the occupied regions, were discovering that the annihilation campaign had obliterated their own families. Private Grigorii Uszpol, a twenty-one-year-old artilleryman from a rural village near Święciany in the formerly Polish Wilno district,[106] passed near his hometown with his unit during summer 1944. He related his experience to an interviewer from the Mints Commission[107] in June 1945:

> I was told[108] that my parents had perished, but they didn't let me go there, because bandits were still in the area, and they could kill [me]. In the town of Głębokie, which we were passing through, I saw a burnt-out quarter where the ghetto had been, in the middle of which was a smouldering synagogue and the bones of several thousand Jews. There I was told about my family. My father was shot on the third day after the Germans arrived.[109] Together with eight Jews, Komsomol members, and others he had been tossed away, his hands tied to a shovel. My mother, my sisters, and my brothers had been driven into the ghetto, where in 1942 they had been shot at [the military training ground known as] Poligon in Nowe Święciany.[110] [The news] devastated me. I cried for the first time in my life.[111]

The news also gave him renewed motivation to fight: "I decided to kill as many as I could." He made good on his resolution and did not hold back. In the fierce battles that took place between Tilsit (Sovetsk) and Klaipėda he took the place of a wounded gunner, firing some two hundred shells over three days of fighting, destroying a German Elefant ("Ferdinand") supertank, along with three personnel carriers, one light tank, and one heavy tank.

On the battle's first day, Uszpol's gunnery crew repelled fourteen counterattacks by German forces trying to break through along a highway; on the second day it threw back nine similar attacks, and on the third it destroyed nearly an entire infantry battalion.

In honor of his battlefield achievements Uszpol was promoted to the rank of corporal, named a Hero of the Soviet Union, and sent to be trained as a political officer. These acts solidified his attachment to the USSR. He told his interviewer that he didn't believe he would be recognized as a Soviet Hero: "I thought, 'I'm a Jew, so they won't give it to me.'" But they did, and they invited him to Moscow to receive the award. "I enjoyed the ceremonial atmosphere in the Kremlin. . . . I was at the Bolshoi Theatre. I saw Prince Igor. At the Yiddish theatre [I saw] Tevye the Dairyman. Now I could see for myself that there is no national oppression here. I am proud. I don't hear the word 'Jew' [spoken with contempt]."[112] Earlier in the interview he had explained that he had heard the word often while growing up in interwar Poland; it had told him that he was not equal and often served as grounds for his fellow schoolboys to tear into him. "In Wilno," where his parents had sent him to study in a yeshiva, he remembered, "we weren't able to go out into the streets; we would be attacked."[113] Those memories may have pushed him, despite his religious background, to join Komsomol after the Soviets first arrived. After receiving his award he took another step pointing to renewed Soviet commitments: he changed his last name to the Lithuanian Ušpolis.[114]

Major Wolf (Vulf) Vilenskii had a similar story. Born in Kaunas, like Uszpol from a traditional Jewish family and educated in a yeshiva, he too learned of German massacres of Jews as his unit passed close to his family home.[115] At the end of August 1944 he was given a two-day leave to go to Kaunas, to see if he could find out something about the fate of his relatives. He had just turned twenty-five. He found his family home, a wooden house of forty-three square meters, still standing—the last one in the Kaunas ghetto. The furniture was intact, too. The new owner, a certain Pole, tried to keep Vilenskii out. Vilenskii had to restrain himself in order not to shoot the man on the spot. "I had no doubt," he later recalled, "that this man standing before me . . . must surely have lent a hand to the rapid liquidation of the ghetto, the expropriation of our property, and first of all our house." Vilenskii left. The next morning he returned to find only two steps remaining. The Pole had pulled the house apart overnight and vanished without a trace. Vilenskii had no time to search for him. He didn't locate him even after the war ended.[116]

During his visit Vilenskii learned that almost all of his relatives had been killed. When he returned to his unit he told the officers, among whom were many Jews, about what he had heard—stories about how the Germans had massacred the Jews of Kaunas, including the children. Hearing his account, the battalion commander remarked that German soldiers should not be taken prisoner at all. "My subordinates took the phrase literally, like an order," Vilenskii later wrote, adding with candor that "they began to carry it out flawlessly."[117] Word of the battalion that took no German prisoners quickly spread beyond his division, and Vilenskii was nearly brought before a tribunal, until the commander of the front, General Ivan Bagramian, personally intervened, and the entire matter was hushed up. But Vilenskii's own fighting ardor only grew. On 14 October 1944 he led a single company to attack an advancing German force from the rear; when a machine gunner fell, he personally took over the weapon, mowing down no small number of enemy soldiers before he was wounded so severely that he was left for dead. He recovered, however, and for his bravery he was named a Hero of the Soviet Union in March 1945. Having been honored earlier with the Alexander Nevskii Order, two Orders of the Red Banner, one Order of the Patriotic War First Class, and one Order of the Red Star, he was the Red Army's most highly decorated Lithuanian Jew.[118]

Another highly decorated Baltic Jew, thirty-two-year-old political officer Ruvin Amdur from Riga, entered his hometown on 17 October 1944. In late June 1945, the war concluded, Amdur told the Mints Commission what he had seen:

> I had never felt such happiness and such excitement as I did when I entered Riga. . . . I thought, "There I have both relatives and friends." But I was so disappointed when I entered. I did not run into anyone [I knew]. The first thing I did was go to my apartment. . . . Of course, the apartment was empty; the Germans had been living there, and they had looted everything, leaving nothing behind. I had so many relatives, but no one remained. I have a father and a mother and sisters with children. Every single one had been killed.

Soon he learned how they had met their deaths. He described for his interviewer his feelings upon hearing the tragic report. His emotional state while relating what he had been told was similarly palpable:

> When the neighbors told me how they were sent to the ghetto, when they told me about my mother, I didn't cry, but it was as if I had been cut with a knife. My older brother (who later fell at the front), when he was going away [into evacuation] with his family on 27 June 1941, told our mother that he would take her. She said, "No, I'm going to look for my younger son'—that is, for me.... Neighbors said that when everyone left, she wanted to go to my wife's parents. She went to them and they fed her, but they didn't have any bread either. A Latvian neighbor met my mother on Dvinskaya Street[119] when she was on her way to her sister. The neighbor said ... that mother looked as awful as a corpse. When the neighbor told me this, I had such a strange feeling. Later they took my mother, my sister, and my sister's daughter. They took them away on 30 November [1941] to Ludinskaya Street.[120] Twelve thousand women were shot, and the next morning the corpses were piled on the cart like firewood, taken ... into the forest, and buried there. My sister's neighbor who lives there said that they heard the cries and the groans.
>
> My father, 73 years old, a good old guy, lived alone. On 1 July [1941], when the Germans arrived, the female building superintendant and one of the tenants told the Germans that this old man had two communist sons, both of whom had run off with the Reds.[121] Then two policemen came, took my father, and while leading him to the station beat him to death with a pistol. Everyone beat him over and over, and he bled to death.
>
> I have seen a lot, to be sure, but after I heard enough of such stories, the city seemed completely alien to me, not my native town.[122]

Amdur placed heavy responsibility for the annihilation of Latvian Jewry upon the Latvian people and their prewar nationalist bent. He told his interviewer that he had found only 152 Jews remaining in Riga: some had survived with Latvian help, while others had hidden in underground bunkers or bribed their captors. Most of the survivors told him that they had encountered at best an attitude of indifference among the Latvians and at worst happiness over the Jews' plight, "because they could rob until their pockets were full."[123] While they professed to condemn what the Germans had done, he maintained, "They related to the extermination of the [Jewish] population in extremely cold-blooded fashion." Amdur attributed this attitude to their having been "educated in the spirit of the most uncompromising chauvinism," learning that "only we are people, while all the rest are some sort of scum." Had Latvians received a Soviet education, he suggested, their wartime behavior would surely have been different.[124]

Esther Mankova, a military nurse from Ludza, a town in the Latgale region of Latvia on the Riga-Moscow highway, drew somewhat different conclusions from her encounter with her former neighbors following the end of the German occupation. Demobilized due to pregnancy, she shared living quarters in Riga with a Latvian woman who was a doctor and former comrade from her division. Years later she recalled that although she had heard about the extermination of Latvian Jewry, she continued to hold out hope that her parents had survived. She learned of their death only during a visit to her hometown. It turned out that her family had been murdered in their own home by coworkers of her father, an accountant in a shoemaking *artel*. The murderers had included her former teachers, neighbors, and good friends with whom she had played as a young girl.[125] Yet the alienation Mankova felt upon observing that some of the people who had ridiculed Jews in their final moments—and had perhaps even participated in the murders continued to live in prosperity—was only compounded by the kindness that her roommate's family showed her. That feeling was brought home to her at the family's Christmas celebration:

> The more this family gave me attention, the clearer it became to me that [their way of life] was not mine. They have a family, songs, a language, a culture. This is their Christmas, their tree. . . . Here, in the USSR, I have no family, and I will never have my language, my songs, my holidays. And what will my son become?[126]

Indeed, the last question was not an idle one for her: her roommate's mother, a Latvian peasant, advised her frankly that if she did not want to bring misfortune upon her son, she should not raise him as a Jew. She left Riga in 1946 with an underground Zionist organization, bound for Palestine, which she reached "after two and a half years of rough wandering."[127]

Certainly not all Jewish soldiers who came face-to-face with the awful outcome of the German war against the Jews drew such far-reaching operative conclusions from their encounter. But many appear to have begun to see the Jewish victims of that war as their own people in a way they hadn't before. Lieutenant Grigorii Pomerants, for example, a political officer, had, by his own admission, heard reports about the Nazi extermination campaign, but he had not paid them much heed. He had felt himself far too Russian, far too urbane to care about the *shtetl* Jews—people "not like me"—whom he assumed had borne the brunt of the Nazi onslaught. The well-educated Jews of the intelligentsia, he hoped, had managed to escape in the evacuation. In any case, in a war in which millions were perishing, he saw no reason to sort out the dead by nationality.[128] But his attitude changed radically when, returning from Germany, he stopped at the former Majdanek killing center in Poland, where he was taken aback by the sight of children's shoes piled together in a heap. He now "felt the dead as if they were my own children, and for the first time . . . experienced the words of Ivan Karamazov: the little children who are guilty of nothing."[129]

Boris Tartakovskii took an even more pronounced turn. The army political instructor who had once recoiled from the sight of Jews in sidelocks and condemned efforts to maintain "national habits"[130] did an about-face in 1944 after helping drive German forces from the Soviet southwest. In Zhmerinka, which had been part of Romanian-occupied Transnistria, he encountered Jews who had remained beyond the Germans' reach. When he arrived there in early May, as he noted in his diary, "The city was full of people returning to life:"

> For the first time in two and a half years they were able to walk down the street with heads held high, free and independent, without the humiliating yellow star on their chest. The poles with barbed wire have been cut clean away. There is no longer a threatening border [of a ghetto]. It was a touching sight. . . . And for the first time in my life I regretted that I did not know the Yiddish language.[131]

As a result of their experience at the front, at least some Soviet-style "new Jews" were discovering dimensions of themselves that before the war they had dismissed as insignificant.

For some of those Jews, the process of rediscovery unfolded within the framework of an ongoing Soviet experiment in managing the relations among the USSR's multiple ethnic groups.

Grigorii Uszpol, Wolf Vilenskii, Ruvin Amdur, and Esther Mankova all served in so-called National Military Formations (*Natsionalnye voinskiie formirovaniia*) of the Red Army. These units (mainly divisions or regiments) constituted a new incarnation of what had been a long-standing Soviet and Imperial Russian practice of grouping soldiers of similar ethnic background together under a single command. Their existence had long been controversial, and they had been abolished in 1938; but German efforts to stoke domestic discord and to recruit collaborators from among the USSR's non-Russian national groups,[132] along with the urgent need to mobilize thousands of mostly Central Asian and Transcaucasian Soviet citizens whose meager command of the Russian language would otherwise render them unsuitable for service, impelled the Soviet leadership to resurrect the concept.[133] In the Baltic regions annexed by the USSR in 1940 the Soviets were especially concerned with high levels of German recruitment among the local population, which, they worried, might undermine the commitment of their newfound Western allies to maintaining recently imposed Soviet rule once Germany was defeated. Consequently, hoping no doubt to generate a perception that substantial numbers Lithuanians, Latvians, and Estonians supported the Soviet cause, they began during summer and fall 1941 to establish a series of national units from the new Baltic SSRs.[134] The 201st Latvian Rifle Division was the first: organized on 3 August 1941,[135] its personnel came mainly from the estimated forty-thousand inhabitants of Latvia who successfully fled the German occupation during the opening weeks of the war or from former Latvian residents who had migrated across the pre-1940 international border with the USSR, along with soldiers from the Baltic region who had retreated in the face of the German invasion.[136] The Sixteenth Lithuanian Rifle Division, a formation of similar structure, purpose, and composition, was created on 18 December 1941.[137] Both were formed in the Moscow military district, with recruits brought in from as far away as Central Asia.[138]

These units were notable for their relatively high concentrations of Baltic Jews. Seventeen percent of the 10,348 soldiers mustered into the 201st Latvian Division during the first four months of its existence were Jews, as were at least 22 percent in the initially much smaller Sixteenth Lithuanian Division.[139] These proportions were approximately three times greater than the percentages of Jews in the populations of both countries between the two world wars.[140] The presence of Jews was especially pronounced in medical battalions.[141] The ethnic composition of the national divisions may have been to a degree a result of recruitment procedures, which filtered potential inductees according to their prewar background and included a set of political-ideological questions; Jews may have made up a disproportionately large share of the candidates deemed politically reliable.[142] Whatever the case, though, these divisions, along with a handful of other national units—like the 308th Latvian Rifle Division, created toward the end of the war—were virtually the only military formations in which Jews had such visible presence. Yiddish speech and Yiddish-language songs were commonly heard in the ranks. In fact, Jews stood out so prominently that upon reviewing a portion of the 201st Latvian Division shortly after its establishment, a high-ranking official in the Latvian SSR is said to have asked in unpleasant surprise, "Is this a Jewish regiment?"[143]

There were no Jewish regiments in the Red Army, but some Jews pushed to establish them. In December 1941 a veteran Jewish Party member, Yosef Kalmanovich, wrote to Solomon Mikhoels, director of the Moscow State Yiddish Theatre,[144] that "in this great campaign of ours . . . it is our right to show that in the Soviet state our [Jewish] people's heroism has been reborn."[145] He believed that designated Jewish divisions were the best vehicle for such a demonstration. Other leading Jewish cultural figures encountered similar suggestions throughout the war. Some who approached them argued, as Lieutenant Shimon Grinshpun wrote to Ilya Ehrenburg in March 1944, that "there is not a Jew who, in addition to the general account that the entire [Soviet] people has with fascism, does not also have a personal account with the fascist beast"—an account that would make them fight with special ferocity.[146] Others insisted that Jews were no less a nation than the Latvians or Estonians who had been awarded their own divisions, not to mention the Polish and Czech refugees who had been organized into exile forces fighting alongside the Red Army under their own command.[147] One, a political officer, was even reportedly overheard venturing Zionist sentiments—speech that he knew might cost him dearly.[148] Indeed, even the more modest proposals for an identifiably Jewish military unit had no chance to materialize.[149]

How service in a Lithuanian or a Latvian national military division affected the self-understanding of Baltic Jews is difficult to determine. It is tempting to posit a connection between such service and the prominent role Jews from the Baltic SSRs later played in the movement for emigration to Israel.[150] However, analysis of postwar testimonies by Jewish veterans of those units has revealed multiple subsequent trajectories. Some of those veterans affirmed a Soviet internationalist outlook, some became active in the so-called national communist factions that developed during the 1950s, and some drew Jewish nationalist conclusions.[151] It seems that these fighters, like Jewish Red Army soldiers in general, shared no single typical wartime experience.

Some Jews—there is no telling how many—appear to have had no particularly "Jewish" experiences at all.

Much is known, for example, about Sergeant Elena Deichman, a second-year student at Moscow State University and chair of her department's Russian Red Cross Society, who enlisted in March 1942 and served as a nurse and a combat medic before falling in battle in Slovakia in February 1945. Deichman carried on a voluminous wartime correspondence with friends and family.[152] The daughter of upwardly mobile migrants who had left the former Jewish Pale for the Soviet capital—her mother, Sofia Barenboim, had become a prominent trauma surgeon at a Moscow hospital; her father, Isaak Deichman, was a party functionary who had run afoul of the regime and been sentenced to imprisonment in a penal colony in the Russian Far East—her letters lack any mention of Jews or Jewish affairs.[153] Elena described in detail her efforts to join the army,[154] her work to secure her father's release from prison,[155] her situation as a military woman and her relationships with men,[156] and her daily life at the front;[157] however, any special concern she might have had about any of these matters as a Jew appear to have been absent from her consciousness. As far as their wartime exchanges reveal, she and her family were Soviet people before all else.[158] Nothing suggests that her motivation to fight was influenced in any way by knowledge of or worry about the special plight or fate of Jews under German occupation.[159]

Deichman's combat path took her far to the south in the Red Army's westward advance, through the Carpathians and Slovakia, somewhat removed from the most horrible signs of the Jewish fate. How a different set of assignments might have affected her perspective cannot be known. However, a similar lack of attention to Jewish matters is noticeable in the wartime writings of other Jewish soldiers who fought their way through Poland and on to Berlin. Two of them, Major Anna Marants, a medical corps pathologist, and Lieutenant Elena Kagan, a translator for the Soviet counterintelligence agency SMERSH,[160] actually came (literally) face to face with the corpse of Adolf Hitler. They were part of a small special forensic unit charged with making a positive identification of the charred cadavers that had been discovered in Berlin in the bunker complex under the Reich Chancellery garden by a soldier from Soviet military intelligence, Private Ivan Churakov.[161] Marants performed the autopsies and found one body—Hitler's—with jaws and teeth surprisingly intact; these became the basis of identifying the remains of the Nazi *Führer*. The teeth were removed and, with no safer means of storage available, placed in a burgundy-colored box, which was entrusted to Kagan.[162] The two people who came closest to Hitler in death—one who dug deep into his entrails, the other who preserved the final traces of his identity—were two Soviet Jewish women.[163]

Marants and Kagan, like Deichman, were quintessential "new" Soviet Jews. But lack of interest in Jewish matters was displayed by Jewish soldiers with stronger and deeper roots in the Yiddish language and in the affairs of the Jewish world. Perhaps the most notable of these "older" Jews was Captain Emmanuil Kazakevich, a highly decorated intelligence officer who distinguished himself in commando operations behind German lines. Born in 1913 in Kremenchug—a town on the Dnieper River in which Jews, according to the 1926 Soviet census, made up half of the sixty thousand residents—his father, Henekh Kazakevich, was a prominent Yiddish-language writer, translator, journalist, and editor who had long identified with the Bolshevik cause. In 1930 he and his family moved to the Jewish Autonomous Region centered in Birobidzhan, where his father edited the regional Yiddish newspaper, *Birobidzhaner shtern*, and Emmanuil became director of the Birobidzhan State Jewish Theatre. During his time in what the Soviet government touted as the new Jewish homeland, he also began to publish poems in Yiddish and to translate works by Soviet playwrights and classical Russian writers. When repressions began to decimate the Jewish leadership of Birobidzhan in 1937, Kazakevich managed to escape to safety outside of Moscow, where he, his wife, and their children remained until the threat of arrest had passed.[164]

His close brush with Stalinist terror does not appear to have cooled his ardor for the Soviet homeland. Though nearsighted to the point of disqualification for military service, when war broke out in 1941 he volunteered for the Moscow People's Militia (*Narodnoe opolchenie*)—units created urgently in the wake of the German invasion to mobilize the initial defenses of major cities.[165] After three months he was transferred to the regular army, incurring wounds during his effort to break out of encircled Moscow in search of a unit in which to enlist. In training courses he demonstrated leadership capabilities, but his background as a writer got him assigned to his training brigade's newspaper. He sought combat, however, to the point where in June 1943 he deserted his post and headed for the front. In a letter he left for his commanding officers, military and political, he explained his act:

> An ardent and irresistible desire to be at the front, to fight actively for our cause in the ranks of the front-line soldiers—a desire about which I have told you many times—that is the reason for my sudden departure. From the perspective of everyday existence my life here has been wonderful. But I have some big scores to settle with the Germans—I am a communist, a commander, a writer. It's time for me to start settling those scores.[166]

"A communist, a commander, a writer"—not a Jew.

Kazakevich barely escaped a court-martial for his self-reassignment. As a result, and with the help of his first training officer, who had spotted his military talent, he managed to attach himself to a series of infantry intelligence units, soon attaining increasingly responsible command positions. In April 1944 he became chief of intelligence of the Seventy-Sixth Army Division; he was wounded three months later but recovered to become assistant head of intelligence for the entire Forty-Seventh Army. Throughout his time in the intelligence service his units fought through parts of the former Pale of Settlement before moving on to Poland and then to Germany. It was there that he wrote a letter to his sister containing perhaps his sole mention of what had befallen his fellow Jews:

> We are continuing to fight. That's how I ended up abroad, amidst the countryside and the cities of Germany, with their churches, their tiled roofs, and cobblestone streets. The churches are enormous, cold and empty, with the

> obligatory grand organ along the back wall and the obligatory Luther Bible in large folio format. This is the picture of the Germany about which we have read and thought so much since childhood; but now to that picture we are adding a moving scene: the Fritzes who have been killed, the Fritzes who have been frightened to death, and the old Fritzes. Sometimes I feel pity standing and looking at these people, especially the children, but then you remember the ditch at Kerch,[167] Majdanek, the murdered women and children, the extermination of the Jews throughout Europe, whose sole guilt was belonging to this nation, and you begin to think that it is just, and it can't be and shouldn't be otherwise.[168]

Who can say which aspects of his being—the writer, the soldier, the communist, the Jew—shaped Captain Kazakevich's sense of justice more or less profoundly? What is known is that in 1946 he left the Red Army and resumed writing, which he had abandoned during his years of service.[169] The war was a central theme in his early postwar literary corpus. In particular, his book *Zvezda* (The Star), about a military intelligence unit like his own, became a standard work of Soviet war literature; between 1947 and 1951 it was published in twenty editions with a circulation of several million copies, and in 1949 a film version was produced.[170] A Yiddish version of the story followed shortly after the Russian, but from then on Kazakevich wrote exclusively in the Russian language. Following a 1961 visit with Yiddish poet Hirsh Osherovich, he explained why:

> Osherovich . . . read me his poems, one about Spartacus, another about the exodus from Egypt, a third about Hiroshima. They are ably written, with talent and skill in places. The only problem—nobody needs them. One can write well or poorly in a living language, one that people—workers and peasants—actually speak and use to produce real material value; but in a language that is dying or already dead after the tragedy that the people and the language lived through, [the writing] has to be brilliant—otherwise nobody needs it. But— here is the dialectic at work—brilliant writing is possible only in a living, developing language. When literature becomes a personal affair for 50 or 500 people it loses its main function; it stops being a means of communication and for improving society. Once it has lost this quality, it stops being literature.[171]

The war, it seems, had relegated his Jewish self (or at least the part that expressed itself in Yiddish) to the past.[172]

Writing in Russian gave Kazakevich and several of his fellow Jewish Red Army veterans who did not know Yiddish—including David Kaufman (Samoilov), Boris Slutskii, and Elena Kagan, who, under the pseudonym Elena Rzhevskaia (from the horrific Battle of Rzhev,[173] in which she took part), became a widely read fictional chronicler of life and death at the front[174]—a platform from which they helped shape Russian memories of the war for generations after. Other Jewish writers served as military journalists; they helped shape Soviet perceptions of the war in real time. Foremost among them was Ilya Ehrenburg, already well known both for his fiction and for his reporting as *Izvestiia*'s Paris correspondent during the 1930s.[175] In June 1941 Ehrenburg, already fifty years old, inaugurated a regular column in the Red Army newspaper, *Krasnaia zvezda* (The Red Star); over the next four years more than two thousand of his articles appeared in the Soviet press.[176] He was arguably the most widely read writer at the front, thanks no doubt in part to his insistence upon embedding himself among the fighters, over his editors' objections, so that he could, as he expressed it, "put into words what the men at the front are thinking."[177] Soviet leaders recognized his immense value as motivator and morale booster: Foreign Minister Molotov reportedly reckoned that he was worth an entire military division.[178] Ehrenburg himself later reflected on his task and its aim:

> Like everybody else, I was filled with anxiety and, like everybody else, I was liberated from doubts by the sheer demands of the situation. Never in my life have I worked so hard: every day I wrote three or four articles; at home I sat at my typewriter, in the evening I went to the *Red Star* office, prepared an article for the next issue, read German documents and intercepted radio messages, edited translations and wrote captions for photographs . . . I found arguments to prove that we were bound to win. I believed in victory, not because I relied on our resources or on the Second Front,[179] but because I needed to believe: for me in those days, as for all other Soviet citizens, there was no alternative.[180]

A younger fellow reporter for *Krasnaia zvezda*, Berdichev native Vasilii Grossman, was less well known than Ehrenburg at the outset of fighting, but his vivid, insightful, and brutally honest descriptions of life and death on the battlefield during the German advance on Moscow quickly earned him an avid readership. His circle of readers became even larger in 1942, when the Red Army newspaper began to publish installments of his novel *Narod bessmerten* (The People Immortal), written the previous autumn while covering fighting in Ukraine after the Germans abandoned plans for an immediate assault on the Soviet capital.[181] Frontline soldiers quickly acclaimed the work as the first accurate and honest depiction of their experience; the confidence in him that resulted gave him unparalleled access to sources.[182] Later that year he was awarded the Orders of the Red Banner and the Red Star. The citation underscored his surpassing status:

> The writer Grossman, carrying out his duties as a correspondent, on more than one occasion took part in combat, in the process of which he demonstrated valor and courage. He made his way into the most advanced units, right up to those keeping an eye on the enemy's movements, during the tensest days of military activity. At present he is the only writer who is participating in the fighting for Stalingrad, and he often goes into the city with battalions and companies, where he collects literary material.[183]

Ehrenburg and Grossman were the outstanding examples of Jewish writers who turned their military service into a vehicle for giving voice to the suffering, the trepidation, the courage, the exhaustion, the resilience, and the day-to-day grind of the millions of young Soviet citizens who put their lives on the line for family, home, and homeland; but they were hardly the only ones to do so. They did not know Yiddish, but the prominence in the Moscow militia of Jews who wrote not only in Russian but in Yiddish testifies to the readiness of the Jewish intellectual elite to put their literary and linguistic talents to use for the benefit of the Soviet war effort. Some gave their lives in defense of their homeland. Buzi Olevski was a promising Yiddish-language literary scholar, children's author, short-story writer, and poet, lately from Birobidzhan. Olevski, whose service in the Red Army began in 1939, attained the rank of lieutenant and commanded a machine-gun company before being killed during the early days of fighting. The same fate soon awaited his colleagues Aaron Gurshtein, Shmuel Rosin, Meir Viner, and Shmuel Godiner. The Yiddish poet Shmuel Rosin's wife was killed in fall 1941 while delivering parcels of food and warm clothing to the front on behalf of the Military Commission of the Soviet Writers Union.[184] The aspiring Russian-language poet Pavel Kogan, a friend of Slutskii and Samoilov and the estranged husband of Elena Kagan, died in battle near Novorossiisk in September 1942.

Some of the more prominent Yiddish writers and artists, along with Ehrenburg and Grossman, also seized upon an unlikely chance to serve as a voice for Soviet Jews. Over the course of the war they would form a new, quasi-official Soviet Jewish communal leadership. Their efforts, accomplishments, failures, and interactions with the regime would add yet another dimension to the war's impact upon the future shape of Soviet Jewry.

5

LEADERSHIP

The chance for a group of prominent Jewish (mostly Yiddish) writers to serve as a collective voice for a Soviet Jewish community emerged during summer 1941.

To an extent the opportunity was the result of their own initiative. On 16 August, eight major figures on the Soviet Jewish literary scene—novelist David Bergelson; poets Ezra Finenberg, Shmuel Halkin, Leyb Kvitko, and Peretz Markish; actor-director Solomon Mikhoels, journalist Shakhne Epstein, and critic Isaac Nusinov—requested permission from the Soviet government "to organize a Jewish rally aimed at the Jews of the USA and Great Britain, and also at Jews in other countries . . . , to mobilize world Jewish public opinion in the struggle against fascism and for its active support of the Soviet Union in its Great Patriotic War of liberation."[1] The move was audacious. To begin with, its suggested appeal was not specifically to the Jewish working class, as official Soviet ideology dictated, but to "world Jewish public opinion"—a term tacitly encompassing Jews of all ideological and religious convictions, including the "clerical" and "Zionist" elements that the regime had long condemned.[2] Moreover, the petitioners were hardly in a strong position of public influence. Despite having enjoyed notable support from the Soviet state during the first two postrevolutionary decades, Yiddish in the USSR, like in other countries, had lost substantial ground during the previous decade. In the 1939 census only 39 percent of Ashkenazic Jews declared Yiddish to be their mother tongue, but even that number did not necessarily use Yiddish as their primary language of oral and written communication.[3] In 1938 the government had gone so far as to liquidate the Soviet Yiddish-language school system, except in the so-called Jewish Autonomous Region (administratively centered in the town of Birobidzhan), whose Jewish population numbered fewer than eighteen thousand.[4] To be sure, most of the country's leading Yiddish writers—including Bergelson, Leyb Kvitko, Markish, and the poet David Hofstein, all of whom had previously tasted life abroad and could easily have been suspected of espionage on that basis—had come through the Stalinist purges untouched.[5] In fact, in 1939 Hofstein, Kvitko, and Markish, along with Halkin and fellow poet Itsik Fefer, received high state honors, giving them the exalted (and remunerative) status of "order-bearers" (*ordenonostsy*).[6] Scores of Yiddish fiction writers, playwrights, poets, essayists, and translators continued to belong organizationally to the Jewish (or, more precisely, the Yiddish-language[7]) sections of the Soviet Writers' Union, a highly influential and privileged state-controlled organization created in 1934. Some of their works were translated into Russian and other languages, giving them fame beyond Yiddish-reading circles.[8] But their readership in Yiddish was vanishing: the state-determined print runs of Yiddish books and periodicals had been cut back steadily since the mid-1930s, and the country's leading Yiddish newspaper, Moscow-based *Der Emes* ("The Truth"—i.e., *Pravda*) had been shut down in 1938. In a short time, it seemed, Yiddish writers would lose their raison d'etre.[9]

Yet their application succeeded. Only a week after submitting their petition, on 24 August, a mass gathering took place in Gorky Park, Moscow's premier outdoor recreation and cultural space, featuring speeches by four of the petitioners, as well as by Ilya Ehrenburg, famed film director Sergei Eisenstein, internationally renowned physicist Piotr Kapitsa, and other prominent members of the Soviet intelligentsia, Jewish and non-Jewish, with presumed cachet abroad. The event was filmed and broadcast over Soviet radio. The next day *Pravda*, *Izvestiia*, and other newspapers reported approvingly that "representatives of the Jewish people" (*narod*) had "called . . . with emotion and passion . . . on Jews of the entire world to join in the sacred struggle against the fascist murderers and oppressors who were inundating entire cities and villages of Europe with the blood of their inhabitants."[10] The texts of the main speeches were published, as was a public call to "fellow Jews the world over" (*bratia evrei vsego mira*) to join "the great, freedom-loving Soviet people and its legendary Red Army" in avenging "the blood of Jews tortured in the burning synagogues of Rotterdam . . . [and] the thousands of unmarked graves in the towns and villages of Poland" and in defeating "Hitler's bloody regime, [which] has brutally planned the complete and unconditional annihilation of the Jewish people by all means available."[11] For a regime that had worked assiduously over the previous decade to reduce Jewish visibility among the USSR's constituent nationalities, to denigrate the religious dimensions of Jewish existence, and to circumscribe Soviet Jews' connections with Jews in other lands, such treatment in the media augured a notable reversal of direction.[12]

Surviving film footage of the rally suggests what likely drove the reversal. It features fragments from speeches by Mikhoels, Markish, Bergelson, Ehrenburg, and Eisenstein (son of a baptized Jewish father and a Russian mother). Markish and Bergelson spoke in Yiddish, Mikhoels and Ehrenburg in Russian, and Eisenstein in heavily accented English. The choice of Eisenstein to deliver an address in a Western language—a decision made by high-ranking officials of the regime, who approved the texts of all the speeches[13]—pointed to the audience the Soviets hoped primarily to reach and the reasons why this choice was important. Ehrenburg, whose years in Paris decades before had given him not only keen insight into Western society but near-native command of French, could easily have delivered his remarks in that language. Eisenstein, by contrast, was better known in the English-speaking world and had many admirers in Hollywood, where he had spent time in 1930 under a contract (eventually annulled by mutual consent) to make a film in the United States. Though not a Jew himself, his connections in the American film industry, with its heavily Jewish presence, evidently made him the most desirable presenter to address the international audience as far as the regime was concerned.[14]

Indeed, it was the imagined potential for exploiting presumed Jewish solidarity and influence in the English-language press, radio, and cinema that most likely commended the Yiddish writers' proposal to Soviet policymakers.[15] In the face of the German invasion, those policymakers looked upon favorable publicity in Britain and the United States as a commodity of inestimable value. Caught unprepared by the German surprise attack, one of the USSR's first strategic goals was to consolidate a military alliance with the one remaining power—Britain—standing in the anti-Nazi struggle and to secure material support from Britain's indispensable supplier, the United States. Neither could be taken for granted.[16] An initial Anglo-Soviet agreement was signed in Moscow on 12 July, but although it obligated Britain not to conclude a separate peace with Germany, it was silent about any specific affirmative British aid that might be forthcoming.[17] Negotiations with the United States, still officially neutral in the European conflict, to obtain war matériel under the American Lend-Lease program began the day after fighting commenced, but they continued inconclusively for weeks thereafter.[18] In that context, a public in both countries favorably disposed toward the Soviet cause surely appeared to Soviet leaders an invaluable resource. But, over the previous two years, the Ribbentrop-Molotov Pact, the joint German-Soviet liquidation of Poland, and the USSR's annexation of the Baltic states had made the Soviets seem to many in the Western democracies far more antagonists of ostensible shared Anglo-American values than true allies.[19] Amplifying the cries of some of the Nazi regime's most notable victims could, Soviet planners evidently concluded, help repair their country's tarnished image.

Burnishing the Soviet image abroad was one of the primary tasks entrusted to the newly formed Soviet Information Bureau (*Sovinformburo*), created on 24 June 1941, less than three days following the German attack. This agency, called into being by a joint decision of the Council of People's Commissars and the Communist Party Central Committee, issued regular press and radio bulletins for foreign and domestic audiences, held press briefings for foreign journalists, and placed stories by Soviet reporters and columnists with major newspapers, newsreel services, and broadcast media outlets abroad.[20] It was directed by Aleksandr Shcherbakov, a founding member of the Soviet Writers' Union, with a Jew, Solomon Lozovskii, deputy foreign minister and one of the oldest members of the Party Central Committee, as vice-chairman. Lozovskii was the recipient of the Yiddish writers' request of 16 August.[21] In the margin he penned a note to Shcherbakov: "It seems to me that such a rally should be organized."[22]

For their part, the Yiddish writers no doubt sensed a propitious moment to restore their recently attenuated public function. They may have been looking for ways to do so ever since Markish, Mikhoels, and Nusinov had met with colleagues from newly annexed Western Byelorussia in February 1940 and had subsequently stressed to Stalin the need to cultivate the loyalty of the mostly Yiddish-speaking Jews from the former Polish lands that the Soviets planned to incorporate into the USSR.[23] In effect, they had argued that the Yiddish language could serve as a bridge to masses of Jews who were not already committed communists. The German invasion brought a new effort in a similar direction. On 18 July 1941 Markish and Nusinov were joined by Bergelson, Fininberg, Halkin, and Kvitko in a letter to Sovinformburo asking to renew publication of *Der Emes*, on the grounds that the German conquests in Western Byelorussia and Western Ukraine had destroyed the Soviets' ability to communicate with the region's Jews in their own language. A Yiddish newspaper published in Moscow, they maintained, could mitigate that deficit. The idea of a public rally was put forward only after this earlier proposal had been rejected.[24] After the rally they tried again, explaining now that a new *Der Emes* would help publicize the regime's messages both among the growing numbers of Yiddish-speaking refugees and evacuees heading into the Soviet interior and among the large communities of Jewish emigrants from eastern Europe in Britain and the United States. This time they achieved an agreement, although the evacuation from Moscow in mid-October scuttled implementation for many months.[25]

Nevertheless, it is not clear that the agreement pointed to a new interest within the regime in enhancing the status of *Yiddish* men of letters in particular, let alone in making them into the *internal* spokesmen for Soviet Jewry. To be sure, the apparent success of the rally on 24 August appears to have set high-ranking officials to thinking about how best to cultivate connections with Jews abroad. But their thinking led them at first away from the Yiddish writers who had proposed the rally. Instead, they looked toward two individuals who, however improbably, seemed for a moment to offer a much different path to the West.

The two individuals were Henryk Erlich and Wiktor Alter, senior Jewish political figures from Poland whom the Soviets had incarcerated in 1939 as their campaign against that country drew to a close.[26] Both had been leaders of the Jewish socialist party the Bund and enjoyed notable stature in socialist circles worldwide. Following their arrest on charges of anti-Soviet activity they were kept (separately) in prison without trial for nearly two years. Only after the German invasion was their case heard in court, with predictable results: Alter was sentenced to death on 20 July 1941, Erlich on 2 August. However, within two days Alter's sentence was commuted to ten years' imprisonment. Erlich was given a similar commutation on 22 August. Three weeks later, on 12 and 13 September, the Soviet authorities abruptly set both of them free.[27]

The police files concerning the two leaders provide no hint about the reasons for the authorities' behavior. Perhaps the two were released as part of the general amnesty for deported or imprisoned Polish citizens in the USSR that accompanied the conclusion of an alliance between the Soviets and the London-based Polish government-in-exile on 30 July 1941. The move's precise timing, though, suggests that other considerations of Soviet raison d'état may also have been in play.[28] Inquiries about Erlich and Alter's fate from socialist and trade union organizations and personalities had been received in Moscow from 1939.[29] Even before the Polish-Soviet agreement had been signed, Britain's ambassador to the USSR, Stafford Cripps, a former Labour MP and Popular Front advocate with considerable public following in his country, had expressed his government's concern for the two leaders; following the agreement's conclusion he raised the issue a second time.[30] Poland's newly appointed ambassador to Moscow, Stanisław Kot, included their names in a list of Polish political figures whose immediate release was a priority for his government.[31] Freeing Erlich and Alter thus offered the Soviets, at a minimum, a chance for a low-cost gesture of goodwill toward both the British and the Polish governments and toward Western public opinion.

It appears, though, that some key figures within the Soviet regime, foremost among them Lavrentii Beria, deputy premier and chief of the NKVD,[32] saw possibilities for much more than the minimum gain. Beria most likely believed that the two Polish Jews' extensive political relationships abroad, recently demonstrated by multiple interventions on their behalf, potentially offered the Soviets the most effective access possible to the influential Western circles they desired to reach—certainly more effective than the Soviet Jewish cultural figures behind the rally of 24 August could provide. As former Polish citizens who owed the Soviet Union no allegiance, as long-standing critics of communism and opponents of communist political aspirations outside the USSR, and especially as recent victims of the Soviet apparatus of political repression, their enlistment on behalf of the Soviet war effort stood to make a powerful impression upon the many political figures in Britain and the United States who had greeted the prospect of alliance with the bastion of world communism with undisguised distaste.[33] In any event, the NKVD made certain that Erlich and Alter were not only released from prison but treated in a fashion clearly designed to present the USSR in a different light from the one the pair had known during the previous two years. Erlich described his release and its aftermath in an undated letter to a Bundist colleague in New York:

> On 9 September [1941] I was brought in a second class compartment to Moscow. 11 September I was released and given a room in one of Moscow's richest hotels.[34] The friendliness and attentiveness that we [Alter and I] are both being shown is indescribable. They are constantly trying to convince us that we have been released not on the basis of the agreement with Poland but because they have been persuaded that we were done an injustice, and now they want to right all the wrongs that have been done to us.[35]

Soon, however, the Bund leaders learned that Soviet beneficence came with strings attached. By the beginning of October (and perhaps earlier), the NKVD approached them "about propaganda services, especially in America."[36] On 10 October Erlich and Alter informed the Polish embassy in Moscow that the desired services involved establishing a "Jewish Anti-Hitlerite Committee."[37] During the same month they wrote to Beria, indicating that "pursuant to the conversation with [him]," they had "worked out details" for "the establishment of a Jewish Anti-Hitler Committee" and requested "permission to establish such a committee on the territory of the Soviet Union."[38] Beria in turn advised the pair to submit their proposal directly to Stalin. They did so promptly, writing that Jews in all countries were certain to "participate in the struggle against Hitler with particular vigor and with a special spirit of self-sacrifice."[39] Their committee would, they ventured, "stimulate and organize the energy of the masses of the Jewish people and, insofar as possible, of Jewish society in its entirety, in all countries, for a struggle against Hitlerism using all means and all of the power" at world Jewry's disposal.[40] Specifically they promised, among other things, to "launch a campaign" for "maximum assistance by the United States for the Soviet Union in military equipment and ammunition, maximum credit for the Soviet Union . . . , establishment of a legion of citizens of the United States and other countries who would enlist directly in the ranks of the Red Army . . . , [and] participation by the Jewish population of the United States in defraying (with money and goods) the costs of aid to the Jewish refugees . . . located on Soviet territory."[41] The committee was to consist of ten people: seven delegates representing countries under Nazi occupation and one each representing the USSR, the United States, and Great Britain. Erlich was to serve as committee chair, Alter as secretary, and Solomon Mikhoels as a third member of the Presidium.[42]

While Stalin considered the plan, Erlich and Alter also maintained close contact with the Polish embassy, serving at times as go-betweens for the Poles and the Soviets on matters concerning the welfare of Polish citizens covered by the amnesty agreement between the two states.[43] It was the Poles, not the Soviets, who arranged for the two to be evacuated with the embassy staff when the Soviets, fearing imminent German conquest of Moscow, removed their government institutions to Kuibyshev on 16 October 1941. Conditions in their new location were not nearly as comfortable as they had been in the capital; they were housed at Polish expense together with a third Bundist leader, Lucjan Blit, in one room of a hotel patronized mainly by foreign correspondents and diplomatic personnel.[44] In retrospect it seems that their downgraded status signaled that Stalin was already inclined to reject their proposal. Indeed, for the next six weeks they heard nothing from their NKVD contacts. Then, on 3 December 1941, they received a telephone call from the NKVD administration that one of those contacts wished to meet with them late that night. Erlich recorded what transpired in a complaint he submitted to the Supreme Soviet of the USSR on 27 December:

> We went convinced that the end of our inactivity was finally at hand. We came and, after waiting for twenty hours, [the person who had brought them to the meeting location] announced that he had received instructions from Moscow to arrest us. He admitted there might have been a misunderstanding and this should be clarified in a day or two, but in the meantime he was obliged to detain us.
>
> We were separated and placed in the internal prison [of the Kuibyshev *oblast*], and I have been here in solitary confinement now for three and a half

> weeks. I have not been given the reason for my arrest even now, and even orally I have received no explanation as to what I am accused of.[45]

He never did. Nor did Alter. None but their captors would see them alive again. Erlich was confined until 14 May 1942, when he took his own life. Alter's captivity lasted until 17 February 1943. On that day he was executed by shooting.[46]

The available documents reveal no reason for their fall from grace. Much speculation has centered around their contacts with the Polish embassy, with British and American diplomats in Kuibyshev, and with socialist comrades abroad, through which they distributed graphic accounts of their initial captivity and negative impressions of the Soviet regime that surely did not comport with what their NKVD handlers expected or wished.[47] Beria's son retrospectively attributed the reversal to his father's lack of due diligence: "My father did not know that [Ehrlich and Alter] had formerly been critics of Stalin. . . . When Stalin saw their names on the lists of future members of the Committee he became violently angry . . . , and he ordered their arrests."[48] But whatever the case, the Soviets evidently decided that the task of enlisting Jews in the West on behalf of the Soviet war effort had to be entrusted only to Soviet citizens. The Yiddish writers who had inspired the rally of 24 August 1941 thus appeared now the most politically reliable vehicle for advancing the regime's propaganda aims. Accordingly, the regime turned back to them.

Beria's failure does not appear to have cost him personally, at least in any way that was immediately apparent. Nevertheless, in its wake the mission of recruiting Jews worldwide to the Soviet cause was taken from Beria's NKVD and placed squarely in the hands of *Sovinformburo*. Henceforth the operation's chief supervisor would be Deputy Foreign Ministry Lozovskii. A veteran Bolshevik (despite having been expelled from the party for two years following the Bolshevik seizure of power), Lozovskii was the son of a Hebrew teacher who had taught him the fundamentals of that language. He commanded Yiddish as well. He had spent most of the decade before the revolution in Paris, where, among other activities, he had organized a trade union of Jewish hatmakers. Between 1937 and 1939 he had headed the

State Publishing House for Belles-Lettres, where he had gotten to know a number of Yiddish writers. The Jewish, Russian-born, London-based journalist Alexander Werth, who spent the war years as the British Broadcasting Corporation's Moscow correspondent, noted that Lozovskii was perceived, like Maxim Litvinov before him, as "more sympathetic to the West than Molotov": he was distinguished by his command of French and by "his *barbiche* and carefully cut clothes," which made him appear "rather like an old *boulevardier*, whom one could well imagine on the terrace of the [Café] Napolitain during *la belle époque*."[49] Indeed, his assumption of the role of chief government spokesperson facing the foreign press pointed to a deliberate return to the diplomatic style of the Litvinov era.[50]

Perhaps to differentiate his approach from that of Erlich and Alter, Lozovskii changed the name of the Jewish propaganda organization to the Jewish Anti-Fascist Committee. He also placed it alongside four other Anti-Fascist Committees—an "All-Slavic" one and one each of Soviet women, Soviet youth, and Soviet scientists—thereby presenting the Jewish group as a constituent member of a broad front of civilian Soviet citizens actively working on their country's behalf.[51] His first step regarding the Jewish committee was to recruit Solomon Mikhoels to be its chairman. This move stood as well to solidify the committee's patriotic bona fides. Mikhoels held the highest Soviet decoration, the Order of Lenin; he was one of only two figures among the Jewish cultural elite to have been given such a prestigious award.[52] He had also been named a People's Artist of the USSR and a deputy of the Moscow City Council in 1939 and been designated a Master Class Professor of Acting in 1941.[53] In October 1941 he had been called to lead a Front Theater for entertaining the troops.[54] He was also well known beyond the relatively narrow circles of Yiddish readers and theatergoers, having appeared in two recent popular films *The Circus* (1936), one of the most widely viewed Soviet musical comedies, and *The Family Oppenheim* (1938), based on a novel by German Jewish writer Lion Feuchtwanger describing the persecution of Jews in Nazi Germany.[55] It is thus not surprising that Lozovskii regarded Mikhoels as the person best suited for this highly responsible position. Accordingly, on 15 December 1941, the deputy foreign minister wired the Jewish actor notifying Mikhoels that he had been "confirmed as chairman of the Jewish Anti-Fascist Committee" and instructing him to "maintain direct daily contact with us."[56]

However, Mikhoels was not to be permitted to direct the committee on his own. Shortly after his appointment, another of the initiators of the August 1941 rally, Shakhne Epstein, was named the incipient group's secretary. Epstein, a former Bundist and labor activist in the United States, appears to have operated abroad as a Soviet agent during the 1920s and 1930s. He may even have been involved in a likely NKVD assassination carried out in New York in 1937.[57] His attachment to the committee indicates that the NKVD still sought to maintain a watchful eye over Lozovskii's doings. Eventually the agency also recruited one of the committee's best-known figures, the poet Itsik Fefer, to inform on the activities of other committee members.[58] Other members may have had ties to the NKVD as well. In a society that had come to fear virtually all contact with foreigners, anyone involved in an activity aimed at cultivating precisely such contact could not have operated without the knowledge and approval of the secret police.

Indeed, all who became members of the Jewish Anti-Fascist Committee were carefully selected and vetted by the party and state apparatus on the basis of both professional and political criteria. Fefer described his involvement as the result of having been "called upon to work at" the committee.[59] Markish, too, recalled that he and other writers "were summoned to the Central Committee" in 1941.[60] On 4 May 1942 Kvitko wrote a friend from his refuge in Alma-Ata that he was leaving for Kuibyshev after having "been summoned to work at the Jewish Anti-Fascist Committee."[61] Volunteers were not encouraged to become committee members; random applications to join were rejected.[62] It thus seems that the committee was never intended to become a mass organization. By 1944 its membership consisted of sixty-four handpicked authors (mainly, but not only, Yiddish writers), officers and generals (including Yakov Kreiser[63]), actors, artists, physicians, scholars, and representatives of the Jewish Autonomous Region of Birobidzhan.[64] Perhaps as a reflection of the government's more tolerant attitude to religious practices, Rabbi Shlomo Shliffer, who in 1943 filled the vacant position of chief rabbi of the Moscow Choral Synagogue (his predecessor was executed in 1938), was also allowed to take part in committee activities.[65]

Meanwhile, though, during winter 1942 Mikhoels and Epstein took on the preparatory work for launching the committee. In early February they formulated for Lozovskii a list of fifteen goals, including

> to collect concrete information about the situation of Jews in occupied European countries and areas in the USSR temporarily seized by Hitler's gangs; to collect detailed information about the role and participation of Jews in the Great Patriotic War . . . ; to promote, in every way possible, the creation of Jewish anti-fascist committees abroad . . . ; to publish illustrated collections on the theme 'The fascists are annihilating the Jewish people . . . ; to collaborate with film companies in the USSR and abroad in producing a series of films about fascist atrocities against the Jewish population and about the struggle of the Jewish masses against fascism . . . ; [and] to organize a campaign for financial contributions, especially in the United States, to buy medicine and warm clothing for the Red Army and [for] people evacuated from regions occupied by the Germans."
>
> Lozovskii found the last aim the most important; when he submitted the list to Shcherbakov for approval, he noted that "we could receive millions of dollars in medicine and warm clothing for the evacuated population, for very little work indeed.[66]

Still, it took nearly three more months for Shcherbakov to permit Lozovskii to announce the committee's creation.[67] Perhaps he was finally persuaded by a direct appeal from Epstein two weeks earlier, in which the committee's designated secretary recounted in detail how "former enemies of the Soviet government" in Britain, the United States, and Palestine had, in response to the August 1941 rally, "expressed enthusiastic support for the heroic struggle of the Red Army against the fascist invaders" and "called on Jews the world over, no matter what their political or religious views, to aid the Soviet Union in every way possible." "Even a reactionary organization such as the American Jewish Congress,"[68] Epstein pointed out, "represented by the well-known American Zionist leader and inveterate enemy of the Soviet government, Rabbi Dr. Stephen Wise,"[69] had not only "sent greetings to the Moscow rally" but had "promised to send assistance to the Red Army."[70] In fact, more than promises were already forthcoming from Zionist circles. Epstein might also have mentioned what the Soviets undoubtedly already knew—that during that same month the leadership of the Jewish community in Palestine had announced the formation of the "V-League (for Victory) for the Benefit of Soviet Russia" and had launched a fundraising campaign to purchase an ambulance and medicines to be sent to the

USSR. Pointing out that "every Red Army victory, every town returned to its hands, means saving Jews," the League called upon Palestinian Jewry to "overcome all hesitancies and doubts and to fulfill its elementary obligation to render active and concrete assistance in the common struggle . . . whose outcome is liable to determine the fate of humanity and of the entire world." The first steps toward its formation had been taken in response to the August 1941 rally.[71] That rally, Epstein argued, had been highly effective; hence the time had come "to expand and speed up the growing movement of international Jewish solidarity with the Soviet Union." In order to do so he recommended "to raise the prestige and authority of the Jewish Anti-Fascist Committee abroad by publicizing its composition."[72] The recommendation was tacitly accepted when the Jewish Anti-Fascist Committee was officially proclaimed on 25 April 1942.

In his memorandum to Shcherbakov, Epstein had recommended that the committee undertake three primary activities: "to organize a second all-Jewish anti-fascist radio rally in Moscow or Kuibyshev in the near future; to broadcast a half-hour radio program in Yiddish, once a week . . . , aimed at audiences abroad; [and] to begin the immediate publication of a Yiddish newspaper, as the organ of the Jewish Anti-Fascist Committee, at least twice a month."[73] The rally was staged in short order. In it the same themes around which the August 1941 rally had centered were voiced in much the same terms by many of the same speakers, with the addition of the announcement of concrete goals for Jewish assistance: one thousand tanks and five hundred airplanes for the Soviet military.[74] It was a fleeting event; it did not develop into the regular Yiddish radio broadcast Epstein had urged. Epstein's call for a Yiddish newspaper, by contrast, received a favorable response. *Eynikayt* (Unity), with Epstein as editor, began publication every ten days beginning 7 June 1942. On 1 September it morphed into a weekly, and beginning 22 February 1945 it appeared three times weekly, with ten thousand copies printed.[75] After a four-year hiatus, a regular Yiddish serial publication reappeared in the USSR.

The Jewish Anti-Fascist Committee maintained that *Eynikayt* was aimed at the "mass Jewish reader brought up and reeducated" in the Soviet Union, and also at Jews in the recently annexed territories "who had not attended the Soviet school of life."[76] For most Soviet Jews, however, the newspaper itself does not seem to have been especially meaningful. *Eynikayt*'s relatively small circulation, coupled with the Anti-Fascist Committee's lack of any territorial network for news gathering and distribution apart from the newspaper's correspondents in some localities across the country, makes it safe to assume that many (if not most) Soviet Jews never saw the newspaper. Many may not have known even that the committee existed, despite occasional coverage of its activity in the general press. Significantly, the majority of Soviet Jews outside the annexed territories could not read Yiddish, while the Jews in those territories, all of which had been occupied by the Germans, were hardly in a position to read a Soviet newspaper in any language. Yiddish was also entirely alien to non-Ashkenazic Jews. The committee showed no interest in developing connections with speakers of Judeo-Tadzhik, Judeo-Tat, or Georgian. Jewish writers in these languages were not given any tangible organized role to play during the years of the Second World War. The Judeo-Tadzhik (Bukharian Jewish) section of the Writers Union of Uzbekistan had been closed in 1939.[77] In Dagestan, the section of Judeo-Tat (Mountain Jewish) writers remained inactive during the war, and its members had no contact with the committee.[78] But most importantly, the committee was not allowed to publish a Jewish periodical in Russian, the main language of Soviet Jews. To be sure, toward the end of the war, in March 1945, the committee's leaders appear to have recognized the urgency of having a Russian-language journal; they even decided to raise the matter with Lazar Kaganovich, a deputy prime minister and the highest-ranking Jew in the Soviet hierarchy.[79] But nothing positive came of the conversation.

It appears more likely, then, that the Soviet regime meant *Eynikayt* to connect the committee with world Jewry instead of with Jews in the USSR.[80] Indeed, the newspaper's name—"Unity"—reflected that orientation. The writers who guided the committee and provided the primary copy for the newspaper understood that in the circumstances of war the Soviets needed to appear as champions of a supra-ideological unity transcending class and ideological divisions. That situation allowed them space to disregard what had once been an iron postulate of Soviet doctrine: that bourgeois Jewish ideologists, most prominently Zionists, had fabricated the idea of a worldwide Jewish nation. They had been able, even encouraged, to express a different line at the August 1941 rally, where their speeches had been vetted by

Lozovskii's office. Peretz Markish proclaimed to world Jewry that "we are one people, and now we are one army."[81] David Bergelson echoed the sentiment, speaking of the need to "demonstrate to the whole world that Jews, regardless of their dispersal, are a unified nation."[82] Soon afterward Bergelson reached out to Chaim Zhitlovsky—a prominent Russian-born Jewish socialist (not communist) intellectual who had lived in New York since 1908 and had become known since the 1880s as a theorist of a secular Jewish nationalism—to promote the new conception of a unified Jewish world. However, Bergelson and his fellow Soviet Yiddish writers also understood that that conception was not to be promulgated within their country's borders and that their license to flirt with a worldwide Jewish unity would expire once the war ended. Indeed, in 1945 the Jewish Anti-Fascist Committee addressed a letter to Stalin suggesting that the name *Eynikayt* be changed to *Heymland* (Homeland)—surely more than a cosmetic shift alone.[83]

Actually, though, the committee's impact on the foreign press may have been rather limited. By its own account, during the war years it prepared 23,125 texts. About half of these were short information pieces sent around the world by telegraph; the rest were longer articles, distributed to 264 periodicals in 13 countries, but mostly in the United States (145) and Palestine (74).[84] No data have been compiled showing to what use the committee's material was put outside the USSR. In particular it is not known how the 1938 Foreign Agents Registration Act in the United States[85] affected the distribution of committee publications in that country. There is evidence, however, that American officials limited distribution of at least some Soviet publications. On 3 March 1943, Ambassador Litvinov[86] delivered a memorandum to the US Department of State drawing attention to the repeated "non-delivery, destruction and return to the senders by the American postal authorities of Soviet newspapers and books, sent from the Soviet Union and addressed to American scientific, cultural and other organizations and persons" and concluding that "printed matter on the Soviet Union may be allowed for circulation in the United States only if it does not contain any data or if it does not even allow any inferences favorable to the Soviet Union or its Government; or when it contains criticism and adverse information about the Soviet Union, its leaders and organizations."[87] There is also evidence that American and British periodicals were sometimes reluctant to accept pieces from Soviet sources for journalistic reasons. "Large American newspapers don't print materials from Sovinformburo," Litvinov advised Moscow in April 1942, because "the articles contain few or no concrete facts" and "are, as a rule, too long." According to the ambassador in Washington, "the newspapers prefer to print material received from their [own] correspondents in the USSR." Ambassador Ivan Maiskii in London also observed the same disinclination of British newspapers to publish pieces of more than five hundred to seven hundred words. He urged shorter articles written in a livelier style and better translated than was standard Soviet practice.[88] To be sure, materials prepared by the Jewish Anti-Fascist Committee may have been accepted more readily, since Epstein and several other committee staff members had worked in the American Yiddish press and knew its requirements well. Nevertheless, in May 1944 the committee began to release its materials not through Sovinformburo but through a new Jewish Soviet Press Agency headed by Leyb Kvitko. Most likely this move was made in order to make the committee's materials appear less subversive to American censors.[89]

But in many ways, Soviet censors may have been more dangerous. From the outset the Jewish Anti-Fascist Committee, the only one of the five antifascist committees representing a single Soviet nationality, had to guard itself against repeated accusations that it produced "nationalist" materials. Evidently stories that praised the readiness of Jews as Jews to sacrifice their lives for the Soviet homeland and to do their utmost on the labor front to help bring about victory over the enemy could be regarded as suspicious. In fact, it appears that one of the ongoing tasks of Epstein and Fefer, the committee members most closely tied to the NKVD, was to push the state and party ideological watchdogs to expand the boundaries of permissible topics as far as possible.[90] In November 1943 Epstein wrote to Shcherbakov trying to explain and justify the committee's ostensible strategy, in an effort to cool the watchdog's ire:

> Our difficulties in propagating truthful information about our country stem from the fact that the overwhelming majority of the world Jewish press, with the exception of a few communist publications, is imbued with a narrow-minded nationalist and counterrevolutionary Menshevik spirit and is under the direct influence of Zionists or the most traitorous elements of the Second [Socialist] International.[91] This is the source of its anti-Soviet character. Our Committee

> was faced with the task of somehow breaking the "blockade" against the Soviet Union in the world Jewish press without in any way accommodating ourselves to its views and attitudes. In order to do this it was essential to make use of the specific characteristics of the Jewish press so that under the cover of Jewish themes we could give the Jewish national masses abroad the most vivid view of the many-faceted creative life of the Soviet Union in all areas; the heroic struggle of the Soviet peoples against the fascist invaders on the battlefields; their selflessness on the work front and in cultural construction; and also the infamy and danger which fascism represents for all mankind. As a result, Jewish themes do not dominate our materials, but merely serve as a means to demonstrate the many aspects of our count[r]y's greatness and might.... It is typical that not only the Jewish press, but even the communist press asks us to provide material exclusively about the life of Jews in the USSR, because Hitler's agents abroad are using every means to spread vile lies showing, on one hand, that Jews don't fight, and on the other hand, that anti-semitism is raging in our country. The fact that our materials describe the active participation of Jews not only in the Patriotic War, but in all areas of economic and cultural construction, not isolated and cut off, but rather against the common background of friendship among all our peoples, serves as a most potent antidote to malicious anti-Soviet propaganda.[92]

Epstein's memorandum responded to complaints that the committee's materials "were over-emphasizing the Jews" and were "accommodating... to Zionism,"[93] as well, no doubt, as to charges that it had taken it upon itself to intervene with state and party agencies on behalf of Soviet Jews who had written it about their wartime difficulties.[94] The regime, it appears, was determined not to permit the Jewish Anti-Fascist Committee to represent Soviet Jewry as a particular interest group within Soviet society.

And yet, in spite of all the regime did to prevent it, the committee eventually evolved de facto into a central Jewish organization, albeit one with little leeway for independent decision making. Driving the evolution in significant measure, it seems, was a growing sense, common to committee members and the many Soviet Jews who sought contact with it, that public vituperation toward Jews had become a widespread phenomenon among wartime expressions of Soviet popular opinion.[95] Disquiet over this development is attested in the many thousands of letters (arriving at a pace of some five hundred per week by March 1943[96]), many of them addressed personally to Mikhoels, that the committee and *Eynikayt* received from ordinary Jews throughout the USSR over the course of the war. For example, an inspector of military factories who traveled extensively because of his work wrote that he was "struck by the tremendous increase in antisemitism and antisemitic attitudes in many parts of our Union . . . where this never existed before."[97] A collective farmer from the Stalindorf District—one of the five former Jewish national districts in prewar Ukraine and Crimea that had been deprived of the right to be called "Jewish national" by 1939—complained about the hostile environment in which Jewish residents found themselves upon their return from evacuation. Other letters spoke about ugly incidents in eastern areas of the country that did not fall under the occupation.[98] Indeed, those areas, which saw a dramatic increase in the Jewish population as a result of the evacuation, faced a cultural clash. Their names, facial features, and ways of speaking often bewildered many local residents. Evacuees from the recently annexed territories in the far west no doubt looked and sounded particularly alien. Jewish and "Jewish-looking" functionaries and members of the intelligentsia were often associated with the repressive policies of the Soviet regime. Violence against Jews took place in many different localities.[99]

Of particular concern was the accusation that Jews shirked military service, a charge often encapsulated in the phrase "Jews fight in Tashkent" (a place thousands of kilometers from the front lines).[100] Sometimes the committee assisted Jews who requested their aid to join a front-line unit. Thus, for example, Aron Gitelman, a twenty-five-year-old senior lieutenant serving as an instructor at an artillery school in Penza, western Russia, wrote on 13 April 1944 that eleven days earlier he heard the radio broadcast of a committee rally. This encounter with the committee led Gitelman, whose parents had been killed in Odessa, to turn to Mikhoels, requesting his help in being accepted for service at the front. Whether thanks to Mikhoels's intervention or not, Gitelman did join a combat unit, distinguished himself in battle, and was awarded the Order of the Red Banner.[101]

In reaction to the charges of shirking, many Jews devoted themselves to collecting facts and statistics demonstrating the true extent and nature of Jewish participation in the war effort. The Jewish Anti-Fascist Committee and its members played a central role in trying to bring those facts and statistics to the knowledge of the broader Soviet public. *Eynikayt* made it a matter of editorial policy to highlight Soviet Jewish valor. To that end it enlisted the writer and journalist Shmuel Persov, who even before the war had published Yiddish-language pamphlets about two heroic Soviet Jewish aviators, Yakov Moshkovski and Yakov Shmushkevitsh.[102] Persov continued to publish in this vein throughout the war. In 1944 the Moscow Yiddish publishing house Der Emes released a compilation of his documentary stories about Jewish partisans, under the title *Dayn nomen iz folk* (Your Name is People).[103] In October of that year Itsik Fefer reported in *Eynikayt* that 55,767 Jews had received awards for gallantry in battle, a greater number than all Soviet ethnic groups except the far more populous Russians, Ukrainians, and Byelorussians.[104]

At the same time, committee leaders fought to include information about Jewish war heroes in official Soviet publications. In April 1943 Mikhoels and Epstein wrote to Shcherbakov complaining about an article in the tone-setting party journal *Bolshevik*. Whereas the article reported the ethnic breakdown of Red Army soldiers and officers decorated for bravery, no figure was given for Jews.[105] The committee chairman and secretary stressed that "concealment of the exact number of decorated Jewish soldiers and officers plays into the hands of hostile elements in the USSR and abroad" and could be "picked up by Hitlerite agents, who have been spreading malicious rumors that 'Jews are not fighting.'"[106] Their efforts may have borne some fruit, for a year later the academic publication *Istoricheskii zhurnal* (The History Journal) published the ethnic breakdown of decorated Red Army troops as of 1 January 1944. Those figures showed that Jews continued to hold fourth place, with 32,067 medals, not far behind the 37,036 awarded to Byelorussians.[107]

The committee seems to have been especially interested in promoting stories about Jewish cavalry soldiers. Since the mid-1930s, when the USSR reestablished special cavalry divisions designated as "Cossack," the valor of Cossack-style horsemen had become a yardstick of Jewish bravery and, more generally, of Jews' adoption of Soviet values and mores. The use of that measure was ironic because historically no love had been lost between Jews and Cossacks—members of Russian or Ukrainian communities of warriors who over the centuries had participated in numerous instances of violence against Jews. In order to smooth over historical enmities, Soviet works of art from the 1930s celebrated Jewish-Cossack friendship, depicting, for example, happy marriages between young people from the two once-hostile groups.[108] To be sure, if statistics existed about the ethnic breakdown of the Red Army's Cossack cavalry units, they would probably reveal relatively low numbers of Jews.[109] Nevertheless, the units included a number of Jewish career officers, along with newly mobilized doctors, political instructors, and other reserve officers. *Eynikayt* featured their stories. Journalist Moyni Shulman introduced readers to Colonel Chaim (Efim) Popov, commander of a Cossack regiment, although his text, probably sanitized at some point in the editorial process, said nothing about Popov's Jewishness, which was clear only from his name.[110] The Jewishness of another cavalry commander, General Vladimir Tsetlin, received greater emphasis in a story by Shmuel Persov. Persov mentioned that Tsetlin grew up in a proletarian Jewish family in Odessa and spoke Yiddish.[111]

Sometimes Jewish writers tried to claim Jewish heroes whose Jewishness was actually doubtful. Perhaps the most significant case was that of the fabled General Lev Dovator, commander of a cavalry corps, whose Jewish legend began to circulate soon after (or perhaps even before) his death in the battle for Moscow in December 1941. In early 1942 Solomon Mikhoels announced that his theater, which had recently been evacuated from Moscow to Tashkent, would stage a play devoted to Dovator's exploits:

> I cherish the dream of producing very shortly the heroic epic of General Dovator. A son of the Jewish people, the Red Army commander showed himself to be a hero and a patriot.... In choosing General Dovator as the subject of the play, we could hardly find a figure more noble and colorful than this Jewish cavalryman and brave general who commanded regiments of Cossacks who in Czarist Russia were used by reactionary forces for bloody pogroms against innocent Jews.[112]

A year later the Soviet embassy in Washington released an information bulletin quoting Mikhoels to the effect that "the popular Jewish playwright, David Bergelson, is writing a play for us about the talented Jewish cavalry general, Lev Dovator, who covered his name with glory in the present war."[113] However, the plan never materialized. Dovator was most likely born into a family of Byelorussian peasants, and the Soviet propaganda machine evidently preferred to present him in this light.[114] This fiasco surely disappointed the committee, for it threw a wrench into their effort to highlight the brave deeds of Jewish cavalrymen.[115]

Indeed, this aspect of the committee's strategy did not comport well with regime policy. During fall 1943, when the Red Army was retaking Ukraine from the German occupiers, Stalin and his advisors sought to send an encouraging message to Ukrainians, the second-largest ethnic group in the Soviet population. Accordingly, in October 1943, the Red Army introduced the Order of Bogdan Khmelnitskii, named for the leader of the seventeenth-century uprising by a Cossack host and Ukrainian peasants against the ruling Polish nobility in the southeastern portions of the Polish-Lithuanian Commonwealth. The revolt had made Khmelnitskii (Ukrainian: Khmelnytsky) a Ukrainian national hero, but Jews viewed him as a monstrous personality responsible for the wholesale annihilation of Jewish communities, whom his troops associated invidiously with Polish domination.[116] Khmelnitskii became the eponym for the only Soviet military order named after a non-Russian historical personality; however, the use of his name was a searing insult to Jews, who by tradition accompanied any mention of it with the curse, "May his name be blotted out." To make matters worse in Jewish eyes, the Soviets renamed the Ukrainian town of Pereiaslav, where in 1654 Khmelnitskii had pledged fealty to the Muscovite Tsar Aleksei I, for the Cossack leader. The town was also the birthplace of the classic Yiddish writer Sholem Aleichem, making its new designation an especially bitter pill for Jews to swallow. It likely did not occur to Soviet leaders that their act would resonate negatively in Jewish circles all over the world. It resonated negatively with the Jewish Anti-Fascist Committee as well: *Eynikayt* conspicuously never once referred to the decrees relating to the use of the name issued by the Supreme Soviet.[117]

The committee tried to respond to the expressed needs and sensibilities of Jews concerning a broad range of other matters as well. Yakov Eidelman, a military journalist, who knew Mikhoels personally from his prewar days as a student at a Jewish theater school in Kiev and then as a theater critic in Moscow, wrote his acquaintance in April 1944 urging the committee to send representatives to the recently liberated city of Kamenets-Podolskii, in western Ukraine,[118] where thousands of Jews, whom he described as "the last of the Mohicans of western Jewry," desperately needed help. Expelled by the Romanians from Bessarabia and Bukovina, the survivors, he observed, found themselves in extremely difficult circumstances.[119] Another letter came from a Krimchak Jew,[120] Mark Piastro, who described the tragic destiny of his small group.[121] The committee was usually not in a position to render direct material aid to survivors, but it did work to collect and to publish materials about German atrocities against the Jewish population in the USSR. In this context it became involved in the *Black Book* project, which occupies a special place in the committee's later history. The evolution and eventual fate of this project revealed many of the limitations the committee faced in trying to give voice to the perceptions and sensibilities of the Soviet Jewish population.

It appears that the idea for the *Black Book* project originated in the United States at the end of 1942, when Albert Einstein, best-selling Yiddish author Sholem Asch, and Ben-Zion Goldberg, a Yiddish journalist (and a son-in-law of Sholem Aleichem), who more than a year earlier had formed a Committee of Jewish Writers, Artists, and Scientists in support of the Soviet war effort, proposed a joint publication by the Anti-Fascist Committee, the World Jewish Congress, and the Jewish National Council of Palestine, in preparation for which each organization would collect and share materials about German anti-Jewish crimes.[122] The book was to be issued simultaneously in English, Yiddish, Russian, and Hebrew. Negotiations evidently proceeded for several months, but on 27 July 1943 *Eynikayt* mentioned agreement to the American Jewish proposal and appealed to anyone who had materials about fascist crimes against Jews to submit them to the committee.[123]

In conjunction with this international project, the committee appointed an editorial board, chaired by Mikhoels and consisting almost exclusively of Yiddish writers. However, the committee soon crossed purposes with Ilya Ehrenburg, who formed a second editorial board, which he dubbed a "literary commission," for the purpose of publishing a Russian-language book of testimony about atrocities that combined documentation with literary representations. This board was made up primarily of Russian-language authors.[124] In the end, a short book, consisting of excerpts of materials Ehrenburg's group had gathered, along with Ehrenburg's introduction, was published in Yiddish by the Der Emes publishing house in April 1944 under the title *Murderers of Peoples: Materials about the Murders by the German Invaders in the Temporary Occupied Soviet Territories.*[125] A second part came out in 1945. The committee leaders were unhappy with the publication. They had envisioned the *Black Book* as an exhaustive compilation of documents, reaching perhaps a thousand pages, unlike Ehrenburg's short, largely literary work. For his part, Ehrenburg objected to including his work in the larger international *Black Book* project to which the committee had agreed. Ehrenburg and the committee broke relations with one another in spring 1945, although Vasilii Grossman, who had been part of Ehrenburg's team, continued to work with the Yiddish writers.[126]

At the same time the Soviet regime appears to have been having second thoughts about the entire *Black Book* enterprise. During the war Ehrenburg and the committee (to which communications to Ehrenburg were often addressed) had received numerous letters from Jews, many in response to Ehrenburg's reportage, expressing extreme hatred toward Germans. A Jewish officer wrote, for example, "We keep killing them without mercy, but it is not enough for us, Comrade Ehrenburg. For the Germans, death is not a punishment but a chance to be saved from the people's severe judgment. They have to be sentenced to a living death for what they have been doing in our country." Ehrenburg himself wrote in reply to one such letter, "I don't like Germans (not only the Nazis, but the nation at whole)."[127] This attitude was evidently not acceptable to the highest reaches of the Soviet hierarchy. On 14 April 1945 *Pravda* published an article by party ideologist Georgii Aleksandrov entitled "Comrade Ehrenburg Simplifies." Written on the personal order of Stalin himself, the piece argued that "Comrade Ehrenburg writes in his articles that there is no Germany, only a '*colossal gang*.' If one accepts the point of view of Comrade Ehrenburg as correct, it follows that the entire population of Germany should share the fate of the Hitlerite clique." Aleksandrov's criticism was received quite negatively by many frontline soldiers: Ehrenburg wrote in his memoirs that never in his life had he received such warm letters as from writers who openly took a stance against the new line of the Central Committee.[128]

Eventually the Soviet government scuttled both Ehrenburg's conception of the project and that of the Anti-Fascist Committee, explaining that each of them deviated from a proper representation of the fate of Jews under German occupation.[129] Evidently government readers determined that both overemphasized the Nazis' animus and cruelty toward Jews as such. Ironically, though, the committee's writers, Ehrenburg and Grossman, had long been speaking of Jews as but the first in a long line of Nazi victims that would eventually encompass all the peoples of German-occupied lands. As early as the August 1941 rally Bergelson had declared that "we Jews will be first to be thrown into the fire."[130] In October 1941 Ehrenburg wrote in the army newspaper *Krasnaia zvezda* that the invaders aimed to annihilate one half of the people of the Soviet Union and to make slaves of the other half. "The Germans," he warned, "hate all peoples except the Germans and despise all races except the German race."[131] Grossman accommodated the official Soviet interpretation in his 1943 short story, "*Staryi uchitel*'" (The Old Teacher), one of the first works of fiction about the Nazi Holocaust in any language. Grossman's protagonist, the aging intellectual Boris Rosenthal, meets death praising his non-Jewish compatriots: "The Fascists . . . meant to unleash hatred, but what has been born is compassion." His recapitulation of their miscalculation essentially denied the uniqueness of what the Nazis had done to Jews:

> The Fascists have created an all-European system of forced labor and, to keep the prisoners obedient, they have constructed a huge ladder of oppression. The Dutch are worse off than the Danes, the French are worse off than the Dutch, the Czechs are worse off than the French. Things are still worse for the Greeks and the Serbs, worse still for the Poles, and last of all come the Ukrainians and Russians. These are the rungs of the ladder of forced labor. . . . And then, at the very bottom of this huge, many-storied prison is the abyss to which the Germans have condemned the Jews. Their fate has to terrify all the forced laborers of Europe, so that even the most terrible fate will seem happiness in comparison with that of the Jews.[132]

Grossman and other Jewish Anti-Fascist Committee members also tended to undermine traditional Jewish categories for confronting tragedy. They celebrated the heroism of Jewish soldiers and resistance fighters in the occupied territories but were loath to write about any Jewish behavior that smacked of *kiddush-hashem* (sanctification of God's name by martyrdom) and its associated readiness to die without showing any resistance. Indeed, soon after the end of the war, Peretz Markish would write to his old friend, the American Yiddish writer Joseph Opatoshu: "Our literature will have to sum up and reevaluate the notion of *kiddush-hashem* as an eternal national category, which, in fact, helped Fascism and eased the annihilation of our people."[133]

Evidently such expressions were insufficient for the watchdogs. No matter how closely they chimed with the ethos of the new Soviet Jew, by the end of the war the Soviet regime had come to suspect that the Jewish Anti-Fascist Committee had overstepped its mark.

That suspicion was reinforced by the history of the committee's international activities.

International contacts across the ideological spectrum were central to the group's raison d'être. In April 1944 the Boston *Jewish Advocate* wrote that the committee "has been the agency through which the Jews of the Soviet Union have re-established contact with the Jews of the rest of the democratic world, after an estrangement of a quarter of a century."[134] The US State Department considered the committee to be one of a host of organizations whose mission was to replace the Moscow-centered Communist International (Comintern), dissolved in 1943 at the behest of the USSR's Western allies, in spreading communist ideology worldwide.[135] But the returns the Soviets received in this regard were problematic.

The reaction in the West to the committee's formation exposed deep fissures within Jewish communities there. Following the August 1941 rally, with its appeal for unity among "fellow Jews the world over,"[136] the influential American Yiddish daily *Forverts* (Forward), a stronghold of socialist, notably Menshevik and Bundist, anti-Sovietism, ran a pithy negative editorial entitled, "A Photo with an Appeal and Salt on Jewish Wounds."[137] In other Jewish circles, by contrast, the appeal found a diametrically different response. On 11 September 1941, Chaim Zhitlovsky initiated a meeting that resulted in the establishment of the Soviet-sympathetic Committee of Jewish Writers, Artists, and Scientists (CJWAS).[138] From 29 November 1942 the CJWAS published a Yiddish-language periodical, *Eynikayt*, indicating its affinity with the Jewish Anti-Fascist Committee in Moscow.[139]

Tensions among Jews abroad, especially among Jewish socialists, were exacerbated in February 1943, when Ambassador Litvinov informed William

Green, president of the American Federation of Labor, that Henryk Erlich and Wiktor Alter had been executed for "hostile activities [to the Soviet Union], including appeals to the Soviet troops to stop bloodshed and immediately to conclude peace with Germany."[140] The announcement, made at a time when the attention of Jews throughout the free world was focused on recently publicized reports of Nazi mass murders in Poland and in occupied Soviet territories and when Soviet prestige in the West was especially high following the victory at Stalingrad, called forth vigorous protests and condemnations in Jewish communities around the world.[141] Rumors even circulated implicating Mikhoels in the arrest and subsequent death of the two Bundists.[142] The primary mission the Jewish Anti-Fascist Committee had been created to fulfill had now clearly suffered a setback.

Palliating the outrage in the wake of the announcement about Erlich and Alter was surely one of the factors Soviet officials considered when they decided shortly thereafter to send a Jewish delegation to the United States, Mexico, Canada, and Great Britain.[143] Such an unprecedented move[144] appears to have been first suggested by Albert Einstein in a conversation with Litvinov, who relayed the idea to Moscow. A formal invitation followed from Einstein's Committee of Jewish Writers, Artists, and Scientists and a parallel, more broadly based organization, the Jewish Council for War Help to Russia. The Anti-Fascist Committee initially hoped to send six of its members, but in the end only two—Mikhoels and Fefer—were dispatched.[145] The criteria for selection can only be surmised. Both Mikhoels (especially) and Fefer had good oratorical skills in Yiddish, a lingua franca of the targeted audiences. Fluency in English would undoubtedly have been useful as well, but evidently no suitable candidates with such language skills were available.

Mikhoels and Fefer traveled from Moscow to New York under difficult wartime conditions, which necessitated a route through Tehran, Cairo, and Khartoum and extended the length of their journey to forty days. Fefer, who was introduced throughout as a lieutenant colonel instead of simply a poet, declared that he was going abroad bearing "a manifesto of Communist Jewish pride."[146] He was referring, no doubt, to his poem, "Ikh bin a yid" (I am a Jew), first published in *Eynikayt* on 27 December 1942, which has since become one of the most frequently anthologized samples of Soviet Jewish patriotism. Fefer described himself in the poem as "a Jew who drank from

Stalin's magical cup of happiness," but he also presented a Soviet Jewish genealogy that included such figures as Simon Bar Kokhba,[147] King Solomon, Baruch Spinoza, and Karl Marx, along with classical Russian landscape painter Isaac Levitan, Soviet Russia's first head of state Yakov Sverdlov, and Stalin's trusted lieutenant Lazar Kaganovich.[148] Yet not all Jews abroad turned out to have been quite as proud of Fefer's Jewish communist lineage as Fefer proclaimed himself to be. The only Yiddish writers to receive him in New York as part of the official welcoming committee were Sholem Asch and Peretz Hirschbein, both of whom had visited the Soviet Union in the late 1920s and returned with qualified sympathetic impressions about Jewish life in the country.[149] Asch's participation in particular was criticized by some of his colleagues. Though a star writer for the socialist but staunchly anticommunist *Forverts* during the previous quarter of a century, his stature with the paper and its readers had fallen sharply after the English translation of his novel, *The Nazarene* (based on the life of Jesus) became a bestseller in the United States in 1939, leading to accusations that he had betrayed the national interest of the Jewish people.[150] His role as a host of the Soviet delegation added fuel to the fire. For example, the journalist Tsivion (Benzion Hoffman), a popular *Forverts* columnist, reminded Asch that Fefer had called his 1931 novel *Moscow* "a work by a fascist who looks at Moscow with the eyes of an interventionist." He also reprinted a satirical poem in which Fefer had ridiculed Asch as a loyal servant of capitalist reaction, like Hitler. Tsivion sarcastically commented on Asch's forgiveness: "According to the teacher from Nazareth, if someone strikes you on one cheek, turn to him the other also." Tsivion, a lifelong anti-Zionist, also castigated the welcoming enthusiasm of leading Zionist supporters, writing that the Zionist leadership was disappointed with the British and American attitude to establishment of a Jewish state and hoped that "salvation would come from Stalin."[151]

Even a mass public rally of forty-seven thousand people in honor of Mikhoels and Fefer's visit, held at New York's largest outdoor stadium, the Polo Grounds, on 8 July 1943—hailed in the Soviet press as the greatest manifestation of sympathy for the USSR ever organized in the United States to date[152]—did not stimulate American Jews to close ranks behind the delegates from Moscow, as its organizers had hoped it would. Some, to be sure, celebrated the message of unity that Mikhoels and Fefer carried for months after their mission had ended.[153] But other spokesmen and journalists who met with the pair tried to put serious questions to them about the future of Soviet Jewry: What were the prospects for Soviet Jewish participation in postwar international Jewish life? Had Soviet Jewish activists and the Soviet government changed their attitude toward Zionism and Palestine? What was the status of Jewish culture in the USSR? The Soviet delegates could only brush these queries aside, asking their interlocutors to concentrate exclusively on issues that could facilitate victory in the war effort. In Fefer's words, "When the house is on fire, one must [first] extinguish the fire, and only then comes the moment to think about installing doors and windows."[154]

Lazar Fagelman, one of *Forverts*' most serious and respected journalists, wrote that the visit of Mikhoels and Fefer had actually revealed an abyss dividing the Soviet and American Jewish worlds. Fagelman had no doubt that the different ideological and cultural environments in the two countries played a much more significant role than the physical distance between them in creating that chasm. Inevitably, he argued, a wall had appeared between the two communities: American Jews and Soviet Jews, especially from the younger generations, had begun to speak essentially different languages, even though both spoke Yiddish. "Now we have to understand that Soviet Jews differ from us: their habits, values, and manners are different; their vision of life is different; they have a different attitude to people, to the world, and to all political, economic, and moral problems."[155]

For their part, the Soviet delegates also felt estrangement, both from their Jewish hosts and from America in general. While in Chicago, Fefer wrote a poem he called "In a Strange Land":

Af yene lipn—nit undzer shmeykhl.	On those lips—not our smile,
In yene moykhes—nit undzer seykhl,	In those brains—not our wisdom,
Nit undzer veyts in yene stoygn,	Not our corn in those ricks,
Nit undzer flam in yene oygn,	Not our flame in those eyes,
Nit undzer landish ...	Not our lily of the valley ...
Di zelbe zun, di zelbe shtern,	The same sun, the same stars,
Nor epes andersh.	Yet somewhat different.

For both Mikhoels and Fefer, Soviet people through and through, America remained synonymous with all of the dark aspects of capitalist society. The young American diplomat Frederic Barghoorn, who served in the US

Embassy in Moscow during the 1940s, later summarized his impressions of Mikhoels's published American travelogues and of a public lecture the actor gave in April 1944:

> In general, Mikhoels' observations on America were a mixture of admiration and ridicule.... Mikhoels' approach was that of a prominent Soviet intellectual hewing closely to the party line. The impressions he received of American life were certainly highly distorted. He followed the conventional Soviet political formula which selected and exaggerated the least appealing aspects of American life while overlooking and probably not understanding its major currents.... In one important respect his impressions were probably sincere and personal. He was not at all impressed by the impact of the war on the lives of Americans, and he indicated that they were not making sacrifices comparable to those experienced by the Soviet people.[156]

After six months abroad, Mikhoels and Fefer came back riding high. They reported that their rallies and meetings had attracted hundreds of thousands of people and had helped raise millions of dollars for the Soviet Union.[157] They also brought a symbolic gift—a fur coat for Stalin, made by members of the communist-controlled International Fur and Leather Workers Union. Mikhoels and Fefer also received similar coats.[158]

Upon their return both delegates felt themselves in a new position. Their public and private encounters with a broad variety of individuals and groups had taken them into the orbit of international and specifically Jewish politics. The trip, which was dramatically consequential for the Jewish Anti-Fascist Committee institutionally and for its members and associates personally, had inspired their comrades with more confidence than ever that they had been placed in a position to act beyond the remit of a merely propagandistic bureau, to make real history for Soviet Jewry. Even before Mikhoels and Fefer's trip abroad, members of the committee had been profoundly concerned with their frequently conflicting roles of loyal Soviet appointees on one hand and of Jewish activists on the other. Some of them had called for openly broadening the scope of the committee's activities by responding directly to the requests for help concerning the many problems and grievances that dogged Jews who, beginning in 1943, were returning from evacuation and even being liberated from German occupation. Such opinions had been aired during the committee's plenary session in February 1943. At that meeting Markish even carefully ventured to endorse the idea of forming separate Jewish units in the Red Army, an idea that had been presented to Mikhoels more than a year earlier.[159]

Mikhoels was cautious. Summing up the discussion, he observed that "only one issue caused a dispute. The functions and scope of the Jewish Anti-Fascist Committee's activity were not, apparently, understood by everyone as they should have been. Some wanted to add even more functions." However, he stressed, "it was lost sight of that the Jewish Anti-Fascist Committee is a fighting unit, which has a single purpose, to consolidate all its forces for the struggle against fascism. This is its only task." But on the other hand, he recognized that "there are many people suffering because of the war, and we cannot turn away from them, and say that they are no concern of ours. We must take part in their fate, raise a question about them, but all this is still a side issue."[160] Accordingly, the committee's official published reports never mentioned its activities beyond the propaganda sphere. That they focused instead exclusively on the achievements reflected its narrow remit (and that of the other antifascist committees) of turning out thousands of texts of various size, provenance, and scope for publication in hundreds of foreign periodicals.[161]

But as time went on Mikhoels faced conflicting pressures from within and without. Particularly outspoken among the leading committee members was Boris Shimeliovich, the medical director of Moscow's Botkin Hospital. In October 1944, during a meeting of committee leaders, he even called their organization "the so-called Jewish Anti-Fascist Committee" for its reluctance to address tasks beyond producing and distributing propaganda materials.[162] Shimeliovich, whose brother, Iulius, was a legendary Bolshevik—Mikhoels had played him in the Moscow Jewish State Theater's production of M. Daniel's 1931 play *Fir Teg* (Four Days)—surely did not believe that this attitude reflected any weakening of his Soviet loyalty and patriotism. Like many people, he seems to have convinced himself that the war had created an environment more conducive to independent Jewish initiative, and that the wartime Jewish tragedy permitted the committee to cross previously uncrossable lines.

The impressive figures about the placement of propaganda materials in the foreign press that the committee marshaled in its reports were undoubtedly meant to prove the committee's continued usefulness to the regime, thereby creating a space in which it could take up a Jewish advocacy role while being safeguarded against liquidation after the war. Ultimately the calculation failed. The forced end of the *Black Book* project was but one indication of that failure. Others would follow. In January 1948 Mikhoels met death in Minsk, his assassination disguised as a hit-and-run accident. The committee, *Eynikayt*, the publishing house Der Emes, the Jewish sections of the Writers Union, and most other remaining institutions of cultural activity in Yiddish disappeared shortly thereafter. Wartime possibilities for a new Jewish leadership proved short-lived indeed.

Herman Kruk. Photo Credit: Archives of the YIVO Institute for Jewish Research, New York.

Bundist leaders during a meeting in Warsaw. Left to right: Yisroel Lichtenstein, Yitskhok Rafes, Henryk Ehrlich, Yekusiel Portnoy, Bella Shapiro. The Yiddish banner reads: "Bund in Poland. Proletarians from all lands unite!" Photo Credit: Archives of the YIVO Institute for Jewish Research, New York.

Yiddish writers and poets in Vilna. The poets Shmerke Kaczerginski and Abraham Sutzkever are seated in the middle. Photo Credit: Archives of the YIVO Institute for Jewish Research, New York.

Jewish partisans on the day Wilno was liberated. Photo Credit: Yad Vashem Photo Archives.

A view of the pit in Ponary in Lithuania where Jews were rounded up before their murder, surrounded by SS men, German policemen, and Lithuanian collaborators. This photograph was taken in July 1941 by Otto Schroff, a member of the 96th Infantry Division of the *Wehrmacht*, who witnessed the killing of around four hundred Jews at Ponary on three consecutive days. Photo Credit: Yad Vashem Photo Archives.

Wartime photo of Hersz Smoliar. Photo Credit: Yad Vashem Photo Archives.

Vladimir Gelfand in Berlin, with the damaged Reichstag building behind him. Photo Credit: Courtesy of Vitaly Gelfand.

Sergeant Elena Deichman. Photo Credit: Courtesy of Oleg Budnitskii.

Jews being marched through the streets of Lwów. Photo Credit: United States Holocaust Memorial Museum, courtesy of Leonard Lauder.

A street view of the synagogue in Białystok. Photo Credit: United States Holocaust Memorial Museum, courtesy of Tomasz Wisniewski.

Abraham Sutzveker stands in front of the Wilno ghetto school ruins after the liberation of the city. Photo Credit: United States Holocaust Memorial Museum, courtesy of the Sutzkever Family.

Three Jewish partisans in the former Wilno ghetto soon after the city's liberation. From left to right: Yosef Harmatz; Valia Pszewalska and Avraham Sabrin (the last commander of the partisan LaNitsahon battalion). Photo Credit: United States Holocaust Memorial Museum.

Jewish refugee children from Poland performing on stage in Polish folk costumes in Kazakhstan. Photo Credit: United States Holocaust Memorial Museum, courtesy of Shlomo Adler.

Jewish refugees boarding the Rosja–Polska train to return home from Bukhara, Uzbekistan. Photo Credit: United States Holocaust Memorial Museum, courtesy of Shlomo Liwer.

Three Jewish girls, Zlata, Chaya, and Maria Gerchikova, in a photograph from before the war in Chechersk, Belarus. When the war started, the Gerchikov family fled to Uzbekistan, where Zlata, Chaya, and their grandmother died of malnutrition. Maria worked in a textile factory in Fergana and survived the war. Photo Credit: United States Holocaust Memorial Museum, courtesy of Maria Gerchikova Maymina.

Polish Jewish refugees celebrate the circumcision of a newborn according to Jewish ritual. Jonas Markowicz and Rywka Welnern fled Poland in 1939 and arrived in Uzbekistan in 1941. In 1942, Rywka gave birth to a son, and a local Bukharian Jew circumcised the baby. The couple returned to Poland in 1946 to find that all of the family that had stayed in Poland had perished in the Holocaust. Photo Credit: United States Holocaust Memorial Museum, courtesy of Pessia Polak.

A group of Polish Jews standing in front of a mud hut in Kazakhstan. Photo Credit: United States Holocaust Memorial Museum, courtesy of Helena Jacobs.

Polish Jews photographed near a train car on their way back home to Poland. The train exterior bears the Russian rendition of USSR above a hammer and sickle device, the white eagle of the Polish Coat of Arms, and a portrait of Stalin. Photo Credit: United States Holocaust Memorial Museum, courtesy of Aaron Yermus.

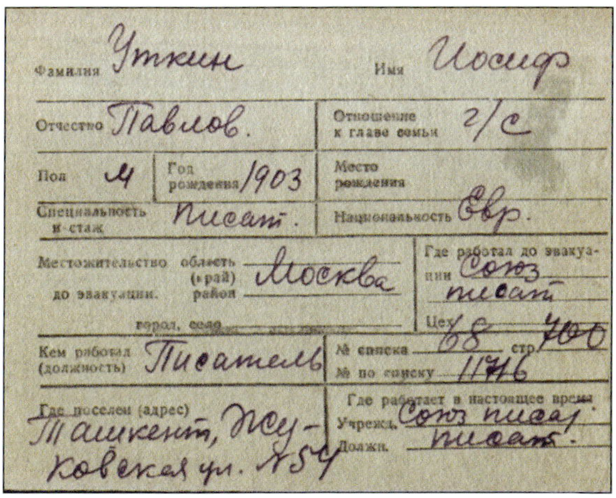

Фамилия Уткин Имя Иосиф
Отчество Павлов. Отношение к главе семьи г/с
Пол м Год рождения 1903 Место рождения
Специальность и стаж писат. Национальность Евр.
Местожительство до эвакуации область (край) район Москва город, село
Где работал до эвакуации Союз писат
Цех 68 700
Кем работал (должность) Писатель № списка стр. № по списку 1176
Где поселен (адрес) Ташкент, Жуковская ул. № 54
Где работает в настоящее время Учрежд. Союз писат. Должн. писат.

Evacuation registration card of a Jewish refugee in Uzbekistan. The text reads: *Iosif Utkin*. Ethnicity: *Jew*. Profession: *Writer*. Place: *Tashkent*. Photo Credit: United States Holocaust Memorial Museum Archives.

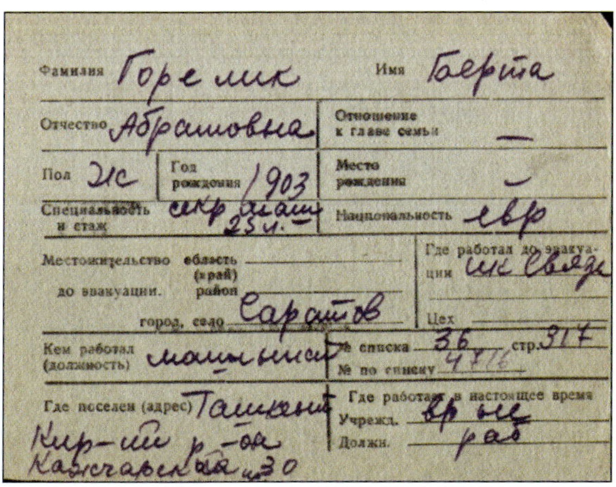

Фамилия Горелик Имя Берта
Отчество Абрамовна Отношение к главе семьи —
Пол ж Год рождения 1903 Место рождения —
Специальность и стаж секр. маш. 25 л. Национальность евр
Местожительство до эвакуации область (край) район город, село Саратов
Где работал до эвакуации
Цех
Кем работал (должность) машинист № списка 36 стр. 317 № по списку 4716
Где поселен (адрес) Ташкент Кир-ий р-он
Где работает в настоящее время Учрежд. Должн.

Evacuation registration card of a Jewish refugee in Uzbekistan. The text reads: *Berta Gorelik*. Ethnicity: *Jew*. Place: *Tashkent*. Photo Credit: United States Holocaust Memorial Museum Archives.

Polish Jewish refugee children pose with drawings in their school in Uzbekistan. One drawing depicts a train with words *Buchara Warszawa*. Photo Credit: United States Holocaust Memorial Museum, courtesy of Zvia Levy.

General Kreiser in Sevastopol. Photo Credit: The Russian State Library, IZO.

Boris Komskii in Allenstein, Prussia. Photo Credit: The Blavatnik Archive.

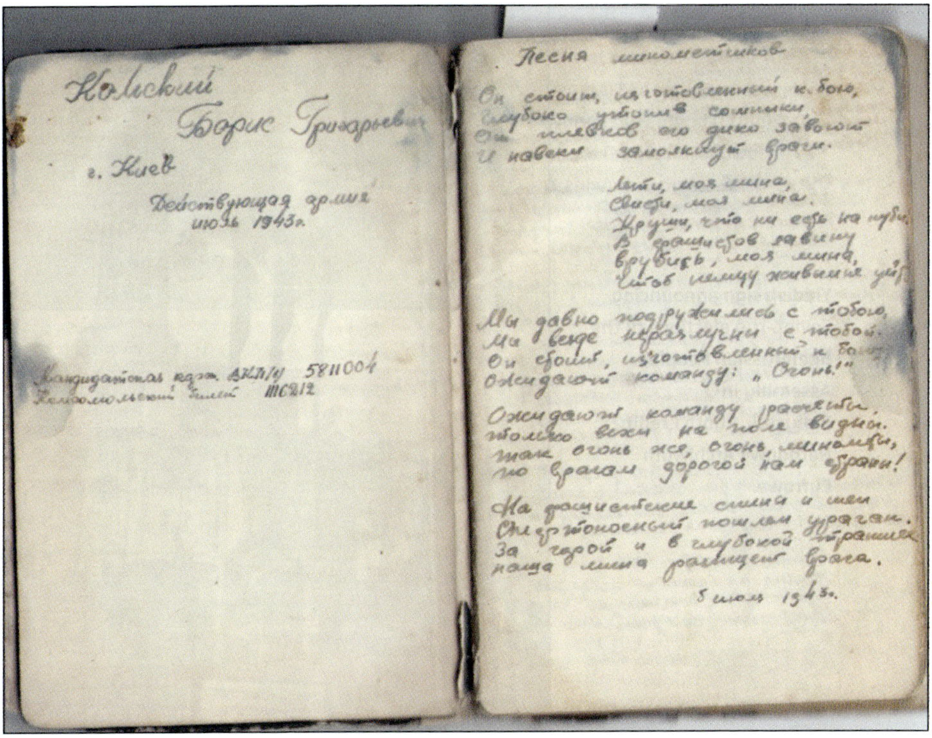

The opening pages of Boris Komskii's diary, with his signature and song lyrics. Photo Credit: The Blavatnik Archive.

Kiev Jews marching to Babii Yar. Photo Credit: Staatsarchiv Amberg, Staatsanwaltschaft Regensburg 9294/32.

Portrait of Naum Rosenberg. Photo Credit: Courtesy of Marianna Litvinova.

Ruvin Amdur in military uniform. Photo Credit: State Archives of Latvia.

Jewish refugees eat in a canteen in Wilno. Photo Credit: JDC Archives.

David Kaufman (Samoilov) in military uniform. Photo Credit: Courtesy of Alexander Kaufman (Davydov).

David Kaufman (Samoilov) in military uniform, on the left, with a fellow soldier. Photo Credit: Courtesy of Alexander Kaufman (Davydov).

שאבעס 1 פעב

№ 14 (420)
שאבעס
1
פעווראל
יאר 1947

פרייז 30 קאפ.

איינקייט

ארגאן פונעם יידישן אנטיפאשיסטישן קאמיטעט אין ססר

«ЭЙНИКАЙТ» (Единение) «EINIKAIT» (Unity)

ОРГАН ЕВРЕЙСКОГО АНТИФАШИСТСКОГО КОМИТЕТА В СССР

די אומבאזיגבארע קראפט פון דער לעניניש־סטאלינישער נאציאנאלער פאליטיק

דער ארמיי־גענעראל ...

דער העלד פון ד...

A front page of the newspaper *Einikayt*. Photo Credit: Memorial International Archive.

Alfred Rosenberg giving a speech. Photo Credit: Scherl/Süddeutsche Zeitung Photo / Alamy Stock Photo.

Maxim Litvinov gives a speech during the banquet at the Conference on Disarmament. Photo Credit: Scherl/Süddeutsche Zeitung Photo / Alamy Stock Photo.

Vasilii Grossman in Schwerin, Germany. Photo Credit: Alamy Stock Photo.

Ilya Ehrenburg in Warsaw, Poland. Photo Credit: PAP / Alamy Stock Photo.

The Red Army entering Chişinău in 1940. Photo Credit: Alamy Stock Photo.

Itsik Fefer (left) and Solomon Mikhoels (right) walk with Albert Einstein during their visit to the United States. Photo Credit: Sovfoto\UIG via agefotostock.

The Jewish Anti-Fascist Committee, a group of Jewish artists, writers, and musicians, signing an appeal to the Jews of the world. Photo Credit: Sovfoto\UIG via agefotostock.

Ilya Ehrenburg (center, wearing beret) with Jewish partisans after entering Wilno with the Red Army. Photo Credit: Sovfoto\UIG via agefotostock.

6

THE REAR

The Jewish Anti-Fascist Committee operated in a zone the Soviets called the "rear" (*tyl*)—the vast expanse of the country that did not fall under German occupation. The large majority of Jews who lived through the war survived there.[1] Every person who ended up in the Soviet rear, either via an organized evacuation or a spontaneous escape, has a story. These stories form a crucial chapter of the history of Jewish life and death in the Soviet Union during the Second World War.

Many Soviet people remember that the first day of the war on Soviet soil—Sunday, 22 June 1941—started with a devastating announcement on the radio. Viacheslav Molotov, vice-chairman of the Council of People's Commissars, and anchor Yuria Levitan informed the public that at four o'clock that morning German troops had attacked the USSR's western border. For the most part, however, residents of the country's western territories, most of whom had come under Soviet rule only after September 1939, did not need to hear a radio broadcast; they had already awakened to the sounds of bombs, vehicles, shootings, and—in border cities like Brest (Brześć)—German being spoken in the streets. The fortress of Brest is well known in Soviet history and hagiography as the site of one of the first battles of the Soviet-German war. Less well known is that nearly 50,000 residents of the town, of whom 17,574 were Jews, fell under German rule in a matter of hours—so quickly that none of them was able to follow instructions given by Soviet officials only half a day later.

The process of "evacuation," during which an estimated 16.5 million Soviet citizens traveled to the country's interior, began the same day as the German invasion of Brest and lasted, for the most part, into the second half of 1941.[2] In the context of the wartime Soviet Union, the term "evacuation" refers colloquially to a multitude of upheavals experienced by civilians, including departures organized by employers, self-initiated escapes, and panicked flights by civilians hearing the sounds of gunfire and fighter planes.[3]

By the end of 1941 between 1.2 million and 1.25 million Jews had fled the area that German forces occupied.[4] From July through October 1941 much of the Jewish population of Moscow and Leningrad, having correctly assessed the nature of the threat, took advantage of any opportunity for evacuation or flight.[5] The process of escape and survival was not straightforward, organized, or simple. In some cases, it involved a double evacuation. Some people left in July 1941 and fled again in December 1941, after German troops had advanced further east. Thousands of people were evacuated to Stalingrad, only to leave a few months later for Kazakhstan or for Ufa in Bashkiria (Bashkortostan). Similarly, some people who fled to Stavropol and to other locations in the North Caucasus by the end of 1941 were evacuated again in 1942.[6] Equally important are cases of unsuccessful evacuation. It has been estimated that of almost two million (1,969,000) Jews who lived in the annexed Soviet territories, between 140,000 and 170,000 escaped initially, but only between 75,000 and 100,000 managed to reach the unoccupied Soviet territories.[7]

Confusion, chaos, and uncertainty reigned in the Soviet western territories during the first days of the war. When German troops entered Wilno on 24 June 1941, approximately sixty thousand Jews lived in the city. In the previous two days about three thousand of them had managed to escape. Soviet officials, including Jews, had greater access to transportation and to other crucial resources; by 23 June they could leave, before the Germans arrived. But even for them the process of escape was not straightforward.

Here, for example, is how Esfir A.—born in Orshad, Byelorussia, in 1908 and married to a high-ranking Communist Party functionary stationed in Wilno—described her escape from the city shortly after the onset of war:

My husband was an appointed state official in Vilnius in February 1941. When we saw the first bombs, I went home and packed some of the most important photographs and all our documents. Then it became clear that my husband would not be able to join his regiment, so he received an order to evacuate what was necessary for the army, namely food. He received a truck, and he was told to bring dried bread, butter, and herring to military posts. . . . He also had to prepare food and send it to Russia. The troops that were located there did not have any weapons and were waiting for pistols. Meanwhile, they had to be fed, so my husband brought bread to them.

We were in Vilnius, and we learned from Polish refugees what the Germans did to the Jews. There were many family members of military personnel, women and children, and we all wanted to leave. But our husbands had state orders, and [they] could not give us trucks. We all stood on the roadsides with little children and tried to hitchhike. When we saw a bomb, we would run into a building.

Suddenly, I saw an officer with a truck. But he was filling his truck with his furniture, clothes, and then his wife came in and sat in the truck. I realized that he received the truck to evacuate all of us, but he took his family and his furniture. . . . I approached him, and said: "We can't leave, we are hitchhiking but nobody takes us." That man ignored me.

Then I saw my husband, who came back with the herring. He came down from the truck, and said, "Here, women, have some herring and bread!" I told him, "We do not need herring. We need to get out of here. You have to save us." He said, "There is nothing I can do." Then I cried and said, "You brought me here, and you have to be a human being, and save us all! Throw the herring out from the truck and put us on it. The soldiers will not die without herring; they already ate!"

My husband had two soldiers, who helped him. He ordered [them]: "Take all the food down!" They threw the boxes on the ground. But the truck was small, so he said: "I will only take women with children, and pregnant women. Others should go by foot." We were only allowed to take our documents, nothing else. I helped the women to get on that truck. We loaded everyone. I was the last one. I was then seven months pregnant, so there was no place for me in this truck. The soldier said, "Fira, there is no place for your belly here. Go sit on your husband's lap." I came to the front cabin, and told my husband, who was sitting next to the driver. I said, "There is no space left for me. I can only go if I push

> out the baby." So I sat on his lap. . . . With great adventures, I gradually made my way to Tula [south of Moscow].[8]

In the middle of the first day of the invasion, 22 June 1941, the Presidium of the Supreme Soviet of the USSR declared large sections of the country—the former Polish *kresy* and Baltic states, Bessarabia, and Northern Bukovina, along with all of Byelorussia and parts of eastern Ukraine—under martial law. Any entry or exit from those areas was forbidden. These were the areas where the majority of Soviet Jews lived.[9] Officially the declaration meant that anybody caught by Soviet authorities trying to flee the designated region would face a military tribunal. Not everyone knew about the order, however, including local government officials, many of whom, sensing the absence of strong central leadership and the rapid disintegration of Soviet punitive organs, assumed unprecedented power. Many in government positions or their family members used this power to flee eastward, even as some of them felt they should try to prevent others from doing so as well. Esfir A. and her husband belonged to an extremely privileged group, with greater access to transportation (and other crucially important resources) than most residents of Wilno, including its sixty thousand Jews, but early confusion made the process of escape far from straightforward even for them.

Many evacuees interpreted seemingly inconsistent, arbitrary behavior on the part of local officials to be the result of personal decisions to help or not to help them escape. Some recalled with resentment that the same agents of the regime who prevented their flight in the name of preventing panic used their privileged position to save themselves. Twenty-year-old Etya G., from Kopai in the Vinnitsa region of Ukraine, remembered trying to get away several times, but each time the local party leader stopped her. She never made it to the rear:

> Once we heard about the war, I wanted to flee. I heard that some factories and their workers were being relocated, and I wanted to go with them. My son was only two years old at the time. I went to the party leader and explained that. He said: "If you leave, we will consider you a deserter. How can you believe that the Germans will make it this far? Go to work and be a good Soviet citizen." The next day, he fled. I, on the other hand, could not squeeze onto the train. I

> tried four times. My husband was in the army. In the end, I stayed, and ended up in a ghetto in Kopai. It is a miracle that my son and I survived.[10]

Stories of local officials preventing people from leaving by not issuing them train tickets or by suggesting that flight would lead to arrest are common. On the other hand, cases have been noted in which officials actually bent the ostensible rules in order to help people board trains or at least did not try to stop them from finding their own means of transportation. In any event, many officials probably sought to carry out what they understood to be orders from Moscow (often based on rumors, on instructions from the prewar period, or on their notion of party ideology) and to interpret them creatively in situations that seemed to them particularly dangerous. The bureaucrats themselves did not know how the German invasion would progress. Nor did they know precisely what might constitute a criminal violation of regime policy. In the absence of firm direction from above, they were forced to improvise, often creating an impression of capriciousness among the people whose fate they directly influenced.

The territories under martial law included a high proportion of Jews, especially in cities and towns.[11] Some undoubtedly knew from the outset that the stakes of local officials' behavior were especially high for them, as Esfir A. and her husband understood. Retrospectively the consequences of that behavior appeared clear to most everyone. Those later perceptions colored views of the Soviet administration. Indeed, many Jews later credited local officials with their survival, while simultaneously holding them responsible for their grandparents' deaths.

Attitudes toward the central Soviet leadership developed within the context of Soviet evacuation policy and its evolution. On 24 June 1941, Stalin appointed an eight-member Supreme Evacuation Council, chaired by Lazar Kaganovich.[12] On 27 June the council, together with party officials, decided "to evacuate and relocate quotas of persons and assets of value," giving priority to "factories that produce military wares along with the metallurgical and chemical industries."[13] Two days later, the government and the Party Central Committee instructed that "trains should be evacuated during the withdrawal" and that "the enemy should not be left with even a kilogram of grain or a liter of fuel."[14] Stalin himself repeated the gist of this message in his radio address of 3 July,[15] indicating in effect that evacuating physical objects and institutions was more important in the regime's eyes than evacuating civilians. Civilians were to be evacuated only to the extent that they were deemed necessary for the Soviet war effort. These were, in the first instance, skilled workers, engineers, and other employees of enterprises designated for removal to the rear, along with young people fit for military service and state and party leadership cadres.[16] The academies of Sciences of the various Soviet Republics, research institutes, universities and other institutions of higher education, and theaters were also marked for evacuation, together with the scientists, scholars, and cultural figures who staffed them.[17] The question of what to do with certain categories of civilians who did not work at strategically important institutions, such as family members of enlisted soldiers, was not considered until 5 July. Only then, nearly two weeks after the German invasion had begun, did the Supreme Evacuation Council decree the establishment of evacuation stations (*evakopunkty*), where both official evacuees (people connected with institutions officially designated for removal eastward) and refugees (people who had fled spontaneously on their own) could be registered, receive food, and be assigned to transport.[18]

The delay arguably cost the large majority of Jews in the western borderlands their lives. Once evacuation stations began to be established, the ability to reach them often meant the difference between life and death. They were far from ubiquitous; refugees had to find their way to them on foot, by bicycle, or with a horse and wagon (for those lucky enough to possess them). Moreover, the way to them was liable to be encumbered. For example, the parents of fifteen-year-old Fira B. first tried to run away from Berdichev on 27 June 1941 but were stopped by Soviet officials. Two days later they tried again. They managed to reach an *evakopunkt* only in mid-July. There they were placed on a train that took them to Saratov on the Volga River.[19] Altogether around ten thousand people, mostly Jews, were evacuated or managed to escape from the city, which the German army overran on 7 July. By the end of 1941 almost all the remaining Jews of Berdichev had been killed.[20]

In any case, evacuating civilians from places such as Berdichev does not seem to have been a priority for the regime. The Evacuation Council divided Soviet territory into three distinct zones, each with a different degree of precedence. One zone was deemed in immediate danger of occupation; another included territories within seventy-five to one hundred kilometers of the fighting. With the German army's rapid advance, the areas of both zones changed daily. The third zone included five major urban population centers—Moscow, Leningrad, Minsk, Kiev, and Odessa. The authorities placed their greatest emphasis on moving people out of these cities at the expense of provincial regions. Moscow was most important of all: 44 percent of all trains deployed for evacuation during the first two months of war served the capital. Leningrad was allotted 17 percent. The rest of the country had to make do with what remained.[21]

Initial plans called for settling evacuees in central Russia, but the Evacuation Council soon extended the zone of resettlement to include Siberia, Central Asia, and Kazakhstan. The council drew graphs illustrating exactly how many trains would go to which destinations. Workers from Leningrad were to be evacuated to the Kirov, Iaroslav, and Ivanovo regions; people from western Ukraine would be sent to places along the southern Volga, the North Caucasus, and Kazakhstan.[22] Most Moscow-based institutions, including the executive branches of government, were evacuated to Kuibyshev, whereas some party institutions, as well as archives and units of the Soviet Academy of Sciences, ended up elsewhere in the eastern parts of Russia. Many industrial enterprises were sent to the Ural area, as were people from throughout the USSR's western regions. About three hundred thousand residents of Moldova were moved to Kazakhstan.[23] In total, by the end of 1942, as many as twelve million Soviet citizens had been evacuated.[24] After German forces, contrary to Soviet expectations, reached the North Caucasus, Kuban, and the southern Volga region in the summer and fall of 1942, some 4.5 million people were added to that total. Many were evacuees for the second time, having been moved to those areas during the previous year.[25]

Remarkably, in light of subsequent events, neither Uzbekistan in general nor Tashkent in particular figured among the reception sites designated for evacuees in the Evacuation Council's original plans. In the immediate aftermath of the invasion, authorities in Moscow did not imagine that places so far away from the front lines would be required for resettlement. In light of the Red Army's rapid retreat, however, the designated zones were substantially enlarged, until Tashkent became a privileged destination. Many prestigious cultural and scientific institutions, including the Moscow Jewish State Theater, were eventually relocated there.[26]

Jews made up at least 8 percent of the total number of evacuees, perhaps as many as 19 percent.[27] In many respects their experiences converged with those of other civilians, but in other respects they diverged. To begin with, although Jews were not specifically designated for evacuation, they made especially great efforts to leave the occupied zone. They did so through self-evacuation or by being included in the lists of critically important workers designated for removal to the rear. Even after they had found a place on an evacuation transport or had managed to make their way east on their own, however, they faced many challenges, dangers, and opportunities unique to them. Such features would help shape a set of perceptions and memories of Jewish life in the rear, notably different in emphasis from those of their non-Jewish fellow Soviet citizens.

Evacuee stories usually unfold in three chapters: before leaving, during the journey, and arriving in a new location.

Regarding the first phase, the narratives point to three broad patterns, both of behavior and of retrospective perception. The first pattern is typical of people who possessed documents that entitled them to board an evacuation train legally. These people describe a system that helped rescue them thanks to the professional positions they or their parents held. By and large, they do not mention Jewish ethnicity as a factor affecting their escape in any way. Evacuation presented them with other challenges, such as dealing with small children, deciding what possessions to take, finding a new job, and obtaining appropriate clothing for a new climate. But none of the challenges that stood out in their minds was specifically related to being a Jew.

A second pattern concerns Jews without evacuation documents or orders but with an independent means of transportation, such as a horse, a bicycle, or a wagon, that gave them a degree of flexibility in deciding whether, when, and how to flee. Eyewitness accounts often mention members of this group using their vehicles to make money by helping others run away instead of escaping themselves. Fifteen-year-old Basia Chaika from Kiev, for example, remembered some of her neighbors working around the clock to take other residents of the city to the train station, where they would try to board any train headed east. One of those neighbors, Lyova, evidently did not sense sufficient danger to give up what had become a profitable business: "[His] mom says to him, 'Why are you not leaving? Take your family, your three little kids, and go!' He answers, 'Mama, I am making money!'" His decision had tragic consequences; as Chaika recalled, "Some families from [our] courtyard ended up in Babi Yar. Lyova did, too."[28]

The third pattern is displayed by the greatest number of fleeing Jews, who possessed neither official eligibility for evacuation nor transport of their own. Their perceptions of evacuation often begin with an assessment of the difficult choices they had to make in deciding whether to stay or go.[29] Some of those choices depended on personal circumstances, such as which family members were able to travel and which would need to be left behind. Others involved how to interpret available information coming from the sources most readily at hand: rumors, official Soviet statements about the dangers of fascism from before the Ribbentrop-Molotov Pact, and German anti-Jewish propaganda released during the invasion. Still other choices concerned estimating the likely behavior of neighbors. All turn out to have had a particularly Jewish dimension that stuck in the memories of many Jewish evacuees.

Among many factors that influenced the decision to leave was whether a person believed that the German invasion would be dangerous specifically for their families. Rumors about Nazi treatment of Jews beyond the USSR flourished in the late 1930s. They stemmed from many sources—newspaper articles that left details vague, leaks from high-ranking officials ostensibly sworn to secrecy, and (after September 1939) tales brought by refugees from Nazi-occupied Poland. Rumors from Polish refugees, however, were often dismissed as inaccurate or false. There were several reasons for skepticism. First, refugees were rarely seen as sources of trustworthy information; their personal motives were suspect.[30] Second, stories from Polish refugees often clashed with beliefs that had been deeply inculcated through the Soviet media. Even the 1938 Soviet film *Professor Mamlock*, despite its chilling depiction of Nazi persecution of German Jews, was seen by many viewers less as a warning sign for the future than as a reminder of Soviet Jews' favorable situation. That, at least, was what Frida S. recalled thinking after seeing the film in Kiev's Khreshchatyk Theater:

> My husband and I could not find a babysitter, and we took our child with us. Later, he [the child] was terrified, as these horrible events of how Jews were being killed were shown in the film. My child had nightmares. He was then five or six years old. Now we understand that this film was the first sign. But then we did not think that it was relevant to us. I had no associations with any possible danger. All propaganda, all of the press, and all of the media only said that even if war broke out, it would never happen in our country. I worked in a school and saw a map in the teacher's room. During recess, the geography teacher would approach the map, and say: "Look, German troops are already here: Poland, France, Norway.... Look how fast they move, this is scary." But even he did not think that they would ever get to us.[31]

The message that "the war will take place on foreign soil," disseminated regularly by the Soviet press, radio, and cinema before June 1941 appears to have been widely internalized among Jews. Basia Chaika remembered the message as a source of encouragement:

> Once a week, our school had a lecture about international politics. We knew everything.... People believed that our country was so strong that it would not allow any incidents.... We were not afraid of war. First, we knew about the peace treaty with Germany.... And we thought that even if Germany attacked, our army would not let them onto our territory. Everyone was confident in this, adults and children. Well, maybe adults thought differently, but children were sure.... And when we were leaving, my father said, "Do not take anything along, we will be back in a month."[32]

Chaika's words accurately reproduce the rhetoric of the contemporary Soviet media. That message was regularly reinforced by local Soviet officials, who tried to persuade citizens that the prospect of war was hypothetical and would not affect their daily lives. Iosif A., fifteen years old in 1941, recalled that his father took that line as authoritative:

> It was never even mentioned as a possibility that the war would take place on our soil. Those who suggested that a foreign army could come and invade were seen as traitors and were immediately silenced. What I remember was constant talk that "the war will take place on foreign soil" and that "no enemy will enter our land." When war broke out, my grandfather went to his rabbi, who said to stay put, as Germans had been nice to Jews during the first war. My father did not take the rabbi seriously, but he believed Soviet officials. As a result we all stayed, and almost perished a few months later.[33]

Some downplayed reports of German atrocities against Jews in the context of the Great Terror. Natalia Chepur remembered that after hearing "rumors that Jews in Poland were being taken somewhere and . . . shot," she thought: "Here [in the Soviet Union] enemies of the people were shot . . . , but it would be impossible to shoot everyone."[34] Others, especially those who had suffered from Soviet economic policies, were prepared to credit positive rumors about the German army, in the belief that a change of regime would be beneficial.[35] Faina G. from Byelorussia (born 1918) noted such an attitude in her father:

> Rumors circulated that when the Germans come, they will destroy the collective farms. They will give everyone land. They will help create new jobs. They will arrest communists and Jews. My father said that antisemites came up with this [last point about arresting Jews]. He knew Germans when they came during World War I. He remembered them as cultured, polite people; some of them had even been Jews. "No," he said. "The neighbors do not like Jews; that is why they come up with these rumors." However, he did believe all the positive information. Because of this, we did not hurry to evacuate, and when we wanted to, it was too late.[36]

General dissatisfaction with Soviet economic management provided fertile ground for optimism about what a German conquest might bring. Efim G., from Parichi in Byelorussia (born 1918), ventured that "had I not been Jewish, I would have awaited the German army as well. The Soviet Union destroyed the lives of peasants, and [the peasants] hoped the Germans would give them back their soil."[37] The question facing Jews who thought this way was: how differently from their non-Jewish neighbors could they expect to be treated once the Germans arrived? At the time they could not imagine how great the divergence would be.

Soviet Jews worried not only about the German invaders but also about how the local non-Jewish population would treat them in the absence of Soviet rule. On the whole, in fact, the fear of violence against them by their own neighbors and colleagues appears to have been greater than the threat they perceived from the Germans. Many were concerned that only Soviet law stood between them and potential attackers and that the collapse of Soviet rule would inevitably expose them to the wrath of the local population.[38] Liza L. from Kharkov, for one, named fear of neighbors as the primary reason her family fled:

> We left because we were afraid of the locals. My mother survived pogroms, and she remembered different armies: Whites, Greens, Reds. She saw women being raped all the time. She said, "I have two girls, who are 16 and 17, and we have to leave. . . ." When we came to the railway station, it was crowded with people. We spent all day there but could not find a train, so we went back home. . . . But when we came back, our neighbors had already moved their stuff into our house. We had to go back to the station, as we had no place to sleep. The next day, we managed to get on a cargo train.[39]

On the other hand, some people were persuaded by non-Jewish neighbors and friends to remain in their houses. Fira B. from Berdichev recalled that her high-school boyfriend's Ukrainian family offered to hide her in their cellar until the Germans established their rule and things "calmed down." The only reason Fira gave for not accepting the offer was that she "did not really like this boy so much and wanted to be with her own family."[40] Twenty-year-old Golda R. told a similar story but with a different reason for rejecting aid:

> In school, my best friend's name was Natasha. Her father was the deputy director of a factory. When the war began, and conversations started about leaving, her mother came to my mother and said, "We have a nice big cellar; we will hide you there until things settle down." My mother was worried, though, and

> made sure that we left. She gave her golden ring to a man with a horse and cart, who took us to the railway station in Shepetivka.[41]

In these stories the neighbors appear to have been offering protection both against the German army and from potentially hostile local residents. It seems that they saw local enmity as the greater danger. In fact, it may be that some Jews, most likely older ones, were induced not to flee by the thought that they could purchase safety by bribing people whom they had known for many years. Running away into uncertainty, or even dealing with crowds at chaotic train stations, seemed a much riskier choice for people with impaired health. However, as Golda R.'s testimony shows, other people—younger ones, the ones with teenage children—chose to use whatever property they possessed, including jewelry, gold coins, silver forks, and even farm animals, in order to get themselves onto a train headed east.

Some Jewish residents of Moscow and Leningrad often looked at their non-Jewish neighbors from a somewhat different vantage point. Those Jews were not under quite the urgent pressure to run for their lives as were their fellow Jews farther west, but many of them did sense that colleagues, friends, and fellow residents had begun to look upon them as alien to the Soviet people's community.[42] As a result, offensive remarks and attitudes, coupled with rumors about Nazi treatment of Jews and a widespread sense among non-Jews that the Germans were likely to target only Jews and communists, created an atmosphere of anxiety and uncertainty for Jews in the USSR's two largest urban centers. Disquiet over the generally bad news from the front was compounded by fears that neighbors would abandon them to an especially egregious fate should German forces prevail. For some, taking flight seemed to play into invidious stereotypes. Still, out of 450,000 Jews listed as residents of the two cities in 1939, between 250,000 and 300,000 evacuated.[43]

In short, those Jews from throughout the USSR who managed to make their way to an embarkation point for evacuation already carried with them a host of powerful, recently formed emotions involving themselves, their families, their relationship to the Soviet state, and their place in Soviet society—emotions that stemmed from their Jewishness no less than from their Soviet citizenship.

Nearly every Soviet Jewish family has a story of parents or grandparents who chose not to flee. A reason frequently cited is good German behavior toward Jews during the First World War. Here, for example, is how Liza L. from Kharkov (born 1923) explained why her grandfather did not evacuate with the rest of the family:

> My grandfather did not want to leave. He had all of his possessions there, and he did not think that the Germans represented a danger to him. Even before the war, when a young woman from Poland came to synagogue and told us that Germans persecute and kill Jews, no one believed her. My father survived World War I, and he remembered Germans then. He said they were civilized people, and [stories of German atrocities] could not be true.[44]

Such narratives about older family members who did not trust reports of German atrocities because of their own positive experiences with the German army earlier in the century are so common that they are easily taken as the principal reason why members of the older generation chose to stay home in 1941. It is likely, however, that the story is more complex. There was no government policy to evacuate the elderly, and for the first few weeks of war it was officially illegal for any civilians to leave their homes without explicit state authorization. In that context, the assertion of disbelief in reports of German cruelty could well have been an excuse offered by older family members who feared jeopardizing their children's or grandchildren's chances for successful escape and survival. If so, narratives that recall an older person's positive attitude toward the Germans actually serve as an example of how a difficult history was preserved in popular memory.

The children of older people who remained behind sometimes had to make a choice between their parents and their own children. For Jews the results of that choice were never happy. The relatively few Jewish survivors of German occupation were mostly young and strong, not old and frail. Older people were abandoned to their fate. The first to abandon them was the Soviet regime, whose evacuation policies prioritized industry over people, but some families had to leave them as well, making horrific choices to save their younger members. Stories of family solidarity and self-sacrifice by the old for the sake of the young thus may have helped Jews who returned from evacuation cope with the pain and anger of loss and with the consequences of their decisions.[45]

Nearly every Soviet Jewish family also carried memories of children born in 1939, 1940, or 1941 who "never made it." Those memories are usually expressed not in stories but in silences. Still, some accounts of parents abandoning infants or toddlers who encumbered their escape have been preserved. Two were collected as part of the *Black Book* project.[46] Emilia Kotlova and Raisa Zelenkova, both mothers, reported how they left their small children with strangers in order to try to save their own lives. Kotlova could not leave Kiev with the evacuation because her daughters had measles. At first she stayed home to care for them, but later, hoping to pass with her "non-Jewish looks," she went into hiding, leaving the children in a succession of locations—with neighbors, with peasants, and even in a Nazi-run children's house.[47] Zelenkova, from the Ukrainian village of Piatigory, near Uman, similarly hesitated to run away because of her infant daughter.[48] Eventually she had to forsake her. She later described her feelings in a poem in a mixture of Ukrainian and Russian that she sent to Ilya Ehrenburg:

Okh! Iaka zh tse smert' strashnaia	Death is so scary
Dni i dniamy dozhydat'	So is waiting for it, day and night,
Okh! iak obidno i dosadno	It is devastating and sad,
Za shcho mushu pogibat'?	Why should I die?
Ty, dytiako, ne shchasliva	You, the baby, are so unfortunate
Ty ostaesh'sia sirota	You will remain an orphan
Ne plach, ne plach i ne zhurisia	Do not cry though
Ha Ukraini ty ne odna.	You are not alone, in Ukraine
Koly ty vyrostesh' velika	If you grow up
Dobrei liudi razskazhut	People will tell you
Sho matir tvo ubyvaly	That your Mama was killed
Za to, shcho bula vona "Iud"!	Because she was a "Yud"!
Okh! Liudi dobrei, priimeti pokoianiia	Oh, dear people, forgive me my sins,
Prosit Vas neshchasna mat'	Forgive the miserable mother
Na Vas ia dochku zamishaiu,	I will leave my dear baby to you
Proshu ii neie obizhat'![49]	I beg you not to hurt her![50]

Leaving children with neighbors, with strangers, or even on the side of the road seems to have been a fairly frequent occurrence, both when people tried to save children from shootings or run away to save their other children.[51]

Although as yet there has been no comprehensive research on what happened to Soviet Jewish children during the Holocaust, numerous accounts exist of children losing their parents in the chaos of evacuation, if only temporarily. According to data from the Soviet Ministry of Internal Affairs, in 1942 there were 212,705 registered homeless children. In 1944, the number grew to 596,121, with the understanding that many other such children were not registered.[52] According to one government juvenile affairs account, more than 190,000 Soviet children lost touch with their parents between mid-1941 and May 1943.[53] Most of these children lost their parents to combat or were accidentally lost in the chaos of escape. How many of them were Jewish is not known. But it is hard to find a Soviet Jewish family that did not lose a small child during the war due to punishing circumstances.

Arriving at a train station and getting on a train are important parts of evacuation narratives. In those narratives, "chaos" is a typical description of the scene. Yet despite the disorder, trains kept moving, carrying millions of evacuees eastward while also bringing soldiers and resources westward to the front. Indeed, the transports managed to bring most would-be escapees successfully to the rear.

Reaching a station was often a struggle; so was managing at the station before boarding a train. Stories tell of people with children and the elderly sitting on their bags, often made of sheets, drinking the ubiquitous boiled water (*kipiatok*), and anxiously watching the world pass by as they waited for places on a train to become available. Sometimes the waiting crowds panicked, creating confusion so overwhelming that people seeking to travel together, including parents and children, became separated, sometimes never to be united again. Others lost their possessions.[54]

Many trains, especially those departing from Moscow, reflected existing hierarchies of privilege within Soviet society. Some groups and enterprises received their own train cars, which they reserved for employees and their families. Some trains assigned seats to ticket holders, while others, especially ones departing from Ukraine and Byelorussia, resembled cattle cars. Bribery could improve chances for boarding. All cars, privileged or not, were overcrowded, and none of them (save a very small number of first-class compartments reserved for high-ranking officials and elite writers) were equipped with water, let alone with toilets.[55] Tatiana Lugovskaia, sister to Vladimir Lugovskoi, *Pravda* journalist, wrote that she was allowed to evacuate from Moscow with Vladimir himself, their disabled mother, and their nanny, who was registered as an "aunt." They shared a sleeping car with poet Iosif Utkin, who also traveled with his mother. Although these were the most comfortable seats on the train, neither Utkin nor Lugovskaia had a place to sit. They were tending to their mothers and sat at their feet. Other people in the car shared seats designed for one person.[56]

The infrastructure of railway stations was not designed to accommodate tens of thousands of daily passengers. No stations had hot food. Hot water was often not available in sufficient amounts, and the dry food supply was inadequate. At any given moment hundreds of people waited in lines to pick up *kipiatok* or food or to use the bathroom. Communities formed on trains. People took turns bringing water, watching each other's possessions, and saving seats for traveling companions needing to go to the station.[57] The bonds that formed helped passengers cope with their uncertain situation. Many people became sick during the journey, especially young children and the elderly. Many small children died from infections. One memo about a train that arrived at Alma-Ata on 5 December 1941 from Voronezh stated that of 879 people on board, 23 of them, mostly children, were sick with dysentery. Shortly after their arrival four of them died.[58]

When trains were bombed passengers tried to get off. Survivors then waited together for a new train to collect them.[59] Sometimes trains were delayed, and sometimes they had to be rerouted, forcing evacuees off one train and onto another or into stations where they would have to wait for days.[60]

Evacuees could not be sure of their final destination. Decisions were made en route in response to the changing circumstances of the war and the need to deploy rolling stock most efficiently. Many early destinations became overwhelmed, forcing local officials to redirect arrivals on their own authority. Trains initially bound for Sverdlovsk, Omsk, and Novosibirsk, for example, were redirected to regions not originally intended for evacuees. Officials in the Georgian SSR sent evacuees arriving in Batumi and

Sukhumi to Central Asia. Authorities in the Turkmen SSR diverted arriving trains to Uzbekistan.[61]

Evacuees also knew that upon arrival they would not be guaranteed jobs, places to live, or the means to exist. Even those who did not worry about the immediate discomforts of the journey remember their anxiety about the future. Some tried to make connections with fellow passengers in hopes of securing something—a place to live or even a job at the unknown destination. Some evacuees were wealthier, and fellow passengers would try to stay close to them in case they would be "hiring." Physician Berta Gorelik, wife of film director Ioisif Gorelik, who was eligible for evacuation because of her husband's high status, recalled that people wanted to be close to her, as they wanted to tell her all about their ailments: "The only conversations on the boat were about where to live and what to live on." From the conversations it became clear to her that many people had money with them. Others hoped that family members at the destination would help them.[62]

Some passengers left their transports before they reached their designated final stop. There were even instances in which passengers who did not like where they had been sent raised money to bribe a railroad worker to dispatch them to a more desirable location.[63] Evacuees, especially from big cities, tended to prefer urban destinations to villages. Tashkent, known for its mild winters and general hospitality, was an attractive destination for many, even though evacuation authorities had not originally thought to send travelers there.[64]

It was during the evacuation journey that many Jews first noticed that their experiences and perceptions differed from those of non-Jews. Fourteen-year-old Naum A. from Kherson recalled that his moment of realization came on a train headed for Saratov, pursued by German planes dropping flyers:

> The Germans were throwing down proclamations. Everyone was grabbing them. So they were reading them with approval. . . . The plane was flying low. It wasn't a combat plane; it was . . . more like a glider, I don't know. . . . And the proclamations were everywhere, everywhere. So I grabbed one, too. And a guy, a Russian guy, he was older and stronger, he took it. He comes up to me and says, "Look what it says here . . . : Beat the communists, there, the Jews, the commissars. . . ." Well, I don't remember the contents any more. It's malicious

> that they could write that, damn their entire race. There. And he looked at me like this: "You see, but we don't touch you. That's how it is." He let me know that he knows nothing: "See, you should thank us that we don't bother you." So I moved away from him.[65]

At that moment Naum and his fellow traveler stopped being two Soviet boys and became instead a Jew and a non-Jew talking to one another. Such incidents were common. Sometimes they led to hostility; sometimes they did not. But the sense that two people on the same train could be running from a different sort of danger helped make shared ethnicity, as much as place of origin and social class, a bonding factor for Jews and a basis for community formation. Naum remembered the process:

> Mainly there were Jews on the train, but also Russians and Ukrainians. Some were refugees. Yiddish saved us then. It helped in everyday survival. People had their things, their valuables. In Yiddish one could quietly ask to look after these things. Jews trusted other Jews, in Yiddish, because if you ask someone else, who knows what they will do?[66]

Some evacuees later recalled that it was during their journey away from the front lines that they first came face to face with the depth of popular hostility toward Jews. They remembered that non-Jews had not wanted to help them or even to sell them food because they thought Jews deserved to be punished. One woman reported being in a crowd of evacuees looking to cross the Dnieper River to escape the German army. She heard boatmen saying not to take Jews across but to bring them to the villages, where the Germans would pay a handsome bounty for Jewish heads.[67]

By contrast, other Jews encountered kindness from other evacuees and passing soldiers. Still, they were not eager to be identified as Jews. Faina M., a young woman who fled Proskurov with her friend's family by pretending to be her sister, told a complex story of goodwill and prejudice together:

> It was July, and we took the train and got to the station in Bakhmach, in the Kiev region [*sic*].[68] Bombings began. The bombings were so strong that eighteen trains were hit. There were so many corpses that I could not look. Then

military people came and helped us out. They were going to Berlin, but because there were bombings they were stationed there.[69] I was barefoot and wearing a light summer dress, because it was hot outside. I had nothing else. They gave me food and then asked me where I was going. I explained that I had nowhere to go, because Basia's family had all been killed. They began to write down addresses for me to go to. One had family in Moscow, another one in Gorkii, and then another one to Ordzhonikidze. I said I would not go to a city. Then one young man, a short man, asked me if I wanted to go to a village. I said that would be easier. He gave me an address [in the] Gorkii region. I decided to go there, as I was.

I took the first train in that direction. I was so hungry. What could I have done? I pretended to be mute, so I stretched my hand when people began to eat, I begged. I was not in a passenger train but in a cargo train. It took me eleven days to get to that village. At one point, I found myself by a commercial ship. They gave me some food there and an old shirt. Then I took off, went by foot through the forest, then some truck gave me a lift, then some horses. But most of the time I walked, mostly through forest. When I finally got there, all doors were closed. I went to sleep in the street. I had a piece of sugar that I got at the commercial ship. I could suck on it, so I was happy. Then an old man asked me who I was. I said, "I arrived here from the front line." He then asked, "Why did you come here?" I said, "I have brought regards from Sasha Soshnikov to his parents." Then Sasha's mother came, started crying, kissing me. All the villagers came together. They all brought something: one brought eggs, others brought milk. We sat down to talk.

They asked me all different questions. Then they asked what ethnicity I was. I said I was a Jew. They said, "How could it be, you speak Russian, you look like a nice girl, you can't be Jewish." Meanwhile, the hostess made potatoes. Then she saw through the window that her neighbor's chickens came to eat at her vegetable garden. She took a potato to throw at them and screamed, "You cursed Jews!" It was after I said that I was Jewish. Then she tells me, "You can't be Jewish. You are Russian." I said, "Why are you telling me that I am Russian, I know I am a Jew." She said, "You do not speak Yiddish." I said, "Who should I speak with? With you?" She said, "No, say at least a word!"

You see, they never saw Jews before, they thought that Jews had swollen eyes, long noses, and had nonhuman faces. I did not look like this, so they did not believe me that I was a Jew.[70]

Faina's story is a narrative of some of the most disadvantaged evacuees and refugees. She was a young woman, traveling alone, pretending first to be related to someone who is not family, then supporting herself by begging, going to a stranger's house at a village in the Gorkii region, and finally revealing who she was (although that part of the story could have been invented). What is not imagined is the lack of the state's involvement in Faina's journey. She may have forgotten some details, but it is clear that no agency was in charge of her well-being. She managed the journey more or less as a refugee, running for her life, rather than as a Soviet citizen going through an organized evacuation.

The trajectories and paths of refugees and evacuees merged frequently during this time. Sometimes evacuees from the pre-1939 USSR found themselves in the same train cars with Jews from the recently annexed western territories. Often, Yiddish was the only vehicle for communication between the two groups. Both Faina and Naum spoke about this fact in their testimonies. Similarly, Esfir A., the wife of a Soviet officer who fled from Wilno in a train containing both local Jews and the families of Soviet officials, reported that her Yiddish improved significantly during her journey.

Although some evacuees did not know their exact destination, most were allowed (or ordered) to travel so that they could resume working in one of thousands of strategically crucial industries being relocated to the Soviet rear. Their job, essentially, was to build the home front that would support the Soviet war effort. During the first year of war, between July 1941 and first half of 1942, 2,110 industrial units were evacuated to the Soviet rear, including 761 factories from Ukraine, 44 from Belarus, and 1,288 from Russia. Most of these industries ended up in eastern parts of Russia, in places such as Kuibyshev, Molotov, Tiumen, Izhevsk, and Kazan. Some went to Kazakhstan, while the rest went to Georgia and to other republics of Central Asia.[71]

Landscapes of the cities that hosted industries changed dramatically during the second part of 1941. The population of Ufa, for example, the capital of Bashkiria, expanded from 250,000 people to 382,000 in 1945. The city now housed more than a hundred industrial plants. Forty of them had been evacuated from the western part of Russia, along with more than a dozen research institutions working on applied solutions for weapons production and other army needs.[72] Alma-Ata, the capital of Kazakhstan, now housed numerous shooter training fields and modern warfare equipment. Eleven nursing schools and twenty-six intensive nursing schools were set up, as well as thirty-seven sanitary posts. Schools for training snipers, telegraph operators, truck drivers, and specialized soldiers appeared all over the city. By the end of 1941, a tailoring plant, a fur-processing plant, a meat-processing plant, and an industrial bakery were built. A tram line was opened. Some plants made coats, military uniforms, pants, underwear, and hats for the army. Others made fur coats and shoes, again for the army, both for winter and warmer seasons. Between 1941 and 1943, thirty-four factories, plants, and workshops became fully operational, including those for tractor manufacturing, wagon repair, cotton processing, and many other industries.[73]

Small, almost rural, towns suddenly became industrial centers. For example, the small town of Krasnoufimsk in the Barnaul region, which formerly lacked a single plant, became home to ten new ones. These included a transplanted Moscow wagon-repairing factory, Kharkov's mechanical factory, and factories from Rostov, the Kolomenskii District, and Riazan. As they were strategically important, many of the factories became operational before roofs were even built. They functioned in the open air.[74] The town also absorbed fifteen thousand evacuees. Similarly, the town of Troitsk in the Cheliabinsk region, with a local prewar population of fewer than forty-thousand people, became home to some of the largest military plants, including the Thirty-Fourth Aircraft Factory. Within a few weeks, the number of residents in the town reached four hundred thousand. Evacuees took central roles in coordinating the rebuilding of these industries.

Setting up industries on such a scale, with many workers absent because of being drafted into the army, presented a major challenge. The industries were expected to provide the army and the rest of the country with weapons, food, and clothes. Twelve- to fourteen-hour-long shifts of unqualified workers, including children—all living under extremely difficult conditions—typified daily life on the Soviet home front. Many industries had to rely on less than 40 percent of their usual workforce. Many had to improvise with resources. Manganese, for example, normally excavated near Nikopol, in Ukraine, was not available in the rear, leading to the construction of new mines in Kuybyshev and in Kazakhstan.[75] Similarly, because the Soviet Union lost its coal mines in Donbass, new ones were built in the Ural, Kuzbass, and Karaganda regions. By the end of 1941, forty-four new mines were opened.

Although historical accounts are often written without mentioning ethnicity, many of the high-profile players in industry at the rear were Jews, including scientists and other highly specialized workers. In Ufa, where the Ukrainian Academy of Science had been evacuated, Ilia Khrizman was in charge of resettling academic institutions from Ukraine. Academician Alexander Brodsky headed the physics and chemistry research branch of the Ukrainian Academy of Science.[76] One of the key people in setting up such research in Kazakhstan, especially galvanic cell research, was Vladimir Layner. In Troitsk, Cesar Fainberg was appointed chief engineer of a Cheliabinsk tractor factory. Yevsei Kusheleevich ran an agricultural plant in that same city. A key figure in the Soviet tank-making industries was Isaac Zaltsman. After being demoted from the position of the Deputy Commissar of the Tank Industry, he was appointed as head of the Comintern Tank-Manufacturing Plant number 183. Located in Nizhnii Tagil in the Sverdlovsk region, the plant produced T-34 tanks. Zaltsman was known as the "King of Tanks."[77] Countless other Jews worked in these factories without holding positions of power.[78] These people and many others were among thousands of highly specialized and talented individuals of Jewish origin who helped to establish industries that within months worked to provide steel and metal to the entire country.

Soviet industries also needed workers who could be quickly trained to produce high-quality goods. Many not only learned a new trade or skill but also moved from white-collar jobs to manual work in plants, forests, and mines. They had to adapt to noisy environments, long working hours, and—especially—unfamiliar work cultures. For refugees without experience working in the Soviet Union, the cultural challenges were among the hardest, as they were not used to Soviet hierarchies, to say nothing of the Russian language, which many of them had to learn quickly. Both evacuees and refugees were often injured. Some remained permanently disabled.[79]

In the Yiddish newspaper *Eynikayt*, journalists regularly highlighted the extraordinary motivation and efficiency of Jewish workers producing tanks and airplane parts, working in mines, making uniforms for soldiers, and preparing food for the army.[80] Individual stories, however, reveal the complexities and challenges that stood behind the cheerful portrayals.

British journalist Alexander Werth, describing the Soviet war effort in the rear, emphasized the heroic efforts of the people who rebuilt Soviet industrial output in the context of their living and working conditions. For example, people often walked five to eight kilometers to work, one way. Even in frigid Siberia, factory walls were made of wood to save steel and cement for military needs, which meant buildings were poorly heated and barely suitable for work.[81] Dora D., a twenty-five-year-old single mother evacuee, found a job as a quality controller at a foundry in Gurievsk, in Russia's Kemerovo region. Responsible for ensuring the quality of explosive mines that the factory produced, she had to make sure that the cast-iron shells had no defects. Her training lasted only one week, and the stakes were high. One mistake and she could be fired and deprived of rations for herself and her daughter. Before the war Dora had worked as a kindergarten teacher.[82]

Sometimes, people learned three different professions in the course of a few months. Grigori Husid was a seventeen-year-old high school senior from Zinovievsk in Ukraine. He was a talented young man, whose work trajectory may be seen either as chaotic or as the seizing of any opportunity to advance. In June 1941 he learned how to operate a bulldozer while working in a *kolkhoz*, then how to plow a field with oxen. Upon his arrival in Kuibyshev he worked briefly as a draftsman (*chertezhnik*). Toward the end of 1941 he got a job as a lathe operator at Airplane Factory No. 34, forming part of the assembly line for helicopters, also known as "Black Death Choppers." Afterward he was promoted to the motor-making shop at the same factory, and later he learned how to repair airplanes. He had progressed through all these jobs by the end of 1942.[83]

Young evacuees often accepted challenges eagerly and excelled spectacularly. An example was Roza Levenberg, a twenty-one-year-old woman from Uman, Ukraine. She worked at a tank-making plant in Stalingrad,[84] but she always wanted to be a writer. During her shift she stood next to a boy who worked as a lathe operator. He was so short that he needed to stand on a wooden crate to reach the grinder, but he worked well with his hands and could make especially nuanced and complicated parts. Levenberg wrote a short article about him for the factory's newspaper. Her writing skills turned out to be more valuable than her manual work:

> Whenever they needed an article about how motivated people are to work, they asked me to write it. When the position of deputy leader in the Komsomol bureau opened up, they asked if I was interested. I accepted the position. Before that, I had been coming to work at 7 a.m. and leaving at 8 p.m. I worked like that for months. If bombings began, I never even left the factory. Whenever bombs hit the walls and injured someone, the casualties would be removed, but the work would continue. I was able to write the story about the boy only because I was at the factory at 4 a.m., when many of the workshops were empty. People slept on the floor. There was a big oven there, where they dried some parts, so it was warm, and people slept there. Many people did not have heat at home. But this child never went home. He was always at the factory and he kept working. I still have the pass from that factory, and it says "0 to 24:00," because sometimes I, too, never went home.[85]

Most work in the rear involved serious physical strength and endurance. Genrietta F., a twenty-two-year-old evacuee from Odessa, worked twelve-hour shifts at the brick-making factory in Tashkent. Her forty-five-year-old mother also worked there taking inventories. Genrietta's job involved receiving carts with raw bricks and placing them in the oven. The room was poorly ventilated, and fires—often with injuries—were common. Only women worked in that room, and according to Genrietta they all looked as "thin as sticks" and "black covered with dust and pebbles."[86]

Strenuous work was not the only challenge. Evacuees also had to learn how to function in a Soviet workplace, an environment where, on the one hand, supervision over work production was severe, and, on the other hand, everyone was trying to steal something, either for their own household or to sell on the black market. Genrietta recalled:

> There was no soap. We needed it to wash ourselves, or at least to wash our hands. So at the factory people stole wooden planks [to sell for soap], boards that served as holders for drying bricks. My mother would take the ones that were already fully black. She was caught three times.[87]

Just as common as stealing was denouncing those who stole, often with the goal of personal gain. In his memoirs of the evacuation, artist Vladimir Sidur recalled the following incident:

> Next to a mechanical workshop, there was a smaller workshop where they made buttons. They also made combs from horns. Hoofs and bones were used to make buttons for soldier's shirts. This was all for the military. In charge of the room was an old Jew with a long, cared-for beard. At the lunch break, he would always go home to eat with his wife. He would carry soup to her from the canteen in a pot. He would never take the main course. Only soup. Once, the guards stopped the old man. They dumped the soup on the ground and found combs on the bottom. There were about fifteen of them. These were made out of horns, polished ones. Each one sold on the market for no less than 40 rubles. The old man got five years in prison. Rumors said it was his student protégé who denounced him. After the old man was gone, the protégé became the head of the button-making workshop.[88]

Figuring out the culture of the workplace, finding the balance between working, stealing, trusting the right people, and distrusting others, was a central part of adapting to the industrial workplace. For refugees who had not lived in the Soviet Union before the war and who did not speak Russian fluently, the challenge was especially hard to overcome. In her memoirs detailing her ordeal in the Soviet Union, Betty Rich explained that the hardest thing to learn was not the language but the culture, both of work and of communication.[89] Younger refugees figured things out more quickly than did older ones. A man named E. G., a refugee from Warsaw who found employment in an ice-cream plant in Leninabad, Tajikistan, quickly became involved in a "business-on-the-side" deal. As recounted by a scholar who heard his story, "His superior, the deputy director of the plant, whom E.G. identified as 'a Jew from Leningrad,' co-opted him into using less than the allotted quantity of sugar for the ice cream in order to sell off the remaining sugar at the market and make some extra money on the side."[90]

Narratives of Jewish evacuees and refugees who worked in the Soviet industrial complex in the rear illustrate a number of things about their lives. First, the stories provide a sense of what it took for Soviet industry to function efficiently, given that many workers were not trained to do the job they were asked to do. Second, they open a window onto how people functioned in the workplace—how they built their social networks and survived long work hours under tough working conditions. They are Soviet stories, of course, but they are also stories of Jewish individuals who were never allowed to forget about being Jewish at their workplace and who lived their everyday lives in the rear both as evacuees and as refugees. Some of the younger people among them—generally healthier than others, more able to take risks and see chances even in the midst of never-ending work—found opportunities they might not have enjoyed in their former homes. Notable among the opportunities was higher education.

Institutions of higher education—known colloquially in Russian by the acronym VUZy (*vysshiie uchebniie zavedeniia*) were prioritized for evacuation. In 1940–1941 there were 817 VUZy in the Soviet Union, with 811,700 enrolled students and 50,000 faculty members. The sudden onset of the war meant that it was too late for some VUZy to relocate despite prioritization. Only six out of twenty-six, for example, were able to leave Byelorussia. By the end of 1941, 334 institutions of higher education had been destroyed or had ceased to function. By the 1942–43 academic year only 460 institutions continued to operate in the Soviet Union.[91]

VUZy that continued to function in unoccupied territories and that survived the evacuation had problems getting students to finish their programs and difficulty enrolling new students. Many students and faculty members were drafted into the army, and some left to work in industry. As a result, in the academic year 1941–42, only 59 percent of the usual number of freshmen began their studies. To encourage enrollment, especially for priority professions such as engineering, a special government directive was issued in 1942, eliminating entrance exams for high school students with high grades.[92] In some institutions students were also newly entitled to dormitories and some food rations, usually provided through canteens. In addition, the length of study was reduced by one year. Five-year programs were squeezed into four years, four-year programs into three.[93]

Some young people in the rear took advantage of these changes. Fira G., born in the Ukrainian Jewish agricultural colony of Efingar in 1925, recalled how her determination to escape cold and starvation accidentally set her on the path to becoming a distinguished medical scientist:

> I went to study in Perm.[94] One neighbor harnessed horses and took me there in a sled. I didn't have a coat. It had been stolen from me, so I borrowed a

> jacket, covered my feet with cotton balls, wrapped them with ropes, and took a forest dirt road to Perm. When I got to Perm, I first went to the department of literature at the university. I really wanted to study literature, because I wrote. I wanted to be a writer. I arrived and the director of the university came out and said, "If you pass the exams, we will settle you in the dormitory." I said, "Give me a roof over my head." Then he said, "We have already finished [teaching] the Old Slavonic language, and you don't know it." I said, "True, I don't know it." He said, "Then study it, pass the tests, and come back." I understood that it wasn't going to work out. Then the old man who drove me said, "What shall we do, girl? I brought you here alive through the forest for 120 kilometers. What are you going to do?" I said to him, "Take me to the Medical Institute. I'll definitely get in. My mother is a paramedic." And so he took me to the medical school, and they accepted me. They took everyone after the eighth grade, without exams.[95]

Roza K. from Zhitomir, born in 1922, recalled a similar experience. She fled with her mother on foot for more than two hundred kilometers and boarded a train for Alma-Ata, where her mother ("miraculously," she said) found employment on the cleaning staff of the local hospital. The job gave the family a card for food rations—a stroke of particularly good fortune, since Roza and her mother had lost their suitcase containing their personal documents and education records, including Roza's high-school diploma. Even though Roza could not demonstrate eligibility to study at a university, a combination of economic pressure, daring, good fortune, and loose requirements (something she did not mention herself) opened a new educational path for her:

> I found out from a newspaper that the Moscow Geological Exploration Institute had moved to Semipalatinsk,[96] a town a hundred kilometers from us. But before the war I had dreamed about [attending] the Mendeleev Institute [of Chemical Engineering]. So we can't think about our dreams. . . . We have to think that we have nothing. We are the poorest of the poor, we are beggars, we are homeless. . . .
>
> Yet we got the nerve to dream that I would go to Semipalatinsk. They organized preparatory courses there for the Geological Exploration Institute. We didn't have anything—no clothes, no shoes. But I was going. Yes! I wrote to

the director of the institute that the documents had been in the suitcase, that we lost them during the war. And that I had lost everything, my clothes, my shoes, the means to exist, all of it, except for my desire to study. Imagine my cheekiness! And we received an invitation from the director, complete with the money to buy the ticket. You can't imagine how happy everyone was in the hospital [where my mother worked]. The director wrote in his letter that I needed a note, signed by two witnesses, that I had indeed finished ten classes. Can you imagine finding witnesses in Kazakhstan that I finished school with a gold medal? But get this, people are people. Miraculous, kind, nice people.... They all ran to me and said, "I would sign, I would sign." ... They wrote the note together. Then I received an invitation (at that time you could not buy a ticket without an invitation). They also wrote that they would give me a dorm room. I set off. I arrived a month after classes had started. But nevertheless, I got admitted to the hydrogeological department. I could study. But I realized that I didn't have anything to wear in that cold climate, I had nothing to eat, nothing to use as a blanket at night. I wrote a letter to my mother saying, "Get me out of here."

My mother arranged for the hospital chief to send a telegram, which said, "Get here urgently, your mother is sick." I took the telegram to the director of the institute. I asked him for permission to go there and return. That convinced him that I would indeed come back, and he gave me permission to leave and money for the ticket. I went back to that hospital to be with my mother. I never returned.

In 1945, I went to Moscow, where my father's relatives lived. My mother and I had nothing—no home, no shelter, no clothes, no shoes, nothing. I came to Moscow so I could study and work. But no one would hire me without a *propiska* [residence registration permit], or admit me to an institute. Then someone advised me to try the Institute of Economics. I didn't want to go there. It was my least favorite option. My father used to say, "Don't go there." But I went there because I decided that I would study there for a year, get a Moscow [residence] registration, then find work, then finally get into my preferred Mendeleev Institute.[97]

Despite poverty and other circumstances that seemed to push her down, Roza associated her time in Kazakhstan with a chance to get ahead. Some Jewish refugees from Poland were able to follow a similar trajectory. Like

Roza and Fira, these young adults sometimes had access to education or training that helped them rise above their previous status. For example, Ann Benjamin-Goldberg, a refugee of working-class background from eastern Poland, was accepted into a medical program in the Soviet rear.[98]

It is hard to say whether Jews embracing opportunities for higher education in the rear is more a Jewish than a Soviet story. But it is clear that many Jewish evacuees and refugees speak with pride of their decision to study and attribute it to their strong desire to live and succeed despite the war. Indeed, opportunities were available to the most resourceful and ambitious evacuees and refugees. Others, less connected and less fortunate, lived through the war with their status downgraded, not upgraded. They ended up being settled in rural localities and assigned to work in collective farms. Those who were educated often had to forget their existing skills and learn new ones.

In addition to providing the country with industry to support the war effort, the Soviet rear had to build up its agricultural production. Evacuating livestock and farming equipment was a priority mainly because, before June 1941, the entire Soviet Union relied on its western regions, especially Ukraine, for food production. Before 1941, 33 percent of all wheat, 84 percent of sugar, and 38 percent of livestock (including 60 percent of pigs) were produced there. Between the end of June 1941 and midsummer 1942, the majority of food production capacity, for both the army and the rest of the country, moved to the Volga region, the Urals, Western Siberia, and Kazakhstan.[99]

Evacuating the agricultural sector saved some Jewish lives. For example, at Efingar, in the Nikolaev region of Ukraine, the two collective farms Rakosha and Molotov were ordered, on 5 August 1941, to move livestock away from the front. Centralized help with logistics was not available, but one directive, issued in late July 1941, specified that "livestock cannot be moved on the same roads as the troops." Instead, it recommended that herdsmen leaving Crimea or Ukraine move livestock across fields.[100] Evacuation of livestock was a strenuous exercise. Cows needed to be milked, fed, and herded in the right direction. Here is what Tatiana Pasik remembered about the process using a road:

> Although we were not too far from the Dnieper River, we walked for a long time. We shared the road with refugees and retreating army units. We saw people, equipment, carts, livestock, everyone was moving slowly to the East. German planes dropped bombs and shot at us with machine guns. Animals panicked and tried to run away. With difficulty we managed to get them back and continue walking. Sometimes we got to listen to the radio, and every day we heard bad news about surrendering cities. Everyone was anxious. . . . On the way we saw Jews from Novopolatava and Dobrin, our neighbors. They were walking back, in the opposite direction from us, because they had lost hope of being able to cross the Dnieper. We kept going and finally got to Berislav. . . . We got in line. The rumors spread that soon dams would open and we would get flooded. Finally, it was our turn. We crossed the Dnieper on ferries and boats. Some people swam. Then we would return and take the next group of cows. This is how we moved the entire herd. After that, we delivered them to the next organization and were free to evacuate.[101]

Pasik and her family made it to the rear and so, it seems, did most of the livestock that she helped to evacuate. All other residents of Efingar—those not ordered to leave—were murdered on 10 September 1941.[102] Similarly, women and older men who evacuated livestock from a settlement with the Esperanto name Voyo Nova (New Way), in the Eupatoria region of Crimea, were the only survivors of the German invasion in October 1941.[103] They walked three hundred kilometers before reaching the Crimean city of Kerch, from where they were evacuated in a more organized manner.[104]

For agricultural workers the initial escape was often harder than for those from the cities, but adapting to a new location was sometimes easier. Urban evacuees were poorly prepared to jump right into collective farm living, with its early waking, long days of physical labor, and primitive living conditions. For farmers the transition tended to be easier. Take, for example, Semyon Vernovsky, born in 1927 on the collective farm of Lenin Veg (Lenin's Way) in Crimea. In his 2015 autobiography he recalled an evacuation full of hardship. His father had been drafted, and in September 1941 he, with his mother and two siblings and two other families, had to deliver their livestock to Kerch. His job was to push a cart carrying family possessions. One of the other families could not handle the difficulties of walking in the rain under bombardments and amid the general uncertainty. They returned to their village and a few weeks later were all murdered. Vernovsky's family made it to Kerch and received permission to evacuate. The family ended up in Nevinnomysk, on the shore of the Kuban River. They were settled at a nearby collective farm, where the family, accustomed to agricultural conditions, began work the next day.[105] Unfortunately, the Germans approached Kuban a few weeks later, and Verkhovsky's family had to be evacuated again. They ended up in Irtyshsk, near Omsk. In his autobiography Verkhovsky described the evacuations as grueling but did not once complain about the hard agricultural work.[106]

Other evacuees remember life on farms in the Soviet rear as more traumatic, not just for the strenuous physical work but for the unfamiliar work culture and hierarchies. As one former evacuee recalled: "Mama worked in the collective farm. Every worker was under surveillance. If a local brigade leader noticed that an evacuee took a carrot or something, they were immediately written up and reported."[107] Some evacuees could not work in a *kolkhoz* because they had no shoes or clothes that they could wear in such a harsh climate. Others were sick. For example, of the twenty thousand evacuees from Bessarabia who arrived in western Kazakhstan, only about seven thousand were able to start working right away because the others did not have appropriate boots. By 1 January 1942 the majority of evacuees in the Zelenovsky district who settled in the collective farm, Day of the Red Army, lived in barns and without stoves. No other accommodation existed for them.[108]

One evacuee, twenty-eight-year-old Bella Gold, from Rzhev of the Kalinin region in Russia, recalled her life on a collective farm in Kosobrodsk, in Russia's Kurgan region in the Urals:

> Children got sick with measles. My sister's kids survived, but my daughter, who was one year and nine months old, died. I was devastated. Before she died, I worked very hard. I worked as a cleaner. I had no proper clothes. I did not have boots, gloves, or a coat. I had a light hat and only fashionable boots. I would wrap myself in rags just to get warm. In the evening collective farmers would sometimes share bread with my children. Every morning at 4 am, I had to go to the well. The well was surrounded by ice. The temperature was minus forty-five degrees. I had to walk to the well, carry a barrel of water, and prepare it for farmers. It was so heavy that, every time, I was terrified that I would fall with it into that well. By 6 am, two big ovens had to be lit so that farmers could put

> their potato pots on them. If I could not light the oven, they would yell at me: "Muscovite, you are useless!" I used to get upset because of this. One young man especially would yell at me: "Muscovite, look at our women, learn from them!" He played balalaika. To this day, I hate the sound of the balalaika. He played and sang songs about *zhidy* (Jews), that we do not like to work, that we are bums, and about why we came there. He harassed me so much that I cried. I worked so hard. I had to clean those huge rooms. I cleaned and cried. My eyes were puffy, and I was bent all day, but at least I was alone most of the day and did not have to interact with him or other farmers.[109]

To urban teenagers whose parents had experienced little hard physical labor, life on a *kolkhoz* seemed especially tough. Among them, those from recently acquired Soviet territories seemed to suffer the most. Writer Grigorii Kanovich, for example, arrived in Kazakhstan and began to work at a collective farm in 1941. Soon he was copying some of the other boys who worked there by stealing small spikes of leftover wheat (*koloski*). A guard caught Grigorii and beat him nearly unconscious. Kanovich described the episode in his memoirs, recalling it as a moment of almost unbearable fear and horror. He also said the beating probably saved him from a more formal prison sentence.[110]

Polish Jewish refugees who ended up at collective farms in Siberia, Chuvashia, or Kazakhstan left some of the most devastating memoirs. Even official reports reveal a frequent and consistent pattern of harassment and violence toward Jewish refugees. For example, a district attorney named Poluektov reported the following incident in a secret communication to Bochkov, chief attorney of the USSR:

> A worker Goyzhe has routinely beaten Jewish citizens, humiliated them, and called for ethnic hostility. Every time he would stage a public beating, a crowd would gather. Many screamed: "Beat Jews! All Russians are at the front, but *zhidy* came to hide in Zhambul. They do not want to work and do not want to go to collective farms."[111]

The State Archives of Kazakhstan are full of letters of complaint about local authorities. Here is an official reply from the executive committee of the Alma-Ata district council:

> Thirty-three Polish families (eighty-three people) arrived in our district. All received a place to live, most were provided with employment, and many received help in purchasing food. Polish citizens, who live in the collective farm "Red Worker," complained that the chairman of the Frunze village council, Comrade Akhmetov, and the *kolkhoz* chair, Comrade Eltsov, do not show compassion for the Polish citizens and do not give them work or food. The complaint was urgently verified. On 12 December 1941, both comrades Akhmetov and Eltsov were disciplined and urged to accommodate them as much as possible.
>
> All chairmen of kolkhoz and village councils are asked to fully accommodate and employ Polish citizens and create normal living conditions for them.[112]

Although material conditions were indeed harsh, some younger Polish Jewish refugees adapted well. For example, Tova Passal and Sara Burak, two friends from Poland who ended up at a *kolkhoz* in Uzbekistan, managed to learn Russian and Uzbek quickly, earning the trust of both the Soviet authorities and the local population. Passal soon became a deputy town head of Kokand, and Burak was transferred from the fields to work as a teacher. Eventually he became a director of the school.[113] Still, most memories of life in a *kolkhoz* are associated with hunger, disease, and hardship. Polish Jewish comedian Szymon Dzigan, who ended up first in a labor camp, then in Tashkent, made the following joke: "What is the difference between a *kolkhoz* and *kol-nidre* [a prayer said on the Jewish Day of Atonement]? When you say *kol-nidre*, you do not eat for a day. When you say *kolkhoz*, you don't eat for a year."[114]

Regulating access to food was one of the major ways of mobilizing and controlling the civilian population in the Soviet rear. In July 1941 rations were introduced for essential food items such as bread in the Moscow and Leningrad regions. Gradually other food items were rationed, too, and rations were instituted in 197 other regions of the Soviet Union.[115] In 1941, 12 kinds of ration cards existed. By 1942, 51 cards existed; there were 112 by 1943, and as many as 135 by 1944. On 13 November 1942, the People's Commissariat of Trade issued a memo dividing urban residents into four groups, each with its own proportion of food rations: (1) Workers (including qualified workers, scientists, doctors, teachers, artists, and blood donors); (2)

civil servants; (3) dependents; and (4) children younger than twelve. The first category was entitled to the highest allowance (800 grams of bread per day and 800 grams of sugar per month), whereas civil servants received 600 grams of bread per day and 600 grams of sugar per month, and dependents and children got 400 grams of bread per day and 400 grams of sugar per month.[116]

Rations were dispensed monthly. They were acquired with coupons (*talony*), which could be used only on a specific day. Expired *talony* would not be honored. Some workers were also eligible for hot lunches in canteens, which counted toward *talony*. Some workplaces had canteens that sold cooked meals without *talony*. Each work group was entitled to its "norm." The first group (workers) was entitled to 2,200 grams of fish or meat per month, whereas group three received only 1,200 grams. Children received less. Party officials, council chairpersons, and Komsomol administrators all technically belonged to group one, but in practice they, too, were divided into three categories, each with greater or lesser privileges. Regional bosses ranked higher than urban ones, and district bosses ranked lower than urban ones.[117] The first category of officials was entitled to 9,400 grams of fish or meat per month and 3,100 grams of candy. The third (or lowest) group received 3,600 grams of meat or fish and 800 grams of candy. Workers not in the official category got no candy at all. Some industries advocated for their workers to receive additional goods and provided bonuses and prizes for workers who produced above the norm. However, without a doubt, a party official of even the lowest rank enjoyed a much better situation than even the best and most committed worker. Some exceptions applied. Workers in some cases were rewarded for exceptional work with additional rations. For example, architect Valentin Feldshteyn recalled that workers could get a coupon for an additional two hundred grams of bread and a hot meal at the canteen.[118]

Figuring out how to receive the ration, how to go up a category, how to use expired *talony*, and how to exchange bread *talony* for dairy *talony* became crucial survival skills in the rear. Routinely, inspectors (who could be bribed) revealed that parents received *talony* for children older than twelve, when children older than twelve were expected to work to earn their rations themselves. One inspection at Tailor Plant No. 7 revealed that two workers obtained rations for their older children, a sixty-eight-year-old woman acquired a children's ration, and fired workers kept all their rations. There was no inventory of rations. One worker illegally obtained a ration for his wife, claiming that she was his dependent, although she was able-bodied and was supposed to work for her ration.[119]

Reports of starvation came from all areas of the Soviet rear, especially in 1941. One report to the Kremlin, for example, stated that a group of evacuated students from Kiev University sustained themselves solely on rice while housed in a *kolkhoz* called International, in the Sar-Darnitskoy district of the Kzyl-Orda region of Kazakhstan. With no access to vegetables, many fell ill with scurvy. Another report stated that ninety-five evacuated families had not seen bread in a long time, as they had no resources to buy it.[120] One woman wrote to her husband on active military duty: "It is so hard to live here. I regret leaving Leningrad. I would rather be killed by a bomb than die here, in stages, from starvation."[121]

Polish Jewish refugees often did not have official job assignments and had to rely on themselves to find a job, leaving them especially vulnerable to hunger and disease. A number of centrally issued directives, including some signed by Viacheslav Molotov himself, ordered that Polish citizens be provided with flour, grain, sugar, and a small sum of money.[122] Every person who lived through the evacuation has a story about food shortages and hunger. Starvation became the greatest cause of death in the industrial cities, as the food crisis came to envelop not only children, the elderly, and the sick but also the best-fed population sector in the rear: male industrial workers.[123] People lived their lives juggling rations, selling some and buying others, working on getting access to canteens, and figuring out how to eat things that were barely edible, such as peels, stems, and wheat by-products.[124]

Alexander Berman, who survived the war in evacuation as a teenager and who later spent decades collecting stories from former evacuees and refugees, observed that people forever remembered the figures of 800 and 400 (800 grams of bread for "workers" and 400 grams for "dependents"). Many decades later, some people spoke of the rush of happiness they experienced when they got to hold a piece of bread in a store and take a small bite.[125] For example, during an interview in 1992, Victor Rozenzaft, evacuated from Poltava to Uralsk, recalled the taste of bread in remarkable detail:

> Throughout the winter of 1943 I stood in line for bread, lining up in the evening the day before. Once, someone stole my bread card for the entire week. I am still grateful to my mom's colleagues who each gave me a little crumb. I still remember the taste of that bread—something gooey, wood-like—pure joy. Baked potato peel—enjoyment. When the spring came, my mom used to make soup from nettles.[126]

Others remember humiliation. For example, Jusef Vaidenfeld recalled: "We waited in line for hours to receive 400 grams of bread. The line was long. The bread was awful, clay-like, and we waited all day and all night."[127] Residents of the Soviet rear seemed to have spent a lot of time in lines. They lined up to redeem their coupons, then lined up to buy food or supplies. Families assigned duties to different members, including small children, who, like Jusef, kept a place in line to buy food supplies. To pass the time, many people engaged in casual (but long!) conversations with strangers about politics, local news, and other topics. An NKVD report documented an argument in line. One citizen argued that Jews were not fighting on the front lines and that food shortages were all caused by Jews. He said so in the presence of a Jewish amputee, who had lost his leg in the Red Army. A militia man was present but chose to say nothing.[128]

In food lines many Jews experienced, some for the first time, casual hostility directed at them both as Jews and as evacuees. In the minds of many, starvation, hunger, lines, and hostile conversations became blurred into one never-ending experience of the evacuation. They also endured extremely crowded and often unsuitable accommodation.

Finding a place to live for sixteen and a half million people in a few months would be a challenging enough task in peacetime. Doing so in the midst of a full-scale war, in conditions that required resettled people to start working as soon as possible, verged on the impossible. Already, most city inhabitants of the Soviet rear were living in crowded conditions, often in communal apartments.

As the evacuation was not planned, no new accommodation could be built in time. State officials executed a number of strategies to settle newcomers. They prioritized strategically important personnel, people in charge of establishing industries and working there, and moved others, including local residents who did not work in such industries to other, mostly rural locations. The agricultural sector needed workers who could be taught what to do, whereas industries needed a qualified workforce. Many groups that were considered unreliable, such as former prisoners or formerly deported ethnic groups, were moved again—also to rural locations.[129] Such relocations happened in Alma-Ata, Stalingrad, Molotov, Kuibyshev, Barnaul, and many other larger cities in the rear. Following the same logic, evacuees who were mostly urban but whose expertise was not immediately needed in the cities were sent to villages. Such policies led to large-scale hostility against evacuees, and especially against Jews, who were often overrepresented among evacuees resettled into people's apartments.

Exacerbating difficulties was the frequent unwillingness of local residents to take refugees in. Most people simply did not have extra floor space, to say nothing of a room, to accommodate the newcomers. Many residents devised strategies to keep refugees away. Some demanded exorbitant rents, knowing few evacuees could afford them. Others, prodded by local officials to charge reasonable fees, harassed renters so that they would leave. One landlord in the village of Gvardeiskoe, in the Penza region of Russia, forced the children of evacuees to remain outside while their mothers were at work, even in the dead of winter, with temperatures as low as minus 30°C. A landlord in the Dubovo-Umet district of the Kuybyshev region is reported to have forced tenants to sleep on a floor that had been coated with urine. Another is said to have allowed a sheep into the house while children were sleeping.[130] In a village called Gory, in the Guryev region, every room was made to accommodate seventeen or more people. All had to sleep on the floor without sheets, blankets, or pillows.[131] In a *kolkhoz* named after Lenin's wife, Nadezhda Krupskaia, in the Chimkent region of south Kazkhstan, fifty-six people lived in twelve apartments, but of those apartments only three were considered habitable. The others lacked heating or doors.[132] In the Belebeev district of the Ufa region, residents refused to settle evacuees once they discovered they were Jews.[133]

Evacuation destinations were almost universally overcrowded. A 1943 report about conditions in Tashkent noted that "at present each inhabitant has on average 2.6 square meters of living space," a situation that "does not meet even the most elementary demands that have been placed on available housing stock."[134] Even that figure may have overestimated the space available to newcomers. Factory workers were typically housed in dormitories where ten or more people shared a single room, with beds for half of them or fewer.[135] Architect Valentin Feldshteyn recalled that although he personally was involved in record-speed construction projects—building hospitals and industrial plants in the village of Chernikovka near Ufa in Bashkortostan—most workers lived in tents situated around open boilers. Not until 1943 did workers begin to move into dorms and apartments.[136]

The accommodation shortage created widespread homelessness, especially in larger evacuation centers, such as Alma-Ata, Ashkhabad, Samarkand, and Tashkent. Many people had no shoes or clothes suitable to the harsh climate. Others were too sick to work. Typhus and other infectious diseases spread rapidly in overcrowded conditions with poor sanitation. Evacuated students lived in dugouts, which were not heated or ventilated. Almost all students caught lice.[137] Writer Nadezhda Mandelstam recalled "sick people all around."[138]

Children were a priority evacuation group, according to early directives of the Soviet Evacuation Council. Many were evacuated with parents, mostly mothers who worked at eligible industries. Others accompanied their parents on so-called spontaneous evacuations or escapes. Still others were evacuated unaccompanied by family members; they left with their kindergartens, orphanages, and sometimes summer camps. On 19 August 1941, 10,550 such children were evacuated from Moscow to the Cheliabinsk and Molotov regions. One month later, 60,000 children from Moscow boarding schools followed. By the end of 1942, 188,364 children were evacuated from western parts of Russia and Ukraine to the eastern parts of the Russian Federation.[139] Kazakhstan accepted the relocation of 104 orphanages with 12,859 children and sixteen Moscow boarding schools with 2,304 children.[140] In Tashkent, special evacuation centers were established for children traveling alone. By the summer of 1943, 33,921 children were registered at Tashkent evacuation centers, about half of them unaccompanied.[141] Overall, Uzbekistan received about 200,000 children of different ethnic groups, of whom 4,500 were placed in Uzbek families.[142] In 1942, 15,649 children lived in orphanages, and by 1945, this number had risen to 31,000.[143] Similarly, a large number of orphans ended up in Siberia, especially in the Omsk, Chkalov, Cheliabinsk, Kuibyshev, Kirov, Sverdlovsk, and Novosibirsk regions. In general, children constituted about 40 percent of all evacuees (excluding Polish citizens, for which statistics are harder to obtain).

All the difficulties that adults suffered in the rear children suffered as well: starvation, disease, and terrible living conditions, made worse for children because they could not always advocate for themselves. The settlement of orphans and unaccompanied minors, let alone social and institutional support for them, constituted one of the major challenges of the evacuation. It was also very much a topic of wartime discussion—how to care for orphans, who will raise them, who will pay their expenses and how? These were issues discussed in the press and in everyday conversations. The experiences of some segments of the orphan population, such as evacuated children from Leningrad, are well known. The stories of the vast majority, however, remain obscure.[144]

There is no precise estimate of how many evacuated children were Jews, but their number was significant, probably around the same proportion as the rest of the evacuees—between 5 percent and 19 percent. Jewish children and teenagers were arguably much more exposed than other evacuees of their own age to bigoted comments and to negative attitudes because they spent most of their day not with their own families but with other people, at school, at work, and in lines for food.[145]

Although the number of Jewish orphans in the Soviet rear is unknown, the archives of the Yiddish-language newspaper *Eynikayt* provide some information. For example, one article states that in 1945 there were about nine hundred Jewish orphans in Kazakhstan. When Soviet authorities engaged in building a state-of-the-art orphanage for Jewish children in Birobidzhan, they asked orphanage directors to identify Jewish children who could speak Yiddish so that they could send them there. About a hundred Jewish orphans were identified in the Omsk area, but none of them spoke Yiddish.[146]

As for the significance of the experience of Jewish children in the Soviet rear, a few factors stand out. First, the children spent their formative years with an acute awareness of their ethnicity. Many of them learned the words "Jew" and *zhid* simultaneously. This factor alone may have shaped how the children, as adults, understood being Jewish.[147] In other words, they formed the first generation of Soviet Jews who understood that being Jewish was a disadvantage to be overcome, a cornerstone of Soviet Jewish urban identity for decades.

Second, this is the generation that told the story of their evacuation, both to audiences in Russia and abroad. It is this generation's experience that has been recorded in oral history projects by the Shoah Foundation, Kiev's Institute for Judaica Studies, Anna Shternshis's oral history project, and many others. Through activism and outreach, this generation insisted that their story belonged to the history of the Holocaust and needed to be known in Israel, the United States, Germany, and Canada. It is through the lens of their stories that an alternative to Soviet-sponsored surveys and documents has been acquired, as well as to memoirs written by intellectuals, which had previously served as the only sources for outside knowledge about the Jewish experience in the Soviet rear.

Women accounted for nearly two-thirds of the evacuees from the pre-1939 Soviet territories.[148] Those among them who wrote memoirs or gave interviews emphasized that the months they spent fleeing to and living in the rear were the most difficult of their lives. They took responsibility for supporting their children and their elderly parents physically, psychologically, and financially under circumstances of extraordinary hardship. They had to prepare food, to stand in line for ingredients and for coal or wood, to care for the sick, and to make and mend clothes, all while working long hours at difficult jobs. Women without jobs or with poor-paying ones, or who lacked bread-ration cards, or who had no savings—the actual situation of most evacuees—were often unable to put sufficient food on the family table. Yet somehow women were expected to hold their families together. To do so they required assistance from communities of mutual support, consisting mostly of other women.

Dealing with various aspects of life in the rear engendered culture shock. Something as routine and simple as standing in line could turn into a hostile encounter, both because the women were Jews and because they were women. Vladimir Sidur, for example, recalled that in Stalinabad women had to stand in separate, longer lines for rations, compared to men.[149] Similarly, some refugees were surprised by the ritualized division of labor between men and women in Uzbek villages. One observer noticed: "When they walk together, [Uzbek] women follow men, just like Hassidim do."[150] The behavior of evacuee women often came off as entitled or standoffish. Their urban clothes, manner of speaking, and expectations seemed unreasonable to local residents. In the Molotov region, for example, these women are remembered as being dressed in "European" clothes, looking to buy a "little chicken" (*kurochku*) at the market.[151]

Hostility against evacuee women was three-fold: as evacuees, as women, and as Jews. When it came to domestic issues, including violence, women endured much abuse, and their complaints were often dismissed as "entitled." A woman who complained about her landlord—a party functionary who, after beating his own wife and child, harassed the woman's sister, broke her door, and tried to attack her—was told, "Damn you, Odessa Jews!"[152] At a public event one local official said that "many party comrades are hiding from doll-like orangutans with long nails and painted faces."[153] What were the concerns about "entitlement" that provoked such reactions? Here is an example from Kazakhstan. A woman wrote to an official pleading for help: "I am an evacuated woman, and I do not have clothes or shoes," she said. "In winter, I asked you to help me buy shoes, but you refused me. Now I ask you to fire me from my job, because when summer comes, I will go and live in a *sovkhoz* (Soviet state farm). I have no access to the canteen here in the city. I live solely on rations."[154]

To get a sense of specific challenges that women experienced, recall what happened to Esfir A., the pregnant wife who fled Wilno on her husband's lap in the passenger seat of a truck.[155] Her story offers a window onto the ways in which gender and Jewishness intersected in wartime USSR. She was seven months pregnant. She made it to a train that took her to Tula, an industrial city some two hundred kilometers south of Moscow, where her non-Jewish sister-in-law lived. Being in a place where she had relatives made her feel able to give birth in safety. She was mistaken:

> My sister-in-law lived in Tula. I asked her to register me with her so that I could go to the hospital later to give birth. She refused. She was afraid. But I met a friend and she registered me. She herself was evacuated so the registration was temporary, only for the duration of her permit.... The sister-in-law was village-like (*derevenskaia*), so she was afraid.

The sister-in-law had actually come from a nearby village, Savino, where Esfir's parents-in-law continued to reside. Esfir decided to go to them, even though she was not certain how they would react: "After all, I was pregnant with their baby [grandchild]. So I hitchhiked on a truck and got a ride to their village." The people in the village received her with kindness: "Many saw me and offered to let me stay with them for no money. They offered me food." But her troubles were far from over:

> I did not feel well. When we were running from the German attacks [on the way to the village], we were hiding in the forests, and there was no water. We drank water from puddles. We sort of filtered it with hankies. There was not enough water, so we gave what we could to children. And I drank some. So probably I got infected and infected my baby.
>
> When I arrived in the village, I started getting contractions. They took me to Serpukhov [a town midway between Tula and Moscow]. I suffered for seven days. I could not give birth. Probably the baby was fighting. He got sick with toxic dyspepsia. The doctor said I did not get sick because I was so stressed that my body mobilized its entire immunity to fight it. Otherwise, we would have both died from all this.
>
> So I spent seven days in the hospital. There was one professor there, who finished [his training] at the Leningrad Academy. He was told that I needed surgery. They wanted to do a C[aesarian] section on me. Someone said to him, "A refugee woman from Vilnius [*sic*] is suffering there. She ran from Vilnius, but she is from Leningrad. She is so beautiful, such a shame and pity on her. Now they will do a C-section...."
>
> He dropped everything and ran to the operating room. I was already prepped, covered with a sheet. Ten students came in to see how to do a C-section. He approached me, took off the sheet, looked at me. I was indeed very beautiful [shows picture]. The picture does not do justice. He looked at me and said, "Such a woman, and you will take such a risk. She will have so many children. Leave her alone. Bring a thick bath towel." And then he simply squeezed the baby [out] with it. But you see, when he squeezed him out, he understood, this baby would not live. His face color....

But to the doctor's surprise, the baby lived. The doctor was kind to Esfir, bringing her rolls and butter to eat and flowers every morning during the two weeks she remained in the hospital. But following her discharge, more problems appeared:

> I nursed the baby all the time.... Twenty-four hours [a day] he suckled, but it all came out immediately. I realized he was sick. I read books. I knew.
>
> I picked him up and wanted to take him to Serpukhov, to the hospital. No one would admit me, so I walked with him on the road, the Moscow-Tula road. It was already bombed. One plane circled around me, and the pilot tried to shoot me. I held the baby. I still remember the face of that pilot—his red hair—he was laughing and shooting. He saw I had a baby.

Esfir walked the twenty-five kilometers from the village to Serpukhov, holding her baby and nursing him along the way. Without a diaper, he was covered in excrement. Because of German bombings, what would ordinarily have been a five-hour journey lasted ten hours. It was 10 p.m. when she reached the hospital:

> The hospital was closed, and all the doctors had gone home. Someone opened the door, I showed them the baby.
>
> The nurse called a doctor. The doctor said, "Do not touch this baby, he won't live." ... I ask them, "Let me stay the night, and in the morning I will go to the doctor who delivered him." I believed he would save my baby. I believed it.
>
> But they were afraid. I probably looked scary. My clothes were all torn up. I had been running from the plane. The baby looked scary. We were covered in poop. They said, "No, she might leave the baby here. Do not let her in."

She sat outside the hospital and cried. A Russian woman saw her and took her in, washing both baby and mother even though she had no bath. The woman made cloth diapers for the baby and gave Esfir a dress and some underwear. The following morning Esfir returned to the hospital, where she brought her baby to "her" professor:

> He unwrapped the child and said, "My dear girl, you will have children. You are so beautiful. You will have lots of children. You will not save this child. If I save him, you will not thank yourself. And he won't thank me...." He said, "You

> see, his mouth and his eyes are open all the time. It means his brain is infected. If I save him, he won't be normal. Why do it for him, or for your sake? He is little, he does not understand anything. I don't even know if I can save him. His illness is advanced. He probably got sick while you were still pregnant. Plus your delivery was so long and complicated."

The baby screamed and screamed until he was given a painkiller. He died three days later.

At first glance this haunting narrative of a desperate mother witnessing the cruel death of her infant child appears silent about how being Jewish may have influenced the outcome. However, a close reading reveals details suggesting that at several points Jewishness played a key role. To begin with, it is plausible that Esfir's sister-in-law refused to register the desperate mother because she did not approve of her brother's choice of a wife. Maybe they did not get along. Or maybe she did not approve because Esfir was a Jew.

Second, the refusal to admit a woman to the hospital with her sick baby no doubt points to the nurses' worry that an exhausted mother would simply abandon her child and leave him in the hospital's care. This was a common phenomenon. Evacuee and refugee mothers figured that if something bad happened to them, at least their children would be in good hands. Esfir did not mention that Jewish women were suspected of abandoning their children more than others, but it may well be that her Jewishness was a factor in her being turned away.[156] In this regard it appears significant that she received help from the hospital only after she was able to clean herself and put on a village dress, thereby looking less like a Jewish refugee. In any event, the subject remained so painful that even decades later it could be narrated only between the lines.

Jews constituted a minority of evacuees overall, but at some receiving centers they formed a majority. In late 1941, for example, 63 percent of Tashkent's evacuee population,[157] 62 percent of evacuees in Alma-Ata,[158] about 22 percent of evacuees in the Urals,[159] and between 20 and 30 percent in Ufa[160] were Jews. The social environment in the Soviet rear was much more ethnically diverse than in places most evacuees had left. Soviet media were keen to portray mutual friendships and enrichment among many cultures. Newspapers published photographs of Solomon Mikhoels performing at the National Uzbek Theater, along with stories about writer Aleksei Tolstoi incorporating Uzbek folklore into his prose and Uzbek families adopting Ukrainian, Byelorussian, and Bessarabian Jewish orphans.[161] Yet in their recollections evacuees, especially Jews, reported brutal, overwhelming, ubiquitous hostility and distrust toward them as among their greatest problems.

In the decision to leave, or the train journey, or finding a place to live in a small village in the Urals or a big city in Uzbekistan, being Jewish mattered for many people. Although there are documented cases of mutual support and astonishing kindness among Jews, mostly it mattered in a negative way. The bigotry some Jews encountered was to some degree typical of the prejudice faced by evacuees in general, but it also featured stereotypical accusations against them in particular. Initially, some of the bigotry may have been perpetuated by non-Jewish evacuees from places of heavy Jewish settlement. Later, wounded soldiers demobilized to the rear exacerbated the problem by spreading the lie that Jews were underrepresented at the front.[162] Party observers listened to complaints about Jewish evacuees taking up resources while sitting out the war and did nothing to counter such expressions of hatred.[163] During (mandatory) public lectures, speakers were often asked whether it was true that Jews were cowards.[164] In the Molotov region, expressions such as "Tashkent Front" entered common speech to refer to deserters, cowards, and cheaters—allegedly mostly Jews sitting out the war in the deep rear.[165]

Faina M. from Proskurov, Ukraine, became ethnically aware when she tried to explain to otherwise friendly villagers that Jews were not the grotesque creatures the villagers imagined. Never having been forced to think about her ethnicity in the past, she suddenly understood that she represented her entire nation in the eyes of people who claimed never to have seen Jews before.[166] Many Jews who spent their time at the rear in villages in Uzbekistan or Kazakhstan spoke about being the first Jews that their new neighbors had ever encountered. Like Faina, many of them found nothing offensive or mean in the stereotyped images. They interpreted them instead as a sign of backwardness. Nevertheless, once she was defined as a Jew by others, Faina had to explain to herself what being a Jew meant:

> This Russian woman, she knew that I was Jewish, but she did not care, she just never saw Jews before. She thought they had horns. Why else would she call bad chickens Jewish? They were wild in this village in general. I remember it was June or July, and it was really hot. They used to wear *valenki* (fur boots) and *kaloshi* (overshoes) and old-fashioned clothes. They had an accordion and sang, "We will sing, we will sing, we won't let you sleep." I would stand inside, put a handkerchief on and look at them. My landlady would tell me, "Go with them, dance and sing." I would answer, "I will not go. I can see everything from here." Of course, I never went out with them. They were village people, and I was from a good Jewish family.[167]

Jewishness for Faina was evidently measured against the local rural population. She felt superior to these people. Like Faina, some Jews remembered abuse and discrimination in the evacuation, but they also distrusted their new neighbors and looked down on them.

Why did bigotry surface in the rear to such an extent? First, wartime anywhere is fertile ground for conspiracies and rumors. With the future uncertain and policies anything but transparent, people offset their discomfort by reviving the old image of a Jew—Christ killer, merchant, dealer, traitor—similarly to how people had coped during the First World War.[168] Seeing well-dressed evacuees, often entitled to rations and sometimes to an apartment, did not help. Nor did the rumor that "Germans kill only Jews, and the war is taking place only to fight for Jews." Locals were not the only ones to express hostility to Jews. Non-Jewish evacuees did so as well, questioning why some Jews had better clothes and more money than locals and received parcels of food.[169]

Soviet authorities closely surveyed such expressions, which were also perceived as criticisms of Soviet patriotism.[170] Moreover, offenders were often punished. The fact that punishments existed is important in light of what was going on at the same time in Nazi-occupied Europe. On the other hand, people living with bigotry, discrimination, and verbal assaults did not evaluate their situation within that context, and, for many, experiencing abuse was a turning point in their lives.

One of the unintended by-products of life for Jews in the Soviet rear was that Jews from four important centers of cultural production in the Yiddish language—Lithuania, Poland, Romania, and the USSR—found themselves together in the same general location and in the same circumstances. Interactions among them resulted in a temporary blossoming of Jewish cultural and religious life, featuring theatrical performances in Yiddish, concerts of Jewish music, literary events, and even the establishment of a Hasidic yeshiva in the Uzbek city of Samarkand.[171] Shakhne Epstein observed in 1942 that "Uzbekistan now houses over 400,000 Jews, [and] Yiddish is heard in the streets." Tashkent, he declared, had become "the most Jewish of all cities in the Soviet Union."[172] Indeed, during the month of April 1943 alone, the thirty thousand Jews living in the Uzbek capital could see a Yiddish play starring Ida Kamińska, hear three concerts of Yiddish songs (including one featuring Cantor Misha Alexandrovich from Riga), attend a reading of Sholom Aleichem's stories, and listen to readings of the poetry of Peretz Markish. Polish Zionists held meetings. Two synagogues operated. Passover *matsot* could be purchased from a local bakery. More broadly, at least twenty-eight professional Yiddish theaters and musical collectives performed in all areas of Soviet Central Asia and even in Siberia between 1941 and 1944.[173]

The richness of Jewish cultural life in the rear was due largely to the deliberate, state-sponsored evacuation, along with their Russian counterparts, of important Soviet Jewish cultural institutions. As a result of the effort to preserve them, by the end of 1941 the cream of the Yiddish-speaking Soviet intelligentsia and their families, including Peretz Markish, Itsik Fefer, David Bergelson, Isaac Nusinov, Shakhne Epstein, and Der Nister (Pinhas Kaganovich), were living in the Soviet interior. Almost all Soviet Yiddish theaters were reassembled. The Moscow Jewish State Theater and the Odessa Yiddish Theater found new bases in Tashkent, where they performed alongside a local Yiddish theater established in 1933. The Kiev Jewish Theater and the Kharkov Jewish Drama Theater regrouped in the town of Fergana in Uzbekistan. The Byelorussian Jewish Theater was based in Novosibirsk. Joining them were Yiddish actors from Poland who had fled to the USSR in 1939, including Ida Kamińska, who performed regularly with Soviet Yiddish troupes. Among other members of the Jewish intelligentsia from the recently annexed areas who found refuge in the Soviet rear were many

Wilno-based workers of YIVO (*Yidisher visnshaftlekher institut*—Yiddish Scientific Institute). They evacuated to Fergana, where they collected folklore while working as teachers. Also, the Moldavian Jewish Jazz Orchestra, from the former Romanian Bessarabia, worked in Samarkand.[174]

Eynikayt published numerous short articles between 1942 and 1945 describing a veritable Jewish renaissance in the Volga region, Central Asia, and Siberia. Often, the stories stressed that ethnically mixed audiences attended and appreciated the performances. For scholars today, the reports offer basic descriptions of the events and make it possible to gauge the remarkable extent of Jewish cultural activity during the period. The reports alone offer little insight into what this cultural activity meant to the people who patronized and took part in it. The addition of oral histories, however, now allows for precisely such interpretation.

Here, for example, is an account of a concert given by singer Roza Plotkina in Saratov in early 1942.[175] It was related by Zoya Lichtman, born in Kiev in 1919. At the time Lichtman was an aspiring pianist who had almost completed her studies at the Kiev Conservatory of Music. Evacuated with her mother to Saratov, she had found employment as a pianist at the conservatory in that city. As Lichtman recalled, she was at her lodgings with her mother when she heard a knock on the door. Opening it, she saw a tall, beautiful brunette with bright eyes. The woman asked for Lichtman by name:

> My mother gave her food and drinks. She ate well and cried. At the end, she told us that she came from Byelorussia, she had walked on foot to Saratov. She said she did not know if her family was still alive. Her husband was at the front. He is a famous Yiddish writer, Moisei Teif, the poet.[176]
>
> I said to her, "How can I help you?"
>
> She said, "I was a student at the Minsk conservatory. I would like to study in Saratov's conservatory. They will give me a dorm, but to take the test I need a pianist to accompany my singing."
>
> I asked her to sing and played for her. I saw that she could sing, but she was in no shape to perform.
>
> I said to her, "Don't worry, they will take your situation into consideration. But maybe, dear Roza (Rozochka), you should sing a folk song, a Byelorussian folk song."

She said, "I know some Byelorussian songs, I sing them together with our songs, my songs."

I asked, "What do you mean, 'my songs?'" She said, "I sing Jewish folk songs in Byelorussia."

"What do you mean, 'Jewish?'" I asked.

"Yes, Jewish songs. I have a huge repertoire. And people like it. I participated in the competition of folk songs in Byelorussia. I won a prize. My husband introduced me to all the Jewish writers: Fefer, Peretz Markish, Mikhoels, Kvitko, Hofshtein. All of them came to visit us when they came to Minsk. I sang for them, and they all liked me."

I asked her to sing a Jewish song. She began to sing. It was magic.

During the exam, Roza performed Jewish songs. When they heard her, they admitted her to the conservatory on the spot.

Later, I helped her to organize an entire concert of Yiddish songs in Saratov. I played piano for her. We did not know if people would come, but we decided to try. Someone made her a concert dress from old theater decorations.

The huge Saratov Conservatory Hall was sold out. People cried. I don't know if the hall was full with Jews. It is impossible that Saratov had so many Jews who were interested in this concert. I didn't believe it, you understand? But nevertheless, there was a full concert hall. It was the beginning of 1942. Maybe the public was mixed, maybe the conservatory public was there. She was extremely successful. The public screamed. She sang several encores.

She sang dance songs and lullabies, a song by Leib Kvitko entitled "Fidele," many children's songs.

After that concert, she performed Yiddish songs a lot, also in Moscow, and at the frontlines for soldiers.[177]

How can the interest and the enthusiastic response of what is described as a largely non-Jewish audience in a town on the Russian Volga to a concert of Yiddish music from Byelorussia be explained? Of course, at the time of that concert, about seven thousand Jews lived in Saratov, and some of them could have come to listen. Another explanation could be that for the audience in Saratov and other parts of the Soviet rear, Yiddish music signified the ultimate expression of anti-German resistance. Evacuees surely blamed the German army for disrupting their lives, but they also had to be aware that Jews had been targeted by the invaders for special suffering.[178] Jews thus represented the antithesis of the Germans and all they stand for. In their overwhelming majority, Soviet citizens from all social strata hoped and worked actively for a German defeat. Although war and evacuation had brought with them heightened expressions of antipathy toward Jews within some segments of Soviet society, along with efforts by the state to distance itself from any association with particular Jewish interests,[179] the sentiments that gave rise to such expressions appear to have been counterbalanced to a degree among evacuees by a sense that continued public performances of Jewish culture represented a supreme act of defiance to German designs. The Red Army apparently found such performances so inspiring to soldiers that it sponsored hundreds of them, as recorded in the archive of the Jewish Anti-Fascist Committee. Roza Plotkina was sent to perform at the front. The actor Emmanuel Kaminka entertained combat troops with an evening of readings from the stories of Sholom Aleichem in Russian translation.[180] These and other evacuee Jewish artists were selected for such assignments after demonstrating their ability to engage the non-Jewish public at a major evacuation site.

Meanwhile, the popularity among Jews of Yiddish literature and music as performed by such artists as Plotkina and Kaminka grew alongside their non-Jewish interests, perhaps even because of it. Even the most highly assimilated Soviet Jews, who had made a practice of distancing themselves from Jewish culture, began to pay increased attention to things Jewish. After all, they could not easily have remained altogether unaffected by the fate of Jews in Byelorussia and in Ukraine, a fate that began to come into increasing focus beginning in 1943.[181] In that context, Yiddish became a vehicle for affirming Jewishness even among the majority of Soviet Jews who did not habitually use the language.

Moreover, the type of Jewish affirmations advanced by Yiddish theaters in evacuation included expressions of a particularistic Jewish consciousness that deviated at times from earlier Soviet norms. For example, the Kharkov Jewish Drama Theater performed the drama *Shvue* (Oath), written by the prolific Soviet Yiddish literary critic and playwright Yehezkel Dobrushin.[182] The play told the story of a heroic Jewish soldier who would not give up fighting because of the oath he swore to defend his country. A review prepared for *Eynikayt* of a performance in Samarkand reported that the play contained unapologetically Jewish elements, including expressions of pride in Jewish heritage and history, along with a few words in Hebrew, a sympathetic portrayal of Jewish rituals and customs, and even satire at the expense of some communist characters.[183] During the 1930s such features might well have brought severe consequences, perhaps even arrest. At the time, however, censors appear not to have noticed. In any event, the reviewer reported that the viewing public was delighted with the result.[184] For evacuee Jewish audiences these plays articulated a triple motivation: to fight the German invasion, to cope with the extreme hardships of evacuation, and to retain hope for the future of their people.

The reviewer also noted that the play's cast consisted of Jewish actors from Poland. Soviet Yiddish theaters in evacuation often hired such actors. It is possible that the play's more particularistic Jewish elements reflected the participation of Polish Jews, often characterized as "more conservative, more stubbornly Jewish, less inclined to give up their own way of life," than Jews who had undergone two decades of Soviet socialization.[185] Indeed, cultural institutions appear to have been the places where Jews from the pre-1939 USSR and Jews from the territories annexed in 1939 and 1940 interacted with one another most readily.[186] Soviet Yiddish writers and Jewish activists often recalled playing a role in helping Polish Jewish colleagues survive in the Soviet rear. For example, Esther Markish, widow of Peretz Markish, described how her husband assisted Yiddish writers from Poland:

> Markish would visit Tashkent on short visits; he would escape for a couple of days from Moscow or from the front. As soon as he would turn up in Tashkent, Jewish writers, mainly from Poland, would immediately approach him. They were so much worse off than the others; they needed assistance and protection. Once a man came who looked like his own shadow: skin and bones, in rags, in a torn soldier's overcoat, holding his pants up with a piece of rope. Markish didn't recognize him. It turned out to be [Yehezkel] Keitelman, a Yiddish writer from Poland. Indeed, he was on the verge of death from hunger, from despair.... Markish gave him his own clothes, gave him money, took him "under his wing." After Markish left for Moscow, Keitelman continued living with us for a while. Later he went off somewhere, disappeared. I knew nothing about him until I left for Israel [in 1972]. Here [in Israel] Keitelman's widow found me. He had died fairly recently. She recounted that her late husband

> had often told her about meeting Markish in Tashkent. He said that he owed [Markish] his life. At the time many Jews passed through the "Markish home." You won't remember all of them. Many of those Jews were saved. They came to Israel. And now strangers or people I have forgotten find me often, and they tell me how Markish helped them, gave them courage and hope, saved them.[187]

In a similar manner, Alla Zuskin Perelman, daughter of Veniamin Zuskin, the lead actor of the Moscow Jewish State Theater, mentioned numerous contacts between the theater and Polish Jewish actors who were looking for work and asked for help.[188] All in all, the Soviet, the newly Soviet, and the Polish Jewish elites seem to have been in contact with one another.

The perceived increased demand for culture in Yiddish invigorated writers and artists, turning them into true leaders of the Soviet Jewish community. Ida Kamińska, for example, got to perform in front of the largest audiences of her career to date. She found new celebrity, and her work mattered not only to Soviet Jews but also to refugees. In many ways, Yiddish culture actually created a new community as another form of resistance.

With regard to those between writers, actors, and other intellectuals, relations between Soviet and Polish Jews were much more strained. The Soviet press portrayed Polish Jews as poor, lost, abandoned, sick, and miserable. At the same time, their contributions to the Soviet war effort were reported widely. Such stories often came to *Eynikayt* in the form of letters and article submissions from Polish Jews themselves. In the words of one such submission, sent to *Eynikayt* in 1942, "Warsaw Jews ran away to Western Byelorussia and then evacuated to the Saratov region—20 people, liked by collective farmers. They worked on tractors, combines; a tailor became a driver; all are winners of Stakhanovite competitions."[189]

Discussing Polish Jews and the horrors they lived through enabled journalists from *Eynikayt* to discuss openly the destruction of the Jews. In fact, Polish Jews were portrayed as people rescued by the Soviet Union from destruction, which in the newspaper's portrayal was happening almost exclusively on Polish soil. Yiddish and Russian versions of these reports differed. Consider, for example, an article submitted for publication in 1943 by a Polish Jewish author:

> I left my home with heavy feelings—Jews have a hard fate, they are eternal exiles, sent around the world, they are like the leaves which fell off a tree, and now they always travel to strange new lands. But they learned to resist and now their energy, initiative, inborn qualities of these people, helped them to survive. Hitler killed their families, houses, possessions; they became lonely, and now they fight for their motherland.[190]

Resistance and fighting for the motherland are presented here as a direct consequence of the attack on Jews. In preparing the Russian translation of this piece, however, the editors took drastic measures, writing, "All these people, ordinary workers, found their place among participants in the great fight against the human enemy—the German Fascists."

During their interviews about the war, few former evacuees and deportees spoke of thriving Yiddish culture. A possible explanation for the omission is that at the time of the interviews, in the 1990s, Soviet Jews believed that this aspect of their life story would not be of interest to the interviewer. Instead, they wanted to focus on hardships, heroism, tribulations of everyday life, and strength of spirit that they and their parents maintained throughout the ordeal. Yiddish cultural life seemed secondary to most, and this perception effectively led to the omission of one of the most fascinating chapters in Jewish cultural history during the Second World War.

After the German advance was finally stopped in late 1942, and the USSR began reclaiming its territories in 1943 and 1944, evacuees began returning home. The earliest to come back were those who had been evacuated as part of an organized group or enterprise. Their organization or employer took care of their return as part of its resumption of operations at its prewar location. Some Soviet evacuees began to return to Moscow, Kharkov, Kiev, Leningrad, and Odessa. Those who had fled on their own, including most Jews, had to wait longer. Their path back was more difficult, as they had to petition the authorities for permission. Some petitioners were denied, leaving them effectively in a state of permanent exile in Siberia or Central Asia.[191] Many women had lost husbands in combat; they were stranded because they needed a man to file a petition on their behalf.[192] Those whose petitions were granted could not be certain that their former apartment would be waiting for them, or even a bed in a shelter, or a couch in a relative's room.

A significant number of evacuees chose to remain in Central Asia and Siberia after the war for a variety of reasons (e.g., better living conditions, professional advancement, the knowledge that their families did not survive, etc.). They did not consider their stay in Central Asia as an exile but rather as a second home. These were mostly Soviet-educated professionals (doctors, engineers, university professors, artists). By and large they were welcomed by local Soviet authorities, who were short of professionals and in dire need of educated people in various fields. After the war and before the collapse of the Soviet Union, many of these former evacuees were instrumental in the development of the local economy and in medical and educational institutions.

Jews, especially those from western parts of the country, faced additional challenges and hurdles. Over the course of the war, attitudes toward them had changed, in many ways for the worse. Public expressions of hostility had become more common, and the regime had become less keen to take action against them.[193] Some officials now appeared to many Jews to be using their power to deny them permission to return.[194] The Jewish Anti-Fascist Committee took up the struggle on behalf of the denied Jews with a petition of its own, sent to Molotov in May 1944:

> The Committee . . . has information that working Jews, whom the Soviet authorities temporarily evacuated to areas deep in the interior of the country, are encountering obstacles in their reevacuation [*sic*] to their native areas. Despite the fact that there are skilled cadres among the evacuees who could be extremely useful in reconstructing ruined cities and villages, they are not given the opportunity to return. . . . In view of the above, we consider it appropriate to . . . provide the opportunity to evacuated working Jews to return to their native towns, eliminating all obstacles created by certain organs of the local authorities.[195]

The committee received what Solomon Mikhoels termed "not a real answer." To be sure, no document has been uncovered suggesting that the Soviet government as a whole mandated or even encouraged discrimination of the type the committee alleged. But by the same token, local officials who engaged in the discrimination do not appear to have been rebuked, let alone to have had their decisions overturned.[196]

Overall, the return was much easier and shorter than the journey to the rear had been. Most people traveled in passenger cars with some money and food. In fact, many remember their trip home as a pleasurable experience, a time when they were filled with hope and anticipation of arrival. They were excited about victory, about expectations of seeing friends and family again, and about a return to normalcy. For most returnees, however, such expectations were quickly dashed. In addition to a generally more hostile public climate than the one they had left, and in the face of official interference in their efforts to reclaim erstwhile dwellings and possessions,[197] they came back to hometowns that the German war had emptied of their fellow Jews. Many had lost parents, grandparents, and children to the German murder campaign. Upon returning, they would listen in shock as they learned how their loved ones had died. They did not anticipate that their lives would be forever changed. They had to learn to live as a stigmatized minority. They had to mourn the killing of almost all members of their families and go on to experience job insecurity, public humiliations, denial of housing, and much more.

Yet these were the most fortunate of all Soviet Jews. Germany had marked them for death. Thanks to eclectic Soviet policies and their own heroic actions, they had remained alive, defying the heaviest of odds. With a mix of gratitude, resentment, and anxiety, they assumed their roles at the foundation of the postwar Soviet Jewish community.

ACKNOWLEDGMENTS

This book, like all the present and future volumes in the larger *Jews in the Soviet Union* project, is the product of a group effort. Its beginnings lie in a 2008 conference entitled "Soviet Jewish Soldiers, Jewish Resistance, and Jews in the USSR during the Holocaust," sponsored by the Skirball Department of Hebrew and Judaic Studies at NYU and the United States Holocaust Memorial Museum. The authors of this book were among the conference presenters, as were several other participants in the current project. That project was catalyzed by a 2015 grant, which enabled NYU's newly created Global Network for Advanced Research in Jewish Studies to undertake a comprehensive history of Soviet Jewry from the beginning to the end of the USSR. The Global Network, led by Lawrence Schiffman, Judge Abraham Lieberman Professor of Hebrew and Judaic Studies at NYU, assembled an international team of authors, advisers, archivists, and librarians, whose collective expertise is reflected in this and in the other volumes of *Jews in the Soviet Union*. Professor Schiffman's steady leadership has kept the project moving through pandemic and war, bringing it to the point where its first fruits may now be celebrated.

Drafts of various chapters were read by the authors of other volumes in the project: Elissa Bemporad, Zvi Gitelman, Deborah Yalen, and Arkadi Zeltser, as well as by four additional expert advisers: Vadim Altskan, David Fishman, Benjamin Nathans, and Jeffrey Veidlinger. All provided important criticisms and suggestions. A research support team, including, most notably, Alexander Frenkel, Efim Melamed, and Alexander Ivanov, helped procure archival and other materials from diverse locations in the former Soviet Union, including in particular documents from the Commission of the Soviet Academy of Sciences on the History of the Great Patriotic War (the Isaac Mints Collection). Ludmilla Gordon was instrumental in finding illustrations and in obtaining permission for their use.

The editorial team at NYU Press, led by Ellen Chodosh, Jennifer Hammer, Martin Coleman, and Jonathan Greenberg, showed immense patience and skill in working with the authors, as did the support staffs of the Global Network and Skirball Department, especially Kirsten Howe and Shayne Figueroa. A project of international, multilingual scope presents formidable academic, administrative, and legal challenges. These behind-the-scenes players met them all with the utmost professionalism and aplomb.

Of course, neither the authors nor any of the people mentioned above would have been able to play their roles without the surpassing encouragement and support of Eugene Shvidler, who not only underwrote Jews in the Soviet Union financially but insisted throughout on the project's scholarly independence and adherence to the highest academic standards.

Our heartfelt thanks to all.

APPENDIX

HOW MANY JEWS SERVED IN THE RED ARMY DURING THE GREAT PATRIOTIC WAR?

In Russia, until very recently, information about the ethnic composition of the Red Army has been classified. The reasons for secrecy, in general, are clear. The myth that the friendship and brotherhood of the Soviet peoples during the Second World War was one of the most important sources of victory became one of the most enduring creations of Soviet propaganda. As a result, the estimates of the number of Jews in the Soviet armed forces often cited in the historical literature—varying from 450,000 to 520,000 in the Soviet army and navy[1]—were actually logical inferences derived from statistical calculations. The most widely cited estimates—450,000 to 470,000—are based on calculations made by Yitzhak Arad,[2] which rest in turn on information about the overall size of the Red Army and its losses during the war provided by Russian historians who are part of the military and have access to the archives of the Ministry of Defense and the General Staff.[3] Civilian historians remain dependent upon the data these uniformed historians feed them from time to time.

The data come from records that despite official secrecy appear to preserve information about the ethnic composition of Red Army personnel. Those records have led a team of uniformed historians to determine that on 1 January 1943 the number of Jews in the Red Army, *excluding* the border forces (*pogranichniie voiska*) and internal security troops (*vnutrenniie voiska*), came to 130,134, or 1.54 percent of the army's personnel roll at the time. At that time 7,651 additional servicemen "of Jewish nationality" were undergoing treatment in hospitals; they made up 1.23 percent of troops in hospital care. Two years later, on 1 January 1945, there were 201,529 Jews in uniform, *including* the border forces and internal security troops. They now accounted for 1.6 percent of all soldiers. Another 10,206 were receiving treatment in hospitals—1.1 percent of the total.[4] In addition, in the study that yielded these figures, the historians placed the number of Jewish soldiers killed during the war at 138,700.[5] Assuming that the figures for 1 January 1945 did not change significantly during the final four months of the war, the total number of Jews who served in the Red Army at any time during the Great Patriotic War would come to 350,435.

However, matters are not so simple. To begin with, this estimate does not account for Jews who left military service during the war because of disability. The study that generated these figures reported a total of 2,576,000 discharged war invalids overall.[6] The basis for calculating the number of Jews among them is not obvious. Should it be the percentage of Jews among soldiers treated in hospitals or the percentage of Jews among soldiers overall? And in either case, what date should be taken as the baseline? Using the average of the percentages of Jewish soldiers in hospitals in 1943 and in 1945—1.16 percent—suggests that 29,881 Jews fell into the category of medical dischargees. By contrast, using the overall percentage of Jewish soldiers in 1945—1.6 percent—yields a figure of 41,216. Adding each figure to the estimated 350,435 Jews who had either been killed or continued to wear a uniform as of 1 January 1945 brings the total number of Jews who served at any time during the war to between 380,000 and 392,000.

In any event, it makes sense to assume that the percentage of Jews in the armed forces did not remain constant but fluctuated significantly according to the progress of the war. Month-by-month estimates contained in a study of two hundred rifle divisions of the Red Army in 1943 list Jews as making up 1.50 percent of personnel on 1 January 1943, 1.56 percent on 1 April, 1.35 percent on 1 July, and 1.28 percent on 1 January 1944.[7] The reason for the reduction is clear: as Ukraine was liberated during 1943, the population of formerly German-occupied areas was drafted into the army. There were virtually no Jews among the local population, for nearly all of them had been killed by the Nazis and their collaborators. Accordingly, the proportion of Ukrainians among soldiers serving in the divisions in question rose notably, from 11.62 percent on 1 July 1943 to 22.27 percent on 1 January 1944.[8]

However, such assumptions are no longer necessary. As this book was being prepared for publication, newly declassified data on the ethnic composition of the Red Army have finally been made available. It turns out that information about the composition of military personnel according to sociodemographic indicators was presented to the state's top leadership twice a year. The following table shows data on the number of Jews in the Red Army and their proportional share for each date:[9]

	1 January 1941	1 July 1942	1 January 1943	1 July 1943	1 January 1944	1 July 1944	1 January 1945
No. of Jews	66,279	178,152	172,118	208,925	196,576	201,039	200,552
Percentage	1.84	1.83	1.91	1.8	1.74	1.68	1.64

These data are for ground and air forces. Information about the national composition of the Soviet Navy remains unavailable. It is known, however, that the number of naval personnel ranged from 351,622 in June 1941 to 527,707 on 1 January 1945.[10] If we assume that the share of Jews in the navy was roughly the same as in the other two branches, then we should add between 6,500 and 8,700 to the figures in the table. Several thousand more Jews may have been drafted into the army or the navy between January and May 1945. For the most part, however, these additions do not drastically change the picture concerning Jews in the Soviet armed forces during the war years.

The number of Jews in the army grew by more than thirty thousand between January 1939 and the beginning of 1941. Two factors explain this sharp increase. First, the universal conscription law of 1 September 1939 canceled deferrals for university students, lowered the draft age for high school graduates to eighteen years, and eliminated exemptions from military service for social reasons. Secondly, in 1940 residents of the annexed former Polish territories were drafted. Their number included between ten thousand and thirteen thousand Polish Jews.

There are no data on the ethnic composition of the Red Army during the first year of the war. In the catastrophic defeats of 1941 and the first half of 1942, in which millions of soldiers were encircled and taken prisoner, the relevant documents were evidently either destroyed or fell into enemy hands.

It is noteworthy that until mid-1944 the proportion of Jews in the Red Army exceeded their proportion in the country's prewar population, even though the mass murders of the Nazi Holocaust led to a substantial reduction of the mobilization base.[11] The fact reflects first of all the loss of Byelorussia and Ukraine to German occupation, which kept Byelorussians and Ukrainians from joining the army. As a result, the share of the various peoples in the ranks changed significantly. As the Germans were expelled from the two republics (especially from Ukraine) during the later years of the war, the situation gradually became more "normal," and the proportion of Jews decreased. Moreover, Jews were quite heavily represented among command and control officers. In January 1939 these officers accounted for some 40 percent of Jewish servicemen.[12] Calculations based upon various declassified reports of the Ministry of Defense intended for official use along with the most recent publications show that their share was no lower over the course of the war.[13] It may have reached even 50 percent, as happened, for instance, in the Sixtieth Army of the First Ukrainian front, which liberated Auschwitz.[14]

The data in the table do not, however, allow for an exact figure of the total number of Jews who served in the Red Army during the war years because there is no indication of how many entered service during the course of the war and how many left due to death or injury. These figures are difficult to ascertain. A study by uniformed historians, based on military casualty lists, placed the number of Jews killed while serving in the Red Army at 142,500.[15] The publishers of this estimate explained that the investigators made their determination "using proportionality coefficients (in percentages) . . . derived from the roll of Red Army servicemen according to sociodemographic characteristics as of 1 January 1943, 1944, and 1945."[16] The sociodemographic characteristics were not specified. Nor was it explained why, knowing the number of soldiers listed in the personnel roll on three specific dates, the investigators saw fit to extrapolate their estimates concerning Jews for the entire period of the war. Clearly they took the share of Jews in the army as of 1 January 1945 (1.64 percent, as indicated in the table), multiplied it by the total number of Red Army personnel killed (8,668.400), and came up with the rounded figure of 142,500.

Needless to say, the estimate is extremely rough. Jewish losses may have been higher or lower by a considerable amount. It appears, for example, on the basis of data concerning the wounded and sick in hospitals, that during the years 1943–1945 Jewish casualties were below average. On 1 January

1943 Jews accounted for 1.23 percent of the hospitalized, 1.47 percent on 1 January 1944, and 1.19 percent on 1 January 1945.[17] The proportion of the Jewish wounded was significantly lower than the proportion of Jews in the army on each of these dates. Since the ratio of wounded or sick to killed was approximately 2.5:1, it is safe to assume that the percentage of Jewish dead was lower as well. That assumption is bolstered by the exceptionally high proportion of officers among Jewish soldiers. Officers among killed or missing soldiers amounted to about 8 percent, in contrast to 17.6 percent for sergeants and 74.4 percent for privates.[18]

There are no available data concerning losses among Jewish servicemen during the first year and a half of the war—precisely the interval when the Red Army suffered its greatest number of casualties. According to official Russian figures, irrecoverable losses (killed and missing) between 22 June and 31 December 1941 came to 3,137,673, including 2,335,482 missing (an overwhelming number of them taken prisoner), with an additional 3,258,216 during 1942 (1,515,221 missing). The number of prisoners was undoubtedly much higher: German sources, more reliable on this point, report that by mid-December 1941, 3.35 million Red Army soldiers had been taken captive, more than a million more than noted in Soviet documents.[19] The figures about prisoners are significant because, although the fate of Soviet prisoners in general was tragic enough—nearly 60 percent perished—Soviet Jewish POWs were annihilated altogether. Of more than 1.5 million Soviet prisoners who returned home by 1 March 1946 there were only 4,762 returning Jews.[20] If we assume that the proportion of Jews among Soviet POWs in 1941 and 1942 corresponded to the share of Jews in the army on 1 January 1941 (1.84 percent), then the number among them who died may have ranged from seventy thousand (using the lower Soviet figures) to ninety thousand (using the German figures). However, it would be more correct to calculate the percentage of Jews in the Soviet military in 1941–1942 without taking Polish Jews into account, because on 22 July 1941 these soldiers, along with other military personnel from the annexed territories who were conscripted in 1939 and 1940, were transferred to labor battalions. Removing those Jews from the equation would yield a share of Jews in the army of around 1.5 percent, meaning that the number of Jews killed after being taken captive could have reached seventy-two thousand or more, with total Jewish military losses (killed in battle and died in captivity) in 1941–1942 alone exceeding a hundred thousand. In any event, it is clear that the greatest losses among Jewish soldiers and officers in the Red Army came during the first eighteen months of the war.

Toward the beginning of the war, Jews also served in several volunteer or quasi-volunteer formations. The largest of these was the People's Militia (*narodnoe opolchenie*).[21] The ranks of the People's Militia in the four large cities of Moscow, Leningrad, Odessa, Kiev, together with the cities and towns of Byelorussia, numbered 413,000 people, of whom nearly half lived in Moscow (160,000) and Leningrad (135,000).[22] No statistics on the nationality distribution of *opolchenie* members have survived; membership lists were destroyed in 1941. Nevertheless, the available fragmentary information permits a fairly confident inference that the proportion of Jews in these units was significantly higher than the Jewish conscription norm for the military as a whole. To begin with, the Jewish recruitment pool was markedly greater. At the beginning of the war the four large cities were home to more than a million Jews, who accounted for 7.35 percent of their combined populations, as opposed to only 1.78 percent in the USSR overall.[23] Moreover, the militia drew upon volunteers who were beyond conscription age; some, especially in Moscow and in Leningrad, received training in militia units that were eventually incorporated into the regular army. Notably, Jewish students were heavily concentrated in those two cities, and they made up an even higher percentage of the population there than did Jews in general.[24] Students were among the most prominent volunteers for the *opolchenie* during the first weeks of the war.

In sum, it appears that around four hundred thousand Jews served in the Red Army during the years of the Great Patriotic War.

NOTES

The symbol (E) denotes an online resource that can be found in the Electronic Repositories and Resources section of the Bibliography.

PROLOGUE

1 "Khronika," *Pravda*, 4 May 1939, 6. The front page of the same day's newspaper contained, in the lower left-hand corner, the three-line text of an "Order of the Presidium of the Supreme Soviet … Concerning the Appointment of Comrade V. M. Molotov as People's Commissar for Foreign Affairs." The order was dated 3 May 1939. "Ukaz prezidiuma Verkhnogo Soveta SSSR … ," *Pravda*, 4 May 1939, 1.

2 Maiskii, *Diaries*, 526. See also Nekrich, *Pariahs*, 106–10; Holroyd-Doveton, *Litvinov*, 355–56.

3 According to the 1897 Imperial Russian Census, of Belostok's 62,993 residents, 41,905 (nearly two-thirds) were Jews.

4 Pope, *Maxim Litvinoff*, 37–38.

5 Pope, *Maxim Litvinoff*, 38–40, 45–46, 51–54, 72–77, 84–87, 96–97, 102–13. See also Phillips, *Between the Revolution and the West*, 1–15.

6 Two Jews had served as heads of government in major European powers—Luigi Luzzatti in Italy (1910–1911) and Léon Blum in France (1936–1938). Two others—Otto Bauer in Austria (1918–1919) and Walter Rathenau in Germany (1922)—had been foreign ministers. The Belgian statesman Paul Hymans, son of a Jewish father and a Protestant mother, had enjoyed a long career as his country's foreign minister (1918–1920, 1924–1925, 1927–1935) and as president of the Assembly of the League of Nations (1920–1921, 1932–1933).

7 The argument was made obliquely in 1937 by the Columbia University historian Salo Baron, who compared the Jewish situation in the USSR with the one in the United States: "Were there no political discrimination, the Jews might hope to

obtain a very large part of . . . governmental appointments. . . . Indeed, in the Soviet Union, where no discrimination is practiced, they constituted in 1926 fully one-twelfth of Russian officialdom. . . . In the United States, the recent more active participation of the Jews in public affairs has aroused exaggerated suspicions concerning the number of Jewish officials. The conspicuous positions occupied by the Secretary of the Treasury [Henry Morgenthau, Jr.] and two Supreme Court justices [Louis Brandeis and Benjamin Cardozo] must not blind us to the fact that in the lower ranks the Jewish share is much smaller. Were statistics available, they would probably show that the total share of the Jews among the federal, state, and municipal employees is less than 4 percent." Baron, *Social and Religious History*, 2:373–74. One other Jew had previously held a cabinet appointment in the United States—Oscar Straus, secretary of commerce and labor in the administration of Theodore Roosevelt, 1906–1909. Both American cabinet secretaries were members of prominent, wealthy families and received elite educations (unlike Litvinov, who did not complete secondary school).

8 Haslam, *Soviet Foreign Policy*, 2–4, 12–13, 118–20; Gorodetsky, "Formulation of Soviet Foreign Policy," 41–42.

9 Uldricks, "Russia and Europe," 80–83.

10 A Russian translation of Hitler's *Mein Kampf* was distributed to Soviet politburo members in the spring of 1933, shortly following the Nazi consolidation of power. On the reception of the book's aggressive tone toward the USSR, see Nekrich, *Pariahs*, 70–82. See also Haslam, *Soviet Union*, 6–10; Govrin, *HeHebet haYehudi*, 69–72.

11 Uldricks, "Soviet Security Policy," 71.

12 Litvinov explained the line at a meeting of the USSR Central Executive Committee in December 1933: "Insuring peace cannot depend on our efforts alone; it requires the cooperation and assistance of other states. While striving therefore to establish and maintain friendly relations with all states, we pay special attention to strengthening relations to the maximum with those among them who, like us, give an indication of their ardent desire to preserve peace and who are prepared to oppose violators of peace. . . . In Germany a *coup d'état* has brought to power a new party . . . , [whose] conception of foreign policy is . . . expand eastward by fire and sword." "Vystuplenie Narodnogo Komissara Inostrannykh Del SSSR M. M. Litvinova na IV sessii TsIK SSSR 6-go sozyva," 29 December 1933, *DVP 1933*, 16:786, 791–92.

13 Haslam, *Soviet Union*, 1–2.

14 Fischer, *Men and Politics*, 130; Roberts, "Maxim Litvinov," 376–77. For a selection of speeches, see Litvinov, *Against Aggression*.

15 This has long been how most historians have explained Litvinov's fall. Since the opening of Soviet archives, additional considerations have been noted. Some scholars have argued that the dismissal indicated only a change in tactics, not in strategy; it was intended as a warning to Britain and France, whose faith in appeasement was already on the wane, that the Soviets had the option of seeking rapprochement with Germany against them. Others have noted changing

political dynamics within the Soviet regime. For various views, see Roberts, "Fall of Litvinov;" Reiss, "Fall of Litvinov;" and the comments by Gabriel Gorodetsky in Maiskii, *Complete Diaries*, 2:527–29.

16 Born in a small town some eight hundred kilometers northeast of Moscow, Molotov (originally Skriabin) had little experience with Europe at the time of his appointment and commanded no language besides Russian. From the early 1920s he had been closely allied with Stalin. In 1930 he had been named chairman of the Council of People's Commissars (effectively the head of government of the USSR). In that position he had been deeply implicated in the state-directed violence of agricultural collectivization and the purges. The most accessible recent scholarly biography is Watson, *Molotov*.

17 Quoted in Watson, *Molotov*, 155. For Molotov's views on Jewish matters, see Watson, *Molotov*, 41, 151.

18 [Molotov], *Molotov Remembers*, 192.

19 According to some accounts, Stalin made this understanding explicit in his conversation with Litvinov that resulted in the foreign minister's dismissal. Holroyd-Doveton, *Litvinov*, 356. For hints of Soviet consideration of a German alliance before 1939, see Nekrich, *Pariahs*, 63–114.

1. NEW LANDS, NEW SUBJECTS

1 On 3 February 1933, less than a week after becoming Germany's chancellor, Hitler told his top military commanders that once the new regime consolidated power, it would likely work toward "conquering new living space (*Lebensraum*) in the East and its ruthless Germanization." "Ausführungen des Reichskanzlers Hitler von den Befehlshabern des Heeres und der Marine . . . ," 3 February 1933, in Vogelsang, "Dokumente," 435. For parallel accounts of this speech, see Wirsching, "'Man kann nur Boden germanisieren'."

2 Weinberg, *Hitler's Foreign Policy*, 52–61.

3 Müller, *Enemy in the East*, 33–38; Karski, *Great Powers*, 170–72; Kamiński and Zacharias, *Polityka zagraniczna*, 156–57, 192–93. Germany had lost several of its eastern provinces to the newly-established Polish Republic as a result of the 1919 Treaty of Versailles. Revision of the treaty, including its border with Poland, had been the centerpiece of Germany's foreign policy between the two world wars.

4 Cienciala, "Foreign Policy," 130–39; Karski, *Great Powers*, 212–18.

5 Melzer, *Ma'avak*, 289–94, 313–38.

6 Melzer, *Ma'avak*, 55. See also Trębacz, *Nie tylko Palestyna*.

7 The most comprehensive treatment of these themes from both Polish and Jewish perspectives is Melzer, *Ma'avak*, 165–360. On violence, see Żyndul, *Zajścia antyżydowskie*.

8 "Note Concerning Ambassador Lipski's Conversation with Reich Minister of Foreign Affairs von Ribbentrop," 24 October 1938, in Jędrzejewicz, *Diplomat in Berlin*, 453. In return Germany had asked the Polish government to

recognize German sovereignty in the Free City of Danzig and to allow German extraterritorial control of a highway linking Danzig with East Prussia across Polish territory. The Anti-Comintern Pact was an agreement between Germany, Japan, Italy, and Spain for mutual consultation in the event of threatening activity in any of them by the Communist International (Comintern), an association of communist parties from throughout the world, directed from Moscow.

9 Cienciala, *Poland*, 5–8; Kamiński and Zacharias, *Polityka zagraniczna*, 233.

10 "Statement by the Prime Minister in the House of Commons," 31 March 1939, Avalon Project (E), 20th Century Documents, British War Blue Book.

11 See, for example, the statement by British Prime Minister Neville Chamberlain in the House of Commons, 23 March 1939: "His Majesty's Government have already made clear that the recent actions of the German Government have raised the question whether that Government is not seeking by successive steps to dominate Europe, and perhaps even to go further than that.... [W]e cannot submit to a procedure under which independent States are subjected to such pressure under threat of force as to be obliged to yield up their independence, and we are resolved by all means in our power to oppose attempts, if they should be made, to put such a procedure into operation" "United Kingdom, Parliament (E), Commons, 23 March 1939 (Volume 345), Oral Answers to Questions, European Situation, column 1462.

12 Reference to Stalin's speech to the Eighteenth Congress of the Communist Party of the Soviet Union, 10 March 1939, in which he advised to "take care not to allow warmongers who are used to stoking the fire with someone else's hands to drag our country into conflicts." "Otchetni doklad t. Stalina na XVIII s'ezde partii o rabote TsK VKP(b)," [Union of Soviet Socialist Republics], XVIII S'ezd, 15. In most English versions "warmongers" are described as being "accustomed to have others pull the chestnuts out of the fire for them."

13 "The German Chargé in the Soviet Union (Tippelskirch) to the German Foreign Office," 4 May 1939, in Sontag and Beddie, *Nazi-Soviet Relations*, 2–3.

14 Roberts, *Soviet Union*, 72–81.

15 The negotiations are described in detail in Watson, "Molotov's Apprenticeship."

16 "The German Ambassador in the Soviet Union (Schulenberg) to the German Foreign Office," 4 August 1939, in Sontag and Beddie, *Nazi-Soviet Relations*, 41.

17 The commander-in-chief of the Polish Armed Forces, Edward Rydz-Śmigły, explained Poland's position: "The entrance of the Soviet army into our territory does not by itself guarantee its active participation in the war, yet it is certain that it would never leave those territories. The Red Army would be followed by the whole [Soviet] administration.... The *passage* would immediately lead to the occupation of a part of the country and our complete dependence upon the Soviets." Quoted in Kornat, "Choosing," 785. Some scholars argue that the Polish attitude merely provided the Soviets with a pretext to do what they had already decided to do—conclude an agreement with Hitler. For an exposition of this position, including an exhaustive alternate reconstruction of Soviet thinking, see Cienciala, "Nazi-Soviet Pact."

18 Watson, "Molotov's Apprenticeship," 715.

19 "Treaty of Nonaggression Between Germany and the Union of Soviet Socialist Republics," 23 August 1939, in Sontag and Beddie, *Nazi-Soviet Relations*, 76–77.

20 See, for example, *Keesing's Contemporary Archives* 3 (no. 8, August 1939):3693 ("Increasing Gravity of Political Situation"); *Los Angeles Times*, 24 August 1939 ("Nazi-Soviet Pact Signed: Europe on War Brink"); *Japan Times and Mail*, 23 August 1939 ("Soviet-Reich Pact Shocks All Europe").

21 For assessments of Germany's strategic situation, see Rossino, *Hitler*, 6–9; Müller, *Enemy in the East*, 148–54. For a contemporary description of popular attitudes see Shirer, *Berlin Diary*, 138–39 (24 August 1939).

22 *New York Times*, 18 September 1939 ("Russians Drive 40 Miles into Poland, Defense Weak"). See also Erickson, "Red Army's March," 12–16.

23 Watson, *Molotov*, 169; Roberts, *Soviet Union*, 89–91.

24 "Secret Additional Protocol," in Sontag and Beddie, *Nazi-Soviet Relations*, 78. Lithuania was assigned to the German sphere, while Latvia and Estonia were assigned to the Soviets. The protocol also listed Finland as one of the Baltic states in whose political future the USSR had an interest, as it did the Romanian province of Bessarabia.

25 Roberts, *Soviet Union*, 92–100. The Soviets justified their invasion, in Molotov's words, as a move to protect their "blood brothers, the Ukrainians and White Russians living on Polish territory," who had been "abandoned to their fate" and "left without protection"—studiously avoiding any hint that it was the Germans from whom those "blood brothers" now needed protection.

26 "German-Soviet Boundary and Friendship Treaty," 28 September 1939, Avalon Project (E), Document Collections, Nazi-Soviet Relations 1939–1941. Among other things, the treaty moved Lithuania into the Soviet sphere of influence.

27 The Polish census of 1931 counted 1.079 million people in the affected territories who claimed Yiddish as their mother tongue and 1.269 million who listed their religion as "Mosaic." The number of Jews was generally estimated to have grown to approximately 1.25–1.3 million by 1939. An additional 145,000–300,000 Jews are estimated to have fled the German-occupied regions into the Soviet zone during the first months of the war. See Edele and Warlik, "Saved," 98; Żaron, *Ludność polska*, 66–73; Altshuler, *Soviet Jewry* (1998), 323–26; Lestschinsky, *Dos sovetishe Idntum*, 366; Arad, *Toledot haSho'ah*, 1:106; Karpenkina, *Sovetizatsiia*, 70–71.

28 The Ukrainian National Republic controlled territories of the former Russian Empire intermittently from late 1918 through late 1919, when it went into exile. The West Ukrainian National Republic claimed sovereignty over the former Habsburg East Galicia. It was able to establish local administrations and to sustain military action against its Polish rivals during approximately the same interval, after which it, too, formed an exile government. Subtelny, *Ukraine*, 360–62, 368–75.

29 Zweig, *Poland*, 31–33; Gorecki, *Poland*, 21–23.

30 On difficulties of definition see Tomaszewski, "Stosunki narodowościowe," 146–54. For examples of liminal cases, see Snyder, *Reconstruction*, 54–56, 123–32.

31 The analogy between the Polish state and a corporation was drawn in some detail by one of Poland's best-known historians, Olgierd Górka, in 1937. Górka, *Naród a państwo*, 66–98.

32 Whereas in Poland peasants accounted for slightly more than 50 percent of the population, in the *kresy wschodnie* nearly three quarters of the inhabitants belonged to the peasantry. Żarnowski, *Społeczeństwo*, 342. For additional indicators of the borderlands' relative underdevelopment compared to areas west of the Polish "ethnographic frontier" see Sword, "Soviet Economic Policy," 86.

33 See Landau and Tomaszewski, *Zarys historii gospodarczej*, 289–90. It is not certain that willful discrimination was the primary cause of the region's poverty. Disparities between west and east in industrial development and the capitalization of agriculture began in the nineteenth century as a result of differences in the economic policies of the three partitioning powers. See Gerschenkron, "Russia;" Bujak, "Rozwój gospodarczy." Political relations in the Second Polish Republic impeded measures to mitigate the imbalance. Kagan, "Agrarian Regime."

34 Soviet spokesmen designated three quarters as Ukrainian or Byelorussian, with Poles and Jews making up a scant 8 percent each. "Extracts from Commissar Molotov's speech on the partition of Poland and Soviet Foreign Policy made at the V extraordinary session of the Supreme Council of the USSR," 31 October 1939, *Documents on Polish-Soviet Relations* 1:68. Polish prewar figures gave Poles a plurality of 43 percent. Żaroń, *Ludność polska*, 67.

35 See Martin, *Affirmative Action Empire*, 9–13.

36 Following the revolution of October 1917, separate Bolshevik parties took power in Russia, Ukraine, and Byelorussia (as well as in Armenia, Azerbaijan, and Georgia). In December 1922 the Bolshevik-dominated workers' councils in those locations agreed to form a union of purportedly equal states: the Union of Soviet Socialist Republics. The constitution of the USSR, adopted in 1924, guaranteed each of the constituent republics the right to secede, thereby acknowledging their theoretical sovereignty.

37 In the Byelorussian Republic, Polish and Yiddish had also been designated official languages, offering legal recognition of the unit's ethnically mixed character.

38 See Roberts, *Soviet Union*, 92–100.

39 For details of the annexation see, inter alia, Marples, *Stalinism in Ukraine*, 25–26. In the newly created National Assembly of Western Ukraine, ethnic Ukrainians accounted for more than 90 percent of the deputies; the equivalent body in the more ethnically mixed Western Byelorussia was composed two-thirds of ethnic Byelorussians, with the remaining third divided among Poles, Jews, Ukrainians, Russians, and others. Wróbel, "Class War," 29. Despite annexation, residents of the new western regions of the two republics could not cross the old border except with NKVD permission. Karpenkina, *Sovetizatsiia*, 54.

40 Subtelny, *Ukraine*, 455. Byelorussian was introduced as a language of elementary and secondary instruction; Żaroń, *Ludność polska*, 99.

41 Marples, *Stalinism in Ukraine*, 27–33.
42 Karpenkina, "'Kvartirnyi vopros'"; Gross, *Revolution*, 189–90.
43 Estimates of the number of Poles deported vary widely. In February 1940 anywhere between 140,000 and 220,000 civilians were dispatched in boxcars to remote settlements in Siberia and the Arctic regions of European Russia. Most of the deportees were Polish landowners or state officials. At least 180,000 more civilians, and perhaps as many as 860,000, were carried off in the three later expulsions (April 1940, June 1940, and June 1941). These included mainly the families of deportees from the first action, together with businessmen, professionals, and refugees from German-occupied western Poland. For divergent figures and discussion of the sources from which they are derived see Jolluck, *Exile and Identity*, 9–16; Hryciuk, "Victims;" Wróbel, "Class War," 21–28; Kochanski, *Eagle Unbowed*, 133–39; Litvak, *Pelitim*, 136–37. The last three deportations encompassed varying numbers of Jews, along with some Ukrainians and Byelorussians. On the Jewish deportees, see below, at nn. 193-207. The ethnic distribution for all for deportations has been estimated at 52 percent Poles, 30 percent Jews, and 18 percent others. See Karpenkina, *Sovetizatsiia*, 104. Several hundred thousand more Poles, including prisoners of war, victims of mass arrest sentenced to labor camps, and voluntary migrants in search of employment, also left the annexed territories during the same time period. See Gross, *Revolution*, 145–51, 190–95; Żaroń, *Ludność polska*, 117–36. About twenty-thousand Ukrainians from the annexed territories were also moved by force to older parts of Soviet Ukraine in order to compensate for labor shortages there. See Marples, "Ukrainians in Eastern Poland," 239. On the role of deportations in Soviet policy in the annexed territories, see Karpenkina, *Sovetizatsiia*, 99–100.
44 Beginning in 1933 the Polish minority in the original (eastern) Ukrainian and Byelorussian Soviet republics had been subjected to vicious measures, including mass executions, arguably aimed at eliminating the Polish populations from those lands altogether. More than 140,000 Poles (nearly one quarter of the entire Polish minority in the USSR) were arrested in the so-called Polish Operation of 1937–1938, of whom more than 111,000 were put to death. See Snyder, *Bloodlands*, 89–105.
45 This is not to say that ethnic considerations did not influence Soviet actions. See Wróbel, "Class War," 40–42.
46 Molotov, *Soviet Union*, 25.
47 Molotov, *Soviet Union*, 70.
48 "Tretii piatiletnii plan razvitiia narodnogo khoziaistva SSSR (1938–1942 g.g.)," in *Vazhneishie resheniia*, 3.
49 Marples, *Stalinism in Ukraine*, 29–41.
50 Viola, *Peasant Rebels*, esp. 234–41; Subtelny, *Ukraine*, 409–13.
51 Marples, "Ethnic Issues," 42–45. On the famine, see Snyder, *Bloodlands*, 24–58.
52 Shkandrij, "Ukrainization, Terror, and Famine," 433.
53 Engel, *Assassination*, 94–95; Motyl, *Turn to the Right*, 174–75.

54 Such attitudes were reflected in a collection of Ukrainian testimonies assembled in Lwów in fall 1941, shortly following the German conquest of the city, and published in Rudnytska, *Zakhidnia Ukraina*. See also Rozenblat, "Zapadniie oblasti," 53–54.

55 See Melzer, *Ma'avak*, 128–32, 303–12; Żarnowski, *Społeczeństwo*, 391–95.

56 For an expanded discussion see, inter alia, Levin, *Tekufah*, 24–34.

57 For an early effort at comparison, see Lestschinsky, *Dos sovetishe Idntum*, 374–76.

58 Beginning in 1933, Soviet citizens carried obligatory internal identity documents (passports) that listed their "nationality" (*national'nost'*). The term was an ethnic designation, not a political one: Soviet citizens were divided into more than one hundred "nationalities," of which "Jew" was one. Other "nationalities" included Chechen, Tatar, Kalmyk, Bashkir, and Volga German, along with Russian, Ukrainian, and Byelorussian. National status did not necessarily carry with it any organized, recognized representation of the group vis-à-vis the state.

59 See p. 6.

60 Most of the evidence comes from contemporaneous and retrospective Jewish first-person accounts. A comprehensive archival analysis illuminating the manner in which the Soviet blueprint was implemented from the perspective of Soviet policymakers and officials has yet to be undertaken. For preliminary work regarding Western Byelorussia, see Karpenkina, *Sovetizatsiia*, 132–38.

61 Mahler, *Yehudei Polin*, 42. "Occupationally active" people were defined as those not dependent upon support from their families. Marcus, *History*, 32.

62 For details, see Mahler, *Yehudei Polin*, 37.

63 Marcus, *History*, 439. These and subsequent figures are for the entire Polish Republic. For the category definitions, see Marcus, *History*, 30–34.

64 Mahler, *Yehudei Polin*, 51.

65 Marcus, *History*, 440. Others measures suggested that Jewish income per capita was slightly higher than that of non-Jews. On the difficulties of measuring and reasons for the discrepancies among different measures, see Marcus, *History*, 43–47.

66 Mahler, *Yehudei Polin*, 194.

67 Marcus, *History*, 47.

68 For a description of this group, with emphasis on Jewish industrialists from Białystok, see Lestschinsky, *Oyfn rand*, 218–32.

69 Levin, *Tekufah*, 74.

70 Klementynowski, "Dos idishe lebn," 84. In 1921, 89 percent of Białystok factories were owned by Jews. Wróbel, "Na równi pochyłej," 169.

71 Kahan, *Unter di sovietishe himlen*, 19; Bender, *Mul mavet*, 74. Similar behavior was noted elsewhere in the newly acquired territories; Lestschinsky, *Sovetishe Idntum*, 373; Levin, *Tekufah*, 74–75. Figures for Jews actually arrested as class enemies have yet to be located, but preliminary indications point to a very low number. Of 31,629 indexed testimonies at the USC Shoah Foundation Institute for Visual History and Education in which the interviewee mentioned the word "Soviet," 17,287 contain the words "Soviet" and "deportation." Of

those, only six contain the additional word "capitalist" and one the additional word "bourgeois." Nine testimonies contain the words "Soviet," "arrest," and "capitalist"; three mention "Soviet," "arrest," and "bourgeois." No testimony employs the phrase "class enemy." The total number of Jews arrested in Western Ukraine and Western Byelorussia for any reason before June 1941 was 23,600; Edele and Warlik, "Saved," 105. For reasons discussed below, it seems likely that most of these involved political behavior.

72 Weiss, "Some Problems," 82; Weiss, "Borysław," 93; Weiss, "Drohobycz," 163. The oil industry centered in the two towns had been a major force in the global petroleum market before the First World War, providing upward of 5 percent of total global production. Marcus, *History*, 74. On the reorganization of production and distribution under the Soviets, see Baran, "Ekonomicheskiie preobrazovaniia," 161–62.

73 Nazaroff, "Soviet Oil," 81–82.

74 Spector, *Sho'at yehudei Vohlin*, 33; Klevan, "Rovnah," 197.

75 For examples of varying approaches see Levin, *Tekufah*, 75–76; Weiss, "Some Problems," 85–88; Fatal-Knaani, *Zo lo otah Grodnah*, 86–89; Bender, *Mul mavet*, 74; Bartov, *Anatomy*, 142–43; Redlich, *Together*, 85.

76 Rozenblat, "Zapadniie oblasti," 48.

77 Karpenkina, *Sovetizatsiia*, 154–58; Lestschinsky, *Sovetishe Idntum*, 373.

78 Baran, "Ekonomicheskiie preobrazovaniia," 169–70; Weiss, "Some Problems," 85; Bender, *Mul mavet*, 73; Fatal-Knaani, *Yehudei Rovnah*, 85.

79 Levin, *Tekufah*, 76; Yonas, *Ashan*, 55; Sword, "Soviet Economic Policy," 88–89.

80 Estimates of the real difference in purchasing power range from 7:1 (Sword, "Soviet Economic Policy," 87) to 12:1 (Marples, *Stalinism*, 26). For the prewar exchange rate, see Baran, "Ekonomicheskiie preobrazovaniia," 156.

81 Weiss, "Some Problems," 86; Cholawski, *Al neharot haNieman*, 40; Sword, "Soviet Economic Policy," 88; Rozenblat, "Zapadniie oblasti," 55–56.

82 See, for example, the testimony of Eliahu Damesek, a printer from Lida in Byelorussia, whose shop was combined with four others to form a single state-run printing house. Damesek helped supervise the process. Yad Vashem Archives, Jerusalem, Israel, O3/981, 7.

83 Soviet industrial investment in Western Ukraine between annexation and the German invasion in June 1941 totaled 700 million rubles ($132 million at the time, equivalent to $2.3 billion in 2018). Baran, "Ekonomicheskiie preobrazovaniia," 162. On training courses, see Levin, *Tekufah*, 96–97.

84 Weiss, "Some Problems," 91–93. In Lwów, 13,500 Jews are reported to have sought work in the Donets Basin (ought of a total Jewish population of one hundred thousand). See also Jolluck, *Exile and Identity*, 291–92n25.

85 Levin, *Tekufah*, 92–96.

86 Karpenkina, *Sovetizatsiia*, 160; Weiss, "Some Problems," 97–98.

87 For excerpts from contemporary letters see Fatal-Knaani, *Yehudei Rovnah*, 127–31; Levin, *Tekufah*, 100–101. Memoirs that dwell extensively on economic hardship include Zak, *Knekht*, 1:88–91; Kahan, *Unter di sovietishe himlen*, 20–22.

88 For data on wages and prices, see Weiss, "Some Problems," 100–103; Levin, *Tekufah beSograyim*, 98, 103; Fatal-Knaani, *Zo lo otah Grodnah*, 91; Karpenkina, *Sovetizatsiia*, 86.

89 Karpenkina, *Sovetizatsiia*, 138–54.

90 Karpenkina, "'Kvartirnyi vopros'," 84, 88–92. For an extended description of the experience of a family forced to share its home with a Soviet administrator, see Banet, *BeTsel korato*, 84–88.

91 Levin, *Tekufah*, 101–102.

92 Fuks, *A vanderung*, 52. See also Weiss, "Some Problems," 102–103. Data for estimating the extent to which women entered the workforce have yet to be compiled. It is also not clear how great a change this phenomenon represented for Jewish society in the region, as women there had long played an active role in economic life. See Hyman, "Gender and the Jewish Family," 31–34.

93 The following assessment, offered in 1943 by two brothers from the town of Głębokie, in what had been the far northeast corner of Poland, appears fairly typical of Jewish testimonies offered in close temporal proximity to the events described: "The greater portion of the Jews falls into line right away in the *arteli*, in the bureaucracy, in the economic units, etc. The richer Jews see their real estate nationalized . . . , but even they fall into line, and things aren't so bad. Life becomes normal (*dos lebn naturalizirt zikh*)." Rajok and Rajok, "Khurbn Glubok," 37–38. Cf. the comments of a Jew from Łomża, in the westernmost reaches of the annexed territories, on conditions in the vicinity during the period of Soviet rule: "The lodgings of the wealthy were confiscated and emptied of their residents. Only the poor were favored. . . . The movable belongings of the wealthy were seized as well. But everyone who wanted to work for [the Soviets] found work. The salary was meagre, to be sure, sufficient for a spare, hand-to-mouth existence. . . . [But the Soviets] didn't make their regime too onerous and were not too severe. Basically, they demanded work. 'If you work, you'll live,' was their slogan. [If you did,] you could arrange your life and behave as you saw fit." Scharfstein, "BeSevivot Lomzah," 73.

94 Lestschinsky, *Sovetishe Idntum*, 373. The observer was a prominent Jewish statistician and demographer who grew up near Kiev and left the Soviet Union in 1921. His remarks were part of a 1941 study of conditions for Jews in the USSR commissioned by the Institute for Jewish Affairs in New York, the research arm of the World Jewish Congress. They were based mainly on close reading of the Soviet press, including Yiddish-language publications.

95 The figure of one-third has been proposed for all of Poland, but it is tenuous; see Heller, *On the Edge*, 324n1. Jews from the *kresy* tended on the whole to be more religiously conservative than Jews from central and western Poland.

96 See Pipes, *Russia*, 337–68.

97 Gershoni, *Yehudim*, 148–49; Levin, *Tekufah*, 177.

98 Levin, *Tekufah*, 178–79. Local variations have been noted. According to a report from Łomża, for example, "Orthodox Jews who wished to observe the commandments were not persecuted [at work] . . . and were not discriminated

against in favor of the irreligious who had given up observance. There was one very observant young man, for example, who did not wish to violate the Sabbath by working; he was given a job as a building watchman." Scharfstein, "BeSevivot Lomzah," 73.

99 Article 124 of the 1936 Constitution of the USSR stipulated that "the church in the USSR is separate from the state" and that "freedom to maintain religious cults and freedom of antireligious propaganda is recognized for all citizens." "Konstitutsiia (Osnovnoi zakon) Soiuza Sovetskikh Sotsialisticheskikh Respublik . . . ," 5 December 1936, Russian Federation, Sait konstitutsii (E), Istoriia, Konstitutsii SSSR i RSFSR (1918–1978).

100 Levin, *Tekufah*, 180. In some places the redirection of synagogues to alternate uses was carried out in response to an ostensible demand from local Jews, instigated by town authorities. See, for example, Nadav, "Pinsk," 294.

101 Levin, *Tekufah*, 178, 182. On the status of Jewish religious communities under Polish rule see Ringel, "Ustawodawstwo," 245–46.

102 Each slaughterer in a state-owned house was issued an individual stamp for all meat prepared under his supervision. Local Jews knew whose stamp indicated a kosher process. See Levin, *Tekufah*, 184.

103 Possibilities also existed for importing *matsot* from abroad. See Levin, *Tekufah*, 184. The writer Moshe Grossman recalled that before Passover 1940, women could be seen in the streets of Białystok carrying *matsot* in small baskets. He did not say how they had been obtained, but he noted that a kilogram cost twenty-eight rubles. Gris, *In farkisheftn land*, 1:82.

104 Levin, *Tekufah*, 185; Gershoni, *Yehudim*, 147.

105 Levin, *Tekufah*, 186.

106 Levin, *Tekufah*, 185–86. Legality meant that no criminal penalties were attached to conducting or participating in these ceremonies. See Gershoni, *Yehudim*, 94–95. However, the state did not recognize Jewish marriages, and rabbis were not empowered to register Jewish births. Also, the forced closure of ritual baths hindered observance of the immersion requirements of the marriage ritual.

107 Gershoni, *Yehudim*, 146; Levin, *Tekufah*, 180.

108 Gershoni, *Yehudim*, 146–47. In some places Soviet security forces appear to have believed that synagogues and Hasidic courts were convenient places for unlawful political discussions and periodically questioned rabbis and *rebbes* about who attended and what they discussed. Levin, *Tekufah*, 181, 187.

109 For example, Evyon, "Shetei peredot," 690: "Old people still wore *kapotes* and prayed in the synagogue, but the young people, and even many of the middle-aged, refrained from going, even though no official pressure was brought upon them."

110 Levin, *Tekufah*, 182–83; Gershoni, *Yehudim*, 145–47.

111 For an example of the former, see the letter by a woman from a village near Białystok, 21 October 1940, quoted in Levin, *Tekufah*, 179; for one of the latter, see Frum, "Geto Lomzah," 79.

112 Epstein, "Mir," 116–17; Seidman, "Yeshivat 'Ets Hayim,'" 238.

113 Rabinowicz, "Yeshivat Lomzhah," 226–27; Ben-Mordechai, "Metivta rabta," 335; Bauer, "Jewish Baranowicze," 103.
114 For a description of these institutions and the range of their activities see Marcus, *History*, 123–62.
115 Levin, *Tekufah*, 181. NKVD (*Narodnyi komissariat vnutrennikh del'*—People's Commissariat for Internal Affairs) controlled all law enforcement in the USSR, including the secret police, for which its name frequently functions as a metonym.
116 Yehezkeli, *Hatsalat haRebbe*, 17–22.
117 Rozenblat, "My, religioznye evrei," 378, 380.
118 See Frost, *Schooling*, 23–26.
119 "Konstitutsiia (Osnovnoi zakon) Soiuza Sovetskikh Sotsialisticheskikh Respublik . . . ," 5 December 1936, Russian Federation, Sait konstitutsii (E), Istoriia, Konstitutsii SSSR i RSFSR (1918–1978).
120 The greatest number of pupils ever recorded in Yiddish-language schools in all of interwar Poland did not exceed 23,000; by the 1934–1935 school year the number had dwindled to around 12,000, with anywhere between 5,000 and 12,000 more studying in private bilingual (Polish-Yiddish) schools. Frost, *Schooling*, 38, 50; Marcus, *History*, 151, 153. By contrast, during the first semester of the 1939–1940 school year upward of 100,000 children were enrolled in Yiddish-language schools in Western Byelorussia (55,000) and Western Ukraine (45,000). Levin, *Tekufah*, 109–11. Cf. Pinkus, *Yehudei Rusiyah*, 327; Kostyrchenko, *Tainaia politika*, 191.
121 Levin, *Tekufah beSograyim*, 147. Cf. Gris, *In farkisheftn land*, 1:26. For wages in other fields of employment, see Weiss, "Some Problems," 101. Not all found the stipends sufficient to maintain their desired standard of living.
122 Levin, *Tekufah*, 153, 158.
123 Levin, *Tekufah*, 163–66.
124 For descriptions see Kaminska, *My Life*, 114–21; Dzigan, *Der koyekh*, 159–61; Broderzon, *Mayn laydns-veg*, 24–25; Fuks, *A vanderung*, 60–61; Bender, *Mul mavet*, 93–96; Yonas, *Ashan baHolot*, 67–71.
125 Fishman, *Book Smugglers*, 25.
126 For figures see Frost, *Schooling*, 35–47.
127 On these changes see Levin, *Tekufah*, 105–106, 116–18.
128 See, for example, Sherman, "HaGimnaziyah," 2:128; Gessen, *Belostok*, 30–32; testimony of Yitshak Durczyn in Avatihi, *Stolin*, 109.
129 On the other hand, a teacher in a small-town Jewish school requested to teach non-Jewish students in order "not to appear a turncoat before Jewish children." Evyon, "Shetei peredot," 689.
130 See the figures in Levin, *Tekufah*, 110–11.
131 Levin, *Tekufah*, 111–12. For a description of the transition from Yiddish to Ukrainian in a Jewish school, see Fuks, *A Vanderung*, 92–93.
132 See the descriptions in Fuks, *A vanderung*, 69; Broderzon, *Mayn laydns-veg*, 20.
133 Estraikh, "Missing Years," 180.

134 Broderzon, *Mayn laydns-veg*, 20.

135 See Gris, *In farkisheftn land*, 1:35–36, 43. In spring 1941, shortly before the German invasion, a second newspaper, *Lemberger shtern*, began daily publication. Fuks, *A vanderung*, 104–106.

136 Kaminska, *My Life*, 115–20.

137 Dzigan, *Der koyekh*, 162.

138 Gris, *In farkisheftn land*, 1:27; Estraikh, "Missing Years," 179.

139 Broderzon, *Mayn laydns-veg*, 23–24.

140 Broderzon, *Mayn laydns-veg*, 21.

141 Broderzon, *Mayn laydns-veg*. The writer described the situation in Białystok. Cf. Fuks, *A vanderung*, 68, which portrays a brief "honeymoon" in Lwów before the onset of "some jealousy, some hatred, and grudges held for no apparent reason" (*glat azoy nisht fargineray*) within literary circles.

142 Kahan, *Unter di sovietishe himlen*, 27. His feeling was that under Soviet rule, "writing, even for the drawer, was impossible." Kahan, *Unter di sovietishe himlen*, 26.

143 Fuks, *A vanderung*, 55; Gregorek, "Biography."

144 Levin, *Tekufah*, 148. Seymour Levitan, "Rokhl Hering Korn," Jewish Women's Archive (E), Encyclopedia.

145 Kamińska, *My Life*, 127–29. See also Levin, *Tekufah*, 62.

146 Gris, *In farkisheftn land*, 1:35, 80, 85.

147 Dzigan, *Der koyekh*, 159–60.

148 Dzigan, *Der koyekh*, 158–64.

149 See Mendelsohn, *Jews*, 21–22.

150 Mendelsohn, "Polin," 207–208; cf. Marcus, *Social and Political History*, 264.

151 See Engel, *Zionism*, 1.

152 Miller, "Soviet Theory," 50–60.

153 Alter was arrested on 26 September 1939, Erlich on 4 October. The two had fled Warsaw on 7 September following evacuation of the city by the Polish government. They moved eastward, away from invading German forces. They could not have known at the time that the Soviets would attack from the east ten days later. On the flight of Jews eastward, see p. 29.

154 Blatman, *Lema'an herutenu*, 53–55.

155 Blatman, *Lema'an herutenu*, 56–58; Perlis, *Tenu'ot haNo'ar*, 53–59; Tsur, *Lifnei bo haAfelah*, 331–39. On Zionist attitudes toward the Soviet regime during its first two decades see also Shapira, *HaHalikhah*, 262–85; Tsur, "HaRadikalizatsiyah haKomunistit;" Garncarska-Kadary, *BeHipusei derekh*, 301–25. On Bund attitudes, see Gechtman, "Rise of the Bund," 38–40. For an different analysis by a contemporary, see [Engel], "Moshe Kleinbaum's Report," 282–84.

156 Foremost among imprisoned Zionists were Emil Sommerstein, president of the Zionist Federation of East Galicia and a former member of the Polish Sejm, and Menachem Begin, head of the Revisionist Zionist youth organization Betar in Poland. Litvak, *Pelitim*, 128–29; Begin, *BeLeilot Levanim*, 7–16. Begin was arrested following the Soviet annexation of Lithuania. On the annexation see

below. For a Zionist leader banished from his home, see Lidowski, *USheviv haEsh*, 48–52. See also Perlis, *Tenu'ot haNo'ar*, 53–85. For names of additional political arrestees, see Litvak, *Pelitim*, 134.

157 Avraham Stupp and Anshel Reiss to Ignacy Schwarzbart, 16 December 1940, Yad Vashem Archives, M2/599.

158 For specific information on several locations in Western Byelorussia, see Żbikowski, *U genezy Jedwabnego*, 134–37.

159 See Rossino, *Hitler*, 1–2, 90–92, 264–65n10.

160 Nesselrodt, *Vernichtung*, 41–42.

161 Litvak, *Pelitim*, 22.

162 See above, n. 27. Non-Jews also fled from the German to the Soviet zone, but Jews made up 80–90 percent of their number. Karpenkina, "'Kvartirnyi vopros'," 74.

163 Litvak, *Pelitim*, 27–41; Karpenkina, *Sovetizatsiia*, 71–73.

164 Harrowing descriptions of the journey and of crossing the border occupy a conspicuous place in many refugee memoirs, suggesting lasting trauma. See, among many others, Fuks, *A vanderung*, 38–43; Gris, *In farkisheftn land*, 1:8–20; Broderzon, *Mayn laydns-veg*, 13–18; Kaminska, *My Life*, 96–111; Temkin, *My Just War*, 3–4, 11–12; Warhaftig, *Refugee*, 32–37; Zarnowitz, *Fleeing*, 29–43; Zerubavel, *Na veNad*, 38–65.

165 With rare exceptions, the Soviets refused to allow Jewish organizations to bear the burden. It was evidently more important to them to redirect Jewish assets than to alleviate the refugees' distress. See Levin, *Tekufah*, 196–97.

166 Bender, *Mul mavet*, 68, 36. Cf. Karpenkina, "'Kvartirnyi vopros'," 86.

167 See p. 20; Zerubavel, *Na veNad*, 70–71. The number of *vostochniki* in Białystok reached 12,396 in October 1940—more than a third the number of refugees. Karpenkina, *Sovetizatsiia*, 82.

168 For an alternate analysis of the refugee situation see Pinchuk, *Yehudei Berit-haMo'atsot*, 37–45.

169 Levin, *Tekufah*, 199–200.

170 Karpenkina, *Sovetizatsiia*, 162–65. At the time the USSR may have been the world's only country where no legal restriction prevented nonresidents from working. Officials evidently did not regard competition for jobs as a significant aspect of the refugee problem. Litvak, *Pelitim*, 98.

171 Litvak, *Pelitim*, 99–100; Rozenblat, "'Chuzhdyi element,'" 30.

172 Shtokfish, *In rod*, 36. The author noted "long lines of men and women" at the registration office.

173 Estimates range from forty thousand to fifty-three thousand. Edele and Warlik, "Saved," 105–106. For documented figures for Western Byelorussia see Karpenkina, *Sovetizatsiia*, 165. See also Litvak, *Pelitim*, 101–104; Altshuler, "Distress," 95–98. Many who took jobs in the interior—mainly in collective farms, factories, and mines—found themselves unsuited for these positions. Rozenblat, "'Chuzhdyi element,'" 31. For descriptions of conditions, see Temkin, *My Just War*, 21–27; Shtokfish, *In rod*, 42–44.

174 On this hope, see Browning, *Origins*, 24–28, 106–110. Germans also periodically expelled Jews into Soviet territory. Karpenkina, *Sovetizatsiia*, 72.

175 Minc, *HaMetsukot*, 268–95. On the treaty, see p. 9.

176 "German-Soviet Boundary and Friendship Treaty," 28 September 1939, Avalon Project (E), Document Collections, Nazi-Soviet Relations 1939–1941.

177 See, for example, "Memorandum by the State Secretary," 5 December 1939, *Documents on German Foreign Policy*, Series D, 8:489: "The expulsion of Jews into Russian territory . . . did not proceed as smoothly as had apparently been expected." For the Soviet perspective, see Karpenkina, *Sovetizatsiia*, 100.

178 Polian, "Hätte der Holocaust . . . ," 14–15. They also left thousands of Jews stranded between the German and Soviet realms. See Arad, *Toledot haSho'ah*, 1:107.

179 Polian, "Hätte der Holocaust . . . ," 13–14. Maxim Litvinov was a member of the commission.

180 Kostyrchenko, *Tainaia politika*, 186–89. Birobidzhan was a district in Soviet East Asia, designated the Jewish Autonomous Region in 1934.

181 Longerich, *Holocaust*, 158. During the first half of 1940 German attention concentrated mainly on Madagascar. Germany would revisit the USSR as a destination for European Jewry after June 1941. See chapter 2, at nn. 18–29.

182 That passportization involved intentional deceit, with a mind to entrapping candidates for deportation, is suggested by a memorandum from NKVD Commissar for Ukraine, I. A. Serov, describing a scheme for duping refugees wishing to leave the USSR into boarding trains ostensibly bound for the German side but actually headed to the Soviet interior. Serov to L. P. Beria, 4 June 1940, Haluzevyi derzhavnyi arkhiv Sluzhby bezpeky Ukrainy, 16/1/397/7–9.

183 Litvak, *Pelitim*, 105. The Ukrainian territories were incorporated on 1 November, the Byelorussian territories on 2 November.

184 Karpenkina, *Sovetizatsiia*, 53. Refugees who arrived after the border closing were subject to arrest for illegal entry.

185 For further information about passports, see above, n. 58.

186 For details regarding refusal to accept a passport, see Karpenkina, *Sovetizatsiia*, 169.

187 Litvak, *Pelitim*, 114. About sixteen hundred Jews managed to return to Poland, presumably with transports repatriating "persons of German descent." Edele and Warlik, "Saved," 108.

188 Litvak, *Pelitim*, 116–17. Many who applied for passports revealed information that made them suspect in Soviet eyes. They received documents with an endorsement (Paragraph 11) forbidding residence in certain controlled zones, including border cities, where large concentrations of refugees had settled. Those with such documents often had to look for new residences in smaller towns farther from the frontier. See Karpenkina, *Sovetizatsiia*, 169–73. For an account by a Jew who received a Paragraph 11 passport and had to move from Białystok to Słonim, see Korzec, "Fragmenty," 29–31.

189 Rozenblat, "'Chuzhdyi element'," 33–39.

190 Litvak, *Pelitim*, 126–27. Some spoke of 90 percent; others (hyperbolically) of "the whole town." Zak, *Knekht*, 1:136; Fuks, *A vanderung*, 79. In early 1940 Zionist leader Moshe Kleinbaum took an informal poll in Lwów and Łuck; he reported three quarters wished to leave the USSR. [Engel], "Moshe Kleinbaum's Report," 284. An NKVD document from June 1940 mentioned "up to 35,000 refugees" in Lwów, "clogging all railroad stations, spending the night on benches in public squares, awaiting transfer to German territory," with another five thousand in "other districts" nearby. Serov to L. P. Beria, 4 June 1940, Haluzevyi derzhavnyi arkhiv Sluzhby bezpeky Ukrainy, 16/1/397/7–9. See also Adler, *Survival*, 90–91.

191 I. A. Serov, quoted in Kostyrchenko, *Tainaia politika*, 188.

192 Fuks, *A vanderung*, 79. The patch was actually a blue star on a white background. According to Fuks, "Rumors were already circulating about something called ghettos, about yellow patches."

193 Fuks, *A vanderung*, 80.

194 Zak, *Knekht*, 1:136.

195 For example, Moshe Grossman; see Gris, *In farkisheftn land*, 1:35, 80, 85. Women and children were well represented among the refugee population. Adler and Aleksiun, "Seeking Relative Safety," 46–53; Rozenblat, "'Chuzhdyi element'," 31.

196 Zerubavel, *Na veNad*, 21–23.

197 Zak, *Knekht*, 1:137.

198 Gris, *In farkisheftn land*, 1:84.

199 Some appear to have understood the situation even earlier. Writing in 1943, a young engineer from a town near Warsaw who fled to the Soviet side recalled that he chose to return home in October 1939 after hearing a warning from his aunt: "You [Jews in the German zone] have it so good. The Germans will leave, and you'll have Poland again, but we [in the Soviet area] will be under Bolshevik domination for the rest of our lives." Perechodnik, *Spowiedź*, 18. Jewish assessments of the situation could be fluid, and some crossed the border back and forth multiple times before the Soviets required them to make a permanent choice. Adler, "Hrubieszów," 21–22.

200 [Engel], "Moshe Kleinbaum's Report," 280. The joke, which dates from no later than October 1939 (Levin, "Yerushalayim deLita," 222), should be understood as an assessment of the two occupiers' theoretical, long-range inclinations. It does not reflect awareness of a German policy that called for the death of all Jews. Refugees who applied to return to the German zone evidently believed that although Germans may have wanted to kill Jews en masse, they were unlikely to have a chance to fulfill that desire.

201 For more on considerations behind the choice, see Adler, *Survival*, 90–94.

202 Edele and Warlik, "Saved," 105–106; Altshuler, "Distress," 88. The deportation order had already been issued on 20 April 1940. Karpenkina, *Sovetizatsiia*, 101. For additional categories deported see Litvak, *Pelitim*, 137–38.

203 Litvak, *Pelitim*, 146–52; Sword, *Deportation*, 22–25. On the place and operation of the two types of exile within the broader Soviet penal and surveillance system, see Polian, *Ne po svoiei vole*, 95–102.
204 Kaplan, *Megilat yisurin*, 82.
205 Kaplan, *Megilat yisurin*, 83. The diarist was evidently unaware of the border closure.
206 Unlike prisoners, whose sentences were finite, exiles were exiled indefinitely.
207 Gris, *In farkisheftn land*, 1:105; Zak, *Knekht*, 1:156.
208 Fuks, *A vanderung*, 74.
209 Roberts, *Soviet Union*, 103–105.
210 Liekis, *1939*, 115–76. Germany did not give up its claim. In January 1941, after the Soviet annexation of Lithuania, the USSR paid Germany for the disputed territory.
211 Border crossing was legal until 15 November, but substantial movement continued illegally until mid-January 1940, when the Soviets implemented stricter controls and winter impeded the flow. Arad, "Concentration," 204–207.
212 Levin, "Perakim," 78; Bauer, "Rescue," 215. The figure also included some twenty-four hundred extruded by Germany from Suwałki in Poland to Lithuanian Suvalkija. According to Warhaftig, *Refugee*, 50, "The vast majority [of refugees] came from the Soviet zone."
213 Warhaftig, *Refugee*, 52–57. On the other hand, cases are known in which Jews from the Wilno district departed for territories elsewhere in the USSR for fear of reprisals by the local Lithuanian and Polish populations. Karpenkina, *Sovetizatsiia*, 74.
214 Bauer, "Rescue," 218–23. Cf. American Jewish Joint Distribution Committee, *Aiding Jews*, 27, 39.
215 Roberts, *Soviet Union* 119–20.
216 For a detailed description of the process in Lithuania, see Levin, *Bein haPatish vehaMagal*, 31–56.
217 Deletant, *Hitler's Forgotten Ally*, 12–15; Hitchens, *Rumania*, 445–47. Bessarabia had belonged to the Russian Empire; the Soviet Union had never recognized Romanian sovereignty there.
218 Figures derived from Arad, *Toledot haSho'ah*, 1:99–100; Levin, *Tekufah*, 24; Kaganovitch, "Estimating the Number," 465–68. Finnish territories, with about three hundred Jewish residents, were also annexed in March 1940. Together with virtually all of the local population of 420,000, those Jews were relocated to Finnish-controlled areas. Kostanick, "Soviet Territorial Annexations," 16; Shinedling, "Finland," 309.
219 Kaganovitch, "Estimating the Number," 465.
220 *American Jewish Year Book* 42 (1940–41): 601–605.
221 Levin, *Tekufah*, 87, 146.
222 Kaganovitch, "Estimating the Number," 465.
223 A young woman from Bukovina recalled, "When the Soviets occupied Czernowitz [Cernăuţi] ... my parents' bourgeois world collapsed. My father

was placed under surveillance and persecuted as a capitalist and a Zionist, stripped of his property and left without employment. We lived in two small rooms that we sublet. But the Soviet occupation also freed us young people from the oppression of petty bourgeois existence that hemmed us in." Shmueli, *Ein Kind*, 69.

224 Bessarabia and Northern Bukovina included significant Ukrainian minorities. The Soviets used this fact justify their demand that Romania "return" the former and "transfer" the latter to Soviet rule. See "Ultimativnaia nota sovetskogo pravitelstva rumynskomu pravitelstvu," 26 June 1940, in Iakovlev, *Bessarabskii vopros*, 64–65.

225 Senn, "Sovietization," 123.

226 Levin, *Tekufah*, 303, 305;[Anonymous,] "Yehudei Latvia," 313–15; Angrick and Klein, *"Final Solution"*, 24–26.

227 Murphy, *What Stalin Knew*, 37–41.

228 Figures: Latvia (5,000)—Angrick and Klein, *"Final Solution"*, 26; Lithuania (7,000)—Levin, "Perakim," 83; Romania (9,000–10,000)—Kaganovitch, "Estimating the Number," 468.

229 On the expulsions of Polish citizens see above, n. 43. Precise figures are unavailable, but calculating from the estimate by the Polish government-in-exile that approximately 30 percent of the total of deportees in all four expulsions were Jews, the number may have exceeded twenty-five thousand. *Report on the Relief* 3. Cf. Gross, *Revolution*, 196; Edele and Warlik, "Saved," 105.

230 Such, at least, was the impression of observers watching the scene closely. Statistical data from these years are lacking. See Lestschinsky, *Sovetishe Idntum*; Zinger, *Dos banayte folk*.

231 Lestschinsky, *Sovetishe Idntum*, 15. The words were written in October 1940.

232 Kostyrchenko, *Tainaia politika*, 196–218. On the resolution, see the Prologue to this volume.

233 For details see Budnitskii, "Evrei," 3–9. Maiskii's mother was not Jewish.

234 In fact, Jews continued to enjoy prominence in many walks of Soviet life during the period of rapprochement. When, for example, listeners across the USSR learned of the German invasion in June 1941, they heard the news from Yurii Levitan, Stalin's handpicked (Jewish) voice of Radio Moscow. Throughout the war Levitan was the principal source of news for millions of Soviet residents. He broadcast the announcement of victory in 1945. See Budnitskii, "Evrei," 39–61.

235 Quoted in Nekrich, *Pariahs*, 168.

236 Above, n. 26.

237 Minc, *HaMetsukot*, 287–98; Pinchuk, *Yehudei Berit-haMo'atsot*, 63–67.

238 Hicks, *First Films*, 18–43. *Professor Mamlock* was based on a play of the same title by German playwright Friedrich Wolf. It tells the story of a gifted German Jewish surgeon, a veteran of the First World War, who, despite saving the life of a high Nazi official, is persecuted, beaten, and eventually killed by police after a call for resistance to Hitler's regime. On reception of the film by Soviet Jews see pp. 217–18. There are indications that already at the onset of German-Soviet

negotiations in May 1939 Soviet officials prevented dissemination of works deemed unfavorable to Germany, including an original play scheduled to be performed at the Moscow Jewish State Theater. Altshuler, "Distress," 76.

239 Gris, *In farkisheftn land*, 1:35–36.

240 On applications to return to the German zone, see pp. 31–32.

241 See chapter 2.

242 See Michman, *Emergence*, 77–82. On food supply, see Ungar, *Lodz*, 143–48.

243 Gutman, *Yehudei Varshah*, 82.

244 For a fuller discussion, see chapters 3 and 4.

245 See Levin, *Tekufah*, 241–55; Altshuler, "Distress," 92–95.

246 Facsimile in Levin, *Tekufah*, [250]. Cf. Fitzpatrick, "Annexation," 138–39.

247 On attenuation efforts, see the observations of Deborah Yalen and Arkadi Zeltser in volume 2 of this series.

248 Lestschinsky, *Sovetishe Idntum*, 368.

249 See Altshuler, "Distress," 107–12.

250 The number of these officials and their family members has been estimated at twelve thousand to eighteen thousand. Altshuler, "Distress," 92. On the variety and extent of their activities among Jews, see Karpenkina, *Sovetizatsiia*, 82–83.

251 Levin, *Tekufah*, 236–41.

252 Quoted in Levin, "Response," 100.

253 Levin, "Response," 100.

254 Bronfman, *Zvezda*, 54–55.

255 One example among many, reported by a Palestinian Jewish woman who had been visiting Warsaw, was caught by the German invasion, and fled to Białystok: "There is an orphanage for Christian children, run by nuns. A group of homeless Jewish refugee children was sent there [by the Soviet authorities]. The nuns . . . screamed . . . and threw them out, claiming that theirs was a home for Christian children only, and no Jews would be admitted. Soldiers came, threw the nuns out, and let the Jewish children in, together with a Jewish teacher. The Soviet soldiers simply could not grasp how one could make a distinction between children: Christian or Jewish, what difference did it make? They are first and foremost *children*!" Zerubavel, *Na veNad*, 68.

256 Levin, *Tekufah*, 257, 335.

2. DISFIGUREMENT

1 For "new living space," see chapter 1, n. 1. For the timeline and the thinking behind it, see Weinberg, *World*, 179–88.

2 Roberts, *Soviet Union*, 136–39; Glantz and House, *Titans*, 44–51, 57.

3 Glantz and House, *Titans*, 34, 367.

4 Evans, *Third Reich at War*, 179.

5 See Tooze, *Wages*, 466–80.

6 Glantz and House, *Titans*, 390–91. Totals are for both sides.

7 Barber and Harrison, "Patriotic War," 226.

8 Barber and Harrison, "Patriotic War," 226.

9 Arad, *Toledot haSho'ah*, 2:1014.

10 The maximum figure includes an estimated twenty thousand Jewish partisans; Arad, *BeTsel haDegel*, 431–32. For considerations suggesting a figure closer to the minimum, see Appendix.

11 Since the 1990s numbers have been revised upward, as a result both of new techniques of approximation and of the opening of Soviet archives. For analyses, see Maksudov, "Jewish Population Losses"; Kupovetsii, "Liudskie poteri" (1995), esp. 145, 150–52; Arad, *Toledot haSho'ah*, 2:1005–15. For earlier estimates, see Ainsztein, "Soviet Jewry," 297–98. Similar techniques and discoveries have led to a parallel upward revision of overall Soviet casualty figures; Weinberg, *World*, 894.

12 In Western and Eastern Byelorussia, most of whose territories were occupied by Germany for a full three years, 20 to 25 percent of the total population perished, compared with nearly three quarters of the Jewish population. Gerlach, *Kalkulierte Morde*, 762. Figures for Ukraine are 10 percent of the total population and 65 percent of the Jewish population. Kruglov, "Jewish Losses," 286–87.

13 Ehrenburg was a member of the Jewish Anti-Fascist Committee, about which see chapter 5. On 24 August 1941, in a committee-sponsored radio address, he stated, "I am a Russian writer.... But the Hitlerites have reminded me of something else: . . . I am a Jew." Quoted in Rubenstein, *Tangled Loyalties*, 201. For more on Ehrenburg's wartime journalism, see chapter 4.

14 Ehrenburg, *War*, 191–92. Cf. Rubenstein, *Tangled Loyalties*, 225–26; Goldberg, *Ilya Ehrenburg*, 214–15.

15 For a list of Soviet armies destroyed or disbanded, see Glantz and House, *Titans*, 369. An additional offensive in summer 1942 brought Germany to the lower Volga River and the Caucasus Mountains. On events regarding Leningrad and Moscow, see pp. 83–86.

16 See Pohl, *Herrschaft*, 152–53.

17 See Browning, *Origins*, 213–14.

18 The fullest and clearest explication of these ideas remains Jäckel, *Hitler's World View*, esp. 87–107.

19 Quoted in Browning, *Origins*, 215–16.

20 See, for example, the directive by General Erich Hoepner, commander of the Fourth Panzer Army, dated 2 May 1941: "The war against Russia is ... the old battle of the Germanic against the Slav peoples, of the defence of European culture against Moscovite-Asiatic inundation, and the repulse of Jewish Bolshevism. The objective of this battle must be the destruction of present-day Russia.... Every military actiion must be guided in planning and execution by an iron will to exterminate the enemy mercilessly and totally.... No adherents of the present Russian-Bolshevik system are to be spared." Quoted in Förster, "German Army," 18.

21 "Richtlinien für das Verhalten der Truppe in Rußland," 4 June 1941, quoted in Browning, *Origins*, 222–23.

22 Goebbels diary entry, 4 June 1941, quoted in Herf, *Jewish Enemy*, 90. On 27 June, five days after the invasion began, Goebbels and Dietrich released a pamphlet entitled *Warum Krieg mit Stalin*, which named members of the Soviet "Jewish leadership clique." Herf, *Jewish Enemy*, 96–97.

23 Calculated from "Protokoll der 'Besprechung "uber die Endlösung der Judenfrage," 20 January 1942, Haus der Wannsee-Konferenz (E), Konferenz, Dokumente zur Wannsee-Konferenz.

24 Browning, *Origins*, 36–43.

25 Fritz, *Ostkrieg*, 55, 93.

26 Minc, *HaMetsukot*, 269–72; Arad, *Toledot haSho'ah*, 1:108.

27 See p. 30. Nor had a series of subsequent internal German projects for a "territorial final solution of the Jewish question" borne any fruit. Browning, *Origins*, 43–110.

28 Aly, *Final Solultion*, 171–76.

29 "Unterredung des Führers mit Marschall Kvaternik," 21 July 1941, quoted in Hillgruber, *Germany*, 87: "The Jews are the scourge of mankind.... If the Jews had free reign, as in the Soviet paradise, they would put the most outrageous schemes into practice. That was how Russia became a plague for mankind.... Even if only one state, for whatever reason, were to tolerate a Jewish family in it, this would become the bacillus for renewed decay. The unity of the European states would no longer be disturbed if there were no more Jews in Europe. It doesn't matter where one sends the Jews, to Siberia or Madagascar. I shall approach each state with this demand." On Madagascar, see chapter 1, n. 180. At the time Hitler spoke, Madagascar had been abandoned as a possible destination; only Soviet territory was under active consideration.

30 Browning, *Origins*, 222–23.

31 The *Einsatzgruppen* were made up of personnel from various SS branches, including the Secret State Police (*Geheime Staatspolizei*—Gestapo, charged with keeping watch over the Third Reich's political enemies), the Criminal Police (*Kriminalpolizei*—Kripo, charged with investigating nonpolitical crimes), the Order Police (*Ordnungspolizei*—Orpo, a uniformed police and civil defense force that served also as a military reserve), and the Armed SS (*Waffen-SS*, tactical combat units). Beginning in July 1941, additional Orpo and Waffen-SS units were assigned to kill Jews through a chain of command within the SS but separate from that of the *Einsatzgruppen*. The personnel of these units eventually outnumbered the *Einsatzgruppen*. See below, also Browning, *Origins*, 229–34; Browning, *Ordinary Men*, 4–11; Curilla, *Deutsche Ordnungspolizei*, 95–99.

32 Quoted in Browning, *Origins*, 215–16. *Einsatzgruppen* had also operated in Poland for several months following the German conquest. The task forces created in March 1941 were a new incarnation of the name. On their command structure, place within the SS, and relations with the military, see Hilberg, *Destruction*, 1:274–90.

33 Quoted in Arad, Krakowski, Spector, *Einsatzgruppen Reports*, iv-v. "Administrative measures" is a translation of the German *Exekutivmassnahmen*,

which alternatively could be rendered "executive measures." See Hilberg, *Destruction*, 1:284.

34 Browning, *Origins*, 217.

35 Halder diary entry, 6 May 1941, quoted in Browning, *Origins*, 219.

36 Quoted in Arad, *Toledot*, 1:147. Keitel was the highest-ranking officer in the German Armed Forces.

37 In postwar trials six *Einsatzgruppen* officers testified that on the eve of the invasion they had received an oral order from a high-ranking SS official to kill all Jews they encountered in the USSR, but their testimonies did not withstand scrutiny. See Hilberg, *Destruction*, 1:290; Browning, *Origins*, 226–27.

38 "Heydrichs nachträgliche schriftliche Einweisung der vier Höheren SS- und Polizeiführer im Osten," 2 July 1941, in Klein, *Einsatzgruppen*, 324. See also Arad, Krakowski, and Spector, *Einsatzgruppen Reports*, viii.

39 Such, at least, appears to have been the understanding of the commander of *Einsatzgruppe* A, Franz Walter Stahlecker, expressed in a comprehensive report on the activities on his unit through mid-October 1941: "According to general orders, the Security Police were supposed to undertake the work of purging [the occupied territories] with the aim of eliminating Jews as completely as possible." "Report by SS Brigadeführer Stahlecker...," 15 October 1941, in International Military Tribunal, *Trial*, 37:687. In postwar testimonies from the late 1950s two *Einsatzgruppe* unit commanders reported attending a briefing with Heydrich on 17 June 1941, five days before the beginning of Operation Barbarossa, at which they were instructed that Jews in the captured territories needed to be eradicated. According to one witness, "It was impossible to understand anything except that all Jews needed to be eradicated, without regard to age or sex." The other could not recall whether Heydrich had referred only to "Jews" or to "all Jews." There is no way to determine the accuracy of the two witnesses' understanding or the extent to which their recollections were influenced by knowledge of subsequent events. Quoted in Szarota, *U progu zagłady*, 212–13. See also Breitman, *Architect*, 169–70.

40 Matthäus, "Die 'Judenfrage,'" 58–59.

41 Aly, *Final Solution*, 114–15; cf. Bartov, *Germany's War*, 92.

42 Hilberg, *Destruction*, 1:289.

43 Streit, "German Army," 4. In fact, the army leadership pushed back against the High Command's instruction regarding shooting POWs. On 24 July 1941, Army Quartermaster-General Eduard Wagner (second in command to Army Chief of Staff Halder) ordered that "Asians (in terms of race), Jews, [and] German-speaking Russians" who were not "politically intolerable and suspicious elements, commissars and agitators" were to be held separately from other prisoners. Förster, "German Army," 21.

44 See, for example, Blachetta, *Das wahre Gesicht*, 7–13. The author maintained that Lithuanian residents of the Wilno region were victims of Poland's 1922 annexation of Wilno ("the true capital of Lithuania," which "Lithuanians will never relinquish") and its surrounding area. In general, he claimed, Poland had

displayed "an intolerant attitude toward Lithuanians and Byelorussians" and imposed "bloody terror" upon Ukrainians.

45 Matthäus and Bajohr, *Political Diary*, 7; Rosenberg Diary, 2 April 1941 (evening), 20 April 1941, in Matthäus and Bajohr, *Political Diary*, 234–36, 241. For biographical details see Rosenberg's testimony at Nuremberg, 15 April 1946, in International Military Tribunal, *Trial*, 11:446.

46 "Rede des Reichskanzlers A. Rosenberg von den engsten Beteiligten am Ostproblem," 20 June 1941, in International Military Tribunal, *Trial*, 26:616 (Document 1058-PS). The phrase "all these peoples" referred to Ukrainians, Balts, Finns, and the indigenous inhabitants of the Caucasus region.

47 From a report to the head of the German Security Police and Security Service in Kraków, 20 October 1939, quoted in Struve, *Deutsche Herrschaft*, 133.

48 Details in Struve, *Deutsche Herrschaft*, 133–35.

49 Quoted in Pohl, *Nationalistische Judenverfolgung*, 38.

50 "Excerpts from four policy texts by [Alfred] Rosenberg's office . . . ," spring 1941, in Matthäus and Bajohr, *Political Diary*, 373.

51 Matthäus and Bajohr, *Political Diary*, 373–74. Cf. Struve, *Deutsche Herrschaft*, 131–32; Kangeris, "Die Nationalsozialistischen Pläne," 169–70.

52 "Rede des Reichskanzlers A. Rosenberg von den engsten Beteiligten am Ostproblem," 20 June 1941, in International Military Tribunal, *Trial*, 26:616–25 (Document 1058-PS).

53 Matthäus and Bajohr, *Political Diary*, 373.

54 Matthäus and Bajohr, *Political Diary*, 374.

55 Abbreviations for *Sicherheitspolizei* (Security Police) and *Sicherheitsdienst* (Security Service). In practice these were parallel bureaucracies. The former was originally an arm of the German state, the latter of the Nazi Party. In September 1939 they were both placed under the supervision of the Main Reich Security Office (*Reichssicherheitshauptamt*—RSHA), a division of the SS. Heydrich, one of whose titles was Chief of SP and SD, supervised both, as well as RSHA overall. For details see Hilberg, *Destruction*, 1:275–80.

56 "Fernschreiben Heydrichs an die Einsatzgruppenchefs," 29 June 1941, in Klein, *Einsatzgruppen*, 318–19.

57 "Heydrichs nachträgliche schriftliche Einweisung der vier Höheren SS- und Polizeiführer im Osten," 2 July 1941, in Klein, *Einsatzgruppen*, 324. See also Arad, Krakowski, and Spector, *Einsatzgruppen Reports*, viii.

58 Franz Stahlecker, commander of *Einsatzgruppe A*, appears clearly to have understood this policy demand, as revealed in his account of the activities of his unit during their first four months of operation: "Considering that the population of the Baltic countries suffered the most during the period of their incorporation into the USSR under Bolshevik-Jewish rule, it was assumed that after they were liberated from foreign rule, they would take it upon themselves to render harmless those enemies who remained behind following the withdrawal of the Red Army. The task of the security police was supposed to be to set the self-purging efforts in motion and to channel them in the proper direction,

so that the goal for cleansing that had been established could be reached as quickly as possible. No less essential was making it appear as established and demonstrable fact that the liberated population had of its own volition taken up the severest measures against the Bolshevik and Jewish enemies, without leaving any trace that German authorities ordered them to do so." See "Report by SS Brigadeführer Stahlecker ...," 15 October 1941, in International Military Tribunal, *Trial*, 37:687.

59 See "Heydrichs nachträgliche schriftliche Einweisung ...," 2 July 1941, in Klein, *Einsatzgruppen*, 325–26: "The self-purging efforts of anticommunist and anti-Jewish circles in the newly-occupied territories should ... be encouraged, with allowing these local 'self-defense' circles later to be able to call for arrangements or acknowledgment of political promises."

60 On these compilations, their sources, and their structure, see Headland, *Messages*, 37–50.

61 "Operational Situation Report USSR No. 24," 16 July 1941, in Arad et al., *Einsatzgruppen Reports*, 27–28.

62 "Operational Situation Report USSR No. 31," 23 July 1941, in Arad et al., *Einsatzgruppen Reports*, 42.

63 "Operational Situation Report USSR No. 43," 5 August 1941, in Arad et al., *Einsatzgruppen Reports*, 68. Cf. Arad et al., *Einsatzgruppen Reports*, 73: "A spark of ... the deep, insurmountable conflict between the Ukrainians and Jews ... survives ... with the present Ukrainian older generation. But they will not expend the energy, given their present mood, to proceed towards the total destruction of the remaining Jews."

64 "Operational Situation Report USSR No. 47," 9 August 1941, in Arad et al., *Einsatzgruppen Reports*, 79.

65 "Operational Situation Report USSR No. 81," 12 September 1941, in Arad et al., *Einsatzgruppen Reports*, 131.

66 "Tätigkeits- und Lagebericht Nr. 6 der Einsatzgruppen der Sicherheitspolizei und des SD in der UdSSR (Berichtszeit v. 1.10–31.10.1941)," in Klein, *Einsatzgruppen*, 229. Stahlecker's report of 15 October 1941 offered a more complex picture. Stahlecker noted that in Kaunas, Lithuania's de facto capital during the interwar years, action by Lithuanians in late June 1941 had rendered thirty-eight hundred Jews "harmless" (*unschädlich*). Nevertheless, he explained, "it was, surprisingly, not easy at first to set a progrom [*sic*] against the Jews in motion on a larger scale." In the end it was not the populace at large that rose up against the Jews but a Lithuanian militia acting "on the basis of information supplied him by the small German advance detachment that had been stationed in Kaunas." Nevertheless, Stahlecker pointed out, that unit, along with similar ones in other places in Lithuania, had eventually had to be disarmed. Once that happened, "The self-purging actions inevitably came to an end." Hence, according to Stahlecker, "It was self-evident from the outset that only the first days after occupation offered the possibility for carrying out progroms [*sic*]." Moreover, "It proved considerably more difficult to set similar cleansing

actions … in motion in Latvia." "Report by SS Brigadeführer Stahlecker …," 15 October 1941, in International Military Tribunal, *Trial*, 37:682–83.

67 The two most thorough and inclusive data sets are *Pinkas haKehillot* and *Encyclopedia of Camps and Ghettos 1933–1945*, compiled by Yad Vashem (the official Holocaust memorial authority of the State of Israel) and the United States Holocaust Memorial Museum (USHMM), respectively. The volumes of *Pinkas haKehillot* concerning areas occupied by Germany in 1941 were published between 1980 and 2005; those of the USHMM *Encyclopedia* appeared in 2012. The latter work employs a broader source base than the former, including much material from former Soviet and Soviet-bloc archives. The former, by contrast, makes more extensive use of materials in the Yiddish and Hebrew languages. The USHMM *Encyclopedia* provides data for all areas occupied by Germany in 1941, whereas (to date) *Pinkas haKehillot* confines its attention to German-occupied areas that were added to the USSR in 1939 and 1940 (i.e. formerly Polish, Estonian, Latvian, Lithuanian, and Romanian territories), excluding lands within the Soviet Union's pre-1939 boundaries. On the other hand, *Pinkas haKehillot* offers data from a far greater number of Jewish settlements; the USHMM *Encyclopedia* considers only those locations where ghettos (defined as places where "the German authorities ordered the Jews to move into a designated area, where only Jews were permitted to live") or forced labor camps (places of confinement "based in factories, at other work sites, or at some distance from previous Jewish settlements") were established (2A:XLIII). The differences between the two compilations make precise statistical calculations impossible. The findings presented here use both data sets in tandem to achieve rough estimates. For another set of estimates, based on data derived from different sources and on different criteria for classifying and counting violent events, see Kopstein and Wittenberg, *Intimate Violence*. That study is confined to the former Polish *kresy*. With regard to those territories, its principal findings regarding the proportional incidence and geographical distribution of violence—especially its conclusion that violent attacks by local civilians upon their Jewish neighbors "were relatively rare events" (2)—mostly comport with those presented here. On the different classification criteria, see n. 68.

68 The figure includes places where organized armed bands not associated with any political group and claiming no local authority not derived from the German occupiers (like the one organized by Algirdas Klimaitis in Kaunas) were noted as prominent perpetrators but not places where the primary perpetrators appear to have belonged to local militias advancing autonomous political claims (what Heydrich called "*permanent* self-defense associations with a central leadership") or to armed units of nationalist organizations (like the Organization of Ukrainian Nationalists or the Lithuanian Activist Front). On the latter category see pp. 58–61. Scholarly literature generally does not employ this distinction; instead it tends to analyze all violent "anti-Jewish incidents" under the single rubric of "pogroms." Different authors have employed different definitions of "pogrom,"

but no definition has taken into account differentiations that the German occupiers and their superiors in Berlin appear to have regarded as crucial. See, inter alia, Hilberg, *Destruction*, 1:310; Dieckmann, *Deutsche Besatzungspolitik*, 300; Mędykowski, *W cieniu gigantów*, 25–30, 372; Kopstein and Wittenberg, *Intimate Violence*, 45–46. A categorization that differentiates local violence according to criteria employed by Germans at the time aids in understanding shifts in German practice that profoundly affected the manner in which millions of Jews in the post-1939 Soviet Union lived and died. As a result, the discussion that follows does not employ the term "pogrom" and eschews the analytical category it habitually defines.

It is not always possible to distinguish between the two categories from the digests in the data sets, or even from the testimonies on which they are based. In some places it appears that both types of violence occurred. The approximations regarding mob violence include dubious cases in order to estimate the most favorable appraisal German observers could have been expected to make.

69 Numerical estimates are extremely uncertain, for most accounts of violence offer no numbers at all, and the minority that do generally provide only rounded figures. Where multiple accounts exist, the numbers often differ. No doubt this situation has deterred many scholars who have studied the events in question from proposing any estimates of their own. The highest conjectures cited in the scholarly literature count no more than sixty thousand Jewish victims of attacks by local populations in any form, including not only mobs but also auxiliary forces under German command and militias acting on their own authority. Polonsky, *Jews*, 3:491. Cf. Polonsky and Michlic, *The Neighbors Respond*, 26–27. For lower estimates that also encompass all forms of local violence see, inter alia, Pohl, "Anti-Jewish Pogroms," 306; Arad, *Toledot haSho'ah*, 1:209; Spector, *Sho'at yehudei Vohlin*, 60–61; Weiss, "Jewish-Ukrainian Relations," 413. Some of the figures are for a limited region of the areas under German occupation. The figure given here relates only to mob violence, and it pertains to all areas under German occupation.

70 See p. 64. Estimated Jewish deaths during the so-called pogrom epidemic associated with the Russian Civil War and the Polish-Soviet War range between fifty thousand and two hundred thousand, but these figures relate to a period of between two and five years. Whether deaths during any three-month interval between 1917 and 1922 approached thirty thousand cannot be determined on the basis of available evidence. In any event, the large majority of the deaths resulted from actions not by mobs but by armies or militias contending for political power. For details see Engel, *Assassination*, esp. 58–59.

71 "Excerpts from four policy texts by [Alfred] Rosenberg's office . . . ," spring 1941, in Matthäus and Bajohr, *Political Diary*, 373.

72 Not to be confused with the larger Galician town Tłuste, located approximately forty kilometers south-southwest of Touste.

73 Wein and Dąbrowska, "Touste," 253.

74 Levin and Klevan, "Wąsosz," 188. Cf. Żbikowski, "Pogromy," 169–71.

75 Levin and Klevan, "Radziłów," 423. Cf. Żbikowski, "Pogromy," 231–59; Gross, *Neighbors*, 57–69; Bender, "Not Only in Jedwabne," 23–26.

76 Abramski-Bligh, "Jedwabne," 243. Cf. Gross, *Neighbors*, 90–104. Much ink has been spilled over the violence in Jedwabne, Radziłów, and vicinity, with debate centered largely upon the precise number of victims and the relative responsibility of Germans and Poles for the events. For a sample, see Polonsky and Michlic, *The Neighbors Respond*. Neither issue is of consequence for the discussion here, which is concerned primarily with how the German occupiers assessed the strategic benefit they gained from the violence. The Germans expected to be involved in setting aggressive local crowds in motion; a mob attack upon Jews that they encouraged was neither more nor less useful to them than one launched without their involvement. They were also more concerned with rough percentages of Jewish targets killed than with precise casualty figures. Nor did they bother much with the ethnic identity of mobs: whether crowds were composed of Poles, Ukrainians, Lithuanians, or others did not affect their strategic calculations. They regarded Poles, whose upper classes they had earlier tried to kill off in the Polish areas they conquered in 1939, as suitable perpetrators of anti-Jewish and anticommunist violence no less than members of the national groups Poles had purportedly oppressed. See "Heydrichs Einsatzbefehl Nr. 2," 1 July 1941, in Klein, *Einsatzgruppen*, 320. For that reason the ethnic identity of perpetrators is not designated here.

77 Abramski-Bligh, "Wizna," 190; Bender, "Not Only in Jedwabne," 23. Some came to Jedwabne, where they presumably perished in the barn. Others headed for Łomża, where no local violence was recorded.

78 Spector, "Ignatowka," 42.

79 Spector, "Włodzimierzec," 85; Kruglov and Fishman, "Włodzimierzec," 1495.

80 Jakubowicz and Dąbrowska, "Bóbrka," 67; Kruglov and Vaisman, "Bóbrka," 750. Additional details in Struve, *Deutsche Herrschaft*, 496–500.

81 Rozin, "Anykščiai," 154; Dean, "Anikščiai," 1040. Additional details in Garfunkel, *Yahadut Lita*, 4:247.

82 Levin, "Viekšniai," 273; Kruglov and Dean, "Viekšniai," 1141.

83 According to the most expansive accounting possible—that is, the ones that could have supported the most favorable German assessment of the strategy of Rosenberg and Heydrich—death tolls ranged from some 5 percent of the Jewish population in Lwów and Kaunas to approximately 50 percent in Złoczów. Most reported figures are lower than the highest ones used for these calculations. For details and estimates regarding the events in Kaunas see Dieckhoff, "Lithuania," 355–61; Dieckhoff, *Deutsche Besatzungspolitik*, 319–25; Szarota, *U progu zagłady*, 226–66. On the Galician sites see, inter alia, Struve, *Deutsche Herrschaft*, 247–432 (Lwów), 566–85 (Złoczów), 591–632 (Tarnopol). On Lwów see also Mick, *Lemberg*, 288–93.

84 On the largest of these incidents and patterns, see below.

85 Arad, *Toledot haSho'ah*, 1:201.

86 From a characterization by an SS official of the attitude of Thunder Cross, 20 March 1941, quoted in Kangeris, "Kollaboration," 182. On 11 July 1941 the same organization pledged to work together with the Nazi regime to achieve "the liberation of Latvia from the Jews and in principle also from the Russians and the Poles;" see Kangeris, "Kollaboration," 183. On Thunder Cross see also Ezergailis, *Holocaust in Latvia*, 81–84. For LAF statements see Dieckmann, "Lithuania," 370–73. For Estonian Liberation Committee pronouncements, see Kangeris, "Kollaboration," 182. For statements by OUN, see, inter alia, Carynnyk, "Foes of Our Rebirth," 328–34. There does not appear to have been any comparable organization in Byelorussia; see Rozenblat, "Polacy;" Gerlach, *Kalkulierte Morde*, 254.

87 Szarota, *U progu zagłady*, 221.

88 Rossoliński-Liebe, "'Ukrainian National Revolution'," 95–97. Founded in 1929, OUN split into two factions in February 1940. The minority, called OUN-M (after its leader, Andrii Melnyk) sought German assistance for the promotion of Ukrainian national aims and was prepared to subordinate its demands to the larger German political program. The majority, led by Stepan Bandera and known accordingly as OUN-B, pushed for Ukrainian independence even without German endorsement. Subtelny, *Ukraine*, 459–60. *Wehrmacht* was the name of the German army. The Austrian governor's residence in Lwów (initially the palace of a Polish nobleman) had been purchased in the late nineteenth century by *Prosvita*, an organization promoting Ukrainian language and literature, widely regarded as an initiator of the Ukrainian national movement.

89 Slovak and Croatian nationalists had proclaimed independence shortly after Germany had dismantled Czechoslovakia (March 1939) and Yugoslavia (April 1941), respectively, and Germany had recognized the governments they had established.

90 Szarota, *U progu zagłady*, 222.

91 Dieckmann, *Deutsche Besatzungspolitik*, 313.

92 Struve, *Deutsche Herrschaft*, 305–306 (on the militia: 298–394).

93 Himka, "Lviv Pogrom," 211–15.

94 Struve, *Deutsche Herrschaft*, 252.

95 Himka, "Lviv Pogrom," 210–11, 215–16. Rapes of women were also reported; Himka, "Lviv Pogrom," 213.

96 The term refers here to anti-Soviet guerillas.

97 "Report by SS Brigadeführer Stahlecker…," 15 October 1941, in International Military Tribunal, *Trial*, 37:677–78.

98 International Military Tribunal, *Trial*, 682–83. Stahlecker did not mention that the Klimaitis group had been extraordinarily vicious in their work, including bludgeoning, mutilation, and decapitation of victims. For a description, see Kassow, "Inside," 13.

99 See Dieckmann, *Deutsche Besatzungspolitik*, 467–79.

100 Rossoliński-Liebe, "'Ukrainian National Revolution,'" 96.

101 "Operational Situation Report USSR No. 10," 2 July 1941, in Arad et al., *Einsatzgruppen Reports*, 2–3.

102 Rossoliński-Liebe, "'Ukrainian National Revolution,'" 100.

103 Posivnych, *Bandera*, 126. Bandera was released from prison shortly thereafter, but in 1942 he was incarcerated in the German concentration camp at Sachsenhausen, where he remained until 1944. Toward the end of the war the Germans freed him, hoping he would mobilize Ukrainians to fight against the Soviet march westward.

104 Rossoliński-Liebe, *Bandera*, 218.

105 In August 1941 Germany awarded another part of the pre-1939 Ukrainian SSR, the area between the Dniester and the Southern Bug rivers, including Odessa, to Romania. Romania called the territory "Transnistrian Government." On the experience and fate of Jews there, see p. 73.

106 Shkandrij, *Ukrainian Nationalism*, 59–60.

107 Himka, "Lviv Pogrom," 220–21. On the process of subordination see Struve, *Deutsche Herrschaft*, 387–89.

108 "Operational Situation Report USSR No. 11," 3 July 1941, in Arad et al., *Einsatzgruppen Reports*, 4.

109 "Operational Situation Report USSR No. 24," 16 July 1941, in Arad et al., *Einsatzgruppen Reports*, 31. These residents appear to have included not only Ukrainians but Poles as well, an ethnic mix that further dampened the Ukrainian nationalist thrust of the violence. Struve, *Deutsche Herrschaft*, 353. Ethnic Poles comprised a majority of the city's population.

110 Struve, *Deutsche Herrschaft*, 394–402; 418–28.

111 Ezergailis, *Holocaust in Latvia*, 177–78, 180–83; Angrick and Klein, *"Final Solution"*, 66–67.

112 "Report by SS Brigadeführer Stahlecker . . . ," 15 October 1941, in International Military Tribunal, *Trial*, 37:683, 688.

113 Angrick and Klein, *"Final Solution"*, 68–77; Ezergailis, *Holocaust in Latvia*, 188–90.

114 Angrick and Klein, *"Final Solution"*, 76.

115 On Ukrainian, Lithuanian, and Latvian nationalist connections with German military intelligence, as well as with other agencies of the Nazi regime, and on messages about Jews transmitted via those connections, see, inter alia, Rossoliński-Liebe, "'Ukrainian National Revolution,'" 91–92; Golczewski, "Kollaboration," 158–61; Torzecki, "Rolle," 241–50; Dieckmann, *Deutsche Verwaltungspolitik*, 246–61; Kangeris, "Baltische Emigranten," 168–74, 176–86; Ezergailis, *Holocaust in Latvia*, 121–23. Poles were in a different position, as Germans did not offer them comparable connections. Nevertheless, reports from Polish underground sources concerning opinion among Poles in the Soviet-occupied parts of the country compiled during 1940 point not only to widespread identification of Jews with the Soviet regime but also to a pervasive feeling that Jews had betrayed Poland in September 1939 by welcoming the Soviet invaders and by supporting its efforts to suppress Polish resistance. Such

feelings appear to have been known and shared by Poles living under German occupation, and Germans were undoubtedly aware of them. See Engel, *In the Shadow*, 60–64.

116 See Hanebrink, *Specter*, 28–37.

117 Budnitskii, *Russian Jews*, 216.

118 See p. 298n70. For casualty estimates see Engel, *Assassination*, 59–60. On attacks in Ukrainian, Byelorussian, and Russian lands that became part of the Soviet Union in 1922, see Miliakova, *Livre des pogroms*. On violence in territories that became part of the Second Polish Republic, see Hagen, *Anti-Jewish Violence*. The Baltic states appear to have witnessed only isolated, small-scale violent incidents; Ezergailis, *Holocaust*, 64–65; Sirutavičius and Staliūnas, "Lithuania," 146.

119 United States Holocaust Memorial Museum, Washington, DC, RG-31.023 (quotations from items 105, 107). See also Koval, "Nazi Genocide," 52.

120 "Operational Situation Report USSR No. 24," 16 July 1941, July 1941, in Arad et al., *Einsatzgruppen Reports*, 28; "Operational Situation Report USSR No. 106," 7 October 1941, in Arad et al., *Einsatzgruppen Reports*, 171.

121 See, for example, the descriptions of the interactions between Jews, Poles, and Ukrainians in Redlich, *Together*, 44–70.

122 Zinger, *Dos banayte folk*, 27–31.

123 Altshuler, *Soviet Jewry* (1998), 74–76.

124 Testimony of Fedot Petrenco, quoted in Dumitru, *State*, 130. The informant described an area of the USSR that fell under Romanian control after June 1941; see below, at n. 171. For indications of mitigated tensions between Jews and non-Jews in other areas and assessment of additional factors driving the trend, see Zeltser, "Ethnic Conflict," 181–82; Dekel-Chen, "Defusing the Ethnic Bomb," 191–98.

125 There is evidence that some German observers shared this perception. See, for example, the comment from the Propaganda Task Force of Army Group Center, 11 August 1941: "Efforts to bring about progroms [*sic*] against the Jews have failed. The reason is that, in the eyes of the average Russian, the Jew has a proletarian lifestyle and is therefore not a suitable object of attack." Quoted in Pohl, *Herrschaft*, 245.

126 See, for example, Redlich, *Together*, 91. For a different view, see Rozenblat, "'Contact Zones.'"

127 Gross, *Revolution from Abroad*, 126–30; Redlich, *Together*, 84–85; Żaroń, *Ludność polska*, 98–116.

128 See, inter alia, Brakel, "Was there a 'Jewish Collaboration'?"; Kopstein and Wittenberg, *Intimate Violence*, 5–7; Levin, *Tekufah beSograyim*, 48–63, 68–70; Polonsky, *Jews*, 3:389–94.

129 One study has identified a correlation in six prewar Polish districts between incidence of local civilian violence and certain voting patterns by Jews and non-Jews during the 1920s. See Kopstein and Wittenberg, *Intimate Violence*, esp. 62–72, 81–83, 94–104. The correlation has yet to be tested for other parts of the USSR that fell under German occupation. More important, it is hardly

obvious that such a correlation should be causative by itself. Much changed in Poland during the 1930s, but the study did not seek correlations with the same variables as they expressed themselves during that decade, let alone with even a significant portion of the range of possible variables. Moreover, the study did not distinguish among incidents according to number of deaths or percentage of Jews killed, nor between violence pursued through what the Germans regarded as "proper channels" and violence conducted outside of those channels.

130 In at least two dozen locations, evacuating Soviet forces, unable or unwilling to provide transport for prisoners in their custody, chose to execute prisoners who had been incarcerated by the NKVD as politically suspect instead of allowing them to be freed by the Germans. The best-documented estimates of the number of prisoners killed range from ninety-four hundred to twenty-four thousand. Hryciuk, "Victims," 183–84; Struve, *Deutsche Herrschaft*, 215–16. Jews and Poles appear to have been overrepresented among those imprisoned for security reasons. Executions took place mostly in East Galicia and Volhynia; most of those executed in these provinces appear to have been ethnic Ukrainians, with Poles comprising about a quarter of the victims. Jews were evidently also among the victims. Struve, *Deutsche Herrschaft*, 253. Places where the discovery of the bodies of the executed prisoners was followed by local attacks upon Jews included Lwów, Tarnopol, Złoczów, Borysław, Brzeżany, Krzemieniec, Sambor, Stryj, and Telšiai.

131 A relatively large number of violent attacks occurred during the interregnum between Soviet withdrawal and the establishment of German rule. See Mędykowski, *W cieniu gigantów*, 164–82; Rozenblat, "Polacy," 65–66.

132 The importance of personal connections is illustrated in approximately a dozen cases in which local non-Jews, including the foreman of a local dairy, a church organist, an attorney, and Catholic or Orthodox priests are reported to have faced down aggressive crowds or dissuaded would-be attackers from harming Jews. In some instances the motivation for action is said to have stemmed from previous favorable personal connections with local Jewish leaders.

133 Testimony of Rachel Shimonovitsch, Institute of Contemporary Jewry, Oral History Division, Hebrew University, Jerusalem, 51–9/13.

134 Testimony of Zillia Tokarski, Institute of Contemporary Jewry, Oral History Division, Hebrew University, Jerusalem, 51–2/1. Cf. Lidowski, *USheviv haEsh*, 55.

135 Shternsis, "Between Life and Death," 494–96; Schneier, "Giluyei haAntishemiyut," 88.

136 This long-contested region had belonged to the Hungarian part of Austria-Hungary between 1867 and 1918. Following the Austro-Hungarian collapse at the end of the First World War, Hungarian, Ukrainian, and Czech-Slovak forces fought for control. The 1919 Treaty of St. Germain, which disposed of the territories of the former Austro-Hungarian Empire, created the autonomous territory of Subcarpathian Rus' (*Podkarpatská Rus*) within the new Czechoslovak state. With the progressive dismemberment of that state following

the Munich Peace Pact, Hungary took control of the province in two stages, the first in November 1938, the second in March 1939. With the German and Hungarian defeats in 1945, the region became a district of the Ukrainian SSR.

137 The USSR established a Republic of Moldova on 2 August 1940. In addition to parts of Bessarabia seized from Romania, it also included pre-1939 Soviet territory designated since 1924 as the Moldavian Autonomous Soviet Socialist Republic, an ostensibly self-governing unit within Soviet Ukraine.

138 Ancel, *Toledot haSho'ah*, 2:757–59; Hitchens, *Romania*, 471–74; Cornelius, *Hungary*, 171–73.

139 The incident involved two or three unidentified airplanes that dropped bombs on the former Slovakian city of Košice (Hungarian Kassa), which Hungary had taken over in 1938. On the incident and on broader Hungarian military and diplomatic considerations concerning participation in the war against the USSR, see Macartney, "Hungary's Declaration;" Cornelius, *Hungary*, 129–52; Weinberg, *World at Arms*, 379–80.

140 Arad, *Toledot haSho'ah*, 1:207–208. On the other hand, Hungarian troops participated in securing the site of a mass German execution of Jews in Kamenets-Podolskii in late August 1941. Arad, *Toledot haSho'ah*, 1:312–13. See also pp. 80–81.

141 Beginning in 1938 the Hungarian government did adopt a series of discriminatory laws against Jews, including a decree of 2 August 1941, modeled after Germany's 1935 Nuremberg Laws, prohibiting marital and sexual relations between Jews and non-Jews. However, the leaders of the Hungarian government regarded those laws more as a sop to its German allies and to its domestic challengers from the radical political right than as an expression of their own personal animus toward Jews. See Braham, *Politics of Genocide*, 24–25.

142 The statement applies to the year and a half following the launching of Operation Barbarossa. Romanian-German cooperation in Jewish matters broke down in late 1942. In March 1944 Germany occupied Hungary, inducing official Hungarian cooperation in the rapid mass deportation of the country's Jews over the next four months.

143 *Conducător*, a Romanian calque of the Italian *Duce* and the German *Führer*.

144 Hitchens, *Romania*, 453–58, 471–73; Deletant, *Hitler's Forgotten Ally*, 48–51, 79–82. Ironically, Romania had also recently lost territory to Hungary and to Bulgaria under German and Italian pressure, but its capitulation merely highlighted the degree to which Germany held the key to its future borders.

145 The Romanian census of 1930 counted 756,930 Jews. According to an estimate by the Romanian Interior Ministry in 1939, the number had grown to 765,000. Following territorial losses to the USSR, Hungary, and Bulgaria only 302,000 remained under Romanian rule. Ancel, *Toledot haSho'ah*, 1:7, 2:1347.

146 For details, see Ioanid, *Holocaust*, 18–31. On at least one occasion Antonescu spoke of ghettoization and expulsion as desirable means for ending "promiscuity between kikes (*jidani*) and Romanians." Florian, "Antonescu Regime," 101–2.

147 Hostile, even violent sentiments toward foreigners had long figured in the speeches and writings of revered Romanian cultural and political figures. Weber, "Romania," 504–8.

148 Solonari, "Model Province," 485–87.

149 Ioanid, *Holocaust*, 37–43; Ancel, *Toledot haSho'ah*, 1:175–200.

150 "Extras din discursul lui Mihai Antonescu . . . ," 3 July 1941, in Carp, *Cartea neagră*, 3:91.

151 "Extras din discursul lui Ion Antonescu . . . ," 8 July 1941, in Carp, *Cartea neagră*, 3:92. Cf. the more extensive extract in Arad, *Toledot haSho'ah*, 1:416, in which the Leader is recorded as having spoken of "merciless extermination" and as having promised to absolve soldiers of all legal responsibility for shooting Jews. Some sources ascribe the speech to Mihai Antonescu. See Ancel, *Toledot haSho'ah*, 1:540–41. In any case, Ion Antonescu had already indicated a week earlier that Jews from Bessarabia and Bukovina were engaged in sabotage against Romanian forces and ordered that "all those who act in any way against the army and against the interests of the nation be executed on the spot." Quoted in Solonari, "Patterns," 57.

152 Quoted in International Commission, *Final Report*, 128. For details, see Ancel, *Toledot haSho'ah*, 1:547–48.

153 *Einsatzgruppe* D was the smallest of the *Einsatzgruppen* and the last to be formed. Browning, *Origins*, 225; Hilberg, *Destruction*, 289. These facts may reflect a German belief that Romanian elements could be counted upon to carry the major burden of killing in the south. See Angrick, "Einsatzgruppe D," 88; Longerich, *Holocaust*, 201–203.

154 For detailed discussion of local civilian involvement in the countryside, see Dumitru, *State*, 143–60.

155 Mahler, "Bucovina," 574; Vago, "Romanian Jewry," 33.

156 Solonari, "Patterns," 61.

157 Lavi, "Ciudei," 2:486.

158 International Commission, *Final Report*, 129.

159 Ancel, "Noua-Suliță," 368, 371. Cf. Ancel, *Toledot haSho'ah*, 1:550; Arad, *Toledot haSho'ah*, 1:418.

160 Ancel, "Hotin," 356.

161 Schaary, *Yahadut Bukovina*, 285. Arad, *Toledot haSho'ah*, 1:418 offers an estimate of two thousand killed among fifty-five thousand Jewish residents.

162 Carp, *Cartea neagră*, 3:36. For population estimates, see Ancel, "Kishinev," 1093; Ancel, "Chişinău," 411. An unknown number of Jews, reaching perhaps several tens of thousands, fled the city following the Soviet evacuation, making the number killed by Romanian forces an even higher percentage of the Jewish population.

163 Knowledge of the killings comes mainly from postwar Romanian and Soviet trials of perpetrators. Those trials exposed incidents only in places where the particular defendants on trial served. Killings perpetrated by people who did not stand trial often escaped judicial notice, leaving no record.

164 International Commission, *Final Report*, 177. Other estimates range from 10,000 (Hilberg, *Destruction*, 2:771) to 150,000–160,000 (Ancel, "German-Romanian Relations," 67).

165 When Operation Barbarossa was launched, Bessarabia was estimated to contain 160,000 to 165,000 Jews, Northern Bukovina 70,000. Arad, *Toledot haSho'ah*, 1:416. On relative degrees of Romanian and German participation in killing, see Longerich, *Holocaust*, 201–202.

166 Ancel, "German-Romanian Relations," 65–66; cf. "Operational Situational Report USSR" Nos. 19 (11 July 1941), 22 (14 July 1941), 25 (17 July 1941), 40 (3 August 1941), 61 (23 August 1941).

167 For clarification of the ideological background and practical implications of this goal, see Solonari, "Model Province," 473–85.

168 For an overview of the July-August deportations, see Deletant, *Hitler's Forgotten Ally*, 150–52. For descriptions and varying estimates of numbers deported and killed in the deportation of 24–25 July, see Ioanid, *Holocaust*, 116; International Commission, *Final Report*, 135–36; Arad, *Toledot haSho'ah*, 1:422.

169 See in particular the eyewitness testimony of Solomon Shapira, quoted in Arad, *Toledot haSho'ah*, 1:423; also Ioanid, *Holocaust*, 116–22.

170 International Commission, *Final Report*, 137.

171 Deletant, *Hitler's Forgotten Ally*, 152–53.

172 "Heydrichs nachträgliche schriftliche Einweisung der vier Höheren SS- und Polizeiführer im Osten," 2 July 1941, in Klein, *Einsatzgruppen*, 324. See also Arad, Krakowski, and Spector, *Einsatzgruppen Reports*, viii.

173 Ancel, *Toledot haSho'ah*, 2:757, 786. The difference also includes an undetermined number who fled successfully.

174 Except Odessa, which the Soviets were still defending, with heavy casualties on both sides.

175 For details, see Deletant, *Hitler's Forgotten Ally*, 184–86.

176 Ancel, *Toledot haSho'ah*, 2:798.

177 Deletant, *Hitler's Forgotten Ally*, 186–87. By comparison, mortality in Europe's largest ghetto, Warsaw, stood at 10 percent during the year before the beginning of systematic liquidation in July 1942.

178 Quoted in Deletant, *Hitler's Forgotten Ally*, 178. For the number of Jews under Isopescu's supervision, see International Commission, *Final Report*, 146.

179 See the descriptions in Ioanid, *Holocaust*, 182–87; International Commission, *Final Report*, 146–50; Deletant, *Hitler's Forgotten Ally*, 180–82.

180 According to the 1939 census, Kiev counted 224,236 Jews, some 10 percent more than Odessa's 200,961. Altshuler, *Distribution*, 20–21. However, a greater percentage of Kiev Jews than Odessa Jews escaped before occupation. For details, see below, at n. 225.

181 Borovoi, "Gibel'," 119; Ancel, *Toledot haSho'ah*, 2:758, 786

182 Ancel, *Toledot haSho'ah*, 2:890.

183 Deletant, *Hitler's Forgotten Ally*, 171; International Commission, *Final Report*, 150.

184 The Romanian army set up its command post in what had been the offices of the NKVD. The explosive booby trap had probably been set by NKVD personnel before evacuation.

185 Antonescu's orders of 23 and 24 October quoted in Ioanid, *Holocaust*, 179–80.

186 Ioanid, *Holocaust*, 179–80; Borovoi, "Gibel'," 121–24. One of the warehouses was blown up, perhaps in symbolic retaliation for the bomb that killed the Romanian soldiers. International Commission, *Final Report*, 152.

187 "Za chto?" (recollections of Lidia Slipchenko), in Arad et al., *Nieizvestnaia chernaya kniga*, 100–101. The written text was composed before 1944. The author was a female Jewish doctor married to a Ukrainian man. She escaped Slobodka by ruse thanks to her connections among Ukrainians in the medical world.

188 Arad et al., *Nieizvestnaia chernaya kniga*, 99.

189 In a radio address of 3 July 1941 Stalin had called for guerilla warfare against the occupiers.

190 "File Memorandum, 16 July 1941 . . .," in International Military Tribunal, *Trial*, 38:87, 88, 92.

191 Jews as such were not mentioned explicitly in the meeting, but Heydrich's instruction to the *Einsatzgruppen* of 2 July 1941 (p. 48) had linked "Jews in Party and State employment" with "other radical elements (saboteurs, propagandists, snipers, assassins, inciters, etc.)." The standard Nazi identification of Jews with Bolshevism encouraged the rhetorical treatment of all Jews as "partisans." See Büchler, "*Kommandostab*," 14.

192 "File Memorandum, 16 July 1941 . . .," in International Military Tribunal, *Trial*, 38: 93.

193 On the organizational relationship between the SS and the Order Police, see p. 293n31.

194 Browning, *Ordinary Men*, 10–11.

195 Hartmann, *Wehrmacht*, 653.

196 Büchler, "*Kommandostab*," 15. On the implications of the Rastenburg meeting for the campaign against the Jews, see Breitman, *Architect*, 181–84.

197 Browning, *Origins*, 310.

198 Estimate compiled from figures in Longerich, *Holocaust*, 196–201. The figure of "at least 62,805 persons" killed by *Einsatzgruppen* before the end of July offered in Headland, "*Einsatzgruppen*," 406 actually includes "all categories of victims of the *Kommandos* [including Higher SS and Police units] as well as statistics of pogroms" (412, n. 58). The first executions of Jews, by *Einsatzkommando Tilsit*, a police unit attached to *Einsatzgruppe A*, took place in the Lithuanian towns of Gargždai, Kretinga, and Palanga on 24–27 June 1941. A total of 526 Jews were shot during these operations. See Kwiet, "Rehearsing," 4. The combined Jewish population of the three locations at the time of the German invasion was likely between two thousand and twenty-three hundred.

199 See, for example, "Operational Situational Report USSR No. 21," 13 July 1941, in Arad et al., *Einsatzgruppen Reports*, 22: "The Lithuanian Ordnungsdienst

[Security Police] which was placed under the Einsatzkommando after the Lithuanian political police [of LAF] had been dissolved... arrested the Jews and put them into concentration camps where they were subjected the same day to Special Treatment [execution]."

200 Dieckmann, *Deutsche Besatzungspolitik*, 325–31.

201 Dieckmann, *Deutsche Besatzungspolitik*, 342–45, 353–61; Arad, *Vilnah*, 65–78. For the high estimate of numbers killed see Longerich, *Holocaust*, 199. For descriptions of similar operations in other towns and regions in the territories of *Einsatzgruppen A*, *B*, and *C*, see, inter alia, Kwiet, "Rehearsing," 5–8; Gerlach, *Kalkulierte Morde*, 791–92; Cholawski, *BeSufat haKilayon*, 184–96; Lower, *Nazi Empire-Building*, 73–74.

202 For details see Bender, *Mul mavet*, 105–108; Curilla, *Deutsche Ordnungspolizei*, 510–18.

203 Bender, *Mul mavet*, 110–11; Browning, *Ordinary Men*, 14–15.

204 Testimony of Heinrich (last name not given), a member of Police Battalion 307, in Gitelman, *Bitter Legacy*, 281–83. For additional details and varying numerical estimates see Garrard and Garrard, "Barbarossa's First Victims," 19–23; Bauer, *Rethinking*, 153–54; Browning, *Nazi Policy*, 119–21.

205 A week before the massacre, a unit of *Einsatzgruppe A* had executed two hundred Jewish men, only to move on with the advancing front. Garrard and Garrard, "Barbarossa's First Victims," 18.

206 "Operational Situation Report USSR No. 94," 25 September 1941, in Arad et al., *Einsatzgruppen Reports*, 158.

207 Calculated from incomplete figures compiled in Browning, *Ordinary Men*, 17.

208 Gerlach, *Kalkulierte Morde*, 794.

209 Pohl, *Herrschaft*, 157; Nadav, "Pinsk," 295.

210 See pp. 68–69.

211 Segal, *Genocide*, 6.

212 Segal, *Genocide*, 75–76.

213 Segal, *Genocide*, 73; Pohl, "Murder," 29. The difference between Germany's willingness to assign Soviet territory to Romania and its unwillingness to do the same for Hungary no doubt reflected its assessment of the two states' contributions to its war effort. In addition, Germany, having twisted Romania's arm a year earlier to cede northern Transylvania to Hungary, now found occasion to compensate it at Soviet expense. As far as Germany was concerned, Hungary merited no compensation.

214 Quoted in Pohl, "Murder," 29.

215 Pohl, *Herrschaft*, 257.

216 Pohl, *Herrschaft*, 257–58; Pohl, "Murder," 30–32.

217 See p. 48.

218 Altshuler, *Soviet Jewry* (1987), 4; "Statistics of Jews," *American Jewish Year Book* 48 (1946–47): 599–604.

219 The words belonged to Stahlecker. See "Stahlecker's Answer to [Hinrich] Lohse's Guidelines on Treatment of Jews in the Ostland," 6 August 1941, in

Ezergailis, *Holocaust*, 378–80. For analysis of this document, and for additional evidence that in summer 1941 Germany's leaders envisioned the complete annihilation of Soviet Jews, not only in Stahlecker's domain but throughout the USSR, see Browning, *Path*, 101–11.

220 Weinberg, *World at Arms*, 367.

221 Fritz, *Ostkrieg*, 111–12.

222 Fritz, *Ostkrieg*, 114–22 (quotations 121); Weinberg, *World at Arms*, 371–72.

223 See "File Memorandum," International Military Tribunal, *Trial*, 38:88.

224 Fritz, *Ostkrieg*, 124–34; Tooze, *Wages*, 487–89.

225 For detailed descriptions, see Levitas, "Babyn Yar," 95–98; Breitman, *Architect*, 211–12.

226 During its most intensive operation, the murder of 435,000 Jews deported from Hungary between 15 May and 9 July 1944, killings at Auschwitz-Birkenau averaged approximately 8,000 per day, less than half that at Kiev. Treblinka was most active between 23 July and 21 September 1942, when gassings reached upward of 4,000 daily.

227 Pohl, *Herrschaft*, 259–60; Arad, *Toledot haSho'ah*, 1:324–28; Levitas, "Babyn Yar," 108–12. See also the statistical tables in Zabarko, *Holocaust*, 388–89.

228 The 1939 Soviet census counted 250,181 Jews in the city. Altshuler, *Distribution*, 28. An estimate for early 1941 put the Jewish population at 430,000. *American Jewish Year Book* 43 (1941–1942): 319. Any population increase was doubtless due mainly to an influx of Jewish refugees and evacuees from the German-occupied regions.

229 Glantz and House, *Titans*, 393.

230 Fritz, *Ostkrieg*, 145–62.

231 The 1939 Soviet census counted 201,542 Jews in Leningrad. Altshuler, *Distribution*, 30. For the higher 1941 estimate, see *Congress Weekly*, 9 January 1942 [11–13].

232 See p. 289n218.

233 For various estimates, see Bidlack and Lomagin, *Leningrad Blockade*, 270–73. Death tolls from suburbs within the siege area bring the total to around nine hundred thousand.

234 For details, see Bidlack and Lomagin, *Leningrad Blockade*, 239–43.

235 The estimate implies an average mortality among Jews of 1,400 to 2,500 per month over the siege's twenty-nine-month interval. By comparison, German restrictions on food supplies in the Warsaw ghetto in Poland induced a monthly average of 4,300 Jewish deaths during the twelve months between June 1941 and May 1942, before active mass murder in the ghetto began. Gutman, *Yehudei Varshah*, 82.

236 Figures in Altshuler, *Distribution*, 9–12. The count encompasses the following administrative regions (*krai*, *oblast*, or ASSR) of the Russian SFSR: Cheliabinsk, Gorkii, Irkutsk, Khabarovsk (including the Jewish Autonomous Region of Birobidzhan), Krasnoyarsk, Kuibyshev, Novosibirsk, Omsk, Primorye, Saratov, Sverdlovsk, Tatar ASSR, and Iaroslavl, each with five thousand to thirty-one

thousand Jews, along with twenty-four additional regions with forty-nine hundred Jews or fewer.

237 On these activities, see chapters 4 and 6.

238 For calculation of the numbers, see Arad, *Toledot haSho'ah*, 1:200–202. The listed total of between 1.122 and 1.173 million does not include 100,000 to 125,000 Jews from former Polish, Romanian, and Baltic states territories deported to the Soviet interior in 1940 and 1941 (see pp. 33 and 37) or some 250,000 to 300,000 Jews evacuated from Moscow and Leningrad in summer and fall 1941. Altogether between 1,450,000 and 1,550,000 Jews had left their homes for the interior by the end of 1941. See Dubson, "Toward a Central Database," 102; Dubson, "On the Problem," 38.

239 Estimates range between seven and twenty-five million. For an evaluation and justification of a low estimate, see Dubson, "Toward a Central Database," 96, 103–108. For justification of the estimate of 16.5 million, see Belsky, *Encounters*, 3. On the state's evacuation program and the categories of people encompassed by it, see Manley, *To the Tashkent Station*, 33–41. There does not appear to be any basis for determining how many Jews were evacuated as part of the official program and how many fled of their own initiative.

240 Levin, *Tekufah*, 332.

241 Of course, leaving did not guarantee survival. Some who took to the roads found their paths blocked and were forced to return; others perished in German artillery or air bombardments. Figures for the entire Soviet Union are not available. A study of evacuation from Eastern Byelorussia estimated that 181,000 of the 384,000 Jews of the region reached areas beyond the German occupation. 133,000 were escapees or civilian evacuees, 48,000 military draftees. Of these, 160,000 to 170,000 remained alive at the end of the war. Altshuler, "HaPinnui," 150–51.

242 Figures compiled from Altshuler, "Escape," 91–99; Arad, *Toledot haSho'ah*, 1:183–98. See also Pinchuk, *Yehudei Berit-haMo'atsot*, 92–124. For a fuller discussion of the evacuees and their experiences, see chapters 3 and 6.

243 "Operational Situation Report USSR No. 73," 4 September 1941, in Arad et al., *Einsatzgruppen Reports*, 120–21.

244 Arad, *Toledot haSho'ah*, 1:353–56. For details on personnel involved in the killing operation, see Radchenko, "Znyshchennia kharkivs'kikh evreiv."

245 See Beorn, *Marching*, esp. 92–118.

246 Gerlach, *Extermination*, 99n11.

247 See p. 47.

248 Arad, *Toledot haSho'ah*, 1:215–19. See also p. 121.

249 Except in regional capitals (Białystok, Kaunas, Minsk, Riga, Wilno), these initial steps did not include segregation of Jews in closed residential quarters (ghettos). Hundreds of ghettos were established in the occupied USSR, but most followed compulsory marking and the appointment of Jewish councils by weeks or months and were ordered by SS or civilian officials. On reasons for eventual ghettoization see Michman, *Emergence*, 110–21.

250 "Report by the Economic Staff East, Group Agriculture," 23 May 1941, in International Military Tribunal, *Trial*, 36:148, 154. See also Tooze, *Wages*, 479; Gerlach, *Extermination*, 218–19.

251 They envisioned a residual force of sixty divisions, which was a third the size of the invasion army (or less). Mazower, *Hitler's Empire*, 134. Once conquest was complete, resources would be sent to Germany and its allies before local inhabitants were allowed to claim them, leaving an estimated twenty to thirty million locals to starve. Tooze, *Wages*, 476–80. Cf. "Report...," 23 May 1941, in International Military Tribunal, *Trial*, 36:145–47.

252 The same calculation applied to Red Army prisoners of war. See, inter alia, Fritz, *Ostkrieg*, 166–69.

253 Dieckmann, "HaMilhamah," 290–300.

254 Testimony of Mikhael Potashnik, in Bankier and Kilbansky, *Expulsion*, [MS 137–38]. For a description of a shooting operation in the North Caucasian town of Mineralnye Vody in 1943, based on eyewitness testimony, see pp. 159–60.

255 On 1 December 1941 the commander of *Einsatzkommando 3*, Karl Jäger, reported killing 133,346 people in Lithuania between 4 July and 25 November. 1,898 of these were not Jews. Another 4,934 were Jews who had been deported to Kaunas from Germany and Austria. "The only remaining Jews," he stated, "are laborers and their families: in Shavli [*sic*] ca. 4,500; in Kovno [*sic*] ca. 15,000; in Vilna [*sic*] ca. 15,000." Text in Hilberg, *Documents*, 47–57. For somewhat larger estimates, including five hundred in Święciany, see Dieckmann, *Deutsche Besatzungspolitik*, 1009, 1014. Small numbers of Jews also remained in other provincial towns in the Wilno district, including Michaliszki, Oszmiana, and Soły. Arad, *Vilnah*, 290. Between forty-five hundred and fifty-five hundred Jews remained in Riga after a major killing operation on 8 December; Ezergailis, *Holocaust*, 248. Virtually all of the one thousand Jews in Estonia who did not flee eastward before the German invasion were killed between October 1941 and January 1942. Weiss-Wendt, "Holocaust," 130.

256 Dieckmann, *Deutsche Besatzungspolitik*, 649–50, 1009–13; Arad, *Vilnah*, 127–31, 151–57; Ezergailis, *Holocaust*, 221–30, 247–48, 271–302.

257 Mendelsohn, *Jews*, 225–26, 244–45.

258 See Bubnys, "Holocaust," 209–11; Arad, "Murder," 187–89.

259 Dieckmann, *Deutsche Besatzungspolitik*, 951–56; Ezergailis, *Holocaust*, 239–61. In his report of 1 December (see above at note 255), Karl Jäger indicated that the ability to cooperate with Lithuanian "partisans" had been necessary for mass killing to succeed.

260 Cholawski, *Al neharot haNieman*, 18–20; Cholawski, *BeSufat haKilayon*, 17–18.

261 *Pinkas haKehillot* lists 588 locations of Jewish residence in prewar Lithuania and another 114 in Estonia and Latvia, as opposed to 204 throughout the prewar Polish provinces of Białystok, Nowogródek, and Wilno. The three Polish provinces were home to nearly 300,000 Jews in September 1939, the three Baltic States to 260,000.

262 Dieckmann, *Deutsche Besatzungspolitik*, 519–20; Dean, *Collaboration*, 64. So great was the imbalance that in October 1941 the Twelfth Lithuanian *Schutzmannschaft* Battalion was transferred from Kaunas to the Minsk area to assist in mass executions. Dean, *Collaboration*, 62–63.

263 These are stereotypes typically associated with Jews.

264 "Daklad Lidskaha hebitskamisara majora Chanvieha . . . ," 8 April 1943, in Majsiejonak, "Daklad." At the time the report was written, about forty-five hundred Jews remained alive in Lida, approximately half the number present at the time of the German occupation. Nearly six thousand had been killed in a mass murder operation in May 1942, but several thousand Jews had come to the town from surrounding villages and from the Wilno district, where the threat of death appeared more immediate. See Spector, "Lida," 393. On the reasons for initiating selective killing in 1942, see below.

265 Arad, *Toledot haSho'ah*, 1:298.

266 Arad, *Toledot haSho'ah*, 1:288. Cf. Gerlach, "Einsatzgruppe B," 58.

267 Arad, *Toledot haSho'ah*, 1:288; Lenn, "Slonim," 504; Beorn, *Marching*, 1–2, 135–48.

268 Gebietskommissar Sluzk to Generalkommissar Minsk, 30 October 1941, in International Military Tribunal, *Trial*, 27:4–5.

269 "Report from an Armament Inspector in the Ukraine to General Thomas Personally," 2 December 1941, in International Military Tribunal, *Trial*, 32:73.

270 "Excerpts from Rosenberg's 'Statement . . . Regarding the Relationship between the Reich Minister for the Occupied Eastern Territories and the *Reichsführer-SS*,'" in Matthäus and Bajohr, *Political Diary*, 393. Emphasis in source.

271 See "Report," 2 December 1941, in International Military Tribunal, *Trial*, 32:74–75. He also wondered about the economic consequences of allowing prisoners of war to perish and large parts of the local population to die of hunger.

272 In Volhynia and Podolia (*Generalkommissariat Wolhynien und Podolien*) some 63,000 Jews were killed in 1941, out of approximately 400,000. Of these, approximately 23,500 were Jews from Równe, murdered on 7–9 November 1941. In *Distrikt Galizien* of the Polish *Generalgouvernement*, 56,000 perished out of 570,000. All together, upward of 441,000 Jews in areas of present-day Ukraine under German or Romanian control were killed in sixty-four shooting actions between 1 September and 31 December 1941, but more than twice as many remained alive. In *Distrikt Bialystok* of East Prussia German forces appear to have killed about 25,000 of 150,000 Jews. Figures compiled from Kruglov, "Jewish Losses," 278–79; USHMM *Encyclopedia*, IIa:744, 858–60; IIb:1315. For *Generalkommissariat Weißruthenien*, see p. 93. For Ukraine, see also Burds, *Holocaust*, 20–22. For tabulations by Soviet republic, see Altman, *Zhertvy*, 303.

273 Friedländer, *Prelude*, 303–14.

274 The Soviets retook only a few positions to the west of Moscow. Glantz and House, *Titans*, 108–18; Fritz, *Ostkrieg*, 205–15; Evans, *Third Reich*, 209–14.

275 See Tooze, *Wages*, 504–23.

276 On the dual aims, see pp. 46–47.

277 Herf, *Jewish Enemy*, 83–91, 122–33.
278 "Top-Secret Memorandum by Rosenberg on his Discussion with Hitler," 14 December 1941, in International Military Tribunal, *Trial*, 27:279.
279 Against this background, Rosenberg's statement of early January 1942 (p. 94) should be read as an argument for active efforts to minimize difficulties, recognizing that the aim itself had acquired top-priority status.
280 See p. 312n271.
281 See, for example, Angrick, "Annihilation."
282 Dean, "German *Gendarmerie*," 175–83; Dean, *Collaboration*, 60; Hilberg, *Destruction*, 1:368–70.
283 Arad, *Toledot haSho'ah*, 1:503–18; Arad, *Mivtsa Reinhard*, 169–76. During the final year of occupation, Jews from other parts of Byelorussia and Ukraine met their deaths in similar fashion at three other killing centers—Sobibór, Majdanek, and Auschwitz-Birkenau.
284 Kruglov, "Jewish Losses," 280–81; Gerlach, *Kalkulierte Morde*, 918, 928; Arad, *Toledot haSho'ah*, 2:562, 1008–13. The figure excludes approximately 150,000 Jews in Transnistria, Bukovina, and Bessarabia, who were under Romanian rule. See Ioanid, *Holocaust*, 199–201. About three quarters of the remaining Jews under German rule were concentrated in *Distrikt Galizien*. Mass killings there were coordinated with the administration of the *Generalgouvernement* of Poland, where a different set of considerations from those affecting the other occupied Soviet territories led to wholesale liquidations being spread over a longer interval. See Pohl, *Judenverfolgung*, 179–210.
285 Their number has been estimated at anywhere between thirty-five thousand and seventy-five thousand. See Feferman, *Holocaust*, 230; Altman, *Zhertvy*, 286; Arad, *Toledot haSho'ah*, 1:520–35, 2:1007. The total also includes some forty-two hundred Jews from the Crimean port city Sevastopol, which capitulated to the Germans in early July 1942 after eight months under siege.
286 For numerical estimates see Feferman, *Holocaust*, 293, 297, 307–308; Arab, *Toledot haSho'ah*, 1:535. The name *Gorskie Evrei* was invented for them by nineteenth-century tsarist bureaucrats. See Goluboff, "Jews or Asians?" 117. The thirty-five thousand to forty thousand Mountain Jews were concentrated mainly in Azerbaijan and Dagestan, which did not fall under German occupation.
287 On Karaites under Nazi rule, see Friedman, *Roads*, 153–75. Most Soviet Karaites lived in Crimea, with smaller communities (numbering no more than a few hundred each) in Lithuania, Latvia, Galicia, and Volhynia.
288 For details see Feferman, *Holocaust*, 296–305. On the other hand, a similar group of fifty-five hundred to seven thousand Jews, the Krimchaki of the Crimean Peninsula, indigenous to the region, who spoke a religiolect of the Tatar language and until recently had refused to intermarry with Ashkenazi Jews, was annihilated along with the other thirty thousand to thirty-five thousand Jews of the Peninsula between November 1941 and June 1942. Feferman, *Holocaust*, 171, 280–92; Berlin, "Istoriia krymskoi tragedii;" Loewenthal, "Extinction," 135–36.

289 "Order by Himmler for the Liquidation of the Ghettos of Ostland," 21 June 1943, in Arad et al., *Documents*, 456–57.

290 For details, see, inter alia, Angrick and Klein, *"Final Solution"*, 366–94; Arad, *Vilnah*, 321–35; Bender, *Mul mavet*, 259–92; Pohl, *Nationalsozialistische Judenverfolgung*, 331–61; Yones, *Ashan*, 182–88. Following promulgation of the order, the SS and Organisation Todt established a series of camps in Estonia, designed to employ up to fifty thousand prisoners in the quarrying of shale and the extraction of oil from the rock. Dworzecki, *Mahanot*, 66.

291 Most of these survived in Transnistria, where Romania had ceased active killing operations after the first six months of its rule. In late 1942, sensing eventual German defeat, Romania decided to refuse further cooperation with Germany in its war against the Jews. See Ancel, *Toledot haSho'ah*, 2:1258–61.

292 Arad, *Toledot haSho'ah*, 2:1007–1014. The figure of 103,000 to 119,000 total survivors (1014) includes workers taken to Germany in the last stages of the war and liberated there.

293 Milch, *Testament*, 278–79.

3. SPACES FOR SURVIVAL

1 See p. 310n238.

2 Margalit, "Yoman," 353–54. Jews traditionally called the town "Ludmir."

3 Korczak, *Lehavot*, 8–9. Cf. the contemporary description by the Soviet war correspondent Konstantin Simonov: "Jewish refugees from the vicinity of Bialystok, from Lida, and from hundreds of Jewish towns made their way along the roads . . . [,] elderly people, whom I had never encountered, with sidelocks and beards . . . [,] fatigued women who had aged prematurely and children . . . [,] on each cart six, eight, and ten dark-eyed children." Quoted in Altshuler, "Evacuation," 70.

4 Tory, *Surviving*, 6.

5 Tory, *Surviving*, 6.

6 See, for example, in *Pinkas haKehilot: Polin*, the entries for Buczacz, Dobromil, Drohobycz, Przemyślany, Sambor, and Drohobycz (East Galicia); Drohiczyn, Łuck, and Szumsk (Volhynia and Polesie); Grodno, Ilja, Jeziory, Swisłocz, Szarkowszczyzna, and Zabłudów (Wilno, Białystok, and Nowogródek Districts). See also Bankier and Kilbansky, *Expulsion*, [MS 57–58, 74]; Arad, *Horet*, 53–54; Kless, *Gevulot*, 34; Altshuler, "Evacuation," 71; Spector, *Sho'at yehudei Vohlin*, 47–48; Levin, *Tekufah*, 319.

7 *Pinkas haKehilot* records Jews encountering such interference while attempting to flee Dawidgródek, Łunieniec, Nowogródek, Pińsk, Sarny, and Šiauliai, among others. For additional examples see Levin, *Tekufah*, 326–27. Border enforcement appears to have been up to individual commanders. See Kless, *Gevulot*, 35–36; Cholawski, *Al neharot haNieman*, 95–96; Altshuler, "HaPinnui," 120. The same is true regarding enforcement of martial law, proclaimed by the Supreme Soviet

on the day of the invasion in territories on both sides of the former border. See pp. 213–14.

8 Such was the case especially in the newly annexed territories, which had not benefited from the Soviet rail expansion of the 1920s and 1930s. Hence, for example, the situation in Święciany (in Poland until 1939), as described retrospectively by a Jewish teenager: "There were no means of transportation at the disposal of those who wanted to flee except for carts or bicycles, which only a few had." Arad, *Horet*, 52.

9 See p. 314n3.

10 Kaminska, *My Life*, 144–50 (quoted words on 149).

11 Kaminska, *My Life*, 151–59.

12 See, inter alia, the testimonies quotes in Altshuler, "Evacuation," 59–60; Maksudov, "Evacuation," 121–22; Cholawski, *BeSufat haKilayon*, 45–48.

13 See p. 27.

14 Manley, *To the Tashkent Station*, 33–36; Shveibish, "Evakuatsiia," 37–41.

15 Levin, *Tekufah*, 329–30. There are indications that during the first three months following the German invasion, Jews comprised a greater proportion of evacuees, both official and unofficial, than their percentage of the population in the areas occupied during that time. Altshuler, "Evacuation," 68. The disproportion is probably best explained by Jews' increasing entry into Soviet economic, political, and cultural elites during the previous two decades, combined with a wider feeling among Jews of an urgent need to leave. In any event, there does not appear to have been official policy awarding Jews priority in evacuation. See Kaganovitch, "Jewish Refugees," 88–93; Pinchuk, *Yehudei Berit-haMo'atsot*, 86–92, 125–30; Cholawski, *BeSufat haKilayon*, 51–53.

16 Smoliar, *Yehudim*, 15; Broderzon, *Mayn laydns-veg*, 32.

17 Altshuler, "HaPinnui," 126. For additional details on official Soviet evacuation policy, see pp. 213–16.

18 Manley, *To the Tashkent Station*, 52–54.

19 Testimony of Shlomo Mann and Yisrael Glazer, in Dror, "HaAh'vah," 227.

20 Alexander, "My Life," 8.

21 See Altshuler, "Evacuation," 59–60; Dror, "HaAh'vah," 226–28; Kless, *Gevulot*, 36–37; Levin, *Tekurah*, 330.

22 Altshuler, "Evacuation," 68.

23 Levin, *Tekufah*, 326. Women and children do not appear to have been favored as a matter of general policy, but in some places local authorities afforded them preference. Manley, *To the Tashkent Station*, 36–37.

24 Fuks, *A vanderung*, 112.

25 Dzigan, *Der koyekh*, 196. The author and his theater company were actually touring by train when war broke out, but they needed to entice railroad workers in Kharkov to attach their cars to an evacuation transport heading for Tashkent. See also Altshuler, "Evacuation," 71.

26 See pp. 26–27.

27 Broderzon, *Mayn laydens-veg*, 33.

28 Testimony of Shlomo Mann and Yisrael Glazer, in Dror, "HaAh'vah," 227.
29 Kless, *Gevulot*, 36; Maksudov, "Evacuation," 121.
30 Levin, *Tekufah*, 331.
31 Altshuler, "Evacuation," 70; Shternshis, "Between Life and Death," 490. See also p. 221.
32 See, for example, Naftali Kamienicki, "Di yidishe Lide in fayer un untergang," Yad Vashem Archives, M1E/954/802. See also Levin, *Tekufah*, 321.
33 See p. 24.
34 Dzigan, *Der koyekh*, 195.
35 "Conversation of the writer A. A. Bek with Comrade Iakov Borisovich Gertsovich," 18 November 1941, in Matthäus, *Jewish Responses*, 130. See also Levin, *Tekufah*, 320; Cholawski, *Al neharot haNieman*, 95.
36 See, inter alia, Mędykowski, *W cieniu gigantów*, 83–102, 110–14.
37 Shternshis, "Between Life and Death," 494–97. For additional examples see pp. 220–21. On German evaluations of such talk and their implications for Soviet Jews, see p. 49.
38 Shechner, *Mot haZeman*, 38–39.
39 Quoted in Levin, *Tekufah*, 321.
40 Milch, *Testament*, 102–103. When the last Soviet troops departed Tłuste on 6 July 1941, peasants killed some Jews in surrounding villages. By some accounts, local priests prevented attacks within the city. Weiss, "Tłuste," 269. Milch provided no details of these events. Cf. Shechner, *Mot haZeman*, 40–41.
41 Shechner, *Mot haZeman*, 39.
42 Quoted in Levin, *Tekufah*, 321. Shkolnik did not see his family for several months.
43 See p. 314n3; Smoliar, *Yehudim*, 12.
44 From a memoir by Ezra Rivlis, quoted in Cholawski, *BiSufat haKilayon*, 51.
45 From a memoir by Ezra Rivlis, quoted in Cholawski, *BiSufat haKilayon*, 51.
46 Cholawski, *Al neharot haNieman*, 95; Levin, *Tekufah*, 318.
47 For cases of both types see Smoliar, *Vu bistu?*, 166; Arad, *Horet*, 54; Altshuler, "Evacuation," 58. And cf. Kruk, *Last Days*, 58–60.
48 Dzigan, *Der koyekh*, 191.
49 Arad, *Horet*, 53–54. Rudnicki was unpersuaded. He had run from German-occupied Warsaw for the Soviet zone in 1939, leaving his parents behind to experience the ghetto regime that his uncle pronounced preferable to leaving. By his account, he was the only one among his friends and family in Święciany to have tasted German rule firsthand; the taste made him press for flight. In the end, however, after traveling for eight kilometers with two friends and a group of about twenty retreating Soviet soldiers, "We were suddenly fired upon from the edge of a nearby forest. A few soldiers at the head of the column were wounded. The group split apart.... [At] a crossroads near a village ... we found the naked corpses of five young men from our area. They had apparently been killed shortly before by villagers or by Lithuanian militias. The sight of the bodies had a strong effect upon us. We decided to return to our town, Święciany." On the

other hand, there is evidence of refugees from the German zone who advised against flight on the grounds that the Soviets had proved themselves the less desirable of the two masters. See Spector, *Sho'at yehudei Vohlin*, 47.

50 Shternshis, "Between Life and Death," 491–92; Cholawski, *Al neharot haNieman*, 96; Altshuler, "Evacuation," 71–72. About half of the overall post-1941 Soviet Jewish population was old enough in 1939 to have living memory of the war. Nove and Newth, "Jewish Population," 144. The percentage was greater in the regions where fighting had actually taken place. For additional examples see pp. 218–20.

51 Kahane, "Mikulińce," 78.

52 Agin, "BeMilhemet haOlam," 2:730. Apparently, even after two decades of Soviet rule, this religious Jew continued to identify his place of residence as appropriately "Jewish," unlike points east, which belonged to "them."

53 Testimony of Yitshak Gordon, quoted in Cholawski, *Al neharot haNieman*, 96. See also Levin, *Tekufah*, 324.

54 Kruk, *Last Days*, 46.

55 Even the most sensitive and sympathetic observers of the plight of Jews under Nazi rule to that point did not predict unprecedented suffering, let alone annihilation. In 1940, from his vantage point in Moscow, Peretz Markish composed a forty-poem cycle bemoaning the tragedy that had befallen the Jews of Poland. It was filled with foreboding: "Gold stolen, jewelry scattered / On the threshold an empty cradle / The stake to burn you has been lit / Your love for the world will cost you your life." The poet addressed the Jewish people, figured as a female dancer. But in the end he saw nothing that the Jewish people had not endured many times before in the past: "The Jordan cut your feet like glass / You flooded the rivers of Babylon with your tears / And when they burned you along the Rhine / Did the heavenly stars not come out for you?" He was certain the "heavenly stars" would shine upon the Jews once more: "The muddled day covers your body like sackcloth / The Swastika fans out above your head / There is no sword that has not been sharpened against you / There is no sword that will not break upon you." Markish, *Tsu a yidisher tentserin*, 28, 36, 38. The poem remained unpublished until well after Markish's execution in 1952, most likely because of its harsh depiction not only of Nazi Germany but of the USSR.

56 See p. 107; additional examples in Levin, *Tekufah*, 123–24; Manley, *To the Tashkent Station*, 86–88.

57 See p. 30.

58 Arad, *Horet*, 44, 53–54.

59 See p. 39.

60 What the Soviets knew and understood of German plans for Jews awaits systematic study in Soviet archives.

61 Quoted in Zimmerman, *Polish Underground*, 88.

62 See the extensive discussions in Altshuler, "Escape," 83–91; Altshuler, "HaPinnui," 127–34.

63 Arad, *Horet*, 54; Shechner, *Mot haZeman*, 39.

64 Spector, *Sho'at yehudei Vohlin*, 49–50.
65 Calculation from figures in Mahler, *Yehudei Polin*, 22; Levin, *Tekufah*, 393; Altshuler, "HaPinnui," 149–50.
66 Altshuler, "HaPinnui," 150–58. Cf. Dobson, "On the Problem," 51, which claims four times as many successful escapes in areas occupied during the first two weeks of July 1941 than in areas occupied in June.
67 Calculation from figures in Mahler, *Yehudei Polin*, 22; Levin, *Tekufah* 393.
68 Dean, "Zhytomyr Region," 1510.
69 On the chronological and geographical progression of German mass murder operations during 1941, see pp. 80–84. Soviet archives have yet to reveal definitively how quickly, how far, and in which directions news of the first killings spread. General assessments that Jews in Byelorussia and Ukraine were "being subjected to merciless annihilation," exemplified by reports of shootings of up to four hundred Jews, circulated among high-ranking Soviet officials from mid-August 1941, but only individual incidents were afforded press coverage. See Berkhoff, *Motherland*, 135, 140. The Polish underground appears to have learned of the massacre that occurred in Białystok on 27 June 1941 (see p. 79) some two weeks after the fact, and of the wholesale liquidations of Jewish communities in Lithuania, which began in August, only in October. Puławski, *W obliczu zagłady*, 45–46. Shechner reported learning of the late August murder in Kamenets-Podolskii (see p. 81) shortly after the fact "from official Hungarian sources and from [Hungarian] soldiers stationed" there, as well as from "a tiny number of small children [who] managed to escape from the killing site." He also described "people returning from the front" who told of "mass killing of Jews in cities, towns, and villages." Shechner, *Mot haZeman*, 43–44, 46. None of these examples provides evidence of news crossing the battle front from the German to the Soviet side.
70 On Jews' reception of information about systematic killing on a scale greater than "murders with many victims," see pp. 133–34.
71 For examples, see Shternshis, "Between Life and Death," 494–94; Manley, *To the Tashkent Station*, 85–86.
72 On the quantity of transports, see Dubson, "On the Problem," 47–48. The greatest number of trains were available to evacuees in the war zone during the second half of July. Before and after that interval more trains were allocated to Moscow and Leningrad. Dubson, "On the Problem," 52–53. However, evacuations for most places of Jewish settlement in areas that fell to the Germans in August and later had already been carried out during late July. Altshuler, "Escape," 97–98; Altshuler, "HaPinnui," 140–43.
73 Also, fewer aircraft were available. The German air force had lost some two-thirds of its planes during the first two months of the war. Glantz and House, *Titans*, 98.
74 See especially Feferman, "'Jews' War'," 580–81.
75 Feferman, "Jews' War," 581–82.
76 See p. 32.

77 Fuks, *A vanderung*, 151.

78 In a sense, differing perspectives on evacuation exacerbated a divergence that had arguably begun during the 1920s. See Slezkine, *Jewish Century*, 242–75.

79 "Vystuplenie po radio...V. M. Molotova, 22 iyunia 1941 goda," *Pravda*, 23 June 1941, 1.

80 For a description of the process among young Soviet Ukrainians, see Weiner, *Making Sense*, 369–74. Dzigan noted a similar collapse of confidence among his fellow refugees in Poland: "We observed Soviet life, its awful administration, the hardships, the scarcity....We refugees were certain that the army's...needs must be swallowing all others because it has to be strong, an iron wall. It turned out that it too was a victim of Soviet poverty. Only then did a lot of Red enthusiasts among us begin to understand that the misfortune was rooted in the failed system...." Dzigan, *Der koyekh*, 195.

81 See the extensive discussion in Manley, *To the Tashkent Station*, 77–111.

82 Even veteran Jewish communists were among the disgruntled. David Lifschitz, one-time editor of the Minsk Jewish communist newspaper *Oktiabr*, later chairman of the state-run Byelorussian Association of Journalists, reportedly accused the state and party leadership of treachery: "They betrayed us...They ran away like cowards, deserters, without even giving us a warning...They ordered us to dig ditches and anti-tank trenches. We were disciplined party members, so we obeyed. But they escaped, and what's more, instead of loading up their trucks with people they used them to take their personal belongings." Smoliar, *Yehudim*, 29–30.

83 From a confidential German Propaganda Ministry press directive, 25 June 1941, quoted in Herf, *Jewish Enemy*, 95. On dissemination see Altshuler, "Escape," 89. In early July 1941 Panteleimon Ponomarenko, first secretary of the Communist Party of Byelorussia, wrote to Stalin that all enemy agitation "is being conducted under the banner of a struggle with Jews and communists, which are treated as synonyms." Quoted in Kostyrchenko, *Tainaia politika*, 222.

84 See p. 64.

85 Budnitskii, "Great Patriotic War," 782–83; Manley, *To the Tashkent Station*, 112.

86 Quoted in Fitzpatrick, "Annexation," 141.

87 Quotations in Manley, *To the Tashkent Station*, 113–14. For similar statements see Budnitskii, "Great Patriotic War," 782. On the other hand, Jews in evacuation, and especially performances of Jewish culture, also became a symbol of anti-German resistance. For details see pp. 258–59.

88 Manley, *To the Tashkent Station*, 112–13. A contemporary report spoke of a maintenance man at a Moscow motorcycle plant, a Mr. Nekrasov, who "led a counterrevolutionary group demonstration near the factory garage with a pogrom-like character and called upon the workers to annihilate the Jews." *Moskva voiennaia*, 118. The writer Arkadi Perventsev recorded in his diary an encounter with a violent crowd, one of whose members told him, "Comrade Perventsev, we are looking for Jews to beat." He likened the crowd to the prerevolutionary "Black Hundreds," the monarchist movement known for

fomenting and carrying out violence against Jews as part of its campaign to prop up the tsarist autocracy. References provided by Oleg Budnitskii.

89 See p. 39.

90 Korey, "Legal Position," 97–98; Slezkine, *Jewish Century*, 249; Lestschinsky, *Dos sovetishe Idntum*, 259.

91 The records are from the Cheliabinsk Regional Court, in the Ural region; they concern cases of hostility toward and mistreatment of Jewish evacuees. For details see Starkov, "Bor'ba."

92 Budnitskii, "Great Patriotic War," 782.

93 Manley, *To the Tashkent Station*, 112, 113.

94 Sometimes even high-ranking officials were willing to paint Jews in a negative light in order to deflect criticism from their own handling of the war emergency. Thus, for example, Ponomarenko explained to Stalin in early July 1941 that the disorganized flight from Byelorussia during the first days after the invasion "can be explained to a certain extent by the large Jewish element in the cities, which was seized with an animal fear of Hitler and instead of fighting ran away." Quoted in Kostyrchenko, *Tainaia politika*, 222–23. Actually, Ponomarenko and other officials in Byelorussia gave off mixed signals regarding evacuation during the early weeks of the war. See Manley, *To the Tashkent Station*, 26; Kaganovitch, "Jewish Refugees," 88–89. Ponomarenko himself withdrew with the Central Committee of the Byelorussian Communist Party from Minsk to Gomel (which remained unoccupied until 21 August), where he became a member of the Military Council for the Western Front. Many who evidently knew only that he had left his post in Minsk condemned his move. A Jewish witness recalled much accusatory graffiti, including one death wish, a rhyme playing on his first name: "*Panteleimon—dusha s tebia von*" (Panteleimon, may your soul leave [your body]). Smoliar, *Yehudim*, 30.

95 See Branderberger, "'. . . It is Imperative,'" 276–78; Hosking, "Second World War," 170–73.

96 "Sovetskii narod idiot na pobedonosnuiu, otechestvennuiu voinu za rodinu, za chest', za svobodu," *Pravda*, 23 June 1941, 2.

97 "Vystuplenie po radio . . . J. V. Stalina, 3 iyulia 1941 roda," *Pravda*, 23 June 1941, 3 July 1941, 1.

98 See p. 114.

99 For examples of comments intercepted by the NKVD to the effect that German aims were limited to rooting out those two groups, see Budnitskii, "Great Patriotic War," 782–83; Brandenberger, "'. . . It is Imperative,'" 277. For further evidence of the pervasiveness of this belief see Manley, *To the Tashkent Station*, 83–85; Kostyrchenko, *Tainaia politika*, 225.

100 The only larger group unmentioned was Kazakhs. In later speeches Stalin did make occasional incidental references to Nazi designs upon Jews. On these references, see p. 157.

101 Arad, *BeTsel haDegel*, 163; Schwartz, *Yidn*, 119–21; Gilboa, *Black Years*, 32–33. The number of Jews who served in the Red Army appears to have been

approximately equal to what would have been expected based upon their percentage of the total Soviet population after adjustments for age, gender, and geographical distribution. On calculating the figure, see Appendix. A greater proportion of Jewish soldiers than of any other Soviet ethnic group was killed in the course of military service. Arad, *BeTsel heDegel*, 36, 431–32. On the experience of Jewish soldiers during their service, see chapter 4.

102 Thus, for example, in September 1941 *Pravda* published excerpts from the diary of Emil Goltz, a recently killed German soldier, which had been recovered by Soviet forces. The original diary, located in the former archive of the Central Committee of the Communist Party of the Soviet Union (currently the Russian State Archive of Socio-Political History), contains two references to killing actions against Jews in Byelorussia in late June and early July. The references were excised from the published version. "Ot sovetskogo informbiuro," *Pravda*, 23 September 1941, 1; original text in Kostyrchenko, *Tainaia politika*, 229. See also Berkhoff, *Motherland*, 140–41.

103 Killings of Jews did receive mention in a handful of Soviet Foreign Ministry communications intended mainly for consumption abroad. The most prominent was a diplomatic note from Molotov to the governments of all states with whom the USSR maintained relations "concerning widespread robbery, plunder, and monstrous acts of brutality by the German authorities on the Soviet territories they have occupied," dated 6 January 1942. This lengthy text of over eleven hundred lines, which took up nearly two full printed newspaper pages, contained a twenty-two-line description of a "frightening slaughter and pogrom" in which "52,000 . . . Ukrainians, Russians, Jews, or people discovered to belong to the Soviet regime" were shot to death in Kiev. An additional sentence noted that "unarmed, defenseless Jewish workers" were among the chief targets of killings in other Ukrainian towns. The only other mention of Jews came in passing, in a list of "other peoples," some of whose "individual persons" lived on the territories of seven occupied republics where the Germans had demonstrated no compunction about "insulting their national feelings." The peoples were "Jews, Georgians, Armenians, Uzbeks, Azeris, Tadzhiks, and other representatives of the Soviet peoples who are welded together by a feeling of brotherly friendship and cooperation in the Soviet Union." "Nota Narodnogo Komissara Inostrannykh Del' tov. V. M. Molotova o povsemestnykh grabezhakh, pazorenii naseleniia i chudovishchnykh zverstvakh germanskikh vlastei na zakhvachonnykh imi sovetskikh teritoriiakh," *Pravda*, 7 January 1942, 1–2. The description of the murder in Kiev merely repeated a report of 25 November 1941, probably from a Polish source, that had already been published in the Western press. Laqueur, *Terrible Secret*, 68. By contrast, during certain intervals, beginning in late 1941, some Soviet newspapers intermittently published reports about killings of Jews in particular locations. On these reports see chapter 4.

104 See the extensive discussion in Berkhoff, *Motherland*, 134–66.

105 In November 1942 the government established a special agency to gather information about such policies and practices—the Extraordinary State

Commission (*Chrezvichainaia gosudarstvennaia komissiia*) for the Establishment and Investigation of the Crimes of the Fascist German Invaders and their Accomplices, and the Damage They Caused to Citizens, Collective Farms, State Enterprises, and Institutions of the USSR. The commission received numerous testimonies describing the total systematic murder of Jews in many locations and distinguishing it from atrocities committed against other groups, but its published reports mentioned Jews only occasionally and in passing, preferring to subsume all victims under the label of "peaceful Soviet citizens." For details see Feferman, "Soviet Investigation," 590–98; Sorokina, "People and Procedures," 829. See also pp. 158–59. A month after the commission was created, the Polish government-in-exile offered the Soviets, along with the governments of the United Kingdom, United States, and nine German-occupied countries, its assessment that "the German authorities aim with systematic deliberation at the total extermination" of Jews in Poland and beyond. An earlier report of the Polish government, indicating that "one of the war aims of Hitler's regime . . . is a complete extermination of Jews wherever the rapacious hand of German Fascism made its way," was quoted in the Western press in early December 1942. On 17 December the USSR joined other allied governments in condemning the Germans' "bestial policy of cold-blooded extermination" of Europe's Jews, noting that "the German authorities . . . are now carrying into effect Hitler's oft-repeated intention to exterminate the Jewish people in Europe" and that Jews "from all of the occupied countries" were being "massacred in mass executions." Engel, *In the Shadow*, 197–200; Gilbert, *Auschwitz and the Allies*, 100, 104. *Pravda* published the declaration in full, without comment. "Sovmestnaia deklaratsiia . . . o provodimom Gitlerovskimi vlastiami istreblenii evreiskogo naseleniia Evropy," *Pravda*, 18 December 1942, 1. This statement and a follow-up published the next day by the Information Bureau of the Foreign Ministry were the only ones devoted exclusively to the murder of Jews to which the Soviet government attached its name. On the follow-up, see p. 158. On the continuation beyond the conclusion of the war of the line that subsumed the murder of Jews within the panoply of German murders of Soviet civilians see Gitelman, "Soviet Reactions;" Hirszowicz, "Holocaust."

106 Tory, *Surviving*, 7.

107 Redlich, *Together*, 93, 104–5.

108 Kahane, *Yoman*, 30.

109 See p. 59. On the duration of the action see Himka, "Lviv Pogrom," 215.

110 Agin, "BeMilhemet-haOlam," 2:730.

111 Allerhand diary entry no. 1, in Gutterman, *BeVo haEimah*, 31. Cf. Struve, *Deutsche Herrschaft*, 307–308.

112 See Struve, *Deutsche Herrschaft*, 307–50; Himka, "Lviv Pogrom," 210–21. Allerhand learned later the same day that his son had been taken to Brygidki, where he had been forced to participate in the exhumation of the corpses of prisoners murdered by the Soviets. He still did not mention that some Jews (who

were not as fortunate as his son) had been executed on the spot. Allerhand diary entry no. 3, in Gutterman, *Be Vo haEimah*, 35–36.

113 Text of the report in Gutterman, *Be Vo haEimah*, 63–65.

114 Allerhand diary entry no. 2, in Gutterman, *Be Vo haEimah*, 34.

115 Gutterman, *Be Vo haEimah*, 34–35. Allerhand, who identified as a Pole by ethnicity and a Jew by religion, did not mention Poles among the Jews' attackers.

116 See p. 89.

117 In his diary entry for 4 July 1941, Herman Kruk hinted that an analogous encounter had taken place that day in Wilno, but he provided no details beyond the outcome—the sexton of the Great Synagogue had been ordered "to set up a Jewish representative body." Kruk, *Last Days*, 52.

118 See p. 78.

119 Jews commonly called the suburb Slobodka. It was home to a number of important Jewish institutions, including the famous Slobodka yeshiva, the flagship of the *musar* movement, which had remained open under Soviet rule.

120 Tory, *Surviving* 10. Avraham Golub, who quoted the commander, was not present at the meeting; his account was composed on the day the meeting took place following conversations with the Jews involved.

121 Tory, *Surviving* 10.

122 They tried to negotiate both during and after the meeting; Tory, *Surviving*, 10, 14–16.

123 Evidently the Jewish leaders did not realize that their interlocutor, Karl Jäger, besides serving as Gestapo commander in Lithuania, also headed the *Einsatzkommando* that ordered the murders at the Seventh Fort.

124 Some Jews seem to have been confused about whether the ghetto was a German or a Lithuanian project. Golub attributed the creation of the ghetto, and subsequently of the Kaunas *Ältestenrat*, to Lithuanian initiative. On 4 August he called the ghetto "one of the first acts of the restored Lithuania, of the renewed independence," and he ascribed the *Ältestenrat* order to a Lithuanian municipal official. Tory, *Surviving*, 24, 25.

125 Tory, *Surviving*, 13. Allerhand also appears to have thought that Ukrainians controlled the situation in Lwów. See his diary entry no. 6, 4 July 1941, in Gutterman, *Be Vo haEimah*, 37.

126 Tory, *Surviving*, 26.

127 See pp. 317–50. Haika Grossman, a Zionist youth movement activist originally from Brześć, recalled how it was common for parents, "on Friday and on Saturday after tea," to "tell tales about the First World War, when taskmaster followed taskmaster, when the 'Russian' left and the 'German' came." Grossman, *Anshei haMahteret*, 9. The stereotype may also be a source of the frequently expressed notion that once Soviet authority vanished, non-Jews felt free to show what were supposedly their true colors. See p. 68.

128 See the documents in Tory, *Surviving*, 16–18.

129 Kassow, "Inside," 20.

130 Tory, *Surviving*, 26–27.

131 Friedman, *Roads*, 250. The sum is equivalent to nearly $70 million in 2018.

132 Text in Gutterman, *BeVo haEimah*, 38.

133 Gutterman, *BeVo haEimah*, 38–39, 41–42.

134 Two major exceptions were Berdichev and Zhitomir, where no Jewish councils were constituted. Lower, "Facilitating Genocide," 121.

135 Lower, "Facilitating Genocide," 122–41; Michman, *Emergence*, 1114–21.

136 The USHMM *Encyclopedia of Camps and Ghettos 1933–1945* lists 784 locations throughout the German-occupied territories in which ghettos were established. *Pinkas haKehillot* contains data about thirteen hundred Jewish communities in the annexed territories alone. The total number of discrete communities with entries in at least one of the compilations exceeds seventeen hundred. In the two divisions defined by more or less identical boundaries in each compilation (East Galicia/Distrikt Galizien and Latvia [plus Estonia]) *Pinkas haKehillot* lists 307 communities, in which the USHMM *Encyclopedia* located 89 ghettos or camps. Among communities in which no ghetto was established were Chernigov, Dniepropetrovsk, Kiev, Poltava, Simferopol, Voroshilovgrad, and Zaporozhye in Ukraine; Svisloch and Telekhany in Belarus; and Briansk, Orel, and Rostov-on-Don in Russia.

137 See pp. 78 and 80.

138 An anonymous diarist from Lwów, a clerk in the Jewish council, offered another interpretation when forty-one intellectuals and suburban residents were arrested during the night of 6–7 August 1941: "If someone managed to escape, the police didn't come back to get him.... In other words, this was a campaign of mass terror, not of individual repression. In that sense the Gestapo campaign resembled the campaigns of the NKVD." Text in Gutterman, *BeVo haEimah*, 151.

139 See p. 78.

140 See, for example, the testimony of Mark Dworzecki, a physician from Wilno, relating the story of a woman who sought treatment from him in September 1941: "She described how, on the night of 31 August 1941, she was brought [to Ponary] together with about ten thousand Jews." She said she had been wounded in a mass shooting operation but had escaped. "I saw the wound," Dworzecki reported, "the bullet hole, and ants were crawling in the hole—ants of the forest. Then I realized the truth about Ponary.... I turned to the Jews and said: 'Jews, Ponary is not a labor camp—in Ponary they are killing Jews.' And they said to me: 'Doctor, you ... are creating a panic.... How could it be that they should simply take Jews and kill them?" Israel, *Trial*, 1:447–48.

141 See Porat, *MeEver laGashmi*, 82–83. These observations, concerning Wilno, appear to be applicable to many Jewish communities both large and small throughout the annexed territories. The situation within the pre-1939 Soviet territories is less clear, mainly because the extant traces of Jewish thinking that have been identified and studied to date are few and far between. The only available source material of sufficient volume to provide even the most tenuous grounds for generalization comes from Minsk. However, Minsk was unusual

in that a ghetto was decreed there already in July 1941. This move apparently marked the earliest establishment of a ghetto in the pre-1939 USSR. It came months before similar moves in most other veteran Soviet locations where ghettos eventually arose. It also preceded initial German killing operations. Moreover, unlike in the annexed territories, Germans did not use Byelorussian auxiliaries to prepare executions; instead it imported auxiliaries from elsewhere, mainly from Lithuania. As a result, Minsk Jews may have been less inclined than Jews in many places in the annexed territories to attribute the most violent aspects of occupation to their neighbors instead of to the Germans. In testimonies, survivors from Minsk often referred idiosyncratically to killing operations as "pogroms," perhaps suggesting that they understood them to have been initiated by the governing authority. See, for example, testimony of Devora Trebnik, Institute of Contemporary Jewry, Oral History Division, Hebrew University, Jerusalem, 51–1/2; testimony of Tsvi Rubenchik, Institute of Contemporary Jewry, Oral History Division, Hebrew University, Jerusalem, 51–17/4. On the other hand, some associated "pogroms" with "Ukrainians"; testimony of Hinde Tasman, Institute of Contemporary Jewry, Oral History Division, Hebrew University, Jerusalem, 51–11/8. Cf. Epstein, *Minsk Ghetto*, loc. 1506.

142 Druker, "Kakh nitharvah ayaratenu," 276.

143 Severe penalties and fear that violations were likely to be discovered also impelled Jews to register with the authorities when required. See, for example, Kruk, *Last Days*, 75 (26 August 1941); Shechner, *Mot haZeman*, 68.

144 See, for example, the description of home invasions in Lwów recorded in the diary of Samuel Czortkower, 8 November 1940 [*sic*, actually 1941], in Gutterman, *BeVo haEimah*, 70–71. For Minsk, see testimony of Miriam Tokarski, Institute of Contemporary Jewry, Oral History Division, Hebrew University, Jerusalem, 51–3/1. Herman Kruk wrote of Wilno on 11 July, "the Snatchers come into the courtyards and drag people right out of their apartments. They search and rummage around in the beds, under the beds, in the closets, in the attics." Kruk, *Last Days*, 62. See also Korczak, *Lehavot*, 10; Spector, *Sho'at yehudei Vohlin*, 88; Fatal-Knaani, *Zo lo otah Grodnah*, 119–21.

145 Kruk, *Last Days* 61 (10 July 1942). Cf. Tory, *Surviving*, 37–38 (4 October 1941); Smoliar, *Yehudim*, 43; Milch, *Testament*, 115.

146 Kahane, *Yoman*, 58. The quoted words are from Deuteronomy 32:25. They recall the poetic portion of Moses's farewell address, which warned of deadly divine wrath as punishment for infidelity. It is not clear whether Rabbi Kahane understood contemporary events as fulfillment of a prophecy or merely availed himself of a biblical figure of speech.

147 Shechner, *Mot haZeman*, 59–63, 70.

148 Rudashevski, *Diary*, 30. The entry, dated "the end of the summer of 1941," is placed before the entry for 6 September, the date Wilno Jews were forced into a ghetto. It was likely written retrospectively, probably a year later.

149 Smoliar, *Yehudim*, 38.

150 Cf. the testimony Kamieniecki and Ganusowitsch, "Di yidishe Lide," 8: "There was no time to think. Each person was held back by the basics of daily life, the struggle for a piece of bread. This drove out thought."

151 Rosenberg, *To Tell*, 21. Between twenty thousand and thirty thousand Jews lived in Kołomyja in 1941.

152 Kahane, *Yoman*, 58. The quoted words are from Deuteronomy 32:25. They recall the poetic portion of Moses's farewell address, which warned of deadly divine wrath as punishment for infidelity. It is not clear whether Rabbi Kahane understood contemporary events as fulfillment of a prophecy or merely availed himself of a biblical figure of speech.

153 Shechner, *Mot haZeman*, 63–64.

154 Shechner, *Mot haZeman*, 63–64.

155 The word is attested in Polish dictionaries since at least 1902 as a designation for a thieves' lair. Most likely it entered the language from central European underworld slang, much of which was built from Hebrew sources. Thus, ironically, it may have been derived from the Hebrew root *lun*—"to spend the night"—as in the twentieth-century coinages *malon* (hotel) and *melunah* (kennel).

156 Kruk, *Last Days*, 62–63. The date is less than three weeks after German occupation of Wilno and nearly two months before a ghetto was established.

157 Redlich, *Together*, 94.

158 Institute of Contemporary Jewry, Oral History Division, Hebrew University, Jerusalem, 51–3/4–5.

159 Redlich, *Together*, 94.

160 Korczak, *Lehavot*, 42–43.

161 Kruk, *Last Days*, 63.

162 Arad, *Horet*, 59. Święciany was part of the region the Soviets transferred to Lithuania in October 1940 (see p. 35). As a result, the Lithuanian-Byelorussian border was only ten kilometers away. Święciany was a hundred kilometers from the 1939 Riga line.

163 Arad, *Horet*, 59–70.

164 Arad, *Horet*, 59.

165 For example, Kamieniecki and Ganusowitsch, "Di yidishe Lide," 7; testimony of Fejga (Tzipora) Reznik Berkowicz (Barkai), Yad Vashem Archives, Jerusalem, O3/2827, 3.

166 There are scattered hints about other areas. A Polish observer in Lwów, for example, noted that when a ghetto was announced in late October 1941, "many left, especially women. Warsaw now became the city of dreams for all of the refugees." Zaderecki, *BiMeshol tselav haKeres*, 241. For reports about movement among locations in Volhynia, see Fatal-Knaani, *Yehudei Rovnah*, 292.

167 Kamieniecki and Ganusowitsch, "Di yidishe Lide," 9–10.

168 For examples of difficulties in Lithuania, see Bankier and Klibanski, *Expulsion*, 229–31 (cited from a manuscript in the author's possession).

169 See the discussion in Fatal-Knaani, *Yehudei Rovnah*, 290.

170 Redlich, *Together*, 95: "One night my mother took me by the hand and we walked into a neighboring village.... We knocked on a few doors, but nobody wanted to let us in. We returned to [our hiding place in] the attic and stayed there."

171 See at n. 40.

172 Zaderecki, *BiMeshol tselav haKeres*, 240. In early September 1941 a Nazi Polish-language daily reported that "4,000 Jews in Lwów have applied to the Roman Catholic church for conversion." Quoted in Yones, *Ashan*, 228.

173 Borwicz, *Arishe papirn*, 1:41–60; Grossman, *Anshei haMahteret*, 19–23.

174 Kaczerginski, *Ikh bin geven a partizan*, 17–24 (quoted words from 17, 18, 21). Because he spoke Polish with a notable Jewish accent, his documents presented him as a deaf mute. Surely the inability to speak and the need to feign deafness added to his burden.

175 The regions included mainly the former Polish *kresy*; the pre-1939 Soviet territories included in *Generalkommissariate* Weißruthenien, Wolhynien und Podolien, and Shitomir; and a handful of larger towns in the Baltics and in southeastern Ukraine. See pp. 92–94. Some locations within those regions had seen only single instances of selective, relatively small-scale killings during summer and fall 1941. In some of these, collective, community-oriented responses appear to have crystallized earlier. See, for example, Bauer, "Baranowicze," 106–107.

176 Schalkowsky, *Clandestine History*, 160.

177 Kruk, *Last Days*, 170, 172.

178 A survivor testimony characterized Krzemieniec as a "disintegrating town." Bauer, "Buczacz," 268–69. See also Bauer, *Death*, 75–76; Vaysman, "Krzemieniec," 1395–96; Klevan, "Kremenets," 186. In 2016 no country's crude death rate (including all causes, not only starvation) exceeded fifteen per thousand. For figures on food allocation in other Jewish communities see Arad, *Toledot haSho'ah*, 2:827–28.

179 Bauer, "Jewish Baranowicze," 110–12; Kless, "*Judenrat*;" Lidowski, *USheviv haEsh*, 80.

180 Rudashevski, *Diary*, 40.

181 Smoliar, *Yehudim*, 42.

182 Such was arguably the primary message even of Yiddish works produced in the USSR during the 1930s. See Shneer, *Yiddish*, 215–19.

183 Smoliar, *Yehudim*, 42.

184 See pp. 28–29.

185 See Bauer, *Death*, 81–88. In the annexed territories German officials tended to locate council members among employees and elected officers of erstwhile Jewish communal organizations or in municipal governments. In some places refugees from western Poland were chosen, no doubt on the assumption that they would enjoy little local support, making their authority entirely dependent on their German handlers. In several locations, most notably Kaunas, Jews selected their own council members. Spector, *Sho'at yehudei Vohlin*, 122–29; Cholawski, *Al neharot haNieman*, 247; Arad, "HaYudenratim," 80–84; Friedman,

Roads to Extinction, 251–52, 544. Little is known about council composition within the pre-1939 Soviet boundaries. Sometimes rabbis were selected. In other cases—Minsk is the most prominent—knowledge of German may have been a decisive factor. Smoliar, *Yehudim*, 32–33.

186 It is not known whether the expression was coined by Jews or by others, under German rule or post factum, and what connotations it initially carried.

187 "Protokol fun der algemayner farzamlung...," 9 November 1941, in Blumenthal, *Darko shel yudenrat*, 81.

188 "Protokol fun der algemayner farzamlung...," 21 June 1942, in Blumenthal, *Darko shel yudenrat*, 203–205.

189 For overviews see Trunk, *Yudenrat*, 358–63; Arad, *Toledot haSho'ah*, 2:844–47. For specific communities, see Bender, *Mul mavet*, 136–47; Arad, "HaYudenratim," 90–91; Kassow, "Inside," 27–31; Anonymous, "Geto Shavli," 205–206; Fatal-Knaani, *Zo lo otah Grodnah*, 147–50; Fatal-Knaani, *Yehudei Rovnah*, 249–51.

190 See Arad, *Toledot haSho'ah*, 2:827–30, 841–43. The economics of rescue through work in the Soviet territories have not been studied in detail. Some raw material for such a study of Wilno can be found in Balberyshski, *Shtarker*, 313–26. At present the system's workings can best be inferred from the most thoroughly investigated case, Łódź, in the German-annexed portion of Poland. See Löw, *Juden*, 118–24; Horwitz, *Ghettostadt*, 57–59; Unger, *Lodzh*, 326–41. Łódź, however, continued to be beset by widespread hunger.

191 Arad, *Toledot haSho'ah*, 2:835–40; Arad, *Vilnah*, 262–66. On the Wilno library see Balberyshski, *Shtarker*, 433–42; Fishman, *Book Smugglers*, 42–50.

192 Trunk, *Yudenrat*, 367–68. On the divisions, see pp. 92–94.

193 Quoted in Fishman, *Book Smuggleres*, 47.

194 On labor camp transfers, see p. 98. About twenty-three thousand Jews who had been removed from ghettos in Wilno, Kaunas, and Šiauliai to labor camps in Estonia in late 1943 and 1944 were sent to the Stutthof concentration camp in West Prussia days before German forces departed. Arad, *Toledot haSho'ah*, 2:603. This number of Jews removed to Germany proper was more than half of the approximately forty thousand to forty-five thousand Jews found by the Red Army in Soviet territories that had been under German occupation. It is not known how many of them lived until the Red Army reached the camp in May 1945.

195 Arad, *Vilnah*, 286–88; Bender, *Mul mavet*, 226–29.

196 Kruk, *Last Days*, 490.

197 Kruk, *Last Days*, 506–507 (entries from 8–9 April 1943).

198 For the estimated number, see Arad, *Vilnah*, 202.

199 Quoted in Arad, *Vilnah*, 196.

200 See Porat, *MeEver laGashmi*, 23–39.

201 Quoted in Korczak, *Lehavor baEfer*, 49–52. At the time, Kovner was virtually alone in his appraisal. His interlocutors believed that the mass killings in Lithuania during fall 1941 were the result of local factors and that evidence

for Kovner's prediction was absent. Kovner agreed that he could not prove his claim. Nevertheless, he argued, "We must choose to act as if we were certain, despite the doubts" in order to be ready for the worst.

202 Quoted in Arad, *Vilnah*, 199.

203 Quoted in Korczak, *Lehavot*, 52.

204 Quoted in Korczak, *Lehavot*, 51.

205 There is no complete enumeration for the entire area. Cholawski, *Al neharot haNieman*, 333–37 lists 64 groups in Western Byelorussia, with a total of 2,065 members. Another 40 have been noted in East Galicia and central Volhynia. However, many of these planned not to defend their communities but to join Soviet partisan units. Bauer, *Death*, 121–23.

206 Bauer, *Death*, 121–51.

207 Arad, *Toledot haSho'ah*, 2:870–75. In Białystok, on 16 August 1943, some two hundred members of the ghetto's Antifascist Combat Organization attacked German forces sent to liquidate the ghetto. Hardly any of the ghetto's thirty thousand remaining residents joined the fight, and the revolt was easily quashed. Bender, *Mul mavet*, 268–79.

208 Arad, *Vilnah*, 328–31.

209 Arad, *Vilnah*, 317; Porat, *MeEver laGashmi*, 107. In his radio address of 3 July 1941 (see pp. 115–16), Stalin declared that "in enemy-occupied areas it is necessary to establish partisan detachments . . . [and] diversionary groups to fight enemy units . . . , to blow up bridges, roads, telephone and telegraph connections. . . ." From the first weeks of German occupation, bands of Red Army soldiers who had escaped capture roamed heavily forested areas, ambushing German troops who crossed their path. During 1942 the Communist Party and the Soviet government gradually established control over these groups, organized them into a coordinated command structure, and supplied them by air. See Cholawski, *Meri*, 20–21.

210 Porat, *MeEver laGashmi*, 125–26.

211 "Berurim laTakanon," 4 April 1943, in Korczak, *Lehavot*, 147. The document also declared that "going to a *melina* is *treason* under all circumstances." Emphasis in source.

212 The commander of the Antifascist Combat Organization in the Białystok ghetto, Mordechai Tenenbaum, favored a plan similar to the one of FPO, but beginning in late 1942 many members left to join partisan units. See Bender, *Mul mavet*, 195–96.

213 Elsewhere the most conspicuous exponents of a partisan-based strategy were centered in Brody, on the East Galicia-Volhynia border—a forested island in a larger region of steppe vegetation. See Weiler, "HaIrgun haYehudi."

214 Smoliar, *Yehudim*, 46–48.

215 Epstein, *Minsk Ghetto*, locs 1620–1941, 2713–2762; Cholawski, *BeSufat haKilayon*, 139–63.

216 Overall survival rate calculated from Arad, *Toledot haSho'ah*, 2:1010, 1014. The high rate did not reflect a larger underground; the number of members in

Minsk did not exceed 450, smaller than FPO in relation to Jewish population. Arad, *Toledot haSho'ah*, 2:854. Only about twenty-five Jews from Minsk who did not flee to the forest were alive when the Soviets entered. Cholawski, *BeSufat haKilayon*, 237–38.

217 Arad, *Toledot haSho'ah*, 2: 871–72; Epstein, *Minsk Ghetto*, loc 3728.

218 For an overview and numerical estimates see Arad, *Toledot haSho'ah*, 2:893–961. For a comprehensive listing of units in Byelorussia, see Cholawski, *Meri*, 521–38.

219 Atlas fell in battle in December 1942; Bielski survived the war. Cholawski, *Meri*, 186–92; Tec, *Defiance*, 55–85.

220 Tec, *Defiance*, 110–11.

221 Tec, *Defiance*, 112; Arad, "Mahanot," 278.

222 Arad, "Mahanot," 276–81.

223 A major killing action took place in early July 1941, three more in August, two in November, and one each in March, April, July, and October 1942. Between these operations the ghetto was subject to raids nearly every night.

224 Smoliar, *Yehudim*, 48.

225 See p. 130; also Epstein, *Minsk Ghetto*, loc 1634–51.

226 See the map in Arad, *Toledot haSho'ah*, facing 895.

227 Geography may explain in part why fewer Jews escaped to the forest from Kaunas than from the significantly smaller towns of Baranowicze, Lida, and Słonim. In the latter three places, thick forests were within a day's journey on foot; in Kaunas, walking would have taken two or more days. See Epstein, *Minsk Ghetto*, locs 276, 3728.

228 Leikina, "Yemei haSho'ah," 100.

229 Kahane, *Yoman*, 76–77, 135–36.

230 Redlich, *Together*, 97–98.

231 See, for example, testimony of Fejga (Tzipora) Reznik Berkowicz (Barkai), Yad Vashem Archives, Jerusalem, O3/2827.

232 Bartov, *Anatomy*, 232–45 (quotation 233).

4. THE FRONT

1 Milch, *Testament*, 279. See pp. 98–99.

2 The number of Jews serving in the Red Army with the rank of major as of 1 May 1944 was 6,578 (excluding the central administrative offices of the People's Commissariat of Defense). They composed 8.38 percent of all Red Army officers at that rank. All told, as of this date, there were 8,595 Jewish senior officers (majors, lieutenant colonels, and colonels) in the army, 7.87 percent of the total. Bezugolnyi, *Opyt*, 597.

3 Germany had assumed control of Cernăuţi in February 1944, in the face of the Soviet advance through Northern Bukovina. German authorities planned to deport the city's Jews on 20 March, but their scheme was foiled by the Red Army's arrival a day before.

4 Quoted in Arad, *BeTsel haDegel*, 112–13. The journalist Tania Fuks, who had made her way from Lwów to Cernăuţi shortly before the German invasion and survived in the city's ghetto, recalled a similar scene: "We look out of the windows and see how a few people, slowly, with great caution, are making their way outside. We recognize our Jewish neighbors.... Yes, they are here ..., our saviors, our deliverers, the Russian army.... Slowly a crowd surrounds a group of Red Army soldiers. The arrivals had out cigarettes, chocolate for the children.... They are like our own, like brothers.... A blessing upon them.... Our front has ended, theirs not yet. They moved on." Fuks, *A vanderung*, 257.

5 For extended discussion of numerical estimates and the data on which they are based, see Appendix.

6 Arad, *BeTsel haDegel*, 432.

7 This subject is treated by Anna Shternshis in volume 4 of this series.

8 On the conscription order, see Stanislawski, *Tsar Nicholas I*, 13–34; Petrovsky-Shtern, *Jews*. On reflections in Jewish literature, see Litvak, *Conscription*.

9 In 1912 fifty senior military commanders responded to a questionnaire concerning "the professional and moral qualities of lower-ranking soldiers of the Jewish confession." All replied that the presence of Jews in the ranks was harmful. Thirty-four indicated a desire to remove Jews from the army altogether; twenty-eight of these stated that it was necessary to do so "categorically." Litvin, "Generaly."

10 Between the introduction of universal conscription as part of the military reform of Count Dmitry Miliutin in 1874 and the overthrow of the tsarist autocracy in 1917, only nine Jews (or twelve, according to another account) were commissioned as officers. Eight of them were children of leading bankers. All of these commissions were issued before 1886. Raskin, "Evrei," 173; Zaionchkovskii, *Samoderzhavie*, 201–2.

11 Shneer, *Plen*, 2:11–12; Budnitskii, *Russian Jews*, 385–86. In the Red Army, commissars were officers holding military rank but reporting directly to a civilian chain of command. They were appointed to make certain that field commanders, most of whom had served under the tsar and whose loyalties were often to political parties allied with the Bolsheviks instead of to the Bolshevik leadership, would follow official Bolshevik military policy. For details see Pipes, *Russia*, 53–58.

12 Budnitskii, *Russian Jews*, 356–63 (quotation 359). By "antisemitic" the authors of this text appear to have meant not simply discriminatory or hostile attitudes toward Jews but actual murderous intent.

13 Budnitskii, *Russian Jews*, 366–69, 404–5. See also the discussion of this issue by Elissa Bemporad in volume 1 of this series.

14 For an incomplete list of Jews who held military and political command posts in the Red Army during the civil war, including at the regimental, divisional, and brigade levels, see Abramovich, *V reshaiushchei voine*, 1:49–61.

15 Nauchnyi arkhiv Instituta russkoi istorii Rossiiskoi Akademii Nauk (henceforth NA IRI RAN), f. 2, razd. IV, d. 3a, l. 2. The interview was conducted in

Ufa on 2 September 1942 as part of a project supervised by the Commission of the USSR Academy of Sciences on the History of the Great Patriotic War. The commission, commonly known as the Mints Commission (after its leader, Isaak Izraelevich Mints) was established in January 1942 and continued its work through December 1945. Under its direction, professional historians recorded more than four thousand interviews concerning the wartime experiences of soldiers, partisans, and Soviet citizens who had lived under German occupation. On the history of the commission and the fate of its archive, see Budnitskii, "Harvard Project." On Mamontov and his attacks upon Jews during the civil war see idem., *Russian Jews*, 222, 271.

16 Altshuler, *Soviet Jewry* (1998), 19–20. The Jewish level of service was achieved even though *lishentsy* (persons denied the right to vote because of their class background) were generally not drafted, and Jews were disproportionately represented in this disfavored group. On Jews among the *lishentsy*, see the discussion in volume 1.

17 Altshuler, *Soviet Jewry* (1998), 194n8; Penslar, *Jews*, 282n118. Out of 49,018 commanders of combat units (as opposed to administrative, political, or medical officers), Jews numbered 958 in 1926 (nearly 2 percent). They ranked fourth numerically among the Soviet ethnic groups, behind Russians (36,042), Ukrainians (4,496), and Byelorussians (2,585), ahead of Latvians (793). Bezugolnyi, "Prizyvnoe zakonodatelstvo," 111.

18 Altshuler, *Soviet Jewry* (1998), 20.

19 Sverdlov, *Evrei-generaly*, 262–69. The rank of general was introduced into the Red Army only in 1940. See also Cherushev, "Vmeste so Stalinym," 89–94. For a list of general officers repressed during the Terror, including their ethnic (national) identification, see Cherushev and Cherushev, *Rasstreliannaia elita*.

20 All told, sixty-eight of the council's eighty-five members were shot, two died by suicide, one was beaten to death during interrogation, one more perished in a camp, two survived camp imprisonment, and two more were released after short prison terms. Only nine remained untouched. "Sostav voennogo soveta pri narkome oborony SSSR," *Izvestiia TsK KPSS* 1989, no. 4, 74–80.

21 Calculation based on data from Sverdlov, *Evrei-generaly*.

22 Altshuler, *Soviet Jewry* (1998), 156.

23 Altshuler, *Soviet Jewry* (1998), 21.

24 One particularly striking indication among many of the massive population redistribution brought about by this migration: in June 1939 more than 450,000 Jews were counted in the two largest Soviet cities, Moscow and Leningrad, a full 20 percent more than the 375,000 Jews who resided in the entire Byelorussian SSR. Altshuler, *Soviet Jewry* (1998), 13–15, 220–22.

25 Altshuler, *Soviet Jewry* (1998), 277.

26 See pp. 112–13. See also Slezkine, *Jewish Century*, 217–42.

27 "Sovetskii narod idet na pobedonosnuiu, otechestvennuiu voinu za rodinu, za chest', za svobodu," *Pravda*, 23 June 1941, 2.

28 Samoilov, *Podennye zapisi*, 1:47 (29 November 1935).
29 Samoilov, *Podennye zapisi*, 1:61 (6 March 1936).
30 "Boris Tartakovskii," Yad Vashem (E), Research, Jews in the Red Army, 1941–1945.
31 The reference is to the main character in Ilya Ehrenburg's 1922 novel, *Neobychainye pokhozhdeniia Khulio Khurenito i ego uchenikov* (The extraordinary adventures of Julio Jurenito and his disciples). Chapter 11 of the book concerns "the fate of the Jewish people."
32 Tartakovskii, *Iz dnevnikov*, 32–33.
33 For biographical information, see Budnitskii, "Jews at War," 65–66.
34 Shumelishskii, *Dnevnik*, 37.
35 Quoted in Gitelman, "Soviet Jewish Veterans," 8.
36 Soldiers (other than professional writers) were not permitted to keep diaries at the front or to take notes; their letters, which tended to be short and strictly factual, were censored. Altshuler, "Jewish Combatants," 16–18; Budnitskii, "Jews at War," 58.
37 For details see Budnitskii, "Jews at War," 75–79.
38 For biographical details, see "Boris Slutskii," Yad Vashem (E), Research, Jews in the Red Army, 1941–1945.
39 They appeared posthumously: Slutskii, "Zapiski."
40 Slutskii, "Zapiski," 122.
41 Slutskii, "Zapiski," 107–17. Cf. the English version: Slutskii, "Story."
42 Slutskii, "Zapiski," 117–18.
43 Slutskii, "Zapiski," 118–21.
44 There is no evidence that such was in fact the case; see Appendix. In addition to the army corps in which Slutskii claimed a significant Jewish presence, Jews also played prominent roles in the navy and the air force, as well as in the medical corps and the intelligence services. For details see Arad, *BeTsel haDegel*, 141–55.
45 Slutskii, "Zapiski," 122–23.
46 Slutskii, "Zapiski," 128.
47 Slutskii, *Stikhi*, 121.
48 English by Marat Grinberg, in Grinberg, *"I Am to Be Read . . . ,"* 139–40.
49 "Vladimir Gelfand," Yad Vashem (E), Research, Jews in the Red Army, 1941–1945.
50 Gelfand, *Dnevnik*, 123 (entry from 29 December 1942).
51 Cf. his entry for 23 October 1941, while he was still a civilian evacuee in Yessentuki in the North Caucasus (he joined the Red Army in May 1942: "All through the streets and in the park, in the bakery and in the queue for kerosene—you can hear the whisper everywhere, quiet, ferocious, merry, but hateful. They are talking about the Jews. . . . Jews are thieves. A certain Jewish woman stole this or that. The Jews have money. . . . The Jews don't like to work. The Jews don't want to serve in the Red Army. The Jews are living [here] without proper documents. . . . In short, the Jews are the cause of all misfortune. I have heard all this more than once. . . ." Gelfand, *Dnevnik*, 44.

52 Gelfand, *Dnevnik*, 44.
53 Gelfand, *Dnevnik*, 97 (28 July 1942).
54 Gelfand, *Dnevnik*, 164 (9 April 1943).
55 "Iakov Forzun," Yad Vashem (E), Research, Jews in the Red Army, 1941–1945.
56 Altshuler, *Soviet Jewry* (1998).
57 NA IRI RAN, f. 2, razd. IV, d. 1255, l. 10.
58 Details from NA IRI RAN, f. 2, razd. IV, d. 1255, l.
59 Budnitskii, "Jews at War," 62.
60 Gelfand, *Dnevnik*, 164 (9 April 1943).
61 "Iakov Forzun," Yad Vashem (E), Research, Jews in the Red Army, 1941–1945.
62 "Boris Komskii," Yad Vashem (E), Research, Jews in the Red Army, 1941–1945.
63 For excerpts see Budnitskii, "Jews at War," 67–69.
64 See pp. 8–9.
65 Probably in a shooting action conducted by an *Einsatzgruppe* unit, by a German police battalion, or by a local auxiliary force; see chapter 2, at nn. 199–205.
66 A soldier in the so-called Russian Liberation Army (*Russkaia osvoboditelnaia armiia*), a pro-German force commanded by former Red Army General Andrei Vlasov, who had defected to the German side in July 1942 after being taken prisoner in an abortive effort to break the siege of Leningrad.
67 A quotation from the well-known 1932 novel by Nikolai Ostrovskii, *Kak zakalialas stal* (How the steel was tempered). Yakov Forzun mentioned this book in his 1945 interview as one of the Russian books he had read.
68 Komskii, "Dnevnik," 66 (7 January 1945). The specific phenomena designated by the word "antisemitism" beyond discrimination against Jews seeking advancement are not elucidated in this text.
69 Komskii, "Dnevnik," 64 (16 December 1944).
70 Komskii, "Dnevnik," 65.
71 See Yad Vashem, "Boris Komskii," Yad Vashem (E), Research, Jews in the Red Army, 1941–1945.
72 Budnitskii, "Jews at War," 81.
73 "Rozenberg, Naum Lazarevich," Mezhdunarodnyi obedinnennyi biograficheskii tsentr (E), Galereia veteranov.
74 Diary of N. L. Rosenberg (MS), 19 November 1943, Permski gosudarstvennyi arkhiv noveishei istorii, f. 6827, op. 1, d. 292.
75 Diary of N. L. Rosenberg (MS), 6 March 1944.
76 Diary of N. L. Rosenberg (MS), 20 April 1944. Krzemieniec was taken by the Red Army on 19 March 1944. The actual prewar Jewish population was about eight thousand; only some twenty remained when the Soviets arrived. Bauer, "Buczacz and Krzemieniec," 252; Klevan, "Kremenets," 186.
77 Diary of N. L. Rosenberg (MS), 6 March 1944.
78 Diary of N. L. Rosenberg (MS), 6 March 1944.
79 Diary of N. L. Rosenberg (MS), 1 January 1945.
80 See Biograph, "Rozenberg, Naum Lazarevich," Mezhdunarodnyi obedinnennyi biograficheskii tsentr (E), Galereia veteranov.

81 A copy of the letter was sent to Oleg Budnitskii by Finenko's great-granddaughter, Inna Dmitrievna Lysenko, on 20 June 2017. A handwritten transcription of the original by Finenko's daughter, Anna, is preserved in the family archive.
82 See n. 81.
83 Entries from the diary of N. K. Verzhbitskii recounted events of 25–27 October 1941, *Moskva voiennaia*, 482–83. For the testimony of a Jew who had fought at Viazma and taken prisoner by the Germans, see "The Story of M. Sheynman, Former Prisoner of War," in Ehrenburg and Grossman, *Black Book*, 503–18.
84 Slavgorodskii, *Frontovoi dnevnik*, 115. He rendered the name "Abgash[a]."
85 Slavgorodskii, *Frontovoi dnevnik*, 182. Cf. his comment on "Jewish features," Slavgorodskii, *Frontovoi dnevnik*, 142.
86 Slavgorodskii, *Frontovoi dnevnik*, 85.
87 The adjective was a standard derogatory description for Jews throughout eastern Europe.
88 "Frontovoi dnevnik N. F. Belova," www.booksite.ru/fulltext/vol/ogd/atwo/19.htm#27.
89 Perhaps he was of mixed German-Russian origin, or perhaps entirely Russian, like the fictional Dr. Werner in Mikhail Lermontov's classic 1840 novel, *Geroi nashego vremeni* (A hero of our time). (Book V, chapter 2: "This morning the doctor came to see me. His name is Werner, but he is a Russian. What is there surprising in that? I knew a man named Ivanov, who was a German.")
90 Another example of hostile prejudice driving the behavior of non-Jewish soldiers toward their Jewish comrades comes from the reminiscences of Sergeant Viktor Zalgaller. He recalled how at the beginning of September 1941, near Leningrad, a lieutenant in command of a group of soldiers trying to escape encirclement by the Germans could not find the way out. Zagaller took charge of the column. After a while he heard one of the soldiers say, "Why follow him, a Jew?" Eventually, though, they all followed him and returned to their own lines. V. Zagaller, "Byt voiny," *Vestnik*, 22 May 2001.
91 See chapter 3, at nn. 85–93. At least one scholar has argued that some high-ranking Communist Party officials, led by Aleksandr Shcherbakov, head of the Red Army Political Directorate, determined to slow the promotion of Jewish officers and to limit decorations awarded to Jewish soldiers. Arad, *BeTsel haDegel*, 162. Documentary evidence of such a policy has not been discovered. In any case, these alleged efforts do not appear to have resulted in underrepresentation of Jews in higher military ranks or among medal recipients.
92 See Lomagin, *Neizvestnaia blokada*, 196. The text is recalled in numerous memoirs.
93 "XXIV godovshchina Velikoi Oktiabrskoi sotsialisticheskoi revoliutsii: Okonchanie doklada tovarishcha I. V. Stalina," *Pravda*, 7 November 1941, 2.
94 See p. 116.
95 Rostov fell to the Germans on 21 November 1941 and reconquered by the Soviets on 29 November. Germany occupied the city for a second time on 23 July 1942.

On 11–12 August a German killing squad, supported by Ukrainian auxiliaries and by a number of turncoat Soviet POWs who had volunteered to assist, murdered most of the 15,000–18,000 Jews (of a prewar Jewish population of 27,000) who had not escaped or been evacuated. Some Jews were killed in gas vans. By the time the Red Army drove the Germans from the city again, on 13 February 1943, only a handful of Jews remained. Arad, *Toledot haSho'ah*, 1:370, 522. The killings in Rostov were the most extensive of any Jewish community in the RSFSR.

96 See chapter 2 at nn. 180–88, 225–27.

97 E. Vilenskii, "Po piatam vraga: V osvobozhdennom Rostove," *Izvestiia*, 2 December 1941, 3.

98 See pp. 321–22n105.

99 "Ob ocushchestvlenii gitlerovskimi vlastiami plana istrebleniia evreiskogo naseleniia Evropy," *Pravda*, 19 December 1942, 1. The text also appeared on the same day in *Izvestiia*, *Vecherniaia Moskva*, *Komsomolskaia pravda*, *Krasnaia zvezda*, and *Krasnyi flot*, all on the front page. The figures for Łuck and Sarny were reasonably accurate; cf. Snyder and Dean, "Łuck," 1413; Kruglov and Fishman, "Sarny," 1464. The others were significantly mistaken. In Riga about thirty thousand local Jews had been enclosed in a ghetto in August 1941; all but five thousand were killed by the end of the year. However, more than twenty thousand Jews from Germany, Austria, and the Protektorat had been sent there between late fall 1941 and mid-1942; most of them remained alive in the ghetto until late 1943. Reichelt and Dean, "Riga," 1920–22. On Wilno and Święciany see p. 311n255.

100 See pp. 321–22n105.

101 A. Tolstoi, "Korichnevyi durman," *Pravda*, 5 August 1943, 2. The same issue of the newspaper contained a lengthy report by the Extraordinary State Commission that made passing mention of the murder of Jews in Kislovodsk and in other North Caucasian cities.

102 See pp. 116–17.

103 Zeltser, "Kholokost," 50. On Ehrenburg see chapter 6.

104 NA IRI RAN, f. 2, op. 16, d. 7, l. 68f. The interview was conducted 18 May 1943. Epstein continued: "One answered me, 'There are no Jews.' I asked, 'Why?' he said, 'It doesn't matter to me, it's all the same, but they don't take [Jews]. I said, 'Look, I'm a Jew and a commander in the Russian army.' So he became a little different."

105 Itenberg, "Pisma," 326.

106 "Grigorii Ushpolis," Yad Vashem (E), Research, Jews in the Red Army, 1941–1945.

107 See pp. 321–22n15.

108 He did not indicate by whom.

109 The German army entered Głębokie on 2 July 1941.

110 See p. 126.

111 NA IRI RAN, f. 2, razd. IV, d. 930, l. 5–6. The interview was conducted on 22–23 June 1945.

112 NA IRI RAN, f. 2, razd. IV, d. 930, l. 6–7.
113 NA IRI RAN, f. 2, razd. IV, d. 930, l. 1.
114 "Grigorii Ushpolis," Yad Vashem (E), Research, Jews in the Red Army, 1941–1945.
115 "Wolf Vilenskii," Yad Vashem (E), Research, Jews in the Red Army, 1941–1945.
116 Vilenskii, *Povoroty sud'by*, 11–12.
117 Vilenskii, *Povoroty sud'by*, 288–89.
118 http://podvignaroda.ru/?#id=1350540928&tab=navDetailManCard.
119 In Latvian: Daugavpils iela, a street in the center of the Riga ghetto.
120 In Latvian: Ludzas iela, one of the streets bordering the so-called small ghetto of Riga, an area enclosed with barbed wire on 27 November 1941 in order to separate able-bodied workers from the rest of the ghetto population. Three days later, on 30 November, more than eleven thousand Jews were taken from all parts of the ghetto to the Rumbula forest, about ten kilometers away, and shot to death. The testimony most likely used the street name as a metonym for the assembly point from which the victims were taken to Rumbula. For details see Ezergailis, *Holocaust*, 247–56 (map on p. 252).
121 Amdur was a so-called June communist, a resident of one of the Baltic states who joined the Communist Party after the Soviet takeover in June 1940.
122 NA IRI RAN, f. 2, razd. I, op. 16, d. 29, l. 6–7. The interview took place on 28 June 1945.
123 Amdur suggested that Latvian attitudes toward Jews may have improved as the front approached: "One guy [told me] that in 1942 they fed the Jews with sticks, in 1943 they sometimes started throwing out crusts of bread, and in 1944 they were already starting to bring sandwiches, because the Red Army was coming closer and closer." NA IRI RAN, f. 2, razd. I, op. 16, d. 29, l. 5.
124 NA IRI RAN, f. 2, razd. I, op. 16, d. 29, l. 7. One year later the Mints Commission sent a delegation to Riga to investigate the annihilation of Latvian Jewry. Amdur met with the delegation. In that interview he related what a peasant had told him about the murder of the entire Jewish population of the venerable Latvian town of Preiļi. The peasant reportedly did not know that Amdur was a Jew, for Amdur spoke a pure Latvian. He maintained that the Germans had forced the local peasants to shoot the Jews under pain of death. All together they killed about five hundred Jews. Amdur quoted the peasant: "It's a bad business, but what could you do, you had to save your own life." Although the peasant claimed to have heard the story from his cousin, Amdur was certain that he had taken part in the in the shooting operation himself. NA IRI RAN, f. 2, razd. I, op. 16, d. 41. The interview was conducted on 2 June 1946.
125 Fain, *Po dorogam*, 257–60.
126 Fain, *Po dorogam*, 256, 261.
127 Fain, *Po dorogam*, 296.
128 Pomerants, *Zapiski*, 86.
129 Fain, *Po dorogam*, 158. Cf. *The Brothers Karamazov*, book 5, chapter 4: "Listen! I took the case of children only to make my case clearer. Of the other tears of

humanity with which the earth is soaked from its crust to its center, I will say nothing. I have narrowed my subject on purpose. I am a bug, and I recognize in all humility that I cannot understand why the world is arranged as it is. Men are themselves to blame, I suppose; they were given paradise, they wanted freedom, and stole fire from heaven, though they knew they would become unhappy, so there is no need to pity them. With my pitiful, earthly, Euclidian understanding, all I know is that there is suffering and that there are none guilty; that cause follows effect, simply and directly; that everything flows and finds its level—but that's only Euclidian nonsense, I know that, and I can't consent to live by it! What comfort is it to me that there are none guilty and that cause follows effect simply and directly, and that I know it?—I must have justice, or I will destroy myself. And not justice in some remote infinite time and space, but here on earth, and that I could see myself." Translated from the Russian by Constance Garnett; available at Project Gutenberg (www.gutenberg.org). It seems characteristic of a Russian Jewish intellectual to claim that the tragedy of the Jewish people allowed him to penetrate the thought of a great Russian writer, especially when spoken by the hero of the Dostoevskii novel most offensive to Jews.

130 See pp. 144–45.

131 Tartakovskii, *Iz dnevnikov*, 171. Tartakovskii contrasted the scene in Zhmerinka with what he observed in Kamenets-Podolskii: "Once these regions were populated largely by Jews. At first the Germans turned the Old City into an authentic ghetto; later they destroyed all its inhabitants and the city itself. [Now only] footsteps echo across the grassy town squares, the broken windows of the houses watch in silence, scraps of wallpaper can still be seen on what remains of the destroyed walls. Rarely will a human being pass by, only a lost dog will run around. Silence." Tartakovskii, *Iz dnevnikov*, 176.

132 See pp. 159–61 and 113–14.

133 On the prewar history of Soviet national military formations see Herspring, *Russian Civil-Military Relations*, 37–51; Shoigu, *Velikaia otechestvennaia voina*, 3:9–10. On conscription of Central Asian and Transcaucasian nationalities see Schechter, "People's Instructions," 109–16.

134 See Valleau and Cherkasov, "Baltic States," 96–97; Arad, *BeTsel haDegel*, 38.

135 Herspring, *Russian Civil-Military Relations*, 52.

136 Yu and Terushkin, "Heroes," 3; Merritt, "In the Fight," at n. 4; Levin, *Lohamim*, 49. On the number of evacuees from Latvia, see "Migrations of Latvians during W[orld] W[ar] 2," Roots = Saknes (E), Ethnicity, Latvians, WW2.

137 Levin, *Lohamim*, 48.

138 Levin, *Lohamim*, 49–50.

139 Valleau and Cherkasov, "Baltic States," 97; Yu and Terushkin "Heroes," 1. In the 201st Latvian Division, 51 percent of soldiers were ethnic Latvians, 26 percent Russians. In the Sixteenth Lithuanian Division, 39 percent were Russians and 32 percent Lithuanians. Levin, *Lohamim*, 59, has estimated 45 to 50 percent Jews, 25 to 30 percent Lithuanians, and 20 to 25 Russians in the Lithuanian

Division, while Arad, *BeTsel haDegel*, 38, has proposed that the percentage of Jews in the Latvian Division may have reached one third. Percentages varied over time. The percentage of Jews appears to have declined markedly as the war progressed, reaching as low as 10 percent in the Lithuanian division and 5.6 percent in the Latvian. Levin, *Lohamim*, 59; Merritt, "In the Fight." The decline may indicate a disproportionate percentage of Jewish casualties.

140 Jews constituted a bit more than 5 percent of the population of interwar Latvia and about 7.25 percent in Lithuania. Mendelsohn, *Jews*, 244, 225.

141 Merritt, "In the Fight."

142 Levin, *Lohamim*, 49–50.

143 Merritt, "In the Fight."

144 In 1940 Mikhoels had advocated for the Soviet government to address the plight of Jews in the German occupation zone of Poland. See p. 41. He would eventually become chairman of the Jewish Anti-Fascist Committee; see chapter 5.

145 Quoted in Arad, *BeTsel haDegel*, 39.

146 Arad, *BeTsel haDegel*, 40.

147 Arad, *BeTsel haDegel*, 41. Several thousand Jews who had managed to flee to the USSR from German-occupied Poland and Czechoslovakia and had been deported or escaped to the Soviet interior served in the Polish and Czech exile armies (commanded by Colonel Zygmunt Berling and General Ludvik Svoboda, respectively) that formed on Soviet soil and fought alongside the Red Army during its westward advance. For details see Nussbaum, *VeHafach lahem leRo'ets*, 102–56, 233–77; Kulka, "Jews," 389–426. Several thousand more Jews also served in the first Polish exile army under General Władysław Anders, which was evacuated from the USSR in 1942. See, inter alia, Engel, *In the Shadow*, 132–40.

148 Arad, *BeTsel haDegel*, 40–41.

149 Not only the Soviets were averse to creating such units. The only military unit bearing a Jewish insignia to be formed during the Second World War was the Palestinian Jewish Infantry Brigade Group, established within the British Army in September 1944.

150 See Gennady Estraikh's observations on this matter in volume 5 of this series.

151 Merritt, "In the Fight," following n. 16. "National communist" movements developed after the Second World War in some of the non-Russian Soviet republics and in a number of Eastern Bloc countries in opposition to the claims of the Soviet regime to control the actions of communist movements worldwide. They maintained that local circumstances in each republic or state demanded different paths to communist realization from those dictated by Moscow and sought to pursue independent domestic and foreign policies.

152 The correspondence, along with other family documents, was held for decades by the Deichman-Barenboim family. Following the death of the last family member, Elena's sister Galina Deichman, in 2013, the family archive was transferred to the International Center for the History and Sociology of World

War II and its Consequences at the Moscow Higher School of Economics. Galina Deichman had previously published a selection of her sister's letters: Deichman, *Sto pisem.* The published version is sometimes marred by inaccurate dates or transcriptions of handwriting. Consequently, all citations here refer to the original document, giving sender, recipient, and date.

153 She received three letters from friends in which the word "Jew" appeared in passing, two of them in a negative context: Boris Kanevskii to Deichman, 17 October 1941; Boris Kanevskii to Deichman, 8 December 1941. She also wrote a letter on the eve of her induction in which she described a dream: "I had no things, no home, no relatives, no friends. . . . ; like a bird, I would be free and would wander like the Eternal Jew. And how very light and bright this thought made me." Elena Deichman to Aleksander Nemirovsky, 18 March 1942.

154 During the first month of the war she, her mother, and her sister had been exiled to Troitsk in the Ural Mountains, probably because the regime automatically suspected the loyalties of family members of political convicts like her father. Enlistment offered her escape from a life she described as an "orphaned existence" that she could "bear no longer." Elena Deichman to Aleksander Nemirovsky, 18 March 1942. She misrepresented her training and experience in order to gain entry into the army. Once accepted, she wrote to her mother: "Mama, you wanted to raise me as a member of Komsomol, as a good worker, as a patriot, didn't you? Now that I'm already in place, [I can say that] it's good that I accomplished this by myself and that I am going as a volunteer and with great desire for work. . . . Do you understand, mommy, I simply couldn't do without being here; for my entire life I wouldn't be able to forgive myself for not taking part in the war now." Elena Deichman to Sofia Barenboim, 27 May 1942.

155 See, for example, Elena Deichman to Sofia Barenboim, 21 April 1944: "I have written to [Soviet President Mikhail] Kalinin, to the State Prosecutor, and to the GULAG [*Glavnoe upravlenie lagerei*—Main Camp Office], all in Moscow. . . . I wrote about the state of Father's health, about the term of his sentence, about myself, attaching certificates that I have been wounded [in October 1943, in fighting along the Dnieper River], [military] decorations [I have received], and about you—a doctor and professor of surgery. Will it do any good?" Her efforts were to no avail. On 14 July 1944 she wrote her mother, "I have received three statements from Moscow about Papa, three denials."

156 Around a half million women served in the Red Army and the Soviet Navy, out of a total of some 34.5 million military personnel. Their service was not easy for them because the military was not adapted to women's needs. To begin with, uniforms and boots were not normally cut and sized to fit women, forcing women to look for ways to alter them. Moreover, their relatively small number frequently forced them into a flirtatious and sometimes overtly exploitative sexual atmosphere. Sometimes commanding officers compelled them to cohabit. For greater detail see Budnitskii, "Muzhchizny." Deichman's letters reflected these circumstances. See, for example, Elena Deichman to Izaak Deichman, 13 January 1944: "Most of the girls—and they include good people

and [good] workers—have married the officers who live with them and take care of them, but still these are temporary, unstable, frivolous marriages, because every one of [the officers] has a family and children at home, whom they are not about to leave. It is simply difficult for someone to live at the front alone and without affection.... Many men here say that after the war they won't start a conversation with a military girl. If [the women] have medals, [the men] say they know ... how they got them. It is very difficult to know that many girls have earned that attitude with their behavior." Deichman herself eventually became pregnant from a romance with a married captain. She described her pregnancy and her difficulties arranging an abortion in a letter to her mother, 18 July 1944. Nowhere in her correspondence did she indicate that Jewishness played any role in her situation or in how she responded to it. Nor did she indicate that Jewish women in general faced circumstances peculiar to them.

157 For example, Elena Deichman to Galina Deichman, 22 April 1943, requesting items to relieve boredom in the hospital to which she had been assigned: "The poems you chose [have arrived], but I am dreaming about [Russian symbolist poet Aleksandr] Blok. [Can you send] a book by parcel post? Shakespeare would be good. If this is possible, then pack inside the book a pair of stockings. Color and quality don't matter (stockings and boots are a disaster here)." Cf. Elena Deichman to Izaak Deichman, 19 January 1944, from the front: "How good it is for me here! I'm very friendly with everyone, and I'm treated well."

158 Her letters betray not even the slightest hint of resentment toward the Soviet regime. To be sure, the letters were subject to censorship, but they provide no basis for taking the sentiments she expressed in them at anything less than face value. Deichman appears to have had no doubt that the Soviet state needed to be defended and that she needed to play her personal part in its defense.

159 In addition to straightforward patriotic motives, Deichman may have believed that heroic service at the front could aid her father's political rehabilitation. A hint is found in Nadia Rasheeva to Elena Deichman, 5 October 1941.

160 A portmanteau of the Russian *smert' shpionam* ("death to spies"), the agency was created in April 1943 with the aim of consolidating counterespionage and disinformation activities. Jews, including Lieutenant General Isai Babich and Major General Grigorii Bolotin, occupied high-ranking positions within the organization.

161 On the circumstances of the discovery of Hitler's corpse see Bezymenskii, *Operatsiia "Mif"*; Kozlov, *"Gde Gitler?"*

162 Rzhevskaia, *Berlin*, 170–73.

163 Marants wrote nothing personal about the episode or about her military service more generally. Kagan kept a wartime diary, which is currently in the possession of her granddaughter, Liubov Summ, who has also preserved her military records. After the war Kagan became a writer, using the pseudonym Elena Rzhevskaia. She published a war memoir in 1965 (Rzhevskaia, *Berlin*). Nothing in these writings focuses on matters of particular Jewish concern. On her postwar writings, see below.

164 "Emmanuil Kazakevich," Yad Vashem (E), Research, Jews in the Red Army, 1941–1945. On repressions in Birobidzhan, see volume 2 in this series. Kazakevich's ability to save himself from arrest by moving to a different place reflected practical difficulties that the NKVD faced in tracking down its targets. See Estraikh, *Evreiskaia literaturnaia zhizn'*, 215–16.

165 http://www.armchairgeneral.com/rkkaww2/formation/DNO.htm contains a list of People's Militia units throughout the USSR. In Moscow, enrollment of volunteers was carried out through various social, economic, and political organizations. Kazakevich enrolled through the Moscow branch of the Union of Soviet Writers, to which he had been admitted in 1940. Volunteers via the Union made up a so-called writers company within the Moscow militia's Eighth Division. Approximately one hundred writers joined this company, about one third of them Jews. For details see Budnitskii, "Moskovskoe narodnoe opolchenie"; Budnitskii, "Writers' Company"; Lévesque, "Moscow 1941."

166 Quoted in Ruben, "Za svoiei zvezdoi."

167 In November 1941 German forces occupied the Crimean port city of Kerch; in January 1942 Soviet forces expelled them. Upon entering the city they discovered the bodies of some seven thousand people, mostly Jews, whom the Germans had shot to death in a ditch. The event was widely reported in the Soviet press, although often in a manner that obscured the fact that Jews were the primary victims. Those reports, along with accompanying photographs, offered the Soviet public a shocking early encounter with what were officially dubbed "German (or fascist) atrocities." For details see Shneer, *Grief*, 31–56.

168 Ruben, "Za svoiei zvezdoi."

169 Upon leaving, he penned a verse to the Army chief of staff: "Seeing that I am blind as an owl, / And that I walk on my wounded legs like a goose, / I'm barely, barely suited for war / But I'm not suited for peacetime at all. / Besides, I confess, open and direct, / That I have no military sense at all. / I ask that you let me go home / Immediately upon receipt."

170 The film script was written by Pavel Furmanskii, who had served with Kazakevich in the writers' company of the Moscow People's Militia. The film was released only in 1953, after Stalin's death. It seems that Stalin did not like that all of the heroes in the film died. Another film based on the story was shot in 2002. It became a Russian blockbuster.

171 Quoted in Frezinskii, "Tragediia."

172 For additional details about Kazakevich's literary output, see, inter alia, Kazakevich and Ruben, *Vospominaniia*; Bocharov, *Emmanuil Kazakevich*; Bocharov, *Slovo*; Telman, *General i poet.*

173 The fighting lasted for fourteen months, from January 1942 through March 1943. It resulted in German withdrawal from a strategically important point threatening Moscow, but not before hundreds of thousands of soldiers on both sides had been killed. The battle quickly became known in Soviet popular consciousness as the "Rzhev meatgrinder" (*Rzhevskaia miasorubka*). For details see, inter alia, Gerasimova, *Rzhev Slaughterhouse*; Glantz, *Zhukov's Greatest Defeat.*

174 Among her stories: "Ot doma do fronta" (From home to the front, 1964); "Fevral': krivye dorogi" (February: Crooked roads, 1975); "Voroshenyi zhar" (Turning up the heat, 1982–1983); "Blizhnie podstupy" (Nearby approaches, 1985); and "Dalekii gul" (A distant rumble, 1988). These and other war tales can be found in Rzhevskaia, *Izbrannoe.*

175 On Ehrenburg's prewar career see Rubenstein, *Tangled Loyalties.*

176 For details see Rubenstein, *Tangled Loyalties.*

177 Ehrenburg, *War*, 74.

178 Rubenstein, "Il'ia Ehrenburg," 36.

179 A reference to military engagements in southern and western Europe between German and Allied forces. Throughout the war the USSR demanded that Great Britain and the United States intensify fighting along the "second front" in order to relieve pressure on the Red Army.

180 Ehrenburg, *War*, 11.

181 See p. 83.

182 For details see Beevor and Vinogradova, *A Writer at War*, esp. xi–xiv, 110–14.

183 'Vasilii Grossman," Yad Vashem (E), Research, Jews in the Red Army, 1941–1945.

184 Gromova, *Stranniki voiny*, 112, 262.

5. LEADERSHIP

1 "A Proposal to Organize a Jewish Rally in Moscow," 16 August 1941, in Redlich, *War*, 173–74.

2 During the 1930s the regime's anticlerical and anti-Zionist inclinations had resulted in virtual eradication of literary and cultural activity in the Hebrew language, accompanied by active repression of those who continued to use Hebrew as a medium for creative expression. See Gilboa, *A Language Silenced*; Greenbaum, "Hebrew Literature;" Halperin, "A Hebrew Writer."

3 Konstantinov, *Evreiskogo naselenie*, 29.

4 Altshuler, *Distribution*, 9.

5 Notable exceptions were poets Moshe Kulbak and Izi Kharik, see p. 26. On Yiddish writers during the purges, see volume 2 of this series.

6 For details, see Estraikh, *Evreiskaia literaturnaia zhizn'*, 184.

7 The Russian languages uses the same word (*evreiskii*) to designate "Jewish" and "Yiddish" (paralleling the practice in the Yiddish language, in which the word *yiddish* signifies both). As a result, the label *evreiskii*, in the sense of "Yiddish," delimited what the regime considered to be legitimate forms of Jewish culture, literature, and education. This practice meant that Jewish-born writers and actors who wrote or performed in Russian, Ukrainian, Byelorussian, or another of the USSR's many languages could never be categorized officially as "Jewish." The notion of a hyphenate Russian-Jewish, Ukrainian-Jewish, or other-Jewish culture did not exist in Soviet discourse. It was shunned as a concept that slowed assimilation and condemned therefore

as a nationalist deviation. Other Soviet minority cultures were also forced into a similar set of procrustean definitions.

8 The best known was perhaps Kvitko's 1938 poem, "*A briv dem khaver Voroshilov*" (A letter to Comrade Voroshilov; in Russian: "*Pismo Voroshilovu*"), in which a schoolboy whose brother has been drafted into the Red Army assures Soviet Defense Minister Kliment Voroshilov that should his brother fall in battle, he will "grow up fast" in order to take his place in the ranks. See Gloster, "Soviet Children's Poetry," 21; Rubenstein and Naumov, *Stalin's Secret Pogrom*, 161–62.

9 Szmeruk, "Soviet Yiddish Publications," 103–106. *Der Emes* was also the name of the Moscow-based publisher of Yiddish-language books.

10 "Pravda Report of the First Jewish Rally," 25 August 1941, in Redlich, *War*, 183. Cf. *Izvestiia*, 25 August 1941 (p. 3: "Bratia evrei vsego mira! Vystupleniia predstavitelei evreiskogo naroda na miting, sostaivshemsia v Moskve 24 avgusta 1941 g.").

11 "An Appeal to World Jewry," 24 August 1941, in Redlich, *War*, 174–77. The appeal also extolled the USSR as a country where "the Jewish people . . . , for the first time in thousands of years, felt at home among their own, equal among equals," and "found its place among the great family of nations of the USSR."

12 On the place of Jews and Jewish affairs in Soviet nationalities policy during the 1930s, see the observations of Deborah Yalen and Arkadi Zeltser in volume 2 of this series.

13 Redlich, *War*, 22. On the high-ranking officials and their position in the regime, see p. 180.

14 Eisenstein's father, famous as a designer of art nouveau buildings in Riga, had converted to Russian Orthodoxy before Eisenstein's birth and married a Russian woman.

15 Some Jewish commentators warned even at the time that the USSR's seeming turn toward world Jewry was rooted in the long-standing invidious "fantasy of Jews as a world power." *Forverts*, 17 July 1943 (p. 8: David Einhorn, "Veys der oylem dem emes vegn der yidish-sovetisher delegatsye?") Cf. comments by the son of NKVD chief Lavrentii Beria: "[Stalin] wanted to use the Jewish lobby to incite the USA to enter the war, because only the influence of that lobby could shift America out of its isolationism." Beria, *My Father*, 109.

16 In the immediate aftermath of the invasion Soviet observers raised the possibility that the German move had been aimed in the first instance (as the USSR's ambassador in London, Ivan Maiskii, wrote in his diary on 27 June 1941) "to revive [Hitler's] glory as 'saviour of European civilization from Bolshevik barbarism,' to cause a split in the public opinion of the 'democracies' and to secure either a favourable peace with them, or, at the very least, their effective withdrawal from the war until he has finished dealing with the Bolsheviks." "So far," Maiskii noted with relief that "this plan has entirely failed," at least as far as Britain and its empire were concerned. Nevertheless, he warned, "some grey areas remain. First, what will England's aid consist of? And will it really be serious? I'm not sure. . . . Second, *bewilderment* is still palpable in the minds of

the public. Psychologically, this is quite understandable. Only recently 'Russia' was considered a covert ally of Germany, all but an enemy. And suddenly, within 24 hours, it has become a friend! This transition was too abrupt, and the British *mentality* has yet to adjust to the new state of affairs." Maiskii, *Diaries*, 367–68 (emphasis in source).

17 The agreement contained two provisions: "1) The two governments mutually undertake to render each other assistance and support of all kind in the present war against Hitlerite Germany. 2) They further undertake that during this war they will neither negotiate nor conclude an armistice or treaty of peace except by mutual agreement." "Agreement between the United Kingdom and the Union of Soviet Socialist Republics," 12 July 1941, Avalon Project (E), Document Collections, World War II Documents 1940–1945.

18 Sumner Welles, Acting US Secretary of State, to Lawrence Steinhardt, US Ambassador to the USSR, 23 June 1941, *Foreign Relations of the United States, 1941*, 767. The Lend-Lease program was inaugurated by act of the US Congress in March 1941. It authorized the US President to "sell, transfer title to, exchange, lease, lend, or otherwise dispose of, to any such government [whose defense the President deems vital to the defense of the United States] any defense article." A Lend-Lease agreement with the USSR was concluded on 7 October.

19 See, for example, the notation in the diary of British MP Harold Nicolson upon hearing of the German invasion: "Most people in England will be delighted. I am not so optimistic. It will have a bad effect on America, where many influential people do not like to see themselves as the allies of Bolshevism. It will have a bad effect on Conservative and Catholic opinion here." Nicolson, *War Years*, 174 (entry for 22 June 1941). Four days earlier, when British intelligence reports raised the possibility of a German move against the Soviets, Nicolson observed, with apparent trepidation, "If it happens then we must be prepared to regard Russia as an ally," while wondering at the same time, "Are we to play the Red Flag on Sundays and so on?" Nicolson, *War Years*, 172 (entry for 18 June 1941). He was referring to the British Broadcasting Corporation's practice to play the national anthems of all of Britain's allies every Sunday before the 9 p.m. news broadcast. The Soviet national anthem, the Internationale (also known in Britain as the Red Flag), was also the hymn of the Communist International (Comintern); playing it would thus indicate British encouragement not only for the Soviet state but for a political movement that all government members, from left to right, anathematized. The British government soon asked Soviet Ambassador Maiskii to suggest an alternate song; Maiskii refused. As he recorded the situation in his diary: "The hair of thousands of British Blimps stands on end when they hear it. It came to blows—in the press, in Parliament, in society.... Churchill himself is behind all this. He declares: I am ready to do anything for Russia, but I will not allow the communists to make political capital from the 'Internationale.'" Maiskii, *Diaries*, 370.

20 For details see Redlich, *War*, 4–6. Sovinformburo provided daily bulletins to be read over Radio Moscow by Yurii Levitan, the station's lead announcer. Levitan

would become known throughout the USSR as "the voice of the war." Between 1941 and 1945 he was arguably the country's best-known Jewish personality and definitely the one with whom the greatest number of Soviet citizens maintained regular (albeit virtual) contact. On Levitan's wartime role see Zakharine, "Speaking," 173.

21 Shcherbakov was soon also named head of the Red Army Political Directorate. For more on Shcherbakov, see chapter 4, n. 91.

22 See Redlich, *War*, 173–74.

23 See chapter 1, at n. 245.

24 Redlich, *War*, 21.

25 Redlich, *War*, 21–22. A different newspaper, *Eynikayt*, began publication in June 1942. See below.

26 See chapter 1, n. 153.

27 For details about the periods of imprisonment and the trials, based upon NKVD records, see Pickhan, "'That Incredible History'," 251–56.

28 Unlike Britain, which, before becoming allied with the Soviets had previously regarded the USSR as a neutral party in its war with Germany, Poland (through a government-in-exile that had been formed in France and removed to Britain following the French capitulation to Germany in June 1940) had been officially at war with the Soviet Union since the Red Army entered its territory in September 1939 and declared that the Polish state had ceased to exist. British policymakers found it unthinkable that two of its allies should be at war with one another. Accordingly they pressed the two states to make peace. The agreement, concluded between Soviet Ambassador Maiskii and Polish Prime Minister Władysław Sikorski in late July, satisfied the Soviets more than the Poles. The USSR (re)recognized Poland, but it did not commit itself, as the Poles had demanded, to returning the Polish territories it had conquered in 1939. It also permitted a Polish army under Polish command to be formed on Soviet soil; however, over Polish objections, the force was to be "subordinated in an operational sense to the Supreme Command of the USSR." The key positive provision for the Poles was the agreement's final sentence: "The Soviet Government grants amnesty to all Polish citizens now detained on Soviet territory either as prisoners of war or on other sufficient grounds, as from the resumption of diplomatic relations." The amnesty officially went into effect on 12 August, but implementation continued for months. For the text of the agreement, see "Polish-Soviet Union Agreements," 30 July 1941, Avalon Project (E), Document Collections, World War II Documents 1940–1945. On implementation see Kochanski, *Eagle*, 173–87; Litvak, *Pelitim*, 174–84.

29 For a list see *Henryk Erlich*, 170–72.

30 Korzec, "Hidat retsihatam," 286.

31 Korzec, "Hidat retsihatam," 286.

32 See chapter 1, n. 115.

33 See n. 19. The explanation for Beria's interest in Erlich and Alter is merely plausible; no document has been located that can confirm or refute it.

34 Hotel Metropol, located on Moscow's Theater Square, close to the Kremlin. During the 1920s many Kremlin personnel had been housed there.
35 Text in *Henryk Erlich*, 185. Cf. Redlich, *War*, 11.
36 As described by Poland's ambassador in Moscow, Stanisław Kot, reporting to the Polish government-in-exile on his own recent meeting with Erlich and Alter, 3 October 1941. Text in Korzec, *Hidat retsihatam*, 299.
37 Quoted in Redlich, *War*, 11.
38 Erlich and Alter to Beria, October 1941, in Redlich, *War*, 165.
39 Erlich and Alter to Stalin, October 1941, in Redlich, *War*, 166.
40 Erlich and Alter to Stalin, October 1941, in *Henryk Erlich*, 190.
41 "Der plan fun unzer arbet," in *Henryk Erlich*, 193.
42 Erlich and Alter to Stalin, October 1941, in *Henryk Erlich*, 191.
43 Korzec, *Hidat retsihatam*, 287.
44 Korzec, *Hidat retsihatam*, 287.
45 "Ehrlich's Complaint to the Presidium of the USSR Supreme Soviet," 27 December 1941, in Redlich, *War*, 168.
46 "Report of Ehrlich's Suicide," 18 May 1942, in Redlich, *War*, 169; "Report of Alter's Execution," 17 February 1943, in Redlich, *War*, 170.
47 Korzec, "Hidat retsihatam," 289–303.
48 Beria, *My Father*, 109–10. The son added: "After this gaffe my father delved into the history of the Bund: I saw Merkulov bring him huge files about it. Any Party could derive inspiration from the Bund's remarkable organisation, he remarked. I heard my father express regret at the deaths of Erlich and Alter." The files concerning the history of the Bund may have included a manuscript history of the organization that Erlich had prepared during his first Soviet prison term. For a description of that work, see Pickhan, "That Incredible History."
49 Werth, *Russia*, 180–81.
50 In fact, shortly after the German invasion Litvinov himself began broadcasting over Radio Moscow's foreign service. In November 1941 he was dispatched to Washington as Soviet ambassador to the United States.
51 On the five Anti-Fascist Committees see Petrova, *Antifashistskie komitety*. On the All-Slavic committee see also Moskovskikh, "Vozniknovenie."
52 The other was Peretz Markish, who headed the Moscow branch of the Jewish section of the Soviet Writers' Union. Of the two, Mikhoels had a more illustrious track record.
53 See *Sovetskoe iskusstvo*, 2 April 1939 (p. 4: Peretz Markish, "Narodnyi artist Mikhoels"); *Pravda*, 13 April 1941 (p. 2: "Prisuzhdenie uchenykh zvanii vydaiushchymsia masteram teatral'nogo iskusstva").
54 *Izvestiia*, 8 October 1943 (p. 3: "Frontovoi teatr").
55 *The Family Oppenheim* had been withdrawn from Soviet cinemas following conclusion of the 1939 German-Soviet agreement. See chapter 1, n. 237.
56 "Appointment of Mikhoels as Chairman of the Jewish Anti-Fascist Committee," 15 December 1941, in Redlich, *War*, 195.

57 Epstein had lived in the United States from 1909 to 1917 and from 1921 to 1929. Between 1917 and 1921 he had held several positions in the *Evsektsiia*, the Jewish section of the Soviet Communist Party, 1918–1930 (see the survey by Elissa Bemporad in volume 1 of this series). During his latter stay in the United States he served as editor of the New York–based Yiddish-language newspaper *Frayhayt*. Suspicions about his connections to Soviet intelligence surfaced at that time. In 1937 he made a trip to New York, during which time his one-time American lover, a known Soviet agent named Juliet Poyntz, was kidnapped and never seen again. According to one version of events, Poyntz had unwisely made known her plans to sever her connections with Soviet intelligence and to expose some of what she knew. Rumors linked Epstein's visit to Poyntz's disappearance and murder. See Epstein, *Jew and Communism*, 391–92; Pozniakov, *Sovietskaia razvedka*, 524–25; Lynn, "Gendered Narratives," 40–50. Epstein may have entered the United States illegally in 1937: according to a US State Department document from June 1945, Epstein was "still wanted on a passport charge in New York." Joseph C. Grew, Acting Secretary of State, to the President [Truman], 27 June 1945, Enclosure: "Possible Resurrection of Communist International, Resumption of Extreme Leftist Activities, Possible Effect on United States," 2 June 1945, *Foreign Relations of the United States, 1945*, 1:275.

58 Estraikh, "Itsik Fefer," 30–31. Fefer's testimony would serve the state during the postwar trials of Committee members, which ultimately engulfed him as well. See the discussion by Anna Shternshis in volume 4 of this series.

59 Rubenstein and Naumov, *Stalin's Secret Pogrom*, 81.

60 Rubenstein and Naumov, *Stalin's Secret Pogrom*, 120.

61 Kvitko and Petrovskii, *Zhizn'*, 268. Kvitko added, "I don't know yet what I'll be doing there."

62 See, for example, Epstein to A. G. Aizenshtadt, 27 July 1943, Gosudarstvennyi arkhiv Rossiiskoi Federatsii (GARF), f. R-8114, o. 1, d. 935, l. 17.

63 See chapter 4, n. 15.

64 Redlich, "Soviet Uses," 139–42. Recruitment proceeded throughout the war, sometimes taking advantage of opportunities presented during the fighting. One opportunistic acquisition was the poet Abraham Sutzkever. In September 1943 Sutzkever and his wife, members of the Wilno *Fareynikte partizaner organizatsye* (FPO—see pp. 133–34), escaped from the ghetto with the last FPO fighters, eventually finding cover in the Narocz forest, two hundred kilometers away, where they made contact with a Soviet partisan unit. Through that unit their whereabouts eventually became known to the Jewish Anti-Fascist Committee. In March 1944, Mikhoels and Epstein wrote to Antanas Sniečkus, first secretary of the Lithuanian Communist Party, who also headed the Lithuanian partisan movement. They asked Sniečkus for help to bring the poet, who had distinguished himself as a member of the resistance movement in the ghetto, to Moscow, along with his wife. The letter characterized Sutzkever as the only surviving Yiddish writer in the German-occupied territories and stressed the

propaganda importance of his participation in a rally of representatives of the Jewish people, scheduled initially for 26 March (it took place in April). Mikhoels and Epstein to Sniečkus, 2 March 1944, GARF, f. R-8114, o. 1, d. 897, l. 22–23. See also Fishman, *Book Smugglers*, 116–18, 129–31.

65 *The Reform Advocate*, 21 April 1944 (p. 4: William Zukerman, "The Moscow Jewish Conference").

66 "Outline of Jewish Anti-Fascist Committee Goals," 5 February 1942, in Redlich, *War*, 196–97.

67 Redlich, *War*, 24.

68 Organization established on a permanent basis in Philadelphia in May 1922 "to speak and to act on behalf of Jews in all matters affecting the welfare of Jews as Jews." Frommer, *American Jewish Congress*, 1:181.

69 American Reform rabbi, Zionist leader, and well-known political commentator and public speaker, prominent in anti-Nazi activities during the 1930s and one of the primary organizers of the World Jewish Congress, established in 1936. Wise's public pronouncements to 1942 included few references to the Soviet Union.

70 "From Epshteyn's Report and Suggestions Concerning the Jewish Anti-Fascist Committee," 13 April 1942, in Redlich, *War*, 200.

71 Liga-V lema'an Rusiyah haMo'atsatit, *Likrat magbit haEzrah liVerit haMo'atsot*, April 1942, Archives of the Israel Labour Movement, Tel Aviv, IV 519. The publication indicated that the campaign was being coordinated with Soviet Ambassador Maiskii in London.

72 "From Epshteyn's Report," Redlich, *War*, 201.

73 "From Epshteyn's Report," Redlich, *War*, 201.

74 Redlich, *War*, 25, 202–206. Jews were promised that the tanks and planes they contributed (or the army units that received them) could be named for Jewish historical figures, including Simon Bar Kokhba, leader of a revolt against Rome in 132 CE. Soviet Jews also appear to have been excited by this idea. In January 1943, for example, the Jewish community of Kuibyshev sent ten thousand rubles to Stalin, accompanied by a telegram of blessing and the suggestion that the money be used for a tank named after Bar Kokhba, the "immortal Jewish hero." *Jewish Telegraphic Agency Bulletin*, 19 January 1943 (p. 3: "Kuibyshev Jewish Community Sends 10,000 to Stalin for 'Bar Kochba' Tank"). To all appearances, a tank carrying this name was never built, even though Bar Kokhba had been "legalized" in the Soviet Union following production of a successful eponymous play by Shmuel Halkin at the Moscow Jewish State Theater in 1938. See Wolitz, "*Shulamis*," 87–104; Veidlinger, *Moscow Jewish State Theater*, 168–73. In 1942 the Byelorussian Jewish State Theater, which had been evacuated to Novosibirsk, included this play in its repertoire. *Literatura i iskusstvo*, 18 August 1942 (p. 1: "Uspekh zaima"). Soviet discourse of the time condoned references to historic Jewish heroes, as, for instance, when describing Jewish soldiers as "the Maccabees of our days." *Eynikayt*, 15 March 1943 (p. 3: "Tsveyter plenum fun yidishn antifashistishn komitet in fssr").

75 "Otchet o deiatel'nosti Evreiskogo antifashistskogo komiteta v SSSR," GARF, f. R-8114, o. 1, d. 1064.
76 Quoted in Zeltser, "How the Jewish Intelligentsia Created the Jewishness," 105.
77 Gitlin, *Istoricheskie sudby*, 653.
78 Dymshits, *Gorskie evrei*, 381, 385.
79 "Povestka dnia prezidiuma Evreiskogo antifashistskogo komiteta," 13 March 1945, GARF, f. R-8114, o.1, d. 1054, l. 306.
80 This conclusion appears true even though only three thousand of the newspaper's ten thousand printed copies were sold abroad. Zeltser, "How the Jewish Intelligentsia Created the Jewishness," 105.
81 Shneer, "Rivers of Blood," 141.
82 Sherman, "David Bergelson," 58.
83 "TsK VKP(b). Tovarishchu Stalinu," GARF, f. R-8114, o. 1, d. 923. Eventually *Heymland* would become the title of a short-lived Yiddish literary almanac (1947–1948), published under the auspices of the Writers Union.
84 Estraikh, "Smertelno opasnoe natsionalnoe edinenie," 335–37.
85 The act (US Code Title 22, Chapter 11, Subchapter II) required, among other things, that any "partnership, association, corporation, organization, or other combination of persons . . . having its principal place of business in a foreign country" and acting "within the United States as a public-relations counsel, publicity agent, information-service employee or political consultant for or in the interests of" a foreign government "file with the Attorney General a true and complete registration statement" including "a detailed statement of every activity which the registrant is performing."
86 See n. 50.
87 Embassy of the Soviet Union to Department of State, 3 March 1943, *Foreign Relations of the United States, 1943*, 830–31.
88 Balandina, "Deiatelnost'," 220–22.
89 See "Protokol Prezidiuma Evreiskogo antifashistkogo komiteta," 11 May 1944, GARF, f. R-8114 o. 1, d. 1053, l. 8. See also Moseikina, "Velikaia otechestvennaia voina," 80.
90 See Zeltser, "How the Jewish Intelligentsia Created the Jewishness," 109.
91 The newspaper that was probably uppermost in the writers' minds was the world's most widely circulated Yiddish-language daily, the New York–based *Forverts*. For more on this newspaper's attitude toward Soviet propaganda efforts aimed at Jews in the United States, see pp. 203–204.
92 "Epshteyn Rejects Accusations against the Jewish Anti-Fascist Committee," 23 November 1943, in Redlich, *War*, 287–88.
93 "From Minutes of a Meeting at the Sovinformburo concerning the Jewish Anti-Fascist Committee," 9 November 1943, in Redlich, *War*, 286.
94 See, for example, "V. Kruzhkov's Criticism of the Jewish Anti-Fascist Committee," 11 May 1943, in Redlich, *War*, 285: "I consider it politically harmful that the leadership of the Jewish Anti-Fascist Committee receives letters with various kinds of petitions of a material/domestic nature from Soviet Jewish

citizens, and then takes it upon itself to satisfy these requests by corresponding with Soviet and Party organs."

95 For further discussion on public opinion of Jews in the USSR, see pp. 112–17.

96 *Eynikayt*, 15 March 1943 (p. 3: "Tsveyter plenum fun yidishn antifashistishn komitet in fssr").

97 Zeltser, *To Pour Out*, 163.

98 Redlich, *Evreiskii antifashistskii komitet*, 105–107.

99 For additional details see chapter 6.

100 See Grüner, "Did Anti-Jewish Mass Violence Exist;" Leibovich, "Antisemitskie nastroenniia;" Manley, *To the Tashkent Station*, 231–32, 264. For figures concerning Jews' service in the military and their deployment, see chapter 4 and Appendix.

101 Redlich, *Evreiskii antifashistskii komitet*, 102. Cf. "Aron Gitelman," Yad Vashem (E), Research, Jews in the Red Army, 1941–1945.

102 Persov, *Yakov Moshkovski*; Persov, *Yakov Shmushkevitsh*.

103 Persov, *Dayn nomen*.

104 *Eynikayt*, 5 October 1944 (p. 2: Itsik Fefer, "Azoy shlogn zikh yidn").

105 As of October 1942, 5,163 Jews had received military awards. They ranked fourth among Soviet ethnic groups, after Russians, Ukrainians, and Byelorussians.

106 See Mikhoels and Epstein to Shcherbakov, 2 April 1943, in Kostyrchenko, *Gosudarstvennyi antisemitizm*, doc. 7.

107 *Istoricheskii zhurnal* 1944, nos. 2–3 (p. 11: "Krasnaia Armiia: armiia boevogo edinstva i druzhby narodov").

108 Such interethnic families appear in the final scenes of the 1936 film *Iskateli schastia* (Seekers of happiness), which portrayed a Jewish family resettling to Birobidzhan, and in the 1940 operetta *Vzaimnaia liubov'* (Mutual love) by the Soviet Jewish composer Sigismund Katz. *Sovetskoe iskusstvo*, 24 June 1940 (p. 3: Viktor Ermans, "Vzaimnaia liubov'"). See also Estraikh, "Jews as Cossacks;" Le Foll, "Image," 240.

109 Not many Jews lived in areas with heavy Cossack populations, where such units were formed. Moreover, except for a relatively small number of enthusiasts, horse riding was not an activity in which Jews had historically engaged.

110 *Eynikayt*, 19 October 1944 (p. 3: Moyni Shulman, "Der kazakisher polkovnik Khaim Popov").

111 *Eynikayt*, 31 May 1945 (p. 3: Shmuel Persov, "Der rumfuler kavalerist").

112 *Jewish Advocate* (Boston), 3 April 1942 (p. 1: Jacob Chernyak, "Soviet-Jewish General to Be Immortalized in Play").

113 Embassy of the USSR in Washington, *Soviet Art in Wartime: Information Bulletin. Special Supplement* (1943), 48.

114 Maksimenko, "Belorusskaia tematika," 144.

115 The Committee also made inquiries into the ethnic origin of General Ivan Cherniakhovskii but was told that he, too, was not Jewish. See Amir et al., "Skeletons."

116 For an attempt to distinguish actual history from subsequent legend see, inter alia, Stampfer, "What Actually Happened."
117 In London, the *Jewish Chronicle* expressed the hope that Soviet Jewish combatants would not "through an act of sheer forgetfulness, be insulted" by decoration with the new order. Nonetheless, a number of Jews did become insulted by offer of the award. There are a couple of unverified cases where Jewish soldiers rejected it. More often, Jews to whom it was presented, as products of a Soviet upbringing, were most likely either unaware of Khmelnitskii's historical record or saw the calamitous event as ancient history, with no direct relevance to their world. See Estraikh, "Jews and Soviet Remythologization."
118 On the massacre of Jews in Kamenets-Podolskii in August 1941 see pp. 80–81.
119 Redlich, *Evreiskii antifashistkii komitet*, 103. In 1950, Eidelman, who made known his Zionist sympathies, would be denounced, arrested, accused of "nationalist activity," and sent to labor camps. Eidelman, *Neokonchennye dialogi*, 9.
120 See chapter 2, n. 288.
121 Zeltser, *To Pour Out*, 92–93. See also Berlin, "Istoriia krymskoi tragedii."
122 See For more information about the Committee of Jewish Writers, Artists, and Scientists, see below, n. 139.
123 Asher, "Black Book," 401–402. See also "A Letter by Mikhoels and Epshteyn to Shcherbakov concerning the Publication of a Black Book," in Redlich, *War*, 347–48.
124 *Dos yidishe folk*, 101–102; "A Letter by Mikhoels and Epshteyn to Shcherbakov concerning the Black Book," 23 August 1944, in Redlich, *War*, 349. See also Rubenstein, "Il'ia Ehrenburg."
125 Ehrenburg, *Merder fun felker*.
126 Asher, "Black Book," 402–403; Altman and Karasik, "Istoriia," 133–38. Cf. "Ehrenburg's Letter to the JAFC [Jewish Anti-Fascist Committee] concerning the Black Book," 30 January 1945, in Redlich, *War*, 354, in which Ehrenburg objected to sharing his work with the international *Black Book* project.
127 Altshuler et al, *Sovetskie evrei pishut*, 124, 135.
128 Budnitskii and Rupp, "Intelligentsia," 633.
129 For details see Redlich, *War*, 100–104.
130 Sherman, "David Bergelson," 58.
131 Berkhoff, "'Total Annihilation,'" 69.
132 Grossman, *The Road*, 99. On the story see Volokhova, "'Staryi uchitel'" (two articles).
133 Quoted in Estraikh, "Anti-Nazi Rebellion," 175.
134 *Jewish Advocate* (Boston), 6 April 1944 (p. 17: Raymond A. Davies, "A 'Jewish Corner' of Soviet Russia").
135 "Possible Resurrection of Communist International" (see n. 57).
136 See "An Appeal to World Jewry," 24 August 1941, in Redlich, *War*, 174–77.
137 *Forverts*, 27 August 1941 (p. 4: "A fotografye mit an oyfruf un zalts oyf yidishe vundn").
138 On Zhitlovsky, see p. 191. On CJWAS, see p. 198.

139 Following Zhitlovsky's death in May 1943, the CJWAS was led by Albert Einstein, honorary president; Sholem Asch, president; Ben-Zion Goldberg, chairman, and the historian Raphael Mahler, vice-chairman. *Eynikayt* (New York), 3 June 1943 (p. 13: "Sholem Ash derveylt prezident fun yidishn shrayber-komitet").

140 Quoted in Engel, *Facing a Holocaust*, 55.

141 See Soyer, "Executed Bundists;" Hirszowicz, "Soviet Union;" Reimann, "Local Brawls."

142 Engel, *Facing a Holocaust*, 82.

143 Another consideration, perhaps more important, was no doubt the need to mobilize Western public opinion in favor of commencing Allied military operations in Europe in order to relieve pressure on Soviet troops.

144 No Soviet Jewish cultural figures had visited America during the entire interwar period. David Bergelson's American sojourn in 1928–1929 was at best an approximation of a Soviet Jewish intellectual's visit, especially as, even though he described himself as a Soviet writer, Bergelson lived at the time in Berlin and held a Lithuanian passport. See Estraikh, "David Bergelson," 205.

145 Redlich, *War*, 74.

146 Soyer, "Executed Bundists," 302.

147 See n. 74.

148 The regime evidently did not have any objection to this representation of Jewish history in 1942. Even before the war, in November 1936, Mikhoels had been rebuked for his allegedly "absurd, harmful point of view" that "the Jewish people, being stateless, had had no history so far." *Literaturnaia gazeta* 26 November 1936 (p. 6: "Vyvody i uroki: Na soveshchanii teatralnykh rabotnikov v Komitete po delam iskusstv, 23 noiabria"). During the same month in which Fefer published his poem, Efim Dyskin, a prewar student at the elite Moscow Institute of Philosophy and Literature who had been awarded the title of Hero of the Soviet Union in April 1942, wrote from his hospital bed, "I am proudly aware that I am a son of the great Jewish people, the people that has given to the world such great men as Marx and Heine, Sholem Aleichem and Einstein, Sverdlov and Kaganovich, Spinoza and [classic Yiddish writer I. L.] Peretz." Zeltser, *To Pour Out*, 234. Even earlier, a poem was published entitled "I am a Jew," written by Gafur Guliam, an Uzbek poet without Jewish roots. *Literature i iskusstvo*, 14 February 1942 (p. 4: "Pisateli na tribune"); *Ogonek*, 4 October 1942 (p. 13: "Poety Uzbekistana"). See also Manley, *To the Tashkent Station*, 223, 230.

149 Estraikh, "From 'Green Fields'"; Estraikh, "Sholem Asch's Moscow Sojourn."

150 See Fischthal, "Abraham Cahan."

151 *Forverts*, 3 July 1943 (pp. 6, 9: Tsevion, "Yidishe interesn").

152 *Pravda*, 15 July 1943 (p. 4: "Miting v Niu-Iorke v chest' Mikhoels i Fefera"). The same article appeared also in *Izvestiia* 15 and 16 July 1943.

153 See, for example, *Harper's Magazine*, April 1944 (pp. 415–16: Eliahu Ben-Horin, "The Soviet Wooing of Palestine").

154 *Forverts*, 8 July 1943 (pp. 4, 6: Mendel Osherovitsh, "An intervyu mit der sovetisher delegatsye").
155 *Forverts*, 12 July 1943 (p. 4: Lazar Fagelman, "Di sovetishe yidn un di amerikaner yidn"). Fagelman would later become the newspaper's editor (1962–1968).
156 Barghoorn, *Soviet Image*, 73–74. Barghoorn would eventually become a leading Sovietologist in the United States. In 1963 Soviet officials arrested him in Moscow on espionage charges and confined him for sixteen days, until the charges were dropped and Barghoorn expelled from the country.
157 Estraikh, "Smertelno opasnoe natsionalnoe edinenie," 329–32.
158 *Daily Worker* (New York), 18 September 1943 (p. 5: Art Shields, "Furriers Here Honor 2 Soviet Delegates"). See also Medvedev, *Moi velikie starukhi*, 159.
159 "From the Minutes of the Second JAFC Plenary Session," 18–20 February 1943, in Redlich, *War*, 210. On the idea of separate Jewish units in the Red Army see chapter 4, nn. 145–48.
160 Redlich, *War*, 213–14.
161 Rubenstein and Naumov, *Stalin's Secret Pogrom*, 64.
162 "Protokol soveshchaniia Evreiskogo antifashistskogo komiteta, 24 October 1944," GARF, f. R-8114, o. 1, d. 1053, l. 4–5.

6. THE REAR

1 For statistics, see chapter 2, n. 238. It is not known how many of these people died during the journey to the rear or after arrival, but it is clear that most survived, making them more than two-thirds and perhaps as much as three quarters of postwar Soviet Jewry.
2 Manley, *To the Tashkent Station*, 1. See also chapter 2, n. 239.
3 For criticism that the term was created and used by Soviet scholarship to "evoke the notion of a planned and organized operation, even when what actually happened was a panic-stricken and spontaneous escape," see Altshuler, "Escape and Evacuation," 78.
4 Dubson, "On the Problem," 38.
5 Of Leningrad and Moscow's 450,000 Jewish residents (according to the 1939 census), between 250,000 and 300,000 evacuated. Consequently, among those evacuated by the end of 1941 there were between 1,450,000 and 1,550,000 Jews. See Dubson, "Toward a Central Database," 102.
6 Feferman, "Soviet Humanitarian Action?"
7 Dubson, "On the Problem," 51.
8 Interview with Esfir A. by Anna Shternshis, Potsdam, Germany, June 2001. On the circumstances of the interview see Shternshis, *When Sonia Met Boris*, 15.
9 Altshuler, "Escape and Evacuation," 78.
10 Interview with Etya G. by Anna Shternshis, New York, 1998.
11 See the tables, graphs, and maps in Żaron, *Ludność polska*, 67–73.
12 Altshuler, "Escape and Evacuation," 78.
13 Quoted in Altshuler, "Escape and Evacuation," 79.

14 Quoted in Altshuler, "Escape and Evacuation," 79. The instruction continued: "It is imperative to destroy any valuable property that cannot be taken."
15 See chapter 3, n. 97.
16 Manley, *To the Tashkent Station*, 34.
17 Manley, *To the Tashkent Station*, 36.
18 Most sources do not distinguish between the two categories, referring to all who left their homes and fled eastward, whether under official auspices or not, as "evacuees." See Altshuler, "Escape and Evacuation," 78.
19 Interview with Fira B. by Anna Shternshis, Berlin, 2002.
20 The 1939 Jewish population of Berdichev was 23,266. Altshuler, *Distribution*, 22. Among the victims was the mother of Vassilii Grossman.
21 Manley, *To the Tashkent Station*, 40.
22 Manley, *To the Tashkent Station*, 136.
23 Kaganovitch, "Jewish . . . Draftees," 468.
24 Manley, *To the Tashkent Station*, 50.
25 Manley, *To the Tashkent Station*, 50. For a significantly lower figure (1–1.5 million), see Borzunova et al., "Migratsiia." It is conventional to speak of a "first evacuation," which began in June 1941 and continued through early 1942, and a "second evacuation," carried out in July and August 1942. In the event, however, many people fled the Germans in more than two stages. A proportion of Jewish evacuees had initially been refugees from Nazi-occupied Poland and had migrated within the USSR before the war. Thus, for some people like Tatiana Remer, the so-called second evacuation actually represented her fourth move since Germany invaded Poland—from Warsaw to Lwów in 1939, from Lwów to Kiev in 1940, from Kiev to Stalingrad in 1941, and from Stalingrad to Kazakhstan in 1942. Interview with Natalia Chepur by Yulia Smilianskaya, Kiev, 2002, "Natalia (Bronislava) Chepur," Centropa (E), Interviews. An additional one hundred thousand Jews had reached the Soviet rear as a result of deportation from the western territories annexed in 1939 and 1940. See pp. 33 and 37.
26 Manley, *To the Tashkent Station*, 137.
27 See chapter 2, nn. 238–39.
28 Interview with Basia Chaika by Tatiyana Chayka, Kiev, 2001, "Basya Chaika," Centropa (E), Interviews.
29 On these choices see Shternshis, "Between Life and Death;" also see chapter 3.
30 See Esses et al., "Uncertainty;" Knox and Kushner, *Refugees*; Wyman, *Paper Walls*.
31 Interview with Frida S. by Anna Shternshis, Moscow, 2002. This recollection runs counter to a scholar's assertion that "the frequency with which the film is mentioned in Holocaust survivor testimonies collected by [the] Steven Spielberg Shoah Foundation suggests that it may have helped Soviet Jews to survive by impressing on them the murderous nature of Nazi antisemitism." Hicks, *First Films*, 29. However, the available evidence does not appear to establish a strong connection between information from the film and the actual decision to flee at the onset of war. On the film, see chapter 1, n. 238.

32 Interview with Basia Chaika by Tatiyana Chayka, Kiev, 2001, "Basya Chaika," Centropa (E), Interviews.
33 Interview with Iosif A. by Anna Shternshis, Toronto, 2008.
34 Interview with Natalia Chepur (above, n. 25).
35 See Altshuler, "Escape and Evacuation," 90.
36 Interview with Faina G. by Anna Shternshis, Toronto, 2007.
37 Interview with Efim G. by Anna Shternshis, New York, 1999.
38 See also chapter 3,at nn. 36–42.
39 Interview with Liza L. by Anna Shternshis, New York, 1999.
40 Interview with Fira B. by Anna Shternshis, Berlin, 2002.
41 Interview with Golda R. by Anna Shternshis, Toronto, 2007.
42 See chapter 3, at nn. 85–88.
43 Dubson, "Toward a Central Database," 102.
44 Interview with Liza L. by Anna Shternshis, New York, 1999.
45 A study of elderly Jews in the Łódź ghetto in Poland uncovered a similar phenomenon. It found that postwar memoirs and testimonies are "more likely to highlight family cohesion in a way that memorializes elderly parents and grandparents," unlike sources generated during the war years, which are "much more forthcoming about familial tensions that, in some cases, resulted in a complete rupture of relationships among family members." Strauss, *"Cast me not off"*, 40. See also Shik, "Infinite Loneliness," 125–26.
46 See pp. 198–99.
47 "Kak ya spaslas' ot Gitlera" (recollections of Emilia Borisovna Kotlova), in Arad et al., *Nieizvestnaia chernaya kniga*, 50–73.
48 "V mestechke Piatigory Kievskoi oblasti (recollections of Raisa Zelenkova)," in Arad et al., *Nieizvestnaia chernaya kniga*, 166–83.
49 The transliteration is an effort to reflect the mixture of Ukrainian and Russian, including all grammatical mistakes. The English translation does not reflect these grammatical errors.
50 From the Ehrenburg papers at Yad Vashem Archives, P21.1, file 223, pp. 5–6.
51 Chepelev, "Soviet Children." On the complexities of parental decisions during the Holocaust, including decisions that could lead to leaving children behind, see Ofer, "Parenthood."
52 Emelin, "Borba."
53 Zadneprovskaia, "Zabota," 68.
54 Manley, *To the Tashkent Station*, 119–21.
55 Manley, *To the Tashkent Station*, 121–25.
56 Lugovskaia, *Kak znaiu*, 288.
57 Gromova, *Evakuatsiia*, 135.
58 Zharkynbaeva et al., "Voennaia povsednevnost'," 100.
59 See chapter 3, at nn. 26–28.
60 Manley, *To the Tashkent Station*, 132.
61 Manley, *To the Tashkent Station*, 138.
62 Gromova, *Evakuatsiia*, 23.

63 Manley, *To the Tashkent Station*, 138–40.
64 See above, at n. 26.
65 Interview with Naum A. by Anna Shternshis, Toronto, 2007. For more on Naum and his escape, see Shternshis, "Between Life and Death," 477–78.
66 Naum A., interview (see previous note).
67 Interview with Basya Ch. by Anna Shternshis, Brooklyn, New York, 1999.
68 Bakhmach is not far from Kiev, but it is in the Chernigov region of Ukraine.
69 Faina was probably referring to the Eighty-Third Battalion of the Fifth Railroad Brigade, stationed in Bakhmach until September 1941. Faina mistakenly referred to these troops as "going to Berlin." For more on the bombing of Basmach and Red Army soldiers' interactions with civilians and evacuees there, see Kabanov. *Stalnye peregony*, 101.
70 Interview with Faina M. by Anna Shternshis, New York, 1999.
71 Mikhailova, "Evakuatsiia," 26–27.
72 Shkurko, "Evakuirovannye evrei."
73 Zharkynbayeva et al., "Voennaia povsednevnost'."
74 Testimony of Garry Feldman, in Levin, *Evreiskie bezhentsy*, 241.
75 Aupyonova, "Zavod No. 517."
76 Shkurko, "Evakuirovannye evrei," 104–105.
77 See www.yadvashem.org/ru/remembrance/jews-red-army/zaltzman.html, accessed 5 March 2022.
78 Testimony of Lubov' Gorelik, in Levin, *Yevreiskie bezhentsy*, 247.
79 Levin, "Evreiskoe naseleniie," 47.
80 One such report, which was never published, claimed that Polish Jewish workers produced five times more parts for tanks than did their colleagues. "Di poylishe yidn in Uzbekistan," GARF (see chapter 5, n. 62), f. R-8114, op. 1, d. 124, l. 18.
81 Werth, *Russia*, 218.
82 Interview with Dora D. by Anna Shternshis, Moscow, 2002.
83 Interview with Grigorii Husid by Ella Orlikova, Kiev, 2002, "Grigoriy Yakovlevich Husid," Centropa (E), Interviews.
84 Snegiriova, "Evakuatsiia."
85 Autobiography of Roza Evseevna Levenberg, "Roza Levenberg," Centropa (E), Interviews.
86 Interview with Genrietta F. by Anna Shternshis. Berlin, 2002.
87 Genrietta F., interview (see previous note).
88 Sidur, *Pamiatnik*, 243. Thanks to Arkady Zeltser for the reference.
89 Rich, *Little Girl*, 83.
90 Belsky, "Fraught Friendships," 166.
91 Speransky, "Vysshaya shkola," 33.
92 Speransky, "Vysshaya shkola," 35.
93 Speransky, "Vysshaya shkola," 35.
94 In the Ural Mountains, some eleven hundred kilometers east of Moscow. Between 1940 and 1957 it was known as Molotov.
95 Quoted in Shternshis, *When Sonia Met Boris*, 100–101.

96 Since 2007, Semey, Kazakhstan.
97 Shternshis, *When Sonia Met Boris*, 102–103.
98 Adler, *Survival*, 168.
99 Werth, *Russia*, 216–17.
100 Perehrest. *Silske gospodarstvo*, 24.
101 Tania Pasik, "Evakuatsiia," Efingar (E), chast' 2.
102 Altman. *Kholokost*, 301.
103 Ia. Pasik, "Katastrofa evreiskogo krestianstva Iuga Ukrainny i Kryma," Evreiskie zemledelskie kolonii (E).
104 Zinovii Bekman, "Ispytaniia i nevzgody," Evreiskie zemledelskie kolonii (E), Vospominaniia.
105 Testimony of Semyon Vernovsky in Levin, *Evreiskie bezhentsy*, 269.
106 Potemkina, "Evakuatsiia," 66.
107 Potemkina, "Evakuatsiia," 67.
108 Savgabaeva, "Evakuatsiia."
109 Interview with Bella Gold by Mikhail Gold, Kiev, 1996.
110 Kanovich, *Liki*, 107–10.
111 Poluektov to Bochkov, 1942, in Levin, *Evreiskie bezhentsy*, 174.
112 Cheremukhin to Sharipov, in Levin, *Evreiskie bezhentsy*, 148.
113 Levin, "Evreiskoe naselenie," 51.
114 Dzigan, *Der koyekḥ*, 178.
115 Orlov, "Kartochnoe snabzhenie," 37.
116 Orlov, "Kartochnoe snabzhenie"; Zinich, *Povsednevnaia zhizn'*, 5.
117 Zinich, *Povsednevnaia zhizn'*, 5.
118 Shkurko, "Evakuirovannye evrei," 106
119 Zinich, *Povsednevnaia zhizn'*, 7.
120 Levin, "Evreiskoie naseleniie," 150.
121 Levin, "Evreiskoie naseleniie," 151.
122 Levin, "Evreiskoie naseleniie," 188.
123 Filtzer and Goldman, *Hunger*, 4.
124 Filtzer and Goldman, *Hunger*, 61. Cf. 73–74: "In 1943, the state launched a major campaign to use a variety of 'invented' foods to supplement the diet. Pine needle extract (*nastoi khvoi*), a bitter concoction made from boiled pine needles containing high amounts of vitamin C, was used as a 'juice' to counteract scurvy. Scientists searching for protein additives discovered yeast extract (*belkovye drozhzhi*), and canteen cooks began adding tons of the foul-tasting stuff to soups and foods. Unions organized workers into large groups to gather edible wild greens, including sorrel, nettles, and dandelion leaves, with high nutritional value. The Union of Workers in Pubic Catering (ROP) taught cooks to boil down the starchy water left after cooking potatoes to create a variety of jelly-like 'desserts' by adding sugar to the potato starch (*krakhmal*)."
125 Alexander Berman, "Zhguchaya pamiat ob evakuatsii," in Levin, *Evreiskie bezhentsy*, 221.
126 Testimony of Viktor Rozenfat, in Levin, *Evreikie bezhentsy*, 264.

127 Wąs, "Kak vosprinimalis drugie," 97.
128 Shkurko, "Evakuirovannye evrei," 120.
129 Zharkynbaeva et al., "Voennaia povsednevnost'," 101.
130 Fedotov, "Evakuatsiia," 57.
131 Levin, "Evreiskie bezhentsy," 149.
132 Levin, "Evreiskie bezhentsy," 150.
133 Shkurko, "Evakuirovannye evrei," 118.
134 Quoted in Manley, *To the Tashkent Station*, 172.
135 Manley, *To the Tashkent Station*, 177.
136 Shkurko, "Evakuirovannye evrei," 106.
137 Levin, "Evreiskie bezhentsy," 150.
138 Quoted in Manley, *To the Tashkent Station*, 193.
139 Belsky, "Evacuated Children," 171.
140 Belsky, "Evacuated Children," 173.
141 Manley, *To the Tashkent Station*, 186.
142 Islamova, "Uzbekistan," 506.
143 Choriev, "K istorii."
144 Nikiforov, "Organizatsiia," 486.
145 Belsky, "Am I a Jew?," 275.
146 B. Slutskii, "Evreiskie siroty v Kazakhstane," GARF, R-8114, op. 1, delo 523, l.178.
147 For this claim see Belsky, "Am I a Jew?," 276.
148 Edele and Warlik, "Saved," 111; Manley, *To the Tashkent Station*, 165. The proportions reflect differing contexts. The majority of refugees from Nazi-occupied Poland to the Soviet zone in 1939 had been men, whereas a large proportion of men from the pre-1939 territories were conscripted into the military.
149 Sidur, *Pamiatnik*, 244.
150 Wąs, "Kak vosprinimalis," 83.
151 Leibovich, "Antisemitskic nastroeniia," 287.
152 Leibovich, "Antisemitskie nastroeniia," 289.
153 Leibovich, "Antisemitskie nastroeniia," 287.
154 Zharkynbayeva et al., "Voennaia povsednevnost'," 102.
155 See Esmir A., interview (above, n. 8).
156 The journalist M. Zheleznova (Ayzerman) prepared a story on the topic for *Eynikayt* in 1943. She recorded an encounter between two female Jewish refugees, one from pre-1939 Poland, the other from the pre-1939 USSR, in which the Polish Jew found it remarkable that the Soviet Jew had three little children with her. "Not many of them saved their kids," Zheleznova wrote. In preparing the story for publication the editor crossed out that line, substituting "many children died during the trip." Stories about Jewish mothers abandoning their children were evidently too much for readers to handle, even in wartime, when they had become accustomed to reports of atrocious violence and cruelty. In the end the story was not published. For the manuscript see M. Zheleznova,

"Evrei evakuirovannye iz zapadnykh oblastei ustroilis' v Kazakhstane," GARF, f. R-8114, op. 1, d. 30, l. 95–96.

157 Manley, *To the Tashkent Station*, 229–30.

158 "Vypiska iz postanovleniia SNK SSSR i TsK VKP[B] o poriadke osvobozhdeniia repressirovannykh polskikh grazhdan," 123 August 1941, in Levin *Evreiskie Bezhentsy*, 194.

159 Potemkina, "Evakuatsiia," 59.

160 Shkurko, "Evakuirovannye evrei," 104.

161 Manley, *To the Tashkent Station*, 220–30.

162 See pp. 155–57. See also Fitzpatrick, "Annexation," 142.

163 Manley, *To the Tashkent Station*, 230–33.

164 Leibovich, "Antisemitskie nastroeniia," 241.

165 Leibovich, "Antisemitskie nastroeniia," 242.

166 See Faina M., interview (above, n. 70).

167 Faina M., interview (above, n. 70).

168 Leibovich, "Antisemitskie nastroeniia," 242.

169 For more details, see Belsky, "Am I a Jew?."

170 See Fitzpatrick, "Annexation," 142–43.

171 For detailed discussion of Jewish religious life in evacuation see Gershoni, *Yehudim ve Yahadut*, 177–82.

172 Sh. Epstein, "Spletenie dvukh pesen evreev" (ms), GARF, f. 8114, op.1, d. 254, l. 169. The phrase "the most Jewish of all cities in the Soviet Union" was stricken from the text as it was prepared for publication.

173 D. Manevich, "Evreiskie nationalnye uchrezhdeniia v SSSR," GARF, f. R-8114, op. 1, d. 89.

174 V. Vismond, "Moldavsko-Evreiskii dzhaz orchestra v Samarkande," GARF, f. R-8114, op. 1, d. 130.

175 A correspondent for *Eynikayt* prepared a brief account, preserved in a Russian manuscript in the archive of the Jewish Anti-Fascist Committee: Fayvl Sito, "Kontsert evreiskich pesen v Saratove," GARF, f. 8114, op. 1, d. 169.

176 Teif had been imprisoned as a "Jewish nationalist spy" from 1938 to April 1941, when he was abruptly released. After escaping eastward at the beginning of the war, he was conscripted into the Red Army in October 1941. He and his wife left a young son behind in Minsk, who later perished. "Moisei Teif," Yad Vashem (E), Research, Jews in the Red Army, 1941–1945.

177 Interview with Zoya Lichtman by E. Tsekhnovitska, Kiev, 2001.

178 For an indication of such awareness and one of its sources, see the account by Naum A., n. 65.

179 See chapter 3, at nn. 85–105.

180 Emmanuel Kaminka, "Der groyser yiddisher klasiker in mayn repertuar," GARF, f. 8114, op. 1, d. 177, l. 73–83.

181 See chapter 4, at nn. 97–101.

182 Viktor Vismond, "'Kliatva' I. Dobrushina v postanovke Kharkovskogo gosudarstvennogo teatra," GARF, f. R-8144, op. 1, d. 122.

183 Viktor Vismond, "Vashever yidishe aktyorn in a kharkover yidisher melukhe teater," GARF, f. 8114, op.1, d. 127, l. 178.
184 At least ten plays written during the years of evacuation portrayed heroic Jewish soldiers who sacrificed everything not only for their country but for their lost families who had been burned alive or otherwise killed during the first months of the war. Lurye, "Sovetskie evreiskie teatry v 1948g.," GARF, f. R-8114, op.1, d. 380.
185 See p. 41.
186 Later interviews with former evacuees, both Soviet and Polish (or Romanian), suggest for the most part that Polish and Soviet Jews had little daily contact with one another, even if they lived on the same street. Nevertheless, there is evidence of Soviet Jews helping Polish Jewish deportees released from detention camps and special settlements by the 1941 amnesty become settled in new surroundings. See Belsky, "Fraught Friendships," 164–66.
187 Markish, *Stol' dolgoe vozvrashchenie*, chapter 12.
188 Zuskina-Perelman, *Travels*, 149–52.
189 V. Mark, "Evreiskie bezhentsy na doske pocheta luchshikh polevykh rabotnikov," GARF, f. R-8114, op. 1. d.23, p. 88.
190 Iona Rozenfeld, "Na prazdnike paskhi sredi tashkentskikh evreev," GARF, f. R-8114, op. 1. d. 124, p. 162.
191 Manley, *To the Tashkent Station*, 248–49. Petitions were often granted or denied depending upon the time of their submission and the destination to which the petitioner sought to return. See Manley, *To the Tashkent Station*, 246–47.
192 Manley, *To the Tashkent Station*, 243–44.
193 See pp. 114–15.
194 For examples, see Manley, *To the Tashkent Station*, 249–50.
195 "An Appeal to Molotov Concerning Jewish Survivors," 18 May 1944, in Redlich, *War*, 243–44.
196 See Manley, *To the Tashkent Station*, 250–51.
197 See, for example, the letter that a Jewish returnee to Odessa sent to Ilya Ehrenburg: "I was in evacuation for three years. I returned to my native city recently. The things and furniture in my apartment had been stolen; my apartment was occupied. I have two sons who are officers defending the motherland, and for seven days I had to sleep in the front entrance before a neighbor felt sorry for me and let me into his apartment. The bureaucrats in the housing division have still not given me an order for an apartment." Quoted in Manley, *To the Tashkent Station*, 263.

APPENDIX

1 Sverdlov, *Evrei-generaly*, 15; Arad, *BeTsel haDegel*, 431–32.
2 Arad, "Soviet Jews," 81.
3 Krivosheev, *Grif sekretnosti*.
4 Gareev et al., *Pamiati pavshikh*, 64.

5 Gareev et al., *Pamiati pavshikh*, 90.
6 Gareev et al., *Pamiati pavshikh*, 90.
7 Artemiev, *Bratskii boevoi soiuz narodov*, 55–59.
8 Artemiev, *Bratskii boevoi soiuz narodov*, 55–59.
9 Bezugolnyi, *Opit*, 591.
10 Krivosheev and Kirilin, *Velikaia Otechestvennaia Voina*, 40 (table 6a).
11 About 900,000 Jews in the German-occupied areas of the pre-1939 USSR, out of a total of 1,112,000 Jews who lived in those territories before the war, perished at German hands—some 30 percent of pre-1939 Soviet Jewry. Kupovetskii, "Liudskie poteri" (2008), 196, 200.
12 Altshuler, *Soviet Jewry* (1998), 20.
13 *Sovetskaia aviatsiia*, 193; *Rukovodiashchii politicheskii sostav*; Bezugolnyi, *Opit*, 595, 597.
14 Among the Jewish soldiers in the Sixtieth Army, 546 were officers and 527 were enlisted men (including 213 sergeants). Jews thus accounted for 1.2 percent of the soldiers of this army and 4.8 percent of the officers.
15 Krivosheev, *Rossiia i SSSR*, 238.
16 Krivosheev, *Rossiia i SSSR*, 238.
17 Bezugolnyi, *Opit*, 306.
18 Krivosheev and Kirilin, *Velikaia Otechestvennaia Voina*, 51, 55, 62. Nevertheless, in absolute numbers, casualties among officers were huge: 631,008 killed; 392,085 missing; and 1,030,721 wounded. Beloborodov, *Voennye kadry*, 130. Rates varied from unit to unit, depending, among other factors, upon function (half of all losses among officers were in the infantry), rank, and role in the military hierarchy.
19 Krivosheev and Kirilin, *Velikaia Otechestvennaia Voina*, 60; Streit, *"Oni nam ne tovarishchi"*, 130. The discrepancy is probably due in the first instance to the fact that the Soviet figures account only for army personnel, not for any other branch of military service.
20 Polian, *Zhertvy*, 527.
21 See chapter 4, n. 165.
22 Kupovetskii, "Liudskie poteri" (2008), 203, n. 46. *Opolchenie* units were formed in other parts of the country as well. In the RSFSR they numbered approximately a million members.
23 Altshuler, *Distribution*, 9.
24 For every thousand Jews over the age of twenty in Moscow and in Leningrad in 1939, 190 possessed higher education. Altshuler, *Soviet Jewry* (1998), 130.

BIBLIOGRAPHY

Abramovich, Aron. *V reshaiushchei voine: Uchastie i rol' evreiev SSSR v voine protiv natsisma.* St. Petersburg: Dean, 1999.

Abramski-Bligh. "Jedwabne." In *Pinkas haKehilot, Polin*, vol. 4: *Varshah vehaGalil*, edited by Abraham Wein, 241–43. Jerusalem: Yad Vashem, 1989.

———. "Wizna." In *Pinkas haKehilot, Polin*, vol. 4: *Varshah vehaGalil*, edited by Abraham Wein, 189–90. Jerusalem: Yad Vashem, 1989.

Adler, Eliyana R. "Hrubieszów at the Crossroads: Polish Jews Navigate the German and Soviet Occupations." *Holocaust and Genocide Studies* 28, no. 1 (2014): 1–30.

———. *Survival on the Margins: Polish Jewish Refugees in the Wartime Soviet Union.* Cambridge, MA: Harvard University Press, 2020.

Adler, Eliyana R., and Natalia Aleksiun. "Seeking Relative Safety: The Flight of Polish Jews to the East in the Autumn of 1939." *Yad Vashem Studies* 46, no. 1 (2018): 41–71.

Agin, Shimon. "BeMilhemet haOlam haSheniyah uleahareiha." In *Bobruisk: Sefer-zikaron leKehilat Bobruisk uVenoteiha*, edited by Yehuda Slutsky, 730–31. Tel Aviv: Yotse'ei Bobruisk beMedinat Yisra'el uveArtsot-haBerit, 1967.

Ainsztein, Reuben. "Soviet Jewry in the Second World War." In *The Jews in Soviet Russia since 1917*, edited by Lionel Kochan, 281–99. Oxford: Oxford University Press, 1978.

Alexander, Saunders P. [= Alexander Prużański]. "My Life Story," unpublished manuscript in author's possession.

Altman, Ilya, ed. *Kholokost na territorii SSSR: Entsiklopediia.* Moscow: ROSSPEN, 2011.

———. *Zhertvy nenavisti: Kholokost v Rosii, 1941–1945.* Moscow: Kovcheg, 2002.

Altman, Ilya, and Olga Karasik. "Istoriia i sudba 'Chernoi knigi': pisateli i dokumenty epokhi." *Filologiia i kultura* 3 (2018): 133–38.

Altshuler, Mordechai. "The Distress of Soviet Jews in the Wake of the Molotov-Ribbentrop Pact." *Yad Vashem Studies* 36, no. 2 (2008): 73–141.

———. *Distribution of the Jewish Population of the USSR 1939*. Jerusalem: Maccabi Press, 1993.

———. "Escape and Evacuation of Soviet Jews at the Time of the Nazi Invasion: Policies and Realities." In *The Holocaust in the Soviet Union: Studies and Sources on the Destruction of the Jews in the Nazi-Occupied Territories of the USSR, 1941–1945*, edited by Lucjan Dobroszycki and Jeffrey S. Gurock, 77–104. Armonk, NY: M. E. Sharpe, 1993.

———. "Evacuation and Escape during the Course of the German-Soviet War." *Dapim: Studies on the Holocaust* 28, no. 2 (2014): 57–73.

———. "HaPinnui vehaMenosah shel haYehudim miByelorussia haMizrahit biTekufat haSho'ah (Yuni-August 1941)." *Yahadut Zemanenu* 3 (1986): 119–58.

———. "Jewish Combatants of the Red Army Confront the Holocaust." In *Soviet Jews in World War II: Fighting, Witnessing, Remembering*, edited by Harriet Murav and Gennady Estraikh, 16–35. New York: Academic Studies Press, 2014.

———. *Soviet Jewry on the Eve of the Holocaust: A Social and Demographic Profile.* Jerusalem: Hebrew University and Yad Vashem, 1998.

———. *Soviet Jewry since the Second World War: Population and Social Structure.* New York: Greenwood Press, 1987.

Altshuler, Mordechai, Yitzhak Arad, and Shmuel Krakowski, eds. *Sovetskie evrei pishut Il'e Erenburgu, 1943–1966*. Jerusalem: Yad Vashem, 1993.

American Jewish Joint Distribution Committee. *Aiding Jews Overseas: A Report of the Work of the Joint Distribution Committee in Bringing Relief to Thousands of Distressed Jews throughout the World during the Year 1940 and the First 5 Months of 1941*. New York: American Jewish Joint Distribution Committee, 1941.

Amir, Dan, Boris Morozov, and Aleksander A. Maslov. "Skeletons in the Closet? On the Chernyakhovsky Controversy." *Journal of Slavic Military Studies* 26 (2013): 81–113.

Ancel, Jean. "Chişinău." In *Pinkas haKehilot, Romania*, edited by Jean Ancel and Theodor Lavi, 2:400–16. Jerusalem: Yad Vashem, 1980.

———. "Hotin." In *Pinkas haKehilot, Romania*, edited by Jean Ancel and Theodor Lavi, 2:353–57. Jerusalem: Yad Vashem, 1980.

———. "German-Romanian Relations during the Second World War." In *The Tragedy of Romanian Jewry*, edited by Randolph L. Braham, 57–76. New York: Columbia University Press, 1994.

———. "Kishinev." In *Entsiklopediyah shel haSho'ah*, edited by Yisrael Gutman, 5:1093–94. Tel Aviv: Sifriyat Po'alim, 1990.

———. "Noua-Suliţă." In *Pinkas haKehilot, Romania*, edited by Jean Ancel and Theodor Lavi, 2:368–72. Jerusalem: Yad Vashem, 1980.

———. *Toledot haSho'ah: Romaniyah*. Jerusalem: Yad Vashem, 2002.

Angrick, Andrzej. "Annihilation and Labor: Jews and Thoroughfare IV in Central Ukraine." In *The Shoah in Ukraine: History, Testimony, Memorialization*, edited by Ray Brandon and Wendy Lower, 190–223. Bloomington: Indiana University Press, 2010.

———. "Die Einsatzgruppe D." In *Die Einsatzgruppen in der besetzten Sowjetunion 1941/42: Die Tätigkeits- und Lageberichte des Chefs der Sicherheitspolizei und des SD*, edited by Peter Klein, 88–110. Berlin: Hentrich, 1997.

Angrick, Andrzej, and Peter Klein. *The "Final Solution" in Riga: Exploitation and Annihilation, 1941–1944*. New York; Berghahn, 2009.

[Anonymous]. "Geto Shavli." In *Yahadut Lita*, vol. 4: *HaSho'ah 1941–1945*, edited by Leib Garfunkel, 185–231. Tel Aviv: Igud yots'ei Lita beYisra'el, 1984.

[Anonymous]. "Yehudei Latvia beGerush Sibir." In *Yahadut Latvia: Sefer zikaron*, edited by M. Eliav, Mendel Bobeh, and Elhanan Kremer, 312–29. Tel Aviv: Igud yotse'ei Latviyah veEstoniyah beYisra'el, 1953.

Arad, Yitzhak. *BeTsel haDegel haAdom: Yehudei Berit haMo'atsot baLehimah neged Germaniyah haNatsit.* Tel Aviv: Ministry of Defense Publishing House, 2008.

———. "Concentration of Refugees in Vilna on the Eve of the Holocaust." *Yad Vashem Studies* 9 (1973): 201–14.

——— [Rudnicki]. *Horet baZikaron: Lohem, Sored, Mantsi'ah.* Jerusalem: Yad Vashem, 2016.

———. "Mahanot haMishpahah baYe'arot: Derekh hatsalah mekorit." In *Nisyonot uFe'ulot hatsalah biTekufat haSho'ah*, edited by Y. Gutman, 276–94. Jerusalem: Yad Vashem, 1976.

———. *Mivtsa Reinhard: Bełżec, Sobibór, Treblinka.* Tel Aviv: Am Oved, 1988.

———. "The Murder of the Jews in German-Occupied Lithuania (1941–1944)." In *The Vanished World of Lithuanian Jews*, edited by Alvydas Nikžentaitis, Stefan Schreiner, and Darius Staliūnas, 175–99. Amsterdam: Rodopi, 2004.

———. "Soviet Jews in the War against Nazi Germany." *Yad Vashem Studies* 23 (1993): 73–125.

———. *Toledot haSho'ah: Berit haMo'atsot.* Jerusalem: Yad Vashem, 2004.

———. *Vilnah haYehudit beMa'avak uveKhilayon.* Tel Aviv: Sifriyat Po'alim, 1976.

———. "HaYudenratim beGeta'ot Lita: Kovnah uVilnah." In *Demut haHanhagah haYehudit beArtsot haShelitah haNatsit 1933–1945*, edited by Y. Gutman, 79–96. Jerusalem: Yad Vashem, 1980.

Arad, Yitzhak, Israel Gutman, and Abraham Margaliot, eds. *Documents on the Holocaust.* Lincoln: University of Nebraska Press, 1999.

Arad, Yitzhak, Shmuel Krakowski, and Shmuel Spector, eds. *The Einsatzgruppen Reports: Selections from the Dispatches of the Nazi Death Squads' Campaign against the Jews, July 1941–January 1943.* New York: Holocaust Library, 1989.

Arad, Yitzhak, T. Pavlova, I. Altman, and Sh. Krakowski, eds. *Neizvestnaia chernaia kniga: Svidetel'stva ochevidtsev o katastrofe Sovetskikh evreei (1941–1944).* Jerusalem: Yad Vashem, 1993.

Artemiev, A. P. *Bratskii boevoi soiuz narodov SSSR v Velikoi Otechestvennoi Voine.* Moscow: Mysl, 1975.

Asher, Harvey. "The Black Book and the Holocaust." *Journal of Genocide Research* 1, no. 3, (1999): 401–16.

Aupyonova A. "Zavod No. 517: Istoriia stanovlenia i razvitia evakuirovannogo promyshleennogo ob'ekta na kazakhstanskoi zemle." In *Istoriia, Pamiat', Liudi:*

Materialy VIII Mezhdunarodnoi nauchno-prakticheskoi konferentsii, edited by L. S. Aktaeva, A. I. Baron, and M. S. Makarova, 229–34. Almaty: Tsentralnyi gosudarstvennyi arkhiv Komiteta informatsii i arkhivov Ministerstva sviazi i informatsii Respubliki Kazakhstan, 2017.

Avatihi, A., and Y. Ben-Zakai. *Stolin: Sefer zikaron leKehilat Stolin vehaSevivah.* Tel Aviv: Stroud, 1952.

Balandina. "Deiatelnost' Sovinformburo za rubezhom v gody Velikoi Otechestvennoi Voiny: Effektivnost' i ideologicheskie prioretety." *Nauchnyi dialog* 3 (2019).

Balberyshski, M. *Shtarker fun ayzn: Iberlebungen in der Hitler-tkufe.* Tel Aviv: Menorah, 1967.

Banet (Markus), Hannah. *BeTsel korato shel haNatsi: Sipur hayehah shel nitsolat sho'ah.* Tel Aviv: Alef, 1987.

Bankier, David, and Ben-Zion Kilbansky. *Expulsion and Extermination: Holocaust Testimonials from Provincial Lithuania.* Jerusalem: Yad Vashem, 2011.

Baran, V. K. "Ekonomicheskiie preobrazovaniia v Zapadnoi Ukrainie v 1939–1941 godakh." In *Zapadnaia Belorussiia i Zapadnaia Ukraina w 1939–1941 gg.: Liudi, sobytiia, dokumenty*, edited by O. V. Petrovskaia and E. Iu. Borisenok, 156–76. St. Petersburg: Aleteiia, 2011.

Barber, John, and Mark Harrison. "Patriotic War, 1941–1945." In *Cambridge History of Russia*, vol. 3: *The Twentieth Century*, edited by Ronald Grigor Suny, 217–42. Cambridge: Cambridge University Press, 2008.

Barghoorn, Frederic C. *The Soviet Image of the United States: A Study in Distortion.* Port Washington, NY: Kennikat Press, 1950.

Baron, Salo W. *A Social and Religious History of the Jews.* New York: Columbia University Press, 1937.

Bartov, Omer. *Anatomy of a Genocide: The Life and Death of a Town Called Buczacz.* New York: Simon & Schuster, 2018.

———. *Germany's War and the Holocaust: Disputed Histories.* Ithaca, NY: Cornell University Press, 2003.

Bauer, Yehuda. "Buczacz and Krzemieniec: The Story of Two Towns during the Holocaust." *Yad Vashem Studies* 33 (2005): 245–306.

———. *The Death of the Shtetl.* New Haven, CT: Yale University Press, 2009.

———. "Jewish Baranowicze in the Holocaust." *Yad Vashem Studies* 31 (2003): 94–151.

———. "Rescue Operations through Vilna." *Yad Vashem Studies* 9 (1973): 215–23.

———. *Rethinking the Holocaust.* New Haven, CT: Yale University Press, 2001.

Beevor, Antony, and Luba Vinogradova, eds. *A Writer at War: Vasily Grossman with the Red Army 1941–1945.* London: Harvill Press, 2005.

Begin, Menachem. *BeLeilot levanim: Korotav shel asir Tsiyon beRusiyah.* Jerusalem: Karni, 1953.

Beloborodov, A. P., ed. *Voennye kadry Sovetskogo gosudarstva v Velikoi Otechestvennoi Voiny 1941–1945 gg.* Moscow: Voennoe izdatel'stvo Ministerstva oborony SSSR, 1963.

Belsky, Natalie. "'Am I a Jew?': Soviet Jewish Youth and Antisemitism on the Home Front during the Second World War." *Holocaust and Genocide Studies* 34, no. 2 (2020): 274–94.

———. "Encounters in the East: Evacuees in the Soviet Hinterland during the Second World War." PhD diss., University of Chicago, 2014.

———. "Evacuated Children: The Difficulties of Survival on the Home Front." *Demograficheskoe obozreenie* 3, no. 2 (2016): 169–79.

———. "Fraught Friendships: Soviet Jews and Polish Jews on the Soviet Home Front." In *Shelter from the Holocaust: Rethinking Jewish Survival in the Soviet Union*, edited by Mark Ederle, Sheila Fitzpatrick, and Atina Grossman, 161–84. Detroit: Wayne State University Press, 2018.

Bender, Sara. *Mul mavet orev: Yehudei Bialystok beMilhemet haOlam haSheniyah 1939–1943*. Tel Aviv: Am Oved, 1997.

———. "Not Only in Jedwabne: Accounts of the Annihilation of the Jewish *Shtetlach* in Northeastern Poland in the Summer of 1941." *Holocaust Studies* 19 (2013): 1–38.

Ben-Mordechai, A. "Metivta rabta 'Ohel Torah' deBaranovitch." In *Mosedot torah beEiropah beVinyanam uveHurbanam*, edited by S. K. Mirsky, 329–35. New York: Ogen, 1956.

Beorn, Waitman Wade. *Marching into Darkness: The Wehrmacht and the Holocaust in Belarus*. Cambridge, MA: Harvard University Press, 2014.

Beria, Sergo L. *My Father: Inside Stalin's Kremlin*. London: Duckworth, 2001.

Berkhoff, Karel C. *Motherland in Danger: Soviet Propaganda During World War II*. Cambridge, MA: Harvard University Press, 2012.

———. "'Total Annihilation of the Jewish Population': The Holocaust in the Soviet Media, 1941–45." *Kritika* 10, no. 1 (2009): 61–105.

Berlin, Boris G. "Istoriia krymskoi tragedii: K voprosu o Kholokoste v Krymu." *Krymskii archiv* 4 (2014): 114–26.

Bezugolnyi, A. Yu. "Opyt stroitelstva vooruzhennykh sil SSSR: Natsionalnyi aspekt (1922–1945 gg.)." PhD diss., Military Academy of the General Staff of the Armed Forces of the Russian Federation, Moscow, 2019.

———. "Prizyvnoe zakonodatel'stvo i komplektovanie raboche-krestianskoi Kra'noi armii predstaviteliami nerusskikh natsional'nostei v 1920-e gg." *Vestnik Kalmytskogo instituta gumanitarnykh issledovanii RAN* 3, no. 3 (2003): 102–13.

Bezymenskii, L. A. *Operatsiia "Mif," ili Skol'ko raz khoronili Gitlera?* Moscow: Mezhdunarodnye otnosheniia, 1995.

Bidlack, Richard, and Nikita Lomagin. *The Leningrad Blockade, 1941–1944: A New Documentary History from the Soviet Archives*. New Haven, CT: Yale University Press, 2012.

Blachetta, Walther. *Das wahre Gesicht Polens*. Berlin: Die Wehrmacht, 1939.

Blatman, Daniel. *Lema'an herutenu veHerutchem: HaBund bePolin 1939–1949*. Jerusalem: Yad Vashem, 1996.

Blumenthal, Nachman. *Darko shel yudenrat: Te'udot miGeto Bialystok*. Jerusalem: Yad Vashem, 1962.

Bocharov, A. G. *Emmanuil Kazakevich: Ocherki tvorchestva*. Moscow: Sovetskii pisatel', 1965.

———. *Slovo o pobediteliakh: Voennaia proza Em. Kazakevicha*. Moscow: Khudozhestvennaia literatura, 1970.

Borovoi, S. Ya., "Gibel' evreiskogo naseleniia Odessy vo vremya Rumynskoi okkupatsii." In *Katastrofa i opir ukrains'koho evreistva (1941–1944): Narysy z istorii Holokostu i oporu v Ukraini*, edited by S. Ya. Elizavets'kyi, 118–53. Kiev: Ukrainian National Academy of Sciences, 1999.

Borwicz, Michał. *Arishe papirm*. Buenos Aires: Unión Central Israelita Polaca en la Argentina, 1955.

Borzunova, T. I., R. V. Manshin, E. M. Moiseeva, G. F. Morozova, G. H. Ochirova, and S. V. Piazantsev. "Migratsiia naseleniia v gody Velikoi Otechestvennoi Voiny." In *Velikaia Pobeda sovetskogo naroda: Sotsialno-politicheskie i demograficheskie aspekty*, edited by S. V. Riazantsev and V. N. Ivanov, 272–90. Moscow: Institut sotsialno-politicheskikh issledovanii, 2020.

Braham, Randolph L. *The Politics of Genocide: The Holocaust in Hungary*. Condensed ed. Detroit, MI: Wayne State University Press, 2000.

Brakel, Alexander. "Was There a 'Jewish Collaboration' under Soviet Occupation: A Case Study from the Baranowicze Region." In *Shared History—Divided Memory: Jews and Others in Soviet-Occupied Poland, 1939–1941*, edited by E. Barkan, E. A. Cole, and K. Struve, 225–44. Leipzig: Leipziger Universitätsverlag, 2007.

Branderberger, David. ". . . It is Imperative to Advance Russian Nationalism as the First Priority': Debates within the Stalinist Ideological Establishment, 1941–1945." In *A State of Nations: Empire and Nation-Making in the Age of Lenin and Stalin*, edited by Ronald Grigor Suny and Terry Martin, 275–99. New York: Oxford University Press, 2001.

Breitman, Richard. *The Architect of Genocide: Himmler and the Final Solution*. Hanover, NH: University Press of New England, 1991.

Brener, Fani. *Di ershte helft lebn*. Tel Aviv: Y. L. Perets, 1989.

Broderzon, Sheyne-Miriam. *Mayn laydns-veg mit Moshe Broderzon*. Buenos Aires: Unión Central Israelita Polaca en la Argentina, 1960.

Bronfman, Naum. *Zvezda na konchike smychka*. New York: Slovo, 2001.

Browning, Christopher R. *Nazi Policy, Jewish Workers, German Killers*. Cambridge: Cambridge University Press, 2000.

———. *Ordinary Men: Reserve Police Battalion 101 and the Final Solution in Poland*. New York: HarperCollins, 1992.

———. *The Origins of the Final Solution: The Evolution of Nazi Jewish Policy, September 1939–March 1942*. Lincoln: University of Nebraska Press, 2004.

———. *The Path to Genocide: Essays on Launching the Final Solution*. Cambridge: Cambridge University Press, 1992.

Bubnys, Arūnas. "The Holocaust in Lithuania: An Outline of the Major Stages and Their Results." In *The Vanished World of Lithuanian Jews*, edited by Alvydas Nikžentaitis, Stefan Schreiner, and Darius Staliūnas, 205–19. Amsterdam: Rodopi, 2004.

Büchler, Yehoshua. "*Kommandostab Reichsführer-SS*: Himmler's Personal Murder Brigades in 1941." *Holocaust and Genocide Studies* 1, no. 1 (1986): 11–25.

Budnitskii, Oleg. "Evrei Stalina." Unpublished paper submitted for the *Comprehensive History of Jews in the Soviet Union* Project, 2017.

———. "The Great Patriotic War and Soviet Society: Defeatism." *Kritika* 15, no. 4 (2015): 767–97.

———. "A Harvard Project in Reverse: Materials of the Commission of the USSR Academy of Sciences on the History of the Great Patriotic War—Publications and Interpretations." *Kritika* 19, no. 1 (2018): 175–202.

———. "The Intelligentsia Meets the Enemy: Educated Soviet Officers in Defeated Germany, 1945." *Kritika* 10, no. 3 (2009): 629–82.

———. "Jews at War: Diaries from the Front." In *Soviet Jews in World War II: Fighting, Witnessing, Remembering*, edited by Harriet Murav and Gennady Estraikh, 57–84. New York: Academic Studies Press, 2014.

———. "Moskovskoe narodnoe opolchenie: Prichiny i osobennosti sozdaniia." *Rossiiskaia istoriia* 3 (2020): 3–20.

———. "Muzhchizny i zhenshchiny v Krasnoi Armii (1941–1945)." *Cahiers du monde russe* 52, nos. 2–3 (2011): 405–22.

———. *Russian Jews between the Reds and the Whites, 1917–1920*. Philadelphia: University of Pennsylvania Press, 2012.

———. "The Writers' Company: Toward a History of Wartime Stalinism." *Cahiers du monde russe* 61, no. 1 (2021): 179–205.

Bujak, Franciszek. "Rozwój gospodarczy Galicji (1772–1914)." In *Wybór pism*, 2:342–97. Warsaw: Państwowe Wydawnictwo Naukowe, 1976.

Burds, Jeffrey. *Holocaust in Rovno: The Massacre at Sosenki Forest, November 1941*. New York: Palgrave Macmillan, 2013.

Carp, Matatias. *Cartea neagră: Suferințele evreilor din România*. Bucharest: Dacia Traiană, 1947.

Carynnyk, Marco. "Foes of Our Rebirth: Ukrainian Nationalist Discussions about Jews, 1929–1947." *Nationalities Papers* 39 (2011): 315–52.

Chepelev, Gueorgui, "The Soviet Children under the Nazi Occupation (1941–1944, Belorussia and Western Russia): Heroes, Victims, Survivors, Communicators." Unpublished paper presented to a conference on Children and War: Past and Present, University of Salzburg, 2013.

Cherushev, N. S. "Vmeste so Stalinym." *Voenno-istoricheskii* no. 2 (1991): 89–94.

Cherushev, N. S., and Yu N. Cherushev. *Rasstreliannaia elita RKKA (komandarmy 1-go i 2-go rangov, komkory, komdivy i im ravnye), 1937–1941: Biograficheskii slovar'*. Moscow: Megapolis, 2012.

Cholawski, Shalom. *Al neharot haNieman vehaDniepr: Yehudei Byelorusiyah haMa'aravit beMilhemet haOlam haSheniyah*. Tel Aviv: Sifriyat Poalim, 1982.

———. *BeSufat haKilayon: Yahadut Byelorusiyah haMizrahit beMilhemet haOlam haSheniyah*. Tel Aviv: Sifriyat Po'alim, 1988.

———. *Meri veLohamah partizanit: Yehudei Byelorusiyah beMilhemet haOlam haSheniyah*. Jerusalem: Yad Vashem, 2001.

Choriev, Sh. "K istorii evakuatsionnykh meropriiatii v Uzbekistane v gody vtoroi mirovoi voiny." In *Istoriia, Pamiat', Liudi: Materialy VII Mezhdunarodnoi nauchno-prakticheskoi konferentsii*, L. S. Aktaeva, A. I. Baron, and M. S. Makarova, 228–34. Almaty: Tsentralnyi gosudarstvennyi arkhiv Komiteta informatsii i arkhivov Ministerstva sviazi i informatsii Respubliki Kazakhstan, 2015.

Cienciala, Anna M. "The Foreign Policy of Józef Piłsudski and Józef Beck, 1926–1939: Misconceptions and Interpretations." *Polish Review* 56 (2011): 111–51.

———. "The Nazi-Soviet Pact of August 1939: When Did Stalin Decide to Align with Hitler, and Was Poland the Culprit?" In *Ideology, Politics, and Diplomacy in East Central Europe*, edited by M. B. B. Biskupski, 147–226. Rochester, NY: University of Rochester Press, 2003.

———. *Poland and the Western Powers 1938–1939: A Study in the Interdependence of Eastern and Western Europe*. London: Routledge and Kegan Paul, 1968.

Cornelius, Deborah S. *Hungary in World War II: Caught in the Cauldron*. New York: Fordham University Press, 2011.

Curilla, Wolfgang. *Die deutsche Ordnungspolizei und der Holocaust im Baltikum und in Weißrußland 1941–1944*. Paderborn: Ferdinand Schöningh, 2006.

Dean, Martin. "Anykščiai." In *Ghettos in German-Occupied Eastern Europe*, vol. 2: *United States Holocaust Memorial Museum Encyclopedia of Camps and Ghettos 1933–1945*, edited by Martin Dean, 1040–41. Bloomington: Indiana University Press, 2012.

———. *Collaboration in the Holocaust: Crimes of the Local Police in Belorussia and Ukraine, 1941–44*. New York: St. Martin's Press, 2000.

———. "The German *Gendarmerie*, the Ukrainian *Schutzmannschaft* and the 'Second Wave' of Jewish Killings in Occupied Ukraine: German Policing at the Local Level in the Zhitomir Region, 1941–1944." *German History* 14, no. 2 (1996): 168–92.

———. "Zhytomyr Region (Generalkommissariat Shitomir)." In *United States Holocaust Memorial Museum Encyclopedia of Camps and Ghettos 1933–1945*, vol. 2: *Ghettos in German-Occupied Eastern Europe*, edited by Martin Dean, 1510–14. Bloomington: Indiana University Press, 2012.

Dekel-Chen, Jonathan. "Defusing the Ethnic Bomb: Resolving Local Conflict through Philanthropy in the Interwar USSR." In *Anti-Jewish Violence: Rethinking the Pogrom in East European History*, edited by Jonathan Dekel-Chen, David Gaunt, Natan M. Meir, and Israel Bartal, 186–203. Bloomington: Indiana University Press, 2011.

Deletant, Dennis. *Hitler's Forgotten Ally: Ion Antonescu and His Regime, Romania 1940–44*. London: Palgrave Macmillan, 2006.

Dieckmann, Christoph. *Deutsche Besatzungspolitik in Litauen 1941–1944*. Göttingen: Wallstein, 2011.

———. "Lithuania in Summer 1941: The German Invasion and the Kaunas Pogrom." In *Shared History—Divided Memory: Jews and Others in Soviet-Occupied Poland, 1939–1941*, edited by E. Barkan, E. A. Cole, and K. Struve, 355–85. Leipzig: Leipziger Universitätsverlag, 2007.

———. "HaMilhamah veRetsah yehudei Lita." In *Mediniyut haHashmadah haNatsit 1939–1945: Mehkar uFulmus baHistoriografiyah haGermanit haHadashah*, edited by Ulrich Herbert and David Bankier, 277–315. Jerusalem: Yad Vashem, 2001.

Documents on German Foreign Policy 1918–1945. Washington: Government Printing Office, 1954.

Documents on Polish-Soviet Relations. 2 vols. London: General Sikorski Historical Institute, 1967.

Dos yidishe folk in kamf kegn fashizm. Moscow: Der Emes, 1945.

Druker, Bela. "Kakh nitharvah ayaratenu Shpola." In *Shpola: Masekhet hayei yehudim baAyarah*, edited by David Cohen, 275–77. Haifa: Irgun yots'ei Shpola beYisra'el, 1965.

Dubson, Vadim. "On the Problem of the Evacuation of Soviet Jews in 1941." *Jews in Eastern Europe* (1999): 37–56.

———. "Toward a Central Database of Evacuated Soviet Jews' Names, for the Study of the Holocaust in the Occupied Soviet Territories." *Holocaust and Genocide Studies* 26, no. 1 2012): 95–119.

Dumitru, Diana. *The State, Antisemitism, and Collaboration in the Holocaust: The Borderlands of Romania and the Soviet Union*. New York: Cambridge University Press, 2016.

Dworzecki, Mark. *Mahanot haYehudim beEstonia*. Jerusalem: Yad Vashem, 1970.

Dymshits, Valerii A., Iu. Muradov, M. A. Chlenov, Yosif Begun, and Mordechai Altshuler. *Gorskie evrei: Istoriia, etnografiia, kultura*. Moscow: Znanie, 1999.

Dzigan, Szymon. *Der koyekh fun yidishn humor*. Tel Aviv: Orli, 1974.

Edele, Mark, and Wanda Warlik. "Saved by Stalin? Trajectories and Numbers of Polish Jews in the Second World War." In *Shelter from the Holocaust: Rethinking Jewish Survival in the Soviet Union*, edited by Mark Ederle, Sheila Fitzpatrick, and Atina Grossman, 95–131. Detroit, MI: Wayne State University Press, 2017.

Ehrenburg, Ilya. *Merder fun felker: Materialn vegn di retsikhes fun di daytshe farkhaper in di tsaytvaylik okupirte sovetishe rayonen*. Moscow: Der Emes, 1944.

———. *The War 1941–45*. London: MacGibbon & Kee, 1964.

Ehrenburg, Ilya, and Vasily Grossman, eds. *The Black Book*. New York: Holocaust Library, 1981.

Eidelman, Iakov N. *Neokonchennye dialogi*. Moscow: Mosty kultury, 1999.

Emelin, S. "Borba s detskoi besprizornostyu i beznadzornostiu v gody Velikoi Otechestvennoi voiny (1941–1945)." *Voprosy yuvenalnoi yustitsii* 2, no. 28 (2010): http://juvenjust.org/.

Engel, David. *The Assassination of Symon Petliura and the Trial of Scholem Schwarzbard 1926–1927: A Selection of Documents*. Göttingen: Vandenhoeck & Ruprecht, 2016.

———. *Facing a Holocaust: The Polish Government-in-Exile and the Jews, 1943–1945*. Chapel Hill: University of North Carolina Press, 1993.

———. *In the Shadow of Auschwitz: The Polish Government-in-Exile and the Jews, 1939–1942*. Chapel Hill: University of North Carolina Press, 1987.

———. "Moshe Kleinbaum's Report on Issues in the Former Eastern Territories, 12 March 1940." In *Jews in Eastern Poland and the USSR, 1939–1946*, edited by Norman Davies and Antony Polonsky, 275–300. London: Macmillan, 1990.

———. "Soviet Jewry in the Thinking of the Yishuv Leadership, 1939–1943: Some Preliminary Observations." In *The Holocaust in the Soviet Union: Studies and Sources on the Destruction of the Jews in the Nazi-Occupied Territories of the USSR, 1941–1945*, edited by Lucjan Dobroszycki and Jeffrey S. Gurock, 111–29. Armonk, NY: M. E. Sharpe, 1993.

———. *Zionism: A Short History of a Big Idea*. Harlow, UK: Pearson Longman, 2009.

Epstein, Barbara. *The Minsk Ghetto, 1941–1943: Jewish Resistance and Soviet Internationalism*. Berkeley: University of California Press, 2008.

Epstein, Melech. *The Jew and Communism: The Story of Early Communist Victories and Ultimate Defeats in the Jewish Community, U.S.A., 1919–1941*. New York: Trade Union Sponsoring Committee, 1959.

Epstein, Yosef D. "Mir." In *Mosedot torah beEiropah beVinyanam uveHurbanam*, edited by S. K. Mirsky, 87–132. New York: Ogen, 1956.

Erickson, John. "The Red Army's March into Poland, September 1939." In *The Soviet Takeover of the Eastern Polish Provinces, 1939–41*, edited by Keith Sword, 1–27. New York: St. Martin's Press, 1991.

Esses, V. M., S. Medianu, and A. S. Lawson. "Uncertainty, Threat, and the Role of the Media in Promoting the Dehumanization of Immigrants and Refugees." *Journal of Social Issues* 69, no. 3 (2013): 518–36.

Estraikh, Gennady. "Anti-Nazi Rebellion in Peretz Markish's Drama and Prose." In *A Captive of the Dawn: The Life and Work of Peretz Markish (1895–1952)*, edited by Joseph Sherman. London: Legenda, 2011.

———. "David Bergelson in and on America." In *David Bergelson: From Modernism to Socialist Realism*, edited by Joseph Sherman and Gennady Estraikh, 205–21. Oxford: Legenda, 2007.

———. *Evreiskaia literaturnaia zhizn' Moskvy, 1917–1991*. St. Petersburg: European University Press, 2015.

———. "From 'Green Fields' to 'Red Fields': Peretz Hirschbein's Soviet Sojourn, 1928–1929." *Jews in Russia and Eastern Europe* 1 (2006): 60–81.

———. "Itsik Fefer: A Yiddish *Wunderkind* of the Bolshevik Revolution." *Shofar* 20, no. 3 (Spring 2002): 14–31.

———. "Jews and Soviet Remythologization of the Ukrainian Hetman: The Case of the Order of Bohdan Khmelnitsky." In *Stories of Khmelnitsky: Competing Literary Legacies of the 1648 Ukrainian Cossack Uprising*, edited by Amelia M. Glaser, 169–81. Stanford, CA: Stanford University Press, 2015.

———. "Jews as Cossacks: A Symbiosis in Literature and Life." In *Soviet Jews in World War II: Fighting, Witnessing, Remembering*, edited by Harriet Murav and Gennady Estraikh, 169–81. New York: Academic Studies Press, 2014.

———. "The Missing Years: Yiddish Writers in Soviet Bialystok, 1939–1941." *East European Jewish Affairs* 46 (2016): 176–91.

———. "Sholem Asch's Moscow Sojourn, 1928." In *Three Cities of Yiddish: St. Petersburg, Warsaw and Moscow*, edited by Gennady Estraikh and Mikhail Krutikov, 56–72. Oxford: Legenda, 2017.

———. "Smertel'no opasnoe natsional'noe edinenie: Evreiskii antifashistskii komitet v SSSR." In *Sovetskaia geniza: Novye arkhivnye razyskaniia po istorii evreev v SSSR*, edited by Gennady Estraikh and Alexander Frenkel, 1:293–350. Boston: Academic Studies Press, 2020.

Evans, Richard J. *The Third Reich at War*. New York: Penguin Press, 2009.

Evyon, Yehudah. "Shetei Peredot meIr-huladti." In *Sefer Dombrovitse/Dombrovitser ondenk-bukh*, edited by L. Losch, 686–94. Tel Aviv: Irgun yots'ei Dombrovitse beYisra'el, 1964.

Ezergailis, Andrew. *The Holocaust in Latvia 1941–1944: The Missing Center*. Riga: Historical Institute of Latvia, 1994.

Fain, E. *Po dorogam, ne nami vybrannym*. London: Overseas Publications, 1990.

Fatal-Knaani, Tikvah. *Yehudei Rovnah 1919–1945: Hayehah veKitsah shel kehillah*. Jerusalem: Yad Vashem, 2012.

———. *Zo lo otah Grodnah: Kehilat Grodnah uSevivatah beMilhamah uvaSho'ah 1939–1943*. Jerusalem: Yad Vashem, 2001.

Fedotov, V. V. "Evakuatsiia i mezhnatsionalnye otnosheniia v gody Velikoi Otechestvennoi voiny (po materialam arkhivov Povolzh'ia)." In *Chelovek i obschestvo v usloviiakh voin i revoliutsi: Materialy II vserossiiskoi nauchnoi konferentsii*, edited by E. Semyonova, 55–58. Samara: Samara University, 2015.

Fefer, Itsik. *Lider, balades, poemes: Oysderveylts*. Moscow: Sovetskii pisatel', 1967.

Feferman, Kiril. *The Holocaust in the Crimea and the North Caucasus*. Jerusalem: Yad Vashem, 2016.

———. "'The Jews' War': Attitudes of Soviet Jewish Soldiers and Officers toward the USSR in 1940–41." *Journal of Slavic Military Studies* 27, no. 4 (2014): 574–90.

———. "A Soviet Humanitarian Action? Centre, Periphery and the Evacuation of Refugees to the North Caucasus, 1941–1942." *Europe-Asia Studies* 61, no. 5 (2009): 813–31.

———. "Soviet Investigation of Nazi Crimes in the USSR: Documenting the Holocaust." *Journal of Genocide Research* 5, no. 4 (2003): 587–602.

Filtzer, Donald A., and Wendy Z. Goldman. *Hunger and War: Food Provisioning in the Soviet Union during World War II*. Bloomington: Indiana University Press, 2015.

Fischer, Louis. *Men and Politics: An Autobiography*. New York: Duell, Sloan, and Pearce, 1941.

Fischthal, Hannah Berliner. "Abraham Cahan and Sholem Asch." *Yiddish* 11, nos. 1–2 (1998): 1–17.

Fishman, David E. *The Book Smugglers: Partisans, Poets, and the Race to Save Jewish Treasures from the Nazis*. Lebanon, NH: University Press of New England, 2017.

Fitzpatrick, Sheila. "Annexation, Evacuation, and Antisemitism in the Soviet Union, 1939–1946." In *Shelter from the Holocaust: Rethinking Jewish Survival in the Soviet Union*, edited by Mark Ederle, Sheila Fitzpatrick, and Atina Grossman, 133–60. Detroit, MI: Wayne State University Press, 2017.

Florian, Radu. "The Antonescu Regime: History and Mystification." In *The Tragedy of Romanian Jewry*, edited by Randolph L. Braham, 77–115. New York: Columbia University Press, 1994.

Foreign Relations of the United States, 1941: General—The Soviet Union. Washington, DC: United States Government Printing Office, 1958.

Foreign Relations of the United States, 1943: The British Commonwealth, Eastern Europe, the Far East. Washington, DC: United States Government Printing Office, 1963.

Foreign Relations of the United States, 1945: The Conference of Berlin. Washington, DC: United States Government Printing Office, 1960.

Förster, Jürgen. "The German Army and the Ideological War against the Soviet Union." In *The Policies of Genocide: Jews and Soviet Prisoners of War in Nazi Germany*, edited by Gerhard Hirschfeld, 15–29. London: Allen & Unwin, 1986.

Frezinskii, Boris. "Tragediia Emmanuila Kazakevicha." *Narod knigi v mire knig* 102 (2013):1–11.

Friedländer, Saul. *Prelude to Downfall: Hitler and the United States, 1939–1941*. New York: Alfred A. Knopf, 1967.

Friedman, Philip. *Roads to Extinction: Essays on the Holocaust.* Philadelphia: Jewish Publication Society, 1980.

Fritz, Stephen G. *Ostkrieg: Hitler's War of Extermination in the East.* Lexington: University Press of Kentucky, 2011.

Frommer, Morris. "The American Jewish Congress: A History 1914–1950." PhD diss., The Ohio State University, 1978.

Frost, Shimon. *Schooling as a Socio-Political Expression: Jewish Education in Interwar Poland.* Jerusalem: Magnes Press, 1998.

Fuks, Tania. *A vanderung iber okupirte gebitn.* Buenos Aires: Unión Central Israelita Polaca en la Argentina, 1947.

Gareev, M. A. *Pamiati pavshikh: Velikaia Otchestvennaia voina (1941–1945).* Moscow: Bolshaia rossiiskaia entsiklopediia, 1995.

Garfunkel, Leib, ed. *HaSho'ah 1941–1945.* Vol. 4 of *Yahadut Lita.* Tel Aviv: Igud yots'ei Lita beYisra'el, 1984.

Garncarska-Kadary, Bina. *BeHipusei derekh: Po'alei Tsiyon Semol bePolin ad milhemet haOlam haSheniyah.* Tel Aviv: Tel Aviv University Press, 1995.

Garrard, John, and Carol Garrard. "Barbarossa's First Victims: The Jews of Brest." *East European Jewish Affairs* 28 (1998): 3–48.

Gechtman, Roni. "The Rise of the Bund as Reflected in the *Naye Folkstsaytung*, 1935–1936." *Gal-Ed* 17 (2000): 29–55.

Gelfand, Vladimir. *Dnevnik 1941–1946*. Edited with an introduction by O. V. Budnitskii. Moscow: ROSSPEN, 2016.

Gerasimova, Svetlana. *The Rzhev Slaughterhouse: The Red Army's Forgotten 15-month Campaign against Army Group Center, 1942–1943.* Solihull, UK: Helion & Co., 2013.

Gerlach, Christian. "Die Einsatzgruppe B 1941/42." In *Die Einsatzgruppen in der besetzten Sowjetunion 1941/42: Die Tätigkeits- und Lageberichte des Chefs der Sicherheitspolizei und des SD*, edited by Peter Klein, 52–70. Berlin: Hentrich, 1997.

———. *The Extermination of the European Jews.* Cambridge: Cambridge University Press, 2016.

———. *Kalkulierte Morde: Die deutsche Wirtschafts- und Vernichtungspolitik in Weißrußland 1941 bis 1944*. Hamburg: Hamburger Edition, 1999.

Gerschenkron, Alexander. "Russia: Agrarian Policies and Industrialization, 1861–1917." In *Continuity in History and Other Essays*, edited by Alexander Gerschenkron, 140–248. Cambridge, MA: Belknap, 1968.

Gessen, Ester. *Belostok-Moskva*. Moscow: AST, 2014.

Gershoni, A. E. *Yehudim ve Yahadut bi Verit haMo'atsot: Yahadut Rusiyah mi Tekufat Stalin ve'ad haZeman haAharon*. Jerusalem: Feldheim, 1970.

Gilbert, Martin. *Auschwitz and the Allies*. New York: Holt, Rinehart, and Winston, 1981.

Gilboa, Yehoshua. *The Black Years of Soviet Jewry*. Boston: Little, Brown, 1971.

———. *A Language Silenced: The Suppression of Hebrew Literature and Culture in the Soviet Union*. Rutherford, NJ: Farleigh Dickinson University Press, 1982.

Gitelman, Zvi, ed. *Bitter Legacy: Confronting the Holocaust in the USSR*. Bloomington: Indiana University Press, 1997.

———. "Soviet Jewish Veterans of World War II Remember: Listening to Oral Histories." *Michigan Jewish History* 40 (2000): 2–15.

———. "Soviet Reactions to the Holocaust, 1945–1991." In *The Holocaust in the Soviet Union: Studies and Sources on the Destruction of the Jews in the Nazi-Occupied Territories of the USSR, 1941–1945*, edited by Lucjan Dobroszycki and Jeffrey S. Gurock, 3–27. Armonk, NY: M. E. Sharpe, 1993.

Gitlin, Semen I. *Istoricheskie sud'by evreev Srednei Azii*. Tel Aviv: Media-Gal, 2008.

Glantz, David M. *Zhukov's Greatest Defeat: The Red Army's Disaster in Operation Mars, 1942*. Lawrence: University Press of Kansas, 1999.

Glantz, David M., and Jonathan M. House. *When Titans Clashed: How the Red Army Stopped Hitler*. Lawrence: University of Kansas Press, 2015.

Gloster, Vladimir. "Soviet Children's Poetry: Some Historical Observations." *Phaedrus* 12 (1986–87).

Golczewski, Frank. "Die Kollaboration in der Ukraine." In *Kooperation und Verbrechen: Formen der "Kollaboraton" im östlichen Europa 1939–1945*, edited by Christoph Dieckmann, Babette Quinkert, and Tatjana Tönsmeyer, 151–82. Göttingen: Wallstein, 2005.

Goldberg, Anatol. *Ilya Ehrenburg, Revolutionary Novelist, Poes, War Correspondent, Propagandist: The Extraordinary Epic of a Russian Survivor*. New York: Viking, 1984.

Goluboff, Sascha L. "Are They Jews or Asians? A Cautionary Tale about Mountain Jewish Ethnography." *Slavic Review* 63, no. 1 (2004): 113–40.

Gorecki, Roman. *Poland and her Economic Development*. London: G. Allen & Unwin, 1935.

Górka, Olgierd. *Naród a państwo jako zagadnienie Polski*. Warsaw: Biblioteka Polska, 1937.

Gorodetsky, Gabriel. "The Formulation of Soviet Foreign Policy: Ideology and *Realpolitik*." In *Soviet Foreign Policy 1917–1991: A Retrospective*, edited by Gabriel Gorodetsky, 30–44. New York: Routledge, 2013.

Govrin, Yosef. *HaHebet haYehudi beYahasei Germaniyah haNatsit im Berit haMo'atsot.* Jerusalem: Magnes Press of the Hebrew University, 1986.

Greenbaum, Alfred A. "Hebrew Literature in Soviet Russia." *Jewish Social Studies* 30, no. 3 (1968): 135–48.

Gregorek, Aniela, and Jerzy Gregorek. "The Biography of Maurycy Szymel." *Asheville Poetry Review* 10 (2003): http://www.ashevillepoetryreview.com.

Grinberg, Marat. *"I Am to Be Read Not from Left to Right, but in Jewish, from Right to Left": The Poetics of Boris Slutsky.* Boston: Academic Studies Press, 2011.

Gris, P. [Moshe Grossman]. *In farkisheftn land fun legendarn Dzugashvili.* 2 vols. Paris: Emes un frayhayt, 1950.

Gromova, Natalia. *Evakuatsiia idet . . . 1941–1944: Pisatelskaia koloniia: Khristopol', Elabuga, Tashkent, Alma-Ata.* Moscow: Sovpadenie, 2008.

———, ed. *Stranniki voiny: Vospominaniia detei pisatelei 1941–1944.* Moscow: Astrel', 2012.

Gross, Jan T. *Neighbors: The Destruction of the Jewish Community in Jedwabne, Poland.* Princeton, NJ: Princeton University Press, 2001.

———. *Revolution from Abroad: The Soviet Conquest of Poland's Western Ukraine and Western Belorussia.* Princeton, NJ: Princeton University Press, 1988.

Grossman, Haika. *Anshei haMahteret.* 2nd ed. Merhavia: Sifriyat Po'alim, 1965.

Grossman, Vasily. *The Road: Stories, Journalism, and Essays.* New York: New York Review Books, 2010.

Grüner, Frank. "Did Anti-Jewish Mass Violence Exist in the Soviet Union?—Anti-Semitism and Collective Violence in the USSR during the War and Post War Years." *Journal of Genocide Research* 11, nos. 2–3 (2009): 355–79.

Gutman, Yisrael. *Yehudei Varshah 1939–1943: Geto, mahteret, mered.* Tel Aviv: Sifriyat Po'alim, 1977.

Hagen, William W. *Anti-Jewish Violence in Poland, 1914–1920.* Cambridge: Cambridge University Press, 2018.

Halperin, Hagit. "A Hebrew Writer in the Soviet Union: The 'Case' of Zvi Preigerzon." *Jews in Eastern Europe* 20 (1993): 5–14.

Hanebrink, Paul. *A Specter Haunting Europe: The Myth of Judeo-Bolshevism.* Cambridge, MA: Harvard University Press, 2018.

Hartmann, Christian. *Wehrmacht im Ostkrieg.* Munich: R. Oldenbourg, 2010.

Haslam, Jonathan. *Soviet Foreign Policy, 1930–1933: The Impact of the Depression.* New York: St. Martin's Press, 1983.

———. *The Soviet Union and the Struggle for Collective Security in Europe, 1933–1939.* New York: St. Martin's Press, 1984.

Headland, Ronald. "The *Einsatzgruppen*: The Question of their Initial Operations." *Holocaust and Genocide Studies* 4, no. 4 (1989): 401–12.

———. *Messages of Murder: A Study of the Reports of the Einsatzgruppen of the Security Police and the Security Service, 1941–1943.* Rutherford, NJ: Farleigh Dickinson University Press, 1992.

Heller, Celia S. *On the Edge of Destruction: Jews of Poland between the Two World Wars.* New York: Columbia University Press, 1977.

Henryk Erlich un Wiktor Alter: A gedenk-bukh. New York: Farlag "Unzer Tsayt," 1951.
Herf, Jeffrey. *The Jewish Enemy: Nazi Propaganda during World War II and the Holocaust*. Cambridge, MA: Harvard University Press, 2006.
Herspring, Dale R. *Russian Civil-Military Relations*. Bloomington: Indiana University Press, 1996.
Hicks, Jeremy. *First Films of the Holocaust: Soviet Cinema and the Genocide of the Jews, 1938–1946*. Pittsburgh: University of Pittsburgh Press, 2012.
Hilberg, Raul. *The Destruction of the European Jews*. 2nd ed. New York: Holmes and Meier, 1985.
Hillgruber, Andreas. *Germany and the Two World Wars*. Cambridge, MA: Harvard University Press, 1981.
Himka, John-Paul. "The Lviv Pogrom of 1941: The Germans, Ukrainian Nationalists, and the Carnival Crowd." *Canadian Slavonic Papers* 53 (2011): 209–43.
Hirszowicz, Lukasz, "The Holocaust in the Soviet Mirror." In *The Holocaust in the Soviet Union: Studies and Sources on the Destruction of the Jews in the Nazi-Occupied Territories of the USSR, 1941–1945*, edited by Lucjan Dobroszycki and Jeffrey S. Gurock, 29–59. Armonk, NY: M. E. Sharpe, 1993.
———. "The Soviet Union and the Jews during World War II: British Foreign Office Documents." *Soviet Jewish Affairs* 3, no. 1 (1973): 73–119.
Hitchens, Keith. *Rumania 1866–1947*. Oxford: Clarendon, 1994.
Holroyd-Doveton, John. *Maxim Litvinov: A Biography*. N.p.: Woodland, 2013.
Horwitz, Gordon J. *Ghettostadt: Łódź and the Making of a Nazi City*. Cambridge, MA: Harvard University Press, 2008.
Hosking, Geoffrey. "The Second World War and Russian National Consciousness." *Past and Present* 175 (2002): 162–87.
Hryciuk, Grzegorz. "Victims 1939–1941: The Soviet Repressions in Eastern Poland." In *Shared History—Divided Memory: Jews and Others in Soviet-Occupied Poland, 1939–1941*, edited by E. Barkan, E. A. Cole, and K. Struve, 173–200. Leipzig: Leipziger Universitätsverlag, 2007.
Hyman, Paula E. "Gender and the Jewish Family in Modern Europe." In *Women and the Holocaust*, edited by Dalia Ofer and Lenore J. Weitzman, 25–38. New Haven, CT: Yale University Press, 1998.
Iakovlev, V. N., ed. *Bessarabskii vopros i obrazovanie Pridnestrovskoi Moldavskoi Respubliki: Sbornik ofitsialnikh dokumentov*. Tiraspol: RIU PGKU, 1993.
International Commission on the Holocaust in Romania. *Final Report*. Bucharest: Polirom, 2004.
International Military Tribunal. *Trial of the Major War Criminals*. Nuremberg: Allied Control Authority for Germany, 1946.
Islamova, S. "Uzbekistan vo vremia vtoroj mirovoj vojny i vklad uzbeksogo naroda v razvitiie obschestva." In *Istoriia. Pamiat', Liudi: Materialy VII Mezhdunarodnoi nauchno-prakticheskoi konferentsii*, edited by L. S. Aktaeva, A. I. Baron, and M. S. Makarova, 505–11. Almaty: Tsentralnyi gosudarstvennyi arkhiv Komiteta informatsii i arkhivov Ministerstva sviazi i informatsii Respubliki Kazakhstan, 2015.

Israel (State of), Ministry of Justice. *The Trial of Adolf Eichmann: Record of Proceedings in the District Court of Jerusalem*. Jerusalem: Yad Vashem, 1993.

Itenberg, B. S. "Pis'ma iz deistvuiushchei armii, 1943–1945 gg." In *V ritme vremeni: Frontovnik, uchitel', istorik—pamiati doktora istoricheskikh nauk B. S. Itenberga, sbornik statei i materialov*, edited by O. V. Budnitskii and V. V. Shelokhaev, 319–33. Moscow: ROSSPEN, 2018.

Jäckel, Eberhard. *Hitler's World View: A Blueprint for Power*. Cambridge, MA: Harvard University Press, 1981.

Jakubowicz, Aharon, and Danuta Dąbrowska. "Bóbrka." In *Galitsiyah haMizrahit*, vol. 2: *Pinkas haKehilot, Polin*, edited by Danuta Dąbrowska, Avraham Wein, and Aharon Weiss, 65–68. Jerusalem: Yad Vashem, 1980.

Jędrzejewicz, Wacław, ed. *Diplomat in Berlin: Papers and Memoirs of Józef Lipski, Ambassador of Poland*. New York: Columbia University Press, 1968.

Jolluck, Katherine R. *Exile and Identity: Polish Women in the Soviet Union during World War II*. Pittsburgh: University of Pittsburgh Press, 2002.

Kabanov, Pavel. *Stalnye peregony*. Moscow: Voenizdat, 1973.

Kaczerginski, Shmerke. *Ikh bin geven a partizan (di grine legende)*. Buenos Aires: Printed by the author, 1952.

Kagan, George. "Agrarian Regime of Pre-War Poland." *Journal of Central European Affairs* 3 (1943): 241–69.

Kaganovitch, Albert. "Estimating the Number of Jewish Refugees, Deportees, and Draftees from Bessarabia and Northern Bukovina in the Non-Occupied Soviet Territories." *Holocaust and Genocide Studies* 27, no. 3 (Winter 2013): 464–82.

———. "Jewish Refugees and Soviet Authorities during World War II." *Yad Vashem Studies* 38, no. 2 (2010): 85–121.

Kahan (Ben Aharon), Jacob. *Unter di sovietishe himlen*. Tel Aviv: J. L. Peretz, 1961.

Kahane, David. *Yoman geto Lvov*. Jerusalem: Yad Vashem, 1978.

Kahane, Leon M. "Mikulintsa—Ireinu haYedidutit." In *Mikulintsa: Sefer yizkor*, edited by Haim Preschel, 77–83. Israel: Irgun yots'ei Mikulintsa beYisra'el uveArtsot haBerit, 1985.

Kamieniecki, Naftali, and Icchak Ganusowitsch. "Di yidishe Lide in fayer un untergang." Unpublished manuscript. Yad Vashem Archives, Jerusalem, M-1/E, 954/802.

Kaminska, Ida. *My Life, My Theater*. New York: Macmillan, 1973.

Kamiński, Marek K., and Michał J. Zacharias. *Polityka zagraniczna II Rzeczypospolitej 1918–1939*. Warsaw: Młodzieżowa Agencja Wydawnicza, 1987.

Kangeris, Kārlis. "Kollaboration vor der Kollaboration? Die baltischen Emigranten und ihre 'Befreiungskomitees' in Deutschland 1941/1941." In *Europa unterm Hakenkreuz: Okkupation und Kollaboration (1938–1945)*, edited by Werner Röhr, 165–90. Berlin: Hüthig, 1994.

———. "Die Nationalsozialistischen Pläne und Propagandamassnahmen im Generalbezirk Lettland 1941–1942." In *Collaboration and Resistance during the Holocaust: Belarus, Estonia, Latvia, Lithuania*, edited by David Gaunt, Paul A. Levine, and Laura Palosuo, 161–86. Bern, Switzerland: Peter Lang, 2004.

Kanovich, Grigorii. *Liki vo t'me: Povest' i rasskazy*. Jerusalem: Ierusalimskaia antologiia, 2011.

Kaplan, Chaim. *Megilat yisurin: Yoman geto Varshah*. Tel Aviv: Am Oved, 1966.

Karpenkina, Yanina. "'Kvartirnyi vopros' v Zapadnoi Belorussii i evreiskoe naselenie, 1939–1940 gg." *Soviet and Post-Soviet Review* 45 (2018): 73–98.

———. "Sovetizatsiia evreiskogo naseleniia Zapadnoi Belorussii (1939–1941 gg.)." PhD diss., Higher School of Economics, 2018.

Karski, Jan. *The Great Powers and Poland 1919–1945: From Versailles to Yalta*. Lanham, MD: University Press of America, 1985.

Kassow, Samuel D. "Inside the Kovno Ghetto." In *The Clandestine History of the Kovno Jewish Ghetto Police*, edited by Samuel Schalkowsky, 1–59. Bloomington: Indiana University Press, 2014.

Kazakevich, G. O., and B. S. Ruben, eds. *Vospominaniia o E. Kazakeviche: Sbornik*. 2nd ed. Moscow: Sovetskii pisatel', 1984.

Khrushchev, Nikita. *Memoirs of Nikita Khrushchev*. Edited by Sergei Khrushchev. University Park: Pennsylvania State University Press, 2004.

Kirschenbaum, Lisa A. "The Meaning of Resilience: Soviet Children in World War II." *Journal of Interdisciplinary History* 47, no. 4 (2017).

Klein, Peter, ed., *Die Einsatzgruppen in der besetzten Sowjetunion 1941/42: Die Tätigkeits- und Lageberichte des Chefs der Sicherheitspolizei und des SD*. Berlin: Hentrich, 1997.

Klementynowski, Dowid. "Dos idishe lebn far der milkhome." In *Der Bialystoker yizkor-bukh*, edited by I. Shmulewitz, 79–89. New York: Bialystoker Center, 1982.

Kless, Shlomo. *Gevulot, mahteret u Verihah: Pe'ilut tsiyonit-halutsit bi Verit-haMo'atsot uKesharim im haYishuv baArets (1941–1945)*. Tel Aviv: Moreshet, 1989.

———. "The *Judenrat* of the Baranovichi Ghetto 1942–1943." www.jewishgen .org.

Klevan, Avraham. "Kremenets." In *Vohlin uPolesia*. Vol. 5 of *Pinkas haKehilot, Polin*, edited by Shmuel Spector, 179–86. Jerusalem: Yad Vashem, 1990.

———. "Rovnah." In *Vohlin uPolesia*, vol. 5: *Pinkas haKehilot, Polin*, edited by Shmuel Spector, 192–200. Jerusalem: Yad Vashem, 1990.

Knox, Katharine, and Tony Kushner. *Refugees in an Age of Genocide: Global, National, and Local Perspectives during the Twentieth Century*. Hoboken, NJ: Taylor and Francis, 2012.

Kochanski, Halik. *The Eagle Unbowed: Poland and the Poles in the Second World War*. Cambridge, MA; Harvard University Press, 2012.

Komskii, B. G. "Dnevnik, 1943–1945." Edited with an introduction by O. V. Budnitskii. *Arkhiv evreiskoi istorii* 6 (2011): 11–70.

Konstantinov, Viacheslav. *Evreiskoe naselenie byvshego SSSR v XX veke: Sotsialno-demograficheskii analiz*. Jerusalem: Lira, 2007.

Kopstein, Jeffrey S., and Jason Wittenberg. *Intimate Violence: Anti-Jewish Pogroms on the Eve of the Holocaust*. Ithaca, NY: Cornell University Press, 2018.

Korczak, Reizl (Różka). *Lehavot baEfer*. 3rd ed. Merhavia: Sifriyat Po'alim, 1965.

Korey, William. "The Legal Position of Soviet Jewry: A Historical Enquiry." In *The Jews in Soviet Russia since 1917*, edited by Lionel Kochan, 78–105. Oxford: Oxford University Press, 1978.

Kornat, Marek. "Choosing Not to Choose in 1939: Poland's Assessment of the Nazi-Soviet Pact." *International History Review* 31 (2009): 771–97.

Korzec, Paweł. "Fragmenty wspomnień." *Białostoccy Żydzi* 1 (1993): 21–52.

———. "Hidat retsihatam shel H. Erlich uW. Alter biYdei haSovietim." *Gal-Ed* 10 (1987): 281–310.

Kostanick, Huey Louis. "Soviet Territorial Annexations in Eastern Europe." *Yearbook of the Association of Pacific Coast Geographers* 13 (1951): 14–18.

Kostyrchenko, Gennday, ed., *Gosudarstvennyi antisemitizm SSSR*, Moscow: MFD, 2005.

———. "Evreiskii Krym: Spekuliatsiia na mirazhe." *Nash sovremennik* 6 (2010).

———. *Tainaia politika Stalina: Vlast' i antisemitizm*. Moscow: Mezhdunarodnye otnosheniia, 2003.

Koval, M. I. "The Nazi Genocide of the Jews and the Ukrainian Population." In *Bitter Legacy: Confronting the Holocaust in the USSR*, edited by Zvi Gitelman, 51–60. Bloomington: Indiana University Press.

Kozlov, V. A. *"Gde Gitler?" Povtornoe rassledovanie NKVD (MVD) SSSR obstaiatelstv ischeznoveniia Adolfa Gitlera (1945–1949)*. Moscow: ROSSPEN, 2016.

Krivosheev, G. F. *Grif sekretnosti sniat: Poteri Vooruzhonykh Sil SSSR v voinakh, boievykh deistviiakh i voennykh konfliktakh—Statisticheskoe issledovanie*. Moscow: Voenizdat, 1993.

———. *Rossiia i SSSR v voinakh XX veka: Poteri vooruzhonnykh sil—Statisticheskoie issledovanie*. Moscow: OLMA-PRESS, 2001.

Krivosheev, G. F., and A. V. Kirilin, eds. *Velikaia Otechestvennaia Voina bez grifa sekretnosti: Kniga poter'*. Moscow: Veche, 2009.

Kruglov, Alexander. "Jewish Losses in Ukraine, 1941–1944." In *The Shoah in Ukraine: History, Testimony, Memorialization*, edited by Ray Brandon and Wendy Lower, 272–90. Bloomington: Indiana University Press, 2010.

Kruglov, Alexander, and Martin Dean. "Viekšniai." In *Ghettos in German-Occupied Eastern Europe*, vol.2: *United States Holocaust Memorial Museum Encyclopedia of Camps and Ghettos 1933–1945*, edited by Martin Dean, 1141. Bloomington: Indiana University Press, 2012.

Kruglov, Alexander, and Samuel Fishman. "Sarny." In *Ghettos in German-Occupied Eastern Europe*, vol. 2: *United States Holocaust Memorial Museum Encyclopedia of Camps and Ghettos 1933–1945*, edited by Martin Dean, 1463–65. Bloomington: Indiana University Press, 2012.

———. "Włodzimierzec." In *Ghettos in German-Occupied Eastern Europe*, vol. 2: *United States Holocaust Memorial Museum Encyclopedia of Camps and Ghettos 1933–1945*, edited by Martin Dean, 1494–96. Bloomington: Indiana University Press, 2012.

Kruglov, Alexander, and Ester-Basya Vaisman. "Bóbrka." In *Ghettos in German-Occupied Eastern Europe*, vol. 2: *United States Holocaust Memorial Museum*

Encyclopedia of Camps and Ghettos 1933–1945, edited by Martin Dean, 750–51. Bloomington: Indiana University Press, 2012.

Kruk, Herman. *The Last Days of the Jerusalem of Lithuania: Chronicles from the Vilna Ghetto and the Camps, 1939–1944*. New Haven, CT: Yale University Press, 2002.

Kulka, Erich. "Jews in the Czechoslovak Armed Forces During World War Two." In *The Jews of Czechoslovakia: Historical Studies and Surveys*, edited by Avigdor Dagan, 3:331–431. Philadelphia: Jewish Publication Society of America, 1984.

Kupershmid, Sh. *Folkslider vegn der foterlendisher milkhome*. Moscow: Der Emes, 1944.

Kupovetskii, Mark. "Liudskie poteri evreiskogo naseleniia v dovoiennykh (na sentiabr' 1939 goda) i poslevoiennykh granitsakh SSSR v gody Velikoi Otechestvennoi Voiny." In *Otritsanie otritsania, ili Bitva pod Aushvitsem: Debaty o demografii i geopolitike Kholokosta*, edited by A. Koch and P. Polian, 179–203. Moscow: Mosty kultury / Gesharim, 2008.

———. "Liudskie poteri evreiskogo naseleniia v poslevoiennykh granitsakh SSSR v gody Velikoi Otechestvennoi Voiny." *Vestnik evreiskogo universitetu v Moskve* 2/9 (1995): 134–55.

Kvitko, Berta, and Miron Petrovskii, eds. *Zhizn' i tvorchestvo L'va Kvitko*. Moscow: Detskaia literatura, 1976.

Kwiet, Konrad. "Rehearsing for Murder: The Beginning of the Final Solution in Lithuania in June 1941." *Holocaust and Genocide Studies* 12 (1998): 3–26.

Landau, Zbigniew, and Jerzy Tomaszewski. *Zarys historii gospodarczej Polski 1918–1939*. 5th ed. Warsaw: Książka i Wiedza, 1986.

Laqueur, Walter. *The Terrible Secret: Suppression of the Truth about Hitler's "Final Solution."* Boston: Little, Brown, 1980.

Lavi, Theodor. "Ciudei." In *Pinkas haKehilot, Romania*, edited by Jean Ancel and Theodor Lavi, 2:486. Jerusalem: Yad Vashem, 1980.

Le Foll, Claire. "The Image of the Jews in Belorussian Soviet Cinema, 1924–1936." In *Visualizing Jews through the Ages: Literary and Material Representations of Jewishness and Judaism*, edited by Hannah Ewence and Helen Spurling, 229–46. New York: Routledge, 2015.

Leibovich, Oleg. "Antisemitskie nastroeniia v sovetskom tylu." In *SSSR vo Vtoroi Mirovoi Voine: Okkupatsiia, kholokost, stalinizm*, edited by Oleg Budnitskii, 280–96. Moscow: ROSSPEN, 2014.

Leikina, Rosa. "Yemei haSho'ah biDnepropetrovsk." In *Sefer Yekaterinoslav-Dnepropetrovsk*, edited by Ts. Harkavy and Y. Goldbort, 93–104. Jerusalem: Irgun yots'ei Yekaterinoslav-Dnepropetrovsk beYisra'el, 1973.

Lenn, Yitshak. "Slonim." In *Mehozot Vilnah, Bialystok, Novogrudek*, vol. 8: *Pinkas haKehilot, Polin*, edited by Shmuel Spector, 492–506. Jerusalem: Yad Vashem, 2005.

Lestschinsky, Jacob. *Dos sovetishe Idntum: Zayn fargangenhayt un kegnvart*. New York: Idisher Kemfer, 1941.

———. *Oyfn rand fun opgrunt: Fun yidishn lebn in Poyln*. Buenos Aires: Unión Central Israelita Polaca en la Argentina, 1947.

Lévesque, Jean. "Moscow 1941: The Rise and Fall of the Soviet People's Militia (*Narodnoe Opolchenie*)." In *The Civilization of War: The Changing Civil-Military Divide, 1914–2014*, edited by Andrew Barros and Martin Thomas, 64–80. Cambridge: Cambridge University Press, 2018.

Levin, Dov. *Bein haPatish vehaMagal: Yehudei haAratsot haBaltiyot tahat haShilton haSovieti beMilhemet haOlam haSheniyah*. Jerusalem: Makor, 1983.

———. *Lohamim veOmedim al nafsham: Milhemet yehudei Lita baNatsim 1941–1945*. Jerusalem: Yad Vashem, 1975.

———. "Perakim beToledot haYehudim beLita." In *Pinkas haKehilot, Lita*, edited by Dov Levin, 1–110. Jerusalem: Yad Vashem, 1996.

———. "The Response of the Jews of Eastern Poland to the Invasion of the Red Army in September 1939 (As Described by Jewish Witnesses)." *Gal-Ed* 11 (1989): 87–102.

———. *Tekufah beSograyim 1939–1941: Temurot beHayei haYehudim baEzorim sheSuphu liVerit haMo'atsot beTehilat milhemet haOlam haSheniyah*. Jerusalem: Institute of Contemporary Jewry, 1989.

———. "Viekšniai." In *Pinkas haKehilot, Lita*, edited by Dov Levin, 270–74. Jerusalem: Yad Vashem, 1996.

———. "Yerushalayim deLita: Shishah shavu'ot beSograyim." *Gal-Ed* 3 (1976): 213–44.

Levin, Shmuel, and Avraham Klevan. "Radziłów." In *Varshah vehaGalil*, vol. 4: *Pinkas haKehilot, Polin*, edited by Abraham Wein, 422–24. Jerusalem: Yad Vashem, 1989.

———. "Wąsosz." In *Varshah vehaGalil*, vol. 4: *Pinkas haKehilot, Polin*, edited by Abraham Wein, 187–88. Jerusalem: Yad Vashem, 1989.

Levin, Zeev, ed. *Evreiskie bezhentsy i evakuirovannye v SSSR, 1939–1946: Sbornik statei, dokumentov i svidetel'stv*. Jerusalem: Asotsiatisya hazit haKavod, 2020.

———. "Evreiskoe naselenie SSSR nakanune natsistskogo vtorzheniia: Deportatsii i nachalo evakuatsii." In *Evreiskie bezhentsy i evakuirovannye v SSSR, 1939–1946: Sbornik statei, dokumentov i svidetel'stv*, edited by Zeev Levin, 23–52. Jerusalem: Asotsiatisya hazit haKavod, 2020.

Levitan, Seymour. "Rokhl Haering Korn." *Jewish Women's Archive*, https://jwa.org.

Levitas, F. L. "Babyn Yar (1941–1943)." In *Katastrofa i opir ukrains'koho evreistva (1941–1944): Narysy z Istorii Holokostu i Oporu v Ukraini*, edited by S. Ya. Elizavets'kyi, 88–117. Kiev: Ukrainian National Academy of Sciences, 1999.

Lewin, Moshe. *The Gorbachev Phenomenon: A Historical Interpretation*. Berkeley: University of California Press, 1991.

Lidowski, Eliezer. *USheviv haEsh lo da'akh*. Tel Aviv: Irgun haPartizanim, 1986.

Liekis, Šarūnas. *1939: The Year That Changed Everything in Lithuania's History*. Amsterdam: Rodopi, 2010.

Litvak, Olga. *Conscription and the Search for Modern Russian Jewry*. Bloomington: Indiana University Press, 2006.

Litvak, Yosef. *Pelitim yehudim miPolin biVerit haMo'atsot 1939–1946*. Jerusalem: Institute of Contemporary Jewry of the Hebrew University, 1988.

Litvin, A. "Generaly i evrei (Dokladnaia zapiska nachal'nika Generalnogo Shtaba Ya. G. Zhilinskogo)." *Vestnik evreiskogo universiteta* 22, no. 4 (2000): 273–90.

Litvinov, Maxim. *Against Aggression: Speeches by Maxim Litvinov*. London: Lawrence and Wishart, 1939.

Loewenthal, Rudolf. "The Extinction of the Krimchaks in World War II." *American Slavic and East European Review* 10, no. 2 (1951): 130–36.

Lomagin, N. A. *Neizvestnaia blokada*. St. Petersburg: Neva, 2004.

Longerich, Peter. *Holocaust: The Nazi Persecution and Murder of the Jews*. Oxford: Oxford University Press, 2010.

Löw, Andrea. *Juden im Getto Litzmannstadt: Lebensbedingungen, Selbstwahrmehmung, Verhalten*. Göttingen: Wallstein Verlag, 2006.

Lower, Wendy. "Facilitating Genocide: Nazi Ghettoization Practices in Occupied Ukraine." In *Life in the Ghettos during the Holocaust*, edited by Eric Sterling, 120–44. Syracuse, NY: Syracuse University Press, 2005.

———. *Nazi Empire-Building and the Holocaust in Ukraine*. Chapel Hill: University of North Carolina Press, 2005.

Lugovskaia, Tatiana. *Kak znaiu, kak pomniu, kak umeiu: Vospominaniia, pis'ma, dnevniki*. Moscow: Agraf, 2001.

Lynn, Denise. "Gendered Narratives in Anti-Stalinism and Anti-Communism during the Cold War: The Case of Juliet Poyntz." *Journal of Cold War Studies* 18, no. 1 (2016): 31–59.

Macartney, C. A. "Hungary's Declaration of War on the U.S.S.R. in 1941." In *Studies in Diplomatic History and Historiography in Honour of C. P. Gooch, C.H.*, edited by A. O. Sarkissian, 153–65. New York: Barnes & Noble, 1961.

Mahler, Rafael. "Bucovina." In *Universal Jewish Encyclopedia*, edited by Isaac Landman, 2:573–74. New York: Universal Jewish Encyclopedia, 1940.

———. *Yehudei Polin bein shetei milhamot haOlam: Historiyah kalkalit-hevratit leOr haStatistikah*. Tel Aviv: Dvir, 1968.

Maiskii, I. M. *The Complete Maisky Diaries*. Edited by Gabriel Gorodetsky. New Haven, CT: Yale University Press, 2017.

———. *The Maisky Diaries: Red Ambassador to the Court of St James's, 1932–1943*. Edited by Gabriel Gorodetsky. New Haven, CT: Yale University Press, 2015.

Majsiejonak, Andrej. "Daklad haŭliajteru Bielarusi Vilhielmu Kuba." *Lidski letapisets* 15 (2002), http://pawet.net/.

Maksimenko, Elena P. "Belorusskaia tematika propagandistskogo fronta Velikoi Otechestvennoi Voiny." *Istoricheskie, filosofskie, politicheskie i iuridicheskie nauki, kul'turologiia i iskustvovedenie* 7 (2011): 141–46.

Maksudov, Sergei. "Evacuation Documentation and Testimonies as Sources for the Study of Soviet Jewish Population Losses during World War II." *Holocaust and Genocide Studies* 26, no. 1 (2012): 120–30.

———. "Jewish Population Losses of the USSR from the Holocaust: A Demographic Approach." In *The Holocaust in the Soviet Union: Studies and Sources on the Destruction of the Jews in the Nazi-Occupied Territories of the USSR, 1941–1945*, edited by Lucjan Dobroszycki and Jeffrey S. Gurock, 207–13. Armonk, NY: M. E. Sharpe, 1993.

Malkin, M. "Voiskovoi razvedchik." In *Vospominaniia o E. Kazakeviche: Sbornik*, edited by G. O. Kazakevich and B. S. Ruben, 162–71. 2nd ed. Moscow: Sovetskii pisatel', 1984.

Manley, Rebecca. *To the Tashkent Station: Evacuation and Survival in the Soviet Union at War*. Ithaca, NY: Cornell University Press, 2009.

Marcus, Joseph. *Social and Political History of the Jews in Poland, 1919–1939*. Berlin: Mouton, 1983.

Margalit [Margolis], Moshe. "Yoman haYagon." In *Pinkas Ludmir: Sefer Zikaron leKehilat Ludmir*, 345–430. Tel Aviv: Irgun yots'ei Ludmir beYisra'el, 1962.

Markish, Esther. *Stol' dolgoe vozvrashchenie: Vospominaniia*. Tel Aviv: publisher not identified, 1989.

Markish, Peretz. *Tsu a yidisher tentserin*. Tel Aviv: Masada, 1976.

Marples, David R. "Ethnic Issues in the Famine of 1932–1933 in Ukraine." In *Holodomor and Gorta Mór: Histories, Memories, and Representations of Famine in Ukraine and Ireland*, edited by Christian Noack, Lindsay Janssen, and Vincent Comerford, 35–49. London: Anthem Press, 2012.

———. *Stalinism in Ukraine in the 1940s*. London: Palgrave Macmillan, 1992.

———. "The Ukrainians in Eastern Poland under Soviet Occupation, 1939–1941: A Study in Soviet Rural Policy." In *The Soviet Takeover of the Eastern Polish Provinces, 1939–41*, edited by Keith Sword, 236–52. New York: St. Martin's Press, 1991.

Martin, Terry. *The Affirmative Action Empire: Nations and Nationalism in the Soviet Union, 1923–1939*. Ithaca, NY: Cornell University Press, 2001.

Matthäus, Jürgen. *Jewish Responses to Persecution*, vol. 3: *1941–1942*. Lanham, MD: AltaMira Press, 2013.

———. "Die 'Judenfrage' als Schulungsthema von SS und Polizei: 'Inneres Erlebnis' und Handlungslegitimation." In *Ausbildungsziel Judenmord? "Weltanschauliche Erziehung" von SS, Polizei und Waffen-SS im Rahmen der "Endlösung,"* edited by R. Breitman, J. F, K. Kwiet, J. Matthäus, and U. Rennert, 35–86. Frankfurt: Fischer, 2003.

Matthäus, Jürgen, and Frank Bajohr. *The Political Diary of Alfred Rosenberg and the Onset of the Holocaust*. Lanham, MD: Rowman & Littlefield, 2015.

Mazower, Mark. *Hitler's Empire: How the Nazis Ruled Europe*. New York: Penguin Press, 2008.

Medvedev, Feliks N. *Moi velikie starukhi*. St. Petersburg: BKhV-Peterburg, 2011.

Meierkevitch, A. *In di khvalyes fun yene zibn yor: A palet in Ratn Farband*. N.p.: A. Meierkevitch, 1998.

Melzer, Emanuel. *Ma'avak medini beMalkodet: Yehudei Polin 1935–1939*. Tel Aviv: Diaspora Research Institute, 1982.

Mendelsohn, Ezra. *The Jews of East Central Europe between the World Wars*. Bloomington: Indiana University Press, 1983.

———. "Polin." In *HaTefutsah: Mizrah Eiropah*, edited by Jacob Tsur, 169–211. Jerusalem: Keter, 1976.

Merritt, Harry C. "In the Fight, Yet on the Margins: Latvian Jewish Red Army Soldiers." *Peripheral Histories*, 11 June 2019, www.peripheralhistories.co.uk/.

Mędykowski, Witold. *W cieniu gigantów: Pogromy 1941 r. w byłej sowieckiej strefie okupacyjnej—kontekst historyczny, społeczny i kulturowy*. Warsaw: Instytut Studiów Politycznych Polskiej Akademii Nauk, 2012.

Michman, Dan. *The Emergence of Jewish Ghettos during the Holocaust*. Cambridge: Cambridge University Press, 2011.

Mick, Christoph. *Lemberg, Lwów, Lviv: Violence and Ethnicity in a Contested City*. Lafayette, IN: Purdue University Press, 2015.

Mikhailova, T., "Evakuatsiia promyshlennosti v gody Velikoi Otechestvennoi voiny i rost gorodov Rossii: Chislennyi analiz," 29 March 2018, DOI: https://dx.doi.org/10.2139/ssrn.3152304.

Milch, Baruch. *Testament*. Warsaw: KARTA, 2001.

Miliakova, Lidia, ed. *Le livre des pogroms: Antichambre d'un génocide—Ukraine, Russie, Biélorussie, 1917–1922*. Paris: Calmann-Lévy, 2010.

Miller, Jacob. "Soviet Theory on the Jews." In *The Jews in Soviet Russia since 1917*, edited by Lionel Kochan, 46–63. 3rd ed. Oxford: Oxford University Press, 1978.

Minc, Matityahu. *HaMetsukot, haTikvot vehaYe'ush shel yehudei Rusiyah haSovietit*. Tel Aviv: Goldstein-Goren Diaspora Research Center, 2015.

Ministerstvo Inostrannykh Del SSSR. *Dokumenty vneshnei politiki SSSR*. Moscow: Izdatel'stvo Politicheskoi Literatury, 1970.

[Molotov, Viacheslav M.]. *Molotov Remembers: Inside Kremlin Politics, Conversations with Felix Chuev*. Edited by Albert Resis. Chicago: Ivan R. Dee, 1993.

———. *The Soviet Union in 1942: The Third Five-Year Plan for the National Economic Development of the U.S.S.R.* New York: Workers Library Publishers, 1939.

Moseikina, Marina N. "Velikaia otechestvennaia voina Sovetskogo Soiuza: rol' antifashistskikh komitetov v organizatsii dvizheniia podderzhki SSSR v stranakh Vostoka i Afriki." In *Mnogolikaia istoriia: k 70-leniiu Tamary Vasil'evny Bataevoi*, edited by N. E. Bekmakhanova and N. M. Moseikina, 76–85. Moscow: Publishing House of the People's Friendship University of Russia, 1997.

Moskovskikh, Irina A. "Vozniknovenie i pervye gody deiatelnosti Vseslavianskogo komiteta v Moskve." *Pravo i obrazovanie* 6 (2004): 210–26.

Moskva voiennaia: Memuary i arkhivnnye dokumenty. Moscow: Mosgorarkhiv, 1995.

Motyl, Alexander. *The Turn to the Right: The Ideological Origins and Development of Ukrainian Nationalism, 1919–1929*. New York: Columbia University Press, 1980.

Müller, Rolf-Dieter. *Enemy in the East: Hitler's Secret Plans to Invade the Soviet Union*. London: I. B. Tauris, 2015.

Murphy, David E. *What Stalin Knew: The Enigma of Barbarossa*. New Haven, CT: Yale University Press, 2005.

Nadav, Mordechai. "Pinsk." In *Vohlin uPolesiyah*, vol. 5: *Pinkas haKehilot, Polin*, edited by Shmuel Spector, 276–99. Jerusalem: Yad Vashem, 1990.

Nazaroff, Alexander. "The Soviet Oil Industry." *Russian Review* 1 (1941): 81–89.

Nekrich, Aleksandr M. *Pariahs, Partners, Predators: German-Soviet Relations, 1922–1941*. New York: Columbia University Press, 1997.

Nesselrodt, Markus. "Die Vernichtung entkommen: Erfahrungen polnischer Juden in der Sowjetunion (1939–1946)." PhD diss., Freie Universität Berlin, 2017.

Nicolson, Harold. *The War Years 1939–1945*. New York: Atheneum, 1967.

Nikiforov, O. "Organizatsiia detskikh domov i internatov Omskoi oblasti v gody Velikoi Otechestvennoi vojny." In *Istoriia, Pamiat', Liudi: Materialy VII Mezhdunarodnoi nauchno-prakticheskoi konferentsii*, edited by L. S. Aktaeva, A. I. Baron, and M. S. Makarova, 483–98. Almaty: Tsentralnyi gosudarstvennyi arkhiv Komiteta informatsii i arkhivov Ministerstva sviazi i informatsii Respubliki Kazakhstan.

Nove, Alec, and J. A. Newth. "The Jewish Population: Demographic Trends and Occupational Patterns." In *The Jews in Soviet Russia since 1917*, edited by Lionel Kochan, 132–67. Oxford: Oxford University Press, 1978.

Nussbaum, Klemens (Kalman). *VeHafach lahem leRo'ets: HaYehudim baTsava haAmami haPolani biVerit haMo'atsot*. Tel Aviv: Diaspora Research Institute, 1984.

Ofer, Dalia. "Parenthood in the shadow of the Holocaust." In *Jewish Families in Europe, 1939–Present: History, Representation, and Memory*, edited by Joanna B. Michlic, 3–25. Hanover, NH: Brandeis University Press, 2017.

Orlov, Igor. "Kartochnoe snabzhenie v 1941–1943 gg: Raschety i proschety." *Sovremennyie problemy servisa i turizma* 3 (2010): 36–42.

Pankowsky, Hanna Davidson. *East of the Storm: Outrunning the Holocaust in Russia*. Lubbock: Texas Tech University Press, 1999.

Penslar, Derek J. *Jews and the Military: A History*. Princeton, NJ: Princeton University Press, 2013.

Perechodnik, Calek. *Spowiedź*. Warsaw: KARTA, 2011.

Perehrest, O. *Silske gospodarstvo Ukrainy v roki Velikoi Vitchiznyanoi vijny (1941–1945 rr)*. Kiev: Institut istorii Ukrainy, 2010.

Perlis, Rivkah. *Tenu'ot haNo'ar haHalutsiyot bePolin haKevushah*. Tel Aviv: HaKibuts haMe'uhad, 1987.

Persov, Shmuel. *Dayn nomen iz folk: Fartseykhenungen vegn yidn partizaner*. Moscow: Der Emes, 1944.

———. *Yakov Moshkovski*. Moscow: Der Emes, 1940.

———. *Yakov Shmushkevitsh: Der doplter held fun Ratnfarband*. Moscow: Der Emes, 1941.

Petrova, Nina K. *Antifashistskie komitety v SSSR, 1941–1945*. Moscow: Nauka, 1999.

Petrovsky-Shtern, Yohanan. *Jews in the Russian Army, 1827–1917: Drafted into Modernity*, New York: Cambridge University Press, 2009.

Phillips, Hugh D. *Between the Revolution and the West: A Political Biography of Maxim M. Litvinov*. Boulder, CO: Westview, 1992.

Pickhan, Gertrud. "'That Incredible History of the Polish Bund Written in a Soviet Prison': The NKVD Files on Henryk Erlich and Wiktor Alter." *Polin* 10 (1997): 247–72.

Pinchuk, Ben-Cion. *Yehudei Berit-haMo'atsot mul penei haSho'ah: Mehkar biVe'ayot haglayah uFin'ui*. Tel Aviv: Diaspora Research Institute, 1979.

Pinkus, Benjamin. *Yehudei Rusiyah uVerit haMo'atsot: Toledot mi'ut le'umi*. Jerusalem: Mosad Bialik, 1986.

Pipes, Richard. *Russia under the Bolshevik Regime.* New York: Vintage, 1994.

Pohl, Dieter. "Anti-Jewish Pogroms in Western Ukraine: A Research Agenda." In *Shared History—Divided Memory: Jews and Others in Soviet-Occupied Poland, 1939–1941*, edited by E. Barkan, E. A. Cole, and K. Struve, 305–13. Leipzig: Leipziger Universitätsverlag, 2007.

———. *Die Herrschaft der Wehrmacht: Deutsche Militärbesetzung und einheimische Bevölkerung in der Sowjetunion 1941–1944.* Munich: R. Oldenbourg, 2009.

———. *Nationalistische Judenverfolgung in Ostgalizien 1941–1944: Organisation und Durchführung eines staatlichen Massenverbrechens.* Munich: Oldenbourg, 1997.

Poliakov, Iu. A. *Vsesoiuznaia perepis' naseleniia 1939 goda: Osnovnye itogi.* Moscow: Nauka, 1939.

Polian, Pavel. "Hätte der Holocaust beinahe nicht Stattgefunden: Überlegungen zu einem Schriftwechsel im Wert von zwei Millionen Menschenleben." In *Besatzung, Kollaboration, Holocaust: Neue Studien zur Verfolgung und Ermordung der europäischen Juden*, edited by Johannes Hürter and Jürgen Zarusky, 1–19. Berlin: Oldenbourg de Gruyter, 2008.

———. *Ne po svoiei vole . . . : Istoriia i geografiia prinuditel'nykh migratsii v SSSR.* Moscow: Memorial, 2001.

———. *Zhertvy dvukh dictator.* Moscow: ROSSPEN, 2002.

Polonsky, Antony. *The Jews in Poland and Russia.* Oxford: Littman Library of Jewish Civilization, 2012.

Polonsky, Antony, and Joanna B. Michlic. *The Neighbors Respond: The Controversy over the Jedwabne Massacre in Poland.* Princeton, NJ: Princeton University Press, 2004.

Pomerants, G. *Zapiski gadkogo utenka.* Moscow: ROSSPEN, 2003.

Pomerantz, Jack, and Lyric Wallwork Winik. *Run East: Flight from the Holocaust.* Urbana: University of Illinois Press, 1997.

Pope, Arthur Upham. *Maxim Litvinoff.* New York: L. B. Fischer, [1943].

Porat, Dina. *MeEver laGashmi: Parashat hayav shel Abba Kovner.* Tel Aviv: Am Oved, 2000.

Posivnych, Mykola. *Stepan Bandera.* Kharkiv: Glagoslav Distribution, 2015.

Potemkina, Marina. "Evakuatsiia i evrei: Strategii vyzhivaniia v voennom sotsiume." In *Evreiskie bezhentsy i evakuirovannye v SSSR, 1939–1946: Sbornik statei, dokumentov i svidetel'stv*, edited by Zeev Levin, 53–76. Jerusalem: Asotsiatisya hazit haKavod, 2020.

Puławski, Adam. *W obliczu zagłady: Rząd RP na Uchodźstwie, Delegatura Rządu RP na Kraj, ZWZ-AK wobec deportacji Żydów do obozów zagłady (1941–1942).* Lublin: Instytut Pamięci Narodowej, 2009.

Rabinowicz, Yisrael. "Yeshivat Lomzhah." In *Mosedot torah beEiropah beVinyanam uveHurbanam*, edited by S. K. Mirsky, 217–27. New York: Ogen, 1956.

Radchenko, Yuri. "Znyshchennia kharkivs'kikh evreiv orhanamy GFP ta SD v roky Druhoi svitovoi viiny." *Visnyk Kharkivs'koho natsional'noho universytetu imeni V. N. Karazina* 42 (2010): 134–44.

Rajok, Michael, and Tsvi Rajok. "Khurbn Glubok." In *Khurbn Glubok, Sharkoyztsene, Dunilowicz, Postow, Droye, Kazan: Dos lebn un umkum fun yidishe shtetlekh in*

Vaysrusland-Lite (Vilne gegent), edited by Shlomo Suskowicz, 9–284. Buenos Aires: Sociedad Residentes de Szarkowszczyzna, Dunilowicze, Postawy y Glubokie en la Argentina, 1956.

Raskin, D. I. "Evrei v sostavie rossiiskogo ofitserskogo korpusa v XIX-nachale XX veka." *Evrei v Rossii* 5 (1998): 170–74.

Redlich, Shimon, ed. *Evreiskii antifashistishkii komitet v SSSR, 1941–1948* Moscow: Mezhdunarodnye otnosheniia, 1996.

———. "Soviet Uses of Jewish Nationalism during World War II: The Membership and Dynamics of the Jewish Antifascist Committee in the USSR," *Nationalities Papers* 5 (no. 2, 1977): 136–66.

———. *Together and Apart in Brzezany: Poles, Jews, and Ukrainians, 1919–1945*. Bloomington, IN: Indiana University Press, 2002.

———. *War, Holocaust and Stalinism: A Documented History of the Jewish Anti-Fascist Committee in the USSR*. London: Routledge, 1995.

Reichelt, Karen, and Martin Dean. "Riga." In *Ghettos in German-Occupied Eastern Europe*. Vol. 2 of *United States Holocaust Memorial Museum Encyclopedia of Camps and Ghettos 1933–1945*, edited by Martin Dean, 1019–23. Bloomington, IN: Indiana University Press, 2012.

Reimann, Aribert. "Local Brawls and Global Confrontation: Transnational Political Violence among the Exiled Left in Mexico City during 1943." *Journal of Iberian and Latin American Research* 23, no. 1 (2017): 1–17.

Report on the Relief Accorded to Polish Citizens by the Polish Embassy in the U.S.S.R., with Special Reference to Polish Citizens of Jewish Nationality, September 1941–April 1943. London: Geo. Barber & Son, [1943].

Resis, Albert. "The Fall of Litvinov: Harbinger of the German-Soviet Non-Aggression Pact." *Europe-Asia Studies* 52 (2000): 33–56.

Rich, Betty. *Little Girl Lost*. Toronto: Azrieli Foundation, 2011.

Ringel, Michał. "Ustawodawstwo Polski Odrodzonej o gminach żydowskich." In *Żydzi w Polsce Odrodzonej: Działalność społeczna, gospodarcza, oświatowa i kulturalna*, edited by I. Schipper, A. Tartakower, A. Hafftka, 2:242–48. Warsaw: Wydawnictwo "Żydzi w Polsce Odrodzonej," [1933].

Roberts, Geoffrey. "The Fall of Litvinov: A Revisionist View." *Journal of Contemporary History* 27 (1992): 639–57.

———. *The Soviet Union and the Origins of the Second World War: Russo-German Relations and the Road to War, 1933–1941*. New York: St. Martin's Press, 1995.

Roberts, Henry L. "Maxim Litvinov." In *The Diplomats 1919–1939*, edited by Gordon A. Craig and Felix Gilbert, 344–77. Princeton, NJ: Princeton University Press, 1953.

Rosenberg, Blanca. *To Tell at Last: Survival under False Identity*. Urbana: University of Illinois Press, 1993.

Rossino, Alexander B. *Hitler Strikes Poland: Blitzkrieg, Ideology, and Atrocity*. Lawrence: University of Kansas Press, 2003.

Rossoliński-Liebe, Grzegorz. *Stepan Bandera: The Life and Afterlife of a Ukrainian Nationalist*. Stuttgart: Ibidem-Verlag, 2014.

———. "The 'Ukrainian National Revolution' of 1941: Discourse and Practice of a Fascist Movement." *Kritika* 12 (2011): 83–114.

Rozenblat, E. S. "'Chuzhdyi element': Evreiskie bezhentsy v Zapadnoi Belorussii glazami sovetskoi vlasti, 1939–1944 gg." *Uroki kholokausta: istoriia i sovremennost'* 1 (2009): 28–43.

———. "'Contact Zones' in Interethnic Relations: The Case of Western Belarus, 1939–1941." In *Shared History—Divided Memory: Jews and Others in Soviet-Occupied Poland, 1939–1941*, edited by E. Barkan, E. A. Cole, and K. Struve, 201–23. Leipzig: Leipziger Universitätsverlag, 2007.

———. "'My, religioznye Evrei, kazhdyi den' dolzhny ozhidat' aresta . . .': Politika sovetskoi vlasti v otnoshenii iudaizma v Zapadnoi Belorussii skvoz' prizmu odnogo dokumenta." *Arkhiv Evreiskoi istorii* 1 (2004): 377–88.

———. "Polacy, Białorusini i Żydzi na Polesiu w pierwszych tygodniach wojny niemiec-radzieckiej." In *Początek wojny niemiecko-sowieckiej i losy ludności cywilney*, edited by J. J. Milewski and Anna Pyzewska, 65–71. Warsaw: Instytut Pamięci Narodowej, 2003.

———. "Zapadniie oblasti Belorussii v 1939–1941 godakh: Okkupatsiia, vossoiedininenie, sovetizatsiia." In *Zapadnaia Belorussiia i Zapadnaia Ukraina w 1939–1941 gg.: Liudi, sobytiia, dokumenty*, edited by O. V. Petrovskaia and E. Iu Borisenok, 42–61. St. Petersburg: Aleteiia, 2011.

Rozin, Yosef. "Anykščiai." In *Pinkas haKehilot, Lita*, edited by Dov Levin, 151–55. Jerusalem: Yad Vashem, 1996.

Ruben, Berngard. "Za svoiei zvezdoi: Dokumentalnaia povest' o E. G. Kazakeviche." *Druzhba narodov* 2010, no. 2: http://magazines.russ.ru/.

Rubenstein, Joshua. "Il'ia Ehrenburg and the Holocaust in the Soviet Press." In *Soviet Jews in World War II: Fighting, Witnessing, Remembering*, edited by Harriet Murav and Gennady Estraikh, 36–56. New York: Academic Studies Press, 2014.

———. *Tangled Loyalties: The Life and Times of Ilya Ehrenburg*. New York: Basic Books, 1996.

Rubenstein, Joshua, and Vladimir P. Naumov, eds. *Stalin's Secret Pogrom: The Postwar Inquisition of the Jewish Anti-Fascist Committee*. New Haven, CT: Yale University Press, 2001.

Rudashevski, Yitskhok. *The Diary of the Vilna Ghetto*. Tel Aviv: Beit Lohamei haGeta'ot, 1973.

Rudnytska, Milena, ed. *Zakhidnia Ukraina pid Bol'shevykamy*. New York: Shevchenko Scientific Society, 1958.

Rukovodiashchii politicheskii sostav upravlenii frontov, flotov, armii, flotilii, korpusov, divizii, soedinenii Voenno-morskogo flota i tankovykh brigad perioda Velikoi Otechestvennoi Voiny 1941–1945 gg. Moscow: Voennaia Akademiia im. M. V. Frunze, 1964.

Rzhevskaia, Elena. *Berlin, Mai 1945: Zapiski voennogo perevodchika*. Moscow: Sovetskii pisatel', 1967.

———. *Izbrannoe*. 2 vols. St. Petersburg: INAPRESS, 2015.

Samoilov, D. *Podennye zapisi*. Moscow: Vremia, 2002.

Savgabaeva, A. N. "Evakuatsiia v Zapadno-Kazakhstanskuiu oblast' v period Velikoi Otechestvennoi voiny 1941–45gg." In *Istoriia. Pamiat' Liudi: IX Mezhdunarodnaia nauchno-prakticheskaia konferentsiia*, edited by K. Sh. Alimgazinov, A. I. Baron, A. Kh. Mustafina, L. A. Prokopenko, and E. V. Chilikova, 167–72. Almaty: Tsentralnyi gosudarstvennyi arkhiv Komiteta informatsii i arkhivov Ministerstva sviazi i informatsii Respubliki Kazakhstan, 2017.

Schaary, David. *Yahadut Bukovina bein shetei milhamot haOlam*. Tel Aviv: Goldstein-Goren Diaspora Research Center, 2004.

Schalkowsky, Samuel, ed. *The Clandestine History of the Kovno Jewish Ghetto Police*. Bloomington: Indiana University Press, 2014.

Scharfstein, Nahman. "BeSevivot Lomzah biYmei ni'uts haNatsizm." In *Sefer zikaron leKehilat Lomzah*, edited by Yom-Tov Lewinski, 72–78. Tel Aviv: Olei Lomza, 1952.

Schechter, Brandon. "'The People's Instructions': Indigenizing the Great Patriotic War among 'Non-Russians.'" *Ab Imperio* (2012–2013): 109–33.

Schneier, Aharon. "Giluyei haAntishemiyut biVerit haMo'atsot biTekufat haSho'ah." *Masu'ah* 29 (2001): 83–107.

Segal, Raz. *Genocide in the Carpathians: War, Social Breakdown, and Mass Violence 1914–1945*. Stanford, CA: Stanford University Press, 2016.

Seidman, Hillel. "Yeshivat 'Ets Hayim' deKletsk." In *Mosedot torah beEiropah beVinyanam uveHurbanam*, edited by S. K. Mirsky, 229–42. New York: Ogen, 1956.

Senn, Alfred Erich. "The Sovietization of the Baltic States." *Annals of the American Academy of Political and Social Science* 317 (1958): 123–29.

Shapira, Anita. *HaHalikhah al kav haOfek*. Tel Aviv: Am Oved, 1989.

Shechner, Yehoshua. *Mot haZeman haYehudi: Kronikah shel hurban haKehilah haYehudit beTluste uveSevivoteiha*. Jerusalem: Yad Vashem, 2017.

Sherman, Haya. "HaGimnaziyah biTekufat haKibush haSovieti." In *Pinsk: Sefer edut veZikaron leKehilat Pinsk-Karlin*, edited by N. Tamir (Mirsky), 2:128. [Tel Aviv]: Irgun yotse'ei Pinsk-Karlin biMedinat Yisra'el, 1966.

Sherman, Joseph. "David Bergelson (1894–1952): A Biography." In *David Bergelson: From Modernism to Socialist Realism*, edited by Joseph Sherman and Gennady Estraikh, 7–78. Oxford: Legenda, 2007.

Shik, Na'ama. "Infinite Loneliness: Some Aspects of the Lives of Jewish Women in the Auschwitz Camps According to Testimonies and Autobiographies Written between 1945 and 1948." *Lessons and Legacies* 8 (2008): 125–56.

Shinedling, Abraham I. "Finland." In *Universal Jewish Encyclopedia*, edited by Isaac Landman, 4:308–309. New York: Universal Jewish Encyclopedia, 1941.

Shirer, William L. *Berlin Diary*. New York: Popular Library, 1941.

Shkandrij, Myroslav. *Ukrainian Nationalism: Politics, Ideology, and Literature*. New Haven, CT: Yale University Press, 2015.

———. "Ukrainization, Terror, and Famine: Coverage in Lviv's *Dilo* and the Nationalist Press of the 1930s." *Nationalities Papers* 40 (2012): 431–51.

Shkurko, Emma. "Evakuirovannye evrei v Bashkirskoi ASSR (1941–45gg): Demograficheskie, kul'turnye i psikhologicheskie aspekty." In *Evreiskie bezhentsy i evakuirovannye v SSSR, 1939–1946: Sbornik statei, dokumentov i svidetelstv'*, edited by Zeev Levin, 104–25. Jerusalem: Asotsiatisya hazit haKavod, 2020.

Shmueli, Ilana. *Ein Kind aus guter Familie: Czernowitz 1924–1944*. Aachen: Rimbaud, 2006.

Shumelishskii, M. G. *Dnevnik soldata*. Moscow: Kolos, 2000.

Shneer, A[ron]. *Plen*. Jerusalem: A. Shneer, 2003.

Shneer, David. *Grief: The Biography of a Holocaust Photograph*. New York: Oxford University Press, 2020.

———. "Rivers of Blood: Peretz Markish, the Holocaust, and Jewish Vengeance." In *A Captive of the Dawn: The Life and Work of Peretz Markish*, edited by Joseph Sherman, 139–56. Oxford: Legenda, 2011.

———. *Yiddish and the Creation of Soviet Jewish Culture 1918–1930*. Cambridge: Cambridge University Press, 2004.

Shoigu, S. K., ed. *Velikaia otechestvennaia voina 1941–1945: Dokumenty i materialy*, vol. 3: *Natsionalnye formirovaniia Krasnoi Armii*. Moscow: Voievoda, 2015.

Shternshis, Anna. "Between Life and Death: Why Some Soviet Jews Decided to Leave and Others to Stay in 1941." *Kritika* 15, no. 3 (2014): 477–504.

———. *When Sonia Met Boris: An Oral History of Jewish Life under Stalin*. New York: Oxford University Press, 2017.

Shtokfish, Shlomo. *In rod fun tsorn: Mayne iberlebungen in tveytn veltkrig*. Tel Aviv: Yisroel-Bukh, 1975.

Shveibish. "Evakuatsiia i sovetskie evrei v gody katastrofy." *Vestnik evreiskogo universiteta v Moskve* 9 (1995): 36–55.

Sidur, Vadim. *Pamiatnik sovremennomu sostoianiiu: Mif*. Moscow: Vagrius, 2002.

Sirutavičius, Vladas, and Darius Staliūnas. "Was Lithuania a Pogrom-Free Zone? (1881–1940)." In *Anti-Jewish Violence: Rethinking the Pogrom in East European History*, edited by Jonathan Dekel-Chen, David Gaunt, Natan M. Meir, and Israel Bartal, 144–58. Bloomington: Indiana University Press, 2011.

Slavgorodskii, G. V. *Frontovoi dnevnik, 1941–1945*. Moscow: ROSSPEN, 2017.

Slezkine, Yuri. *The Jewish Century*. Princeton, NJ: Princeton University Press, 2004.

Slutskii, Boris. *Stikhi raznykh let: Iz neizdannogo*. Moscow: Sovetskii pisatel', 1988.

———. "The Story of Gershel'man, a Jew." In *Soviet Jews in World War II: Fighting, Witnessing, Remembering*, edited by Harriet Murav and Gennady Estraikh, 208–18. Translated by Dariia Kabanova. New York: Academic Studies Press, 2014.

———. "Zapiski o voine." In *O drugikh i o sebe*. Moscow: PROZAIK, 2005.

Smirnov, E. I. *Frontovoe miloserdie*. Moscow: Voenizdat, 1991.

Smoliar, Hersz. *Vu bistu, Khaver Sidorov?* Tel Aviv: I. L. Peretz, 1975.

———. *Yehudim Sovietiyim me'ahorei gidrot haGeto*. Tel Aviv: Sifriyat Po'alim, 1984.

Snegiriova, Liudmila. "Evakuatsiia naseleniia iz Stalingrada v Sibirski tyl v gody Velikoi otechestvennoi voiny (1942 god)." *Vestnik Tomskogo gosudarstvennogo pedagogicheskogo universiteta* 192, no 3 (2018):174–85.

Snyder, Timothy. *Bloodlands: Europe between Hitler and Stalin*. New York: Basic Books, 2010.

———. *The Reconstruction of Nations: Poland, Ukraine, Lithuania, Belarus, 1569–1999*. New Haven, CT: Yale University Press, 2003.

Snyder, Timothy, and Martin Dean. "Łuck." In *Ghettos in German-Occupied Eastern Europe*, vol.2: *United States Holocaust Memorial Museum Encyclopedia of Camps and Ghettos 1933–1945*, edited by Martin Dean, 1411–14. Bloomington: Indiana University Press, 2012.

Solonari, Vladimir. "'Model Province' Explaining the Holocaust of Bessarabian and Bukovinian Jewry." *Nationalities Papers* 34, no. 4 (2006): 471–500.

———. "Patterns of Violence: The Local Population and the Mass Murder of Jews in Bessarabia and Northern Bukovina." In *The Holocaust in the East: Local Perpetrators and Soviet Responses*, edited by Michael David-Fox, Peter Holquist, and Alexander M. Martin, 51–82. Pittsburgh: University of Pittsburgh Press, 2014.

Sontag, Raymond James, and James Stuart Beddie. *Nazi-Soviet Relations 1939–1941: Documents from the Archives of the German Foreign Office*. Washington, DC: United States Department of State, 1948.

Sorokina, M. A. "People and Procedures: Toward a History of the Investigation of Nazi Crimes in the USSR." *Kritika* 6, no. 4 (2005): 797–831.

Sovetskaia aviatsiia v Velikoi Otechestvennoi Voine 1941–1945 gg. v tsifrakh. Moscow: Generalnyi shtab Voenno-vozdushnykh sil, 1962.

Soyer, Daniel. "Executed Bundists, Soviet Delegates and the Wartime Jewish Popular Front in New York." *American Communist History* 15, no. 3 (2016): 293–332.

Spector, Shmuel. "Ignatowka." In *Pinkas haKehilot, Polin, Vohlin uPolesia*, edited by Shmuel Spector, 42–43. Jerusalem: Yad Vashem, 1990.

———. "Lida." In *Mehozot Vilnah, Bialystok, Novogrudek*, vol. 8: *Pinkas haKehilot, Polin*, edited by Shmuel Spector, 387–94. Jerusalem: Yad Vashem, 2005.

———. *Sho'at yehudei Vohlin 1941–1944*. Jerusalem: Yad Vashem, 1986.

———. "Włodzimierzec." In *Vohlin uPolesia*, vol. 5: *Pinkas haKehilot, Polin*, edited by Shmuel Spector, 84–86. Jerusalem: Yad Vashem, 1990.

Speransky, Andrei. "Vysshaia shkola SSSR v 1941–45gg: Ekzameny voiny." *Vestnik Yuzhno-Uralskogo gosudarstvennogo universiteta* 15, no. 3 (2015): 33–38.

Stampfer, Shaul. "What Actually Happened to the Jews of Ukraine in 1648?" *Jewish History* 17 (2003): 165–78.

Stanislawski, Michael. *Tsar Nicholas I and the Jews: The Transformation of Jewish Society in Russia, 1825–1855*. Philadelphia: Jewish Publication Society of America, 1983.

Starkov, Arsenii V. "Bor'ba s antisemitizmom v sovetskom tylu v nachal'nyi period Velikoi Otechestvennoi voiny, 1941–1942." *Soviet and Post-Soviet Review* (2020): 1–31.

Strauss, Elizabeth. "'Cast Me Not Off in My Time of Old Age . . .': The Aged and Aging in the Łódź Ghetto, 1939–1944." PhD diss., University of Notre Dame, 2012.

Streit, Christian. "The German Army and the Politics of Genocide." In *The Policies of Genocide: Jews and Soviet Prisoners of War in Nazi Germany*, edited by Gerhard Hirschfeld, 1–14. London: Allen & Unwin, 1986.

———. *"Oni nam ne tovarishchi . . .": Wehrmacht i sovetskie voennoplennye v 1941–1945 gg*. Moscow: Russkaia panorama, 2009.

Struve, Kai. *Deutsche Herrschaft, ukrainischer Nationalismus, antijüdische Gewalt: der Sommer 1941 in der Westukraine*. Berlin: de Gruyter Oldenbourg, 2015.

Subtelny, Orest. *Ukraine: A History*. 3rd. ed. Toronto: University of Toronto Press, 2000.

Sverdlov, F. D. *Evrei-generaly Vooruzhennykh sil SSSR: kratkie biografii*. Moscow: [Publisher not identified], 1993.

Sword, Keith. *Deportation and Exile: Poles in the Soviet Union, 1939–48*. London: St. Martin's Press, 1994.

———. "Soviet Economic Policy in the Annexed Areas." In *The Soviet Takeover of the Eastern Polish Provinces, 1939–41*, edited by Keith Sword, 86–101. New York: St. Martin's Press, 1991.

Szarota, Tomasz. *U progu zagłady: Zajścia antyżydowskie i pogromy w okupowanej Europie*. Warsaw: Sic!, 2000.

Szmeruk, Ch. "Yiddish Publications in the USSR from the Late Thirties to 1948." *Yad Washem Studies on the European Jewish Catastrophe and Resistance* 4 (1960): 99–133.

Tartakovskii, B. G. *Iz dnevnikov voiennykh let*. Moscow: AIRO-XX, 2005.

Tec, Nechama. *Defiance: The Bielski Partisans*. New York: Oxford University Press, 1993.

Telman, I. G. *General i poet: Dokumentalnaia povest'*. Kiev: Radianskii pismennik, 1971.

Temkin, Gabriel. *My Just War: The Memoir of a Jewish Red Army Soldier in World War II*. Novato, CA: Presidio, 1998.

Tomaszewski, Jerzy. "Stosunki narodowościowe w Drugiej Rzeczypospolitej." In *Polska niepodległa 1918–1939*, edited by Janusz Żarnowski, 139–61. Wrocław: Ossolineum, 1984.

Tooze, Adam. *The Wages of Destruction: The Making and Breaking of the Nazi Economy*. New York: Viking, 2006.

Tory, Avraham [Avraham Golub]. *Surviving the Holocaust: The Kovno Ghetto Diary*. Cambridge, MA: Harvard University Press, 1990.

Torzecki, Ryszard. "Die Rolle der Zusammenarbeit mit der deutschen Besatzungsmacht in der Ukraine für deren Okkupationspolitik." In *Europa unterm Hakenkreuz: Okkupation und Kollaboration (1938–1945)*, edited by Werner Röhr, 239–72. Berlin: Hüthig, 1994.

Trębacz, Zofia. *Nie tylko Palestyna: Polskie plany emigracyjne wobec Żydów 1935–1939*. Warsaw: Żydowski Instytut Historyczny, 2018.

Trunk, Isaiah. *Yudenrat: HaMo'atsot haYehudiyot beMizrah Eiropah biTekufat haKibush haNatsi*. Jerusalem: Yad Vashem, 1979.

Tsur, Eli. *Lifnei bo haAfelah: HaShomer haTsa'ir bePolin uveGalitsiyah, 1930–1940*. Beer Sheva: Ben Gurion University Press, 2006.

———. "HaRadikalizatsiyah haKomunistit shel haNo'ar haTsiyoni: Tenu'at HaShomer HaTsa'ir beGalitsiyah, 1930–1933." *Gal-Ed* 17 (2000): 89–114 (Hebrew pagination).

Uldricks, Teddy J. "Russia and Europe: Diplomacy, Revolution, and Economic Development in the 1920s." *International History Review* 1 (1979): 55–83.

———. "Soviet Security Policy in the 1930s." In *Soviet Foreign Policy 1917–1991: A Retrospective*, edited by Gabriel Gorodetsky, 65–74. New York: Routledge, 2013.

Unger, Michal. *Lodzh: Aharon haGeta'ot bePolin*. Jerusalem: Yad Vashem, 2005.

[Union of Soviet Socialist Republics]. *XVIII S'ezd Vsesoyuznoi Kommunisticheskoi Partii* (b). Moscow: OGIZ, 1939.

Vago, Raphael. "Romanian Jewry during the Interwar Period." In *The Tragedy of Romanian Jewry*, edited by Randolph L. Braham, 29–56. New York: Columbia University Press, 1994.

Vaksberg, Arkady. *Stalin against the Jews*. New York: Alfred A. Knopf, 1994.

Valleau, Annick, and Aleksandr A. Cherkasov. "The Baltic States in the Propaganda Activities of the Third Reich during the Second World War." *Propaganda in the World and Local Conflicts* 4, no. 2 (2015): 95–108.

Vaysman, Ester-Basya. "Krzemieniec." In *Ghettos in German-Occupied Eastern Europe*, vol. 2: *United States Holocaust Memorial Museum Encyclopedia of Camps and Ghettos 1933–1945*, edited by Martin Dean, 1394–98. Bloomington: Indiana University Press, 2012.

Vazhneishie resheniia po sel'skomu khozyaistvu za 1938–1939 gody. Moscow: Gosudarstvennoe Izdatel'stvo Kolkhoznoi i Sovkhoznoi Literatury, 1939.

Veidlinger, Jeffrey. *The Moscow State Yiddish Theater: Jewish Culture on the Soviet Stage*. Bloomington: Indiana University Press, 2000.

Vilenskii, Vulf. *Povoroty sud'by: Kniga vospominanii*. Jerusalem: Kachol-Lavan, 1986.

Viola, Lynne. *Peasant Rebels under Stalin: Collectivization and the Culture of Peasant Resistance*. Oxford: Oxford University Press, 1999.

———. *Stalinist Perpetrators on Trial: Scenes from the Great Terror in the Soviet Union*. New York: Oxford University Press, 2017.

Vogelsang, Thilo. "Neue Dokumente zur Geschichte der Reichswehr 1930–1933." *Vierteljahrshefte für Zeitgeschichte* 2 (1954): 397–436.

Volokhova, Yuliia A. "'Staryi uchitel' V. S. Grossmana: Chetyre varianta odnogo rasskaza." *Vestnik RGGU: Literaturovedenie. Iazykoznanie. Kul'turologiia* 5 (2019): 85–112.

———. "'Staryi uchitel'—zabytaia p'esa V. Grossmana." In *Evrei Rossii, Evropy i Blizhnego Vostoka*, edited by V. G. Vovina and M. O. Meltsin, 132–39. St. Petersburg: Institut iudaiki, 2019.

Warhaftig, Zorach. *Refugee and Survivor: Rescue Efforts during the Holocaust*. Jerusalem: Yad Vashem, 1988.

Watson, Derek. *Molotov: A Biography*. New York: Palgrave Macmillan, 2005.

———. "Molotov's Apprenticeship in Foreign Policy: The Triple Alliance Negotiations in 1939." *Europe-Asia Studies* 52 (2000): 695–722.

Wąs, Maciaj. "Kak vosprinimalis' drugie: Nekotorye nabliudeniia v otnoshenii vospominanii polskikh evreev o prebyvanii v Srednei Azii v gody voiny." In *Evreiskie bezhentsy i evakuirovannye v SSSR, 1939–1946: Sbornik statei, dokumentov i svidetel'stv*, edited by Zeev Levin, 76–103. Jerusalem: Asotsiatisya hazit haKavod, 2020.

Weber, Eugen. "Romania." In *The European Right: A Historical Profile*, edited by Hans Rogger and Eugen Weber, 501–74. Berkeley: University of California Press, 1966.

Weiler, Shmuel. "HaIrgun haYehudi haLohem biBrody." In *Sefer milhamot haGeta'ot*, edited by Y. Cukierman and M. Bassok, 328–31. Tel Aviv: HaKibuts heMe'uhad, 1956.

Wein, Abraham, and Danuta Dąbrowska. "Touste." In *Galitsiyah haMizrahit*, vol. 2: *Pinkas haKehilot, Polin*, edited by Danuta Dąbrowska, Avraham Wein, and Aharon Weiss, 252–53. Jerusalem: Yad Vashem, 1980.

Weinberg, Gerhard. *Hitler's Foreign Policy 1933–1939: The Road to World War II*. New York: Enigma, 2010.

———. *A World at Arms: A Global History of World War II*. 2nd ed. New York: Cambridge University Press, 2005.

Weiner, Amir. *Making Sense of War: The Second World War and the Fate of the Bolshevik Revolution*. Princeton, NJ: Princeton University Press, 2001.

Weiss, Aharon. "Borysław." In *Galitsiyah haMizrahit*, vol. 2: *Pinkas haKehilot, Polin*, edited by Danuta Dąbrowska, Avraham Wein, and Aharon Weiss, 92–99. Jerusalem: Yad Vashem, 1980.

———. "Drohobycz." In *Galitsiyah haMizrahit*, vol. 2: *Pinkas haKehilot, Polin*, edited by Danuta Dąbrowska, Avraham Wein, and Aharon Weiss, 160–171. Jerusalem: Yad Vashem, 1980.

———. "Jewish-Ukrainian Relations in Western Ukraine during the Holocaust." In *Ukrainian-Jewish Relations in Historical Perspective*, edited by Peter J. Potichnyj and Howard Aster, 409–20. Edmonton: Canadian Institute of Ukrainian Studies, 1988.

———. "Some Economic and Social Problems of the Jews in Eastern Galicia in the Period of Soviet Rule (1939–1941)." In *Jews in Eastern Poland and the USSR, 1939–1946*, edited by Norman Davies and Antony Polonsky, 77–109. London: Macmillan, 1990.

———. "Tłuste." In *Galitsiyah haMizrahit*, vol. 2: *Pinkas haKehilot, Polin*, edited by Danuta Dąbrowska, Avraham Wein, and Aharon Weiss, 266–71. Jerusalem: Yad Vashem, 1980.

Weiss-Wendt, Anton. "Holocaust of the Estonian Jews, 1941/42: *Sonderkommando 1a* and the Problem of Collaboration." MA thesis, New York University, 1999.

Werth, Alexander. *Russia at War, 1941–1945*. London: Barrie and Rockliff, [1964].

Wirsching, Andreas. "'Man kann nur Boden germanisieren': Eine neue Quelle zu Hitlers Rede vor den Spitzen der Reichswehr am 3. February 1933." *Vierteljahrshefte für Zeitgeschichte* 49 (2001): 517–50.

Wolitz, Seth L. "*Shulamis*" and "*Bar Kochba*: Renewed Jewish Role Models in Goldfaden and Halkin." In *Yiddish Theatre: New Approaches*, edited by Joel Berkowitz, 87–104. Oxford: Littman Library of Jewish Civilization, 2003.

Wróbel, Piotr. "Class War or Ethnic Cleansing? Soviet Deportations of Polish Citizens from the Eastern Provinces of Poland, 1939–1941." *Polish Review* 59 (2014): 19–42.

———. "Na równi pochyłej. Żydzi Białegostuku w latach 1918–1939: demografia, ekonomika, dezintegracja, konflikty z Polakami." *Studia Podlaskie* 2 (1989): 166–202.

Wyman, David S. *Paper Walls: America and the Refugee Crisis, 1938–1941*. New York: Pantheon, 1985.

Yehezkeli, Moshe [Moshe Prager]. *Hatsalat haRebbe miBelz miGei haHaregah bePolin*. Jerusalem: Yeshurun, 1960.

Yones, Eliahu. *Ashan baHolot: Yehudei Lvov baMilhamah 1939–1944*. Jerusalem: Yad Vashem, 2001.

Zabarko, Boris, ed. *Holocaust in the Ukraine*. London: Vallentine Mitchell, 2005.

Zaderecki, Tadeusz. *BiMeshol tselav haKeres biLvov: Hurban haKehilah haYehudit beEinei mehaber polani*. Jerusalem: Yad Vashem, 1982.

Zadneprovskaia, L. "Zabota partii i pravitelstva o detiakh v gody Velikoi Otechestvennoi voiny." In *Vmeste s armiei i narodom: Sbornik o sovetskoi militsii*, edited by N. E. Adrianov, 64–79. Volgograd: Vysshaia sledstvennaia shkola MVD SSSR, 1970.

Zaionchkovski, P. A. *Samoderzhavie i russkaia armiia na rubezhe XIX–XX stoletii, 1881–1903*. Moscow: Mysl, 1973.

Zak, Abraham. *Knekht zeynen mir geven*. Buenos Aires: Unión Central Israelita Polaca en la Argentina, 1956.

Zakharine, Dmitri. "Speaking for the Soviet Land: Voice and Mediated Communities in the Age of Early Broadcast." *Russian Journal of Communications* 8, no. 2 (2016): 168–82.

Zarnowitz, Victor. *Fleeing the Nazis, Surviving the Gulag, and Arriving in the Free World: My Life and Times*. New York: ABC-Clio, 2008.

Zeltser, Arkadi. "Ethnic Conflict and Modernization in the Interwar Period: The Case of Soviet Belorussia." In *Anti-Jewish Violence: Rethinking the Pogrom in East European History*, edited by Jonathan Dekel-Chen, David Gaunt, Natan M. Meir, and Israel Bartal, 174–85. Bloomington: Indiana University Press, 2011.

———. "How the Jewish Intelligentsia Created the Jewishness of the Jewish Hero: The Soviet Yiddish Press." In *Soviet Jews in World War II: Fighting, Witnessing, Remembering*, edited by Harriet Murav and Gennady Estraikh, 104–28. New York: Academic Studies Press, 2014.

———. "Kholokost glazami krasnoarmeitsev." In *SSSR vo vtoroi mirovoi voine: Okkupatsiia, Kholokost, Stalinizm*, edited by Oleg Budnitskii and Ludmira Novikova, 49–70. Moscow: ROSSPEN, 2014.

———. *To Pour Out My Bitter Soul: Letters of Jews from the USSR, 1941–1945*. Jerusalem: Yad Vashem, 2016.

Zerubavel, Fryda. *Na veNad: Fartseykhnungen fun a pleyte*. Buenos Aires: Unión Central Israelita Polaca en la Argentina, 1947.

Zharkynbaeva, Roza, Nadezhda Dulin, and Evgeniia Anufrieva. "Voennaia povsednevnost' v gorodakh tyla v 1941–1945gg (na primere Alma-Aty)." *Vestnik Volgogradskogo gosudarstvennogo universiteta*. Series 4, 25, no. 1 (2020): 97–108.

Zimmerman, Joshua D. *The Polish Underground and the Jews, 1939–1945*. New York: Cambridge University Press, 2015.

Zinger, L[ev]. *Dos banayte folk: Tsifern un faktn vegn di yidn in FSSR*. Moscow: Der Emes, 1941.

Zinich, M. S. *Povsednevnaia zhizn' naroda v gody Velikoi Otechestvennoi Voiny*. Moscow: IRI RAN, 2019.

Zuskina-Perelman, Alla, and Sharon Blass. *The Travels of Benjamin Zuskin*. Syracuse, NY: Syracuse University Press, 2015.

Zweig, Ferdynand. *Poland between the Two World Wars: A Critical Study of Social and Economic Changes*. London: Seecker & Warburg, 1944.

Żarnowski, Janusz. *Społeczeństwo Drugiej Rzeczypospolitej 1918–1939*. Warsaw: Państwowe Wydawnictwo Naukowe, 1973.

Żaroń, Piotr. *Ludność polska w Związku Radzieckim w czasie II wojny światowej*. Warsaw: Państwowe Wydawnictwo Naukowe, 1990.

Żbikowski, Andrzej. *U genezy Jedwabnego: Żydzi na Kresach Północno-Wschodnich II Rzeczypospolitej wrzesień 1939–lipiec 1941*. Warsaw: Żydowski Instytut Historyczny, 2006.

Żyndul, Jolanta. *Zajścia antyżydowskie w Polsce w latach 1935–1937*. Warsaw: Fundacja im. K. Kelles-Krauza, 1994.

ELECTRONIC REPOSITORIES AND RESOURCES

Avalon Project, Yale University, New Haven, CT (https://avalon.law.yale.edu)

Centropa, Vienna, Austria (www.centropa.org)

Efingar, Nesher, Israel (www.efingar.narod.ru)

Evreiskie zemledelskie kolonii Iuga Ukrainny i Kryma (http://evkol.ucoz.com)

Haus der Wannsee-Konferenz, Berlin, Germany (https://ghwk.de)

Jewish Women's Archive (https://jwa.org)

Mezhdunarodnyi obedinnennyi biograficheskii tsentr, Russia (http://www.biograph.ru)

Russian Federation, Sait konstitutsii Rossiiskoi Federatsii (http://constitution.garant.ru)

Roots = Saknes, Latvia (roots.saknes.lv)

United Kingdom Parliament (https://hansard.parliament.uk)

Yad Vashem, Jerusalem, Israel (www.yadvashem.org)

INDEX

Note: Places are listed according to their official designations in 1939. Alternate place names for most locations whose current or historic names differ from those designations are given in parentheses. Cross-references are provided where an alternate name is substantially different from the name used in the volume. Names of geographical features (such as rivers or mountain ranges) are rendered in the form most likely to be familiar to English readers, which occasionally differs from the current official name.

ABOUT THE AUTHORS

OLEG BUDNITSKII is Professor of History and Director of the Institute for Advanced Soviet and Post-Soviet Studies at HSE University in Moscow, Russia. Budnitskii is the author of *Russian Jews between the Reds and the Whites, 1917–1920* and *People at War* and editor of *Odessa: Life under the Occupation, 1941–1944* and *On the Move: Russian Jewish Émigrés on the Eve and at the Beginning of the World War II, 1938–1941*, among other scholarly monographs and edited volumes. Budnitskii serves as editor-in-chief of the annual *Archive of Jewish History*, and is on the editorial board of the *Russian Review* and *East European Jewish Affairs*. Budnitskii is a recipient of multiple Russian and international grants and awards, including from the US Holocaust Memorial Museum, the Fulbright Program, and the MacArthur Foundation.

DAVID ENGEL is Greenberg Professor of Holocaust Studies, Professor of Hebrew and Judaic Studies, and Professor of History at New York University. He is the author of seven books and more than one hundred scholarly articles on various aspects of Jewish history in the nineteenth and twentieth centuries.

GENNADY ESTRAIKH is Clinical Professor at New York University. He received his doctorate from the University of Oxford. His fields of expertise are Soviet Jewish history, Jewish intellectual history, and Yiddish language and literature. His most recent monograph is *Transatlantic Russian Jewishness* (2020). He won the 2014 National Jewish Book Award for co-editing *1929: Mapping the Jewish World*.

ANNA SHTERNSHIS is the Al and Malka Green Professor of Yiddish Studies and Director of the Anne Tanenbaum Centre for Jewish Studies at the University of Toronto. She is the author of *Soviet and Kosher: Jewish Popular Culture in the Soviet Union, 1923–1939* and *When Sonia Met Boris: An Oral History of Jewish Life under Stalin*.